EVOLUTION OF THE MODERN PRESIDENCY

A BIBLIOGRAPHICAL SURVEY

EVOLUTION OF THE MODERN PRESIDENCY

A BIBLIOGRAPHICAL SURVEY

Fred I. Greenstein
Larry Berman
Alvin S. Felzenberg
with Doris Lidtke

American Enterprise Institute for Public Policy Research
Washington, D.C.

Fred I. Greenstein is Henry Luce professor of law, politics, and society, Princeton University.

Larry Berman is assistant professor of political science, University of California (Davis).

Alvin S. Felzenberg is an advanced graduate student in the Department of Politics, Princeton University.

Doris Lidtke is a computer science specialist at Towson State University.

Price $4.75 per copy

Library of Congress Cataloging in Publication Data

Greenstein, Fred I
   Evolution of the modern presidency.

   (Studies in political and social processes)   (AEI
studies ; 153)
   1. Presidents--United States--Bibliography.
2. United States--Politics and government--1933-1945--
Bibliography.   3. United States--Politics and
government--1945-   --Bibliography.   I.   Berman,
Larry, joint author.   II. Felzenberg, Alvin S., joint
author.   III. Title.   IV. Series.   V. Series:
American Enterprise Institute for Public Policy Research.
AEI studies ; 153.
Z7165.U5G74   [JK511]   016.35303'13   77-8022
ISBN 0-8447-3251-6

AEI studies 153

Printed in the United States of America

CONTENTS

PREFACE

This volume—consisting of approximately 2,500 bibliographical entries, several hundred of them briefly annotated—identifies and classifies significant works bearing on the evolution of the American presidency since 1932. No institution of American government has changed so drastically and with such profound consequences for American society as has the presidency during the years covered. Much has been written about the evolution of the modern presidency, but there remain significant gaps, and no catalogue of existing works has been published. By way of introduction to the compilation of citations that follows, it will be instructive to consider the general contours of historical change in the presidency since 1932, some of the reasons why systematic study of the presidency has not flourished, and the outlines of the present book.

The Rise of the Modern Presidency

Suppose that a learned student of American governmental institutions had played Rip Van Winkle for the half century before the nation's bicentennial. Upon a-wakening in the 1970s, he would have been as amazed as Washington Irving's hero had been when he found himself in a nation led by President George Washington but remembered only a collection of colonies ruled by King George III.

In 1926 President Calvin Coolidge and a handful of White House employees were seeking to minimize the President's impact on the political system. Their approach was exemplified in their attitude toward the Bureau of the Budget (BOB), which had been created by the Budget and Accounting Act of 1921 to enable the President to submit a unified executive budget to the Congress for the first time in American history. The BOB, however, was housed in the Treasury building and was largely preoccupied during its first decade with economy and efficiency in the routine business of government. Although the BOB was officially responsible to the President rather than to the Treasury secretary, its domicile symbolized its disuse as an arm of presidential initiative in matters of policy. The bureau simply perpetuated the political ethos of the time—budgetary parsimony and highly restricted activity by the government in general and the President in particular.

Consider now the presidency of the mid-1970s, battered though it is after the divisive foreign policy of the 1960s, the Nixon impeachment proceedings and resignation, and the statutory innovations designed to limit presidential powers. It is true that the presidency circa 1977 does not prompt the kind of national soul-searching about the "imperial presidency" that went on during the Nixon and Johnson administrations. Nevertheless, even after reforms designed to strengthen Congress, the prediction in some early post-Watergate writings that Congress would become the central focus of the political system and that the presidency would significantly decline in importance proves to have been premature. Congressional government was not the stamp of the Ford administration and is not a likely prospect under President Carter.

The United States has, of course, never been as centrally directed by the executive as other constitutional democracies have been. Beginning with President Franklin D. Roosevelt's "one hundred days," however, the nation underwent a striking shift from Congress-oriented to President-oriented politics and government. This is not to say that the presidency has wholly dominated public policy making since 1932. Throughout the period starting with the New Deal, many major policies have been hatched in Congress or by executive agencies and simply have received a presidential imprimatur; others have been made in the face of presidential opposition. Yet in spite of these signs that the presidency is scarcely omnipotent, the expanded modern presidency is "more equal" than other national political institutions. In contrast to the self-abnegating Calvin Coolidge, who stressed the ceremonial aspects of his office and carried out only a necessary minimum of ministerial duties, each of the Presidents since 1932 has had at his disposal the drastically enlarged role expectations and institutional structure that the presidency acquired beginning in the Great Depression.

The Enlarged Role Expectations of the Presidents. Article II of the Constitution and subsequent legislation provide only a spare description of the President's legal functions. From the Washington to the Hoover administrations the majority of American Presidents allowed congressional leaders to carry the day. From time to time, however, the public's expectations of the President and the President's own claims expanded current notions of what the President was legally entitled to do. The few "activist" Presidents before Franklin Roosevelt—Jackson, Polk, Lincoln, Cleveland, Theodore Roosevelt, and Wilson—established precedents that their successors drew upon to justify unilateral presidential action, or, at any rate, forceful leadership, with respect to such matters as the movement of troops, international agreements, territorial expansion, executive rule making, vigorous use of the veto, and control of the hiring and the firing of executive branch employees.

Except under these assertive leaders, presidential power was generally weak before 1932. In 1885, Woodrow Wilson, then a college instructor, described the source of governmental leadership in the United States during the post-Civil War decades in the title of his first book, *Congressional Government.* In Wilson's lifetime, however, not least in his own period as chief executive, there were numerous instances of presidential autonomy. Moreover, a legal rationale for presidential activism had accumulated, often with the benediction of the Supreme Court. This growing common law that is the basis of the expanded executive power of modern Presidents has been defended most emphatically and consistently during the years since Franklin Roosevelt. In spite of the warnings of a conservative minority, most of those who have written about American government since the 1930s have celebrated presidential autonomy. They have eulogized, for example, Franklin D. Roosevelt's destroyer deal with Great Britain, Harry Truman's unilateral decision to order resistance to North Korea's invasion of South Korea, and John F. Kennedy's performance in the Cuban missile crisis.

The increase in the power that the President exercises and is expected to exercise, needless to say, has not occurred in a vacuum. The bulk of the world's population is ruled by explicitly authoritarian governments, and even in most constitutional democracies the executives have acquired more influence and larger staffs than ever before. The expansion of executive power in democracies has been fostered by the growth of modern governments in general. Their responsibilities have become so vast and complex that it is no longer possible for them to be directed in detail by legislative assemblies. War and international crisis have further encouraged the growth of executive power. In the twentieth century, the dangers of war and the need for central leadership in the international arena have been heightened by extraordinary increases in the speed of communications, in the political and economic interdependency of nations, and in the capacity for military destruction.

The Presidents before Franklin Roosevelt could themselves determine how active a part they would take in decision making. Presidential leadership tended to occur during crises or when the incumbent President was motivated to be a strong leader. Sometimes these factors coincided, as with Woodrow Wilson's leadership in World War I and Abraham Lincoln's in the Civil War. Sometimes a crisis failed to produce leadership (Buchanan), or a leader produced a crisis (Polk), or, in the presence of relatively moderate external stimuli, an activist President was more assertive than other Presidents of his era (Cleveland and Theodore Roosevelt). But from the 1930s onward, as has often been noted, Presidents have had to be leaders whether they chose to be or not.

The Expanding Institutional Presidency. The expansion of what is accepted as the constitutional role of the President is complemented by a second quantum change in the presidency. At the time of the Coolidge administration, the human and organizational resources available to the President were diminutive. Today they have grown into what, in effect, is a presidential *branch* of government, approximately equivalent in personnel and staff support to the modern Congress, with its 535 members and several thousand staff and clerical aides. An institution that was not even a part of the governmental structure in the 1920s, the Executive Office of the President (EOP), has been created, and its staff is directly augmented by resources from outside the EOP—for example, the communications systems provided by the Department of Defense, including Air Force One; the Secret Service, which is officially an arm of the Treasury Department; and White House lawn and garden maintenance provided by the National Park Service.

A brief chronological catalogue of major modern increments in the infrastructure of the presidency might well begin with those initiated by Franklin Roosevelt prior to his taking office. Volume 4 of Frank Freidel's biography of Roosevelt, which deals with the 1932 election, the transition period between the election and the inauguration, and Roosevelt's first year in office, documents how, even before his inauguration in March 1933, Roosevelt had laid the groundwork for adding an advisory component to the presidency. He called on individuals who had worked with him over the years, advisers he had employed as governor of New York, and an added group of university brain-trusters to help him prepare for office and then execute the extraordinary program successfully presented to Congress during his hundred days.[1] Thus, it was clear even before his administra-

---

[1]Freidel's book is cited in the Roosevelt chapter of this bibliography. In that chapter see also Tugwell's *The Brains Trust* and Moley's *After Seven Years.*

tion had formally begun that it was to be far more extensively staffed than preceding ones.

Presidential advisers and aides, of course, are no novelty in American history. Before the Roosevelt administration, there had been, for example, the men described in Louis Koenig's well-titled *The Invisible Presidency*, a book that not only deals with developments since the New Deal but also treats such earlier presidential advisers as Alexander Hamilton in Washington's administration, Martin Van Buren in Jackson's Kitchen Cabinet, and perhaps the most famous White House "grey eminence," Woodrow Wilson's Colonel House. From the start, Roosevelt had many more grey and not-so-grey eminences as advisers and staff assistants than previous Presidents had had, although most of his first two terms elapsed before this unofficial change became formalized in the *United States Code* and the *Federal Register* with the official establishment, in 1939, of the Executive Office of the President.

Following are additional way-stations of significance in the institutional growth of the presidency, all of them documented at least in part in the published literature this book itemizes:

(1) The establishment of formal means of directing and coordinating the agencies and activities that proliferated under the New Deal. Coordination was first attempted through the National Emergency Council. In 1937, however, the Brownlow Committee asserted that "the President needs help," and three years of reorganization politics culminated in the formation of the Executive Office of the President in 1939. The two key components of the EOP were the White House Office (WHO) and the Bureau of the Budget.[2] By the late 1930s, the BOB, which had been mainly an economizing agency (issuing directives even on the use of pencil stubs and on saving paper clips), was beginning actively to synthesize and coordinate the substantive policies of the President and was evaluating and coordinating the agencies' requests for funds and for new legislation. In 1939 the BOB's new role, which would mature during the Truman years, received official recognition with the establishment of the EOP and the appointment of a brilliant bureaucratic entrepreneur, Harold Smith, as Bureau of the Budget director. Its symbolic benediction was the transferral of the BOB from the Treasury building into the neobaroque extravaganza across the street from the west wing of the White House, appropriately renamed the Executive Office Building. (That building, incidentally, had once housed the entire State, War, and Navy Departments.) The establishment of the WHO officially entitled the President to a staff of high-level aides, although the list of White House aides in the 1939 *U.S. Government Organization Manual* is remarkably brief by present-day standards.

(2) World War II, during which FDR's system of loose coordination proved inadequate and gave way to major delegations of authority to the military and to the Office of War Mobilization. No definitive history of this period exists, but important insights can be found in Neustadt's articles on "Planning the President's Program" and Somers's book on the Office of War Mobilization and Recon-

---

[2] For a convenient chart of EOP entities and their life spans, see the appendix to Thomas Cronin, *The State of the Presidency*, cited in chapter four.

version, *Presidential Agency*, as well as in other writings cited in the present volume.

(3) The period after Roosevelt's death, when BOB came into its own as a legislative, as well as financial, clearance agency. During the Truman administration the BOB built upon the foundations laid by FDR and Director Harold Smith and began supplying a far more advanced and comprehensive level of staff support than ever before. BOB became an institution with which congressional leaders could deal in taking account of presidential legislative priorities and to which the President regularly turned for program formation and the issues upon which he would base his next election campaign.

(4) The accumulation of additional EOP agencies, such as the Council of Economic Advisers and the National Security Council. Both of these went through shakedown periods during the Truman administration and a variety of ups and downs in the years to follow. Successive *Government Organization Manuals* show additional EOP agencies, but many of these were of minor significance and short duration. In some cases the EOP has also been a preserve for endangered executive species—innovative agencies like the Peace Corps and the Office of Economic Opportunity that Presidents chose to protect from the bureaucratic complexities and rivalries of cabinet departments. (These "endangered species" agencies within the EOP are not functionally part of the presidency in that they carry out standard line functions of executive departments or bureaus rather than staff functions.)

(5) The growth of executive staff and bureaucratic routines under Eisenhower. In the 1950s a President officially committed to reducing the impact of the presidency but accustomed to military staff procedures chose to increase the size, the formality, and the centralization of the White House staff in the hope of improving management procedures. Eisenhower expanded greatly the size and functions of the National Security Council, formalized the process of legislative liaison, and not only regularly convened the cabinet but also developed a formal cabinet secretariat charged with framing a cabinet agenda and, along with other new White House instruments, with coordinating and implementing policy decisions.

(6) The post-Sputnik establishment of a Presidential Science Adviser and Advisory Council. The official addition of science advising to the presidency began in 1957. This was terminated during the Nixon administration, in the wake of the involvement of members of the President's Science Advisory Council in such controversial issues as whether or not to adopt an antiballistic missile system. It was reinstituted in 1976.

(7) The emphasis in the Kennedy, Johnson, and Nixon White Houses on direct intervention in policy formulation and implementation by White House aides, individually and via task forces. These were initiatives that in the past would have been left to cabinet departments and the BOB. During the Kennedy years, this involvement was not accompanied by expansion of the White House staff. Instead, there was a deliberate dismantling of portions of Eisenhower's ad-

v

ministrative policy apparatus, consistent with Kennedy's administrative philosophy of traveling light and personally coordinating a relatively small group of highly competent aides. In the Nixon and Ford administrations, however, the staff of the White House office grew to a record size and had become inscrutably complex.

Under Nixon and Ford the proliferation of WHO's staff led to major problems of coordination. Especially under Nixon, independent actions were taken by White House staff members who left the impression that they were executing explicit presidential directives. The covert "plumbers" group in the Nixon White House, which extended its mission from the protection of national security secrets to domestic political espionage, was the most notorious example of a WHO accretion during that ill-fated presidency. In general, however, Nixon's White House staff took over functions usually assigned to administrative line agencies. A miniature White House version of the executive branch took shape, most conspicuously in the presidential foreign affairs staff during the period when Henry Kissinger served as both staff adviser and policy maker, far overshadowing the official who was formally second-in-command to the President in foreign affairs, namely, the secretary of state.

Over the years since World War II, the expansion of the presidency has affected the appearance and nomenclature of the vicinity of 1600 Pennsylvania Avenue, just as it has changed organization charts. The metal fence that once surrounded only the White House was extended to bar West Executive Avenue from general traffic and to surround the building that in 1939 became known as the Executive Office Building. More recently this has become the *Old* Executive Office Building, with the construction of a high-rise New Executive Office Building half a block away, one of a number of structures in the Lafayette Square area that house EOP units.

(8) The transformation of the BOB, in its fiftieth year, into the Office of Management and Budget (OMB), different in function and form from the old BOB. Connected with the shift from BOB to OMB mandated in Reorganization Plan Number 2 has been an intricate and continuing readjustment of institutional responsibilities and, in some cases, the growth of overlapping jurisdictions. The Civil Service personnel of OMB had less influence over legislation than their BOB counterparts had had, and presidentially appointed officials were installed in the agency. (By Johnson's time legislative clearance had already begun to be assigned to the White House staff and ad hoc task forces.) During the Nixon years, the head of the OMB occupied an office in the White House and was somewhat isolated from his staff, who dealt with lesser issues. Times had changed since the 1940s and (to a lesser extent) the 1950s, when the Budget Bureau had been a small elite unit composed of experienced individuals who, accurately or inaccurately, thought of themselves as capable of working neutrally for Presidents of varied partisan complexions.

(9) The creation (by the executive order that changed BOB into OMB) of a Domestic Council (DC) ostensibly paralleling the National Security Council. At first, there was no clear demarcation between the DC's policy-shaping functions

and those of OMB, although one effort to link the DC and OMB was the controversial introduction into OMB of White House appointees specifically assigned to advance White House policy goals. OMB and the Domestic Council are clearly in flux at the time of this writing; the Carter administration is expected to abolish the latter in name, though not in function. Although Nixon's innovations have sometimes been described as attempts to impose White House directives on the executive branch, there was a general recognition throughout the 1960s of the need for more domestic-policy analysis in the White House and for a more direct line of control to executive branch agencies. Reorganization Plan Number 2 had bipartisan support.

The Combined Effect of Expanded Role Expectations and Growth. The post-1932 presidency can usefully be called the "modern presidency," in contrast to the earlier "traditional presidency." Its institutional expansion has, of course, coincided with formal and informal expansion in presidential power and in policy initiation and implementation. When Eisenhower announced federal intervention in the school integration controversy in Little Rock, Arkansas, he emphasized the gravity of his action by leaving his vacation spot in order to make the announcement from the White House; he also made use of the facilities in the modern White House that enable Presidents to televise their proclamations, preempting other broadcasting. During the Cuban missile crisis, Kennedy exercised the expanded war powers of modern Presidents, and, largely because of the advanced communications facilities at his disposal, he could maintain a facade of business as usual while the ad hoc policy group in the White House framed a strategy of response. Kennedy took part in midterm congressional campaigns around the country as scheduled until he feigned a mild illness to return to the White House for the famous missile crisis speech.

Johnson and Nixon simultaneously expanded the legal precedents for the exercise of war powers and made use of institutional support facilities to oversee overt and covert military operations abroad. The expansion under Nixon of such spending powers as impoundment and reallocation of funds and Ford's rapid-fire approach to vetoing legislation also illustrate how the physical and the formal changes in the presidency have reinforced one another. Presidents from Washington to Hoover could make similar formal modifications of congressionally mandated policies when their power positions and role conceptions led them to do so. But without the bureaucratic infrastructure of the modern presidency and the general expansion of the executive branch, there were severe limitations on a President's ability to make autonomous decisions about congressionally mandated expenditures or to exercise the veto power.

Presidential initiatives to evaluate legislation, draft veto messages, and issue executive orders are far more feasible now than they once were because of innovations in the 1930s and 1940s in BOB policy analysis activities and other changes in operating procedures. Before the 1930s, a single copy of each bill passed by Congress was transmitted to the White House and was unofficially circulated to what were deemed to be the relevant agencies. Often there was simply insufficient time within the constitutionally stipulated period to make a decision to veto, much less to prepare a veto message. Beginning in the 1930s, however, congressional enactments have been immediately reproduced in multiple copies and circulated to all relevant parties in the executive branch with instructions to veto messages on a contingency basis. Standard procedures also have developed for the discretionary use of presidential spending powers.[3]

The Need for Systematic Knowledge of the Modern Presidency

The foregoing remarks sketch only a few of the more salient departures since 1932 from the tradition of the lightly staffed presidency, which mainly reacted to congressional initiatives, especially in domestic policy. One would think that such a profound change in the structure and function of a central governmental institution in a major world power would have been systematically studied, especially in a nation that also harbors most of the world's political scientists. But this has not been the case.

During the growth of empirical political science in the years since World War II, students of American political processes and institutions have paradoxically treated the modern American presidency like a favorite child and an ignored waif. Possibly the most important reason for the paucity of systematic study of the presidency has been the very popularity of the institution. Until the second half of the 1960s, the bulk of scholarly and popular writing about the presidency, including textbooks and mass media presentations, praised or even glorified the presidency. Academicians and journalists treated it as the fulcrum or mainspring of the American political system and the best of all national political institutions in representing "the national interest"—an institution that, if anything, was too constrained rather than too powerful. Until the Vietnam escalation and the scandals of the Nixon administration, most political commentators were so favorably disposed to the presidency that they treated Congress and most other political institutions largely as obstacles to presidential accomplishment. Even the Supreme Court was so described until the late 1930s, when shifting voting coalitions and the addition of Roosevelt appointees changed the conservative pattern of the Court's decisions.

In retrospect it seems clear that this idealization of the presidency resulted largely from the post-1932 tendency of Presidents (including Eisenhower) to favor more liberal domestic policies and more internationalist foreign policies than did their parties in Congress. Most writing on the presidency, especially by scholars, took for granted the merits of internationalism. During the same years, of course, Presidents were regularly excoriated by political conservatives, including the relatively few scholars of conservative persuasion. But most scholars took seriously Clinton Rossiter's admonition to "leave your presidency alone," expressed in *The American Presidency,* a defense of that institution that had wide circulation in the 1950s. They focused their critical attention on other national political institutions and processes that were in their view more defective.

---

[3]On the spending power the most comprehensive source, Louis Fisher's *Presidential Spending Power,* is cited in the chapter of this bibliography on presidential powers.

Another reason for the lack of scholarship on the presidency is conveyed in the title of Louis Koenig's *The Invisible Presidency*. It has been far too readily assumed that the presidency operates behind closed doors to such an extent that research is virtually impossible. In fact, however, American government is notoriously sieve-like. Moreover, as the presidency itself has become more controversial, revisionist historians and others have demonstrated that the modern presidencies can be studied from primary sources, especially the rich resources of the presidential libraries. Historians' work, along with that of investigative journalists, has made it clearer to students of the presidency that information about "the presidential branch" is available. The sources for fresh research include interviews with aides of chief executives and unpublished archival material, as well as the considerable, sometimes fugitive, published work on the "invisible presidency," much of which is identified in this bibliography. Among published works, government documents—such as the Pentagon Papers and the various Watergate hearings—provide a particularly fertile source of information.

Another impediment to systematic research has been the growth of supporting institutions surrounding the presidency since 1932. This growth has taken place over a short time and on a continuous basis, circumstances that make inevitable a lag between events and knowledge. Furthermore, in regard to the many specific changes in the institution and the practices of the expanded presidency, commentators have gone from one extreme to another, sometimes treating highly specific short-term arrangements as if they were chiseled into Mount Rushmore, at other times writing excessively abstract accounts of the reified entity called *the* presidency.

Then, too, scholars have shied away from comparisons between the modern presidencies out of an awareness that the personal styles of individual Presidents have been highly consequential. Since the study of personality and politics is a controversial area of inquiry, this important side of the presidency has also seemed inaccessible to standard academic techniques. Personal aspects of the presidency have received attention but from journalists more often than from political scientists, historians, or members of the psychological disciplines.

The Nature of the Present Project

The premise of this bibliographical volume is that a major increase in research on the modern presidency is necessary if we are to understand and cope with the dilemmas that face the American political system. Prescriptions to improve the functioning of the presidency abound. Since remedies depend upon accurate diagnoses, however, there is an urgent need for more satisfactory description of the institution and analysis of how it acquired its present shape and dimensions.

The present work was prepared within predetermined time limits and with limited resources. Our aim has been to compile an inventory of selected literature relevant to the issues touched upon in the first sections of this introduction and to do so on a rather rapid schedule. Additions, revisions, and, where necessary, corrections will be supplied in later editions. We found it necessary to make several Procrustean decisions about the limits of the subject if our work was ever to end. I will note these in the course of an overview of what the volume includes.

Another set of time-imposed limitations will be evident to anyone using the bibliography. We have sought to annotate briefly works of special significance and those whose titles are not self-descriptive. But our schedule and other resource considerations prevented us from annotating as many entries as we had originally hoped. Many items of major importance are not annotated, while some less significant items are annotated. There are a variety of reasons for this, including in a few cases simply the ready availability of a summary quotation that could serve as an annotation.

The articles cited in the twenty-one chapters of this book were originally identified in several general and specialized periodical indexes. Each of these indexes has sections that deal with the presidency. The indexes are themselves discussed in Chapter 1 along with other guides to reference sources and books that compile brief factual data on the Presidents. The reader should especially note our annotation to *The Readers' Guide to Periodical Literature,* which covers the more popular periodicals, including weekly news periodicals. Most weekly presidential news reports (including reports in such government serial publications as *The Congressional Record*) have been omitted from this bibliography, but the student will find such references in *The Readers' Guide. The Readers' Guide* and the newspaper indexes are useful not only for particular sequences of events, but also for a general sense of the day-to-day flow of presidential news.

The major exception to our policy of not citing weekly journalism is the authoritative *National Journal,* a periodical that has covered governmental affairs with exceptional depth and comprehensiveness since it began publication in 1969.

The Public Affairs Information Index (PAIS), which cites writings in scholarly journals, books, and government documents, has been particularly valuable in compiling this book. A high proportion of the citations from PAIS found their way into the "short list" of roughly 2,500 publications presented here. Such specialized indexes as *The Business Periodicals Index* and *The Index of Legal Periodicals* also provided many of the citations listed here.

References to the dates, volume numbers, and pages of articles are frequently taken directly from periodical indexes and therefore are not uniform. If an abbreviation needs clarification, it should be checked against the keys contained in the periodical indexes. Periodical titles have in the main been standardized. Several commonly cited periodicals whose titles have been abbreviated in standard form are listed on page 15.

The most comprehensive listing of books on the presidency at our disposal was the *Subject Index to The Library of Congress.* This includes not only books that illuminate the functioning of the presidency but also juvenilia, White House cookbooks, polemics, campaign tracts, and so on. Most such works are not listed here. Many of them, however, have value for social historians; the *Subject Index to the Library of Congress* volume will warrant their attention.

Both in the selection of works in the bibliography and in our annotations, we have given more attention to recent literature and writings on the later modern presidencies than to older works or works concerned with the earlier administrations. Franklin Roosevelt, for example, is the subject of a number of extensively documented biographies and biographies in progress. These either subsume many earlier writings not cited here or direct the reader to them. But there are no authoritative histories of many recent presidencies. Hence the need for a wide range of citations and annotations on those presidencies.

The citations are grouped in twenty-one chapters, several of which are subdivided. Citations are numbered sequentially throughout the book. These numbers (rather than page numbers) are used in the Table of Contents, in cross-references for items that fall into more than one of the book's divisions (these are listed in the "see also" sections at the end of each chapter or chapter subdivision), and in the author index. Items are listed in the chapter to which they most directly apply and cross-referenced as appropriate. Historical works covering several presidencies normally are listed in the chapter on the presidency they discuss first and cross-referenced in the other presidency chapters to which they apply. In some cases, exquisitely subtle but ultimately trivial decisions had to be made about the initial location of a reference.

Chapter 1, as we have indicated, deals with reference sources. Chapter 2, which was compiled by Professor James Fetzer, lists roughly 100 representative sources from the voluminous government-publications literature on the presidency, including continuing publications and key sets of documents. The chapter is subdivided to parallel the entire book, and its entries are cross-referenced on other chapters.

Chapter 3 lists compendia—the many general books of readings on the presidency—and cross-references specialized compendia dealing with particular facets of the presidency, such as relations with Congress. Anthologies are among the more useful starting points for the scholar; moreover, some of them contain writings that are nowhere else available, and many include valuable bibliographies.

The entries in Chapter 4—general works on the presidency—also help to open the gates of presidential study to the novice and at the same time provide the scholar with an inventory of efforts at rounded, synthetic interpretation of the presidency and of its development. In a few instances, we have included pre-1932 literature, citing classic sources that anticipate the growth of the modern presidency and its consequences. Further perspective is provided in Chapter 5 by an inventory of writings that compare the U.S. presidency with the executives in other nations and at other levels of American government and in Chapter 6 by those comparing various American Presidents and their administrations.

Chapters 7 through 13 cover the modern Presidents from Franklin D. Roosevelt to Gerald R. Ford. The same outline is followed in each of these chapters except in the sections on particular events during the seven presidencies: developments under Truman, Eisenhower, Johnson, and Ford are dealt with in sections labeled "domestic," "foreign," and "other" (this last including events with both foreign and domestic elements), whereas the administrations of Roosevelt, Kennedy, and Nixon called for additional subheads such as the New Deal, World War II leadership, the Kennedy assassination, and Watergate.

Chapter 14, on presidential recruitment, deals with the background characteristics and the experiences of individuals who have become President. The sparseness of the listings in Chapter 14 reflects one of the drastic limitations placed on this project in order to complete it within the available time and resources: we have focused on the presidency as a functioning institution during the inter-election period. Thus, we have not attempted to cover writings on the structure of the electoral system, including the nomination processes, campaign management and finance, campaign dynamics, and the nature of electoral behavior. Here we were deterred by the unbounded vastness of the literature and the difficulty of disentangling its presidential and nonpresidential components. The literature on campaigns, voting, elections, and the electoral process shades off in one direction into general treatments of the party system and in another into general literature on voting. Items from this literature are listed in the bibliography because of their bearing on recruitment or on public orientations to Presidents and the presidency. The many good textbooks on American political parties and elections (such as the successive editions of the Polsby-Wildavsky text)[4] will provide an ample bibliographical start for study of these topics. And some future bibliographical work will, we hope, treat the process of becoming President in the detailed way this volume treats the actual functioning of the presidency.

Whereas Chapter 14 deliberately excludes much of the voluminous literature on presidential recruitment, Chapter 15 on presidential personality is much more inclusive, covering even studies of Presidents before Roosevelt. The reason for this emphasis is suggested above: the presidency is notable among political roles for the degree to which it is shaped by the personal qualities of the incumbent. Since scholars traditionally have been hesitant to tackle this obviously important but intellectually controversial topic, we feel it desirable to exhibit the range of efforts at disciplined inquiry in this area. Even generously defined, this category includes more cross-references than primary citations.

Chapter 16 takes account of what we have called the "physical" growth of the presidency, dealing with the many staff components in the EOP and with the general phenomenon of advising the President. We do not include agencies such as the Peace Corps that were placed in the EOP for reasons of administrative politics. Of the presidential staff agencies that reside in the EOP, we omit the Central Intelligence Agency and the intelligence community generally—as with electoral studies, writings on intelligence that deal explicitly with the presidency would be difficult to distinguish from those that do not. In addition, detailed knowledge of the Presidents' use of overt and covert intelligence instrumentalities is only now emerging and is so heterogeneous that we felt this topic also should be left for another bibliography.

---

[4]Nelson W. Polsby and Aaron Wildavsky, *Presidential Elections: Strategies of American Electoral Politics* (New York: Scribner's, 1964, 1968, 1971, 1976).

The advisory-staff institutions that are the subject of Chapter 16 have partial counterparts in the subsections of Chapter 17, which deals with "presidential constituencies." This term, borrowed from Richard Neustadt's *Presidential Power,* refers to the basic components of the President's political environment—public opinion, extragovernmental groups, the other branches of government, and foreign and international entities and their leaders.

Chapter 18, cataloguing presidential powers and restraints, has been inflated in certain of its subcategories (for example, executive privilege, spending power, and impeachment) by such events as the Vietnam War, Nixon's extensive use of impoundment, and Watergate. Chapter 19 deals with that chronically ambiguous office, the vice presidency; Chapter 20 lists writings that advance reform proposals; and Chapter 21 deals with a range of topics that do not fit under the previous headings—varying from presidential transitions to the physical structure, history, and operating logistics of the White House.

As noted above, the published literature on the modern Presidents is richly supported by the primary resources of the presidential libraries. The sections listing writings of the Presidents in the Roosevelt through Kennedy chapters cite the most recent lists of holdings published by the Franklin D. Roosevelt Library, Hyde Park, New York; the Harry S. Truman Library, Independence, Missouri; the Dwight D. Eisenhower Library, Abilene, Kansas; and the John F. Kennedy Library, Waltham, Massachusetts (scheduled to be moved to Boston). Visitors to these libraries will find elaborately indexed finding guides to the documents in each collection of papers that has been cleared for use, oral-history collections of varying degrees of extensiveness, and competent staffs prepared to photostat documents available for release and to process Freedom of Information Act appeals for documents still classified.

The Lyndon B. Johnson Library in Austin, Texas, also has extensive finding guides and a growing oral-history collection, although a general list of its holdings has not yet been published. The status of Richard M. Nixon's papers is still uncertain because of pending litigation.[5] President Ford has donated his papers to the University of Michigan, where a Gerald R. Ford Presidential Library will be established.[6]

Since there is an inevitable arbitrariness in making the selections for a volume of this nature, we urge readers to challenge our decisions, bring omissions and new works to our attention, and apprise us of technical errors in citations or annotations so that any future edition of this work can be appropriately adjusted.

---

[5]For discussions of the Nixon papers see the excellent article on presidential libraries by Clement E. Vose, cited in chapter one, and Karen J. Winkler, "Gaining Access to U.S. Documents: The Struggle Continues" in *The Chronicle of Higher Education,* vol. 14 (February 14, 1977).

[6]See "Donation of the President's Papers to the Government," *Administration of Gerald R. Ford: Presidential Documents,* vol. 12 (week ending December 17, 1976), pp. 1709-1719.

Acknowledgments. My colleagues and I are indebted to the American Enterprise Institute for Public Policy Research, the Ford Foundation, the Henry Luce Foundation, the Woodrow Wilson School of Princeton University, and the Princeton University Computer Center for support in our effort to search out, winnow down, categorize, catalogue, and selectively annotate this list of basic writings on the modern presidency.

The project began with the work of Wesleyan University's reference librarian, Joan Jurale, who supervised a number of able undergraduate research assistants, notably Richard Goodstein and David Weber, in assembling a comprehensive collection of the citations on the presidency listed in the book and periodical indexes discussed above. The book that follows is both expanded and distilled from the document Ms. Jurale and her associates produced. We drew on further citations in works they identified and dropped much of what they found, according to the criteria noted above. Simultaneously we sought to keep track of new publications, a cascade in the case of writings ensuing from Watergate.

The enumeration of citations, cross-referencing, and setting of the bibliography in a form suitable for photo-offsetting were handled by Professor Doris Lidtke, the technical supervisor of this project, who is a computer sciences bibliographer. The authors profited from comments and suggestions by scholars such as James David Barber, James MacGregor Burns, Thomas E. Cronin, Louis Fisher, Henry F. Graff, Alonzo Hamby, Erwin Hargrove, Hugh Heclo, Douglas Kinnard, Richard Neustadt, Michael Riccards, Lester Seligman, Clement Vose, and Aaron Wildavsky, none of whom, however, is to be blamed for any inadequacies of the product. In day-to-day operations we were ably aided by Janet Berman, Ronald Franco, Bruce Olsen, Carol Roan, Elizabeth Schorske, Marion Smiley, Bonnie Tulloss, and Barbara Young. As noted, key government publications were sampled and annotated by James Fetzer, author of Chapter 2.

Fred I. Greenstein
Henry Luce Professor
of Politics, Law and Society
Princeton University

ABBREVIATIONS OF
JOURNAL TITLES

Administrative Science Quarterly	Admin. Sci Q.
American Bar Association Journal	ABAJ
American Historical Review	AHR
American Political Science Review	APSR
Annals of the American Academy of Political and Social Science	Annals
Congressional Quarterly Weekly Reports	Cong. QW Repts.
Federal Bar Journal	Fed. BJ
Journal of Politics	JP
National Journal	National J.
National Review	National R.
Political Science Quarterly	PSQ
Political Quarterly	Political Q
Potomac (Washington Post)	Potomac
Public Opinion Quarterly	POQ
Public Administration Review	PAR
Review of Politics	R. of Politics

Note: For abbreviations not listed here, see lists of abbreviations in periodical guides.

1

BASIC REFERENCE SOURCES

A. GUIDES TO RESEARCH MATERIAL

1 ABC POL SCI. ADVANCE BIBLIOGRAPHY OF CONTENTS: POLITICAL SCIENCE AND GOVERNMENT. SANTA BARBARA: AMERICAN BIBLIOGRAPHICAL CENTER, CLIO PR, 1969--.

A COMPILATION OF ARTICLE TITLES OF INTEREST TO POLITICAL SCIENTISTS. APPEARS EIGHT TIMES YEARLY. FINAL ANNUAL ISSUE PROVIDES A SUBJECT INDEX.

2 BOSTON PUBLIC LIBRARY. THE PUBLIC INTEREST AND THE RIGHT TO KNOW: ACCESS TO GOVERNMENT INFORMATION AND THE ROLE OF THE PRESS: A SELECTIVE BIBLIOGRAPHICAL GUIDE. BOSTON: 1971, PP. 59.

3 BRESSLER, N. A DESCRIPTIVE CATALOGUE OF THE PAPERS IN THE AREA OF TWENTIETH CENTURY AMERICAN STATECRAFT AND PUBLIC POLICY. PRINCETON, N.J.: PRINCETON U LIBRARY, 1972 (REVISED 1974), PP. 50.

4 BUCHANAN, W.W., AND KANELY, E.A. CUMULATIVE SUBJECT INDEX TO THE MONTHLY CATALOGUE OF UNITED STATES GOVERNMENT PUBLICATIONS, 1900-1971. WASHINGTON, D.C.: CARROLLTON PRESS, 1973-.

5 BURKE, J.G. THE MONTHLY CATALOGUE OF U.S. GOVERNMENT PUBLICATIONS: AN INTRODUCTION TO ITS USES. HAMDEN, CONN.: SHOE STRING PRESS, 1973.

6 BUSINESS PERIODICALS INDEX. NEW YORK: WILSON, 1958--.

THE SECTION ON THE PRESIDENCY IN THIS INDEX INCLUDES A MOST THOROUGH COMPILATION OF PRESIDENCY-RELATED ARTICLES FROM BUSINESS AND INTEREST GROUP PUBLICATIONS AS WELL AS POPULAR MAGAZINES. EXCELLENT ON THE PRESIDENT'S RELATIONS WITH THE PRESS AS DISCUSSED IN MEDIA TRADE JOURNALS AND ON RELATIONS WITH SPECIALIZED SEGMENTS OF THE ECONOMY.

7 CALIFORNIA NEWS INDEX. CLAREMONT: CENTER FOR CALIFORNIA PUBLIC AFFAIRS, 1970-,

INDEXES THE <u>LOS ANGELES TIMES</u>, <u>SAN DIEGO UNION</u>, <u>SACRAMENTO BEE</u>, <u>SAN FRANCISCO CHRONICLE</u>.

8 COLE, G.L. "PRESIDENTIAL LIBRARIES." <u>J LIBRARIANSHIP</u> 4 (1972): 115-129.

ON THE HISTORY OF PRESIDENTIAL PAPERS, THE DEVELOPMENT AND FUNCTIONS OF THE PRESIDENTIAL LIBRARY SYSTEM, AND POSSIBLE FUTURE DEVELOPMENTS.

9 CONGRESSIONAL QUARTERLY. <u>CQ GUIDE TO CURRENT AMERICAN GOVERNMENT</u>. WASHINGTON, D.C.. SEMI-ANNUAL 1961 TO PRESENT.

10 COOK, J.F. "'PRIVATE PAPERS' OF PUBLIC OFFICIALS." <u>AMERICAN ARCHIVIST</u> 38 (JULY 1975): 299-324.

11 DREWRY, E.B. "THE ROLE OF PRESIDENTIAL LIBRARIES." <u>MIDWEST Q</u>7:53-65 O '65.

12 FEIS, H. "SOME NOTES ON HISTORICAL RECORD-KEEPING, THE ROLE OF HISTORIANS AND THE INFLUENCE OF HISTORICAL MEMORIES DURING THE ERA OF THE SECOND WORLD WAR." IN <u>THE HISTORIAN AND THE DIPLOMAT</u>, EDITED BY F.L. LOEWENHEIM. NEW YORK: HAR-ROW, 1967: 91-121.

13 <u>GUIDE TO THE NATIONAL ARCHIVES OF THE UNITED STATES</u>. WASHINGTON: NATIONAL ARCHIVES AND RECORDS SERVICE GENERAL SERVICES ADMINISTRATION, 1974.

14 <u>INDEX TO LEGAL PERIODICALS</u>. NEW YORK: WILSON, 1888--.

THE MOST COMPREHENSIVE INDEX OF THE NUMEROUS LAW REVIEWS. ARTICLES ARE LISTED UNDER SPECIFIC PRESIDENCY-RELATED HEADINGS SUCH AS "IMPOUNDMENT," "EXECUTIVE AGREEMENTS," "IMPEACHMENT," AS WELL AS UNDER THE PRESIDENCY ITSELF.

15 <u>INDEX TO THE CHRISTIAN SCIENCE MONITOR</u>. ANN ARBOR: UNIVERSITY MICROFILMS, 1959-.

16 <u>INDEX</u>. FLINT, MICHIGAN: NEWSPAPER INDEXING CENTER, 1970-.

INDEXES THE <u>NATIONAL OBSERVER</u>.

17 JONES, H.G. "PRESIDENTIAL LIBRARIES: IS THERE A CASE FOR A NATIONAL PRESIDENTIAL LIBRARY?" <u>AMERICAN ARCHIVIST</u> 38

(JULY 1975): 325-328.

18 KAHN, H. "THE LONG-RANGE IMPLICATIONS FOR HISTORIANS AND ARCHIVISTS OF THE CHARGES AGAINST THE FRANKLIN D. ROOSEVELT LIBRARY." <u>AMER ARCH</u> 34 (JULY 1971): 265-275.

19 KIRKENDALL, R.S. "A SECOND LOOK AT PRESIDENTIAL LIBRARIES (CONFERENCE PAPER)." <u>AMER ARCH</u> 29:371-86 JL '66.

20 ----------. "PRESIDENTIAL LIBRARIES--ONE RESEARCHER'S POINT OF VIEW." <u>AMER ARCH</u> 25 (OCT 1962): 441-48.

21 <u>LIBRARY OF CONGRESS CATALOG--BOOKS: SUBJECTS</u>. WASHINGTON,D.C.: GPO, 1950--.

BOOKS ON THE PRESIDENCY UNDER "PRESIDENTS" AND INDIVIDUAL PRESIDENTS.

22 MOREHEAD, J. <u>INTRODUCTION TO UNITED STATES PUBLIC DOCUMENTS</u>. LITTLETON, COLORADO: LIBRARIES UNLIMITED, 1975.

23 <u>NEW YORK TIMES INDEX</u>. NEW YORK: N Y TIMES, 1913--.

PUBLISHED CONTINUOUSLY SINCE 1913, THIS ANNUAL INDEX IS THE MOST COMPREHENSIVE RECORD OF ANY NEWSPAPER. SINCE 1967 IT HAS BEEN EXPANDED TO INCLUDE REFERENCE ILLUSTRATIONS AND GRAPHS. SEE SECTIONS ON THE PRESIDENCY; INDIVIDUAL PRESIDENTS, PAST AND PRESENT; REFERENCES TO PRESIDENTIAL ADVISORS AND STAFF AGENCIES; AND PRESIDENCY ENTRIES UNDER "U.S. GOVERNMENT AND POLITICS."

24 <u>NEWSPAPER INDEX: CHICAGO TRIBUNE, LOS ANGELES TIMES, THE NEW ORLEANS TIMES-PICAYUNE, THE WASHINGTON POST</u>. WOOSTER, O.: BELL HOWELL, 1972 -.

PRESIDENCY-RELATED ENTRIES UNDER THE "U.S. GOVERNMENT" CATEGORY AND IN THE "PERSONAL NAMES" SECTION.

25 PATCH, B.W. "ACCESS TO OFFICIAL PAPERS AND INFORMATION." <u>EDITORIAL RESEARCH REPORTS</u> 1 (JUNE 24, 1953): 417-433.

26 <u>PUBLIC AFFAIRS INFORMATION SERVICE ANNUAL CUMULATED BULLETIN (PAIS)</u>. NEW YORK: WILSON, 1914--.

GUIDE TO SCHOLARLY PUBLIC AFFAIRS JOURNALS. SOME MATERIAL FROM THE PRESTIGE PRESS AS WELL AS SELECTED GOVERNMENT

DOCUMENTS, PAMPHLETS, AND SOME LAW REVIEW ARTICLES. MOST
PRESIDENCY ENTRIES CAN BE FOUND UNDER THE "UNITED
STATES-PRESIDENT" SECTION, IN ITS VARIOUS SUBDIVISIONS.
ALSO CHECK FOR ENTRIES ON INDIVIDUAL PRESIDENTIAL ADVISERS
AND EXECUTIVE OFFICE OF THE PRESIDENT AGENCIES.

27 READERS GUIDE TO PERIODICAL LITERATURE. NEW YORK:
WILSON, 1900 --.

INDEXES POPULAR LITERATURE NOT INCLUDED IN PAIS. SEE
"PRESIDENCY, U.S." AND INDIVIDUAL PRESIDENTS.

28 SCHMECKEBIER, L.F., AND EASTIN, R.B. GOVERNMENT
PUBLICATIONS AND THEIR USE. SECOND REVISED EDITION.
WASHINGTON, D.C.: THE BROOKINGS INSTITUTION, 1969.

29 THE NEWSBANK URBAN AFFAIRS LIBRARY. SPRING VALLEY, N.Y.:
ARCATA MICROFILM, 1971-.

INDEXES OVER 150 MAJOR NEWSPAPERS IN OVER 100 CITIES.

30 UNITED STATES CODE ANNOTATED. ST. PAUL, MINNESOTA: WEST,
1967-.

31 UNITED STATES CODE SERVICE, LAWYERS' EDITION. ROCHESTER:
LAWYERS CO-OPERATIVE PUB. CO. SAN FRANCISCO:
BANCROFT-WHITNEY, 1972-.

32 VOSE, C.E. A GUIDE TO LIBRARY SOURCES IN POLITICAL
SCIENCE. WASHINGTON, D.C.: AM POL SCI ASSOC, 1975, PP.
135.

33 ----------. "PRESIDENTIAL PAPERS AS A POLITICAL SCIENCE
CONCERN." PS WINTER 1975, PP. 8-18.

AN ESPECIALLY THOROUGH GUIDE TO THE USES OF THE LIBRARIES
AND THE LITERATURE ON THEM.

B. COLLECTIONS OF SUMMARY INFORMATION

34 ARMBRUSTER, M.E. THE PRESIDENTS OF THE UNITED STATES AND
THEIR ADMINISTRATIONS FROM WASHINGTON TO NIXON. NEW YORK:
HORIZON PRESS, 1973, PP. 378.

35 BEARD, C.A. THE PRESIDENTS IN AMERICAN HISTORY. BROUGHT
FORWARD SINCE 1948 BY WILLIAM BEARD. NEW YORK: MESSNER,
1974, PP. 205.

36 COOKE, D.E. <u>ATLAS OF THE PRESIDENTS</u>. MAPLEWOOD, N.J.: HAMMOND, 1967, PP. 93.

37 DURANT, J., AND DURANT, A. <u>PICTORIAL HISTORY OF AMERICAN PRESIDENTS</u>. 4TH REVISED ED. NEW YORK: A.S. BARNES, 1965, PP. 356.

38 FREIDEL, F. <u>OUR COUNTRY'S PRESIDENTS</u>. WASHINGTON, D.C.: NATIONAL GEOGRAPHIC SOCIETY, 1966, PP. 248. REPRINTED, 1972, PP. 258.

39 HATHAWAY, E.V. <u>THE BOOK OF AMERICAN PRESIDENTS</u>. (REPRINT OF 1933 EDITION) NEW YORK: BOOKS FOR LIBRARIES PRESS, 1970, PP. 399.

40 JENSEN, A.L. <u>THE WHITE HOUSE AND ITS THIRTY FIVE FAMILIES</u>. NEW YORK: MCGRAW, 1970, PP. 321.

41 KANE, J.N. <u>FACTS ABOUT THE PRESIDENTS</u>. NEW YORK, WILSON, 1974, PP. 407.

42 MCCONNELL, B. , AND MCCONNELL, J. <u>PRESIDENTS OF THE UNITED STATES: THE STORY OF THEIR LIVES</u>. NEW YORK: CROWELL, 1970, PP. 383.

43 SOBEL, R. <u>BIOGRAPHICAL DIRECTORY OF THE UNITED STATES EXECUTIVE BRANCH</u>. WESTPORT, CONN.: GREENWOOD, 1972, PP. 491.

44 TAYLOR, T. <u>THE BOOK OF PRESIDENTS</u>. NEW YORK: ARNO, 1972, PP. 703.

45 WHITNEY, D.C. <u>THE AMERICAN PRESIDENTS</u>. GARDEN CITY, N.Y.: DOUBLEDAY, 1975, PP. 470.

46 ----------. <u>THE GRAPHIC STORY OF THE AMERICAN PRESIDENTS</u>. ENLARGED EDITION EDITED BY T.C. JONES. CHICAGO: FERGUSON, 1975, PP.543.

47 WHO'S WHO IN AMERICAN POLITICS: A BIOGRAPHICAL DIRECTORY
    OF UNITED STATES POLITICAL LEADERS. NEW YORK: R.R.
    BOWKER, 1967-.

48 WILSON, V. THE BOOK OF THE PRESIDENTS. BROOKEVILLE,
    MARYLAND: AMERICAN HISTORY RESEARCH ASSOCIATES, 1973, PP.
    79.

    SEE ALSO 341, 631, 645, 835, 928, 1039, 1217, 2347, 2370,
    2431

2

SELECTED GOVERNMENT DOCUMENTS ON THE MODERN PRESIDENCY

James Fetzer

A. BASIC REFERENCE SOURCES

49 CODE OF FEDERAL REGULATIONS. NATIONAL ARCHIVES AND RECORDS SERVICE.

A COMPILATION OF FEDERAL REGULATIONS. PRESIDENTIAL DOCUMENTS, INCLUDING PROCLAMATIONS AND EXECUTIVE ORDERS ARE COMPILED UNDER TITLE 3 THROUGH THE 1971 ISSUE. BEGINNING WITH 1972, PRESIDENTIAL MATERIALS ARE UNDER TITLE 3A.

50 FEDERAL REGISTER. NATIONAL ARCHIVES AND RECORDS SERVICE.

CONTAINS FEDERAL REGULATIONS OF RECENT ISSUE. ESTABLISHED IN 1936, THE FEDERAL REGISTER IS ISSUED DAILY FROM TUESDAY THROUGH SATURDAY OF EVERY WEEK. INDEXES ARE ISSUED MONTHLY, QUARTERLY, AND ANNUALLY. CONTAINS PRESIDENTIAL EXECUTIVE ORDERS AND PROCLAMATIONS.

51 FOREIGN RELATIONS OF THE UNITED STATES. DEPARTMENT OF STATE.

THE PRIMARY COLLECTION OF DOCUMENTS CONCERNING THE FOREIGN POLICY OF THE UNITED STATES. VOLUMES ARE ISSUED BY YEAR AND GEOGRAPHIC AREAS. AS OF 1976 VOLUMES HAVE COVERED MATERIAL THROUGH 1949.

52 MONTHLY CATALOG OF UNITED STATES GOVERNMENT PUBLICATIONS. U.S. GOVERNMENT PRINTING OFFICE.

APPEARING AT THE END OF EACH MONTH THIS CATALOGUE CONTAINS TITLES OF THAT MONTH'S PUBLICATIONS, PRICES, AND INSTRUCTIONS FOR OBTAINING THE DOCUMENTS. INDEXED MONTHLY AND ANNUALLY. THIS IS THE INDISPENSABLE GUIDE TO GOVERNMENT PUBLICATIONS. SEE ALSO THE CUMULATIVE SUBJECT INDEX TO THE MONTHLY CATALOG, WHICH COVERS THE PERIOD 1900-1971.

53 POPULAR NAMES OF U.S. GOVERNMENT REPORTS. LIBRARY OF CONGRESS, 1970.

A CATALOG OF SIGNIFICANT GOVERNMENT REPORTS THAT HAVE BECOME KNOWN BY THE NAME OF A PERSON PROMINENTLY ASSOCIATED WITH THEM. ENTRIES LISTED BY THE POPULAR NAME WITH OFFICIAL TITLE THEN INDICATED.

54 PUBLIC PAPERS OF THE PRESIDENTS OF THE UNITED STATES. NATIONAL ARCHIVES AND RECORDS SERVICE.

INCLUDES THE MAJOR PUBLIC MESSAGES, SPEECHES, AND STATEMENTS OF THE PRESIDENT. THIS SERIES BEGAN WITH THE TRUMAN ADMINISTRATION AND IS COMPILED FOR EVERY ADMINISTRATION THEREAFTER. PUBLISHED ANNUALLY WITH EACH VOLUME COVERING ONE CALENDAR YEAR.

55 THE CONSTITUTION OF THE UNITED STATES OF AMERICA. LIBRARY OF CONGRESS, 1973.

ANALYSIS AND INTERPRETATION OF THE CONSTITUTION THROUGH THE ANNOTATION OF SUPREME COURT DECISIONS. INCLUDES SECTIONS ON ACTS OF CONGRESS AND STATE LAWS HELD UNCONSTITUTIONAL BY THE SUPREME COURT.

56 THE PRESIDENTS OF THE UNITED STATES, 1789-1962. LIBRARY OF CONGRESS, 1963.

SELECTED BIBLIOGRAPHY ON THE PRESIDENTS OF THE U.S. EMPHASIS PLACED ON BIOGRAPHIES, AUTOBIOGRAPHIES, WRITINGS OF THE PRESIDENTS, AND MEMOIRS. COMPILED BY DONALD H. MUGRIDGE.

57 UNITED STATES GOVERNMENT MANUAL. NATIONAL ARCHIVES AND RECORDS SERVICE.

OFFICIAL HANDBOOK OF THE FEDERAL GOVERNMENT. DESCRIBES THE PURPOSES AND PROGRAMS OF MOST FEDERAL DEPARTMENTS AND AGENCIES ALONG WITH LISTING THE TOP PERSONNEL. INCLUDES A SECTION ON THE EXECUTIVE OFFICE OF THE PRESIDENT. FORMERLY ENTITLED U.S. GOVERNMENT ORGANIZATION MANUAL.

58 UNITED STATES REPORTS. U.S. GOVERNMENT PRINTING OFFICE.

THE DECISIONS OF THE U.S. SUPREME COURT. ORGANIZED ACCORDING TO THE TERMS OF THE COURT.

59 UNITED STATES STATUTES AT LARGE. NATIONAL ARCHIVES AND RECORDS SERVICE.

PUBLICATION OF FEDERAL LAWS IN FINAL AND PERMANENT FORM. BEGINNING WITH 1938, EACH VOLUME CONTAINS LAWS ENACTED DURING THE PREVIOUS CALENDAR YEAR. PRE-1938 VOLUMES COVER VARYING TIME PERIODS.

60 UNITED STATES TREATIES AND OTHER INTERNATIONAL AGREEMENTS. DEPARTMENT OF STATE.

ANNUAL PUBLICATION CONTAINING TREATIES AND INTERNATIONAL AGREEMENTS, TO WHICH THE UNITED STATES IS A PARTY, THAT HAVE BEEN SIGNED, PROCLAIMED, OR BY SOME OTHER MEANS FORMALLY EXECUTED.

61 WEEKLY COMPILATION OF PRESIDENTIAL DOCUMENTS. NATIONAL ARCHIVES AND RECORDS SERVICE.

INCLUDES STATEMENTS, PRESS RELEASES, MESSAGES AND EXECUTIVE ORDERS RELEASED BY THE WHITE HOUSE. ESTABLISHED IN 1965. ANNUAL INDEX ISSUED SEPARATELY.

B. COMPENDIA

62 "RESOLVED THAT EXECUTIVE CONTROL OF FOREIGN POLICY SHOULD BE SIGNIFICANTLY CURTAILED." <u>LIBRARY OF CONGRESS HOUSE DOCUMENT 90-298</u>, 90TH CONG., 2ND SESS., 1968.

A COLLECTION OF SCHOLARLY ARTICLES AND SELECT BIBLIOGRAPHY RELATING TO THE NATIONAL COLLEGIATE DEBATE TOPIC, 1968-69. VALUABLE ANTHOLOGY OF IMPORTANT WRITINGS ON PRESIDENT'S POWER IN THE INTERNATIONAL POLITICAL ARENA.

63 "RESOLVED THAT THE FEDERAL GOVERNMENT SHOULD ADOPT PROGRAMS OF COMPULSORY WAGE AND PRICE CONTROLS." <u>LIBRARY OF CONGRESS HOUSE DOCUMENT 91-384</u>, 1970.

ARTICLES ON THE HISTORY, USES, AND RESULTS OF WAGE AND PRICE CONTROLS.

64 "RESOLVED: THAT THE POWERS OF THE PRESIDENCY SHOULD BE CURTAILED." <u>LIBRARY OF CONGRESS HOUSE DOC 97-273</u>, 93RD CONG., 2D SESS., 1974.

AN EXCELLENT COLLECTION OF SCHOLARLY ARTICLES, OTHER RELEVANT DOCUMENTS PLUS A BIBLIOGRAPHY PREPARED FOR THE INTERCOLLEGIATE DEBATE OF 1974-1975, WHICH WAS ON PRESIDENTIAL POWER.

C. MODERN PRESIDENTIAL ADMINISTRATIONS

1. FRANKLIN D. ROOSEVELT

65 "AMERICAN NEUTRALITY POLICY." <u>HOUSE, COMMITTEE ON FOREIGN AFFAIRS</u> HEARINGS, 76TH CONG., 1ST SESS., 1939.

A REVIEW OF THE AMERICAN NEUTRALITY LEGISLATION ENACTED IN THE 1930'S.

66 "NATIONAL INDUSTRIAL RECOVERY." <u>SENATE, COMMITTEE ON FINANCE</u> HEARINGS, 73RD CONG., 1ST SESS., 1933.

SENATE HEARINGS ON THE NATIONAL INDUSTRIAL RECOVERY ACT AND THE NATIONAL RECOVERY ADMINISTRATION. CONSIDERATION OF THE POWERS OF THE PRESIDENT IN RELATION TO THE ECONOMY.

67 <u>PRESIDENTIAL ORDERS PERTAINING TO NATIONAL EMERGENCY</u>. WAR INFORMATION OFFICE, 1942.

CONTAINS THE MAJOR EXECUTIVE ORDERS ISSUED BY PRESIDENT ROOSEVELT IN THE CRUCIAL PERIOD FROM JULY 1, 1939-JULY 1, 1942.

68 "REORGANIZATION OF THE FEDERAL JUDICIARY." <u>SENATE, COMMITTEE ON THE JUDICIARY</u> HEARINGS, PARTS 1-6, 75TH CONG., 1ST SESS., 1937.

SENATE CONSIDERATION OF THE ROOSEVELT "COURT-PACKING" PROPOSAL. CONTAINS SCORES OF STATEMENTS FROM WITNESSES, RANGING FROM CLOSELY REASONED LEGAL BRIEFS TO EXCITED

POLEMICS. EXTENSIVE TESTIMONY BY SUCH LEGAL SCHOLARS AS EDWARD S. CORWIN.

69 "TO PROMOTE THE DEFENSE OF THE UNITED STATES." SENATE, FOREIGN RELATIONS COMMITTEE HEARINGS. 77TH CONG., 1ST SESS., 1941.

THE SENATE HEARINGS ON THE LEND-LEASE BILL.

SEE ALSO 110, 114, 136

2. HARRY S. TRUMAN

70 "ATOMIC ENERGY ACT OF 1946." SENATE, SPECIAL COMMITTEE ON ATOMIC ENERGY HEARINGS, PARTS 1-5, 79TH CONG., 2ND SESS., 1946.

CONSIDERATION OF THE CONTROL OF ATOMIC ENERGY, THE ESTABLISHMENT OF THE ATOMIC ENERGY COMMISSION, AND THE POWERS OF THE PRESIDENT REGARDING CONTROL OF ATOMIC ENERGY.

71 "LABOR RELATIONS PROGRAM." SENATE, COMMITTEE ON LABOR AND PUBLIC WELFARE HEARINGS, PARTS 1-5, 80TH CONG., 1ST SESS., 1947.

HEARINGS ON THE TAFT-HARTLEY ACT.

72 "MILITARY ASSISTANCE PROGRAM OF 1949." SENATE, COMMITTEES ON FOREIGN RELATIONS AND ARMED SERVICES HEARINGS, 81ST CONG., 1ST SESS., 1949.

CONTAINS CONSIDERABLE DISCUSSION OF THE FOREIGN POLICY AND WAR-MAKING POWERS OF THE PRESIDENT AND THE EXECUTIVE BRANCH OF GOVERNMENT.

73 "NATIONAL DEFENSE ESTABLISHMENT (NATIONAL SECURITY ACT OF 1947)." SENATE, COMMITTEE ON ARMED SERVICES HEARINGS. PARTS 1-3, 80TH CONG., 1ST SESS., 1947.

CONGRESSIONAL CONSIDERATION OF LEGISLATION THAT LED TO THE CREATION OF THE NATIONAL SECURITY COUNCIL.

74 "NATIONAL SECURITY ACT OF 1947." HOUSE, COMMITTEE ON EXPENDITURES IN EXECUTIVE DEPARTMENTS HEARINGS, 80TH CONG., 1ST SESS., 1947.

CONGRESSIONAL CONSIDERATION OF LEGISLATION THAT LED TO THE CREATION OF THE NATIONAL SECURITY COUNCIL.

75 "NORTH ATLANTIC TREATY." SENATE, COMMITTEE ON FOREIGN RELATIONS HEARINGS, 81ST CONG., 1ST SESS., 1949.

76 "THE MILITARY SITUATION IN THE FAR EAST." SENATE, COMMITTEES ON ARMED SERVICES AND FOREIGN RELATIONS HEARINGS, 82ND CONG., 1ST SESS., 1951.

THE INVESTIGATION OF THE MACARTHUR DISMISSAL, THE AMERICAN PROSECUTION OF THE KOREAN WAR, AND U.S. POLICY IN EAST ASIA.

77 "THE STEEL SEIZURE CASE." HOUSE, HOUSE DOCUMENT-534 82ND CONG., 2ND SESS., 1952.

CONTAINS BRIEFS FOR THE GOVERNMENT AND STEEL COMPANIES FILED IN THE SUPREME COURT IN THE CASE OF YOUNGSTOWN VS. SAWYER. ALSO INCLUDES LOWER COURT AND AMICUS CURIAE BRIEFS. ALSO INCLUDES PROCEEDINGS IN THE DISTRICT COURT AND COURT OF APPEALS AS WELL AS VARIOUS AMICUS CURIAE BRIEFS.

SEE ALSO 83, 109, 135, 135, 136

3. DWIGHT D. EISENHOWER

78 "TREATIES AND EXECUTIVE AGREEMENTS." SENATE, JUDICIARY COMMITTEE HEARINGS. 82ND CONG., 2ND SESS., 1952, 83RD CONG., 1ST SESS., 1953.

CONSIDERATION OF THE PROPOSED BRICKER AMENDMENT TO THE U.S. CONSTITUTION WHICH SOUGHT TO LIMIT PRESIDENTIAL POWER IN THE MAKING OF TREATIES AND EXECUTIVE AGREEMENTS. IN ADDITION TO TESTIMONY, CONTAINS MANY EXHIBITS AND BRIEFS.

79 "U.S. POLICY IN THE MIDDLE EAST." DEPARTMENT OF STATE, 1957.

A COLLECTION OF DOCUMENTS ON THE SUEZ CRISIS OF 1956. INCLUDES GENERAL STATEMENTS OF POLICY BY U.S. OFFICIALS AND TEXTS OF MESSAGES BETWEEN THE U.S. AND THE SOVIET UNION.

SEE ALSO 83, 109, 136

4. JOHN F. KENNEDY

80 JOHN FITZGERALD KENNEDY, 1917-1963: A CHRONOLOGICAL LIST OF REFERENCES. WASHINGTON: U.S. LIBRARY OF CONGRESS, GENERAL REFERENCE AND BIBLIOGRAPHY DIVISION, 1964, PP. 68.

81 "REPORT OF THE PRESIDENT'S COMMISSION ON THE ASSASSINATION OF PRESIDENT KENNEDY." COMMISSION ON THE ASSASSINATION OF PRESIDENT KENNEDY, 1964.

THE REPORT OF THE WARREN COMMISSION CONTAINS A SUMMARY OF FINDINGS AND THE CONCLUSIONS OF THE COMMISSION. THE APPENDICES OF THE REPORT CONTAIN A LIST OF WITNESSES, A BRIEF HISTORY OF PRESIDENTIAL PROTECTION, DESCRIPTIONS OF COMMISSION PROCEDURES FOR THE TAKING OF TESTIMONY, THE AUTOPSY REPORT, AND A BIOGRAPHY OF LEE HARVEY OSWALD. ALSO SEE THE 26 VOLUMES OF HEARINGS, WHICH CONTAIN TESTIMONY TAKEN BY THE COMMISSION, REPORTS DONE FOR THE COMMISSION, AND THOUSANDS OF EXHIBITS.

82 "TRADE EXPANSION ACT OF 1962." SENATE, COMMITTEE ON

FINANCE HEARINGS, PARTS 1-3, 87TH CONG., 2ND SESS., 1962.

A WAY-STATION IN THE EXPANSION OF PRESIDENTIAL POWER IN MATTERS OF INTERNATIONAL TRADE, TRADE AGREEMENTS, AND TARIFF ADJUSTMENTS.

SEE ALSO 83, 135, 136

5. LYNDON B. JOHNSON

83 "BACKGROUND INFORMATION RELATING TO SOUTHEAST ASIA AND VIETNAM." SENATE, COMMITTEE ON FOREIGN RELATIONS COMMITTEE PRINTS, 91ST CONG., 1ST & 2ND SESS., 1969-1970.

INCLUDES A SUMMARY CHRONOLOGY OF EVENTS IN SOUTHEAST ASIA, 1948-1969, OFFICIAL DOCUMENTS OF U.S.-VIETNAM RELATIONS, STATISTICS ON TROOP STRENGTH AND NUMBER KILLED IN ACTION, 1960-1968, AND DOCUMENTS ISSUED BY NORTH VIETNAM AND THE NLF.

84 "FOREIGN ASSISTANCE ACT OF 1968: PART 1, VIETNAM." SENATE, COMMITTEE ON FOREIGN RELATIONS HEARINGS, 90TH CONG., 2ND SESS., 1968.

TESTIMONY ON VIETNAM BY SECRETARY OF STATE DEAN RUSK.

85 "SUPPLEMENTAL FOREIGN ASSISTANCE FOR FISCAL YEAR 1966 — VIETNAM." SENATE, COMMITTEE ON FOREIGN RELATIONS HEARINGS, 89TH CONG., 2ND SESS., 1966.

A CONSIDERATION OF THE EXTENT AND FUNCTION OF AMERICAN AID TO VIETNAM WITH TESTIMONY BY SECRETARY OF STATE DEAN RUSK, DAVID BELL OF AID, JAMES GAVIN, GEORGE KENNAN, AND MAXWELL TAYLOR. NUMEROUS EXHIBITS.

SEE ALSO 126, 128, 133, 134, 135, 136, 137, 138, 139

6. RICHARD M. NIXON

86 "ANALYSIS OF EXECUTIVE IMPOUNDMENT REPORTS." SENATE, COMMITTEE ON THE BUDGET COMMITTEE PRINT, 94TH CONG., 1ST SESS., 1975.

INCLUDES REPRINTS OF EIGHT REPORTS SUBMITTED BY PRESIDENT NIXON ON PROPOSED DECISIONS AND DEFERRALS.

87 "BRIEFING ON VIETNAM." SENATE, COMMITTEE ON FOREIGN RELATIONS HEARINGS, 91ST CONG., 1ST SESS., 1969.

TESTIMONY BY SECRETARY OF STATE WILLIAM ROGERS AND SECRETARY OF DEFENSE MELVIN LAIRD. CONTAINS DEPT. OF DEFENSE MEMORANDA ON DEVELOPMENTS IN VIETNAM.

88 "CONGRESS AND THE TERMINATION OF THE VIETNAM WAR." LIBRARY OF CONGRESS COMMITTEE PRINT, 93RD CONG., 1ST SESS., 1973.

89 "DR. KISSINGER'S ROLE IN WIRETAPPING." SENATE, COMMITTEE

ON FOREIGN RELATIONS HEARINGS, 93RD CONG., 2ND SESS., 1974.

INVESTIGATION OF THE ROLE OF KISSINGER IN THE WIRETAPPING OF CERTAIN GOVERNMENT OFFICIALS AND NEWSMEN. INCLUDES TESTIMONY BY KISSINGER, ALEXANDER HAIG, JR., CLARENCE KELLY, DEAN RUSK, WILLIAM SAXBE AND ELLIOT RICHARDSON. NUMEROUS MEMORANDA AND LETTERS APPENDED.

90 "FINAL REPORT." SENATE, SELECT COMMITTEE ON PRESIDENTIAL CAMPAIGN ACTIVITIES SENATE REPORT 93-981, 93RD CONG., 2ND SESS., 1974.

REPORT OF THE SO-CALLED SENATE WATERGATE COMMITTEE, CONVENED EARLY IN 1973 AND CHAIRED BY SENATOR SAM ERVIN, JR. CONTAINS CHAPTERS ON THE INVESTIGATIVE PROCEDURES OF THE COMMITTEE AND INDIVIDUAL VIEWS OF COMMITTEE MEMBERS. SEE ALSO THE 25 VOLUMES OF TESTIMONY BEFORE THE COMMITTEE.

91 "IMPEACHMENT OF RICHARD M. NIXON, PRESIDENT OF THE UNITED STATES: REPORT." HOUSE, COMMITTEE ON THE JUDICIARY 93RD CONG., 2ND SESS., 1974.

SEE ALSO THE 43 VOLUME COLLECTION OF MATERIAL DOCUMENTING THE HOUSE JUDICIARY COMMITTEE'S CONSIDERATION IN 1974 OF WHETHER TO RECOMMEND THAT THE HOUSE OF REPRESENTATIVES VOTE TO IMPEACH PRESIDENT NIXON. INCLUDES A MASSIVE "STATEMENT OF INFORMATION" ON NIXON IMPEACHMENT-RELATED MATTERS BY THE COMMITTEE STAFF AND A BRIEFER "STATEMENT OF INFORMATION SUBMITTED IN BEHALF OF PRESIDENT NIXON" (29 VOLUMES), SEVERAL VOLUMES OF TESTIMONY BY EXPERT WITNESSES ON THE FUNCTIONING OF NIXON'S WHITE HOUSE AND ON WATERGATE EVENTS (ON THE FORMER, SEE ESPECIALLY THE TESTIMONY OF ALEXANDER BUTTERFIELD). OTHER VOLUMES CONTAIN THE COMMITTEE'S TRANSCRIPTS OF PREVIOUSLY UNRELEASED TAPE RECORDED CONVERSATIONS AND ITS COMPARISONS OF ITS OWN TRANSCRIPTS WITH THOSE SUBMITTED BY THE WHITE HOUSE, VARIOUS SUMMARY VOLUMES, THE COMMITTEE'S DEBATE AND VOTES ON THE ARTICLES OF IMPEACHMENT, AS WELL AS THE FINAL REPORT OF THE COMMITTEE. A RICH TROVE OF DATA ON THE NIXON PRESIDENCY.

92 "IMPOUNDMENT OF APPROPRIATED FUNDS BY THE PRESIDENT." SENATE, AND THE JUDICIARY HEARINGS, 93RD CONG., 1ST SESS., 1973.

EXTENSIVE TESTIMONY ON EXECUTIVE IMPOUNDMENT. NUMEROUS EXHIBITS INCLUDE PROPOSED LEGISLATION, STATEMENTS AND REPORTS ISSUED BY EXECUTIVE AGENCIES AND CONGRESS, NEWS ARTICLES, AND RELEVANT LITIGATION.

93 "LEGISLATIVE PROPOSALS RELATING TO THE WAR IN SOUTHEAST ASIA." SENATE, COMMITTEE ON FOREIGN RELATIONS HEARINGS, 92ND CONG., 1ST SESS., 1971.

CONSIDERATION OF A VARIETY OF LEGISLATIVE PROPOSALS CONCERNING THE WAR IN SOUTHEAST ASIA. INCLUDED AS EXHIBITS ARE THE TEXTS OF THE PROPOSALS AND SCORES OF ARTICLES AND COMMENTARY.

94 "NOMINATION OF GERALD R. FORD TO BE VICE-PRESIDENT OF THE UNITED STATES." HOUSE, COMMITTEE ON THE JUDICIARY HEARINGS, SERIAL NO. 16, 93RD CONG., 1ST SESS., 1973.

95 "NOMINATION OF HENRY A. KISSINGER." SENATE, COMMITTEE ON FOREIGN RELATIONS HEARINGS, PARTS 1-2, 93RD CONG., 1ST SESS., 1973.

HEARINGS ON KISSINGER'S NOMINATION AS SECRETARY OF STATE. EXTENSIVE QUESTIONING BY THE COMMITTEE.

96 "NOMINATION OF RICHARD G. KLEINDIENST TO BE ATTORNEY GENERAL." SENATE, JUDICIARY COMMITTEE HEARINGS, 92ND CONG., 2ND SESS., 1972.

INCLUDES CONSIDERABLE GENERAL DISCUSSION ABOUT THE PROBLEM OF PUBLIC ACCESS TO EXECUTIVE OFFICIALS AND SPECIFIC MATERIAL ON NIXON ADMINISTRATION DECISIONS ABOUT WHETHER TO CONDUCT ANTI-TRUST PROCEEDINGS AGAINST INTERNATIONAL TELEPHONE AND TELEGRAPH.

97 "RESTORE RURAL WATER AND WASTE DISPOSAL GRANT PROGRAMS." HOUSE, COMMITTEE ON AGRICULTURE HEARINGS, 93RD CONG., 1ST SESS., 1973.

INCLUDES A CONSIDERATION OF THE EXECUTIVE IMPOUNDMENT OF APPROPRIATED FUNDS.

98 "SPECIAL PROSECUTOR." SENATE, COMMITTEE ON THE JUDICIARY HEARINGS, 93RD CONG., 1ST SESS., 1973.

SENATE INVESTIGATION OF THE DISMISSAL OF ARCHIBALD COX AS SPECIAL PROSECUTOR AND CONSIDERATION OF THE ROLE OF THE SPECIAL PROSECUTOR. TESTIMONY BY COX, ELLIOT RICHARDSON, ROBERT BORK, LEON JAWORSKI AND OTHERS.

99 "SPECIAL REPORT: UNITED STATES V. RICHARD NIXON." CONGRESS, JOINT COMMITTEE ON CONGRESSIONAL OPERATIONS COMMITTEE PRINT, 93RD CONG., 2ND SESS., 1974.

A COMPILATION OF MATERIALS OF RECORD BEFORE THE SUPREME COURT IN THE CASE U.S. VS. NIXON.. INCLUDES THE DECISION OF JUDGE SIRICA IN U.S. VS. MITCHELL, THE BRIEFS FILED BY THE PRESIDENT AND SPECIAL PROSECUTOR, THE REPLY BRIEFS OF EACH, A TRANSCRIPT OF ORAL ARGUMENT BEFORE THE COURT, AND THE FULL TEXT OF CHIEF JUSTICE BURGER'S OPINION.

100 "U.S. FOREIGN POLICY FOR THE 1970'S." LIBRARY OF CONGRESS FOR THE HOUSE COMMITTEE ON FOREIGN AFFAIRS COMMITTEE PRINT, 1971-1973.

A COMPARATIVE ANALYSIS OF PRESIDENT NIXON'S FOREIGN POLICY REPORTS TO CONGRESS.

101 "U.S. FOREIGN POLICY FOR THE 1970'S." OFFICE OF THE PRESIDENT, 1970.

A MAJOR FOREIGN POLICY STATEMENT BY THE NIXON ADMINISTRATION.

102 "VIETNAM POLICY PROPOSALS." SENATE, COMMITTEE ON FOREIGN RELATIONS HEARINGS, 91ST CONG., 2ND SESS., 1970.

CONSIDERATION OF A VARIETY OF LEGISLATIVE PROPOSALS CONCERNING THE WAR IN SOUTHEAST ASIA. INCLUDED AS EXHIBITS ARE THE TEXTS OF THE PROPOSALS AND SCORES OF ARTICLES AND COMMENTARY.

103 "WARRANTLESS WIRETAPPING AND ELECTRONIC SURVEILLANCE." SENATE, COMMITTEE ON THE JUDICIARY HEARINGS, 93RD CONG., 2ND SESS., 1974.

SURVEYS THE EXTENT AND LEGALITY OF WIRETAPPING AND ELECTRONIC SURVEILLANCE EMPLOYED BY EXECUTIVE AGENCIES. INCLUDES TESTIMONY, CORRESPONDENCE AND MEMORANDA, NEWSPAPER ARTICLES, AND RELEVANT COURT DECISIONS.

104 "WATERGATE SPECIAL PROSECUTION FORCE REPORT." U.S. DEPARTMENT OF JUSTICE, 1975.

REPORTS ON THE ACTIVITIES OF THE WATERGATE SPECIAL PROSECUTORS, INCLUDING THE STATUS OF CASES HANDLED BY THE OFFICE OF THE SPECIAL PROSECUTOR AND A DESCRIPTION OF THE SPECIAL PROSECUTOR'S RELATIONSHIP WITH OTHER AGENCIES OF THE GOVERNMENT. APPENDIX L IS AN EXCELLENT BIBLIOGRAPHY OF OFFICIAL AND UNOFFICIAL WRITINGS ON WATERGATE. OVERALL THE REPORT IS A GOOD GENERAL HISTORICAL NARRATIVE OF THE EVENTS OF WATERGATE.

105 "WITHHOLDING OF FUNDS FOR HOUSING AND URBAN DEVELOPMENT PROGRAMS." SENATE, COMMITTEE ON BANKING, HOUSING, AND URBAN AFFAIRS HEARINGS, 92ND CONG., 1ST SESS., 1971.

AN EXAMINATION OF THE NATURE AND ECONOMIC IMPACT OF PRESIDENTIAL IMPOUNDMENT OF FUNDS FOR DEPARTMENT OF HOUSING AND URBAN DEVELOPMENT PROGRAMS.

SEE ALSO 121, 122, 126, 128, 133, 137, 138, 139, 155, 157, 160

7. GERALD R. FORD

106 "SEIZURE OF THE MAYAGUEZ." HOUSE, COMMITTEE ON INTERNATIONAL RELATIONS HEARINGS, PARTS 1-2, 94TH CONG., 1ST SESS., 1975.

107 "WAR POWERS: A TEST OF COMPLIANCE." HOUSE, COMMITTEE ON INTERNATIONAL RELATIONS HEARINGS, 94TH CONG., 1ST SESS. 1975.

D. ADVISORY INSTITUTIONS AND PROCESSES

1. GENERAL GROWTH

108 "AUTHORIZATION FOR STAFF SUPPORT IN THE WHITE OFFICE." HOUSE, COMMITTEE ON THE POST OFFICE AND CIVIL SERVICE ANNUAL HEARINGS.

AN INSTRUCTIVE SOURCE OF INFORMATION ON PRESIDENTIAL CLAIMS TO NEED STAFF SUPPORT.

109 "HOOVER COMMISSION REPORTS." COMMISSION ON THE ORGANIZATION OF THE EXECUTIVE BRANCH OF GOVERNMENT 1947-1949, 1953-1955.

THE WORK OF THE TWO HOOVER COMMISSIONS CAN BE DIVIDED INTO TWO BROAD CATEGORIES: COMMISSION REPORTS CONTAINING RECOMMENDATIONS FOR REORGANIZATION OF THE EXECUTIVE AND TASK FORCE REPORTS (STAFF STUDIES MADE IN SUPPORT OF THE COMMISSION REPORTS). FOR A GENERAL OVERVIEW OF THE WORK OF THE COMMISSIONS SEE THE VOLUMES ENTITLED GENERAL MANAGEMENT OF THE EXECUTIVE BRANCH 1949 AND FINAL REPORT TO THE CONGRESS 1955.

110 "INVESTIGATION OF EXECUTIVE AGENCIES OF GOVERNMENT." SENATE, SELECT COMMITTEE TO INVESTIGATE THE EXECUTIVE AGENCIES OF THE GOVERNMENT SENATE REPORT-275, 74TH CONG., 1937.

A DETAILED INVESTIGATION OF THE EXECUTIVE BRANCH. INCLUDES A REPORT ON EXECUTIVE AGENCIES PREPARED BY THE BROOKINGS INSTITUTION ("THE BYRD REPORT").

111 "MODERNIZING THE FEDERAL GOVERNMENT." SENATE, COMMITTEE ON GOVERNMENT OPERATIONS HEARINGS, 90TH CONG., 2ND SESS., 1968.

MATERIAL ON PROPOSALS FOR REORGANIZING THE EXECUTIVE BRANCH. EXHIBITS INCLUDE COPIES OF LEGISLATIVE PROPOSALS AND OF NEWS AND SCHOLARLY ARTICLES.

112 "REORGANIZATION OF EXECUTIVE DEPARTMENTS." HOUSE, COMMITTEE ON GOVERNMENT OPERATIONS HEARINGS, 92ND CONG., 1ST & 2ND SESS., 1971-72.

DETAILED CONSIDERATION OF PROPOSALS FOR REORGANIZATION IN THE EXECUTIVE BRANCH. COPIOUS TESTIMONY BY GOVERNMENT OFFICIALS AND REPRESENTATIVES OF NON-GOVERNMENTAL ORGANIZATIONS.

113 "REPORT ON THE GROWTH OF THE EXECUTIVE OFFICE OF THE PRESIDENT." HOUSE, COMMITTEE ON THE POST OFFICE AND CIVIL SERVICE COMMITTEE PRINT, 92ND CONG., 2ND SESS., 1972.

ONE OF THE RARE STATISTICAL ANALYSES OF EOP EXPANSION.

114 "REPORT WITH SPECIAL STUDIES." PRESIDENT'S COMMITTEE ON ADMINISTRATIVE MANAGEMENT 1937.

PART 1 CONTAINS THE BROWNLOW COMMITTEE'S REPORT TO THE PRESIDENT, PROPOSING WHAT WAS TO BECOME THE EXECUTIVE OFFICE OF THE PRESIDENT. PART II INCLUDES STUDIES ON ADMINISTRATIVE MANAGEMENT AND PERSONNEL ADMINISTRATION IN THE FEDERAL SERVICE, FINANCIAL CONTROL AND ACCOUNTABILITY, THE PROBLEMS ASSOCIATED WITH FEDERAL REGULATORY COMMISSIONS, THE EXERCISE OF RULEMAKING POWER, AND THE PREPARATION OF LEGISLATION BY ADMINISTRATIVE DEPARTMENTS.

115 "TREASURY, POST OFFICE, AND EXECUTIVE OFFICE APPROPRIATIONS." SENATE, COMMITTEE ON APPROPRIATIONS ANNUAL HEARINGS.

ANNUAL HEARINGS WHICH PROVIDE INSIGHT INTO THE DETAILS OF THE ORGANIZATION OF THE WHITE HOUSE AND THE COST OF WHITE HOUSE OPERATION.

116 "TREASURY, POST OFFICE, AND EXECUTIVE OFFICE APPROPRIATIONS." HOUSE, COMMITTEE ON APPROPRIATIONS ANNUAL HEARINGS.

ANNUAL HEARINGS WHICH PROVIDE INSIGHT INTO THE DETAILS OF THE ORGANIZATION OF THE WHITE HOUSE AND THE COST OF WHITE HOUSE OPERATIONS.

2. CABINET

117 "COMMISSION ON THE ORGANIZATION OF THE GOVERNMENT FOR THE CONDUCT OF FOREIGN POLICY (MURPHY COMMISSION)." U.S. GOVERNMENT PRINTING OFFICE FINAL REPORT AND APPENDICES, VOLS. 1-7, 1975.

THE FINDINGS AND RECOMMENDATIONS OF THE COMMISSION LED BY LONG-TIME DIPLOMAT, ROBERT MURPHY, ARE PRESENTED IN THE 1975 FINAL REPORT. A SUMMARY OF THE RECOMMENDATIONS APPEARS AT THE BEGINNING OF THE REPORT. THE APPENDICES WHICH APPEARED EARLY IN 1976 CONSIST OF AN IMPRESSIVE ARRAY OF STUDIES AND ANALYTIC PAPERS SUBMITTED TO THE COMMISSION. THE STUDIES AND PAPERS COVER SUCH SUBJECTS AS POLICY PLANNING, FOREIGN ECONOMIC POLICY, MULTILATERAL DIPLOMACY, BUDGETING AND FOREIGN AFFAIRS COORDINATION, THE INTELLIGENCE FUNCTION, AND PERSONNEL FOR FOREIGN AFFAIRS. LEADING STUDENTS OF PRESIDENTIAL POLITICS, SUCH AS GRAHAM ALLISON AND ALEXANDER GEORGE HAVE CONTRIBUTED MAJOR PAPERS. AN ENTIRE APPENDIX VOLUME DEALS WITH PRESIDENTIAL-CONGRESSIONAL RELATIONS.

SEE ALSO 95, 96

3. FOREIGN AND NATIONAL SECURITY

118 "ADMINISTRATION OF NATIONAL SECURITY." SENATE, COMMITTEE ON GOVERNMENT OPERATIONS STAFF REPORTS AND HEARINGS, 89TH CONG., 1ST SESS., 1965.

AN EXAMINATION OF U.S. FOREIGN POLICY MACHINERY AND THE PERFORMANCE OF FOREIGN POLICY PERSONNEL.

119 "ORGANIZING FOR NATIONAL SECURITY." SENATE, COMMITTEE ON

GOVERNMENT OPERATIONS HEARINGS AND COMMITTEE PRINT, 3
VOLS., 86TH CONG., 2ND SESS., 1960.

THE EXTENSIVE HEARINGS OF THE JACKSON SUB-COMMITTEE ON
UNITED STATES' NATIONAL SECURITY ORGANIZATIONS. VOLUME 2
CONTAINS A BIBLIOGRAPHY ON NATIONAL SECURITY AFFAIRS,
REPORTS ON THE NATIONAL POLICY MACHINERY OF THE SOVIET
UNION AND PEOPLE'S REPUBLIC OF CHINA, AND AN
ORGANIZATIONAL HISTORY OF THE U.S. NATIONAL SECURITY
COUNCIL. VOLUME 3 INCLUDES STAFF REPORTS AND
RECOMMENDATIONS.

120 "U.S. FOREIGN ECONOMIC POLICY: IMPLICATIONS FOR THE
ORGANIZATION OF THE EXECUTIVE BRANCH." HOUSE, COMMITTEE ON
FOREIGN AFFAIRS HEARINGS, 92ND CONG., 2ND SESS., 1972.

4. BUREAU OF BUDGET/OFFICE OF MANAGEMENT AND BUDGET

121 "DISAPPROVING REORGANIZATION, PLAN NO. 2 OF 1970." HOUSE,
COMMITTEE ON GOVERNMENT OPERATIONS HOUSE REPORT 91-1066,
91ST CONG., 2ND SESS., 1970.

SUMMARIZES OBJECTIONS TO THE REORGANIZATION PLAN WHICH,
AMONG OTHER THINGS, CHANGED THE BUREAU OF THE BUDGET TO
THE OFFICE OF MANAGEMENT AND BUDGET AND THEN CONSTITUTED
THE DOMESTIC COUNCIL. APPENDIXES INCLUDE MESSAGE FROM THE
PRESIDENT TRANSMITTING THE PLAN, WHITE HOUSE RESPONSE TO
QUESTIONS ABOUT THE PLAN AND LEGAL OPINIONS EXPRESSED BY
THE ATTORNEY GENERAL, COMPTROLLER GENERAL, AND CIVIL
SERVICE COMMISSION.

122 "REORGANIZATION PLAN NO. 2 OF 1970." HOUSE, COMMITTEE ON
GOVERNMENT OPERATIONS HEARINGS, 91ST CONG., 2ND SESS.,
1970.

CONSIDERATION OF THE CREATION OF THE OFFICE OF MANAGEMENT
AND BUDGET AND THE DOMESTIC COUNCIL. INCLUDES THE
REORGANIZATION MESSAGE FROM THE PRESIDENT AND EXTENSIVE
TESTIMONY ON THE PLAN.

5. DOMESTIC COUNCIL

SEE ALSO 121, 122

6. ECONOMIC

SEE ALSO 121, 122

7. SCIENCE AND TECHNOLOGY

SEE ALSO 70

8. COMMISSIONS, TASK FORCES, ETC.

123 "PRESIDENTIAL ADVISORY COMMITTEES." HOUSE, COMMITTEE ON
GOVERNMENT OPERATIONS HEARINGS, 91ST CONG., 2ND SESS.,
1970.

9. OTHER

   SEE ALSO 110, 112, 114

10. OVERALL ADVISORY PROCESSES

   SEE ALSO 109, 110, 112, 114

11. INDIVIDUAL ADVISERS AND ADVISORY RELATIONSHIPS

   SEE ALSO 95, 96

E. PRESIDENTIAL POWERS AND RESTRAINTS

   1. GENERAL SCOPE OF PRESIDENTIAL POWER

   SEE ALSO 64, 77, 90

   2. FOREIGN RELATIONS AND WAR POWERS

124 "BACKGROUND INFORMATION ON THE USE OF UNITED STATES ARMED
    FORCES IN FOREIGN COUNTRIES." COMMITTEE ON FOREIGN
    AFFAIRS HOUSE REPORT-127, 82ND CONG., 1ST SESS., 1951.

    INCLUDES MATERIAL ON THE POWERS OF THE PRESIDENT TO
    DISPATCH TROOPS TO FOREIGN COUNTRIES.

125 "BACKGROUND INFORMATION ON THE USE OF UNITED STATES ARMED
    FORCES IN FOREIGN COUNTRIES." LIBRARY OF CONGRESS FOR THE
    HOUSE COMMITTEE ON FOREIGN AFFAIRS COMMITTEE PRINT AND
    REVISION, 94TH CONG., 1ST SESS., 1975.

    AN ANALYSIS OF THE PRESIDENT'S AND CONGRESS' POWER TO MAKE
    WAR AND DEPLOY ARMED FORCES ABROAD. INCLUDES A HISTORICAL
    LIST OF INSTANCES OF THE USE OF AMERICAN ARMED FORCES
    ABROAD.

126 "CONGRESS, THE PRESIDENT, AND WAR POWERS." HOUSE,
    COMMITTEE ON FOREIGN AFFAIRS HEARINGS, 91ST CONG., 2ND
    SESS., 1970.

    HEARINGS LEADING TO THE PASSAGE OF THE WAR POWERS
    RESOLUTION OF 1973 (PL-148). INCLUDES EXTENSIVE
    TESTIMONY, LEGISLATIVE PROPOSALS, HISTORICAL REVIEWS OF
    THE EXERCISE OF WAR POWERS, SCHOLARLY ARTICLES, AND COURT
    DECISIONS.

127 "CONGRESSIONAL OVERSIGHT OF EXECUTIVE AGREEMENTS."
    SENATE, COMMITTEE ON THE JUDICIARY HEARINGS, 92ND CONG.,
    2ND SESS., 1972.

    DISCUSSES PROVISIONS FOR CONGRESSIONAL REVIEW OF EXECUTIVE
    AGREEMENTS. INCLUDES EXTENSIVE TESTIMONY, REPRINTS, NEWS
    ARTICLES, PROPOSED LEGISLATION, LEGAL OPINIONS, AND
    SAMPLES OF EXECUTIVE AGREEMENTS. ALSO INCLUDES
    BIBLIOGRAPHY.

128 "DOCUMENTS RELATING TO THE WAR POWER OF CONGRESS, THE PRESIDENT'S AUTHORITY AS COMMANDER-IN-CHIEF, AND WAR IN INDO-CHINA." SENATE, COMMITTEE ON FOREIGN RELATIONS COMMITTEE PRINT, 91ST CONG., 2ND SESS., 1970.

FOCUSES ON THE NATIONAL COMMITMENTS RESOLUTION; INCLUDES POSITION PAPERS ON THE RESOLUTION AND ON THE LEGALITY OF THE WAR IN INDO-CHINA.

129 "EMERGENCY POWER STATUTES." SENATE, SPECIAL COMMITTEE ON THE TERMINATION OF THE NATIONAL EMERGENCY COMMITTEE PRINT, 93RD CONG., 1ST SESS., 1973.

HISTORICAL SKETCH OF THE ORIGINS OF EMERGENCY POWERS: SUMMARY OF THE STATUS OF EMERGENCY POWER STATUTES; CITATIONS OF EMERCENCY POWERS STATUTES IN FORCE.

130 "EMERGENCY POWERS CONTINUATION ACT." HOUSE, COMMITTEE ON THE JUDICIARY HEARINGS, 82ND CONG., 2ND SESS., 1952.

DISCUSSES EMERGENCY POWERS OF THE PRESIDENT. INCLUDES EXHIBITS ON THE STATUTORY BASIS OF EMERGENCY POWERS AND THE VARIOUS USES OF EMERGENCY POWERS.

131 "NATIONAL EMERGENCY." SENATE, SPECIAL COMMITTEE ON THE TERMINATION OF THE NATIONAL EMERGENCY HEARINGS, PARTS 1-3, 93RD CONG., 1ST SESS., 1973.

INCLUDES THE VIEWS OF FORMER ATTORNEYS GENERAL AND CONSIDERATION OF CONSTITUTIONAL QUESTIONS CONCERNING EMERGENCY POWERS.

132 "POWERS OF THE PRESIDENT AS COMMANDER IN CHIEF OF THE ARMY AND THE NAVY OF THE UNITED STATES" LIBRARY OF CONGRESS, 1956.

133 "THE WAR POWERS RESOLUTION: RELEVANT DOCUMENTS, CORRESPONDENCE, AND REPORTS." HOUSE, COMMITTEE ON INTERNATIONAL RELATIONS COMMITTEE PRINT, 94TH CONG., 1ST SESS., 1975.

134 "U.S. COMMITMENTS TO FOREIGN POWERS." SENATE, COMMITTEE ON FOREIGN RELATIONS HEARINGS, 90TH CONG., 1ST SESS., 1967.

AN EXTENSIVE DISCUSSION OF THE FOREIGN POLICY POWERS OF THE PRESIDENT AND THE CONGRESS.

135 "UNITED STATES SECURITY AGREEMENTS AND COMMITMENTS." SENATE, COMMITTEE ON FOREIGN RELATIONS HEARINGS, PARTS 1-10, 91ST CONG., 1ST, 2ND SESS.,1969-1970.

AN EXTENSIVE REVIEW AND INVESTIGATION OF U.S. COMMITMENTS ABROAD. EMPHASIS ON AMERICAN COMMITMENTS IN ASIA AND THE

FOREIGN POLICY POWERS OF THE PRESIDENT.

136 "UNITED STATES-VIETNAM RELATIONS, 1945-1967." HOUSE, COMMITTEE ON ARMED SERVICES COMMITTEE PRINT, BOOKS 1-12, 92ND CONG., 1ST SESS., 1971.

THE FAMOUS PENTAGON PAPERS. BOOKS 1-7 CONTAIN THE DEPARTMENT OF DEFENSE REPORT ON THE ORIGINS AND DEVELOPMENT OF AMERICAN INVOLVEMENT IN VIETNAM. BOOKS 8-12 CONSIST OF A COLLECTION OF U.S. GOVERNMENT DOCUMENTS ON THE DEVELOPMENT OF THE AMERICAN COMMITMENT IN VIETNAM. THE DOCUMENTS ARE ORGANIZED CHRONOLOGICALLY WITHIN EACH PRESIDENTIAL ADMINISTRATION. SEE ARTICLES BY PROFESSORS KAHIN AND WESTERFIELD DISCUSSING THE BIBLIOGRAPHICAL STATUS OF THE PENTAGON PAPERS IN THEIR VARIOUS EDITIONS, AS WELL AS THE PERIODIC DECLASSIFICATION OF FURTHER VOLUMES IN THIS "OFFICIAL" GPO SERIES.

137 "WAR POWERS LEGISLATION." SENATE, COMMITTEE ON FOREIGN RELATIONS HEARINGS, 93RD CONG., 1ST SESS., 1973.

HEARING LEADING TO THE PASSAGE OF THE WAR POWERS RESOLUTION OF 1973 (PL-148). INCLUDES EXTENSIVE TESTIMONY, LEGISLATIVE PROPOSALS, HISTORICAL REVIEWS OF THE EXERCISE OF WAR POWERS, SCHOLARLY ARTICLES, AND COURT DECISIONS.

138 "WAR POWERS LEGISLATION." SENATE, COMMITTEE ON FOREIGN RELATIONS HEARINGS, 92ND CONG., 1ST SESS. 1971.

HEARING LEADING TO THE PASSAGE OF THE WAR POWERS RESOLUTION OF 1973 (PL-148). INCLUDES EXTENSIVE TESTIMONY, LEGISLATIVE PROPOSALS, HISTORICAL REVIEWS OF THE EXERCISE OF WAR POWERS, SCHOLARLY ARTICLES, AND COURT DECISIONS.

139 "WAR POWERS." HOUSE, COMMITTEE ON FOREIGN AFFAIRS HEARINGS, 93RD CONG., 1ST SESS., 1973.

HEARING LEADING TO THE PASSAGE OF THE WAR POWERS RESOLUTION OF 1973 (PL-148). INCLUDES EXTENSIVE TESTIMONY, LEGISLATIVE PROPOSALS, HISTORICAL REVIEWS OF THE EXERCISE OF WAR POWERS, SCHOLARLY ARTICLES, AND COURT DECISIONS.

SEE ALSO 51, 60, 62, 65, 69, 72, 73, 74, 75, 76, 78, 82, 83, 84, 85, 87, 88, 89, 93, 95, 100, 102, 106, 107, 117, 118, 119, 120, 148, 150, 151

3. VETO AND LAW-MAKING POWERS

140 "CONSTITUTIONALITY OF THE PRESIDENT'S 'POCKET VETO' POWER." SENATE, COMMITTEE ON THE JUDICIARY HEARINGS, 92ND CONG., 1ST SESS., 1971.

141 "PRESIDENTIAL VETOES." SENATE, LIBRARY 1969.

PRESIDENTIAL VETOES, 1789-1968. A RECORD OF BILLS VETOED AND SUBSEQUENT ACTION TAKEN BY THE SENATE AND HOUSE OF REPRESENTATIVES.

4. EXECUTIVE ORDERS AND RULE MAKING

142 "EXECUTIVE ORDERS AND PROCLAMATIONS." HOUSE, COMMITTEE ON GOVERNMENT OPERATIONS COMMITTEE PRINT, 85TH CONG., 1ST SESS., 1957.

SEE ALSO 67

5. APPOINTMENT AND DISCHARGE

SEE ALSO 68

6. EXECUTIVE PRIVILEGE, SECRECY, CONFIDENTIALITY

143 "AVAILABILITY OF INFORMATION TO CONGRESS." HOUSE, COMMITTEE ON GOVERNMENT OPERATIONS HEARINGS, 93RD CONG., 1ST SESS., 1973.

CONGRESSIONAL CONSIDERATION OF HOW BEST TO OBTAIN INFORMATION FROM THE WHITE HOUSE AND EXECUTIVE AGENCIES.

144 "EXECUTIVE CLASSIFICATION OF INFORMATION." HOUSE, COMMITTEE ON FOREIGN AFFAIRS HOUSE REPORT 93-221, 93RD CONG., 1ST SESS., 1973.

SUMMARIZES THE RESULTS OF STAFF AND GENERAL ACCOUNTING OFFICE STUDIES OF THE EXISTING CLASSIFICATION PRACTICES AND PROVIDES A HISTORICAL REVIEW OF THE DEVELOPMENT OF THESE PRACTICES.

145 "EXECUTIVE PRIVILEGE." SENATE, COMMITTEE ON THE JUDICIARY HEARINGS, 86TH CONG., 1ST SESS., 1959.

HEARINGS ON THE POWER OF ' THE PRESIDENT AND HIS SUBORDINATES TO WITHHOLD INFORMATION FROM THE CONGRESS. INCLUDES SCHOLARLY ARTICLES, PERTINENT COURT DECISIONS, FEDERAL REGULATIONS, AND LEGAL OPINIONS BY THE DEPARTMENT OF JUSTICE.

146 "EXECUTIVE PRIVILEGE, SECRECY IN GOVERNMENT, AND FREEDOM OF INFORMATION." SENATE, COMMITTEE ON GOVERNMENT OPERATIONS; SENATE, COMMITTEE ON THE JUDICIARY VOLS. 1-3, HEARINGS, 93RD CONG., 1ST SESS., 1973.

EXTENSIVE HEARINGS ON TOPIC. SUPPORTING VOLUME 3 CONSISTS OF LAW REVIEW ARTICLES, STATEMENTS OF LEGAL SCHOLARS, PRESIDENTIAL STATEMENTS, COURT DECISIONS, AND CONGRESSIONAL REPORTS.

147 "FREEDOM OF INFORMATION AND SECRECY IN GOVERNMENT." SENATE, COMMITTEE ON THE JUDICIARY HEARINGS, 85TH CONG., 2ND SESS., 1958.

HEARINGS ON THE POWER OF THE PRESIDENT AND HIS SUBORDINATES TO WITHHOLD INFORMATION FROM THE CONGRESS. INCLUDES SCHOLARLY ARTICLES, PERTINENT COURT DECISIONS, FEDERAL REGULATIONS, AND LEGAL OPINIONS BY THE DEPARTMENT OF JUSTICE.

148 "SECURITY CLASSIFICATION AS A PROBLEM IN THE CONGRESSIONAL ROLE IN FOREIGN POLICY." LIBRARY OF CONGRESS FOR THE SENATE COMMITTEE ON FOREIGN RELATIONS COMMITTEE PRINT, 92ND CONG., 1ST SESS., 1971.

149 "THE RIGHT OF CONGRESS TO OBTAIN INFORMATION FROM THE EXECUTIVE." HOUSE, COMMITTEE ON GOVERNMENT OPERATIONS STAFF REPORT, 84TH CONG., 1ST SESS., 1956.

150 "TRANSMITTAL OF DOCUMENTS FROM THE NATIONAL SECURITY COUNCIL TO THE JOINT CHIEFS OF STAFF." SENATE, COMMITTEE ON ARMED SERVICES HEARINGS, PARTS 1-3. 93RD CONG., 2ND SESS., 1974.

A STUDY OF INSTANCES OF SUCH TRANSMITTALS THROUGH FORMAL AND INFORMAL CHANNELS.

151 "TRANSMITTAL OF EXECUTIVE AGREEMENTS TO CONGRESS." SENATE, COMMITTEE ON FOREIGN RELATIONS HEARINGS, 92ND CONG., 1ST SESS., 1971.

152 "U.S. GOVERNMENT INFORMATION POLICIES AND PRACTICES." HOUSE, COMMITTEE ON GOVERNMENT OPERATIONS HEARINGS, 92ND CONG., 1ST & 2ND SESS., 1971-72.

INCLUDES MATERIAL ON THE PENTAGON PAPERS CASE, THE ADMINISTRATION AND OPERATION OF THE FREEDOM OF INFORMATION ACT, SECURITY CLASSIFICATION PROBLEMS AND CONGRESSIONAL AND PUBLIC ACCESS TO INFORMATION FROM EXECUTIVE AGENCIES.

SEE ALSO 96, 99, 127

7. MANAGEMENT OF THE ECONOMY

153 "BUDGET CONTROL ACT OF 1973." HOUSE, COMMITTEE ON RULES HEARINGS, 93RD CONG., 1ST SESS., 1973.

INCLUDES THE TEXT OF H.R. 7130, ESTABLISHING BUDGET COMMITTEES FOR THE HOUSE AND SENATE AND TESTIMONY BY MEMBERS OF CONGRESS. THE CONGRESSIONAL BUDGET COMMITTEES AND OFFICE ARE DESIGNED TO PROVIDE CONGRESS WITH BUDGETING RESOURCES COMPARABLE TO THOSE OF THE PRESIDENT (E.G. OMB, DOMESTIC COUNCIL).

154 "COMPTROLLER GENERAL'S OPINION OF THE LEGALITY OF EXECUTIVE IMPOUNDMENT OF APPROPRIATED FUNDS." SENATE,

COMMITTEE ON THE JUDICIARY COMMITTEE PRINT, 93RD CONG., 2ND SESS., 1974.

155 "EXECUTIVE IMPOUNDMENT OF APPROPRIATED FUNDS." SENATE, COMMITTEE ON THE JUDICIARY HEARINGS, 92ND CONG., 1ST SESS., 1971.

156 "FEDERAL BUDGET CONTROL BY THE CONGRESS." SENATE, COMMITTEE ON RULES AND ADMINISTRATION HEARINGS, 93RD CONG., 2ND SESS., 1974.

HEARINGS ON THE REFORM OF CONGRESSIONAL HANDLING OF THE FEDERAL BUDGET, INCLUDING THE ESTABLISHMENT OF HOUSE AND SENATE BUDGET COMMITTEES.

157 "IMPOUNDMENT REPORTING AND REVIEW." HOUSE, COMMITTEE ON RULES HEARINGS, PARTS 1-2, 93RD CONG., 1ST SESS., 1973.

CONSIDERATION OF HOW TO LIMIT PRESIDENTIAL IMPOUNDMENT OF APPROPRIATED FUNDS. INCLUDES TEXT OF H.R. 8480, TESTIMONY OF ROY ASH, DIRECTOR OF THE OFFICE OF MANAGEMENT AND BUDGET, AND TESTIMONY BY NUMEROUS MEMBERS OF CONGRESS.

158 "IMPROVING CONGRESSIONAL BUDGET CONTROL." CONGRESS, JOINT STUDY COMMITTEE ON BUDGET CONTROL HEARINGS, HOUSE REPORT -747, 93RD CONG., 1ST SESS., 1973.

INCLUDES TESTIMONY BY FORMER OMB DIRECTOR, CHARLES SCHULTZE, ARTHUR BURNS OF THE FEDERAL RESERVE BOARD, ELMER STAATS OF THE GENERAL ACCOUNTING OFFICE, AND INTERESTED MEMBERS OF CONGRESS.

159 "IMPROVING CONGRESSIONAL CONTROL OF THE BUDGET." SENATE, COMMITTEE ON GOVERNMENT OPERATIONS HEARINGS, PARTS 1-3, 93RD CONG., 1ST SESS., 1973.

IN ADDITION TO TESTIMONY AND FORMAL STATEMENTS, INCLUDES STAFF MEMORANDA AND REPORTS, TEXT OF PROPOSED LEGISLATION, COMMENTS FROM FEDERAL AGENCIES, AND EXCERPTS FROM ARTICLES AND BOOKS ON FEDERAL BUDGET CONTROL.

160 "PRESIDENTIAL IMPOUNDMENT OF CONGRESSIONALLY APPROPRIATED FUNDS." HOUSE, COMMITTEE ON GOVERNMENT OPERATIONS COMMITTEE PRINT, 93RD CONG., 2ND SESS., 1974.

AN ANALYSIS OF COURT DECISIONS CONCERNING THE IMPOUNDMENT OF FUNDS.

161 "PROHIBITING WITHHOLDING OR IMPOUNDMENT OF APPROPRIATIONS." HOUSE, COMMITTEE ON GOVERNMENT OPERATIONS HEARINGS, 85TH CONG., 2ND SESS., 1958.

SEE ALSO 63, 66, 71, 77, 82, 86, 92, 97, 105

8. EXECUTIVE ORGANIZATION AND REORGANIZATION

SEE ALSO 111, 112, 113, 121, 122

9. TENURE IN OFFICE

162 "SELECTED MATERIALS ON THE TWENTY-FIFTH AMENDMENT." SENATE, COMMITTEE ON THE JUDICIARY COMMITTEE PRINT, 93RD CONG., 1ST SESS., 1973.

HOUSE AND SENATE REPORTS ON THE LEGISLATION LEADING TO THE CONGRESSIONAL APPROVAL OF THE TWENTY-FIFTH AMENDMENT PLUS SEVERAL SCHOLARLY ARTICLES.

10. IMPEACHMENT

163 "IMPEACHMENT: SELECTED MATERIALS." HOUSE, COMMITTEE ON THE JUDICIARY COMMITTEE PRINT, 93RD CONG., 1ST SESS., 1973.

INCLUDES SELECTED EXAMPLES OF ARTICLES OF IMPEACHMENT VOTED BY THE HOUSE OF REPRESENTATIVES OVER THE YEARS, PROCEEDINGS OF THE SENATE IN THE TRIAL OF ANDREW JOHNSON, THE REPORT OF THE COMMITTEE APPOINTED TO INVESTIGATE THE ACTIVITIES OF JOHN C. CALHOUN WHILE SECRETARY OF WAR, AND SELECTED SCHOLARLY ARTICLES ON THE POWER OF IMPEACHMENT.

164 "LEGAL ASPECTS OF IMPEACHMENT." DEPARTMENT OF JUSTICE PARTS 1-3, 1974.

WORKING PAPERS PREPARED BY THE JUSTICE DEPARTMENT OFFICE OF LEGAL COUNSEL. INCLUDES DISCUSSION OF WHAT CONSTITUTES AN IMPEACHABLE OFFENSE, A HISTORY OF CONSTITUTIONAL PROVISIONS RELATING TO IMPEACHMENT, AND STATEMENTS MADE AT VARIOUS TIMES IN AMERICAN HISTORY ABOUT EXECUTIVE PRIVILEGE, IMPEACHMENT, AND JUDICIAL REVIEW OF IMPEACHMENT CONVICTIONS.

165 "THE LAW OF IMPEACHMENT." DEPARTMENT OF JUSTICE PARTS 1-2, 1974.

WORKING PAPERS PREPARED BY THE JUSTICE DEPARTMENT OFFICE OF LEGAL COUNSEL. INCLUDES DISCUSSION OF WHAT CONSTITUTES AN IMPEACHABLE OFFENSE, A HISTORY OF CONSTITUTIONAL PROVISIONS RELATING TO IMPEACHMENT, AND STATEMENTS MADE AT VARIOUS TIMES IN AMERICAN HISTORY ABOUT EXECUTIVE PRIVILEGE, IMPEACHMENT, AND JUDICIAL REVIEW OF IMPEACHMENT CONVICTIONS.

SEE ALSO 91

11. SUCCESSION

SEE ALSO 162

F. OTHER

166 "A REPORT ON SIMULTANEOUS TELEVISION NETWORK COVERAGE OF PRESIDENTIAL ADDRESSES TO THE NATION" (BY DENIS S. RUTKUS). THE LIBRARY OF CONGRESS CONGRESSIONAL RESEARCH

SERVICE, 1976, PP. 20.

167 COMPTROLLER GENERAL. PROTECTION OF THE PRESIDENT AT KEY BISCAYNE AND SAN CLEMENTE (WITH INFORMATION ON PROTECTION OF PAST PRESIDENTS). COMPTROLLER GENERAL, 1973.

168 "CONGRESS AND MASS COMMUNICATIONS." LIBRARY OF CONGRESS FOR THE JOINT COMMITTEE ON CONGRESSIONAL OPERATIONS 1974.

ON THE IMBALANCE BETWEEN EXECUTIVE AND LEGISLATIVE MASS COMMUNICATIONS CAPABILITIES. CONSIDERATION OF VARIOUS WAYS IN WHICH CONGRESS MIGHT BETTER PUBLICIZE ITS ACTIVITIES.

169 "COURT PROCEEDINGS AND ACTIONS OF VITAL INTEREST TO THE CONGRESS." CONGRESS, JOINT COMMITTEE ON CONGRESSIONAL OPERATIONS COMMITTEE PRINT, 94TH CONG., 1ST SESS., 1975.

MATERIAL BEARING UPON THE CONGRESSIONAL-EXECUTIVE BRANCH RELATIONSHIP. CONTAINS REPORTS ON THE STATUS OF COURT PROCEEDINGS, CASE BRIEFS, AND THE TEXTS OF DECISIONS. STUDENTS OF THE PRESIDENCY SHOULD BE AWARE OF THE CONTINUING APPEARANCE OF THESE PRINTS, WHICH FREQUENTLY INCLUDE SUCH FUGITIVE MATERIAL AS LOWER COURT DECISIONS, ORAL ARGUMENT TRANSCRIPTS, AND THE FULL ARRAY OF BRIEFS SUBMITTED IN CONNECTION WITH MAJOR COURT DECISIONS.

170 "EXTENT OF THE CONTROL OF THE EXECUTIVE BY THE CONGRESS OF THE UNITED STATES." HOUSE, COMMITTEE ON GOVERNMENT OPERATIONS COMMITTEE PRINT, 87TH CONG., 2ND SESS., 1962.

3

COMPENDIA

A. GENERAL COMPENDIA

171 BACH, S., AND SULZNER, G.T., EDS. <u>PERSPECTIVES ON THE PRESIDENCY</u>. MASSACHUSETTS: D.C. HEATH AND COMPANY, 1974, PP. 411.

ONE OF THE FEW ANTHOLOGIES THAT CONTAIN FULL VERSIONS OF REPRINTED AND ORIGINAL SCHOLARLY ARTICLES, INCLUDING RECENT REEVALUATIONS OF THE PRESIDENCY.

172 CORNWELL, E.E. <u>THE AMERICAN PRESIDENCY: VITAL CENTER</u>. CHICAGO: SCOTT,FORESMAN, 1966, PP. 166.

NOW DATED BUT STILL FASCINATING ANTHOLOGY COMBINING HISTORICAL DOCUMENTS AND SCHOLARLY WRITINGS, INCLUDING SOME USEFUL CONTRIBUTIONS WRITTEN FOR THE ANTHOLOGY. AMONG THE HISTORICAL DOCUMENTS, CORNWELL PRINTS PREVIOUSLY UNPUBLISHED VERBATIM PRESIDENTIAL PRESS CONFERENCES GOING BACK TO WILSON.

173 DUNN, C.W., ED. <u>THE FUTURE OF THE AMERICAN PRESIDENCY</u>. MORRISTOWN, NEW JERSEY: GENERAL LEARNING PRESS, 1975, PP. 363.

A COLLECTION OF BRIEF, POPULARLY WRITTEN ARTICLES ON DIFFERENT FACETS OF THE MODERN PRESIDENCY BY SCHOLARS, JOURNALISTS, AND PUBLIC SERVANTS.

174 HAIGHT, D.E., AND JOHNSTON, L.D., EDS. <u>THE PRESIDENT, ROLES AND POWERS</u>. CHICAGO: RAND MCNALLY, 1965, PP. 400.

175 HIRSCHFIELD, R.S. <u>THE POWER OF THE PRESIDENCY</u>. CHICAGO: ALDINE, 2ND ED., 1973, PP. 395.

A GENERAL COLLECTION.

176 JOHNSON, D.B., AND WALKER, J.L. <u>THE DYNAMICS OF THE AMERICAN PRESIDENCY</u>. NEW YORK: WILEY, 1964, PP. 355.

STRESSES HISTORICAL DOCUMENTS AND EXCERPTS FROM BOOKS RATHER THAN UNEXCERPTED SCHOLARLY STUDIES.

177 POLSBY, N.W., ED. <u>THE MODERN PRESIDENCY</u>. NEW YORK: RANDOM HOUSE, 1973, PP. 236.

THE PERSONAL POLITICAL "STYLES" OF EACH PRESIDENT FROM FDR

THROUGH NIXON AS DESCRIBED BY JOURNALISTS WHO COVERED THEM. (THE FDR EXAMPLE IS BY HISTORIAN ARTHUR SCHLESINGER, JR.).

178 RANKIN, R.S., ED. "THE PRESIDENCY IN TRANSITION: A SYMPOSIUM." JP 11 (FEB 1949): WHOLE ISSUE.

179 ROBERTS, C., ED. HAS THE PRESIDENT TOO MUCH POWER? NEW YORK: HARPER'S MAGAZINE PRESS, 1974, PP. 257.

THE PROCEEDINGS OF A CONFERENCE FOR JOURNALISTS SPONSORED BY THE WASHINGTON JOURNALISM CENTER, OCTOBER 15-18, 1973.

180 THOMAS, N.C., ED. THE PRESIDENCY IN CONTEMPORARY CONTEXT. NEW YORK: DODD, MEAD, 1975, PP. 348.

ANTHOLOGY INCLUDING ORIGINAL CONTRIBUTIONS.

181 TUGWELL, R.G., AND CRONIN, T.E., ED. THE PRESIDENCY REAPPRAISED. NEW YORK: PRAEGER, 1974, PP. 312.

"REVISIONIST" ESSAYS REFLECTING ON THE PRESIDENCY IN THE LIGHT OF VIETNAM AND WATERGATE.

182 WILDAVSKY, A., ED. PERSPECTIVES ON THE PRESIDENCY. BOSTON: LITTLE, BROWN, 1975, PP. 539.

COMPARABLE TO BACH AND SULZNER IN ITS INCLUSION OF SCHOLARLY MATERIAL, MUCH OF IT REEVALUATING CONVENTIONAL WISDOM ABOUT THE PRESIDENCY.

183 ----------. THE PRESIDENCY. BOSTON: LITTLE, BROWN, 1969, PP. 795.

A COMPREHENSIVE SCHOLARLY ANTHOLOGY ATTEMPTING TO ASSEMBLE WHAT THE EDITOR VIEWED AS THE MOST IMPORTANT WRITINGS ON THE PRESIDENCY. INCLUDES ORIGINAL CONTRIBUTIONS.

SEE ALSO 62

B. SPECIALIZED COMPENDIA

SEE ALSO 64, 211, 213, 216, 328, 331, 337, 338, 340, 418, 468, 641, 642, 924, 925, 926, 929, 960, 991, 993, 1003, 1043, 1384, 1411, 1412, 1419, 1433, 1450, 1500, 1590, 1600, 1604, 1790, 1945, 1947, 2076, 2153, 2253

4

GENERAL DISCUSSIONS OF
THE PRESIDENCY

184 ANDREWS, W.G. "THE PRESIDENCY, CONGRESS, AND CONSTITUTIONAL THEORY." IN PERSPECTIVES ON THE PRESIDENCY. EDITED BY A. WILDAVSKY, BOSTON: LITTLE, BROWN, 1975: 24-45.

A REVIEW OF SCHOLARS' SHIFTING VALUE JUDGMENTS OVER THE YEARS AS TO WHICH BRANCH OF GOVERNMENT IS FAVORED AS A SOURCE OF LEADERSHIP INITIATIVE, DEPENDING ON THE WRITERS' EVALUATIONS OF THE SHIFTING SUBSTANTIVE POLICIES FAVORED BY EACH BRANCH.

185 BACH, S., AND SULZNER, G.T. "INTRODUCTION." IN PERSPECTIVES ON THE PRESIDENCY. EDITED BY S. BACH AND G.T. SULZNER, LEXINGTON, MASS.: HEATH, 1974, PP. 1-11.

THREE GENERAL "MODELS," ALL OF THEM IMPERFECT, ARE RELEVANT TO RESTRAINING PRESIDENTIAL AUTOCRACY--RESTRAINT OF PRESIDENTS BY CITIZENS, BY OTHER POLITICAL LEADERS, AND BY THEMSELVES.

186 BELL, J. THE PRESIDENCY: OFFICE OF POWER. BOSTON: ALLYN AND BACON, 1967, PP. 182.

A GENERAL DISCUSSION OF THE PRESIDENCY BY A WASHINGTON JOURNALIST, WITH A FOREWORD BY SENATOR EVERETT M. DIRKSEN.

187 ----------. THE SPLENDID MISERY: THE STORY OF THE PRESIDENCY AND POWER POLITICS AT CLOSE RANGE. GARDEN CITY, N.Y.: DOUBLEDAY, 1960, PP. 474.

188 BINKLEY, W.E. THE MAN IN THE WHITE HOUSE: HIS POWERS AND DUTIES. BALTIMORE: JOHNS HOPKINS, 1958, PP. 310.

A HISTORICALLY ORIENTED ACCOUNT OF THE EVOLUTION OF THE PRESIDENCY, UPDATING BINKLEY'S 1937 BOOK.

189 ----------. THE POWERS OF THE PRESIDENT: PROBLEMS OF AMERICAN DEMOCRACY. GARDEN CITY, N.Y.: DOUBLEDAY, 1937, PP. 332.

190 BROWN, STEWART. THE AMERICAN PRESIDENCY: LEADERSHIP, PARTISANSHIP, AND POPULARITY. NEW YORK: MACMILLAN, 1966, PP. 279.

THE PRESIDENCY DISCUSSED VIA HISTORICAL CASE STUDIES OF PRESIDENTIAL LEADERSHIP.

191 BROWNLOW, L. THE PRESIDENT AND THE PRESIDENCY. CHICAGO: PUBLIC ADMINISTRATION SERVICE, 1949, PP. 137.

A REFLECTIVE WORK BY THE JOURNALIST-PUBLIC ADMINISTRATOR WHO HEADED THE PRESENT EXECUTIVE OFFICE OF THE PRESIDENT. BROWNLOW DRAWS EXTENSIVELY ON PERSONAL RECOLLECTIONS IN DISCUSSION OF THE NATURE OF THE PRESIDENCY, THE SELECTION OF PRESIDENTS, WHAT THE PUBLIC EXPECTS OF PRESIDENTS, AND THE LIMITATIONS OF WHAT PRESIDENTS CAN DO AS WELL AS THE RESOURCES AVAILABLE TO THEM.

192 BURNS, J.M. PRESIDENTIAL GOVERNMENT: THE CRUCIBLE OF LEADERSHIP. BOSTON: HOUGHTON MIFFLIN, 1966, PP. 366.

SETS FORTH THREE "MODELS" OF PRESIDENTIAL GOVERNMENT BASED ON THE THEORIES AND PRACTICES OF ALEXANDER HAMILTON, JAMES MADISON AND THOMAS JEFFERSON. THE AUTHOR PREFERS THE JEFFERSONIAN MODEL, WHICH ENTAILS PRESIDENTIAL ACTIVISM BASED ON THE PRESIDENT'S LEADERSHIP OF HIS PARTY. SUCH AN APPROACH REQUIRES THAT THE PRESIDENT BUILD A POPULAR MAJORITY AND HENCE BOTH AUGMENTS HIS POLICY-MAKING POTENTIAL AND RESTRAINS HIM FROM EXCESS USE OF POWER BY REQUIRING THAT HE CONTINUE TO MAINTAIN PUBLIC SUPPORT.

193 CALIFANO, J.A. A PRESIDENTIAL NATION. NEW YORK: NORTON, 1975, PP. 338.

GENERAL BOOK ON THE NEED FOR AN ACTIVIST PRESIDENCY KEPT RESPONSIBLE BY STRONG COUNTERVAILING INSTITUTIONS, SUCH AS CONGRESS. CALIFANO, JOHNSON'S KEY DOMESTIC POLICY AIDE, OFTEN ILLUSTRATES HIS ABSTRACT ASSERTIONS WITH EXAMPLES FROM HIS OWN WORK IN THE WHITE HOUSE.

194 COMMAGER, H.S. THE DEFEAT OF AMERICA: PRESIDENTIAL POWER AND THE NATIONAL CHARACTER. NEW YORK: SIMON AND SCHUSTER, SECOND EDITION, 1975.

A LIBERAL DEFENDER OF THE "STRONG PRESIDENCIES" INDICATING HIS DISMAY IN PRESIDENTIAL BEHAVIOR IN THE LATE 1960'S AND EARLY 1970'S.

195 COOKE, J.E., ED. THE FEDERALIST. MIDDLETOWN, CONN.:WES U PR, 1961, PP. 672.

AN AUTHORITATIVE EDITION. THE PAPERS ON THE PRESIDENCY ARE NUMBERS 67 THROUGH 77.

196 CORWIN, E.S. PRESIDENTIAL POWER AND THE CONSTITUTION. EDITED BY R. LOSS, ITHACA: CORNELL U PR, 1976, PP. 224.

COLLECTION OF 12 ARTICLES BY CORWIN, COMPOSED FROM 1917 THROUGH 1956, DEALING WITH THE DEVELOPMENT OF PRESIDENTIAL POWER UNDER WILSON, FDR, AND TRUMAN AND WITH HIS OWN CONCEPTION OF LIMITED CONSTITUTIONAL GOVERNMENT. EDITOR'S INTRODUCTION CONTRASTS CORWIN'S WORK WITH THE GENERAL RUN OF PRESIDENTIAL STUDIES PRIOR TO NIXON AND SUGGESTS THAT

IT "CAN ASSIST THE RECOVERY OF A STANDARD EXTERNAL TO PRESIDENTS AND THEIR QUEST FOR POWER." EDITION ALSO LISTS ADDITIONS TO THE MASON-GARVEY BIBLIOGRAPHY OF CORWIN'S WRITINGS.

197 ----------. THE PRESIDENT, OFFICE AND POWERS, 1787-1957: HISTORY AND ANALYSIS OF PRACTICE AND OPINION. NEW YORK: NEW YORK UNIVERSITY PRESS, 1957, PP. 519.

THE FINAL EDITION OF A WORK BY A MAJOR CONSTITUTIONAL SCHOLAR WHO UNLIKE OTHER ACADEMIC WRITERS OF THE TIME WAS CRITICAL OF PRESIDENTIAL "AGGRANDIZEMENT" OF POWER. BASED LARGELY ON THE REASONING IN KEY CONSTITUTIONAL LAW DECISIONS, BUT ALSO DISCUSSES THE POLITICAL CONTEXT OUT OF WHICH THE DECISIONS EMERGED AND THEIR CONSEQUENCES.

198 CORWIN, E.S., AND KOENIG, L.W. THE PRESIDENCY TODAY. NEW YORK: NEW YORK UNIVERSITY PRESS, 1956, PP. 138.

GENERAL CONSIDERATION OF THE NATURE OF MODERN PRESIDENTIAL LEADERSHIP AND OF THE PROBLEMS POSED BY PRESIDENTIAL POWER. ALSO DISCUSSES PRESIDENTIAL PRIMARIES, THE ELECTORAL COLLEGE, THE TRANSITION-PERIOD BETWEEN ADMINISTRATIONS, THE VICE-PRESIDENCY, AND THE THEN (PRE-25TH AMENDMENT) TOPICAL PROBLEM OF PRESIDENTIAL INABILITY.

199 CRONIN, T.E. THE STATE OF THE PRESIDENCY. BOSTON: LITTLE, BROWN, 1975, PP. 355.

FOCUSES ESPECIALLY ON THE IDEALIZATION OF PRESIDENTS IN TRADITIONAL LITERATURE AND ON THE POLITICAL AND ADMINISTRATIVE COMPLEXITIES OF THE WHITE HOUSE OFFICE OF THE PRESIDENT GENERALLY.

200 CUNLIFFE, M. AMERICAN PRESIDENTS AND THE PRESIDENCY. NEW YORK: NEW AMERICAN LIBRARY, 1958, PP. 192. ALSO LONDON: EYRE & SPOTTISWOODE, 1969, PP. 343. SECOND EDITION, NEW YORK: AMERICAN HERITAGE PRESS, 1972, PP. 446.

201 EGGER, R. THE PRESIDENT OF THE UNITED STATES. NEW YORK: MCGRAW, 1972, PP. 198.

A BASIC TEXT.

202 FAIRLIE, H. "THOUGHTS ON THE PRESIDENCY." PUBLIC INTEREST(FALL 1967): 28-48.

AN ENGLISH CONSERVATIVE'S REFLECTIONS ON WHETHER AMERICANS EXPECT TOO MUCH OF THE PRESIDENCY. COMPARE FAIRLIE'S KENNEDY PROMISE.

203 FINER, H. THE PRESIDENCY: CRISIS AND REGENERATION, AN ESSAY IN POSSIBILITIES. CHICAGO: UNIVERSITY OF CHICAGO PRESS, 1960, PP. 374.

PROPOSES A PLURAL EXECUTIVE CONSISTING OF A PRESIDENT AND

A NUMBER OF ELECTED VICE-PRESIDENTS. ASSIGNING "ONE MAN, ONE MORTAL... THE TITANIC AUTHORITY AND TORTURING RESPONSIBILITIES OF THE PRESIDENT CONSTITUTES THE VITAL FLAW IN THE GOVERNMENT OF THE UNITED STATES IN THE TWENTIETH CENTURY."

204 FORD, H.J. THE RISE AND GROWTH OF AMERICAN POLITICS: A SKETCH OF CONSTITUTIONAL DEVELOPMENT. NEW YORK: MACMILLAN, 1898. REPUBLISHED NEW YORK: DA CAPO, 1967, PP. 409.

IN RESPONSE TO GROVER CLEVELAND'S EXPERIENCES IN OFFICE, FORD BECAME ONE OF THE FIRST WRITERS TO CONCEIVE OF THE PRESIDENCY AS THE KEY POLICY-MAKING INSTITUTION IN AMERICAN SOCIETY ("AN ELECTIVE MONARCHY").

205 FURNAS, H. "THE PRESIDENT: A CHANGING ROLE?". ANNALS 280 (NOV 1968): 9-15.

206 GRIFFITH, E.S. THE AMERICAN PRESIDENCY: THE DILEMMAS OF SHARED POWER AND DIVIDED GOVERNMENT. NEW YORK: NYU PR, 1976, PP. 241.

A SIMPLIFIED ACCOUNT OF THE GROWTH OF THE MODERN PRESIDENCY, WHICH ALSO SERVES TO SUMMARIZE THE PAPERS AND THE CONCLUSIONS ARISING FROM A NATIONAL ACADEMY OF PUBLIC ADMINISTRATION CONFERENCE IN 1974 ON THE INSTITUTIONALIZED PRESIDENCY.

207 HARGROVE, E.C. THE POWER OF THE MODERN PRESIDENCY. PHILADELPHIA: TEMPLE UNIVERSITY PRESS, 1974, PP. 353.

A COMPREHENSIVE DISCUSSION OF THE PRESIDENCY AS IT HAD EVOLVED CIRCA WATERGATE, COVERING PRESIDENTIAL PERSONALITY, THE EXPANDING STAFF OF THE PRESIDENCY, AND ALTERNATIVE CONCEPTIONS OF THE PRESIDENT'S ROLE IN THE POLITICAL SYSTEM.

208 HART, J. "THE PRESIDENCY: SHIFTING CONSERVATIVE PERSPECTIVES?" NATIONAL R (NOV. 22, 1974): 1351-1355.

209 HAVARD, W.C. "THE PRESIDENCY: THE OFFICE, THE MAN, AND THE CONSTITUENCIES." VIRGINIA Q R 50 (AUTUMN 1974): 497-514.

STRESSES THE INTERACTION OF THE THREE VARIABLES LISTED IN THE SUBTITLE.

210 HELLER, F.H. THE PRESIDENCY: A MODERN PERSPECTIVE. NEW YORK: RANDOM HOUSE, 1960, PP. 114.

A BRIEF TEXT, STRESSING THE IMPORTANCE OF THE PRESIDENT'S INDIVIDUAL QUALITIES AS A LEADER, BUT EXPRESSING DOUBT AS TO WHETHER ANY PROCEDURE FOR DETECTING APPROPRIATE PRESIDENTIAL QUALITIES CAN BE FOUND.

211 HENRY, L.L., ED. "THE AMERICAN PRESIDENCY: A SYMPOSIUM."

PUBLIC ADMINISTRATION R 29 (1969): 441-480.

212 HIRSCHFIELD, R.S. "THE REALITY OF PRESIDENTIAL POWER."
PARLIAMENTARY AFFAIRS 21 (AUTUMN 1968): 375-383.

213 HOXIE, R.G., ED. THE PRESIDENCY OF THE 1970'S:
PROCEEDINGS OF THE 1971 MONTAUK SYMPOSIUM. NEW YORK:
CENTER FOR THE STUDY OF THE PRESIDENCY, 1973, PP. 196.

TRANSCRIPT OF A DISCUSSION BY INDIVIDUALS WHO HAVE SERVED
AS PRESIDENTIAL AIDES.

214 HOY, J.C., AND BERNSTEIN, M.H., EDS. THE EFFECTIVE
PRESIDENT. PACIFIC PALISADES, CALIFORNIA: PALISADES
PUBLISHERS, 1976, PP.189.

BRIEF PAPERS BY ACADEMICS AND PUBLIC OFFICIALS, DELIVERED
AT A CONFERENCE ON THE PRESIDENCY STIMULATED BY
WATERGATE.

215 HUGHES, E.J. THE LIVING PRESIDENCY. NEW YORK: COWARD,
MCCANN, AND GEOGHEGAN, INC., 1973, PP. 377.

A REFLECTIVE, HISTORICALLY ORIENTED GENERAL DISCUSSION OF
THE PRESIDENCY. A VALUABLE APPENDIX CONTAINS THE
STATEMENTS OF 12 VETERAN PRESIDENTIAL ADVISERS ON PROBLEMS
OF ADVISING PRESIDENTS.

216 HYMAN, S., ED. "THE OFFICE OF THE AMERICAN PRESIDENCY."
ANNALS 307 (SEPT 1956): ENTIRE ISSUE.

217 JAMES, D.B. THE CONTEMPORARY PRESIDENCY. NEW YORK:
PEGASUS, 1969, PP. 187. SECOND EDITION, 1974, PP. 336.

218 JOHNSON, W. 1600 PENNSYLVANIA AVENUE: PRESIDENTS AND THE
PEOPLE SINCE 1929. BOSTON: LITTLE, BROWN, 1959, PP. 390.

LIVELY ACCOUNT OF THE PRESIDENCY DISCUSSING KEY EVENTS IN
THE HOOVER THROUGH EISENHOWER ADMINISTRATIONS. APPROVINGLY
QUOTES THE THEN PRESIDENTIAL CANDIDATE JOHN F. KENNEDY'S
ASSERTION THAT THE PRESIDENT SHOULD BE "A CHIEF EXECUTIVE
WHO IS THE VITAL CENTER OF ACTION IN OUR WHOLE SYSTEM OF
GOVERNMENT."

219 KENYON, C.M., ED. THE ANTIFEDERALISTS. INDIANAPOLIS:
BOBBS-MERRILL, 1975, PP. 455.

COLLECTION OF WRITINGS DURING THE DEBATE ON CONSTITUTIONAL
RATIFICATION BY OPPONENTS OF THE CONSTITUTION. MANY
EXAMPLES OF 18TH CENTURY CRITICISMS OF ARTICLE II.

220 KOENIG, L.W. THE CHIEF EXECUTIVE. NEW YORK: HARCOURT,

BRACE AND WORLD, 1964, PP. 435. THIRD EDITION, 1975, PP. 452.

SINCE 1964, THIS HAS BEEN ONE OF THE MOST WIDELY READ TEXTBOOKS ON THE PRESIDENCY. KOENIG HAS SHIFTED IN SUCCESSIVE EDITIONS FROM STRESSING THE PRESIDENCY'S SINGULAR IMPORTANCE AS AN INSTRUMENT OF NATIONAL LEADERSHIP TO EMPHASIZING THE DESIRABILITY OF A STRONG PRESIDENCY COUNTERBALANCED BY A STRONG CONGRESS AND A STRONG SUPREME COURT.

221 LAMMERS, W.W. PRESIDENTIAL POLITICS: PATTERNS AND PROSPECTS. NEW YORK: HAR-ROW, 1976, PP. 310.

A BASIC TEXT.

222 LASKI, H.J. THE AMERICAN PRESIDENCY, AN INTERPRETATION. HARPER AND BROTHERS, 1940. REPRINTED GREENWOOD PR, 1972, PP. 278.

THIS WORK BY ONE OF THE LEADING INTELLECTUAL SPOKESMEN OF THE BRITISH LABOUR PARTY DRAWS UPON THE EXPERIENCE OF FDR'S "NEW DEAL" LEADERSHIP TO CONCLUDE THAT "THE PRESIDENT...MUST BE GIVEN THE POWER COMMENSURATE TO THE FUNCTION HE HAS TO PERFORM...FOR GREAT POWER ALONE MAKES GREAT LEADERSHIP POSSIBLE; IT PROVIDES THE UNIQUE CHANCE OF RESTORING AMERICA TO ITS PEOPLE."

223 LIPSON, L. "THE DUAL ROLE OF THE AMERICAN PRESIDENT." J PUB ADMIN 2 (JUNE 1939): 59-72.

224 LONG, N. "REFLECTIONS ON PRESIDENTIAL POWER." PUBLIC ADMINISTRATION R 29 (1969):442-450.

ONCE CELEBRATED AS THE "MAINSPRING" OF THE POLITICAL SYSTEM, THE PRESIDENCY CAME IN A RELATIVELY BRIEF PERIOD TO APPEAR TO BE A "BROKEN MAINSPRING." LONG ARGUES THAT AN IDEALIZED VIEW OF THE EFFECTIVENESS OF PARTY LEADERSHIP OF GOVERNMENT BY THE BRITISH EXECUTIVE WAS IMPLICIT IN SUCH AMERICAN ACADEMIC WRITING WHICH STRESSED THE NEED TO BOLSTER RATHER THAN RESTRAIN PRESIDENTIAL LEADERSHIP. THIS VIEW WAS UNDERMINED NOT ONLY BY THE UNPOPULARITY OF JOHNSON'S FOREIGN POLICY, BUT ALSO BY THE DECLINING PERFORMANCE OF GREAT BRITAIN AS A "PATTERN" POLITICAL SYSTEM.

225 LOSS, R. "DISSOLVING CONCEPTS OF THE PRESIDENCY." POL SCI REVIEWER 4 (FALL 1974): 133-168.

ARGUES THAT CORWIN'S DESIRE FOR A RESTRAINED PRESIDENCY STANDS UP BETTER HISTORICALLY THAN THE VIEWS OF SUCH WRITERS AS ROSSITER, NEUSTADT, AND SCHLESINGER. SEE ALSO LOSS'S INTRODUCTION TO HIS COLLECTION OF CORWIN'S ESSAYS ON THE PRESIDENCY.

226 MAIN, J.T. THE ANTIFEDERALISTS, CRITICS OF THE CONSTITUTION 1781-1788. CHAPEL HILL, N.C.: U.OF N.C. PR,

1961, PP. 308.

ON THE VIEWS OF THOSE WHO OPPOSED RATIFICATION OF THE
CONSTITUTION.

227 MCCONNELL, G. THE MODERN PRESIDENCY. NEW YORK: ST.
MARTIN'S PRESS, 1967. PP. 114. SECOND EDITION. NEW YORK:
ST. MARTIN'S PR, 1976, PP. 136.

A BRIEF TEXT CONCLUDING THAT "THERE ARE GENUINE DANGERS IN
OUR DEPENDENCE ON THIS OFFICE AND ON A SINGLE MAN....THE
POSSIBILITY THAT A PRESIDENT MAY ABUSE HIS POWER...THAT HE
WILL NOT USE HIS POWER WISELY OR THAT HE WILL NOT USE IT
AT ALL WHEN IT IS NEEDED."

228 MULLEN, W.F. PRESIDENTIAL POWER AND POLITICS. NEW YORK:
ST. MARTIN'S PR, 1976, PP. 294.

"TOO MUCH HAS HAPPENED IN RECENT YEARS TO BE ATTRIBUTABLE
SOLELY TO THE PERSONALITY FAILINGS OF RECENT INCUMBENTS.
THE OFFICE ITSELF....SEEMED TO MAGNIFY WHAT WAS WORST IN
PRESIDENTS AND TO MINIMIZE THE POLITICAL ACUMEN THAT HAS
ENABLED THEM TO RISE TO POWER....LESS REVERENCE AND AWE
AND A LITTLE LESS SPLENDOR IN THE WHITE HOUSE WOULD
CONTRIBUTE TOWARD BRINGING THE PRESIDENCY BACK TO
EARTH....THE PEOPLE MAY EXPECT FEWER MIRACLES AND NOT
CONTINUALLY BE DISAPPOINTED WITH THE CURRENT INCUMBENT."

229 NEUSTADT, R.E. PRESIDENTIAL POWER: THE POLITICS OF
LEADERSHIP WITH REFLECTIONS ON JOHNSON AND NIXON. NEW
YORK: WILEY, 1976, PP. 324.

THE CORE OF THIS INFLUENTIAL BOOK IS A COMPARATIVE
ANALYSIS, PUBLISHED IN 1960, OF "SUCCESSFUL" AND
"UNSUCCESSFUL" INSTANCES OF DECISION-MAKING BY TRUMAN AND
EISENHOWER, COMBINED WITH AN ANALYTIC DISCUSSION OF HOW
PRESIDENTS CAN BEST ACHIEVE THEIR POLICY AIMS. THE
UP-DATED EDITION INCLUDES A POST-SCRIPT ON THE KENNEDY
PRESIDENCY AND A LONG INTRODUCTORY ESSAY ON HOW THE
PRESIDENCY CHANGED UNDER JOHNSON AND NIXON. FOR AN
EXPLICATION AND CRITIQUE OF NEUSTADT'S GENERAL ANALYTIC
FORMULATION, SEE P. SPERLICH, "BARGAINING AND OVERLOAD."

230 ----------. "THE PRESIDENCY AT MID-CENTURY." LAW AND
CONTEMPORARY PROBLEMS 21 (1956): 609-645.

REFLECTIVE ESSAY ANTICIPATES THE ANALYSIS IN NEUSTADT'S
PRESIDENTIAL POWER. PROVIDES MORE OF NEUSTADT'S
RATIONALE FOR DEFENDING PRESIDENTIAL POLICY-MAKING THAN
DOES HIS BOOK.

231 PATTERSON, C.P. PRESIDENTIAL GOVERNMENT IN THE UNITED
STATES: THE UNWRITTEN CONSTITUTION. CHAPEL HILL, N.C.:
UNIV. OF NORTH CAROLINA PRESS, 1947, PP. 301.

SYSTEMATIC SCHOLARLY DISCUSSION BY AN ADVOCATE OF BALANCE
AMONG THE BRANCHES OF GOVERNMENT.

232 PIOUS, R.M. "THE EVOLUTION OF THE PRESIDENCY: 1789-1932."
CURRENT HISTORY 66 (1974):241-245.

DURING MOST OF THE PRE-FRANKLIN ROOSEVELT YEARS, CONGRESSIONAL RATHER THAN PRESIDENTIAL LEADERSHIP PREVAILED EXCEPT IN CERTAIN LIMITED AREAS SUCH AS TERRITORIAL EXPANSION.

233 REEDY, G. THE PRESIDENCY IN FLUX. NEW YORK: COLUMBIA UNIV. PRESS, 1973, PP. 133.

LARGELY DUPLICATES POINTS MADE IN THE TWILIGHT OF THE PRESIDENCY.

234 ----------. THE TWILIGHT OF THE PRESIDENCY. NEW YORK: WORLD PUBLISHING COMPANY, 1970, PP. 205.

THE BEST KNOWN OF SEVERAL WRITINGS BY THIS FORMER JOHNSON PRESS SECRETARY WHO ARGUES THAT MODERN PRESIDENTS DEVELOP GRANDIOSE, UNREALISTIC VIEWS OF THEMSELVES AND OF THEIR GOALS. A MAJOR CAUSE IS PRESIDENTIAL ISOLATION DUE TO THE RISE OF AN EXTENSIVE WHITE HOUSE STAFF WHICH INEVITABLY TENDS TOWARD SYCOPHANCY.

235 ROGERS, L. "THE AMERICAN PRESIDENTIAL SYSTEM." POLITICAL Q 8 (1937): 517-529.

"IN THE UNITED STATES, THOSE WHO ATTEMPT TO WORK THE PRESIDENTIAL SYSTEM DO NOT HAVE TO PROVE THEMSELVES IN DAY-TO-DAY DEALINGS WITH THE LEGISLATURE. THEY MUST THEREFORE CONVINCE THE PUBLIC OF THEIR STRENGTH BY RESORT TO THE PRESS, THE WIRELESS AND THE CINEMA."

236 ROSSITER, C.L. THE AMERICAN PRESIDENCY. NEW YORK: HARCOURT, BRACE, 1960, PP. 281.

THE UPDATED VERSION OF WHAT WAS PROBABLY THE MOST WIDELY KNOWN GENERAL WORK ON THE PRESIDENCY BY A SCHOLAR DURING THE PERIOD OF LIBERAL CONSENSUS ON THE MERITS OF THE INSTITUTION. ROSSITER WAS EMPHATIC IN HIS CLAIM THAT THE PRESIDENCY FUNCTIONED EXCEPTIONALLY WELL AND SHOULD BE "LEFT ALONE" RATHER THAN REFORMED. ANALYTICALLY, HIS EMPHASIS WAS ON CONCEIVING THE PRESIDENT'S TASK AS A SERIES OF DISTINCT ROLES, SOME OF THEM CONSTITUTIONALLY DEFINED, THE OTHERS ACQUIRED THROUGH HISTORICAL PRECEDENT.

237 RUSK, D. "THE PRESIDENT." (BASED ON ADDRESS) FOREIGN AFFAIRS 38 (APRIL 1960): 353-369.

ADVOCATES STRONG PRESIDENTIAL LEADERSHIP, ESPECIALLY IN FOREIGN AFFAIRS.

238 SCHLESINGER, A.M., JR. THE IMPERIAL PRESIDENCY. BOSTON: HOUGHTON, 1973, REPRINTED WITH EPILOGUE AND APPENDIX: "THE VICE PRESIDENCY: A MODEST PROPOSAL." NEW YORK: POPULAR LIBRARY, 1973, PP. 541.

WIDELY CIRCULATED CRITIQUE OF THE GROWTH OF AUTONOMOUS PRESIDENTIAL POWER, ESPECIALLY WAR MAKING POWER, BY A HISTORIAN AND FORMER WHITE HOUSE AIDE WHOSE BOOKS ON JACKSON, FDR, AND JFK HAD CELEBRATED "STRONG" ACTIVIST

PRESIDENTIAL LEADERSHIP.

239 SELIGMAN, L.G. "DEVELOPMENTS IN THE PRESIDENCY AND THE CONCEPTION OF POLITICAL LEADERSHIP." AMER. SOCIOLOGICAL REVIEW 20 (1955): 706-712.

AN ANALYTIC ACCOUNT OF THE EVOLUTION OF THE PRESIDENTIAL ROLE, CAST IN TERMS OF LEADERSHIP THEORY.

240 ----------. "THE PRESIDENT IS MANY MEN." ANTIOCH R 16 (1956): 305-318.

ON THE EXPANDING NUMBER OF ROLES MODERN PRESIDENTS ARE EXPECTED TO PERFORM.

241 SICKELS, R.J. PRESIDENTIAL TRANSACTIONS. ENGLEWOOD CLIFFS, N.J.: PRENTICE-HALL, 1974, PP. 184.

AN INTRODUCTORY TEXTBOOK, STRESSING THE RELATIONSHIPS BETWEEN THE PRESIDENT AND HIS PARTY, HIS ADVISERS, THE BUREAUCRACY, THE SUPREME COURT, THE CONGRESS, AND THE PUBLIC. THE TERM "TRANSACTIONS" IS DERIVED FROM SOCIOLOGICAL "EXCHANGE THEORY."

242 SMALL, N.J. SOME PRESIDENTIAL INTERPRETATIONS OF THE PRESIDENCY. BALTIMORE: JOHN HOPKINS PRESS, 1932, PP. 208. REPRINTED DA CAPO PR, 1970.

SUMMARIZES CONTRASTING VIEWS OF VARIOUS PRESIDENTS PRIOR TO ROOSEVELT, REGARDING THE GENERAL NATURE OF THE OFFICE AND THE PRESIDENT'S ROLE IN FOREIGN RELATIONS, HIS WAR-POWERS, EXECUTION OF THE LAWS, AND LEGISLATIVE LEADERSHIP.

243 SMITH, A.M. A PRESIDENT IS MANY MEN. NEW YORK: HARPER AND BROTHERS, 1948, PP. 269.

DIGRESSIVE ACCOUNT OF THE COMPLEXITIES OF THE PRESIDENT'S JOB BY A SENIOR WHITE HOUSE CORRESPONDENT, CONTAINING MANY FIRST-HAND ANECDOTAL OBSERVATIONS.

244 SORENSEN, T.C. DECISION-MAKING IN THE WHITE HOUSE: THE OLIVE BRANCH OR THE ARROWS. NEW YORK: COLUMBIA UNIVERSITY PRESS, 1963, PP. 94.

A BRIEF ACCOUNT BY JOHN F. KENNEDY'S LONG-TIME ALTER EGO ADVISOR ON THE NATURE OF PRESIDENTIAL DECISIONS, THE ROLE OF ADVISORS, AND THE IMPORTANCE OF DECISIVENESS ON THE PART OF PRESIDENTS IN RECOGNIZING THAT THE PRESIDENT "MUST BE ATTUNED TO PUBLIC OPINION BUT NOT BOUND BY IT." CONTAINS FOREWORD BY PRESIDENT KENNEDY.

245 SPERLICH, P.W. "BARGAINING AND OVERLOAD: AN ESSAY ON PRESIDENTIAL POWER." IN THE PRESIDENCY, EDITED BY A. WILDAVSKY, PP. 168-192. BOSTON: LITTLE, BROWN, 1969.

WIDELY CITED EXEGESIS OF NEUSTADT'S IMPLICIT MODEL OF LEADERSHIP IN PRESIDENTIAL POWER, STRESSING THAT MODEL'S INCOMPLETENESS, INTER ALIA, FOR INATTENTION TO

NON-BARGAINING INDUCEMENTS TO PERSUASION AND FOR CONCEIVING OF BARGAINING-BASED ROLE-REQUIREMENTS THAT WOULD EXCEED THE PRESIDENT'S LIMITS OF TIME AND ENERGY.

246 STAMPS, N.L. "THE AMERICAN PRESIDENTIAL SYSTEM." POLITICAL Q 25 (1954): 155-165.

THE PRESIDENTIAL SYSTEM IS MORE SUITED TO THE "ENVIRONMENT" AND THE "PECULIAR NEEDS OF AMERICAN SOCIETY" THAN THE PARLIAMENTARY SYSTEM WOULD BE .

247 STOKES, W.S. "WHIG CONCEPTIONS OF EXECUTIVE POWER" PRESIDENTIAL STUDIES QUARTERLY 6 (WINTER AND SPRING 1976): 16-35.

SUMMARIZES THE VIEWS OF THOSE PRE-CIVIL WAR PRESIDENTS WHO PLACED SPECIAL EMPHASIS UPON THE CONSTITUTIONAL RESTRAINTS ON THEIR CAPACITY TO PARTICIPATE IN POLICY-MAKING.

248 STRUM, P. PRESIDENTIAL POWER AND AMERICAN DEMOCRACY. PACIFIC PALISADES: GOODYEAR PUBLISHING COMPANY, 1972, PP. 132.

DRAWS UPON EXAMPLES OF JOHNSON'S AND NIXON'S DECISION-MAKING IN INDO-CHINA IN A GENERALLY CRITICAL ACCOUNT OF "THE DANGERS OF PRESIDENTIAL POWER."

249 TAFT, W.H. OUR CHIEF MAGISTRATE AND HIS POWERS. NEW YORK: COLUMBIA U PR, 1916. REPRINTED AS THE PRESIDENT AND HIS POWERS, 1967, PP. 165.

THE EX-PRESIDENT'S CLASSIC ENUNCIATION OF A CONSTITUTIONALLY RESTRAINED PRESIDENCY.

250 THACH, C.C. THE CREATION OF THE PRESIDENCY, 1775-1789: A STUDY IN CONSTITUTIONAL HISTORY. BALTIMORE: JOHNS HOPKINS PRESS, 1923, PP. 182.

THIS CLASSIC, HISTORICAL EXAMINATION OF THE POLITICS OF THE PERIOD LEADING UP TO THE FRAMING OF THE CONSTITUTION WAS REPRINTED IN 1969 WITH A BRIEF INTRODUCTORY ESSAY BY HERBERT J. STORING.

251 "THE AMERICAN PRESIDENCY." CURRENT HISTORY 66 (1974): ENTIRE ISSUE.

252 "THE POST-WATERGATE PRESIDENCY (A SYMPOSIUM)." COLUMBIA JOURNAL OF LAW AND SOCIAL PROBLEMS 2 (1974):1-34.

253 TOURTELLOT, A.B. THE PRESIDENTS ON THE PRESIDENCY. NEW YORK: DOUBLEDAY, 1964, PP. 505. REPRINTED NEW YORK: RUSSELL, 1970.

A COMPENDIUM OF QUOTATIONS OF ASSERTIONS BY PRESIDENTS

ABOUT VARIOUS ASPECTS OF THE PRESIDENTIAL ROLE AND THE EXPERIENCE OF BEING PRESIDENT.

254 VINYARD, D. THE PRESIDENCY. NEW YORK: SCRIBNER, 1971, PP. 214.

"THE PURPOSE OF THIS VOLUME IS TO PROVIDE THE READER WITH AN INTRODUCTION TO THE AMERICAN PRESIDENCY, SO THAT HE MAY UNDERSTAND THE FUNCTIONS OF THE OFFICE, ITS RELATION TO OTHER PARTICIPANTS IN THE POLICY-MAKING PROCESS AND ITS POWER AND LIMITATIONS."

255 WILDAVSKY, A. "SYSTEM IS TO POLITICS AS MORALITY IS TO MAN: A SERMON ON THE PRESIDENCY." IN PERSPECTIVES ON THE PRESIDENCY, EDITED BY A. WILDAVSKY. BOSTON: LITTLE, BROWN, 1975: 526-539.

ON THE NEED FOR A CONCEPTION OF THE PRESIDENCY THAT WOULD BE PART OF A LARGER VIEW OF THE APPROPRIATE ROLES OF THE VARIOUS INSTITUTIONS IN THE POLITICAL SYSTEM.

256 ----------. "THE PAST AND FUTURE PRESIDENCY." PUBLIC INTEREST 41 (FALL 1975): 56-76.

THE REQUIREMENTS OF AMERICAN POLITICS PLACE INCREASING DEMANDS UPON PRESIDENTS BUT PROVIDE THEM WITH DECREASING RESOURCES WITH WHICH TO MEET THEM.

257 WILSON, W. CONGRESSIONAL GOVERNMENT: A STUDY IN AMERICAN POLITICS. BOSTON: HOUGHTON, 1885. ALSO NEW YORK: MERIDIAN, INTRODUCTION BY WALTER LIPPMAN, 1959.

WILSON ACCURATELY VIEWED THE PREDIDENT AS A WEAK FIGUREHEAD AND CONGRESS AS THE DIRECTING FORCE OF GOVERNMENT IN THIS CLASSIC WORK WRITTEN DURING THE POST-RECONSTRUCTION PERIOD. IN THE 1890S, HAVING OBSERVED THE ASSERTIVE LEADERSHIP OF GROVER CLEVELAND, WILSON ADDED A PREFACE ARGUING THAT A POTENTIAL NOW EXISTED FOR ASSERTIVE PRESIDENTIAL LEADERSHIP.

258 ----------. CONSTITUTIONAL GOVERNMENT IN THE UNITED STATES. NEW YORK: COLUMBIA U PR, 1908. REPRINTED 1964, PP. 236.

WILSON'S FAMOUS REVISION OF HIS THESIS THAT THE AMERICAN PRESIDENCY LACKED LEADERSHIP POTENTIAL. IN THIS WORK, WILSON DEFENDED DECISIVE LEADERSHIP BY A PRESIDENT WHO HOLDS HIMSELF DIRECTLY RESPONSIBLE TO PUBLIC OPINION. WHILE NOT SUBORDINATE TO THE CONGRESS, THE PRESIDENT SHOULD COMPROMISE WHEN THE TWO BRANCHES ARE AT LOGGERHEADS. THE STRESS ON FORCEFUL LEADERSHIP PREDICTED WILSON'S OWN LATER PERFORMANCE IN THE WHITE HOUSE, ALTHOUGH THE REFERENCE TO COMPROMISE PROVED WIDE OF THE MARK IN THE CASE OF WILSON'S COLLISION WITH THE SENATE OVER RATIFICATION OF THE VERSAILLES TREATY.

259 YOUNG, J.S. THE WASHINGTON COMMUNITY, 1800-1828. NEW YORK: COLUMBIA UNIVERSITY PRESS, 1966, PP. 307.

IMPLICITLY TAKING AS HIS MEASURING STICK THE 1950'S AND
EARLY 1960'S LITERATURE ADVOCATING A POLITICALLY
SKILLFULL, POPULARLY BASED, ASSERTIVE PRESIDENCY, YOUNG
ANALYZES THE PRESIDENCIES OF JEFFERSON THROUGH JOHN QUINCY
ADAMS. HE CONCLUDES THAT THE NEW NATION COULD NOT HAVE
ENDURED IF GOVERNMENT BY THE ATOMIZED CONGRESS OF THE DAY
HAD PERSISTED. JACKSON'S EXERCISE OF PRESIDENTIAL AUTONOMY
WAS NECESSARY TO ESTABLISH THE PRECEDENT FOR A
SUFFICIENTLY STRONG EXECUTIVE TO MAINTAIN THE UNION IN THE
MID-NINETEENTH CENTURY CRISIS OF SECESSION.

SEE ALSO 38, 42, 181, 232, 270, 814, 1818, 2024, 2025,
2036, 2037, 2045, 2441, 2451, 2462, 2491

5

COMPARISONS WITH OTHER EXECUTIVES

260 CERNY, P.G. "THE FALL OF TWO PRESIDENTS AND EXTRAPARLIAMENTARY OPPOSITION: FRANCE AND THE UNITED STATES IN 1968." GOVERNMENT AND OPPOSITION 5 (SUMMER 1970): 287-306.

261 CONVERSE, P.E., AND DUPEUX, G. "DE GAULLE AND EISENHOWER: PUBLIC IMAGE OF THE VICTORIOUS GENERAL." IN ELECTIONS AND THE POLITICAL ORDER, EDITED BY A. CAMPBELL, P.E. CONVERSE, ET AL. NEW YORK: WILEY, 1966, PP. 292-345.

SURVEY-RESEARCH ON THE 2 GENERALS-TURNED PRESIDENTS SHOWS THAT THEIR PERSONAL APPEALS WERE TO A WIDER RANGE OF POPULATION-GROUPS THAN IS NORMAL FOR A PARTY-POLITICIAN.

262 GROTH, A.J. "BRITAIN AND AMERICA: SOME REQUISITES OF EXECUTIVE LEADERSHIP COMPARED." PSQ 85 (1970): 217-239.

263 GUEDALLA, P. "ROOSEVELT, CHURCHILL AND HITLER: DO THEY LEAD OR ARE THEY LED?" N Y TIMES MAG (APRIL 20, 1941): 3+.

264 HARGROVE, E.C. "POPULAR LEADERSHIP IN ANGLO-AMERICAN DEMOCRACIES." IN POLITICAL LEADERSHIP IN INDUSTRIAL SOCIETIES, EDITED BY L. EDINGER. NEW YORK: WILEY, 1967.

A COMPARISON OF CULTURAL EXPECTATIONS ABOUT HOW LEADERS IN THE UNITED STATES, BRITAIN, AND CANADA WILL AND SHOULD CARRY OUT THEIR DUTIES.

265 KALLENBACH, J.E. THE AMERICAN CHIEF EXECUTIVE: THE PRESIDENCY AND THE GOVERNORSHIP. NEW YORK: HAR-ROW, 1966, PP. 622.

ONE OF THE FEW ATTEMPTS TO COMPARE THE PRESIDENCY WITH THE EXECUTIVE ROLE AT ANOTHER LEVEL OF AMERICAN GOVERNMENT, NAMELY THE STATE GOVERNORSHIP.

266 ----------. "CONSTITUTIONAL LIMITATIONS ON REELIGIBILITY OF NATIONAL AND STATE CHIEF EXECUTIVES." APSR 46 (1952): 438-54.

267 KING, A. "EXECUTIVES." IN THE HANDBOOK OF POLITICAL SCIENCE, EDITED BY F.I. GREENSTEIN AND N.W. POLSBY, READING, MASS: ADDISON WESLEY, 1975, PP. 173-256.

A GENERAL SURVEY OF THE FUNCTIONS OF EXECUTIVES IN MODERN NATIONS, WITH PARTICULAR ATTENTION TO BRITAIN AND THE U.S.

268 LASKI, H.J. "THE PARLIAMENTARY AND PRESIDENTIAL SYSTEMS." PUBLIC ADMINISTRATION R 4 (1944): 347-359.

A RESPONSE TO PRICE'S 1943 DEFENSE OF THE PRESIDENTIAL OVER A PARLIAMENTARY SYSTEM.

269 NEUSTADT, R.E. ALLIANCE POLITICS. NEW YORK: COLUMBIA U PR, 1970, PP. 167.

ON THE BASIS OF CASE STUDIES OF ANGLO-AMERICAN POLITICAL MISUNDERSTANDINGS, NEUSTADT ARGUES THAT LEADERS OF ALLIANCES WILL FIND THEMSELVES IN UNANTICIPATED DISAGREEMENTS IF THEY DO NOT UNDERSTAND THE DISTINCTIVE REQUIREMENTS OF LEADERSHIP IN THEIR ALLY'S COUNTRY.

270 ----------. "PRESIDENTIAL GOVERNMENT." IN INTERNAT ENCYCLOPEDIA OF THE SOCIAL SCIENCES 1968, VOL. 12, PP. 451-456.

271 ----------. "WHITE HOUSE AND WHITEHALL." PUBLIC INTEREST (WINTER 1966): 55-69.

IN BOTH THE UNITED STATES AND BRITAIN, SKILLED, ENERGETIC STAFF AIDES HAVE BECOME A NECESSARY ADJUNCT TO THE PRESIDENT AND THE PRIME MINISTER. SUCH AIDES TEND TO BE PRESIDENTIALLY APPOINTED MEMBERS OF THE WHITE HOUSE OFFICE STAFF IN THE UNITED STATES AND PROFESSIONAL CIVIL SERVANTS IN BRITAIN.

272 PRICE, D.K. "A RESPONSE TO MR. LASKI." PUBLIC ADMINISTRATION R 4 (1944): 360-363.

THIRD PART OF THE PRICE-LASKI-PRICE EXCHANGE.

273 ----------. "THE PARLIAMENTARY AND PRESIDENTIAL SYSTEMS." PUBLIC ADMINISTRATION R 3 (1943): 317-334.

A WELL KNOWN DEFENSE OF THE AMERICAN SEPARATION-OF-POWERS SYSTEM AGAINST BRITISH-STYLE PARLIAMENTARY GOVERNMENT. TO BE READ IN CONJUNCTION WITH HAROLD LASKI'S REPLY AND PRICE'S REJOINDER.

274 RIES, J. EXECUTIVES IN THE AMERICAN POLITICAL SYSTEM. BELMONT, CALF.: DICKENSON PUBLISHING, 1969, PP. 151.

BRIEFLY CONSIDERS EXECUTIVE ROLES AT ALL GOVERNMENTAL LEVELS.

275 SCARROW, H.A. "PARLIAMENTARY AND PRESIDENTIAL GOVERNMENT COMPARED." CURRENT HISTORY 66 (1974): 264-267.

276 SHAH, C.C. "EXECUTIVE PRIVILEGE TO WITHHOLD INFORMATION FROM THE JUDICIAL BRANCH — A COMPARATIVE STUDY." (U.S. AND U.K.) TEXAS BAR R 30 (1967): 15+.

277 SWINDLER, W.F. "THE EXECUTIVE POWER IN STATE AND FEDERAL CONSTITUTIONS." HASTINGS CONSTIT LAW Q 1 (SPRING 1974): 21-29.

ARGUES FOR DECREASING THE FORMAL POWERS OF THE PRESIDENT AND INCREASING GUBERNATORIAL POWERS.

278 TUGWELL, R.G. THE ART OF POLITICS, AS PRACTICED BY THREE GREAT AMERICANS: FRANKLIN D. ROOSEVELT, LUIS M. MARIN, AND FIORELLO H. LA GUARDIA. GARDEN CITY: DOUBLEDAY, 1958, PP. 295.

SEE ALSO 1554, 2216

6
COMPARISONS OF AMERICAN PRESIDENCIES

279 ADAMS, D.K. "ROOSEVELT AND KENNEDY." BUL BRIT ASSOC AMER STUD 1 (1960): 29-39.

SIMILARITIES BETWEEN THE NEW DEAL AND THE NEW FRONTIER: HOW BOTH CHALLENGED LAISSEZ-FAIRE TRADITIONS, GATHERED INTELLECTUALS IN WASHINGTON, AND HAD THE PROBLEM OF A POLITICAL PARTY WHICH INCLUDED BOTH NORTHERN WORKERS AND SOUTHERNERS.

280 ALBJERG, V. "TRUMAN AND EISENHOWER: THEIR ADMINISTRATIONS AND CAMPAIGNS." CURRENT HISTORY 47 (OCT 1964): 221-228.

281 AMLUND, C.A. "EXECUTIVE - LEGISLATIVE IMBALANCE: TRUMAN TO KENNEDY." WESTERN POLITICAL Q 3 (1965):640-654.

282 BAILEY, T.A. PRESIDENTIAL GREATNESS; THE IMAGE AND THE MAN FROM GEORGE WASHINGTON TO THE PRESENT. NEW YORK: APPLETON-CENTURY, 1966, PP. 368.

CRITICAL ANALYSIS OF THE MANY EFFORTS TO RANK PRESIDENTS IN TERMS OF THEIR "GREATNESS."

283 ----------. "JOHNSON AND KENNEDY: THE TWO THOUSAND DAYS." N Y TIMES MAG (NOV 6, 1966): 30-1+; DISCUSSION, NOV 27, PP. 159-60; DEC 4, P. 22.

284 BORDEN, M. AMERICA'S ELEVEN GREATEST PRESIDENTS. CHICAGO: RAND MCNALLY, 1971, PP. 295.

285 CROSSMAN, R.H. "DID F.D.R. ESCAPE WILSON'S FAILURE? IDEALISM VS. POWER POLITICS IN AMERICAN FOREIGN POLICY." COMMENTARY 8 (NOV 1949): 418-423.

286 FRITCHEY, C. "A TALE OF ONE CITY AND TWO MEN." HARPER'S MAG (DEC 1966): 108-113.

A JOURNALIST'S COMMENT ON THE DIFFERENCES BETWEEN NEW FRONTIER AND GREAT SOCIETY POLITICS.

287 GUERRANT, E.O. HERBERT HOOVER; FRANKLIN ROOSEVELT: COMPARISONS AND CONTRASTS. CLEVELAND: H. ALLEN, 1960, PP. 114.

288 KROCK, A. MEMOIRS: SIXTY YEARS ON THE FIRING LINE. NEW YORK: FUNK AND WAGNALLS, 1968.

LONG-TIME "DEAN" OF WASHINGTON CORRESPONDENTS. PERSONAL ACCOUNT OF HIS ENCOUNTER WITH PRESIDENTS FROM THEODORE ROOSEVELT TO RICHARD NIXON.

289 LAFEBER, W. "KENNEDY, JOHNSON AND THE REVISIONISTS." FOR SERVICE J 50 (MAY 1973): 31-33, 39.

REVIEWS THE REVISIONIST HISTORIANS OF THE KENNEDY AND JOHNSON FOREIGN POLICIES.

290 LINCOLN, E. KENNEDY AND JOHNSON. NEW YORK: HOLT, RINEHART AND WINSTON, 1968, PP. 207.

BY KENNEDY'S FORMER PERSONAL SECRETARY.

291 MARANELL, G.M. "THE EVALUATION OF PRESIDENTS: AN EXTENSION OF THE SCHLESINGER POLLS." J AMER HIST 57 (JUNE 1970): 104-113.

292 MOLEY, R. "FDR--JFK: A BRAIN TRUSTER COMPARES TWO PRESIDENTS, TWO PROGRAMS." NEWSWEEK 57 (APRIL 17, 1961): 32-34+.

293 MOWRY, G.E. "THE USES OF HISTORY BY RECENT PRESIDENTS." J AMERICAN HISTORY 53 (1966):5-18.

STUDIES 7 PRESIDENTS OF WHOM FRANKLIN ROOSEVELT AND JOHN KENNEDY WERE THE MOST HISTORICALLY AWARE.

294 NEUSTADT, R.E. "APPROACHES TO STAFFING THE PRESIDENCY: NOTES ON FDR AND JFK." APSR 57 (1963): 855-864.

295 RAYBURN, S. "THE SPEAKER SPEAKS OF PRESIDENTS." N Y TIMES MAG 4 (JUNE 1961), PP. 32FF.

296 ROSENMAN, S.I., AND ROSENMAN, D. PRESIDENTIAL STYLE: SOME GIANTS AND A PIGMY IN THE WHITE HOUSE. NEW YORK: HARPER AND ROW, 1976, PP. 602.

FIVE CASE-STUDIES OF 20TH CENTURY PRESIDENTS: THEODORE ROOSEVELT, WOODROW WILSON, WARREN HARDING, FRANKLIN

ROOSEVELT, AND HARRY TRUMAN.

297 RUSSELL, R.B. "HOW SENATE DEAN JUDGES SIX PRESIDENTS: EXCERPTS FROM REMARKS." U S NEWS 68 (FEB 12, 1970): 18.

298 SCHLESINGER, A.M., SR. "HISTORIANS RATE U.S. PRESIDENTS." LIFE 25 (NOV 1, 1948): 65-6+.

299 ----------. "OUR PRESIDENT: A RATING BY 75 HISTORIANS." N Y TIMES MAG (JULY 29, 1962).

300 SULZNER, G.T. "THE COLD WAR PRESIDENTS." IN PERSPECTIVES ON THE PRESIDENCY: A COLLECTION, EDITED BY S. BACH AND G.T. SULZNER. LEXINGTON, MASS.: D.C. HEATH AND CO., 1974, PP. 18-34.

CONCISE SUMMARY OF MAJOR ASPECTS OF PRESIDENTIAL FOREIGN AND DOMESTIC POLICY FROM TRUMAN THROUGH EARLY-WATERGATE NIXON, ARGUING THAT, IN THE POST-DETENTE ERA, THE GROWTH OF PRESIDENTIAL POWER WILL REACH A PLATEAU AND CONGRESSIONAL LEADERSHIP OF GOVERNMENT WILL BE ENHANCED.

301 WILLIAMS, W.A. SOME PRESIDENTS : WILSON TO NIXON. NEW YORK: VINTAGE BOOKS, 1972, PP. 122.

COMMENT ON AMERICAN POLITICS AND SOCIETY BY A RADICAL CRITIC.

302 WOODWARD, C.V., ED. RESPONSES OF THE PRESIDENTS TO CHARGES OF MISCONDUCT. NEW YORK: DELL PUBLISHING CO., 1974, PP. 401.

A CHRONOLOGICAL SET OF BRIEF SUMMARIES OF HISTORICAL EPISODES.

SEE ALSO 629, 782, 913, 994, 1196, 1415, 1564, 1568, 1579, 1583, 1615, 1723, 1732, 1878, 2047, 2449

7

FRANKLIN D. ROOSEVELT AND HIS ADMINISTRATION

A. GENERAL HISTORICAL ACCOUNTS AND BIOGRAPHIES

303 BURNS, J.M. ROOSEVELT. 2 VOLS. NEW YORK: HARCOURT, BRACE AND CO., 1956,1970.

FIRST VOLUME, THE LION AND THE FOX, DEALS WITH PRE-WAR DOMESTIC LEADERSHIP. SECOND VOLUME, THE SOLDIER OF FREEDOM, ASSESSES FDR'S PERFORMANCE AS COMMANDER IN CHIEF.

304 CONKIN, P.K. THE NEW DEAL. 2ND ED. NEW YORK: THOMAS Y. CROWELL, 1975, PP. 114.

A CAREFUL SUMMARY SURVEY, DRAWING ON RECENT SCHOLARSHIP AND ON ARCHIVAL SOURCES.

305 DANIELS, J. THE END OF INNOCENCE: FRANKLIN D. ROOSEVELT AND THE ERA OF THE NEW DEAL. PHILADELPHIA: LIPPINCOTT, 1954, PP. 351.

306 FLYNN, J.T. THE ROOSEVELT MYTH. NEW YORK: DEVIN-ADAIR, 1956, PP. 465.

ONE OF THE MANY WORKS BY AN ANTI-FDR POLEMICIST. INTERESTING AS A SPECIMEN OF THE SOCIO-POLITICAL PHENOMENON OF "ROOSEVELT-HATING", AND FOR SPECIFIC POINTS MADE BY FLYNN THAT HAVE BEEN MORE SYSTEMATICALLY ARGUED BY OTHER FDR CRITICS.

307 FREIDEL, F. FRANKLIN D. ROOSEVELT. 4 VOLUMES. BOSTON: LITTLE, BROWN, 1952, 1954, 1956, 1973.

THE MOST COMPREHENSIVE SCHOLARLY LIFE-HISTORY-IN PROGRESS. VOLUME 4 REACHES ROOSEVELT'S FIRST YEAR IN OFFICE.

308 GOLDMAN, E.F. RENDEZVOUS WITH DESTINY: A HISTORY OF MODERN AMERICAN REFORM. NEW YORK: ALFRED A. KNOPF, 1952, PP. 503. REVISED AND ABRIDGED EDITION, NEW YORK: VINTAGE, 1956, PP. 372.

309 GUNTHER, J. ROOSEVELT IN RETROSPECT: A PROFILE IN HISTORY. NEW YORK: HARPER, 1950, PP. 410.

VIVIDLY DESCRIBES FDR'S PERSONAL QUALITIES AND PUBLIC APPEAL.

310 LEUCHTENBURG, W.E. <u>FRANKLIN D. ROOSEVELT AND THE NEW DEAL, 1932-1940</u>. NEW YORK: HARPER & ROW, 1963, PP. 390.

CAREFUL SCHOLARLY STUDY OF FDR'S FIRST TWO TERMS.

311 ROBINSON, E.E. <u>THE ROOSEVELT LEADERSHIP, 1933-1945</u>. PHILADELPHIA: LIPPINCOTT, 1955, PP. 491. ALSO, NEW YORK: DE CAPO PRESS, 1972, PP. 491.

A CONSERVATIVE SCHOLAR'S CAREFULLY DOCUMENTED CRITIQUE OF ROOSEVELT.

312 ROOSEVELT, ELLIOTT, AND BROUGH, J. <u>A RENDEZVOUS WITH DESTINY: THE ROOSEVELTS OF THE WHITE HOUSE</u>. NEW YORK: PUTNAM, 1975, PP. 446.

313 ----------. <u>AN UNTOLD STORY: THE ROOSEVELTS OF HYDE PARK</u>. NEW YORK: PUTNAM AND SONS, 1973, PP. 318.

ONE OF THE 2 ANECDOTAL MEMOIRS BY ONE OF ROOSEVELT'S SONS.

314 ROOSEVELT, J., AND SHALETT, S. <u>AFFECTIONATELY, F.D.R.: A SON'S STORY OF A LONELY MAN</u>. NEW YORK: HARCOURT, BRACE, 1959.

PERSONAL MEMOIRS OF ANOTHER OF ROOSEVELT'S SONS.

315 SCHLESINGER, A.M., JR. <u>THE AGE OF ROOSEVELT</u>. 3 VOLS. BOSTON: HOUGHTON, 1957, 1959, 1960.

VOLUMES TO DATE COVER THE GREAT DEPRESSION AS AN ANTECEDENT OF FDR'S ELECTION AND FIRST TERM.

316 TUGWELL, R.G. <u>F.D.R., THE ARCHITECT OF AN ERA</u>. NEW YORK: MACMILLAN, 1967, PP. 270.

EXPANDS AND GENERALIZES TUGWELL'S EARLIER <u>THE DEMOCRATIC ROOSEVELT</u>. ONE OF MANY BOOKS TUGWELL HAS WRITTEN ON FDR, THIS "POPULAR" WORK EXUDES A SENSE OF TUGWELL'S PERSONAL RESPECT AND ADMIRATION FOR ROOSEVELT THE MAN, AND HIS ACCOMPLISHMENTS.

317 ----------. <u>THE DEMOCRATIC ROOSEVELT: A BIOGRAPHY OF FRANKLIN D. ROOSEVELT</u>. GARDEN CITY: DOUBLEDAY, 1957, PP. 712.

ONE OF THE SEVERAL SYMPATHETIC ACCOUNTS OF ROOSEVELT'S CAREER BY A KEY FORMER ADVISOR.

SEE ALSO 279, 284, 287, 295, 329, 378, 578, 1555, 1564, 1884

B. PRESIDENT'S PAPERS, MEMOIRS

318 DANIELS, J., ED. <u>THE COMPLETE PRESIDENTIAL PRESS</u>

CONFERENCES OF FRANKLIN DELANO ROOSEVELT. 12 VOLUMES. NEW
YORK: DE CAPO PRESS, 1972.

319 JACOBY, R.L. CALENDAR OF THE SPEECHES AND OTHER PUBLISHED
STATEMENTS OF FRANKLIN D. ROOSEVELT, 1910-1920. HYDE
PARK: FRANKLIN D. ROOSEVELT LIBRARY, 1952, PP. 160.

320 MUZZEY, D.S. "PUBLIC PAPERS OF FRANKLIN D. ROOSEVELT."
PSQ 57 (1942): 426-431.

321 ROOSEVELT LIBRARY. HISTORICAL MATERIALS IN THE FRANKLIN
D. ROOSEVELT LIBRARY. HYDE PARK, N.Y.: NATL ARC AND REC
SER, JULY 1975, PP. 17.

322 ROOSEVELT, ELLIOTT, ED. F.D.R.: HIS PERSONAL LETTERS.
NEW YORK: DUELL, SLOAN, 1947-1950, 4 VOLS.

323 ROOSEVELT, F.D. FRANKLIN D. ROOSEVELT AND FOREIGN
AFFAIRS. 3 VOLUMES. EDITED BY E.B. NIXON, CAMBRIDGE,
MASS.: HARVARD U PR, 1969.

324 ----------. LOOKING FORWARD. NEW YORK: JOHN DAY, 1933,
PP. 279.

325 ----------. ON OUR WAY. NEW YORK: DAY, 1934. REPRINTED
NEW YORK: DA CAPO, 1973, PP. 300.

326 ----------. RENDEZVOUS WITH DESTINY: ADDRESSES AND
OPINIONS OF FRANKLIN DELANO ROOSEVELT. SELECTED AND
ARRANGED WITH FACTUAL AND HISTORICAL REFERENCES AND
SUMMARIES BY J.B.S. HARDMAN. NEW YORK: DRYDEN, 1944, PP.
367.

327 ROSENMAN, S.I., ED. THE PUBLIC PAPERS AND ADDRESSES OF
FRANKLIN D. ROOSEVELT. 13 VOLUMES. NEW YORK: RUSSELL,
1938-1950.

EDITOR WAS A ROOSEVELT AIDE.

328 SELIGMAN, L.G., AND CORNWELL, E.E., EDS. NEW DEAL
MOSAIC. EUGENE, OREGON: UNIVERSITY OF OREGON BOOKS, 1965,
PP. 578.

SELECTED, VERBATIM TRANSCRIPTS OF AN EARLY NEW DEAL
COORDINATING COMMITTEE, THE NATIONAL EMERGENCY COUNCIL.

SEE ALSO 54, 329, 653, 2033

C. COMPENDIA AND BIBLIOGRAPHIES

329 BREMER, H.F. FRANKLIN DELANO ROOSEVELT 1882- 1945. DOBBS
FERRY, N.Y.: OCEANA, 1971, PP. 220.

FDR'S CHRONOLOGY, SELECTED PRESIDENTIAL DOCUMENTS, PLUS
BIBLIOGRAPHY.

330 DEGLER, C.N., ED. THE NEW DEAL. CHICAGO: QUADRANGLE
BOOKS, 1970, PP. 242.

331 FREIDEL, F., ED. THE NEW DEAL AND THE AMERICAN PEOPLE.
ENGLEWOOD CLIFFS, N.J.: PRENTICE-HALL, 1964, PP. 151.

332 GRAHAM, O.L., ED. THE NEW DEAL: THE CRITICAL ISSUES.
BOSTON: LITTLE, BROWN, 1971.

333 HAMBY, A.L., ED. THE NEW DEAL. NEW YORK: WEYBRIGHT,
1969, PP. 244.

334 HOLLINGSWORTH, H.M., AND HOLMES, W.F., EDS. ESSAYS ON THE
NEW DEAL. AUSTIN: U OF TEXAS PR, 1969, PP. 115.

335 KIRKENDALL, R.S. "THE NEW DEAL AS WATERSHED: THE RECENT
LITERATURE." J OF AMERICAN HISTORY 54 (1968): 839-852.

SURVEYS SOME 100 STUDIES FROM 1962 TO 1966 AND SUGGESTS
THAT THE NEW DEAL'S HISTORIANS OUGHT NOT TO EXAGGERATE
INNOVATION TO THE POINT OF NEGLECTING CONTINUITY.

336 KIRKENDALL, R.S., ED. THE NEW DEAL: THE HISTORICAL
DEBATE. NEW YORK: WILEY, 1973, PP. 160.

337 LEUCHTENBURG, W.E., ED. FRANKLIN D. ROOSEVELT: A
PROFILE. NEW YORK: HILL AND WANG, 1967, PP. 262.

AN ANTHOLOGY ESPECIALLY STRESSING WORKS ON ROOSEVELT'S
LEADERSHIP AND HIS PERSONAL QUALITIES.

338 ----------. THE NEW DEAL: A DOCUMENTARY HISTORY.

COLUMBIA, S.C.: UNIVERSITY OF SOUTH CAROLINA PRESS, 1968, PP. 263.

339 MAJOR, J., ED. THE NEW DEAL. NEW YORK: B&N, 1967, PP. 261.

340 NASH, G.D., ED. FRANKLIN DELANO ROOSEVELT. ENGLEWOOD CLIFFS, N.J.: PRENTICE-HALL, 1967, PP. 182.

341 STEWART, W.J. THE ERA OF FRANKLIN D. ROOSEVELT, A SELECTED BIBLIOGRAPHY OF PERIODICAL AND DISSERTATION LITERATURE, 1945-1971. NEW YORK: NATIONAL ARCHIVES, 1974, PP. 175.

A LIST OF 2603 WRITINGS ON FDR FROM 1945 TO 1971, MOST ITEMS ANNOTATED.

342 ZINN, H., ED. NEW DEAL THOUGHT. INDIANAPOLIS: BOBBS-MERRILL, 1966, PP. 431.

CONTAINS 72 BRIEF, CONTEMPORARY WRITINGS ON THE NEW DEAL AS WELL AS USEFUL PREFATORY REMARKS BY THE EDITOR.

SEE ALSO 328, 329, 418, 468

D. SELECTED MATERIAL ON PRE-PRESIDENTIAL BACKGROUND

343 BELLUSH, B. FRANKLIN D. ROOSEVELT AS GOVERNOR OF NEW YORK. NEW YORK: COLUMBIA UNIVERSITY PRESS, 1955, PP. 338.

344 FREIDEL, F. "ROOSEVELT'S FATHER." FDR COLLECTOR 5 (1952): 3-10.

345 ----------. "THE EDUCATION OF FRANKLIN D. ROOSEVELT." HARVARD EDUCATIONAL R 31 (1961): 158-67.

346 HOYT, M.H. "ROOSEVELT ENTERS POLITICS." FDR COLLECTOR 1 (1949): 3-9.

ROOSEVELT CONFINED HIS 1910 CAMPAIGN FOR ELECTION TO THE NEW YORK STATE SENATE TO LOCAL ISSUES.

347 KYBAL, V. "SENATOR FRANKLIN D. ROOSEVELT, 1910-1913." FDR COLLECTOR 4 (1952): 3-29.

CONSIDERS CAMPAIGN AND ELECTION OF FDR IN 1910 AND HIS SUBSEQUENT ROLE AS STATE SENATOR IN ALBANY AND LEADER OF

THE INSURGENTS.

SEE ALSO 307

E. ADVISERS AND ADVISORY RELATIONS

348 ALLEN, R.S. "MEN AROUND THE PRESIDENT." HARPER'S 168 (FEB 1934): 267-277.

349 ALSOP, J., AND KINTNER, R. MEN AROUND THE PRESIDENT. NEW YORK: DOUBLEDAY, 1939, PP. 212.

350 BERLE, A. NAVIGATING THE RAPIDS, 1918-1971. NEW YORK: HARCOURT, BRACE, JOVANOVICH, 1973, PP. 859.

351 BIDDLE, F. IN BRIEF AUTHORITY. GARDEN CITY, N.Y.: DOUBLEDAY, 1962, PP. 494.

MEMOIRS OF ROOSEVELT'S ATTORNEY-GENERAL.

352 ----------. "THE WARTIME CABINET." AMER HERITAGE 13 (1962): 64-77.

BIDDLE'S ACCOUNT OF HIS OWN ROLE AND HIS COMMENTS ON ROOSEVELT AND VARIOUS ROOSEVELT AIDES.

353 BLUM, J.M., ED. FROM THE DIARIES OF HENRY MORGENTHAU, JR.. 3 VOLUMES. BOSTON: HOUGHTON MIFFLIN COMPANY, 1959-1967.

A SELECTION FROM THE VERY EXTENSIVE DIARY OF ROOSEVELT'S SECRETARY OF THE TREASURY. THE ORIGINAL IS AVAILABLE AT THE ROOSEVELT LIBRARY IN HYDE PARK.

354 ----------. THE PRICE OF VISION: THE DIARY OF HENRY A. WALLACE, 1942-1946. BOSTON: HOUGHTON MIFFLIN, 1973, PP. 707.

DEALS WITH WALLACE'S YEARS AS VICE PRESIDENT AND HIS PERIOD AS COMMERCE SECRETARY.

355 BUSH, V. PIECES OF THE ACTION. NEW YORK: MORROW, 1970, PP. 366.

COVERS HIS MANY CONTRIBUTIONS TO SCIENCE ADVISING.

356 BYRNES, J.F. ALL IN ONE LIFETIME. NEW YORK: HARPER, 1958, PP. 432.

357 CHARLES, S.F. MINISTER OF RELIEF: HARRY HOPKINS AND THE DEPRESSION. SYRACUSE, NEW YORK: SYRACUSE UNIVERSITY

PRESS, 1963, PP. 286.

358 COIT, M.L. MR. BARUCH. BOSTON: HOUGHTON MIFFLIN, 1957, PP. 784.

ON THE PERENNIAL INFORMAL ADVISOR TO PRESIDENTS.

359 CREEL, G. "THE KITCHEN CABINET." COLLIER'S (JUNE 17, 1933): 17+.

360 CURRENT, R.N. SECRETARY STIMSON: A STUDY IN STATECRAFT. NEW BRUNSWICK: RUTGERS UNIVERSITY PRESS, 1954, PP. 272.

361 DANIELS, J. WHITE HOUSE WITNESS: 1942-1945. GARDEN CITY, N.Y.: DOUBLEDAY, 1975, PP. 299.

JOURNAL OF A PRESS AIDE.

362 DOUGLAS, W.O. GO EAST, YOUNG MAN: THE EARLY YEARS: THE AUTOBIOGRAPHY OF WILLIAM O. DOUGLAS. NEW YORK: DELL, 1974, PP. 493.

INCLUDES MUCH ON PERSONALITIES IN NEW DEAL WASHINGTON.

363 FARLEY, J.A. BEHIND THE BALLOTS. NEW YORK: HARCOURT, BRACE & CO., 1938, PP. 392.

364 ----------. JIM FARLEY'S STORY: THE ROOSEVELT YEARS. NEW YORK: MCGRAW-HILL, 1948, PP. 388.

THE MOST COMPLETE ACCOUNT OF HIS LEADERSHIP OF THE DEMOCRATIC PARTY AS THE DEMOCRATIC COALITION EVOLVED IN THE 1930'S.

365 FENNO, R.F. "PRESIDENT-CABINET RELATIONS: A PATTERN AND A CASE STUDY." APSR 52 (1958): 388-405.

HOW A CONSERVATIVE, ADMINISTRATIVE BRANCH EXECUTIVE, IN BASIC DISAGREEMENT WITH FDR'S GOALS, NEVERTHELESS CONTRIBUTED - AT LEAST FOR MANY YEARS - TO FDR'S OVERALL PURPOSES BY STRENGTHENING FDR'S TIES TO CONGRESSIONAL CONSERVATIVES. FOR PARALLEL EXAMPLES AND A BROADER CONTEXTUAL DISCUSSION SEE FENNO'S BOOK, THE PRESIDENT'S CABINET.

366 FLYNN, E.J. YOU'RE THE BOSS. NEW YORK: VIKING PRESS, 1947.

AUTOBIOGRAPHY OF THE BRONX COUNTY (NEW YORK CITY) LEADER OF THE DEMOCRATIC PARTY, NOTING MANY OF HIS POLITICAL ASSOCIATIONS WITH FDR.

367 FLYNN, J.T. "MR. HOPKINS AND MR. ROOSEVELT." YALE R 28
NO4:667-79 JE '39.

368 FREEDMAN, M. ROOSEVELT AND FRANKFURTER, THEIR
CORRESPONDENCE, 1928-1945. BOSTON: LITTLE,BROWN, 1967,
REPUBLISHED 1968.

369 HARMON, M.J. "SOME CONTRIBUTIONS OF HAROLD L. ICKES."
WESTERN POLITICAL Q 7 (1954): 238-252.

370 HARRIMAN, W.A., AND ABEL, E. SPECIAL ENVOY TO CHURCHILL
AND STALIN, 1941-1946. NEW YORK: RANDOM, 1975, PP. 595.

371 HENRY, L.L. "LOUIS BROWNLOW AND THE GOVERNMENTAL ARTS."
WESTERN POLITICAL Q 8 (1955): 453-464.

372 ICKES, H.L. THE AUTOBIOGRAPHY OF A CURMUDGEON. NEW YORK:
REYNAL AND HITCHCOCK, 1943, PP. 350.

THE INTERIOR DEPARTMENT SECRETARY'S AUTOBIOGRAPHY NEEDS TO
BE READ IN CONJUNCTION WITH HIS FAR MORE INSTRUCTIVE
DIARIES.

373 ----------. THE SECRET DIARY OF HAROLD I. ICKES. 3
VOLS. NEW YORK: SIMON AND SCHUSTER, 1953, 1954, 1955.

374 JAFFE, L.L. "PROFESSORS AND JUDGES AS ADVISORS TO
GOVERNMENT: REFLECTIONS ON THE ROOSEVELT-FRANKFURTER
RELATIONSHIP." HARVARD LAW R 83 (1969): 366-375.

A CRITICAL VIEW OF JUSTICE FELIX FRANKFURTER'S
CONTINUATION AS INFORMAL ADVISOR TO FDR AFTER HIS
APPOINTMENT TO THE SUPREME COURT.

375 KARL, B.D. CHARLES E. MERRIAM AND THE STUDY OF POLITICS.
CHICAGO: U OF CHICAGO PR, 1974, PP. 337.

INCLUDES A DISCUSSION OF MERRIAM'S PARTICIPATION IN THE
ROOSEVELT-APPOINTED COMMITTEE THAT LED TO THE
REORGANIZATION ACT OF 1939.

376 KENNAN, G.F. MEMOIRS 1925-50; 1950-1963. 2 VOLUMES.
BOSTON: LITTLE,BROWN, 1972.

A DISCUSSION OF KENNAN'S LONG SERVICE IN THE DEPARTMENT OF
STATE AS ADVISER ON SOVIET AFFAIRS.

377 KILPATRICK, C., ED. <u>ROOSEVELT AND DANIELS: A FRIENDSHIP IN POLITICS</u>. CHAPEL HILL: UNIVERSITY OF NORTH CAROLINA PRESS, 1952.

ON JOSEPHUS DANIELS, ROOSEVELT'S WORLD WAR ONE MENTOR AS SECRETARY OF NAVY WHEN FDR WAS ASSISTANT SECRETARY. AMBASSADOR TO MEXICO, 1933-41.

378 LASH, J.P. <u>ELEANOR AND FRANKLIN</u>. NEW YORK: NEW AMERICAN LIBRARY, 1971, PP. 1020.

379 LASH, J.P., ED. <u>FROM THE DIARIES OF FELIX FRANKFURTER</u>. NEW YORK: NORTON, 1975, PP. 366.

INCLUDES INFORMATION ON FRANKFURTER'S ADVICE TO ROOSEVELT WHILE HE WAS STILL A HARVARD LAW PROFESSOR AND HIS CONTINUING SERVICE AS AN INFORMAL ADVISER WHILE SERVING ON THE SUPREME COURT.

380 LEAHY, W.D. <u>I WAS THERE: THE PERSONAL STORY OF THE CHIEF OF STAFF TO PRESIDENTS ROOSEVELT AND TRUMAN</u>. NEW YORK: MCGRAW-HILL, 1950.

381 LILIENTHAL, D.E. <u>THE JOURNALS OF DAVID E. LILIENTHAL: VOLUME 1: THE TVA YEARS, 1939-1945</u>. NEW YORK: HARPER AND ROW, 1964, PP. 734.

THE PRIVATE JOURNAL OF THE MAN WHO LED IN THE DEVELOPMENT OF THE TENNESSEE VALLEY AUTHORITY, INCLUDING SELECTIONS FROM HIS EARLIER, PRE-1939 JOURNAL-ENTRIES AS WELL AS THE COMPLETE JOURNAL FOR THE YEARS 1939-1945. FOR THE CONTINUATION OF LILIENTHAL'S CAREER DURING THE TRUMAN ADMINISTRATION, SEE <u>VOLUME II: THE ATOMIC ENERGY YEARS, 1945-1950</u>.

382 MARTIN, G. <u>MADAME SECRETARY FRANCES PERKINS</u>. BOSTON: HOUGHTON, 1976, PP. 589.

THE MOST AUTHORITATIVE BIOGRAPHY OF ROOSEVELT'S SECRETARY OF LABOR.

383 MICHELSON, C. <u>THE GHOST TALKS</u>. NEW YORK: PUTMAN, 1944.

BEHIND-THE-SCENES NEW DEAL ANECDOTES BY A JOURNALIST-TURNED-SPEECH-WRITER FOR ROOSEVELT OFFICIALS.

384 MOLEY, R. <u>AFTER SEVEN YEARS</u>. REPRINTED NEW YORK: DA CAPO, 1971.

385 MOONEY, B. <u>ROOSEVELT AND RAYBURN: A POLITICAL PARTNERSHIP</u>. PHILADELPHIA: LIPPINCOTT, 1971, PP. 228.

386 MORISON, E.E. TURMOIL AND TRADITION: A STUDY OF THE LIFE AND TIMES OF HENRY L. STIMSON. NEW YORK: ATHENEUM, 1964, PP. 565.

387 PERKINS, F. THE ROOSEVELT I KNEW. NEW YORK: VIKING PRESS, 1946, PP. 408. ALSO, NEW YORK: HARPER COLOPHON BOOKS, 1964, PP. 408.

MEMORIES OF ROOSEVELT BOTH AS GOVERNOR AND AS PRESIDENT BY A LONG-TIME ASSOCIATE WHO BECAME HIS SECRETARY OF LABOR AND WHO PROVIDES A PARTICULARLY RICH PICTURE OF ROOSEVELT THE PERSON.

388 PRATT, J.W. CORDELL HULL, 1933-1944. 2 VOLUMES. NEW YORK: COOPER SQUARE, 1964.

389 RICHBERG, D.R. MY HERO: THE INDISCREET MEMOIRS OF AN EVENTFUL BUT UNHEROIC LIFE. NEW YORK: PUTNAM, 1954, PP. 367.

AN ANECDOTALLY RICH MEMOIR BY THE HEAD OF THE EARLY NEW DEAL COORDINATING AGENCY, THE NATIONAL EMERGENCY COUNCIL.

390 ROLLINS, A.B. ROOSEVELT AND HOWE. NEW YORK: KNOPF, 1962, PP. 479.

ON ROOSEVELT'S RELATIONSHIP WITH THE EX-NEWSPAPERMAN WHO SERVED AS HIS PERSONAL POLITICAL ADVISER AND AIDE, BEGINNING WITH ROOSEVELT'S EARLY PERIOD OF POLITICAL ACTIVITY.

391 ROOSEVELT, ELEANOR. THIS I REMEMBER. NEW YORK: HARPER, 1949, PP. 226.

THIS AND MRS. ROOSEVELT'S EARLIER MEMOIR, THIS IS MY STORY, SHOULD BE READ IN THE CONTEXT OF JOSEPH LASH'S COMPREHENSIVE ELEANOR AND FRANKLIN.

392 ----------. THIS IS MY STORY. NEW YORK: HARPER, 1937, PP. 365.

393 "ROOSEVELT'S MEN." LIFE 18 (APRIL 23, 1945): 73-81.

394 ROSEN, E.A. "ROOSEVELT AND THE BRAINS TRUST: AN HISTORICAL OVERVIEW." PSQ 87 (1972): 531-557.

395 ROSENMAN, S.I. WORKING WITH ROOSEVELT. NEW YORK: HARPER,

1952, PP. 560.

ONE OF THE SEVERAL MOST OFTEN CITED MEMOIRES DEALING WITH ROOSEVELT AS A HUMAN BEING. ALSO ESPECIALLY VALUABLE FOR ITS ACCOUNTS OF HOW ROOSEVELT'S SPEECHES WERE WRITTEN.

396 SCHAPSMEIER, E.L., AND SCHAPSMEIER, F. HENRY A. WALLACE OF IOWA: THE AGRARIAN YEARS, 1910-1940. AMES: IOWA STATE PRESS, 1969.

STRESSES WALLACE'S ROLE AS AGRICULTURE SECRETARY.

397 ----------. PROPHET IN POLITICS: HENRY A. WALLACE AND THE WAR YEARS, 1940-1945. AMES: IOWA STATE UNIVERSITY PRESS, 1971.

COVERS WALLACE AS VICE PRESIDENT.

398 SHERWOOD, R.E. ROOSEVELT AND HOPKINS, AN INTIMATE HISTORY. NEW YORK: HARPER AND ROW, 1950, PP. 1002.

THE BULK OF THIS HIGHLY INFLUENTIAL WORK BY THE PLAYWRIGHT WHO SERVED AS A ROOSEVELT-AIDE DEALS WITH HOPKINS' ROLE AS FDR'S EMISSARY TO CHURCHILL AND STALIN DURING WORLD WAR II.

399 STERNSHER, B. REXFORD G. TUGWELL AND THE NEW DEAL. NEW BRUNSWICK, N.J.: RUTGERS UNIV. PRESS, 1964, PP. 535.

400 ----------. "THE STIMSON DOCTRINE: FDR VERSUS MOLEY AND TUGWELL." PACIFIC HISTORICAL R 31 (1962): 281-89.

401 STETTINIUS, E.R., JR. DIARIES OF EDWARD R. STETTINIUS, JR., 1943-1946. ED. GEORGE H. HERRING, JR., NEW YORK: WATTS, 1975.

402 STEVENSON, W. A MAN CALLED INTREPID: THE SECRET WAR. NEW YORK: HARCOURT, BRACE, JOVANOVICH, 1976, PP. 486.

"INTREPID" WAS STEVENSON'S CODE-NAME. HIS SECRET LIAISON-WORK BETWEEN ROOSEVELT AND CHURCHILL PRIOR TO AS WELL AS DURING AMERICAN INVOLVEMENT IN WORLD WAR II REMAINED CLASSIFIED UNTIL THE 1970'S.

403 STILES, L. THE MAN BEHIND ROOSEVELT; THE STORY OF LOUIS MC HENRY HOWE. CLEVELAND: WORLD PUBLISHING COMPANY, 1954, PP. 311.

404 STIMSON, H.L., AND BUNDY, M. ON ACTIVE SERVICE IN PEACE AND WAR. NEW YORK: HARPER, 1948, PP. 396.

SECRETARY STIMSON'S AUTOBIOGRAPHY. WRITTEN IN THE THIRD PERSON WITH BUNDY AS NARRATOR. ALSO SEE CURRENT'S SECRETARY STIMSON.

405 SWISHER, C.B., ED. SELECTED PAPERS OF HOMER CUMMINGS: ATTORNEY GENERAL OF THE UNITED STATES, 1933-1939. NEW YORK: SCRIBNER, 1939, PP. 316. REPRINTED DA CAPO, 1972.

PERHAPS MOST NOTABLE FOR ITS INSIGHT INTO CUMMINGS' ROLE IN THE ABORTIVE EFFORT TO EXPAND THE SUPREME COURT.

406 "THE ROOSEVELT KITCHEN CABINET." LITERARY DIGEST (DEC 13, 1932): 18+.

407 TIMMONS, B.N. GARNER OF TEXAS. NEW YORK: HARPER, 1948.

ROOSEVELT'S VICE-PRESIDENT DURING HIS FIRST 2 TERMS.

408 ----------. JESSIE H. JONES: THE MAN AND THE STATESMAN. NEW YORK: HOLT, 1956, PP. 414.

A BIOGRAPHY OF THE CHAIRMAN OF ROOSEVELT'S RECONSTRUCTION FINANCE CORPORATION AND SUBSEQUENTLY SECRETARY OF COMMERCE.

409 TRANI, E. "CONFLICT OR COMPROMISE: HAROLD L. ICKES AND FRANKLIN D. ROOSEVELT." NORTH DAKOTA Q 36 (WINTER 1968): 20-29.

410 TUGWELL, R.G. THE BRAINS TRUST. NEW YORK: VIKING PRESS, 1968, PP. 538.

THE RECOLLECTIONS OF ONE OF THE 3 COLUMBIA UNIVERSITY PROFESSORS (THE OTHERS BEING RAYMOND MOLEY AND ADOLF BERLE, JR.) CONCERNING THEIR SERVICE AS POLICY-ADVISERS DURING THE PERIOD OF ROOSEVELT'S NOMINATION AND ELECTION CAMPAIGNS AND HIS TIME AS PRESIDENT-ELECT. THE MOST COMPREHENSIVE, SCHOLARLY ACCOUNT OF THIS PERIOD DURING WHICH SO MUCH OF THE POLICY OF THE NEW DEAL DEVELOPED IS TO BE FOUND IN THE LATTER VOLUMES OF FREIDEL'S BIOGRAPHY OF ROOSEVELT.

411 TULLY, G. FDR, MY BOSS. NEW YORK: SCRIBNER, 1949, PP. 391.

RECOLLECTIONS BY PRESIDENT ROOSEVELT'S LONG-TIME PERSONAL SECRETARY.

412 UNOFFICIAL OBSERVER. THE NEW DEALERS. NEW YORK: SIMON AND SCHUSTER, 1934, PP. 414.

JOURNALISTIC SKETCHES OF NUMEROUS OFFICIAL AND UNOFFICIAL ROOSEVELT-ASSOCIATES.

413 WALKER, R.L. E.R. STETTINIUS, JR.. NEW YORK: COOPER

SQUARE, 1965, PP. 423.

A VOLUME IN THE "AMERICAN SECRETARIES OF STATE AND THEIR DIPLOMACIES" SERIES.

SEE ALSO 294, 448, 449, 499, 515, 611, 651, 652, 937, 938, 1706, 1788, 1792, 1805, 2003, 2005

F. SPECIFIC EVENTS, ACTIVITIES AND POLICIES

1. THE NEW DEAL AND OTHER PRE-WAR DOMESTIC TOPICS

414 ALSOP, J., AND CATLEDGE, T. THE 168 DAYS. GARDEN CITY, N.Y.: DOUBLEDAY, 1938, PP. 312.

JOURNALISTIC RECONSTRUCTION OF THE "COURT-PACKING" EPISODE.

415 APPLEBY, P. "ROOSEVELT'S THIRD-TERM DECISION." APSR 46 (1952): 754-65.

ON THE BASIS OF HIS OWN MEMORIES AS ASSISTANT TO THE SECRETARY OF AGRICULTURE, APPLEBY ARGUES THAT ROOSEVELT HAD NOT MADE UP HIS MIND ABOUT WHETHER OR NOT TO RUN FOR A 3RD TERM UNTIL AFTER THE FORMAL VOTE OF THE DEMOCRATIC CONVENTION.

416 AWALT, F.G. "RECOLLECTIONS OF THE BANKING CRISIS IN 1933." BUSINESS HISTORY R 43 (AUTUMN 1969): 347-371.

ON THE COOPERATION BETWEEN HOOVER'S AND ROOSEVELT'S TECHNICAL AIDES IN THE DRAFTING OF THE EMERGENCY BANKING ACT. AT THE TIME, AWALT WAS ACTING COMPTROLLER OF THE CURRENCY.

417 BAKER, L. BACK TO BACK, THE DUEL BETWEEN FDR AND THE SUPREME COURT. NEW YORK: MACMILLAN, 1967, PP. 311.

418 BARNES, W.H., AND LITTLEFIELD, A.W., EDS. THE SUPREME COURT ISSUE AND THE CONSTITUTION. NEW YORK: BARNES AND NOBLE, 1937, PP. 149.

A CONTEMPORARY COMPENDIUM OF CONFLICTING LEGAL VIEWS ABOUT THE CONSTITUTIONAL STANDING OF ROOSEVELT'S PROPOSED EXPANSION OF THE SUPREME COURT.

419 BERNSTEIN, I. THE NEW DEAL COLLECTIVE BARGAINING POLICY. BERKELEY: UC PR, 1950. REPRINTED NEW YORK: DA CAPO, 1975, PP. 178.

420 ----------. TURBULENT YEARS: A HISTORY OF THE AMERICAN WORKER 1933-1941. BOSTON: HOUGHTON-MIFFLIN, 1971.

421 BRENNAN, J.A. SILVER AND THE FIRST NEW DEAL. RENO: U OF NEVADA PR, 1969, PP. 187.

422 CAMPBELL, C.M. THE FARM BUREAU AND THE NEW DEAL: A STUDY OF THE MAKING OF NATIONAL FARM POLICY 1933-40. URBANA: U OF ILL PR, 1962, PP. 215.

423 CONKIN, P.K. FDR AND THE ORIGINS OF THE WELFARE STATE. NEW YORK: CROWELL, 1967, PP. 118.

424 CROWNOVER, A.B. FRANKLIN D. ROOSEVELT AND THE PRIMARY CAMPAIGNS OF THE 1938 CONGRESSIONAL ELECTION. PRINCETON: PRINCETON UNIVERSITY PRESS, 1955, PP. 177.

425 DONAHOE, B.F. PRIVATE PLANS AND PUBLIC DANGERS: THE STORY OF FDR'S THIRD NOMINATION. NOTRE DAME: UNIV. OF NOTRE DAME PRESS, 1965, PP. 256.

426 DROZE, W.H. "THE NEW DEAL'S SHELTERBELT PROJECT, 1934-1942." IN ESSAYS ON THE NEW DEAL, EDITED BY G.M. HOLLINGSWORTH AND W.F. HOLMES, AUSTIN: U TEXAS PR, 1969, PP. 25-48.

427 EVEREST, A.S. MORGENTHAU, THE NEW DEAL AND SILVER: A STORY OF PRESSURE POLITICS. NEW YORK: DA CAPO PRESS, 1973, PP. 209.

428 FEIS, H. "KEYNES IN RETROSPECT." FOREIGN AFFAIRS 29 (JULY 1951): 564-577.

KEYNES EFFECT ON THE U.S.DURING THE NEW DEAL.

429 FEUER, L.S. "AMERICAN TRAVELERS TO THE SOVIET UNION, 1917-1932: THE FORMATION OF A COMPONENT OF NEW DEAL IDEOLOGY." AMER QUAR 14 (SUMMER 1962): 119-149.

AMERICAN VISITORS TO THE SOVIET UNION HAD BROUGHT BACK ENTHUSIASTIC ACCOUNTS OF THE SOVIET SOCIAL EXPERIMENT. ROOSEVELT REGARDED THE SOVIET EXPERIMENT AS AKIN TO HIS OWN.

430 FINE, S. "PRESIDENT ROOSEVELT AND THE AUTOMOBILE CODE." THE MISSISSIPPI VALLEY HISTORICAL REVIEW 45 (JUNE 1958):23-50.

431 GARDNER, L.C. ECONOMIC ASPECTS OF THE NEW DEAL. MADISON: U WISC PR, 1964, PP. 409.

432 GARDNER, R.W. "ROOSEVELT AND SUPREME COURT EXPANSION." CONNECTICUT R 3 (1969): 58-68.

433 GRAHAM, O.L. TOWARD A PLANNED SOCIETY: FROM ROOSEVELT TO NIXON. OXFORD: OXFORD UNIVERSITY PRESS, 1976, PP. 357.

434 GRESSLEY, G.M. "JOSEPH C. O'MAHONEY, FDR, AND THE SUPREME COURT." PACIFIC HISTORICAL R 40 (1971):183-201.

435 GRUBBS, D.H. CRY FROM THE COTTON: THE SOUTHERN TENANT FARMERS' UNION AND THE NEW DEAL. CHAPEL HILL: UNIVERSITY OF NORTH CAROLINA PRESS, 1971, PP. 218.

436 HAWLEY, E.W. THE NEW DEAL AND THE PROBLEM OF MONOPOLY, 1933-39: A STUDY IN ECONOMIC AMBIVALENCE. PRINCETON: PRINCETON UNIVERSITY PRESS, 1966, PP. 525.

437 JACOB, C. LEADERSHIP IN THE NEW DEAL. ENGLEWOOD CLIFFS, N.J.: PRENTICE-HALL, 1967, PP. 101.

438 JONES, B. "A PLAN FOR PLANNING IN THE NEW DEAL." SOCIAL SCIENCE Q 50 (1969): 525-534.

ON THE NATIONAL PLANNING BOARD AS COORDINATOR OF FEDERAL PROJECTS AND INITIATOR OF RESEARCH. AN ANALYSIS OF ITS FINAL REPORT AND ITS REPORT OF DECEMBER 1934.

439 KARL, B.D. EXECUTIVE REORGANIZATION AND REFORM IN THE NEW DEAL, THE GENESIS OF ADMINISTRATIVE MANAGEMENT, 1900-1939. CAMBRIDGE: HARVARD UNIVERSITY PRESS, 1963, PP. 292.

440 KIRKENDALL, R.S. SOCIAL SCIENTISTS AND FARM POLITICS IN THE AGE OF ROOSEVELT. COLUMBIA: UNIVERSITY OF MISSOURI PRESS, 1966.

441 LANDIS, J.M. "THE LEGISLATIVE HISTORY OF THE SECURITIES ACT OF 1933." GEORGE WASHINGTON LAW R 28 (OCT 1959): 29-49.

442 LEUCHTENBURG, W.E. "A KLANSMAN JOINS THE COURT: THE APPOINTMENT OF HUGO L. BLACK." UNIVERSITY OF CHICAGO LAW R 41 (FALL 1973): 1-31.

DESCRIBES THE CONTROVERSY SURROUNDING ROOSEVELT'S APPOINTMENT OF HUGO BLACK TO THE SUPREME COURT, AND THE IRONY OF A "FORMER KLANSMAN BECOMING ONE OF THE CENTURY'S LEADING EXPONENTS OF CIVIL LIBERTIES."

443 ----------. "FRANKLIN D. ROOSEVELT'S SUPREME COURT 'PACKING' PLAN." IN HOLLINGSWORTH, H. AND WHITE, W.F., EDS. ESSAYS ON THE NEW DEAL. AUSTIN, TEXAS: U OF TEXAS PR, 1969, PP. 69-115.

444 ----------. "ROOSEVELT, NORRIS AND THE 'SEVEN LITTLE TVA'S'." JP 14 (1952): 418-441.

445 ----------. "THE CASE OF THE CONTENTIOUS COMMISSIONER: HUMPHREYS' EXECUTOR V. U.S." IN FREEDOM AND REFORM: ESSAYS IN HONOR OF HENRY STEELE COMMAGER. EDITED BY H.M. HYMAN AND L.W. LEVY, NEW YORK: HAR-ROW, 1967: 276-312.

446 MCFARLAND, C.K. ROOSEVELT, LEWIS AND THE NEW DEAL, 1933-1940. FORT WORTH, TEXAS: TEX. CHRISTIAN UNIV. PRESS, 1970, PP. 132.

447 MCKINZIE, R.D. THE NEW DEAL FOR ARTISTS. PRINCETON, N.J.: PRINCETON UNIVERSITY PRESS, 1973, PP. 203.

448 MOLEY, R. AFTER SEVEN YEARS. NEW YORK: HARPER, 1939, PP. 446.

449 ----------. THE FIRST NEW DEAL. NEW YORK: HARCOURT, BRACE & WORLD, 1966, PP. 577.

THE SECOND OF MOLEY'S TWO BOOKS ON HIS EXPERIENCES AS AN ADVISOR TO FDR, WRITTEN WITH MORE HISTORICAL PERSPECTIVE THAN HIS 1930'S BOOK.

450 MOLEY, R., ET AL. "SYMPOSIUM: EARLY DAYS OF THE NEW DEAL." IN THE THIRTIES: A RECONSIDERATION IN THE LIGHT OF THE

AMERICAN POLITICAL TRADITION, EDITED BY M.J. FRISCH AND M. DIAMOND, DEKALB, ILL.: NORTHERN ILLINOIS U PR, 1968: 124-143.

451 MOORE, J.R. "SOURCES OF NEW DEAL ECONOMIC POLICY: THE INTERNATIONAL DIMENSION." J AMER HIST 61 (1974): 728-44.

452 NIXON, E.B. FRANKLIN D. ROOSEVELT AND CONSERVATION. NEW YORK: ARNO PRESS, 1972.

453 O'BRIEN, D.J. AMERICAN CATHOLICS AND SOCIAL REFORM: THE NEW DEAL YEARS. NEW YORK: OXFORD U PR, 1968, PP. 287.

454 O'CONNER, J.F.T. THE BANKING CRISIS AND RECOVERY UNDER THE ROOSEVELT ADMINISTRATION. CHICAGO: CALLAGHAN, 1938, PP. 167. REPRINTED DA CAPO, 1971.

455 PARMET, H.S., AND HECHT, M.B. NEVER AGAIN: A PRESIDENT RUNS FOR A THIRD TERM. NEW YORK: MACMILLAN, 1968, PP. 306.

456 PATENAUDE, L.V. "GARNER, SUMNERS AND CONNALLY: THE DEFEAT OF THE ROOSEVELT COURT BILL IN 1937." SOUTHWESTERN SOCIAL SCIENCE Q 74 (JULY 1970): 36-51.

ON THE IMPORTANCE OF THESE 3 MEN'S OPPOSITION TO THE COURT BILL.

457 PATTERSON, J.T. CONGRESSIONAL CONSERVATISM AND THE NEW DEAL: THE GROWTH OF THE CONSERVATIVE COALITION IN CONGRESS, 1933-1939. LEXINGTON: U OF KY PR, 1967.

458 ----------. THE NEW DEAL AND THE STATES: FEDERALISM IN TRANSITION. PRINCETON: PRINCETON UNIVERSITY PRESS, 1969, PP. 226.

459 ----------. "THE NEW DEAL AND THE STATES." AHR 73 (1967): 70-84.

460 POLENBERG, R. REORGANIZING ROOSEVELT'S GOVERNMENT. CAMBRIDGE: BOSTON UNIV. PRESS, 1966, PP. 275.

ON THE EARLY VICISSITUDES OF THE PROPOSAL BY ROOSEVELT'S COMMITTEE ON ADMINISTRATIVE MANAGEMENT TO REORGANIZE THE FEDERAL EXECUTIVE, ESPECIALLY STRESSING THE 1938 DEFEAT OF THE EXECUTIVE REORGANIZATION BILL.

461 PRICE, C.M., AND BOSKIN, J. "THE ROOSEVELT PURGE: A REAPPRAISAL." JP 28 (1966): 660-670.

ON THE ODDS FACED BY FDR IN HIS ATTEMPT TO OUST INCUMBENTS WHERE HE HIMSELF HAD ONLY WEAK LOCAL SUPPORT. ROOSEVELT'S ATTEMPT WAS A FAILURE BUT THE EXTENT OF THE FAILURE HAS BEEN EXAGGERATED.

462 RAUCH, B. THE HISTORY OF THE NEW DEAL. NEW YORK: CREATIVE AGE, 1944, PP. 369.

463 RESZIN, M. "THE DIES COMMITTEE, 1938." IN CONGRESS INVESTIGATES: A DOCUMENTED HISTORY, VOL. 4, EDITED BY A.M. SCHLESINGER, JR., AND R. BURNS, NEW YORK: CHELSEA HOUSE, 1975, PP. 2923-3112.

464 ROSS, H. "ROOSEVELT'S THIRD-TERM NOMINATION." MID-AMERICA 44 (APRIL 1962): 80-94.

AN ACCOUNT OF THE RESISTANCE TO FDR'S 3RD TERM. "IF THE NEW DEALERS HAD NOT DIRECTED AN INTENSIVE NATIONWIDE DRIVE FOR THIRD TERM DELEGATES, THE PROBABILITY IS THAT THE WILL OF THE ANTI-THIRD TERM MINORITY WOULD HAVE PREVAILED."

465 SALMOND, J.A. THE CIVILIAN CONSERVATION CORPS, 1933-1942: A NEW DEAL CASE STUDY. DURHAM: DUKE UNIVERSITY PRESS, 1967, PP. 240.

STRESSES THE LINKS BETWEEN THE NEW DEAL'S CCC AND SUBSEQUENT LIBERAL PROGRAMS TO FIGHT POVERTY AND/OR FIND OUTLETS FOR YOUNG PEOPLE'S ENERGIES, E.G., THE JOB CORPS AND THE VISTA PROGRAMS OF THE 1960'S.

466 SIREVAG, T. "ROOSEVELTIAN IDEAS AND THE 1937 COURT FIGHT: A NEGLECTED FACTOR." HISTORIAN 33 (1971): 578-595.

FDR'S UNWILLINGNESS TO COMPROMISE DURING THIS FIGHT WAS NOT JUST A MATTER OF STUBBORNESS.

467 STEIN, C.W. THE THIRD-TERM TRADITION. NEW YORK: COLUMBIA UNIVERSITY PRESS, 1943.

468 WARREN, F.A., AND WRESZIN, M., EDS. THE NEW DEAL: AN ANTHOLOGY. NEW YORK: CROWELL, 1968, PP. 254.

SELECTIONS FROM A NUMBER OF MAJOR WRITINGS ON NEW DEAL DOMESTIC POLITICS AND POLICIES.

469 WICKER, E. "ROOSEVELT'S 1933 MONETARY EXPERIMENT." J AMERICAN HISTORY 57 (1971): 864-79.

ON THE CIRCUMSTANCES THAT DREW FDR TO GEORGE WARREN'S THEORY THAT DOMESTIC PRICES WOULD RISE IF THE GOVERNMENT PURCHASED GOLD AT FREQUENT INTERVALS AND THE RESULTS OF THE GOLD-BUYING PROGRAM.

470 WILSON, W.H. "THE TWO NEW DEALS: A VALID CONCEPT?" HISTORIAN 28 (FEB 1966): 266-288.

REVIEWS REACTIONS TO BASIL RAUCH'S ARGUMENT THAT ROOSEVELT MADE A CALCULATED CHANGE FROM CONSERVATIVE PROGRAMS FOR RECOVERY TO LIBERAL POLICIES FOR REFORM IN THE YEARS 1934-1935.

471 WOLFSKILL, G. "NEW DEAL CRITICS: DID THEY MISS THE POINT?" IN ESSAYS ON THE NEW DEAL, EDITED BY H.M. HOLLINGSWORTH AND W.F. HOLMES, AUSTIN: U OF TEXAS PR, 1969: 49-68.

SEE ALSO 66, 68, 304, 304, 328, 331, 331, 339, 357, 373, 375, 381, 436, 438, 458, 459, 462, 465, 470, 471, 591, 597, 597, 1934, 2003, 2005

2. PRE-WAR FOREIGN AND NATIONAL SECURITY

472 BAKER, L. ROOSEVELT AND PEARL HARBOR. NEW YORK: MACMILLAN, 1970, PP. 356.

473 BARRON, G.J. LEADERSHIP IN CRISIS: FDR AND THE PATH TO INTERVENTION. PORT WASHINGTON, N.Y.: KENNIKAT PRESS, 1973, PP. 145.

474 BEARD, C.A. AMERICAN FOREIGN POLICY IN THE MAKING, 1932-1940: A STUDY IN RESPONSIBILITIES. NEW HAVEN: YALE U PR, 1946, PP. 336.

CRITIQUE OF ROOSEVELT'S POLICIES.

475 ----------. PRESIDENT ROOSEVELT AND THE COMING OF THE WAR, 1941: A STUDY IN APPEARANCES AND REALITIES. NEW HAVEN: YALE U PR, 1948. REPRINTED HAMDEN, ARCHON BOOKS, 1968, PP. 614.

476 BISHOP, D.G. THE ROOSEVELT-LITVINOV AGREEMENTS. SYRACUSE: SYRACUSE U PR, 1965, PP. 297.

477 BORG, D. THE UNITED STATES AND THE FAR EASTERN CRISIS OF

1933-1938: FROM THE MANCHURIAN INCIDENT THROUGH THE INITIAL STAGE OF THE UNDECLARED SINO-JAPANESE WAR. CAMBRIDGE, MASS.: HARVARD U PR, 1964, PP. 547.

478 ----------. "NOTES ON ROOSEVELT'S 'QUARANTINE' SPEECH." PSQ 72 (1957): 405-433.

479 BRANDENBURG, E. "FRANKLIN D. ROOSEVELT'S INTERNATIONAL SPEECHES." SPEECH MONOGRAPHS 16 (1949): 21-41.

480 COLE, W.S. "AMERICAN ENTRY INTO WORLD WAR II: A HISTORIOGRAPHICAL APPRAISAL." MISS VALLEY HIST R 43 (MAR 1957): 595-617.

481 DIVINE, R.A. THE RELUCTANT BELLIGERENT: AMERICAN ENTRY INTO WORLD WAR II. NEW YORK: WILEY, 1965, PP. 172.

482 DONOVAN, J.C. "CONGRESSIONAL ISOLATIONISTS AND THE ROOSEVELT FOREIGN POLICY." WORLD POLITICS 3 (1951): 229-316.

483 ESTHUS, R. "PRESIDENT ROOSEVELT'S COMMITMENT TO BRITAIN TO INTERVENE IN A PACIFIC WAR." THE MISSISSIPPI VALLEY HISTORICAL REVIEW 50 (JUNE 1963):28-38.

484 FEHRENBACH, T.R. F.D.R.'S UNDECLARED WAR, 1939 TO 1941. NEW YORK: D. MC KAY CO., 1967, PP. 344.

485 FEINGOLD, H.L. THE POLITICS OF RESCUE: THE ROOSEVELT ADMINISTRATION AND THE HOLOCAUST, 1938-1945. NEW BRUNSWICK, N.J.: RUTGERS U PR, 1970, PP. 394.

486 FEIS, H. THE ROAD TO PEARL HARBOR. PRINCETON, N.J.: PRINCETON U PR, 1950, PP. 356.

487 ----------. "WAR CAME TO PEARL HARBOR: SUSPICIONS CONSIDERED." YALE R 45 (1956):378-390.

488 GOODHART, P. FIFTY SHIPS THAT SAVED THE WORLD: THE FOUNDATION OF THE ANGLO-AMERICAN ALLIANCE. GARDEN CITY, N.Y.: DOUBLEDAY, 1965, PP. 267.

489 HERRING, G.C., JR. AID TO RUSSIA, 1941-1946: STRATEGY, DIPLOMACY, THE ORIGINS OF THE COLD WAR. NEW YORK: COLUMBIA U PR, 1973, PP. 365.

490 KIMBALL, W.F. THE MOST UNSORDID ACT: LEND LEASE, 1939-41. BALTIMORE: JOHNS HOPKINS, 1969, PP. 281.

491 LANGER, W.L., AND GLEASON, S.E. THE UNDECLARED WAR, 1940-1941. NEW YORK: HARPER, 1953, PP. 963.

492 MORISON, S.E. "DID ROOSEVELT START THE WAR? HISTORY THROUGH A BEARD." ATLANTIC 182 (AUG. 1948):91-97.

REVIEW OF CHARLES BEARD'S PRESIDENT ROOSEVELT AND THE COMING OF THE WAR, 1941, CRITICIZING BEARD.

493 MORTON, L. "PEARL HARBOR IN PERSPECTIVE: A BIBLIOGRAPHICAL SURVEY." USN INST PROC 81 (APR 1955): 461-68.

494 NICHOLS, J.P. "ROOSEVELT'S MONETARY DIPLOMACY IN 1933," THE AMERICAN HISTORICAL REVIEW 56 (JANUARY 1951):295-317.

495 RAUCH, B. ROOSEVELT, FROM MUNICH TO PEARL HARBOR: A STUDY IN THE CREATION OF A FOREIGN POLICY. NEW YORK: CREATIVE AGE PRESS, 1950, PP. 527. ALSO, NEW YORK: BARNES AND NOBLE, 1967, PP. 527.

496 STEELE, R.W. "PREPARING THE PUBLIC FOR WAR: EFFORTS TO ESTABLISH A NATIONAL PROPAGANDA AGENCY, 1940-41." AHR 75 (OCT 1970): 1640-1653.

497 STROMBERG, R.N. "AMERICAN BUSINESS AND THE APPROACH OF WAR 1935-1941." J ECON HISTORY 13 (WINTER 1953): 58-78.

498 TANSILL, C.C. BACK DOOR TO WAR: THE ROOSEVELT FOREIGN

POLICY, 1933-1941. CHICAGO: REGNERY, 1952, PP. 630.

499 TUCHMAN, B.W. STILWELL AND THE AMERICAN EXPERIENCE IN CHINA, 1911-45. NEW YORK: MACMILLAN, 1971, PP. 621.

500 WALLACE, W.V. "ROOSEVELT AND BRITISH APPEASEMENT, 1938." BUL BRIT ASSOC AMER STUD 5 (1962):4-30.

501 WALLER, G.M. PEARL HARBOR: ROOSEVELT AND THE COMING OF THE WAR. BOSTON: HEATH, 1953, PP. 112.

502 WEISS, S.L. "AMERICAN FOREIGN POLICY AND PRESIDENTIAL POWER: THE NEUTRALITY ACT OF 1935." JP 30 (1968):672-695.

503 WHITEHEAD, D.F. THE MAKING OF FOREIGN POLICY DURING PRESIDENT ROOSEVELT'S FIRST TERM. CHICAGO: UNIVERSITY OF CHICAGO, 1951.

504 WOHLSTETTER, R. PEARL HARBOR: WARNING AND DECISION. STANFORD: STANFORD U PR, 1962, PP. 426.

505 ----------. "CUBA AND PEARL HARBOR: HINDSIGHT AND FORESIGHT." FOREIGN AFFAIRS 43 (1965):691-707.

     SEE ALSO 65, 67, 69, 339, 402, 513, 524, 2087, 2109, 2125

3. WAR-TIME LEADERSHIP

506 ARMSTRONG, A. UNCONDITIONAL SURRENDER: THE IMPACT OF THE CASABLANCA POLICY ON WORLD WAR II. NEW BRUNSWICK, N.J.: RUTGERS U PR, 1961, PP. 304.

    A STUDY OF THE POLICY OF UNCONDITIONAL SURRENDER'S EFFECTS ON THE WAR AND ON THE ANTI-NAZI RESISTANCE IN GERMANY, CRITICIZING IT FOR SUBORDINATING DIPLOMACY TO STRATEGY.

507 BERNSTEIN, B.J. "THE UNEASY ALLIANCE: ROOSEVELT, CHURCHILL, AND THE ATOMIC BOMB, 1940-1945" WESTERN POLITICAL Q 29 (JUNE 1976): 202-230.

508 BLUM, J.M. V WAS FOR VICTORY: POLITICS AND AMERICAN

CULTURE DURING WORLD WAR II. NEW YORK:HARBRACEJ, 1976, PP. 372.

509 CATTON, B. THE WAR LORDS OF WASHINGTON. NEW YORK: HARCOURT, 1948, PP. 313.

510 CORWIN, E.S. "AMERICAN GOVERNMENT IN WARTIME: THE FIRST YEAR (PART 1. THE WAR AND THE CONSTITUTION: PRESIDENT AND CONGRESS)." APSR 37 (1943):18-25.

511 DALFIUME, R.M. DESEGREGATION OF THE U.S. ARMED FORCES: FIGHTING ON TWO FRONTS, 1939-1953. COLUMBIA, MO.: U OF MO PR, 1969, PP. 252.

512 DALLEK, R. THE ROOSEVELT DIPLOMACY AND WORLD WAR II. NEW YORK: HOLT, RINEHART AND WINSTON, 1970, PP. 125.

513 DIVINE, R.A. ROOSEVELT AND WORLD WAR II. BALTIMORE: JOHNS HOPKINS PRESS, 1969, PP. 107. SECOND EDITION, BALTIMORE: PENGUIN BOOKS, 1972, PP. 107.

A BRIEF, CRITICAL DISCUSSION OF FDR'S HANDLING OF HIS COMMANDER-IN-CHIEF RESPONSIBILITIES IN WORLD WAR II, ARGUING THAT THE SKILLS WHICH MAKE FOR DOMESTIC POLITICAL SUCCESS HAMPER SUCCESSFUL SUPERVISION OF A MILITARY ENDEAVOR.

514 EMERSON, W. "FRANKLIN ROOSEVELT AS COMMANDER-IN-CHIEF IN WORLD WAR II." MILITARY AFFAIRS 22 (1958):181-207.

515 EYRE, J.K. THE ROOSEVELT-MACARTHUR CONFLICT. CHAMBERSBURG: CRAFT PRESS, 1950, PP. 234.

516 FEIS, H. CHURCHILL, ROOSEVELT, STALIN. PRINCETON, N.J.: PRINCETON UNIV. PRESS, 1957, PP. 692. SECOND EDITION, 1967, PP. 702.

517 ----------. THE CHINA TANGLE: THE AMERICAN EFFORT IN CHINA FROM PEARL HARBOR TO THE MARSHALL MISSION. PRINCETON, N.J.: PRINCETON U PR, 1953. PAPER EDITION, 1972, PP. 445.

518 GADDIS, J.L. THE UNITED STATES AND THE ORIGINS OF THE COLD WAR 1941-1947. NEW YORK: COLUMBIA U PR, 1972, PP. 396.

519 GARDNER, L.C. ARCHITECTS OF ILLUSION: MEN AND IDEAS IN AMERICAN FOREIGN POLICY, 1941-1949. CHICAGO: QUADRANGLE BOOKS, 1970, PP.365.

520 GROVES, L. NOW IT CAN BE TOLD: THE STORY OF THE MANHATTAN PROJECT. NEW YORK: HARPER AND ROW, 1962, PP.464.

521 HEATH, J.F. "DOMESTIC AMERICA DURING WORLD WAR II: RESEARCH OPPORTUNITIES FOR HISTORIANS." JOURNAL OF AMERICAN HISTORY 58 (SEPTEMBER 1971): 384-414.

522 HESS, G.R. "FRANKLIN ROOSEVELT AND INDOCHINA." J AMERICAN HISTORY 59 (1972):353-367.

"...ROOSEVELT'S INDOCHINA POLICY WAS TYPICAL OF HIS LEADERSHIP IN FOREIGN POLICY...IT UNDERSCORED HIS LACK OF A SYSTEMATIC AND REALISTIC PLAN FOR THE POSTWAR WORLD."

523 JACOBSEN, H.K. "THE SECOND WORLD WAR AS A PROBLEM IN HISTORICAL RESEARCH." WORLD POLITICS 16 (JULY 1964): 620-641.

524 JAMES, D.C. THE YEARS OF MACARTHUR. 2 VOLS. BOSTON: HOUGHTON MIFFLIN, 1970, 1975.

525 KOLKO, G. THE POLITICS OF WAR: THE WORLD AND UNITED STATES FOREIGN POLICY, 1943-1945. NEW YORK: RANDOM, 1970, PP. 685.

526 LAFEBER, W. "ROOSEVELT, CHURCHILL, AND INDOCHINA: 1942-45." AMER HISTORICAL R 80 (DEC 1975): 1277-1295.

527 LOEWENHEIM, F.L., LANGLEY, H.D., AND JONAS, M., EDS. ROOSEVELT AND CHURCHILL: THEIR SECRET WARTIME CORRESPONDENCE. NEW YORK: SATURDAY REVIEW PRESS, 1975, PP. 805.

528 MAXWELL, J.A., AND BALCOM, M.N. "GASOLINE RATIONING IN THE
UNITED STATES." Q J OF ECON 60 (AUG 1946): 561-587; 61
(NOV 1946): 125-155.

529 MAY, E.R. "THE UNITED STATES, THE SOVIET UNION, AND THE
FAR EASTERN WAR, 1941-1945." PACIFIC HISTORICAL R 24
(MAY 1955): 153-174.

530 MCNEILL, W.H. AMERICA, BRITAIN, AND RUSSIA: THEIR
COOPERATION AND CONFLICT, 1941-1946. LONDON: OXFORD U PR,
1953, PP. 819.

531 MORSTEIN MARX, F., ED. "THE AMERICAN ROAD FROM WAR TO
PEACE: A SYMPOSIUM." APSR 38 (DEC 1944): 1114-1179.

532 MORTON, L. "SOURCES FOR THE HISTORY OF WORLD WAR II."
WORLD POLITICS 13 (APR 1961): 435-453.

533 ----------. "WORLD WAR II: A SURVEY OF RECENT WRITINGS."
AHR 75 (DEC 1970): 1987-2008.

534 NELSON, D.M. ARSENAL OF DEMOCRACY: THE STORY OF AMERICAN
WAR PRODUCTION. NEW YORK: HARCOURT, 1946, PP. 439.
REPRINTED DA CAPO, 1973.

535 O'LEARY, P.M. "WARTIME RATIONING AND GOVERNMENTAL
ORGANIZATION." APSR 39 (DEC 1945): 1089-1109.

536 POLENBERG, R. AMERICA AT WAR: THE HOME FRONT, 1941-1945.
ENGLEWOOD CLIFFS, N.J.: PRENTICE-HALL, 1968, PP. 175.

537 ----------. WAR AND SOCIETY: THE UNITED STATES,
1941-1945. PHILADELPHIA: LIPPINCOTT, 1972.

     INTERACTION OF THE PRESIDENT, WHITE HOUSE AIDES, THE STATE
     DEPARTMENT, THE NAVY, THE JOINT CHIEFS OF STAFF, THE
     MARITIME COMMISSION, THE INTERIOR DEPARTMENT, THE JUSTICE
     DEPARTMENT, AND A CONGRESSIONAL COMMITTEE IN A
     CONTROVERSIAL DECISION ABOUT THE POST-WAR DISPOSITION OF
     GOVERNMENTALLY OWNED TANKERS. ALSO APPEARS IN HAROLD

STEIN, ED. <u>PUBLIC ADMINISTRATION AND DEVELOPMENT: A CASE BOOK</u> (1952).

538 PRICE, D.K. "NOTES FROM THE WAR MEMOIRS." <u>PUBLIC ADMINISTRATION R</u> 10 (SUMMER 1950): 197-207.

539 SCHROEDER, P.W. <u>THE AXIS ALLIANCE AND JAPANESE-AMERICAN RELATIONS</u>. ITHACA: CORNELL U PR, 1958, PP. 246.

540 SMITH, G. <u>AMERICAN DIPLOMACY DURING THE SECOND WORLD WAR, 1941-1945</u>. NEW YORK: WILEY, 1965, PP. 194.

541 STEELE, R.W. <u>THE FIRST OFFENSIVE, 1942: ROOSEVELT, MARSHALL AND THE MAKING OF AMERICAN STRATEGY</u>. BLOOMINGTON: INDIANA UNIV. PRESS, 1973, PP. 239.

542 TSOU, T. <u>AMERICA'S FAILURE IN CHINA, 1941-50</u>. CHICAGO: U OF CHICAGO PR, 1963, PP. 614.

543 VIORST, M. <u>HOSTILE ALLIES: FDR AND CHARLES DE GAULLE</u>. NEW YORK: MACMILLAN, 1965, PP. 280.

544 WILSON, T. <u>THE FIRST SUMMIT: ROOSEVELT AND CHURCHILL AT PLACENTIA BAY</u>. BOSTON: HOUGHTON MIFFLIN, 1969, PP. 344.

SEE ALSO 67, 370, 381, 402, 408, 482, 482, 485, 489, 499, 504, 510, 514, 523, 531, 648, 748, 749, 820, 1779, 2281, 2372

4. NEGOTIATIONS AND PLANS RELATING TO POST-WAR PERIOD

545 BENSON, T.W. "INAUGURATING PEACE: FRANKLIN D. ROOSEVELT'S LAST SPEECH." <u>SPEECH MONOGRAPHS</u> 36 (JUNE 1969): 138-147.

546 CLEMENS, D.S. <u>YALTA</u>. NEW YORK: OXFORD UNIVERSITY PRESS, 1970, PP. 356.

547 CROWELL, L. "THE BUILDING OF THE 'FOUR FREEDOMS' SPEECH." <u>SPEECH MONOGRAPHS</u> 22 (NOV 1955): 266-283.

A STUDY OF THE EVOLUTION, THROUGH 7 DRAFTS, OF FDR'S ADDRESS TO CONGRESS ON JANUARY 6, 1941, SHOWING THE CAREFUL CONSIDERATION GIVEN TO THE TEXT.

548 FENNO, R.F. THE YALTA CONFERENCE. LEXINGTON, MASS.: HEATH, SECOND EDITION 1972, PP. 218.

549 HALPERIN, S. "UNITED STATES IN SEARCH OF A POLICY: FRANKLIN D. ROOSEVELT AND PALESTINE." R OF POLITICS 24:320-41 JL '62.

550 NEUMANN, W.L. AFTER VICTORY: CHURCHILL, ROOSEVELT, STALIN AND THE MAKING OF PEACE. NEW YORK:HAR-ROW, 1967, PP. 212.

551 PAN, S.C.Y. "LEGAL ASPECTS OF THE YALTA AGREEMENT." AMERICAN J OF INTERNATIONAL LAW 66 (1952):40-59.

552 POGUE, F. "THE BIG THREE AND THE UNITED NATIONS." IN THE MEANING OF YALTA: BIG THREE DIPLOMACY AND THE NEW BALANCE OF POWER, EDITED BY J.L. SNELL. BATON ROUGE, LA: LOUISIANA STATE U PR, 1956: 167-187.

553 ROOSEVELT, ELLIOTT. AS HE SAW IT. NEW YORK: DUELL SLOAN, 1945. REPRINTED WESTPORT, CONN.: GREENWOOD PR, 1974, PP. 270.

554 ROSS, D.R.B. PREPARING FOR ULYSSES: POLITICS AND VETERANS DURING WORLD WAR II. NEW YORK: COLUMBIA U PR, 1969, PP. 315.

555 SNELL, J.L. THE MEANING OF YALTA: BIG THREE DIPLOMACY AND THE NEW BALANCE OF POWER. BATON ROUGE: LOUISIANA STATE UNIVERSITY PRESS, 1956.

556 SONTAG, R.J. "REFLECTIONS ON THE YALTA PAPERS." FOREIGN AFFAIRS 33 (1955):615-623.

557 STETTINIUS, E.R., JR. ROOSEVELT AND THE RUSSIANS: THE YALTA CONFERENCE. GARDEN CITY, N.Y.: DOUBLEDAY, 1949. REPRINTED WESTPORT, CONN., GREENWOOD PR, 1970, PP. 367.

558 THEOHARIS, A.G. "ROOSEVELT AND TRUMAN ON YALTA: THE ORIGINS OF THE COLD WAR." PSQ 87:210-41 JE '72.

559 WARNER, G. "FROM TEHERAN TO YALTA: REFLECTIONS ON F.D.R.'S FOREIGN POLICY." INTERNATIONAL AFFAIRS 43 (1967):530-36.

560 WINNACKER, R.A. "YALTA - ANOTHER MUNICH?" VIRGINIA Q R 24 (1948):521-537.

561 WYMON, D.S. PAPER WALLS: AMERICA AND THE REFUGEE CRISIS, 1938-1941. AMHERST: U OF MASS PR, 1969, PP. 315.

SEE ALSO 285, 479, 482, 499, 518, 519, 522, 526, 530, 542, 707, 748, 749

5. PRESIDENT'S ILLNESS AND DEATH; POPULAR REACTIONS

562 ASBELL, B. WHEN F.D.R. DIED. NEW YORK: HOLT, RINEHART AND WINSTON, 1961, PP. 211.

563 BISHOP, J.A. FDR'S LAST YEAR, APRIL 1944-1945. NEW YORK: MORROW, 1974, PP. 690.

564 BRUENN, H.G. "CLINICAL NOTES ON THE ILLNESS AND DEATH OF PRESIDENT FRANKLIN D. ROOSEVELT." ANN INTERN MED 72 (1970):579-591.

MEDICAL REPORT OF FDR'S PHYSICIAN AND CARDIOLOGIST IN 1944-1945 DEFENDS STATE OF ROOSEVELT'S HEALTH AT YALTA.

565 FEIS, H. "WHEN ROOSEVELT DIED." VIRGINIA Q R 46 (1970):576-589.

566 JOHANNSEN, D.E. "REACTIONS TO THE DEATH OF PRESIDENT ROOSEVELT." J OF ABNORMAL AND SOCIAL PSYCHOLOGY 41 (1946): 218-222.

567 MILLER, D.C. "HOW OUR COMMUNITY HEARD ABOUT THE DEATH OF PRESIDENT ROOSEVELT: A RESEARCH NOTE ON MASS COMMUNICATION." AMERICAN SOCIOLOGICAL REVIEW 10 (1945): 691-694.

568 ORLANSKY, H. "REACTIONS TO THE DEATH OF PRESIDENT ROOSEVELT." J SOCIAL PSYCHOLOGY 26 (1947):235-66.

6. OTHER

569 ALEXANDER, A. "THE PRESIDENT AND THE INVESTIGATOR: ROOSEVELT AND DIES." ANTIOCH R 15 (MAR 1955): 106-117.

570 BRADEN, W.W., AND BRANDENBURG, E. "ROOSEVELT'S FIRESIDE CHATS." SPEECH MONOGRAPHS 22 (NOV. 1955):290-302.

HOW FDR USED THE FIRESIDE CHAT AND RESERVED IT FOR CRITICAL ISSUES. THIS STUDY CONSIDERS 5 FIRESIDE CHATS AND INCLUDES A CHRONOLOGICAL LISTING OF 28.

571 BRANDENBURG, E. "THE PREPARATION OF FRANKLIN D. ROOSEVELT'S SPEECHES." Q J OF SPEECH 35 (1949):214-221.

HOW FDR'S SPEECHES WERE PREPARED AND SUPPOSEDLY SPONTANEOUS CHANGES WERE WRITTEN INTO THE MANUSCRIPT.

572 CRIDER, J.H. "THE PRESIDENT'S PRESS CONFERENCE." AMER MERCURY 59 (1944):481-487.

A LIVELY JOURNALISTIC DESCRIPTION OF THE INFORMAL PROCEDURE THAT TYPIFIED ROOSEVELT'S PRESS CONFERENCES.

573 LATHAM, E. THE COMMUNIST CONTROVERSY IN WASHINGTON: FROM THE NEW DEAL TO MCCARTHY. CAMBRIDGE: HARVARD UNIV. PRESS, 1966, PP.446.

574 MATHEWS, J.M. "ROOSEVELT'S LATIN-AMERICAN POLICY." APSR 29 (1935):805-20.

575 POLENBERG, R. "FRANKLIN ROOSEVELT AND CIVIL LIBERTIES: THE CASE OF THE DIES COMMITTEE." HISTORIAN 30:165-78 F '68.

576 RIDDICK, F.M. "CONGRESS VERSUS THE PRESIDENT IN 1944." SO ATLAN Q 44 (1945):308-315.

577 ROSEN, E.A. "INTRANATIONALISM VS. INTERNATIONALISM: THE INTERREGNUM STRUGGLE FOR THE SANCTITY OF THE NEW DEAL." PSQ 81 (1966):274-297.

SEE ALSO 479, 559, 1706, 1950

G. ADDITIONAL ASPECTS AND THEMES

578 ALLEN, R.S. "HOW THE PRESIDENT WORKS." HARPER'S 173:1-14 JE '36.

579 AUERBACH, J.S. "NEW DEAL, OLD DEAL, OR RAW DEAL: SOME THOUGHTS ON NEW LEFT HISTORIOGRAPHY." J SO HIST 35 (FEB 1969): 18-30.

A CRITIQUE OF REVISIONIST INTERPRETATIONS OF THE NEW DEAL AS REFLECTING THE SITUATION OF THE 1960'S RATHER THAN THAT OF THE 1930'S.

580 BEARD, C.A. "ROOSEVELT'S PLACE IN HISTORY." EVENTS 3 (1938):81-86.

581 BERLIN, I. "ROOSEVELT THROUGH FOREIGN EYES." ATLANTIC 196 (JULY 1955):67-72.

582 BRANDENBURG, E., AND BRADEN, W.W. "FRANKLIN D. ROOSEVELT'S VOICE AND PRONUNCIATION." Q J OF SPEECH 38 (1952):23-30.

HOW FDR'S VOICE AND SPEAKING QUALITIES HELPED HIM TO BENEFIT POLITICALLY FROM THE COMING OF RADIO AND THE PUBLIC ADDRESS SYSTEM.

583 BROWN, E.C. "FISCAL POLICY IN THE THIRTIES: A REAPPRAISAL." AMER ECON R 46 (DEC 1956): 857-879.

584 COHEN, J. "SCHLESINGER AND THE NEW DEAL." DISSENT 8 (1961):461-472.

CRITIQUE OF SCHLESINGER'S IMAGE OF ROOSEVELT.

585 EKIRCH, A. IDEOLOGIES AND UTOPIAS: THE IMPACT OF THE NEW DEAL ON AMERICAN THOUGHT. CHICAGO: QUADRANGLE BOOKS, 1969, PP.307.

586 EULAU, H. "NEITHER IDEOLOGY NOR UTOPIA: THE NEW DEAL IN RETROSPECT." ANTIOCH R 19 (1959):523-537.

587 FREIDEL, F. F.D.R. AND THE SOUTH. BATON ROUGE: LA. STATE

UNIV. PRESS, 1965, PP. 102. REPUBLISHED IN 1970.

588 FRISCH, M.J. "ROOSEVELT ON PEACE AND FREEDOM." JP 29:585-96 AG '67.

589 ----------. "ROOSEVELT THE CONSERVATOR: A REJOINDER TO HOFSTADTER." JP 25 (1963):361-372.

590 FUSFELD, D.R. THE ECONOMIC THOUGHT OF FRANKLIN D. ROOSEVELT AND THE ORIGINS OF THE NEW DEAL. NEW YORK: COLUMBIA UNIV. PRESS, 1956, PP. 337. REPRINTED, NEW YORK: AMS PRESS, 1970, PP. 337.

591 GRAHAM, O.L. "HISTORIANS AND THE NEW DEALS: 1944-1960." SOCIAL STUDIES 54 (1963):133-140.

CHALLENGES WRITERS WHO DISTINGUISH BETWEEN A FIRST AND A SECOND NEW DEAL.

592 GREER, T. WHAT ROOSEVELT THOUGHT: THE SOCIAL AND POLITICAL IDEAS OF FRANKLIN D. ROOSEVELT. EAST LANSING: MICHIGAN STATE UNIVERSITY PRESS, 1958, PP.244.

593 HALASZ, N. ROOSEVELT THROUGH FOREIGN EYES. PRINCETON: VAN NOSTRAND, 1961, PP. 340.

594 HOFSTADTER, R. "FRANKLIN D. ROOSEVELT: THE PATRICIAN AS OPPORTUNIST." IN THE AMERICAN POLITICAL TRADITION AND THE MEN WHO MADE IT. NEW YORK: KNOPF, 1948.

595 JONES, A.H. ROOSEVELT'S IMAGE BROKERS: POETS, PLAYWRIGHTS, AND THE USE OF THE LINCOLN SYMBOL. PORT WASHINGTON: KENNIKAT PRESS, 1974, PP. 134.

596 KLUCKHOHN, F.L. "WHEN F.D.R. MAKES A DECISION." N Y TIMES MAG 5 N 2 '41.

597 LEUCHTENBURG, W.E. "THE NEW DEAL AND THE ANALOGUE OF WAR." IN CHANGE AND CONTINUITY IN TWENTIETH-CENTURY AMERICA, EDITED BY J. BRAEMAN, R.H. BREMNER, AND E. WALTERS, COLUMBUS: OHIO STATE U PR, 1964: 81-143.

598 MCNEAL. R. "ROOSEVELT THROUGH STALIN'S SPECTACLES." INTERNATIONAL J 18 (1963):194-206.

599 MILLIS. W. "ROOSEVELT IN RETROSPECT." VIRGINIA Q R 21 (1945):321-330.

600 NEUMANN. W.L. "FRANKLIN DELANO ROOSEVELT: A DISCIPLE OF ADMIRAL MAHAN." U.S. NAVAL INSTITUTE PROCEEDINGS 78 (1952):713-719.

601 PETERSON. M.D. "BOWERS, ROOSEVELT, AND THE NEW JEFFERSON." VIRGINIA Q R 34:530-43 FALL '58.

602 PUSATERI. J. "A STUDY IN MISUNDERSTANDING: FRANKLIN D. ROOSEVELT AND THE BUSINESS COMMUNITY." SOCIAL STUDIES 60:204-11 O '69.

603 ROSSITER. C.L. "POLITICAL PHILOSOPHY OF F.D. ROOSEVELT: A CHALLENGE TO SCHOLARSHIP." R OF POLITICS 11:84-90 JA '49.

604 ROSTEN. L.C. "PRESIDENT ROOSEVELT AND THE WASHINGTON CORRESPONDENTS." POQ 1:36-52 JA '37.

605 SKAU. G.H. "FRANKLIN D. ROOSEVELT AND THE EXPANSION OF PRESIDENTIAL POWER." CURRENT HISTORY 66 (1974):246-248.

606 SMITH. C.W. "PRESIDENT ROOSEVELT'S ATTITUDE TOWARD THE COURTS." KENTUCKY LAW J 31:301-15 MY '43.

607 STEELE. R.W. "THE PULSE OF THE PEOPLE. FRANKLIN D. ROOSEVELT AND THE GAUGING OF AMERICAN PUBLIC OPINION." J OF CONTEMP HIST 9 (OCT 1974): 195-216.

EXAMINES "THE KINDS OF OPINIONS THE PRESIDENT SOUGHT, AND THE WAY IN WHICH HE GATHERED THEM, WHICH DOES SHED SOME LIGHT ON THE WAY HE PERCEIVED THE PUBLIC'S ROLE IN THE CONDUCT OF THE NATION'S AFFAIRS."

608 SUSSMAN, L.A. DEAR FDR: A STUDY OF POLITICAL LETTER-WRITING. TOTOWA: BEDMINSTER PRESS, 1963, PP. 194.

AN EXTENSIVE ANALYSIS BASED ON ROOSEVELT LIBRARY ARCHIVES OF THE DELUGE OF MAIL DIRECTED TO THE WHITE HOUSE DURING ROOSEVELT'S ADMINISTRATION.

609 ----------. "FDR AND THE WHITE HOUSE MAIL." POQ 20 (1956):5-16.

610 THEOHARIS, A.G. THE YALTA MYTHS: AN ISSUE IN U.S. POLITICS, 1945-55. COLUMBIA: UNIVERSITY OF MO. PRESS, 1970, PP. 263.

611 TUGWELL, R.G. IN SEARCH OF ROOSEVELT. CAMBRIDGE: HARVARD UNIV. PRESS, 1972, PP. 313.

612 VENKATARAMANI, M.S. THE SUNNY SIDE OF FDR. ATHENS, OHIO: OHIO UNIV. PRESS, 1973.

613 WANN, A.J. THE PRESIDENT AS CHIEF ADMINISTRATOR; A STUDY OF FRANKLIN D. ROOSEVELT. WASHINGTON: PUBLIC AFFAIRS PRESS, 1968, PP. 219.

614 WATSON, R.L. "FRANKLIN D. ROOSEVELT IN HISTORICAL WRITING, 1950-1957." SO ATLAN Q 57 (1958):104-126.

615 WELLES, S. "THE ROOSEVELT DECISIONS: ONE DEBIT, ONE CREDIT." FOREIGN AFFAIRS 29 (1951):182-204.

616 WILCOX, J. "ANTI-FDR CHECKLIST." FDR COLLECTOR 6 (MAY 1954): 3-18.

617 WOLFSKILL, G., AND HUDSON, J.A. ALL BUT THE PEOPLE: FRANKLIN D. ROOSEVELT AND HIS CRITICS, 1933-1939. NEW YORK: MACMILLAN COMPANY, 1969, PP. 386.

SEE ALSO 292, 297, 301, 564, 782, 1840, 1859, 2304, 2502

8
HARRY S. TRUMAN AND HIS ADMINISTRATION

A. GENERAL HISTORICAL ACCOUNTS AND BIOGRAPHIES

618 ALLEN, R.S., AND SHANNON, W.V. THE TRUMAN MERRY-GO-ROUND. NEW YORK: VANGUARD PRESS, 1950, PP. 502.

CONTEMPORARY JOURNALISTIC PORTRAIT OF TRUMAN AIDES AND ASSOCIATES.

619 COCHRAN, B. HARRY TRUMAN AND THE CRISIS PRESIDENCY. FREEPORT, N.Y.: FUNK & WAGNALLS, 1973, PP. 302.

TRUMAN CRITICIZED BY REVISIONIST CRITERIA, ESPECIALLY AS A COLD WAR INSTIGATOR.

620 DANIELS, J. THE MAN FROM INDEPENDENCE. PHILADELPHIA: LIPPINCOTT, 1950, PP. 384.

FAVORABLE VIEW BY A JOURNALIST WHO SERVED AS A WHITE HOUSE AIDE (LARGELY UNDER FDR.)

621 GOLDMAN, E.F. THE CRUCIAL DECADE AND AFTER: AMERICA 1945-1960. NEW YORK: KNOPF, 1965, PP. 349.

LIVELY POLITICAL HISTORY, STRESSING THE ROLE OF THE PRESIDENT.

622 HAMBY, A.L. BEYOND THE NEW DEAL: HARRY S. TRUMAN AND AMERICAN LIBERALISM. NEW YORK: COLUMBIA UNIV. PRESS, 1973, PP. 635.

"POST-REVISIONIST" MONOGRAPH. USES PRIMARY SOURCES TO SHOW CONTINUITY OF TRUMAN'S POLICIES WITH FDR'S.

623 "HARRY TRUMAN: HIS CAREER, ACHIEVEMENTS, VIEWS." CONG Q W REPT 73 (DEC. 1972): 3164-3167.

DETAILED OBITUARY ESSAY ON TRUMAN'S CAREER.

624 HERSEY, J. "PROFILE: HARRY S. TRUMAN (FIVE PART SERIES)." NEW YORKER APR7-14-21-28-MAY 5, 1951.

BASED ON THE WELL-KNOWN WRITER'S SEVERAL DAYS OF MINUTE-BY-MINUTE OBSERVATION OF TRUMAN AT WORK. GOOD ON WHITE HOUSE AMBIENCE AND TRUMAN'S PERSONAL STYLE. SEE HIS SIMILARLY BASED REPORTING OF PRESIDENT FORD IN ACTION.

625 MARKEL, L. "AFTER FOUR YEARS: PORTRAIT OF HARRY TRUMAN." N Y TIMES MAG 10 APRIL 1949, PP. 7-9+.

626 PHILLIPS, C. THE TRUMAN PRESIDENCY: THE HISTORY OF A TRIUMPHANT SUCCESSION. NEW YORK: MACMILLAN, 1966, PP. 463.

NEW YORK TIMES REPORTER WHO COVERED TRUMAN WHITE HOUSE. INTERVIEW-BASED BIOGRAPHY.

627 STEINBERG, A. THE MAN FROM MISSOURI: THE LIFE AND TIMES OF HARRY S. TRUMAN. NEW YORK: PUTNAM, 1962, PP. 447.

SYMPATHETIC BIOGRAPHY BY A WRITER WHO HAS INTERVIEWED EXTENSIVELY AND HAD GOOD INFORMAL ACCESS TO TRUMAN AND HIS ASSOCIATES.

628 TRUMAN, M. HARRY S. TRUMAN. NEW YORK: POCKET BOOK, 1972, PP. 660.

A DAUGHTER'S AFFECTIONATE PORTRAIT. INCLUDES SOME MATERIAL NOT RELEASED TO SCHOLARS AT THE TIME THE BOOK APPEARED.

629 TUGWELL, R.G. OFF COURSE: FROM TRUMAN TO NIXON. NEW YORK: PRAEGER, 1971, PP. 326.

FDR "BRAIN TRUSTER'S" CRITICAL REVIEW OF POST-FDR PRESIDENCIES.

SEE ALSO 280, 284, 295, 300, 633, 748, 1564, 1568, 1579, 2424

B. PRESIDENT'S PAPERS, MEMOIRS

630 BERNSTEIN, B.J., AND MATUSOW, A.J., EDS. THE TRUMAN ADMINISTRATION: A DOCUMENTARY HISTORY. NEW YORK: HARPER AND ROW, 1966, PP. 518.

631 BROOKS, P.C. "UNDERSTANDING THE PRESIDENCY: THE HARRY S. TRUMAN LIBRARY." PROLOGUE: J OF THE NATIONAL ARCHIVES 1 (1969):3-12.

632 HILLMAN, W. MR. PRESIDENT: THE FIRST PUBLICATION FROM THE PERSONAL DIARIES OF HARRY S. TRUMAN, 32ND PRESIDENT OF THE U.S.A.. NEW YORK: FARRAR, 1952, PP. 253.

633 MILLER, M. PLAIN SPEAKING: AN ORAL BIOGRAPHY OF HARRY S. TRUMAN. NEW YORK: BERKLEY PUBLISHING, 1974, PP. 448.

TAPED TRANSCRIPTS OF THE EX-PRESIDENT'S OFTEN SALTY COMMENTS ON INDIVIDUALS AND EVENTS.

634 SCHNAPPER, M.B., ED. THE TRUMAN PROGRAM: ADDRESSES AND MESSAGES. WASHINGTON, D.C.: PUBLIC AFFAIRS PRESS, 1949, PP. 261.

635 TRUMAN LIBRARY. HISTORICAL MATERIALS IN THE TRUMAN LIBRARY. INDEPENDENCE, MO.: NATL ARC AND REC SER, MARCH 1975, PP. 43.

636 TRUMAN, H.S. MEMOIRS BY HARRY S. TRUMAN. 2 VOLS. YEARS OF DECISIONS. GARDEN CITY, N.Y.: DOUBLEDAY, 1955, PP. 596. YEARS OF TRIAL AND HOPE. GARDEN CITY, N.Y.: DOUBLEDAY, 1956, PP. 594.

637 -----------. MR. CITIZEN. NEW YORK: GEIS ASSOCIATES, 1960, PP. 433.

LOOSELY-CONNECTED, INFORMAL REFLECTIONS BY TRUMAN ON WHAT IT MEANT TO BE PRESIDENT AND OTHER MATTERS.

638 -----------. TRUMAN SPEAKS. NEW YORK: COLUMBIA UNIVERSITY PRESS, 1960, PP. 133.

LECTURE ON THE PRESIDENCY, PLUS TRANSCRIBED QUESTION-AND-ANSWER SESSION. OCCASION WAS A VISIT OF THE EX-PRESIDENT TO COLUMBIA UNIVERSITY.

SEE ALSO 54, 2033

C. COMPENDIA AND BIBLIOGRAPHIES

639 BERNSTEIN, B.J., ED. POLITICS AND POLICY OF THE TRUMAN ADMINISTRATION. CHICAGO: QUADRANGLE BOOKS, 1970, PP. 302.

640 FURER, H.B., ED. HARRY S. TRUMAN, 1884-   : CHRONOLOGY, DOCUMENTS, BIBLIOGRAPHICAL AIDS. DOBBS FERRY: OCEANA, 1970, PP. 155.

641 HUTHMACHER, J.J., ED. THE TRUMAN YEARS: THE RECONSTRUCTION OF POSTWAR AMERICA. HINSDALE, ILL.: DRYDEN PRESS, 1973, PP. 236.

642 KIRKENDALL, R.S., ED. THE TRUMAN PERIOD AS A RESEARCH FIELD. COLUMBIA: UNIVERSITY OF MO. PRESS, 1967, PP.284.

643 -----------. THE TRUMAN PERIOD AS A RESEARCH FIELD, A

REAPPRAISAL, 1972. COLUMBIA: U OF MO PR, 1974, PP. 246.

LIKE KIRKENDALL'S 1967 BOOK OF THE SAME TITLE, THIS
PRESENTS THE OFTEN SHARPLY CLASHING VIEWS OF TRUMAN
SCHOLARS ON SUCH MATTERS AS THE CAUSES OF THE COLD WAR.
INCLUDES AN OUTSTANDING BIBLIOGRAPHY OF SCHOLARSHIP ON THE
TRUMAN PERIOD.

644 KOENIG, L.W., ED. TRUMAN ADMINISTRATION. NEW YORK: N.Y.
UNIV. PRESS, 1956, PP. 394.

645 STAPLETON, M.L. THE TRUMAN AND EISENHOWER YEARS:
1945-1960: A SELECTIVE BIBLIOGRAPHY. METUCHEN, N.J.:
SCARECROW PRESS, 1973, PP. 221.

D. SELECTED MATERIAL ON PRE-PRESIDENTIAL BACKGROUND

646 MCCLURE, A.F., AND COSTIGAN, D. "THE TRUMAN
VICE-PRESIDENCY: CONSTRUCTIVE APPRENTICESHIP OR BRIEF
INTERLUDE?" MISSOURI HISTORICAL R 65 (1971):318-341.

647 RIDDLE, D.H. THE TRUMAN COMMITTEE: A STUDY IN
CONGRESSIONAL RESPONSIBILITY. NEW BRUNSWICK: RUTGERS
UNIVERSITY PRESS, 1964, PP. 207.

648 WILSON, T. "THE TRUMAN COMMITTEE, 1941." IN CONGRESS
INVESTIGATES: A DOCUMENTED HISTORY. VOL. 4, EDITED BY
A.M. SCHLESINGER, JR., AND R. BURNS, NEW YORK: CHELSEA
HOUSE, 1975, PP. 3115-3262.

SEE ALSO 2447

E. ADVISERS AND ADVISORY RELATIONS

649 ACHESON, D. MORNING AND NOON: A MEMOIR. BOSTON:
HOUGHTON-MIFFLIN, 1965, PP. 288.

650 ----------. PRESENT AT THE CREATION: MY YEARS IN THE
STATE DEPARTMENT. NEW YORK: NORTON, 1969, PP.798.

651 BARKLEY, A.W. THAT REMINDS ME. GARDEN CITY, N.Y.:
DOUBLEDAY, 1954, PP. 288.

652 BYRNES, J.F. SPEAKING FRANKLY. NEW YORK: HARPER &

BROTHERS, 1947, PP. 324.

653 CURRY, G. JAMES F. BYRNES. NEW YORK: COOPER SQUARE, 1965, PP. 423.

BYRNES AS SECRETARY OF STATE UNDER TRUMAN. BYRNES HIMSELF DESCRIBES THIS PERIOD IN HIS SPEAKING FRANKLY.

654 FARRAR, R. RELUCTANT SERVANT: THE STORY OF CHARLES G. ROSS. COLUMBIA, MO.: U OF MO PR, 1969, PP. 255.

ON TRUMAN'S FIRST PRESS SECRETARY.

655 FERRELL, R.H. GEORGE C. MARSHALL. NEW YORK: COOPER SQUARE, 1966, PP. 326.

656 FORRESTAL, J.V. THE FORRESTAL DIARIES. NEW YORK: VIKING, 1951, PP. 581.

INCLUDES INSTRUCTIVE INSIGHT INTO THE ACTIONS AND THINKING OF THE FIRST SECRETARY OF DEFENSE.

657 GROSS, B.M. "THE PRESIDENT'S ECONOMIC STAFF DURING THE TRUMAN ADMINISTRATION." APSR 48 (1954):114-130.

A SOMEWHAT GUARDED DISCUSSION OF HOW THE COUNCIL OF ECONOMIC ADVISERS EVOLVED FROM A WOULD-BE SEMI-AUTONOMOUS BODY TO AN AGENCY DIRECTLY RESPONSIVE TO PRESIDENTIAL DIRECTIVES. FOR A GENERAL HISTORICAL ACCOUNT, SEE FLASH'S BOOK ON ECONOMIC ADVISING.

658 LEFBERG, I.F. "CHIEF JUSTICE VINSON AND THE POLITICS OF DESEGREGATION." EMORY LAW JOURNAL 24 (SPRING 1975):243-312.

DISCUSSES VINSON AS A TRUMAN CONFIDANT BOTH BEFORE AND AFTER HE BECAME A SUPREME COURT JUSTICE AND ALSO DISCUSSES VINSON'S PROCLIVITY TO SUPPORT TRUMAN'S POLICIES IN HIS DECISIONS ON THE BENCH.

659 LILIENTHAL, D.E. THE JOURNALS OF DAVID E. LILIENTHAL: VOLUME II: THE ATOMIC ENERGY YEARS, 1945-1950. NEW YORK: HARPER AND ROW, 1964, PP. 666.

THE CONTINUED CAREER OF DAVID LILIENTHAL FROM THE DROPPING OF THE FIRST ATOMIC BOMB UNTIL HIS RETIREMENT FROM THE CHAIRMANSHIP OF THE ATOMIC ENERGY COMMISSION. ON HIS PREVIOUS PERIOD DURING THE ROOSEVELT ADMINISTRATION, SEE VOLUME 1: THE TVA YEARS, 1939-1945.

660 MACARTHUR, D. REMINISCENCES. NEW YORK: MCGRAW-HILL, 1964, PP. 438.

661 "MR. TRUMAN'S WHITE HOUSE." DIAG FORTUNE PP. 47-9+ F '52.

662 PERLMUTTER, O. "ACHESON AND THE DIPLOMACY OF WORLD WAR II." WESTERN POLITICAL Q 14 (1961):896-911.

663 ----------. "THE "NEO-REALISM" OF DEAN ACHESON." R OF POLITICS 26 (1964):100-123.

664 RIDGWAY, M.B., AND MARTIN, H.A. SOLDIER: THE MEMOIRS OF MATTHEW B. RIDGWAY. NEW YORK: HARPER, 1956, PP. 371.

665 ROGOW, A.A. JAMES FORRESTAL: A STUDY OF PERSONALITY, POLITICS, AND POLICY. NEW YORK: MACMILLAN, 1963, PP. 397.

666 SANDER, A.D. "TRUMAN AND THE NATIONAL SECURITY COUNCIL: 1945-1947." J OF AMERICAN HISTORY 59 (1972):369-388.

"PRESIDENT TRUMAN EMPHASIZED THE ADVISORY NATURE OF THE COUNCIL...UNTIL THE STRESSES OF THE KOREAN WAR PROMPTED HIM TO SEEK GREATER ASSISTANCE FROM THE NATIONAL SECURITY COUNCIL IN MEETING THE WAR'S PROBLEMS."

667 SMITH, G. DEAN ACHESON. NEW YORK: COOPER SQUARE, 1972, PP. 473..

AN ACCOUNT AND EVALUATION OF ACHESON'S BACKGROUND, HIS CAREER AS SECRETARY OF STATE, AND OF HIS RELATIONSHIP WITH TRUMAN.

668 THEOHARIS, A.G. "JAMES F. BYRNES: UNWITTING YALTA MYTH-MAKER." PSQ 81 (1966):581-592.

669 WAGNON, W.O., JR. "JOHN ROY STEELMAN: NATIVE SON TO PRESIDENTIAL ADVISOR." ARK HIST Q 27 (AUTUMN 1968): 205-225.

AN ASSESSMENT OF JOHN ROY STEELMAN'S SERVICE AS "THE ASSISTANT" TO PRESIDENT TRUMAN AND OF HOW HIS "EDUCATION AND TRAINING PRIOR TO HIS WHITE HOUSE DAYS" HELPED HIM BE "A KEY FIGURE WITHIN THE TRUMAN FAIR DEAL."

670 WHITNEY, C. MACARTHUR: HIS RENDEZVOUS WITH HISTORY. NEW YORK: KNOPF, 1956, PP. 547.

SEE ALSO 352, 355, 356, 358, 376, 380, 386, 742, 1615, 1633, 1731, 1783, 1788, 1792, 1803, 1891, 2003, 2005, 2013, 2432

F. SPECIFIC EVENTS, ACTIVITIES AND POLICIES

1. DOMESTIC

671 BERMAN, W.C. THE POLITICS OF CIVIL RIGHTS IN THE TRUMAN ADMINISTRATION. COLUMBUS: OHIO STATE UNIVERSITY, 1970, PP. 261.

672 BERNSTEIN, B.J. "ECONOMIC POLICIES." IN THE TRUMAN PERIOD AS A RESEARCH FIELD. EDITED BY R. KIRKENDALL, COLUMBIA, MO.: U OF MO PR, 1967, PP. 87-148.

673 ----------. "THE AMBIGUOUS LEGACY: THE TRUMAN ADMINISTRATION AND CIVIL RIGHTS." IN BERNSTEIN, B.J., ED. POLITICS AND POLICIES OF THE TRUMAN ADMINISTRATION, CHICAGO: QUADRANGLE, 1970, PP.269-314.

674 BILLINGTON, M. "CIVIL RIGHTS, PRESIDENT TRUMAN AND THE SOUTH." J NEGRO HISTORY 58 (APR 1973): 127-139.

675 ----------. "FREEDOM TO SERVE: THE PRESIDENT'S COMMITTEE ON EQUALITY OF TREATMENT AND OPPORTUNITY IN THE ARMED FORCES, 1949 - 1950." J NEGRO HISTORY 51 (1966):262-274.

676 CHRISTENSON, R.M. THE BRANNON PLAN: FARM POLITICS AND POLICY. ANN ARBOR, MICH.: U OF MICH PR, 1959.

677 DAVIES, R. HOUSING REFORM DURING THE TRUMAN ADMINISTRATION. COLUMBIA, MO.: UNIVERSITY OF MO. PRESS, 1966, PP.197.

678 ----------. "SOCIAL WELFARE POLICIES." IN THE TRUMAN PERIOD AS A RESEARCH FIELD, EDITED BY R. KIRKENDALL, COLUMBIA, MO.: U OF MO PR, 1967, PP. 149-186.

679 HAMBY, A.L. "THE VITAL CENTER, THE FAIR DEAL, AND THE QUEST FOR A LIBERAL POLITICAL ECONOMY." AHR 77 (1972):653-678.

680 HARPER, A.D. THE POLITICS OF LOYALTY: THE WHITE HOUSE AND

THE COMMUNIST ISSUE, 1946-1952. WESTPORT, CONN.: GREENWOOD, 1969, PP. 318.

681 HARTMANN, S.M. TRUMAN AND THE 80TH CONGRESS. COLUMBIA: UNIVERSITY OF MISSOURI PRESS, 1971, PP. 241.

682 LEE, R.A. TRUMAN AND TAFT-HARTLEY; A QUESTION OF MANDATE. LEXINGTON: UNIVERSITY OF KENTUCKY PRESS, 1966, PP. 254.

683 ----------. "THE TRUMAN - 80TH CONGRESS STRUGGLE OVER TAX POLICY." HISTORIAN 33 (1970):68-82.

684 ----------. "THE TURNIP SESSION OF THE DO NOTHING CONGRESS: PRESIDENTIAL CAMPAIGN STRATEGY." SOUTHWESTERN SOCIAL SCIENCE Q 44 (1963):256-267.

685 MANN, S.Z. "POLICY FORMULATION IN THE EXECUTIVE BRANCH: THE TAFT-HARTLEY EXPERIENCE." WESTERN POLITICAL Q 13 (1960):597-608.

686 MARSH, J.F., JR. THE FBI RETIREMENT BILL. INTER-UNIVERSITY CASE PROGRAM: BOX 229, SYRACUSE, N.Y., 1949, PP. 26. ALSO REPRINTED IN STEIN, H., ED. PUBLIC ADMINISTRATION AND POLICY DEVELOPMENT: A CASE BOOK. N.Y.: HARCOURT, BRACE, 1952.

687 MATUSOW, A. FARM POLICIES AND POLITICS IN THE TRUMAN YEARS. NEW YORK: ATHENEUM, 1970, PP. 267.

688 MCCLURE, A.F. THE TRUMAN ADMINISTRATION AND THE PROBLEMS OF POST-WAR LABOR: 1945-1948. RUTHERFORD, N.J.: FAIRLEIGH DICKINSON UNIVERSITY PRESS, 1969, PP. 267.

689 NEUSTADT, R.E. "CONGRESS AND THE FAIR DEAL: A LEGISLATIVE BALANCE SHEET." PUBLIC POLICY 5 (1954):351-381.

690 RICHARDSON, E. DAMS, PARKS AND POLITICS: RESOURCE DEVELOPMENT AND PRESERVATION IN THE TRUMAN-EISENHOWER

ERA. LEXINGTON, KY.: UNIVERSITY PRESS OF KENTUCKY, 1973.

691 RUETTEN, R.T., AND MCCOY, D.R. QUEST AND RESPONSE: MINORITY RIGHTS IN THE TRUMAN ADMINISTRATION. LAWRENCE, KAN.: UNIV. PRESS OF KAN., 1973, PP. 427.

692 SITKOFF, H. "HARRY TRUMAN AND THE ELECTION OF 1948: THE COMING OF AGE OF CIVIL RIGHTS IN AMERICAN POLITICS." J OF SOUTHERN HISTORY 35 (1971):597-616.

693 THEOHARIS, A.G. SEEDS OF REPRESSION: HARRY S. TRUMAN AND THE ORIGINS OF MCCARTHYISM. CHICAGO: QUADRANGLE BOOKS, 1971, PP. 238.

694 -----------. "THE ESCALATION OF THE LOYALTY PROGRAM." IN BERNSTEIN, B.J., ED. POLITICS AND POLICIES OF THE TRUMAN ADMINISTRATION, CHICAGO: QUADRANGLE, 1970, PP. 242-68.

695 WILLIAMS, O.P. "THE CREDIT CORPORATION AND THE 1948 PRESIDENTIAL ELECTION." MIDWEST J OF POLITICAL SCIENCE 1 (1957):111-124.

SEE ALSO 71, 77, 433, 711, 743, 771, 1647, 2003, 2005, 2013

2. FOREIGN AND NATIONAL SECURITY

696 ALPEROVITZ, G. ATOMIC DIPLOMACY: HIROSHIMA AND POTSDAM: THE USES OF ATOMIC BOMB AND THE AMERICAN CONFRONTATION WITH SOVIET POWER. NEW YORK: SIMON AND SCHUSTER, 1965, PP. 317.

CONTROVERSIAL REVISIONIST ANALYSIS ARGUING THAT ATOMIC WEAPONS WERE USED AGAINST JAPAN NOT TO SHORTEN THE WAR BUT RATHER AS A WAY OF ESTABLISHING A FAVORABLE POWER POSITION WITH RESPECT TO THE USSR.

697 BERGER, C. THE KOREAN KNOT: A MILITARY-POLITICAL HISTORY. PHILADELPHIA: UNIVERSITY OF PENNSYLVANIA PRESS, 1964, PP. 255.

698 BERNSTEIN, B.J. "AMERICAN FOREIGN POLICY AND THE ORIGINS OF THE COLD WAR." IN BERNSTEIN, B.J., ED. POLITICS AND POLICIES OF THE TRUMAN ADMINISTRATION. CHICAGO:

QUADRANGLE, 1970, PP. 15-77.

699 ----------. "HIROSHIMA AND NAGASAKI RECONSIDERED: THE ATOMIC BOMBINGS OF JAPAN AND THE ORIGINS OF THE COLD WAR, 1941-1945." UNIVERSITY PROGRAMS MODULAR STUDIES, MORRISTOWN, N.J.: GENERAL LEARNING PRESS, 1975, PP. 31.

700 ----------. "SHATTERER OF WORLDS: HIROSHIMA AND NAGASAKI." BULL OF ATOMIC SCIENTISTS (DEC 1975): 12-22.

701 BICKERTON, I.J. "PRESIDENT TRUMAN'S RECOGNITION OF ISRAEL." AMERICAN JEWISH HISTORY Q 58 (1968):170-240.

702 BROWN, D.S. THE PUBLIC ADVISORY BOARD AND THE TARIFF STUDY. INTER-UNIVERSITY CASE PROGRAM: BOX 229, SYRACUSE, N.Y., 1956, PP. 47.

HOW THE MUTUAL SECURITY AGENCY'S PUBLIC ADVISORY BOARD MET THE PROBLEM OF DELIVERING THE TRADE AND TARIFF REPORT ORIGINALLY UNDERTAKEN FOR PRESIDENT TRUMAN TO PRESIDENT EISENHOWER.

703 BROWN, SEYOM. THE FACES OF POWER; CONSTANCY AND CHANGE IN UNITED STATES FOREIGN POLICY FROM TRUMAN TO JOHNSON. NEW YORK: COLUMBIA UNIV. PRESS, 1968, PP.397.

704 CARR, A. TRUMAN, STALIN, AND PEACE. GARDEN CITY, N.Y.: DOUBLEDAY, 1950, PP. 256.

705 DAVISON, W.P. THE BERLIN BLOCKADE: A STUDY IN COLD WAR POLITICS. PRINCETON: PRINCETON UNIVERSITY PRESS, 1958, PP.423.

706 DRUKS, H. HARRY S. TRUMAN AND THE RUSSIANS: 1945-1953. NEW YORK: SPELLER, 1967, PP. 291.

707 FEIS, H. BETWEEN WAR AND PEACE: THE POTSDAM CONFERENCE. PRINCETON: PRINCETON UNIVERSITY PRESS, 1960, PP. 367.

708 ----------. THE ATOMIC BOMB AND THE END OF WORLD WAR II. REVISED EDITION, PRINCETON, N.J.: PRINCETON U PR, 1966, PP. 213.

709 FERRELL, R.H. "TRUMAN FOREIGN POLICY: A TRADITIONAL VIEW." IN THE TRUMAN PERIOD AS A RESEARCH FIELD, EDITED BY R. KIRKENDALL, COLUMBIA, MO.: U OF MO PR, 1974, PP. 11-45.

710 FOGELMAN, E. HIROSHIMA: THE DECISION TO USE THE A-BOMB. NEW YORK: SCRIBNER'S, 1964, PP. 116.

711 FREELAND, R.M. THE TRUMAN DOCTRINE AND THE ORIGINS OF MCCARTHYISM: FOREIGN POLICY, DOMESTIC POLITICS AND INTERNAL SECURITY, 1946-1948. NEW YORK: KNOPF, 1972, PP. 419. REPUBLISHED, NEW YORK: SCHOCKEN, 1974.

712 GADDIS, J.L. "HARRY S. TRUMAN AND THE ORIGINS OF CONTAINMENT." IN MAKERS OF AMERICAN DIPLOMACY: FROM BENJAMIN FRANKLIN TO HENRY KISSINGER. ED. MERLI, F.J., AND WILSON, T.A. NEW YORK: SCRIBNER'S, 1974: 493-522.

713 ----------. "WAS THE TRUMAN DOCTRINE A REAL TURNING POINT?" FOREIGN AFFAIRS 51 (JANUARY 1974): 386-402.

714 GARDNER, L.C. "TRUMAN ERA FOREIGN POLICY: RECENT HISTORICAL TRENDS." IN THE TRUMAN PERIOD AS A RESEARCH FIELD, EDITED BY R. KIRKENDALL, COLUMBIA, MO.: U OF MO PR, 1974, PP. 47-74.

715 GIOVANNITTI, L., AND FREED, F. THE DECISION TO DROP THE BOMB. NEW YORK: COWARD-MCCANN, 1965, PP. 348.

716 GRABER, D.A. "THE TRUMAN AND EISENHOWER DOCTRINES IN THE LIGHT OF THE DOCTRINE OF NON-INTERVENTION." PSQ 73 (1958):321-334.

717 GRAEBNER, N.A. "THE TRUMAN ADMINISTRATION AND THE COLD WAR." CURRENT HISTORY 35 (1958):223-228.

718 GREEN, D. "THE COLD WAR COMES TO LATIN AMERICA." IN BERNSTEIN, B.J., ED. POLITICS AND POLICIES OF THE TRUMAN

ADMINISTRATION, CHICAGO: QUADRANGLE, 1970, PP. 149-95.

719 HALPERIN, M.H. "THE LIMITING PROCESS IN THE KOREAN WAR." PSQ 78 (1963):13-39.

720 HARTMANN, S.M. THE MARSHALL PLAN. COLUMBUS, O.: MERRILL, 1968, PP. 71.

721 HAYNES, R.F. THE AWESOME POWER: HARRY S. TRUMAN AS COMMANDER IN CHIEF. BATON ROUGE: LOUISIANA STATE UNIVERSITY PRESS, 1973, PP. 359.

722 HERZ, M.F. BEGINNINGS OF THE COLD WAR. BLOOMINGTON: IND U PR, 1966, PP. 214.

A COMPENDIUM OF "BASIC TEXTS" BEARING ON THE QUESTION OF RESPONSIBILITY FOR THE BEGINNING OF THE COLD WAR. PASSAGES FROM THE STALIN-HOPKINS CONVERSATIONS, YALTA AND POTSDAM DOCUMENTS AND MEMOIRS, AS WELL AS A GENERAL DISCUSSION BY THE AUTHOR AND A LIST OF 78 QUESTIONS AND ANSWERS BEARING ON THIS HISTORICAL TURNING POINT.

723 HITCHENS, H.L. "INFLUENCES ON THE CONGRESSIONAL DECISION TO PASS THE MARSHALL PLAN." WESTERN POLITICAL Q 21 (1968):51-68.

724 JONES, J.M. THE FIFTEEN WEEKS (FEBRUARY 21-JUNE 5, 1947). NEW YORK: VIKING, 1955, PP. 296.

A PARTICIPANT'S ACCOUNT OF THE FRAMING OF THE MARSHALL PLAN AND TRUMAN DOCTRINE.

725 KOLKO, J., AND KOLKO, G. THE LIMITS OF POWER: THE WORLD AND UNITED STATES FOREIGN POLICY, 1945-1954. NEW YORK: HARPER AND ROW, 1972, PP. 820.

ONE OF THE MOST INFLUENTIAL REVISIONIST CRITIQUES OF POST-WORLD WAR II FOREIGN POLICY. IT INCLUDES A SUBSTANTIAL AMOUNT OF PRIMARY SOURCE MATERIAL.

726 KUKLICK, B. AMERICAN POLICY AND THE DIVISION OF GERMANY. ITHACA, N.Y.: CORNELL U PR, 1972, PP. 286.

727 LAFEBER, W. AMERICA, RUSSIA, AND THE COLD WAR: 1945-1975. NEW YORK: JOHN WILEY, 1976, PP. 328.

728 LECKIE, R. CONFLICT: THE HISTORY OF THE KOREAN WAR: 1950-1953. NEW YORK: PUTNAM'S, 1962, PP. 448.

729 LOFGREN, C.A. "MR. TRUMAN'S WAR: A DEBATE AND ITS AFTERMATH." R OF POLITICS 31 (1969):223-231.

730 MALLALIEU, W.C. "THE ORIGIN OF THE MARSHALL PLAN: A STUDY IN POLICY FORMATION AND NATIONAL LEADERSHIP." PSQ 73 (1958):481-504.

731 MCFADYEN, B.D. THE TRUMAN DOCTRINE: ITS ORIGIN AND EVOLUTION. BOULDER: U OF COLO PR, 1965, PP. 701.

A CLOSELY DOCUMENTED HISTORIAN'S EXAMINATION IN DEPTH OF THE EVENTS DESCRIBED MORE BRIEFLY IN JOSEPH JONES'S THE FIFTEEN WEEKS, AS WELL AS OF THE ANTECEDENTS OF THESE EVENTS.

732 MCLELLAN, D.S., AND REUSS, J.W. "FOREIGN AND MILITARY POLICIES." IN THE TRUMAN PERIOD AS A RESEARCH FIELD, EDITED BY R. KIRKENDALL, COLUMBIA, MO.: U OF MO PR, 1967, PP. 15-85.

733 MEE, C.L. MEETING AT POTSDAM. NEW YORK: M. EVANS AND COMPANY, 1975, PP. 370.

734 OSGOOD, R.E. AMERICA AND THE WORLD: FROM THE TRUMAN DOCTRINE TO VIETNAM. BALTIMORE: JOHNS HOPKINS PR, 1970: PP. 434.

735 PAIGE, G. THE KOREAN DECISION, JUNE 24-30, 1950. NEW YORK: FREE PRESS, 1968, PP. 394.

A HIGHLY DETAILED, SEQUENTIAL RECONSTRUCTION OF EVENTS BASED ON INTERVIEWS WITH PARTICIPANTS AS WELL AS DOCUMENTARY SOURCES. THE AUTHOR HAS A GENERAL INTEREST IN THE NATURE AND DYNAMICS OF DECISION-MAKING.

736 PARK, C.J. "AMERICAN FOREIGN POLICY IN KOREA AND VIETNAM." R OF POLITICS 37 (1975):20-47.

737 PATERSON, T.G. SOVIET-AMERICAN CONFRONTATION: POSTWAR RECONSTRUCTION AND THE ORIGINS OF THE COLD WAR. BALTIMORE: JOHNS HOPKINS, 1973.

738 ----------.   "THE   QUEST   FOR   PEACE   AND   PROSPERITY:
INTERNATIONAL TRADE, COMMUNISM, AND THE MARSHALL PLAN." IN
BERNSTEIN, B.J., ED.,POLITICS AND POLICIES OF THE TRUMAN
ADMINISTRATION, CHICAGO: QUADRANGLE, 1970, PP. 78-112.

739 PRICE, H. THE MARSHALL PLAN AND ITS MEANING. ITHACA,
N.Y.: CORNELL U PR, 1955, PP. 424.

740 QUADE, Q.L. "THE TRUMAN ADMINISTRATION AND THE SEPARATION
OF POWERS: THE CASE OF THE MARSHALL PLAN." R OF POLITICS
27 (1965):58-77.

741 REES, D. KOREA: THE LIMITED WAR. LONDON: MACMILLAN,
1964, PP. 511.

742 RIDGWAY, M.B. THE KOREAN WAR: HOW   WE   MET   THE
CHALLENGE. HOW   ALL - OUT ASIAN WAR WAS AVERTED. WHY
MACARTHUR WAS DISMISSED. WHY TODAY'S WAR OBJECTIVES MUST
BE LIMITED. GARDEN CITY: DOUBLEDAY, 1967, PP. 291.

A MEMOIR BY THE GENERAL WHO WAS ASSIGNED TO REPLACE
MACARTHUR AFTER THE LATTER'S DISMISSAL BY TRUMAN.

743 ROSE, L.A. AFTER YALTA: AMERICA AND THE ORIGINS OF THE
COLD WAR. NEW YORK: SCRIBNER, 1973, PP. 216.

COVERS SIMILAR GROUND TO THE AUTHOR'S DUBIOUS VICTORY.

744 ----------.   DUBIOUS VICTORY: THE UNITED STATES AND THE
END OF WORLD WAR II. KENT, OHIO: THE KENT STATE
UNIVERSITY PRESS, 1973.

A CLOSE EXAMINATION OF THE END OF WORLD WAR II BASED ON
PRIMARY SOURCES ON AMERICAN DECISION-MAKING FROM THE TIME
TRUMAN TOOK OFFICE TO JAPAN'S SURRENDER. IT EXPLICITLY
CONTESTS THE REVISIONIST VIEW THAT AMERICAN POLICY DURING
THAT PERIOD WAS DESIGNED TO PREPARE THE WAY FOR COLD WAR
ANTAGONISMS WITH THE U.S.S.R.

745 ROVERE, R.H., AND SCHLESINGER, A.M., JR. THE GENERAL AND
THE PRESIDENT AND THE FUTURE OF AMERICAN FOREIGN POLICY.
NEW YORK: FARRAR, 1952, PP. 336.

THE COLLABORATION OF A JOURNALIST AND AN HISTORIAN IN A
HIGHLY READABLE ACCOUNT OF THE CONTROVERSIAL DECISION BY
TRUMAN. COMPARE JOHN SPANIER'S   SCHOLARLY ACCOUNT OF
MACARTHUR'S DISMISSAL, LISTED BELOW.

746 RUETTEN, R.T. "GENERAL DOUGLAS MACARTHUR'S 'RECONNAISSANCE

IN FORCE": THE RATIONALIZATION OF A DEFEAT IN KOREA."
<u>PACIFIC HISTORICAL R</u> 36 (1967):79-93.

747 SCHILLING, W.R. "THE H-BOMB DECISION: HOW TO DECIDE
WITHOUT ACTUALLY CHOOSING." <u>PSQ</u> 76 (1961):24-46.

748 SCHOENBERGER, W.S. <u>DECISION OF DESTINY</u>. ATHENS: OHIO U
PR. 1969, PP. 330.

ACCOUNT OF BACKGROUND LEADING TO AND HELPING TO SHAPE
PRESIDENT TRUMAN'S DECISION TO USE THE ATOMIC BOMB.

749 SHERWIN, M.J. <u>A WORLD DESTROYED: THE ATOMIC BOMB AND THE
GRAND ALLIANCE</u>. NEW YORK: KNOPF, 1975, PP. 315.

THE MOST AUTHORITATIVE SCHOLARLY WORK ON THE DEVELOPMENT
AND USE IN WORLD WAR II OF NUCLEAR WEAPONS.

750 ----------. "THE ATOMIC BOMB AS HISTORY: AN ESSAY
REVIEW." <u>WIS MAG HIST</u> 53 (WINTER 1969): 128-134.

751 SNOWMAN, D. "PRESIDENT TRUMAN'S DECISION TO DROP THE FIRST
ATOMIC BOMB." <u>POLITICAL STUDIES</u> OCT. 1966, PP. 365-373.

752 SNYDER, R.C., AND PAIGE, G. "THE UNITED STATES DECISION TO
RESIST AGGRESSION IN KOREA." <u>ADMIN SCI Q</u> 3 (DEC. 1958):
341-378.

A BRIEF SUMMARY OF THE SEQUENCE OF EVENTS DESCRIBED IN
DETAIL BY PAIGE IN <u>THE KOREAN DECISION</u>, WITH ADDITIONAL
EMPHASIS ON THE PROBLEMS OF ANALYZING DECISION-MAKING
PROCESSES.

753 SPANIER, J.W. <u>THE TRUMAN-MACARTHUR CONTROVERSY AND THE
KOREAN WAR</u>. NEW YORK: NORTON, 1965, PP. 311.

ORIGINALLY PUBLISHED IN 1959, THIS STANDARD, SCHOLARLY
STUDY WAS "SOMEWHAT REVISED" IN THE CURRENT EDITION TO
INCLUDE ANALYTIC REMARKS ON THE NOTION OF "TOTAL" VICTORY
AND ON THE LATER LITERATURE ABOUT THE USE OF NUCLEAR
WEAPONS.

754 STEIN, H. <u>THE FOREIGN SERVICE ACT OF 1946</u>.
INTER-UNIVERSITY CASE PROGRAM: BOX 229, SYRACUSE, N.Y.,
1949, PP. 201. ALSO REPRINTED IN STEIN, H., ED. <u>PUBLIC
ADMINISTRATION AND POLICY DEVELOPMENT: A CASE BOOK</u>. N.Y.:
HARCOURT, BRACE, 1952.

755 STIMSON, H.L. "THE DECISION TO USE THE ATOMIC BOMB."
<u>HARPER'S</u> 194 (1947):97-107.

756 TRAVERSO, E. KOREA AND THE LIMITS OF LIMITED WAR. MENLO PARK, CA.: ADDISON-WESLEY, 1970.

757 WILTZ, J.E. "THE MACARTHUR INQUIRY, 1951." IN CONGRESS INVESTIGATES: A DOCUMENTED HISTORY, VOL. 5, EDITED BY A.M. SCHLESINGER, JR., AND R. BURNS, NEW YORK: CHELSEA HOUSE, 1975, PP. 3593-3726.

758 YORK, H.F. THE ADVISORS: OPPENHEIMER, TELLER, AND THE SUPERBOMB. SAN FRANCISCO: FREEMAN, 1976, PP. 175.

AN INSIDER'S ACCOUNT OF THE CONFLICT BETWEEN THOSE GOVERNMENTAL SCIENCE-ADVISERS LED BY EDWARD TELLER, WHO FAVORED DEVELOPMENT OF A HYDROGEN-BOMB, AND THE OPPOSITION GROUP LED BY J. ROBERT OPPENHEIMER. THE AUTHOR CONSIDERS OPPENHEIMER'S POSITION TO HAVE BEEN CORRECT.

SEE ALSO 70, 72, 73, 74, 75, 76, 499, 511, 517, 518, 519, 520, 530, 542, 558, 668, 670, 696, 717, 726, 741, 769, 769, 1753, 2110, 2140

3. OTHER

759 ABELS, J. THE TRUMAN SCANDALS. CHICAGO: H. REGNERY CO., 1956, PP. 329.

760 ANDREWS, R.B. THE RE-AMERICANIZATION OF FOREIGN SERVICE OFFICERS. INTER-UNIVERSITY CASE PROGRAM: BOX 229, SYRACUSE, N.Y., 1970.

761 BANKS, R.F. "STEEL, SAWYER, AND THE EXECUTIVE POWER." U PITTSBURGH LAW R 14:467-537 SUMMER '53.

762 BERNSTEIN, B.J. "RELUCTANCE AND RESISTANCE: WILSON WYATT AND VETERANS' HOUSING IN THE TRUMAN ADMINISTRATION." REGISTER OF THE KENTUCKY HISTORICAL SOCIETY 65 (1967):47-66.

763 ----------. "THE REMOVAL OF WAR PRODUCTION CONTROLS ON BUSINESS, ." BUSINESS HISTORY R 39 (1965):243-260.

764 ----------. "THE TRUMAN ADMINISTRATION AND ITS

RECONVERSION WAGE POLICY." LABOR HISTORY 6
(1965):214-231.

765 ----------. "THE TRUMAN ADMINISTRATION AND THE STEEL
STRIKE OF 1946." J OF AMERICAN HISTORY 52
(1966):791-803.

766 CARIDI, R.J. THE KOREAN WAR AND AMERICAN POLITICS: THE
REPUBLICAN PARTY AS A CASE STUDY. PHILADELPHIA:
UNIVERSITY OF PENNSYLVANIA PRESS, 1968, PP. 319.

HOW INTRA-GOP POLITICS AFFECTED THE DOMESTIC ASPECT OF THE
KOREAN WAR AND VICE-VERSA.

767 CLUBB, O.E. THE WITNESS AND I. NEW YORK: COLUMBIA U PR,
1974, PP. 314.

768 DIVINE, R.A. SINCE 1945: POLITICS AND DIPLOMACY IN RECENT
AMERICAN HISTORY. 3RD ED. NEW YORK: WILEY, 1975, PP.
328.

CHRONOLOGICAL NARRATIVE AS SEEN FROM WHITE HOUSE VANTAGE
POINT AND FOCUSING ON LINKAGE BETWEEN FOREIGN AND DOMESTIC
POLICIES AND EVENTS. EPILOGUE TREATS OF WATERGATE AND THE
RESIGNATION OF PRESIDENT NIXON.

769 ----------. "THE COLD WAR AND THE ELECTION OF 1948." J
AMER HIST 59 (1972):90-110.

770 HAH, C., AND LINDQUIST, R. "THE 1952 STEEL SEIZURE
REVISITED: A SYSTEMATIC STUDY IN PRESIDENTIAL DECISION
MAKING." ADMIN SCI Q 20 (DEC. 1975): 587-604.

A RECONSTRUCTION OF THE PRESIDENT'S DECISION-MAKING IN THE
STEEL SEIZURE IN TERMS OF THE 'LEVELS OF ANALYSIS'
APPROACH DEVELOPED BY GRAHAM ALLISON IN HIS ESSENCE OF
DECISION.

771 KOENIG, L.W. THE SALE OF THE TANKERS. INTER-UNIVERSITY
CASE PROGRAM: BOX 229, SYRACUSE, N.Y., 1950, PP. 184. ALSO
REPRINTED IN STEIN, H., ED. PUBLIC ADMINISTRATION AND
POLICY DEVELOPMENT: A CASE BOOK. N.Y.: HARCOURT, BRACE,
1952.

772 MCCONNELL, G. THE STEEL SEIZURE OF 1952.
INTER-UNIVERSITY CASE PROGRAM: BOX 229, SYRACUSE, N.Y.,
1960, PP. 53.

773 SCHUBERT, G.A. "THE STEEL CASE: PRESIDENTIAL RESPONSIBILITY AND JUDICIAL IRRESPONSIBILITY." WESTERN POLITICAL Q 6 (1953):61-77.

774 SNETSINGER, J. TRUMAN, THE JEWISH VOTE AND THE CREATION OF ISRAEL. STANFORD, CALIF.: HOOVER INST. PRESS, 1974, PP. 208.

DRAWING UPON TRUMAN LIBRARY DOCUMENTS, THE AUTHOR ARGUES THAT TRUMAN VACILLATED ON THE QUESTION OF WHETHER OR NOT TO SUPPORT THE FOUNDING OF ISRAEL. HE WAS TORN BETWEEN STATE DEPARTMENT AND DEFENSE DEPARTMENT ADVICE TO PLACATE ARAB INTERESTS AND DEMOCRATIC PARTY URGINGS TO SUPPORT ZIONIST POLICIES.

775 TANENHAUS, J. "THE SUPREME COURT AND PRESIDENTIAL POWER." ANNALS 307 (1956):106-114.

DEVOTES SPECIAL ATTENTION TO THE YOUNGSTOWN DECISION RULING AGAINST TRUMAN'S STEEL SEIZURE AS A DEPARTURE FROM THE TENDENCY OF THE SUPREME COURT REFLEXIVELY TO SUPPORT PRESIDENTIAL CLAIMS OF POWER.

776 WESTIN, A.F. THE ANATOMY OF A CONSTITUTIONAL LAW CASE: YOUNGSTOWN STEEL AND TUBE CO. VS. SAWYER: THE STEEL SEIZURE DECISION. NEW YORK: MACMILLAN, 1958, PP. 183.

777 WILLIAMS, J. "STEEL SEIZURE--A LEGAL ANALYSIS OF A POLITICAL CONTROVERSY." J PUBLIC LAW 2:29-40 SPRING '53.

778 YARNELL, A. DEMOCRATS AND PROGRESSIVES: THE 1948 PRESIDENTIAL ELECTION AS A TEST OF POSTWAR LIBERALISM. BERKELEY: U OF CAL PR, 1974, PP. 155.

SEE ALSO 573, 659, 702, 2287, 2290

G. ADDITIONAL ASPECTS AND THEMES

779 BERGER, H.N. "PARTISANSHIP, SENATOR TAFT, AND THE TRUMAN ADMINISTRATION." PSQ 90 (SUMMER 1975): 221-237.

A REVISIONIST VIEW OF THE 'NEGATIVE' NATURE OF SENATOR TAFT'S OPPOSITION TO TRUMAN'S POST-WORLD WAR II FOREIGN POLICY.

780 CORNWELL, E.E. "THE TRUMAN PRESIDENCY." IN THE TRUMAN PERIOD AS A RESEARCH FIELD, EDITED BY R. KIRKENDALL, COLUMBIA, MO.: U OF MO PR, 1967, PP. 213-255.

781 DAVIS, E. "HARRY S. TRUMAN AND THE VERDICT OF HISTORY."
REPORTER 3 FEB. 1953, PP. 17-22.

782 HAMBY, A.L. "LIBERALS, TRUMAN AND FDR AS SYMBOL AND MYTH."
J AMER HIST 56:859-67 MR '70.

783 ----------. "THE CLASH OF PERSPECTIVES AND THE NEED FOR
NEW SYNTHESES." IN THE TRUMAN PERIOD AS A RESEARCH
FIELD. EDITED BY R. KIRKENDALL, COLUMBIA, MO.: U OF MO
PR, 1974, PP. 113-148.

784 KILBORN, P. TRUMAN AND THE POSITIVE PRESIDENCY.
CAMBRIDGE, MASS.: DISS. HARVARD U, 1955. NEW YORK, NYU PR,
1956.

785 LEVIERO, A. "HOW THE PRESIDENT MAKES DECISIONS." N Y
TIMES MAG 14-15+ O 8 '50.

786 LORENZ, A.L. "TRUMAN AND THE PRESS CONFERENCE."
JOURNALISM Q 43 (1966):671-679.

787 PATERSON, T.G. COLD WAR CRITICS: ALTERNATIVES TO AMERICAN
POLICY IN THE TRUMAN YEARS. CHICAGO: QUADRANGLE BOOKS,
1971, PP. 313.

788 POLLARD, J.E. "PRESIDENT TRUMAN AND THE PRESS."
JOURNALISM Q 28:457-68 FALL '51.

789 SITKOFF, H. "YEARS OF THE LOCUST: INTERPRETATIONS OF
TRUMAN'S PRESIDENCY SINCE 1965." IN THE TRUMAN PERIOD AS
A RESEARCH FIELD. EDITED BY R. KIRKENDALL, COLUMBIA, MO.:
U OF MO PR, 1974, PP. 75-112.

790 SMITH, G. "'HARRY, WE HARDLY KNOW YOU': REVISIONISM,
POLITICS, AND DIPLOMACY, 1945-54." APSR 70 (1976):
560-582.

A MAJOR BIBLIOGRAPHICAL REVIEW OF RECENT TRUMAN
SCHOLARSHIP, IDENTIFYING SUBSTANTIVE AND IDEOLOGICAL
CONTROVERSIES.

791 STOKES. L. "HARRY TRUMAN, POLITICIAN EXTRAORDINARY." N Y
    TIMES MAG13+ MY 7 '50.

792 STONE, I.F. TRUMAN ERA. NEW YORK: MONTHLY REVIEW PRESS.
    1953, PP. 226.

793 THEOHARIS, A.G. "THE RHETORIC OF POLITICS: FOREIGN POLICY,
    INTERNAL SECURITY, AND DOMESTIC POLITICS IN THE TRUMAN
    ERA, 1945-1950." IN POLITICS AND POLICIES OF THE TRUMAN
    ADMINISTRATION, EDITED BY B.J. BERNSTEIN, PP. 196-241,
    CHICAGO: QUADRANGLE, 1970.

    SEE ALSO 297, 610, 2502

9
DWIGHT D. EISENHOWER AND HIS ADMINISTRATION

A. GENERAL HISTORICAL ACCOUNTS AND BIOGRAPHIES

794 ALEXANDER, C.C. HOLDING THE LINE: THE EISENHOWER ERA, 1952-1961. BLOOMINGTON, IND.: INDIANA U PR, 1975, PP. 326.

A LATTER-DAY ACADEMIC SURVEY OF THE EISENHOWER PRESIDENCY AND ACCOMPANYING SOCIAL HISTORY. TRACES THE STANDARD VIEW STRESSING THE EISENHOWER YEARS AS A PERIOD OF STASIS AND WEAK LEADERSHIP. DOES NOT USE PRIMARY SOURCES, BUT HAS USEFUL BIBLIOGRAPHICAL ESSAY ON THE PUBLISHED LITERATURE ON EISENHOWER AND THE 1950'S IN GENERAL.

795 CHILDS, M. EISENHOWER: CAPTIVE HERO: A CRITICAL STUDY OF THE GENERAL AND THE PRESIDENT. NEW YORK: HARCOURT BRACE, 1958, PP. 310.

796 DONOVAN, R.J. EISENHOWER: THE INSIDE STORY. NEW YORK: HARPER, 1956, PP. 423.

A COMPREHENSIVE PORTRAYAL OF THE ACTORS AND EVENTS THAT SHAPED THE FIRST EISENHOWER ADMINISTRATION. RICH IN INSIGHT INTO EISENHOWER'S STYLE, ATTITUDE TOWARD HIS JOB, AND OPINION OF HIS ASSOCIATES. RECONSTRUCTS CABINET AND NSC MEETINGS FROM A SERIES OF INTERVIEWS WITH LEADING PARTICIPANTS.

797 GRAY, R.K. EIGHTEEN ACRES UNDER GLASS. GARDEN CITY, N.Y.: DOUBLEDAY, 1962, PP. 372.

AN INSIDER'S VIEW OF EISENHOWER'S WASHINGTON WRITTEN FROM THE VANTAGE POINT OF A FORMER CABINET SECRETARY, PRESIDENTIAL APPOINTMENTS SECRETARY, AND AIDE TO SHERMAN ADAMS. RICH IN ANECDOTAL MATERIAL, THIS BOOK IS PARTICULARLY VALUABLE FOR THE APPENDIX DETAILING THE NAMES, POSITIONS, AND DATES OF SERVICE OF EISENHOWER'S STAFF.

798 HUGHES, E.J. THE ORDEAL OF POWER: A POLITICAL MEMOIR OF THE EISENHOWER YEARS. NEW YORK: ATHENEUM, 1963, PP. 372.

MEMOIR BY EISENHOWER SPEECH WRITER. SETS FORTH A LIBERAL CRITIQUE OF EISENHOWER'S LACK OF POLICY INNOVATION.

799 JAMESON, H.B. THEY STILL CALL HIM IKE. NEW YORK: VANTAGE, 1972, PP. 103.

800 LARSON, A. EISENHOWER: THE PRESIDENT NOBODY KNEW. NEW YORK: SCRIBNER, 1968, PP. 210.

LARSON, AN EISENHOWER SPEECH WRITER, THEN DIRECTOR OF USIA, GIVES EISENHOWER HIGH GRADES FOR THE MORALITY AND SINCERITY HE BROUGHT TO THE PRESIDENCY, QUALITIES HE FINDS LACKING IN HIS TWO IMMEDIATE SUCCESSORS. EISENHOWER'S FUNDAMENTAL DISLIKE OF POLITICS IS DEFENDED BY LARSON, WHO PLACES GREAT IMPORTANCE ON SYMBOLIC ASPECTS OF THE OFFICE. OTHER TOPICS DISCUSSED INCLUDE EISENHOWER'S DECISION NOT TO INTERVENE MILITARILY IN INDOCHINA AND HIS PROGRAM TO WIN THIRD WORLD SUPPORT THROUGH ACTION DESIGNED TO PROVIDE AN ALTERNATIVE TO MARXISM.

801 LYON, P. EISENHOWER: PORTRAIT OF THE HERO. BOSTON: LITTLE, BROWN, 1974, PP. 937.

AN ACCOUNT OF EISENHOWER'S MILITARY AND POLITICAL CAREER BASED ON ORIGINAL RESEARCH. HIGHLY CRITICAL OF EISENHOWER, BUT TAKES ISSUE WITH WRITERS WHO DEPRECATE THIS PRESIDENT'S POLITICAL SKILL.

802 PARMET, H.S. EISENHOWER AND THE AMERICAN CRUSADES. NEW YORK: MACMILLAN, 1972, PP. 660.

LENGTHY BIOGRAPHY BASED ON ARCHIVAL SOURCES UNAVAILABLE UNTIL LONG AFTER EISENHOWER LEFT OFFICE. EVALUATION OF HIS PERFORMANCE IN OFFICE IS GENERALLY POSITIVE, BUT BOTH THE AUTHOR'S EVALUATIVE STANCE AND, MORE IMPORTANTLY, HIS ANALYTIC PERSPECTIVE ARE RATHER INEXPLICIT. AS A RESULT, THE BOOK TENDS TO BE LACKING IN ANALYTIC OR INTERPRETIVE PERSPECTIVE.

803 PEAR, P.H. "THE AMERICAN PRESIDENCY UNDER EISENHOWER." POLITICAL Q 28 (1957):5-12.

CONCENTRATES ON EISENHOWER'S IMPLEMENTATION OF THE HOOVER COMMISSIONS' RECOMMENDATIONS FOR ADMINISTRATIVE REFORM.

804 PUSEY, M.J. EISENHOWER, THE PRESIDENT. NEW YORK: MACMILLAN, 1956, PP. 300.

A CAMPAIGN BIOGRAPHY.

805 ROVERE, R.H. AFFAIRS OF STATE: THE EISENHOWER YEARS. NEW YORK: FARRAR, 1956, PP. 390.

A COLLECTION OF ARTICLES WRITTEN BY ROVERE DURING EISENHOWER'S FIRST TERM.

806 SMITH, A.M. MEET MISTER EISENHOWER. NEW YORK: HARPER, 1955.

SEE ALSO 280, 295, 300, 621, 629, 1564, 1568, 1579

B. PRESIDENT'S PAPERS, MEMOIRS

807 BRANYON, R.L., AND LARSEN, L.H., EDS. THE EISENHOWER ADMINISTRATION, 1953-1961: A DOCUMENTARY HISTORY. NEW YORK: RANDOM, 1971, 2 VOLS.

808 CHANDLER, A.D., JR., ED. THE PAPERS OF DWIGHT DAVID EISENHOWER: THE WAR YEARS. BALTIMORE, MD: JOHNS HOPKINS U PR, 1970, 5 VOLS.

809 EISENHOWER LIBRARY. HISTORICAL MATERIALS IN THE DWIGHT D. EISENHOWER LIBRARY. ABILENE, KA.: NATL ARC AND REC SER, APRIL 1975, PP. 57.

810 EISENHOWER, D.D. AT EASE: STORIES I TELL TO FRIENDS. GARDEN CITY, N.Y.: DOUBLEDAY, 1967, PP. 400.

AUTOBIOGRAPHICAL ANECDOTES ABOUT EISENHOWER'S PRE-PRESIDENTIAL YEARS. PROVIDES MORE OF A SENSE OF EISENHOWER'S PERSONAL QUALITIES THAN DO HIS OFFICIAL MEMOIRS.

811 ----------. IN REVIEW: PICTURES I'VE KEPT. GARDEN CITY, N.Y.: DOUBLEDAY, 1969, PP. 237.

812 ----------. PEACE WITH JUSTICE: SELECTED ADDRESSES OF DWIGHT D. EISENHOWER. NEW YORK: COLUMBIA U PR, 1961, PP. 273.

813 ----------. THE WHITE HOUSE YEARS. 2 VOLS. MANDATE FOR CHANGE, 1953-1956. GARDEN CITY, N.Y.: DOUBLEDAY, 1963, PP. 650. WAGING PEACE, 1956-1961. GARDEN CITY, N.Y.: DOUBLEDAY, 1965, PP. 741.

EISENHOWER'S PRESIDENTIAL MEMOIRS.

814 ----------. "SOME THOUGHTS ON THE PRESIDENCY." READER'S DIGEST 93:49-55 N '68.

SEE ALSO 54, 2033

C. COMPENDIA AND BIBLIOGRAPHIES

815 ALBERTSON, D. EISENHOWER AS PRESIDENT. NEW YORK: HILL AND WANG, 1963, PP. 169.

WORKMAN-LIKE COMPENDIUM OF SHORT WRITINGS, LARGELY FROM THE 1950'S. BALANCES CRITIQUES WITH SYMPATHETIC APPRAISALS

AND INCLUDES BIOGRAPHICAL AND BIBLIOGRAPHICAL SKETCHES WRITTEN BY THE EDITOR.

816 VEXLER, R.I. DWIGHT D. EISENHOWER, 1890-1969: CHRONOLOGY, DOCUMENTS, BIBLIOGRAPHICAL AIDS. DOBBS FERRY, N.Y.: OCEANA, 1970, PP. 150.

SEE ALSO 645

D. SELECTED MATERIAL ON PRE-PRESIDENTIAL BACKGROUND

817 AMBROSE, S.E. EISENHOWER AND BERLIN, 1945. NEW YORK: NORTON, 1967, PP. 119.

TAKES ISSUE WITH THE VIEW THAT EISENHOWER COULD AND SHOULD HAVE TAKEN BERLIN BEFORE THE ARRIVAL OF SOVIET TROOPS. WRITTEN IN REACTION TO SUCH POPULAR ACCOUNTS OF THE BIRTH OF THE COLD WAR AS JOHN TOLAND'S THE LAST 100 DAYS, CORNELIUS RYAN'S THE LAST BATTLES.

818 ----------. THE SUPREME COMMANDER: THE WAR YEARS OF GENERAL DWIGHT D. EISENHOWER. NEW YORK: DOUBLEDAY, 1970, PP. 732.

A DETAILED ACCOUNT OF EISENHOWER'S MILITARY YEARS.

819 DAVIS, K.S. SOLDIER OF DEMOCRACY; A BIOGRAPHY OF DWIGHT EISENHOWER. GARDEN CITY, N.Y.: DOUBLEDAY, 1945, PP. 566. SECOND EDITION, 1952, PP. 577.

820 EISENHOWER, D.D. CRUSADE IN EUROPE. NEW YORK: DOUBLEDAY, 1948, PP. 559.

EISENHOWER'S BEST SELLING MEMOIR OF HIS ROLE IN WORLD WAR II.

821 HOBBS, J.P. DEAR GENERAL: EISENHOWER'S WARTIME LETTERS TO MARSHALL. BALTIMORE, MD.: JOHNS HOPKINS PRESS, 1971, PP. 255.

822 KORNITZER, B. THE GREAT AMERICAN HERITAGE: THE STORY OF THE FIVE EISENHOWER BROTHERS. NEW YORK: FARRAR, STRAUSS AND GIROUX, 1955, PP. 331.

RICH IN FAMILIAL MATERIAL. GIVES CLOSE ATTENTION TO THE INFLUENCE OF IDA STOVER EISENHOWER AND HER SONS. A SIMILAR ACCOUNT OF HANNAH NIXON'S INFLUENCE APPEARS IN THE AUTHOR'S BIOGRAPHY OF EISENHOWER'S VICE PRESIDENT.

823 NADICH, J. EISENHOWER AND THE JEWS. NEW YORK: TWAYNE, 1953.

AN ACCOUNT OF EISENHOWER'S WAR-TIME AND POST-WAR

INVOLVEMENT WITH VICTIMS OF NAZI PERSECUTION AND THEIR REPRESENTATIVES.

824 POGUE, F. "SHAEF--A RETROSPECT ON COALITION COMMAND." J MOD HIST 23 (DEC 1951): 329-335.

825 ----------. "WHY EISENHOWER'S FORCES STOPPED AT THE ELBE." WORLD POLITICS 4 (APR 1952): 356-368.

826 SMITH, W.B. EISENHOWER'S SIX GREAT DECISIONS: EUROPE, 1944-1945. NEW YORK: LONGMANS, GREEN, 1956, PP. 237.

A CLOSE EISENHOWER MILITARY AND PRESIDENTIAL ADVISER DESCRIBES THE MOST IMPORTANT DECISIONS EISENHOWER MADE AS A GENERAL: THE INVASION OF NORMANDY, THE ENCIRCLING OF GERMAN FORCES IN NORMANDY, THE BATTLE OF THE BULGE, THE DESTRUCTION OF GERMAN FORCES WEST OF THE RHINE, THE ENCIRCLING OF THE RUHR, AND THE DESTRUCTION OF GERMANY'S CAPACITY TO WAGE WAR.

SEE ALSO 810, 2003, 2005, 2447

E. ADVISERS AND ADVISORY RELATIONS

827 ADAMS, S. FIRSTHAND REPORT: THE STORY OF THE EISENHOWER ADMINISTRATION. NEW YORK: HARPER, 1961, PP. 481.

EISENHOWER'S MOST FAMOUS AND CONTROVERSIAL WHITE HOUSE AIDE ATTEMPTS IN THIS MEMOIR TO "SET THE RECORD STRAIGHT" AS TO THE NATURE OF HIS DUTIES AS ASSISTANT TO THE PRESIDENT AND THE LEADERSHIP QUALITIES OF THE MAN HE SERVED. HIS OPENING CHAPTERS PROVIDE RARE GLIMPSES OF MEN IN TRANSITION: EISENHOWER, FROM A MILITARY TO A POLITICAL LIFE, AND ADAMS' OWN TRANSITION FROM ACCOMPLISHED POLITICIAN (HE WAS A TWO-TERM GOVERNOR, AS WELL AS A CONGRESSMAN), TO PRESIDENTIAL ADVISER. CHAPTERS FOUR AND FIVE, ENTITLED RESPECTIVELY "THE WHITE HOUSE STAFF AND CABINET" AND "AT WORK IN THE WHITE HOUSE" ARE ESSENTIAL READING FOR ANYONE ATTEMPTING TO STUDY PRESIDENTIAL ADVISORY RELATIONS. ADAMS TAKES ISSUE WITH THE WIDELY-PUBLICIZED 1950'S MEDIA PORTRAYAL OF HIM AS ASSISTANT PRESIDENT. HE INSISTS THAT HIS TASK WAS NOT THAT OF ISOLATING THE PRESIDENT FROM BOTH FRIEND AND FOE OR THE MAKING OF TOP-LEVEL POLICY DECISIONS, BUT THE REMOVAL OF ROUTINE ADMINISTRATIVE TASKS FROM EISENHOWER'S IMMEDIATE AGENDA.

828 BEAL, J.R. JOHN FOSTER DULLES: 1888-1959. NEW YORK: HARPER, 1959, PP. 358.

829 BENSON, E.T. CROSS FIRE: THE EIGHT YEARS WITH EISENHOWER. GARDEN CITY, N.Y.: DOUBLEDAY, 1962, PP. 627.

THE MEMOIRS OF EISENHOWER'S CONTROVERSIAL AGRICULTURE SECRETARY.

830 BERLE, A., AND MOOS, M. "THE NEED TO KNOW AND THE RIGHT TO TELL: EMMET JOHN HUGHES, THE ORDEAL OF POWER--A DISCUSSION." PSQ 26 (1964):336-344.

AN EXCHANGE BETWEEN TWO FORMER PRESIDENTIAL ADVISERS ON THE ETHICS OF UNAUTHORIZED MEMOIR WRITING BY WHITE HOUSE AIDES. BERLE TAKES A CONSERVATIVE POSITION AND HIGHLY CRITICAL OF HUGHES, WHILE MOOS CONSIDERS HUGHES' CANDOR A TRIBUTE TO THE KIND OF STAFF EISENHOWER GATHERED AROUND HIM.

831 CHALLENER, R.D., AND FENTON, J. "WHICH WAY AMERICA? DULLES ALWAYS KNEW." AMER HERITAGE 22 (1971):12-13, 84-93.

832 CUTLER, R. NO TIME FOR REST. BOSTON: LITTLE, BROWN, 1966, PP. 421.

PERSONAL MEMOIR OF THE BOSTON BRAHMIN WHO DEVOTED HIS LIFE TO PUBLIC SERVICE. AMONG HIS ACHIEVEMENTS WAS THE SHAPING OF THE ROLE OF THE WHITE HOUSE SPECIAL ADVISER FOR NATIONAL SECURITY, DURING THE EISENHOWER ADMINISTRATION. SUBSEQUENT INCUMBENTS OF THIS ROLE HAVE BEEN: MCGEORGE BUNDY (UNDER KENNEDY AND JOHNSON), WALT ROSTOW (UNDER JOHNSON), AND HENRY KISSINGER (UNDER NIXON AND FORD).

833 DRUMMOND, R., AND COBLENTZ, G. DUEL AT THE BRINK: JOHN FOSTER DULLES' COMMAND OF AMERICAN POWER. GARDEN CITY, N.Y.: DOUBLEDAY, 1960, PP. 240.

834 DULLES, E.L. JOHN FOSTER DULLES: THE LAST YEAR. NEW YORK: HARCOURT, BRACE AND WORLD, 1963, PP. 244.

835 DULLES, J.F. THE JOHN FOSTER DULLES ORAL HISTORY COLLECTION. PRINCETON, N.J.: PRINCETON U LIBRARY, SEPT 1967 (REVISED JUNE 1974), PP. 63.

836 FINER, H. DULLES OVER SUEZ: THE THEORY AND PRACTICE OF HIS DIPLOMACY. CHICAGO: QUADRANGLE, 1964, PP. 538.

A HIGHLY CRITICAL APPRAISAL OF DULLES BY A BRITISH SCHOLAR AND PARTISAN, MAINTAINING THAT DULLES LOST HIS NERVE AT A CRITICAL JUNCTURE.

837 GERSON, L.L. JOHN FOSTER DULLES. NEW YORK: COOPER SQUARE, 1967, PP. 372.

838 GOOLD-ADAMS, R. JOHN FOSTER DULLES: A REAPPRAISAL. NEW

YORK: APPLETON-CENTURY-CROFTS, 1962, PP. 309.

839 GUHIN, M.A. JOHN FOSTER DULLES: A STATESMAN AND HIS TIME. NEW YORK: COLUMBIA UNIVERSITY PRESS, 1972, PP. 404.

840 ----------. "DULLES' THOUGHTS ON INTERNATIONAL POLITICS: MYTH AND REALITY." ORBIS 13 (1969):865-889.

841 HELLER, D., AND HELLER, D. JOHN FOSTER DULLES: SOLDIER FOR PEACE. NEW YORK: HOLT, RINEHART AND WINSTON, 1960, PP. 328.

842 HOLSTI, O.R. "WILL THE REAL DULLES PLEASE STAND UP?" INTERNATIONAL J 30 (1974):34-44.

A REVIEW OF THE VARIOUS INTERPRETATIONS OF DULLES' YEARS AS SECRETARY OF STATE. CONCLUDES WITH A COMPARISON OF DULLES AND KISSINGER.

843 HOOPES, T. THE DEVIL AND JOHN FOSTER DULLES. BOSTON: LITTLE, BROWN AND COMPANY, 1973, PP. 562.

844 HOWARD, N., ED. THE BASIC PAPERS OF GEORGE M. HUMPHREY AS SECRETARY OF THE TREASURY, 1953-1957. CLEVELAND: WESTERN RESERVE HIST SOC, 1975, PP. 644.

845 HYMAN, S. "THE CABINET'S JOB AS EISENHOWER SEES IT." N Y TIMES MAG 20 JULY 1958, PP. 7+.

TRACES EISENHOWER'S ATTEMPTS TO RESURRECT THE CABINET AS A POLICY MAKING INSTITUTION FOCUSING ON THE FORMALIZATION OF MEETINGS AND THE CREATION OF A CABINET SECRETARY.

846 KISTIAKOWSKY, G.B. A SCIENTIST AT THE WHITE HOUSE: THE PRIVATE DIARY OF PRESIDENT EISENHOWER'S SPECIAL ASSISTANT FOR SCIENCE AND TECHNOLOGY. CAMBRIDGE, MA: HARVARD U PR, 1976, PP. 448.

847 MILLER, W.J. HENRY CABOT LODGE: A BIOGRAPHY. NEW YORK: HEINEMAN, 1967, PP. 449.

A THOROUGH INVESTIGATION INTO THE ROLE EISENHOWER'S POLITICAL PROMOTER IN 1952 AND AMBASSADOR TO THE U.N. PLAYED IN THE EISENHOWER, KENNEDY, AND JOHNSON ADMINISTRATIONS.

848 MORROW, E.F. BLACK MAN IN THE WHITE HOUSE: A DIARY OF THE EISENHOWER YEARS BY THE ADMINSTRATIVE OFFICER FOR SPECIAL PROJECTS, THE WHITE HOUSE, 1955-60. NEW YORK: COWARD-MC CANN, 1963, PP. 308.

THE FIRST BLACK TO SERVE AS AN OFFICIAL WHITE HOUSE POLICY ADVISER. MORROW DESCRIBES THE DILEMMA OF MEDIATING BETWEEN AN ADMINISTRATION RELUCTANT TO CHAMPION THE CAUSE OF CIVIL RIGHTS AND BLACK GROUPS SEEKING PRESIDENTIAL ASSISTANCE. WRITTEN IN DIARY FORM, THE BOOK DESCRIBES THE DAY TO DAY OPERATIONS OF THE WHITE HOUSE STAFF AND GIVES CHARACTER SKETCHES OF KEY PERSONNEL.

849 MURPHY, C.J.V. "EISENHOWER'S WHITE HOUSE." FORTUNE JULY 1953, PP. 75-77+.

AN EARLY GLIMPSE INTO EISENHOWER'S OPERATING STYLE. DEVOTES CLOSE ATTENTION TO THE PRESIDENT'S PREFERENCE FOR DELEGATION AND SPECIALIZATION OF FUNCTION.

850 ----------. "THE WHITE HOUSE SINCE SPUTNIK." FORTUNE JAN. 1958.

A DETAILED ACCOUNT OF THE DEVELOPMENT OF A LONG TERM PROGRAM OF MILITARY PREPAREDNESS AND CIVIL DEFENSE DURING EISENHOWER'S ADMINISTRATION.

851 NOBLE, G.B. CHRISTIAN A. HERTER. NEW YORK: COOPER SQUARE, 1970, PP.333.

A BIOGRAPHY OF EISENHOWER'S SECOND SECRETARY OF STATE.

852 STRAUSS, L.L. MEN AND DECISIONS. GARDEN CITY: DOUBLEDAY, 1962, PP. 468.

THE RECOLLECTIONS OF THE FORMER A.E.C. CHAIRMAN AND ILL-FATED COMMERCE SECRETARY DESIGNATE DURING THE EISENHOWER ERA.

853 TAYLOR, M.D. THE UNCERTAIN TRUMPET. NEW YORK: HARPER, 1960, PP. 203.

SEE ALSO 358, 798, 870, 1612, 1615, 1788, 1792, 1805, 2004, 2007, 2011, 2012, 2013, 2432

F. SPECIFIC EVENTS, ACTIVITIES AND POLICIES

1. DOMESTIC

854 BARTLEY, N.V. "LOOKING BACK AT LITTLE ROCK." ARKANSAS HISTORICAL Q 25 (1966):101-116.

RETRACES THE EVOLUTION OF A CRISIS. FOCUSES ON BACKGROUND MATERIAL ON THE LOCAL SCHOOL BOARD AND GOVERNOR FAUBUS RATHER THAN ON EISENHOWER.

855 FINKLE, J.L. THE PRESIDENT MAKES A DECISION: A STUDY OF DIXON-YATES. ANN ARBOR, MICH.: UNIV. OF MICH. INST. OF PUBLIC ADM., 1960, PP. 204.

856 FRIER, D.A. CONFLICT OF INTEREST IN THE EISENHOWER ADMINISTRATION. AMES: IOWA STATE UNIVERSITY, 1969, PP. 238.

857 HOBBS, E.H. "THE PRESIDENT AND ADMINISTRATION-- EISENHOWER." PAR 18 (1958): 306-13.

858 HOLMANS, A.E. "THE EISENHOWER ADMINISTRATION AND THE RECESSION, 1953 - 1955." OXFORD ECONOMIC PAPERS 10 (1958):34-54.

859 HY, R. "PRESIDENTIAL-CONGRESSIONAL DECISION-MAKING: THE DIXON-YATES CONTROVERSY." BUREAUCRAT 3 (JAN. 1975): 489-508.

860 MURPHY, C.J.V. "THE BUDGET AND EISENHOWER." FORTUNE JULY 1957, PP. 96-99, 228-230.

861 SCHER, S. "REGULATORY AGENCY CONTROL THROUGH APPOINTMENT: THE CASE OF THE EISENHOWER ADMINISTRATION AND THE NLRB." JP 23 (1961):667-688.

A CASE STUDY OF THE WAYS IN WHICH A SPECIAL CLIENTELE (LABOR UNIONS) ATTEMPTS TO INFLUENCE PRESIDENTIAL APPOINTMENTS TO A REGULATORY BOARD.

862 SUNDQUIST, J.L. POLITICS AND POLICY: THE EISENHOWER, KENNEDY, AND JOHNSON YEARS. WASHINGTON, D.C.: BROOKINGS INSTITUTION, 1968, PP. 560.

A STUDY OF THE POLITICS OF A NUMBER OF DOMESTIC POLICY ISSUES BETWEEN 1953 AND 1965. TRACES THE GERMINATION DURING THE EISENHOWER YEARS OF FUTURE LEGISLATION (E.G., AID TO EDUCATION AND FEDERALLY AIDED MEDICAL CARE), LARGELY THROUGH A PROCESS OF DEMOCRATIC CONGRESSIONAL INITIATIVE AND PRESIDENTIAL RESISTANCE. DURING THE KENNEDY YEARS, PRESIDENTIAL ADVOCACY OF POLICY ACTION BEGAN, BUT WAS BLOCKED BY JFK'S INABILITY TO OVER-RIDE THE CONSERVATIVE COALITION IN CONGRESS. AFTER JOHNSON'S LANDSLIDE 1964 ELECTION, POLICIES ACTUALLY WERE ENACTED IN THE HITHERTO STALEMATED DOMESTIC POLICY AREAS SUNDQUIST DISCUSSES.

863 WILDAVSKY, A. DIXON-YATES: A STUDY IN POWER POLITICS.
NEW HAVEN: YALE UNIVERSITY PRESS, 1962, PP. 351.

THE MOST COMPREHENSIVE STUDY OF A PROMINENTLY PUBLICIZED
CONFLICT OF INTEREST EPISODE DURING THE EISENHOWER YEARS.

864 WOLK, A. THE PRESIDENCY AND BLACK CIVIL RIGHTS:
EISENHOWER TO NIXON. RUTHERFORD, N.J.: FAIRLEIGH
DICKINSON UNIV. PRESS, 1971.

SEE ALSO 114, 433, 690, 1723, 1987, 2004, 2013

2. FOREIGN AND NATIONAL SECURITY

865 ALIANO, R.D. AMERICAN DEFENSE POLICY FROM EISENHOWER TO
KENNEDY: THE POLITICS OF CHANGING MILITARY REQUIREMENTS,
1957-1961. COLUMBUS: OHIO U PR, 1976.

866 BERNSTEIN, B.J. "FOREIGN POLICY IN THE EISENHOWER
ADMINISTRATION." FOR SERVICE J 50 (MAY 1973): 17-20,
29-31.

A GENERAL DISCUSSION FROM A REVISIONIST STANDPOINT.

867 BLUMBERG, S.A., AND OWENS, G. ENERGY AND CONFLICT: THE
LIFE AND TIMES OF EDWARD TELLER. NEW YORK: G.P. PUTNAM,
1976, PP. 492.

868 BOTTOME, E.M. THE MISSILE GAP: A STUDY OF THE FORMULATION
OF MILITARY AND PRACTICAL POLICY. RUTHERFORD: FAIRLEIGH
DICKINSON U PR, 1971, PP. 205.

869 CAPITANCHIK, D.B. THE EISENHOWER PRESIDENCY AND AMERICAN
FOREIGN POLICY. LONDON: ROUTLEDGE AND KEGAN PAUL, 1969,
PP. 80. ALSO NEW YORK: HUMANITIES PRESS, 1969.

USES EISENHOWER TO ILLUSTRATE THE PROPOSITION THAT A
PRESIDENT'S PERSONALITY CAN INFLUENCE HIS FOREIGN POLICY
EVEN WHEN HIS ROLE CONCEPTION PRECLUDES TAKING AN ACTIVE
PART IN THE POLICY PROCESS.

870 EISENHOWER, M.S. THE WINE IS BITTER: THE UNITED STATES
AND LATIN AMERICA. GARDEN CITY, N.Y.: DOUBLEDAY, 1963,
PP. 342.

THE PRESIDENT'S BROTHER TRACES THE DETERIORATION IN
RELATIONS BETWEEN THE U.S. AND LATIN AMERICA IN THE POST
WORLD WAR II ERA.

871 GARRETT, S.A. "FOREIGN POLICY AND THE AMERICAN
CONSTITUTION: THE BRICKER AMENDMENT IN CONTEMPORARY

PERSPECTIVE." <u>INTERNATIONAL STUDIES Q</u> 16 (1972):187-220.

EXAMINES THE CONTROVERSY IN THE EARLY 1950'S OVER THE BRICKER AMENDMENT, WHICH SOUGHT TO RESTRICT THE POWER OF THE GOVERNMENT TO ENTER INTO TREATIES AND EXECUTIVE AGREEMENTS.

872 HALPERIN, M.H. "THE GAITHER COMMITTEE AND THE POLICY PROCESS." <u>WORLD POLITICS</u>13:360-84 AP '61.

THOUGHTFUL, WELL-DOCUMENTED CASE STUDY OF AN EISENHOWER APPOINTED, OFF-THE-RECORD NATIONAL SECURITY STUDY GROUP THAT BECAME HIGHLY CONTROVERSIAL WHEN ITS RECOMMENDATIONS ON MILITARY POLICY, WHICH WERE CONTRARY TO THOSE OF THE ADMINISTRATION, WERE LEAKED TO THE PRESS.

873 LICKLIDER, R.E. "THE MISSILE GAP CONTROVERSY." <u>PSQ</u> 75 (DEC. 1970): 600-615.

874 PLISCHKE, E. "EISENHOWER'S 'CORRESPONDENCE DIPLOMACY' WITH THE KREMLIN--CASE STUDY IN SUMMIT DIPLOMATICS." <u>J OF POLITICS</u> 30 (1968):137-159.

875 REICHARD, G.W. "EISENHOWER AND THE BRICKER AMENDMENT." <u>PROLOGUE</u> 6 (SUMMER 1974): 88-99.

ARGUES THAT EISENHOWER'S "LARGELY UNRECOGNIZED POLITICAL TALENTS" WERE THE FINAL REASON FOR THE DEFEAT OF THE BRICKER AMENDMENT DESIGNED TO LIMIT THE POWERS OF THE PRESIDENT TO MAKE TREATIES AND ENTER INTO EXECUTIVE AGREEMENTS.

876 SCHICK, J.M. <u>THE BERLIN CRISIS, 1958-1962</u>. PHILADELPHIA: UNIVERSITY OF PENNSYLVANIA PRESS, 1971, PP. 206.

FOCUSES ON THE PATTERN OF DIPLOMATIC BREAKDOWNS AND MILITARY BUILDUPS IN BERLIN DURING EISENHOWER'S AND KENNEDY'S ADMINISTRATIONS.

877 SMITH, A.M. <u>A PRESIDENT'S ODYSSEY</u>. NEW YORK: HARPER, 1961, PP. 272.

878 STRAIGHT, M. "HOW IKE REACHED THE RUSSIANS AT GENEVA." <u>NEW REPUBLIC</u>, AUG.1, 1955.

VIEWS EISENHOWER'S PERSONAL CHARM, FORCE OF CHARACTER, AND PREVIOUS DEALINGS WITH SOVIET LEADERS AS DETERMINANTS OF THE OUTCOME OF THE GENEVA CONFERENCE.

879 SUTHERLAND, A.E. "THE BRICKER AMENDMENT, EXECUTIVE AGREEMENTS, AND IMPORTED POTATOES." <u>HARVARD LAW R</u>67:281-92 D '53.

AN ANALYSIS OF PROPOSED LIMITATIONS UPON THE EXECUTIVE TREATY MAKING POWER. CONSIDERS THE MERITS AND LIMITATIONS IN BRICKER'S AMENDMENT AND SENATE MINORITY LEADER KNOWLAND'S SUBSTITUTE.

880 WISE, D., AND ROSS, T.B. THE U-2 AFFAIR. NEW YORK: RANDOM HOUSE, 1962, PP. 269.

AN EXTENSIVE EXERCISE IN INVESTIGATIVE JOURNALISM, BASED ON NUMEROUS OFF-THE-RECORD INTERVIEWS.

SEE ALSO 78, 703, 716, 725, 727, 728, 734, 836, 1161, 2007, 2011, 2012, 2140

3. OTHER

881 DIBACCO, T.V. "AMERICAN BUSINESS AND FOREIGN AID: THE EISENHOWER YEARS." BUSINESS HISTORY R SPRING 1967, PP. 21-35.

CONSIDERS THE EISENHOWER APPROACH TO FOREIGN AID AS AN INCORPORATION OF TRADITIONAL BUSINESS PREFERENCES FOR SELF REGULATION AND ACCESS TO FOREIGN MARKETS.

882 EDGERTON, R. SUB-CABINET POLITICS AND POLICY COMMITMENTS: THE BIRTH OF THE DEVELOPMENT LOAN FUND. INTER-UNIVERSITY CASE PROGRAM: BOX 229, SYRACUSE, N.Y., 1970.

883 LEAR, J. "IKE AND THE PEACEFUL ATOM." REPORTER, JUNE 12, 1956.

HOW EISENHOWER RESISTED HIS CONSERVATIVE ADVISERS TO NEGOTIATE A PROGRAM OF COOPERATION WITH THE U.S.S.R. INVOLVING SHARED NUCLEAR RESOURCES.

884 REICHARD, G.W. THE REAFFIRMATION OF REPUBLICANISM: EISENHOWER AND THE EIGHTY-THIRD CONGRESS. KNOXVILLE, TENN.: U OF TENN PR, 1975, PP. 303.

QUANTITATIVE CONGRESSIONAL ROLL-CALL ANALYSIS OF SUPPORT FOR EISENHOWER'S PROGRAMS IN THE ONLY 2 YEARS (1953-1954) DURING HIS ADMINISTRATION WHEN THE REPUBLICANS CONTROLLED BOTH HOUSES OF CONGRESS. EISENHOWER EMERGES AS AN ACTIVE PARTY-LEADER, EMBRACING "MAINSTREAM" REPUBLICAN CONSERVATISM, AND OVERWHELMING THE ANTI-INTERNATIONALIST WING OF HIS PARTY BY SYSTEMATICALLY DRAWING ON DEMOCRATIC CONGRESSIONAL VOTING SUPPORT.

885 WALLACE, H.L. "THE MCCARTHY ERA, 1954." IN CONGRESS INVESTIGATES: A DOCUMENTED HISTORY, VOL. 5, EDITED BY A.M. SCHLESINGER, JR., AND R. BURNS, NEW YORK: CHELSEA HOUSE, 1975, PP. 3729-3919.

SEE ALSO 573, 766, 768, 1732, 2287

G. ADDITIONAL ASPECTS AND THEMES

886 "A DAY IN THE LIFE OF THE PRESIDENT." GEORGE WASHINGTON LAW R 24 (1956): 448-64.

887 DE SANTIS, V. "EISENHOWER REVISIONISM." R OF POLITICS 38 (APR 1976): 190+.

SURVEYS LATTER DAY WRITINGS CONTROVERTING THE CONVENTIONAL 1950'S LITERATURE WHICH VIEWED EISENHOWER AS DEFICIENT IN POLITICAL SKILL AND SOPHISTICATION.

888 GRAEBNER, N.A. "EISENHOWER'S POPULAR LEADERSHIP." CURRENT HISTORY 39 (1960):230-236, 244.

GENERAL HISTORICAL DISCUSSION OF EISENHOWER'S PERSONAL APPEAL. FOR AN ANALYSIS THAT USES SURVEY DATA SEE HYMAN AND SHEATSLEY, "THE POLITICAL APPEAL OF PRESIDENT EISENHOWER."

889 HAUGE, G. "ECONOMICS OF EISENHOWER DYNAMIC CONSERVATISM." COMMERCIAL AND FINANCIAL CHRONICLES 182 (1955):1749, 1776-1777.

890 HYMAN, H., AND SHEATSLEY, P.B. "THE POLITICAL APPEAL OF PRESIDENT EISENHOWER." POQ 17 (WINTER 1953-1954): 443-460.

MULTI-FACETED ANALYSIS OF NUMEROUS POST-WORLD WAR II PUBLIC OPINION POLLS SHOWING CONVINCINGLY THAT EISENHOWER EMERGED FROM THE WAR AS AN EXTRAORDINARILY POPULAR NATIONAL HERO AND THAT, UNLIKE OTHER POPULAR WARTIME FIGURES, HIS POPULARITY WAS BROADLY SPREAD ACROSS POPULATION GROUPS OF DIFFERENT SOCIAL STATUSES AND IDEOLOGICAL HUES. HIS APPEAL WAS ESPECIALLY STRONG AMONG NORMALLY DEMOCRATIC VOTERS. THUS THE AUTHORS CONCLUDE THAT EITHER PARTY COULD HAVE NOMINATED EISENHOWER AND WON THE ELECTION IN 1952.

891 KEMPTON, M. "THE UNDERESTIMATION OF DWIGHT D. EISENHOWER." ESQUIRE (SEPTEMBER 1967): 108-109, 156.

AMONG THE FIRST OF THE SO-CALLED "SECOND LOOKS" AT EISENHOWER. ARGUES THAT EISENHOWER'S DISASSOCIATION WITH CONTROVERSY RESULTED FROM A CAREFULLY DEVELOPED STRATEGY.

892 POLLARD, J.E. "EISENHOWER AND THE PRESS: THE FINAL PHASE." JOURNALISM Q SPRING 1961, PP. 181-186.

893 ----------. "EISENHOWER AND THE PRESS: THE FIRST TWO YEARS." JOURNALISM Q 285-300 SUMMER '55.

894 RHODES, R. "IKE: ARTIST IN IRON," <u>HARPER'S</u> JULY 1970 : 70-77.

PROBES THE ORIGINS OF TWO OF EISENHOWER'S MOST PROMINENT CHARACTERISTICS, FRIENDLINESS TOWARD THE WORLD AND TOUGHNESS IN COMMAND. RHODES PUTS FORTH THE THESIS THAT THE KEY TO EISENHOWER'S SUCCESS WAS HIS ABILITY TO SUBORDINATE AN INNER VIOLENCE TO THE CAUSE OF PEACE.

895 ROVERE, R.H. "EISENHOWER OVER THE SHOULDER." <u>AMER SCHOLAR</u> 31:176-9 SPR '62.

PORTRAYS THE EISENHOWER YEARS AS A NECESSARY INTERVAL AFTER PREVIOUS YEARS OF POLITICAL CHANGE AND CONFLICT. EISENHOWER IS PRAISED FOR HIS FIRST TERM FOREIGN POLICY ACHIEVEMENTS, BUT FAULTED FOR HIS FAILURE TO UNDERTAKE BOLD DOMESTIC INITIATIVES IN HIS SECOND TERM.

896 ----------. "EISENHOWER REVISITED: A POLITICAL GENIUS?". <u>N Y TIMES MAG</u>14-15+ F 7 '71; DISCUSSION, P 4+ F28; 12 MR 7 '71.

REVIEW OF THE PRESIDENTIAL YEARS CONTROVERTING BUT NOT FULLY DENYING THAT EISENHOWER'S POLITICAL SKILLS WERE UNDERESTIMATED BY CONTEMPORARY COMMENTATORS.

897 SHANNON, W.V. "EISENHOWER AS PRESIDENT: A CRITICAL APPRAISAL OF THE RECORD." <u>COMMENTARY</u> 26 NOV. 1968, PP. 390-398.

A REPRESENTATIVE SAMPLE OF THE VIEW HELD BY LIBERALS OF EISENHOWER AS A MAN OF GOOD INTENTIONS BUT LITTLE VISION. SHANNON IS CRITICAL OF EISENHOWER FOR LEAVING THE "AMERICAN CONSENSUS" HE INHERITED UNDISTURBED. HE SEES EISENHOWER'S TIME IN OFFICE AS AN ERA OF LOST TIME AND WASTED OPPORTUNITIES.

898 SHOEMAKER, R.J., ED. <u>THE PRESIDENT'S WORDS, AN INDEX</u>. LOUISVILLE:SHOEMAKER AND SHOEMAKER, 1954-1961.

899 STONE, I.F. <u>THE HAUNTED FIFTIES</u>. NEW YORK: RANDOM HOUSE, 1963, PP. 394.

SEE ALSO 261, 297, 301, 610, 823, 1866, 2502

10
JOHN F. KENNEDY AND HIS ADMINISTRATION

A. GENERAL HISTORICAL ACCOUNTS AND BIOGRAPHIES

900 BLAIR, J., AND BLAIR, C., JR. THE SEARCH FOR J.F.K. NEW YORK: BERKLEY, 1976, PP. 608.

EXTENSIVE RESEARCH ON KENNEDY'S LIFE AND CAREER BY TWO INVESTIGATIVE JOURNALISTS.

901 BURNS, J.M. "THE FOUR KENNEDYS OF THE FIRST YEAR." N Y TIMES MAG 14 JAN. 1962. 9+.

902 HEATH, J.F. DECADE OF DISILLUSIONMENT: THE KENNEDY-JOHNSON YEARS. BLOOMINGTON, INDIANA U PR, 1975. PP. 332.

903 HENDERSON, B., AND SUMMERLIND, S. IN MEMORIAM: JOHN F. KENNEDY. NEW YORK: COWLES PUBLICATION, 1968. PP. 243.

904 LASKY, V. J.F.K.: THE MAN AND THE MYTH. NEW YORK: MACMILLAN, 1963, PP. 653.

A CRITICAL ACCOUNT BY A CONSERVATIVE JOURNALIST. COPIES WERE PULLED OFF THE SHELVES AFTER KENNEDY'S DEATH, BUT BEGAN TO REAPPEAR IN THE LATE '60'S. LASKY HAS DONE SIMILAR STUDIES OF ROBERT KENNEDY AND ARTHUR GOLDBERG.

905 MANCHESTER, W.R. PORTRAIT OF A PRESIDENT: JOHN F. KENNEDY IN PROFILE. BOSTON: LITTLE, BROWN, 1962, PP. 238.

AN ACCOUNT OF JOHN KENNEDY'S COMPORTMENT AS PRESIDENT AND OF KENNEDY'S PERSONAL IMPACT ON THE WASHINGTON SCENE. THIS BOOK IS REPORTED TO HAVE INFLUENCED MRS. KENNEDY'S DECISION TO COMMISSION ITS AUTHOR TO RECOUNT THE CIRCUMSTANCES OF HER HUSBAND'S ASSASSINATION IN DEATH OF A PRESIDENT.

906 NEW YORK TIMES, THE STAFF OF. THE KENNEDY YEARS. NEW YORK: VIKING PRESS, 1964, PP. 327.

907 PAPER, L.J. THE PROMISE AND THE PERFORMANCE: THE

LEADERSHIP OF JOHN F. KENNEDY. NEW YORK: CROWN, 1975, PP. 408.

THE MOST EVEN-HANDED, SCHOLARLY, "BALANCE-SHEET" ANALYSIS OF KENNEDY'S GOALS, MEANS, AND ACCOMPLISHMENTS. USES ARCHIVAL SOURCES NOT IN PREVIOUS WRITINGS.

908 SCHLESINGER, A.M., JR. A THOUSAND DAYS: JOHN F. KENNEDY IN THE WHITE HOUSE. BOSTON: HOUGHTON MIFFLIN, 1965, PP. 1087.

THE FIRST SERIOUS HISTORY OF THE KENNEDY YEARS BY AN HISTORIAN WHO WORKED IN THE WEST WING OF THE WHITE HOUSE. A PARTIAL MEMOIR, THE BOOK OUTLINES SCHLESINGER'S ROLE IN THE FORMULATION OF LATIN AMERICAN POLICY.

909 SIDEY, H. JOHN F. KENNEDY, PRESIDENT. NEW YORK: ATHENEUM, 1964, PP. 434.

SYMPATHETIC ACCOUNT BY THE JOURNALIST WHO COVERED THE KENNEDY PRESIDENCY FOR TIME AND WHO HAD COVERED HIS ACTIVITIES DURING THE THREE YEARS HE CAMPAIGNED FOR NOMINATION AND ELECTION.

910 SORENSEN, T.C. KENNEDY. NEW YORK: HARPER, 1965, PP. 783.

VARIOUSLY REFERRED TO AS KENNEDY'S "TOP POLICY AIDE" AND HIS "ALTER EGO," SORENSEN WORKED CLOSELY WITH JFK FROM 1953, WHEN HE WAS HIRED AS A LEGISLATIVE AIDE THROUGH THE END OF THE KENNEDY PRESIDENCY. TRACES THE EVOLUTION OF KENNEDY'S STYLE AS WELL AS SORENSEN'S INFLUENCE UPON THAT STYLE.

911 ----------. THE KENNEDY LEGACY. NEW YORK: MACMILLAN, 1969, PP. 414.

A REVIEW OF THE CAREERS OF JOHN AND ROBERT KENNEDY FOCUSING ON THEIR INSPIRATIONAL CONTRIBUTIONS.

912 WICKER, R. KENNEDY WITHOUT TEARS: THE MAN BEHIND THE MYTH. NEW YORK: MORROW, 1964, PP. 61.

913 WICKER, T. JFK AND LBJ: THE INFLUENCE OF PERSONALITY UPON POLITICS. NEW YORK: MORROW, 1968, PP. 297.

THE TWO PRESIDENTS, BOTH OF WHOM WERE DEEPLY INFORMED ABOUT AMERICAN POLITICS, NEVERTHELESS FAILED, BECAUSE OF PERSONALITY LIMITATIONS, TO ACHIEVE KEY GOALS--KENNEDY IN THE DOMESTIC AND JOHNSON IN THE FOREIGN SPHERE.

SEE ALSO 279, 283, 295, 300, 629, 954, 1555, 1564

B. PRESIDENT'S PAPERS, MEMOIRS

914 CHASE, H.W., AND LERMAN, A.H., EDS. KENNEDY AND THE PRESS: THE NEWS CONFERENCES. NEW YORK: THOMAS Y. CROWELL, 1965, PP. 555.

915 KENNEDY LIBRARY. <u>HISTORICAL MATERIALS IN THE JOHN F. KENNEDY LIBRARY</u>. WALTHAM, MASS.: JOHN F. KENNEDY LIBRARY, JAN 1975, PP. 64.

916 KENNEDY, J.F. <u>PROFILES IN COURAGE</u>. NEW YORK: HARPER, 1956, PP. 266.

JFK'S PULITZER PRIZE WINNING ACCOUNT OF SIX COURAGEOUS SENATORS.

917 ----------. <u>THE BURDEN AND THE GLORY</u>. NEW YORK: HARPER, ROW, 1964, PP. 293.

918 ----------. <u>THE STRATEGY OF PEACE</u>. NEW YORK: HARPER, ROW, 1960, PP. 233.

919 ----------. <u>TO TURN THE TIDE</u>. NEW YORK: HARPER, ROW, 1962, PP. 235.

920 ----------. <u>WHY ENGLAND SLEPT</u>. NEW YORK: FUNK, 1940, PP. 252.

KENNEDY'S HARVARD SENIOR THESIS WITH A FOREWORD BY HENRY LUCE.

921 KLEIN, A.L., ED. <u>TREASURY OF JOHN F. KENNEDY ADDRESSES</u>. 15 CASSETTE SERIES WITH COMPLETE TEXTS OF SPEECHES. NEW ROCHELLE, N.Y.: SPOKEN ARTS. CATALOGUE NO. SAC-JFK-15, N.D.

SEE ALSO 54, 2033

C. COMPENDIA AND BIBLIOGRAPHIES

922 CROWN, J.T. <u>THE KENNEDY LITERATURE: A BIBLIOGRAPHICAL ESSAY ON JOHN F. KENNEDY</u>. NEW YORK: NEW YORK UNIVERSITY PRESS, 1968, PP. 181.

A GENERAL ESSAY AND BIBLIOGRAPHY ON KENNEDY'S OWN WRITINGS AND ON THOSE ABOUT HIM AND HIS PRESIDENCY. A USEFUL START ON KENNEDY RESEARCH IF ONE REALIZES THAT THE SUMMARIES REFLECT THE AUTHOR'S OPINIONS RATHER STRONGLY AND ARE NOT MERELY ABSTRACTS (E.G., MUCH ATTENTION IS DEVOTED TO CONSPIRACY-HYPOTHESES ABOUT KENNEDY'S DEATH. BUT THE VOLUME CONTAINING NUMEROUS POLITICAL-PSYCHOLOGICAL STUDIES OF PUBLIC RESPONSE TO THAT EVENT REPORTED IN THE

GREENBERG-PARKER VOLUME ARE DISCUSSED IN A SINGLE-PARAGRAPH NOTE ON THE ENTIRE VOLUME). THIS BOOK PRECEDES RESEARCH THAT MADE SYSTEMATIC USE OF THE KENNEDY LIBRARY'S ARCHIVES (E.G., LEONARD PAPER'S THE PROMISE AND THE PERFORMANCE).

923 DAVID, J., ED. THE KENNEDY READER. INDIANAPOLIS: BOBBS-MERRILL CO., 1967, PP. 428.

924 DONALD, A.D., ED. JOHN KENNEDY AND THE NEW FRONTIER. NEW YORK: HILL AND WANG, 1966, PP. 264.

AN ANTHOLOGY OF REPRESENTATIVE PRE-1966 JFK LITERATURE.

925 IONS, E.S., ED. THE POLITICS OF JOHN F. KENNEDY. NEW YORK: BARNES AND NOBLE, 1967, PP. 228.

926 LATHAM, E., ED. J.F. KENNEDY AND PRESIDENTIAL POWER. LEXINGTON, MASS.: HEATH, 1972, PP. 296.

AMONG THE MOST COMPREHENSIVE OF THE KENNEDY READERS. DIVIDED INTO CHAPTERS ON POLITICAL STYLE, ECONOMICS, FOREIGN AFFAIRS, AND KENNEDY'S PLACE IN HISTORY, THIS VOLUME PULLS TOGETHER REPRESENTATIVE VIEWS OF LEFT, RIGHT, AND CENTER.

927 ROLLINS, A.B. THE ORAL HISTORY PROJECT OF THE JOHN FITZGERALD KENNEDY LIBRARY; REPORT TO THE HARVARD UNIVERSITY COMMITTEE. CAMBRIDGE: HARVARD UNIVERSITY PRESS, 1965, PP. 195.

928 SABLE, M.H. A BIO-BIBLIOGRAPHY OF THE KENNEDY FAMILY. METUCHEN, N.J.: SCARECROW PRESS, 1969, PP.330.

929 SCHNAPPER, B.N., ED. NEW FRONTIERS OF THE KENNEDY ADMINISTRATION: TEXTS OF THE TASK FORCE REPORTS PREPARED FOR THE PRESIDENT. WASHINGTON, D.C.: PUBLIC AFFAIRS PRESS, 1961, PP. 170.

930 STONE, R.A. JOHN F. KENNEDY, 1917-1963; CHRONOLOGY, DOCUMENTS, BIBLIOGRAGHICAL AIDS. DOBBS FERRY, N.Y.: OCEANA, 1971, PP. 110.

SEE ALSO 960, 991, 992, 993, 1003, 1034, 1043

D. SELECTED MATERIAL ON PRE-PRESIDENTIAL BACKGROUND

931 BURNS, J.M. JOHN KENNEDY: A POLITICAL PROFILE. NEW YORK:

HARCOURT BRACE, 1960, PP. 309.

ALTHOUGH AN AUTHORIZED CAMPAIGN BIOGRAPHY, BURN'S BOOK CONTAINS A RELATIVELY OBJECTIVE APPRAISAL OF JFK'S PRE-PRESIDENTIAL CAREER.

932 CHAMBERLAIN, J. "THE CHAMELEON IMAGE OF JOHN F. KENNEDY," NATIONAL R 23 APRIL, 1960, PP. 41-50.

933 DAMORE, L. THE CAPE COD YEARS OF JOHN FITZGERALD KENNEDY. ENGLEWOOD CLIFFS, N.J.: PRENTICE-HALL, 1967, PP. 262.

934 DINEEN, J. THE KENNEDY FAMILY. BOSTON: LITTLE, BROWN, 1959, PP. 238.

935 DONOVAN, R.J. PT 109: JOHN F. KENNEDY IN WORLD WAR II. NEW YORK: MCGRAW-HILL, 1961, PP. 247.

RE-CREATION OF KENNEDY'S PT 109 EXPERIENCE BY WASHINGTON POLITICAL WRITER WHO INTERVIEWED MEMBERS OF THE CREW. FOR THE FIRST ACCOUNT OF THE STORY, SEE JOHN HERSEY'S "SURVIVAL."

936 HERSEY, J. "SURVIVAL," NEW YORKER (JUNE 17, 1944): 31+.

THE FIRST ACCOUNT OF KENNEDY'S PT-109 EXPERIENCE, LATER REPRINTED IN READER'S DIGEST. A BRIEF VERSION WAS WIDELY DISTRIBUTED DURING HIS FIRST CONGRESSIONAL CAMPAIGN. FOR A LATER ACCOUNT, SEE ROBERT DONOVAN'S PT 109.

937 KOSKOFF, D.E. JOSEPH P. KENNEDY: HIS LIFE AND TIMES. ENGLEWOOD CLIFFS, N.J.: PRENTICE-HALL, 1974, PP.643.

A COMPREHENSIVE TREATMENT OF JOSEPH P. KENNEDY, DRAWING HEAVILY ON PRIMARY SOURCES.

938 WHALEN, R.J. THE FOUNDING FATHER; THE STORY OF JOSEPH P. KENNEDY AND THE FAMILY HE RAISED TO POWER. NEW YORK: NEW AMERICAN LIBRARY, 1964.

THE FIRST SERIOUS STUDY OF JOSEPH P. KENNEDY AND OF HIS INFLUENCE UPON HIS SONS.

939 WHITE, T.H. THE MAKING OF THE PRESIDENT 1960. NEW YORK: ATHENEUM, 1961.

WHITE'S FIRST BOOK ON A PRESIDENTIAL ELECTION. PROVIDES CONCISE SUMMARIES OF THE ORGANIZATION AND STRATEGY OF BOTH CAMPS AND PRESENTS CHARACTER SKETCHES OF THE NOMINEES AND OTHER KEY ACTORS.

SEE ALSO 2447

E. ADVISERS AND ADVISORY RELATIONS

940 EVENING STAR (WASHINGTON, D.C.). THE NEW FRONTIERSMEN: PROFILES OF THE MEN AROUND KENNEDY. WASHINGTON, D.C.: PUBLIC AFFAIRS PRESS, 1961, PP.254.

941 ALSOP, S. "WHITE HOUSE INSIDERS." SAT EVE POST 10 JUNE, 1961.

942 ART, R.J. THE TFX DECISION: MCNAMARA AND THE MILITARY. BOSTON: LITTLE, BROWN, 1968, PP.202.

943 BRADSHAW, J. "RICHARD GOODWIN: THE GOOD, THE BAD, AND THE UGLY," NEW YORK 8 (AUGUST 1975): 29-43.

944 BURLINGHAM, B. "THE OTHER TRICKY DICK: ALL THE MANY THINGS UP THE MANY SLEEVES OF RICHARD GOODWIN." ESQUIRE 84 (NOVEMBER 1975).

A POST-CAMELOT, PERSONALITY SKETCH OF PRESIDENTIAL SPEECHWRITER RICHARD GOODWIN.

945 GALBRAITH, J.K. AMBASSADOR'S JOURNAL. BOSTON: HOUGHTON, 1969, PP. 656.

THE RECOLLECTIONS OF THE NOTED ECONOMIST WHO WAS JFK'S AMBASSADOR TO INDIA.

946 HALBERSTAM, D. THE BEST AND THE BRIGHTEST. NEW YORK: RANDOM HOUSE, 1972, PP. 688.

WELL KNOWN ACCOUNT BY JOURNALIST OF HOW KENNEDY, JOHNSON, AND THEIR ADVISORS ESCALATED THE VIETNAMESE CONFLICT. BASED ON INTERVIEWS AND PUBLISHED SOURCES, BUT FOLLOWS MODE OF "NOT FOR ATTRIBUTION" QUOTATIONS.

947 KAUFMANN, W.W. THE MCNAMARA STRATEGY. NEW YORK: HARPER, ROW, 1964, PP. 339.

948 LINCOLN, E. MY TWELVE YEARS WITH JOHN F. KENNEDY. NEW YORK: D. MC KAY CO., 1965, PP. 371.

THE PERSONAL MEMORIES OF JOHN F. KENNEDY'S PRIVATE SECRETARY. THICK WITH ANECDOTAL MATERIAL.

949 NAVASKY, V.S. KENNEDY JUSTICE. NEW YORK: ATHENEUM, 1971, PP. 482.

AN ACCOUNT OF ROBERT KENNEDY'S TENURE AS ATTORNEY GENERAL, UNDERTAKING A "BEST AND BRIGHTEST" ASSESSMENT OF KENNEDY'S

SUBORDINATES IN THE JUSTICE DEPARTMENT.

950 O'BRIEN, L. NO FINAL VICTORIES: A LIFE IN POLITICS FROM JOHN F. KENNEDY TO WATERGATE. NEW YORK: DOUBLEDAY, 1974.

951 OPOTOWSKY, S. THE KENNEDY GOVERNMENT. NEW YORK: E.P. DUTTON, 1961, PP. 208.

BIOGRAPHICAL CHAPTERS OF THE KENNEDY CABINET WITH A SECTION ON THE WHITE HOUSE STAFF.

952 ROHERTY, J.M. DECISIONS OF ROBERT S. MCNAMARA: A STUDY OF THE ROLE SECRETARY OF DEFENSE. CORAL GABLES: U OF MIAMI PR, 1970, PP. 223.

953 RUSK, D. WINDS OF FREEDOM: SELECTIONS FROM THE SPEECHES AND STATEMENTS OF SECRETARY OF STATE DEAN RUSK, JANUARY 1961-AUGUST 1962. EDITED BY E.K. LINDLEY, BOSTON: BEACON, 1963, PP. 363.

954 SALINGER, P. WITH KENNEDY. GARDEN CITY, N.Y.: DOUBLEDAY, 1966, PP. 301.

AN ANECDOTALLY RICH MEMOIR BY PRESIDENT KENNEDY'S PRESS SECRETARY.

955 SMITH, D. "THE CAMELOTIANS; WHERE THEY ARE NOW." N Y TIMES MAG (NOV. 4, 1973): 38-39+.

REVIEWS THE CAREERS OF FORMER AIDES TO PRESIDENT KENNEDY IN THE YEARS FOLLOWING HIS DEATH.

956 TANZER, L. THE KENNEDY CIRCLE. WASHINGTON: LUCE, 1961, PP. 315.

AN ANTHOLOGY OF CHARACTER SKETCHES OF JFK'S ADVISERS WRITTEN BY A NUMBER OF WASHINGTON JOURNALISTS.

957 TAYLOR, M.D. RESPONSIBILITY AND RESPONSE. NEW YORK: HAR-ROW, 1967, PP. 84.

958 THOMPSON, R.E., AND MYERS, H. ROBERT F. KENNEDY: THE BROTHER WITHIN. NEW YORK: MACMILLAN, 1962, PP. 224.

AN ANALYSIS OF ROBERT KENNEDY'S ROLE AS PRESIDENTIAL ADVISER.

959 TREWHITT, H.L. MCNAMARA: HIS ORDEAL IN THE PENTAGON. NEW YORK: HAR-ROW 1971, PP. 308.

960 WILKINS, B.H., ED. THE ECONOMISTS OF THE NEW FRONTIER: AN ANTHOLOGY. NEW YORK: RANDOM HOUSE, 1963, PP.338.

SEE ALSO 294, 847, 853, 985, 1615, 1783, 1788, 1792, 2004, 2010, 2011, 2013, 2432

F. SPECIFIC EVENTS, ACTIVITIES AND POLICIES

1. DOMESTIC

961 CANTERBURY, E.R. ECONOMICS ON A NEW FRONTIER. BELMONT, CA.:WADSWORTH, 1968.

962 FLEMING, H.C. "THE FEDERAL EXECUTIVE AND CIVIL RIGHTS: 1961 - 1965." DAEDALUS (1965):921-948.

963 GERSHENSON, A.H. KENNEDY AND BIG BUSINESS. BEVERLY HILLS: BOOK COMPANY OF AMERICA, 1964, PP. 256.

964 HARRIS, S.E. THE ECONOMICS OF THE KENNEDY YEARS AND A LOOK AHEAD. NEW YORK: HARPER AND ROW, 1964, PP. 273.

965 HARVEY, J.C. CIVIL RIGHTS DURING THE KENNEDY ADMINISTRATION. JACKSON, MISS.: U PR OF MISS., 1971, PP. 87.

966 HEATH, J.F. JOHN F. KENNEDY AND THE BUSINESS COMMUNITY. CHICAGO, ILL.: UNIV. OF CHICAGO PRESS, 1969, PP. 198.

ESSENTIALLY AN ECONOMIC HISTORY OF JFK'S ADMINISTRATION STRESSING THAT, IN SPITE OF HIS CONFLICT WITH THE STEEL INDUSTRY, KENNEDY HAD INITIATED FRUITFUL COMMUNICATIONS WITH MANY OF THE NATION'S BUSINESS SECTORS.

967 HELLER, W.W. NEW DIMENSIONS OF POLITICAL ECONOMY. CAMBRIDGE, MASS.: HARVARD UNIVERSITY PRESS, 1966, PP. 203.

968 HILLS, R.M. "A CLOSE LOOK AT THREE ADMINISTRATION POLICIES." INDUSTRIAL RELATIONS 3 (FEB 1964): 5-20.

969 HOOPES, R. THE STEEL CRISIS. NEW YORK: JOHN DAY, 1963, PP.314.

970 KNAPP, D. SCOUTING THE WAR ON POVERTY: SOCIAL REFORM POLITICS IN THE KENNEDY ADMINISTRATION. LEXINGTON, MASS.: HEATH LEXINGTON BOOKS, 1971, PP.227.

971 LONGAKER, R.P. "THE PRESIDENT AND THE CIVIL RIGHTS OF NEGROES." IN AMERICAN GOVERNMENT ANNUAL, 1962-1963, EDITED BY I. HINDERAKER, NEW YORK: HR&W, 1962: 53-69.

972 MCCONNELL, G. STEEL AND THE PRESIDENCY, 1962. NEW YORK: W.W. NORTON, 1963, PP. 119.

A DETAILED ACCOUNT OF THE EPISODE IN WHICH KENNEDY INITIATED ACTIONS WHICH LED TO THE RECISION OF A STEEL PRICE INCREASE.

973 O'HARA, W.T. JOHN F. KENNEDY ON EDUCATION. NEW YORK: TEACHER'S COLLEGE PRESS, COLUMBIA UNIV., 1966, PP. 305.

974 ROWEN, H. THE FREE ENTERPRISERS: KENNEDY, JOHNSON, AND THE BUSINESS ESTABLISHMENT. NEW YORK: PUTNAM, 1964, PP. 319.

975 RUKESER, M.S. THE KENNEDY RECESSION. DERBY, CONN.: MONARCH BOOKS, 1963, PP. 220.

976 STERN, J. "THE KENNEDY POLICY: A FAVORABLE VIEW." INDUSTRIAL RELATIONS 3 (FEB 1964): 21-32.

977 TOBIN, J. THE NEW ECONOMICS ONE DECADE OLDER. PRINCETON: PRINCETON UNIVERSITY PRESS, 1974, PP. 105.

FORMER KENNEDY ADVISOR DESCRIBES THE ATTEMPTS OF "NEW ECONOMISTS" TO DEPART FROM THE TRADITIONAL FEAR OF DEFICIT SPENDING AND THE BELIEF IN THE INEVITABILITY OF THE BUSINESS CYCLE. CONCLUDES WITH A DISCUSSION OF ATTACKS AGAINST THE NEW ECONOMICS FROM BOTH THE RIGHT AND THE LEFT.

SEE ALSO 433, 862, 864, 949, 1723, 2004, 2013, 2266, 2287

2. FOREIGN AND NATIONAL SECURITY

978 ABEL, E. THE MISSILE CRISIS. LONDON: MACGIBBON & KEE,

1966, PP. 204; PHILA.: LIPPINCOTT, 1966, PP. 220.

A DAY BY DAY ACCOUNT OF THE MISSILE CRISIS BY A DIPLOMATIC CORRESPONDENT WHO COVERED IT.

979 ALLISON, G.T. ESSENCE OF DECISION: EXPLAINING THE CUBAN MISSILE CRISIS. BOSTON: LITTLE, BROWN, 1971.

A CASE-STUDY OF THE CUBAN-MISSILE-CRISIS SO EXECUTED AS TO ILLUSTRATE 3 DIFFERENT MODES OF ANALYZING POLICY-MAKING, ESPECIALLY IN FOREIGN AFFAIRS. THE NATION CAN BE TREATED AS A SINGLE RATIONAL ACTOR, AS A CONGLOMERATE OF POLICY-MAKING BUREAUCRACIES COMPETING TO CONTROL POLICY-OUTCOMES, OR AS A PROCESS OF INTERPERSONAL BARGAINIG IN WHICH INDIVIDUALS DO NOT INVARIABLY MERELY SPEAK AS BUREAUCRATIC ACTORS. THE MISSILE-CRISIS IS DECOMPOSED INTO 3 OVERLAPPING CASE-STUDIES, EACH ILLUSTRATING ONE OF THE ANALYTIC MODES. THE THIRD MODE FOCUSES ATTENTION ON THE PERSONALITIES OF POLITICAL ACTORS, BUT ALLISON DEVOTES RELATIVELY LITTLE ATTENTION TO KENNEDY HIMSELF, MAINLY ANALYZING THE AD-HOC "EXCOM" ADVISORY GROUP HE EMPLOYED.

980 BAGNALL, J.A. PRESIDENT JOHN F. KENNEDY, A GRAND AND GLOBAL ALLIANCE: THE SUMMONS TO WORLD PEACE THROUGH WORLD LAW. MINNEAPOLIS, MINN.: BURGESS PUB. CO., 1968, PP. 172.

981 BARTLETT, C., AND WEINTHAL, E. FACING THE BRINK: AN INTIMATE STUDY OF CRISIS DIPLOMACY. NEW YORK: SCRIBNER, 1967, PP. 248.

982 BERNSTEIN, B.J. "THE CUBAN MISSILE CRISIS." IN REFLECTIONS ON THE COLD WAR: A QUARTER CENTURY OF AMERICAN FOREIGN POLICY, EDITED BY L.H. MILLER AND R.W. PRUESSEN. PHILADELPHIA: TEMPLE U PR, 1974, PP. 130-133.

983 ----------. "THE WEEK WE ALMOST WENT TO WAR." BULL OF ATOMIC SCIENTISTS 32 (FEB. 1976): 13-21.

984 BOCK, E.A., AND GORVINE, A. PRESIDENTIAL USE OF A SCIENTIFIC PANEL IN FOREIGN AFFAIRS: THE REVELLE REPORT. INTER-UNIVERSITY CASE PROGRAM: BOX 229, SYRACUSE, N.Y., 1976.

985 BUNDY, M. "THE PRESIDENCY AND THE PEACE (EMPHASIS ON THE KENNEDY YEARS)." FOREIGN AFFAIRS 42 (APRIL 1964): 353-365.

986 CHAYES, A. THE CUBAN MISSILE CRISIS; INTERNATIONAL CRISES AND THE ROLE OF LAW. NEW YORK: OXFORD UNIVERSITY PRESS, 1974, PP.157.

ARGUES THAT CONSIDERATIONS OF INTERNATIONAL LAW AND NOT ONLY POWER POLITICS SIGNIFICANTLY INFLUENCED PRESIDENTIAL ACTION DURING THE CUBAN MISSILE CRISIS.

987 CRANE, R. "THE CUBAN MISSILE CRISIS: A STRATEGIC ANALYSIS OF AMERICAN AND SOVIET POLICY." ORBIS (WINTER 1963): 528-563.

988 DEAN, A.H. TEST BAN AND DISARMAMENT: THE PATH OF NEGOTIATION. NEW YORK: HARPER, ROW, 1966, PP.153.

989 DEWART, L. "THE CUBAN MISSILE CRISIS REVISITED." STUDIES ON THE LEFT (SPRING 1965): 15-37.

990 DINERSTEIN, H.S. THE MAKING OF A MISSILE CRISIS: OCTOBER 1962. BALTIMORE: JOHNS HOPKINS U PR, 1976, PP. 320.

A DETAILED RECONSTRUCTION OF THE MISSILE CRISIS DRAWING EXCLUSIVELY UPON THE CONTEMPORARY PRESS ACCOUNTS IN THE VARIOUS NATIONS INVOLVED.

991 DIVINE, R.A., ED. THE CUBAN MISSILE CRISIS. NEW YORK: QUADRANGLE BOOKS, 1971, PP.256.

AN ANTHOLOGY CONTAINING ANALYSES BY JOURNALISTS, SOVIETOLOGISTS, AND POLITICAL PARTICIPANTS.

992 DREIR, J.C., ED. THE ALLIANCE FOR PROGRESS: PROBLEMS AND PERSPECTIVES. BALTIMORE: JOHNS HOPKINS UNIVERSITY PRESS, 1962, PP.146.

993 GALLOWAY, J., ED. THE KENNEDYS AND VIETNAM. NEW YORK: FACTS ON FILE, 1971, PP.150.

994 GEORGE, A., HALL, D.K., AND SIMONS, W.R. THE LIMITS OF COERCIVE DIPLOMACY: LAOS - CUBA - VIETNAM. BOSTON: LITTLE, BROWN, 1971.

INCLUDES EXCELLENT ANALYTIC CASE STUDIES OF KENNEDY POLICY-MAKING VIS-A-VIS LAOS AND THE CUBAN MISSILE CRISIS AND THE KENNEDY-JOHNSON 1964-65 VIETNAM DECISION-MAKING.

995 HARTLEY, A. "JOHN KENNEDY'S FOREIGN POLICY." FOREIGN

POLICY (FALL 1971): 77-87.

996 HILSMAN, R. TO MOVE A NATION: THE POLITICS OF FOREIGN
     POLICY IN THE KENNEDY ADMINISTRATION. GARDEN CITY, N.Y.:
     DOUBLEDAY, 1967, PP. 602.

997 HOLSTI, O.R. "TIME, ALTERNATIVES, AND COMMUNICATION: THE
     1914 AND CUBAN MISSILE CRISES," IN INTERNATIONAL CRISES:
     INSIGHTS FROM BEHAVIORAL RESEARCH. ED. CHARLES F.
     HERMANN. NEW YORK: THE FREE PRESS, 1972, PP. 58-80.

998 KAHAN, J.H., AND LONG, A.K. "THE CUBAN MISSILE CRISIS: A
     STUDY OF ITS STRATEGIC CONTEXT." PSQ (DEC 1972):
     564-590.

999 "KENNEDY AND THE STRATEGY OF AID: THE CLAY REPORT AND
     AFTER." WESTERN POLITICAL Q18:656-68 S '65.

1000 KENNEDY, ROBERT F. THIRTEEN DAYS: A MEMOIR OF THE CUBAN
     MISSILE CRISIS. NEW YORK: W.W. NORTON, 1969.

     ROBERT KENNEDY'S PERSONAL ACCOUNT, WITH INTRODUCTIONS BY
     ROBERT S. MCNAMARA AND HAROLD MACMILLAN. REPRINTED IN
     1971, OMITTING INTRODUCTIONS BUT WITH AN AFTERWORD BY
     RICHARD E. NEUSTADT AND GRAHAM T. ALLISON.

1001 KRAFT, J. THE GRAND DESIGN: FROM COMMON MARKET TO
     ATLANTIC PARTNERSHIP. NEW YORK: HARPER, ROW, 1962,
     PP.122.

1002 LEPPER, M.M. FOREIGN POLICY FORMULATION: A CASE STUDY OF
     THE NUCLEAR TEST BAN TREATY OF 1963. COLUMBUS, OHIO:
     CHARLES E. MERRILL, 1971, PP.191.

1003 MEYER, K.E., AND SZULC, T., EDS. THE CUBAN INVASION: THE
     CHRONICLE OF A DISASTER. NEW YORK: PRAEGER, 1962, PP.160.

1004 NATHAN, J.A. "THE MISSILE CRISIS: HIS FINEST HOUR NOW."
     WORLD POLITICS 27 (1965):256-281.

1005 NUNNERLY, D. PRESIDENT KENNEDY AND BRITAIN. LONDON:

BODLEY HEAD, 1972, PP. 242.

1006 PACHTER, H.M. COLLISION COURSE: THE CUBAN MISSILE CRISIS AND COEXISTENCE. NEW YORK: PRAEGER, 1963, PP.261.

1007 PERLOFF, H.S. ALLIANCE FOR PROGRESS: A SOCIAL INVENTION IN THE MAKING. BALTIMORE, MD.: JOHNS HOPKINS U PR, 1969, PP. 253.

1008 SLUSSER, R.M. THE BERLIN CRISIS OF 1961: SOVIET-AMERICAN RELATIONS AND THE STRUGGLE FOR POWER IN THE KREMLIN, JUNE-NOVEMBER, 1961. BALTIMORE, JOHNS HOPKINS UNIVERSITY PRESS, 1973, PP. 509.

1009 SOBEL, L.A., ED. CUBA, THE U.S. AND RUSSIA, 1960-63. NEW YORK: FACTS ON FILE, 1964, PP. 138.

1010 ----------. DISARMAMENT AND NUCLEAR TESTS, 1960-1963: THE SEARCH FOR A WAY TO ABOLISH WAR, END THE COSTLY BURDEN OF ARMAMENT AND PREVENT THE HORRORS OF RADIOACTIVE CONTAMINATION OF THE ATMOSPHERE. NEW YORK: FACTS ON FILE, 1964, PP.120.

1011 TERCHEK, R.J. THE MAKING OF THE TEST BAN TREATY. THE HAGUE: NIJHOFF, 1970, PP.211.

1012 WALTON, R. COLD WAR AND COUNTERREVOLUTION: THE FOREIGN POLICY OF JOHN F. KENNEDY. BALTIMORE: PELICAN BOOK, 1973, PP. 250.

THIS FIRST REVISIONIST HISTORY OF THE KENNEDY YEARS. CREDITS KENNEDY WITH SEVERAL BOLD INITIATIVES IN THE FIELD OF FOREIGN POLICY BUT SEES KENNEDY'S LEGACY AS A SERIES OF MISCALCULATIONS, OVERREACTIONS, AND LOST OPPORTUNITIES. PAYS CLOSE ATTENTION TO HIS POLICIES REGARDING CUBA, BERLIN, AND VIETNAM.

1013 WEIDNER, E. PRELUDE TO REORGANIZATION: THE KENNEDY FOREIGN AID MESSAGE OF 1961. INTER-UNIVERSITY CASE PROGRAM: BOX 229, SYRACUSE, N.Y., 1969.

SEE ALSO 82, 505, 703, 734, 865, 876, 942, 946, 957, 1138, 1157, 1159, 1162, 1614, 2010, 2011, 2140

3. PRESIDENT'S ASSASSINATION AND ITS AFTERMATH

1014 ASSOCIATED PRESS. THE TORCH IS PASSED: THE ASSOCIATED PRESS STORY OF THE DEATH OF A PRESIDENT. NEW YORK, 1963, PP. 99.

1015 BISHOP, J.A. THE DAY KENNEDY WAS SHOT. NEW YORK: FUNK & WAGNALLS, 1968, PP. 713. ALSO, NEW YORK: BANTAM BOOKS, 1969, PP. 621..

1016 BUCHANAN, T. WHO KILLED KENNEDY? NEW YORK: G.P. PUTNAM'S SONS, 1964.

A JOURNALIST'S BRIEF AND SPECULATIVE CRITIQUE OF THE WARREN COMMISSION.

1017 CORRY, J. THE MANCHESTER AFFAIR. NEW YORK: PUTNAM, 1967, PP. 223.

NEW YORK TIMES REPORTER'S ACCOUNT OF THE CONTROVERSY CONNECTED WITH WILLIAM MANCHESTER'S THE DEATH OF A PRESIDENT.

1018 CUSHMAN, R.F. "WHY THE WARREN COMMISSION?" NEW YORK U LAW R 40 (MAY 1965): 477-503.

1019 EPSTEIN, E.J. INQUEST: THE WARREN COMMISSION AND THE ESTABLISHMENT OF TRUTH. NEW YORK: VIKING, 1966, PP. 224. PAPERBACK, NEW YORK: BANTAM BOOKS, 1966, PP. 193.

A CRITICISM OF THE WARREN COMMISSION'S FINDINGS.

1020 ----------. "MANCHESTER UNEXPURGATED: FROM DEATH OF LANCER TO THE DEATH OF A PRESIDENT; COMPARATIVE STUDY OF SUCCESSIVE VERSIONS OF BOOK." COMMENTARY44:25-31 JL '67.

1021 FORD, G.R., AND STILES, J.R. PORTRAIT OF THE ASSASSIN. NEW YORK: SIMON AND SCHUSTER, 1965.

PRESIDENT GERALD R. FORD WAS A MEMBER OF THE WARREN COMMISSION WHILE A CONGRESSMAN.

1022 FREESE, P.L. "THE WARREN COMMISSION AND THE FOURTH SHOT: A REFLECTION ON THE FUNDAMENTALS OF FORENSIC FACT-FINDING." NEW YORK U LAW R 40 (MAY 1965): 424-465.

1023 GARRISON, J. A HERITAGE OF STONE. NEW YORK: G.P. PUTNAM'S SONS, 1970.

NEW ORLEANS DISTRICT ATTORNEY'S ARGUMENT FOR A CONSPIRACY.

1024 GOODHART, A.L. "THE WARREN COMMISSION FROM THE PROCEDURAL STANDPOINT." NEW YORK U LAW R 40 (MAY 1965): 404-423.

1025 GREENBERG, B.S., AND PARKER, E.B., EDS. THE KENNEDY ASSASSINATION AND THE AMERICAN PUBLIC: SOCIAL COMMUNICATION IN CRISIS. STANFORD, CALIF.: STANFORD UNIV. PRESS, 1965, PP. 392.

1026 JOESTEN, J. OSWALD: ASSASSIN OR FALL GUY?. NEW YORK: MARZANI AND MUNSELL, 1964.

ASSUMES A RIGHT-WING PLOT.

1027 LANE, M. A CITIZEN'S DISSENT: MARK LANE REPLIES. NEW YORK: HOLT, RINEHART AND WINSTON, 1968.

REPLY TO CRITICISM OF RUSH TO JUDGMENT.

1028 LEWIS, R.W. THE SCAVENGERS AND CRITICS OF THE WARREN REPORT. NEW YORK: DELACORTE, 1967, PP. 188.

1029 MANCHESTER, W.R. THE DEATH OF A PRESIDENT: NOVEMBER 20-NOVEMBER 25, 1963. NEW YORK: HARPER & ROW, 1967, PP.710.

THOROUGH ACCOUNT OF THE 4 DAYS CONNECTED WITH KENNEDY'S DEATH. BRINGS INTO THE OPEN THE CONFLICTS BETWEEN THE KENNEDY AND THE JOHNSON GROUPS. ON THE CONTROVERSY CONNECTED WITH ITS PUBLICATION, SEE JOHN CORRY'S THE MANCHESTER AFFAIR.

1030 MEAGHER, S. ACCESSORIES AFTER THE FACT: THE WARREN COMMISSION, THE AUTHORITIES, AND THE REPORT. INDIANAPOLIS: BOBBS-MERRILL,1967.

SCHOLARLY TREATMENT OF THE REPORT AND THE EVIDENCE. CALLS FOR A NEW INVESTIGATION.

1031 ----------. SUBJECT INDEX TO THE WARREN REPORT AND HEARINGS AND EXHIBITS. NEW YORK: SCARECROW, 1966, PP. 150.

1032 PHELAN, J.R. "THE ASSASSINATION THAT WILL NOT DIE. CRITICS OF THE WARREN REPORT HAVE PRODUCED NO HARD NEW EVIDENCE, BUT THEIR IRRESPONSIBLE POLEMICS AND ABSURD THEORIES HAVE LEFT THE PUBLIC MORE DUBIOUS THAN EVER." N Y TIMES MAG (NOV. 23, 1975): 25+.

1033 SAUVAGE, L. THE OSWALD AFFAIR: AN EXAMINATION OF THE CONTRADICTIONS AND OMISSIONS OF THE WARREN REPORT. CLEVELAND: WORLD PUBLISHING CO., 1966.

1034 SCOTT, P.D., ET AL., EDS. THE ASSASSINATIONS: DALLAS AND BEYOND. NEW YORK: RANDOM, 1976, PP. 732.

1035 SHEATSLEY, P.B., AND FELDMAN, J.J. "THE ASSASSINATION OF PRESIDENT KENNEDY. A PRELIMINARY REPORT ON PUBLIC REACTIONS AND BEHAVIOR." POQ 28 NO. 2 (1964): 189-215.

1036 SPARROW, J. AFTER THE ASSASSINATION: A POSITIVE APPRAISAL OF THE WARREN REPORT. NEW YORK: CHILMARK, 1967.

1037 "SYMPOSIUM ON THE WARREN COMMISSION REPORT." NEW YORK LAW R (MAY 1965): PP. 404-524.

1038 THE OFFICIAL WARREN COMMISSION REPORT ON THE DEATH OF PRESIDENT JOHN F. KENNEDY. GARDEN CITY: DOUBLEDAY, 1964, PP. 888.

1039 THOMPSON, W.C. A BIBLIOGRAPHY OF LITERATURE RELATING TO THE ASSASSINATION OF PRESIDENT JOHN F. KENNEDY. SAN ANTONIO: COPY DISTRIBUTING CO., 1968, PP. 28.

1040 U.S. PRESIDENT'S COMM. ON THE ASSASSINATION OF PRES. KENNEDY. REPORT OF THE WARREN COMMISSION ON THE ASSASSINATION OF PRESIDENT KENNEDY. NEW YORK: MCGRAW, 1964, PP. 726.

1041 VANBEMMELEN, J.M. "DID LEE HARVEY OSWALD ACT WITHOUT HELP?" NEW YORK U LAW R 40 (MAY 1965): 466-476.

1042 WHITE, S. SHOULD WE NOW BELIEVE THE WARREN REPORT? NEW YORK: MACMILLAN, 1968.

CONTAINS PREFACE BY WALTER CRONKITE AND TEXT OF CBS DOCUMENTARY.

1043 WOLFENSTEIN, M., AND KLIMAN, G., EDS. CHILDREN AND THE

DEATH OF A PRESIDENT: MULTI-DISCIPLINARY STUDIES. NEW YORK: DOUBLEDAY, 1965, PP. 256.

1044 WRONE, D. "THE ASSASSINATION OF JOHN FITZGERALD KENNEDY: AN ANNOTATED BIBLIOGRAPHY." WISCONSON MAG OF HISTORY (AUTUMN 1972): 21-36.

SEE ALSO 81, 1100, 1843

4. OTHER

1045 JACOBSON, H.K., AND STEIN, E. DIPLOMATS, SCIENTISTS AND POLITICIANS: THE U.S. AND THE NUCLEAR TEST BAN NEGOTIATIONS. ANN ARBOR: UNIVERSITY OF MICHIGAN PRESS, 1966, PP. 538.

1046 LOGSDON, J.M. THE DECISION TO GO TO THE MOON. CAMBRIDGE, MASS.: MIT PR, 1970, PP. 187.

1047 PREEG, W.H. TRADERS AND DIPLOMATS: AN ANALYSIS OF THE KENNEDY ROUND OF NEGOTIATIONS UNDER THE GENERAL AGREEMENT ON TARIFFS AND TRADE. WASHINGTON, D.C.: BROOKINGS INSTITUTION, 1970.

1048 RIPLEY, R.B. "KENNEDY AND CONGRESS." UNIVERSITY PROGRAMS MODULAR STUDIES MORRISTOWN, N.J.: GENERAL LEARNING PRESS, 1972, PP. 25.

SEE ALSO 768, 870, 1732, 1917, 2476, 2498

G. ADDITIONAL ASPECTS AND THEMES

1049 BINGHAM, W., AND JUST, W. "THE PRESIDENT AND THE PRESS." REPORTER (APR. 12, 1962): 18-23.

SYMPATHETIC ACCOUNT OF KENNEDY'S INFORMAL STYLE OF DEALING WITH THE PRESS.

1050 BISHOP, J.A. A DAY IN THE LIFE OF PRESIDENT KENNEDY. NEW YORK: RANDOM HOUSE, 1964, PP. 108.

DESCRIBES JFK'S DAILY ROUTINE AND WORK HABITS.

1051 BRADLEE, B. CONVERSATIONS WITH KENNEDY. NEW YORK: W.W. NORTON, 1975, PP. 251.

BASED ON NOTES DICTATED NORMALLY WITHIN 24 HOURS OF THE

CUNVERSATION, BY A JOURNALIST FRIEND OF KENNEDY'S.
CONTAINS LITTLE NEW HISTORICAL DATA BUT DISPLAYS JFK'S WIT
AND PERSONAL MAGNETISM.

1052 BURNS, J.M. "THE LEGACY OF THE 1,000 DAYS." <u>N Y TIMES</u>
<u>MAG</u> 1 DEC. 1963.

1053 DECTER, M. "KENNEDYISM." <u>COMMENTARY</u> 49 (JUNE 1970):
19-27.

A CRITICAL ACCOUNT OF THE KENNEDY CULT AND WHAT IT
REPRESENTED TO ITS VOTARIES.

1054 FAIRLIE, H. <u>THE KENNEDY PROMISE: THE POLITICS OF
EXPECTATION</u>. GARDEN CITY, N.Y.: DOUBLEDAY & CO., 1973,
PP. 376.

BRITISH JOURNALIST FINDS FAULT IN KENNEDY FOR RAISING
PUBLIC EXPECTATIONS ABOUT GOVERNMENTAL PERFORMANCE TO A
HIGHER LEVEL THAN WAS REALISTIC, THUS SPAWNING CYNICISM,
DISILLUSIONMENT, AND UNCONSTRUCTIVE POLITICAL PROTEST.

1055 ------------. "HE WAS A MAN OF ONLY ONE SEASON." <u>N Y TIMES</u>
<u>MAG</u> NOV. 1965.

1056 FAY, P.B. <u>THE PLEASURE OF HIS COMPANY</u>. NEW YORK: HARPER
AND ROW, 1966, PP. 262.

THE REMINISCES OF JFK'S FORMER PT SHIPMATE, PROVIDING A
RARE GLIMPSE INTO THE PRIVATE SIDE OF KENNEDY'S
PRESIDENCY.

1057 FITZSIMONS, L. <u>THE KENNEDY DOCTRINE</u>. NEW YORK: RANDOM
HOUSE, 1972, PP.275.

1058 FUCHS, L.H. <u>JOHN F. KENNEDY AND AMERICAN CATHOLICISM</u>.
NEW YORK: MEREDITH, 1967, PP. 271.

1059 KATEB, G. "KENNEDY AS STATESMAN." <u>COMMENTARY</u> 41 (JUNE
1966): 54-60.

1060 KAZIN, A. "THE PRESIDENT AND OTHER INTELLECTUALS." <u>AMER
SCHOLAR</u> 30 (1961):498-516.

ATTRIBUTES KENNEDY'S PUBLIC REPUTATION AS AN INTELLECTUAL
TO A POLITICAL STRATEGY DESIGNED TO REDUCE THE PUBLIC
ACCOUNTABILITY OF POLICY MAKERS AND SPECULATES ON THE
REASONS INTELLECTUALS GRAVITATED TO KENNEDY.

1061 KENNEDY, ROSE FITZGERALD. <u>TIMES TO REMEMBER</u>. GARDEN CITY,

N.Y.: DOUBLEDAY, 1974, PP. 536.

THE PERSONAL REMINISCENCES OF THE FAMILIAL TRIUMPHS AND TRAGEDIES BY THE KENNEDY MATRIARCH. CAPTURES THE POLITICAL SETTING OF HONEY FITZ'S BOSTON AND THE PATTERN OF KENNEDY CAMPAIGNS.

1062 KILPATRICK, C. "THE KENNEDY STYLE AND CONGRESS." VIRGINIA Q R 39 (1963):1-11.

1063 KOENIG, L.W. "HARD LIMITS OF GOVERNMENT BY CONSENSUS." N Y TIMES MAG (MAY 7, 1965): 7+.

1064 LESSARD, S. "A NEW LOOK AT JOHN KENNEDY." WASHINGTON MONTHLY (OCTOBER 1971): PP. 8-18.

ARGUES THAT KENNEDY'S PENCHANT FOR THE PRACTICAL FORECLOSED DISCUSSION OF INNOVATIVE ALTERNATIVES IN FOREIGN POLICY.

1065 LEUCHTENBURG, W.E. "PRESIDENT KENNEDY AND THE END OF THE POSTWAR WORLD." AMER R (WINTER 1963): 18-29.

1066 LINCOLN, A.H. THE KENNEDY WHITE HOUSE PARTIES. NEW YORK: VIKING PRESS, 1967, PP. 181.

1067 MAILER, N. THE PRESIDENTIAL PAPERS. NEW YORK: PUTNAM, 1963, PP. 310.

1068 MEYERS, J. JOHN FITZGERALD KENNEDY... AS WE REMEMBER HIM. NEW YORK: MACMILLAN CO., 1965.

THE RECOLLECTIONS OF A NUMBER OF KENNEDY'S ASSOCIATES JUXTAPOSED WITH PHOTOGRAPHS OF JFK AT VARIOUS STAGES IN HIS CAREER.

1069 MIROFF, B. PRAGMATIC ILLUSIONS: THE PRESIDENTIAL POLITICS OF JOHN F. KENNEDY. NEW YORK: DAVID MCKAY, 1976, PP. 234.

A CRITICAL SURVEY OF KENNEDY'S PRESIDENCY WRITTEN FROM LEFT-WING PERSPECTIVE, BUT MAKING LITTLE USE OF THE ARCHIVAL MATERIAL NOW AVAILABLE.

1070 MUNGAR, T.M. "PERSONALITY AND DECISION-MAKING: JOHN F. KENNEDY IN FOUR CRISIS DECISIONS." CAN J POL SCI 2 (JULY 1969): 200-225.

ARGUING THAT DECISION PROCESSES ARE SIGNIFICANTLY INFLUENCED BY THE PERSONALITY DYNAMICS OF CHIEF

EXECUTIVES. MONGAR CITES THE CUBAN MISSILE, STEEL, MEREDITH, AND BAY OF PIGS EPISODES AS INCIDENTS IN WHICH JFK REACTED IN DIFFERENT WAYS TO EVENTS THAT "RESONATED" IN DIFFERENT FASHIONS WITH HIS PERSONALITY.

1071 NEUSTADT, R.E. "KENNEDY IN THE PRESIDENCY: A PREMATURE APPRAISAL." PSQ 79 (1964):321-334.

AN EARLY ASSESSMENT OF PRESIDENT KENNEDY DRAWING UPON THE CRITERIA DEVELOPED BY THE AUTHOR IN PRESIDENTIAL POWER. A CONDENSED VERSION OF THIS ARTICLE APPEARS IN VARIOUS EDITIONS OF THAT BOOK.

1072 O'DONNELL, K., AND POWERS, D. JOHNNY, WE HARDLY KNEW YE. BOSTON: LITTLE, BROWN, 1972.

AN INTIMATE PORTRAIT OF JFK BY TWO LONG-TIME ASSOCIATES. CAPTURES THE SO CALLED "IRISH MAFIA" SIDE OF JFK'S WHITE HOUSE AS WELL AS KENNEDY'S PRIVATE VIEW OF HIS JOB AND HIS ASSOCIATES.

1073 POLLARD, J.E. "THE KENNEDY ADMINISTRATION AND THE PRESS." JOURNALISM Q (WINTER 1964): PP. 3-14.

1074 POLSBY, N.W. "JFK THROUGH RUSSIAN EYES." PSQ 90 (SPRING 1975): 117-126.

REVIEW OF THROUGH RUSSIAN EYES (1973) BY ANATOLI A. GROMYKO OF THE SOVIET ACADEMY OF SCIENCES' USA INSTITUTE. CRITICIZES THE BOOK AS "LITTLE MORE THAN UNFRIENDLY PROPAGANDA," NOT MEETING STANDARDS OF SERIOUS POLITICAL INQUIRY.

1075 RIEMER, N. "KENNEDY'S GRAND DEMOCRATIC DESIGN." R OF POLITICS 27 (1965):3-16.

1076 STOUGHTON, C., CLIFTON, C.V., AND SIDEY, H. THE MEMORIES-1961-JFK-1963. NEW YORK: NORTON, 1973, PP. 200.

1077 WICKER, T. "KENNEDY AS PUBLIC SPEAKAH." N Y TIMES MAG 28 FEB. 1962.

SEE ALSO 286, 289, 290, 292, 297, 301, 1044, 1195, 1494, 1812, 1859, 1866, 1869, 2502

11
LYNDON B. JOHNSON AND HIS ADMINISTRATION

A. GENERAL HISTORICAL ACCOUNTS AND BIOGRAPHIES

1078 BELL, J. THE JOHNSON TREATMENT: HOW LYNDON B. JOHNSON TOOK OVER THE PRESIDENCY AND MADE IT HIS OWN. NEW YORK: HARPER AND ROW, 1965, PP. 305.

STARTS WITH KENNEDY'S DEATH AND ENDS WITH JOHNSON'S ELECTION AND SPECULATIONS ON WHAT HIS EXPERIENCE IN OFFICE WOULD BE.

1079 EVANS, R., AND NOVAK, R. LYNDON B. JOHNSON: THE EXERCISE OF POWER: A POLITICAL BIOGRAPHY. NEW YORK: NEW AMERICAN LIBRARY, 1966, PP. 597.

A BIOGRAPHY BY TWO WASHINGTON JOURNALISTS COVERING THE PERIOD BETWEEN LBJ'S DAYS AS A CONGRESSMAN TO THE MIDPOINT OF HIS PRESIDENCY. PARTICULARLY VALUABLE ON JOHNSON'S STYLE AS SENATE MAJORITY LEADER, INCLUDING HIS HIGHLY PERSONAL MODE OF EXERCISING INFLUENCE.

1080 GOLDMAN, E.F. THE TRAGEDY OF LYNDON JOHNSON. NEW YORK: KNOPF, 1969, PP. 531.

A MEMOIR OF THE EARLY JOHNSON YEARS BY A PRINCETON HISTORIAN WHO SERVED ON THE WHITE HOUSE STAFF. ESPECIALLY INSTRUCTIVE ON JOHNSON'S RELATIONS WITH THE INTELLECTUAL COMMUNITY.

1081 JOHNSON, H.B., AND HARWOOD, R. LYNDON. NEW YORK: PRAEGER, 1973, PP. 187.

A VIVIDLY WRITTEN PROFILE OF JOHNSON THE MAN BY TWO WELL KNOWN WASHINGTON JOURNALISTS.

1082 JOHNSON, S.H. MY BROTHER LYNDON. CHICAGO, ILL.: COWLES, 1970, PP. 278.

MEMOIRS BY JOHNSON'S BROTHER CONTAINING PERSONAL ANECDOTES ABOUT THEIR EARLY YEARS, INFORMAL ACCOUNTS OF CONFLICTS AMONG WHITE HOUSE AIDES, AND A "WART-AND-ALL" CHARACTERIZATION OF LBJ'S PERSONAL QUALITIES.

1083 KEARNS, D. LYNDON JOHNSON AND THE AMERICAN DREAM. NEW YORK: HAR-ROW, 1976, PP. 432.

A LIFE-HISTORY AND PSYCHOBIOGRAPHY OF PRESIDENT JOHNSON, KEARNS' WORK WAS HIGHLY PUBLICIZED BECAUSE JOHNSON HAD TAKEN HER ON AS A CONFIDANT AND RECOUNTED TO HER A NUMBER

OF CHILDHOOD MEMORIES, FANTASIES, AND EVEN RECURRENT NIGHTMARES THAT INTERRUPTED HIS SLEEP DURING TENSE PERIODS DURING THE VIETNAMESE WAR. A DIFFICULT IF NOT IMPOSSIBLE WORK TO VALIDATE AND HENCE EVALUATE, BUT INEVITABLY ONE THAT WILL BE READ BY STUDENTS OF JOHNSON'S ENIGMATIC PERSONALITY.

1084 "LYNDON JOHNSON: 1908-1973." TIME (FEB. 5, 1973): 29-33.

CONSIDERS SOME OF JOHNSON'S ACCOMPLISHMENTS AS PRESIDENT AND HIS HEALTH PRIOR TO DEATH.

1085 SHERRILL, R. THE ACCIDENTAL PRESIDENT. NEW YORK: GROSSMAN PUBLISHERS, 1967, PP. 282.

AN INVESTIGATIVE REPORTER'S HIGHLY CRITICAL PORTRAIT OF LBJ.

1086 SIDEY, H. A VERY PERSONAL PRESIDENCY: LYNDON JOHNSON IN THE WHITE HOUSE. NEW YORK: ATHENEUM, 1968, PP. 305.

ANECDOTAL, PERSONALLY INFORMED PASTICHE OF VIGNETTES ON JOHNSON'S STYLE AND ON THE COURSE OF THE PRESIDENCY BY A WELL KNOWN TIME MAGAZINE JOURNALIST WHO SPECIALIZES IN COVERAGE OF THE PRESIDENCY.

1087 STEINBERG, A. SAM JOHNSON'S BOY: A CLOSE-UP OF THE PRESIDENT FROM TEXAS. NEW YORK: MACMILLAN, 1968, PP. 871.

BASED ON EXTENSIVE RESEARCH, A LIFE-HISTORY FROM JOHNSON'S CHILDHOOD TO HIS ANNOUNCEMENT THAT HE WOULD NOT RUN AGAIN. LBJ "HAD GROWN UP POOR AND SPENT HIS LIFETIME FIGHTING FOR PERSONAL WEALTH AND POWER. ... (HE) HAD LEARNED HOW TO SEIZE AUTHORITY ... (BUT) WAS UNABLE TO GROW IN OFFICE ... TO INSPIRE OTHERS AND GAIN THE AFFECTION AND TRUST OF THE PEOPLE."

SEE ALSO 260, 283, 300, 629, 902, 913, 1107, 1116, 1564, 1568

B. PRESIDENT'S PAPERS, MEMOIRS

1088 JOHNSON, L.B. A TIME FOR ACTION: A SELECTION FROM THE SPEECHES AND WRITINGS OF LYNDON B. JOHNSON, 1953-64. NEW YORK: ATHENEUM, 1964, PP. 183.

1089 ----------. MY HOPE FOR AMERICA. NEW YORK: RANDOM HOUSE, 1964.

1090 ----------. THE CHOICES WE FACE. NEW YORK: BANTAM, 1969, PP. 151.

1091 ----------. THE VANTAGE POINT: PERSPECTIVES OF THE

PRESIDENCY, 1963-1969. NEW YORK: HOLT, 1971, PP. 636.

LBJ'S ACCOUNT OF HIS PRESIDENCY.

SEE ALSO 54, 2033

C. COMPENDIA AND BIBLIOGRAPHIES

1092 BURNS, J.M., ED. TO HEAL AND TO BUILD: THE PROGRAMS OF
PRESIDENT LYNDON B. JOHNSON. NEW YORK: MCGRAW-HILL, 1968,
PP. 506.

A COLLECTION OF JOHNSON'S POLICY-STATEMENTS INTRODUCED BY
BRIEF ESSAYS WRITTEN BY SUCH PUBLIC FIGURES AS CHESTER
BOWLES, DAVID LILIENTHAL, EUGENE ROSTOW, WALTER HELLER,
RALPH ELLISON, STEWART UDALL, MCGEORGE BUNDY, ERIC HOFFER,
AND JAMES MACGREGOR BURNS.

1093 FURER, H.B. LYNDON B. JOHNSON, 1908-_____: CHRONOLOGY,
DOCUMENTS, BIBLIOGRAPHICAL AIDS. DOBBS FERRY, N.Y.:
OCEANA, 1971, PP. 160.

1094 GETTLEMAN, M.E., AND MERMELSTEIN, D., EDS. THE GREAT
SOCIETY READER: THE FAILURE OF AMERICAN LIBERALISM. NEW
YORK: RANDOM, 1967, PP. 551.

1095 GINSBERG, E., AND SOLOW, R.M., EDS. THE GREAT SOCIETY:
LESSONS FOR THE FUTURE. NEW YORK: BASIC BOOKS, 1974, PP.
226.

1096 GROSS, B.M., ED. A GREAT SOCIETY? NEW YORK: BASIC BOOKS,
1968, PP. 362.

1097 LICHTENSTEIN, N., ED. THE JOHNSON YEARS. NEW YORK: FACTS
ON FILE, 1976.

SEE ALSO 1153

D. SELECTED MATERIAL ON PRE-PRESIDENTIAL BACKGROUND

1098 BAKER, L. THE JOHNSON ECLIPSE; A PRESIDENT'S VICE
PRESIDENCY. NEW YORK: MACMILLAN, 1966, PP. 280.

1099 HUITT, R.K. "DEMOCRATIC PARTY LEADERSHIP IN THE SENATE."
APSR 40 (1961):333-344.

A STUDY OF JOHNSON'S PROCEDURES AS SENATE MAJORITY LEADER

BY A POLITICAL SCIENTIST WHO HAD SERVED ON JOHNSON'S STAFF.

1100 WHITE, T.H. THE MAKING OF THE PRESIDENT 1964. NEW YORK: ATHENEUM, 1965, PP. 431.

SHEDS LIGHT ON JOHNSON THE MAN AS WELL AS ON THE 1964 ELECTION.

1101 WHITE, W.S. THE PROFESSIONAL: LYNDON B. JOHNSON. BOSTON: HOUGHTON MIFFLIN, 1964, PP. 273.

A PORTRAYAL OF JOHNSON AS A POLITICAL OPERATOR BY A JOURNALIST SYMPATHETIC TO AND LONG-ASSOCIATED WITH LBJ.

SEE ALSO 939, 1079, 2447

E. ADVISERS AND ADVISORY RELATIONS

1102 "A LOOK AT THE INNER WORKINGS OF THE WHITE HOUSE: INTERVIEW WITH BILL D. MOYERS, TOP AIDE TO THE PRESIDENT." U S NEWS 60 (JUNE 13, 1966): 78-85.

1103 BAGDIKIAN, B.H. "INNER INNER CIRCLE AROUND JOHNSON." N Y TIMES MAG (FEBRUARY 28, 1965): 21+.

1104 FALLOWS, J. "BILL MOYERS: HIS HEART BELONGS TO DADDY." WASHINGTON MONTHLY JULY 1974 PP. 37-50.

ON THE FORMER LBJ AIDE, NEWSPAPER PUBLISHER, AND TELEVISION JOURNALIST. FOLLOWS MOYERS' EXAMPLE OF THE CONSEQUENCES OF TALENTED PEOPLE WHO ATTAIN POSITION THROUGH PATRONS--RATHER THAN ON THEIR OWN.

1105 GOULDING, P.G. CONFIRM OR DENY: INFORMING THE PEOPLE ON NATIONAL SECURITY. NEW YORK: HARPER AND ROW, 1970, PP. 369.

MEMOIR BY AN ASSISTANT SECRETARY OF DEFENSE UNDER MCNAMARA AND CLIFFORD, DISCUSSING THE BACKGROUND OF CERTAIN KEY EVENTS IN THE DECISIONS ON VIETNAM. FOCUSES EXTENSIVELY ON POLICIES OF RELEASING OR SUPPRESSING NEWS.

1106 GRAFF, H.F. THE TUESDAY CABINET: DELIBERATION AND DECISION ON PEACE AND WAR UNDER LYNDON B. JOHNSON. ENGLEWOOD CLIFFS, N.J.: PRENCTICE-HALL, 1970, PP. 200.

A UNIQUELY RICH ANALYSIS OF DECISION-MAKING PROCEDURES BY A HISTORIAN WHO WAS ABLE TO INTERVIEW REPEATEDLY THE PARTICIPANTS IN THE INTIMATE DECISION-MAKING GROUP LBJ USED TO PLAN AND CONDUCT THE CONFLICT IN VIETNAM.

1107 MCPHERSON, H. A POLITICAL EDUCATION. BOSTON: LITTLE, BROWN, AND CO., 1972, PP. 467.

A REFLECTIVE MEMOIR BY A TEXAS LIBERAL WHO SPENT THIRTEEN

YEARS CLOSELY ASSOCIATED WITH LBJ, FIRST AS A MEMBER OF THE SENATE MAJORITY LEADER'S STAFF AND LATER AS SPECIAL COUNSEL TO THE PRESIDENT. THE MOST DEEPLY INTELLECTUAL OF JOHNSON'S LONG-TERM AIDES, MCPHERSON TERMINATED HIS GRADUATE STUDIES TO BECOME A CIVIL LIBERTIES LAWYER. HE DESCRIBES HIS EXPERIENCES, REFLECTS ON THE PRESIDENCY IN GENERAL AND JOHNSON'S IN PARTICULAR AND REACHES AMBIVALENT CONCLUSIONS ABOUT THE CONFLICT BETWEEN PERSONAL IDEALS AND POLITICAL EFFECTIVENESS.

1108 O'BRIEN, L. "LARRY O'BRIEN DISCUSSES WHITE HOUSE CONTACTS WITH CAPITOL HILL." CONGRESSIONAL Q 23 (1965): 1434-1436.

1109 PLISCHKE, E. "THE PRESIDENT'S INNER FOREIGN POLICY TEAM." R OF POLITICS 30 (1968):292-307.

1110 REINERT, A. "WHY JACK VALENTI STILL SLEEPS SOUNDLY." TEXAS MONTHLY 2 (JULY 1974): 68-73.

ARTICLE ON THE FORMER AIDE TO PRESIDENT JOHNSON WHO THEN BECAME PRESIDENT OF THE MOTION PICTURE ASSOCIATION OF AMERICA.

1111 ROBERTS, C. LBJ'S INNER CIRCLE. NEW YORK: DELACORTE PRESS, 1965, PP. 223.

1112 ROCHE, J.P. SENTENCED TO LIFE. NEW YORK: MACMILLAN, 1974, PP. 359.

ESSAYS BY ACADEMIC DESCRIBING HIMSELF AS "AN UNRECONSTRUCTED COLD WARRIOR" WHO WORKED AS AN LBJ AIDE.

1113 ----------. "JIGSAW PUZZLE OF HISTORY." N Y TIMES MAG (JANUARY 24, 1971): 14-15+.

A SPECIAL CONSULTANT TO PRESIDENT JOHNSON COMMENTS ON THE DIFFICULTY OF WRITING "INSTANT HISTORIES" OF A PRESIDENTIAL ERA, PARTICULARLY FOCUSING ON VIETNAM POLICY DURING THE KENNEDY-JOHNSON ERA. REPRINTED WITH ESSAYS IN ROCHE'S SENTENCED TO LIFE.

1114 RUSTOW, W.W. THE DIFFUSION OF POWER: AN ESSAY IN RECENT HISTORY. NEW YORK: MACMILLAN, 1972.

1115 SIDEY, H. "THE WHITE HOUSE STAFF VS. THE CABINET," WASHINGTON MONTHLY FEB. 1969, PP. 2-9+.

1116 VALENTI, J. A VERY HUMAN PRESIDENT. NEW YORK: NORTON,

1975. PP. 402.

A LONG-TIME LBJ AIDE'S ANECDOTES ON JOHNSON'S PERSONAL STYLE AND THE GENERAL AMBIENCE OF THE WEST WING DURING HIS PRESIDENCY. VALENTI WAS PARTICULARLY CONSPICUOUS AS A VOCAL IDEALIZER OF LBJ'S LEADERSHIP QUALITIES.

1117 WATSON, W.M. "THE WHITE HOUSE AT WORK: A MYSTERY EXPLAINED," U S NEWS 60 (FEBRUARY 7, 1966): 36-37.

1118 WICKER, T. "BILL MOYERS: JOHNSON'S GOOD ANGEL." READER'S DIGEST 88 (JANUARY 1966): 72-77.

1119 ----------. "JOHNSON'S MEN: VALUABLE HUNKS OF HUMANITY." N Y TIMES MAG 11 (MAY 3, 1964): 11+.

1120 "43 TOP AIDES HAVE SERVED PRESIDENT JOHNSON SINCE 1963." CONG Q W REPORT 26 (OCTOBER 18, 1968): 2879-2881.

    SEE ALSO 193, 233, 234, 847, 943, 944, 946, 950, 953, 959, 1147, 1164, 1783, 1788, 1792, 1793, 1797, 2004, 2013, 2016, 2432

F. SPECIFIC EVENTS, ACTIVITIES AND POLICIES

1. DOMESTIC

1121 BAILEY, S.K. "CO-ORDINATING THE GREAT SOCIETY." REPORTER 34 (MAY 24, 1966): 39-41.

1122 HARVEY, J.C. BLACK CIVIL RIGHTS DURING THE JOHNSON ADMINISTRATION. JACKSON, MISS.: U PR OF MISS., 1973. PP. 245.

1123 LANDER, B.G. "GROUP THEORY AND INDIVIDUALS: THE ORIGIN OF POVERTY AS A POLITICAL ISSUE." WESTERN POLITICAL Q 24 (SEPT 1971): 514-526.

1124 LANDER, L., ED. WAR ON POVERTY. NEW YORK: FACTS ON FILE, 1967, PP. 167.

1125 LEKACHMAN, R. "DEATH OF A SLOGAN--THE GREAT SOCIETY, 1967." COMMENTARY (JAN. 1967): 56-61.

1126 LEUCHTENBURG, W.E. "THE GENESIS OF THE GREAT SOCIETY." REPORTER (APR. 21, 1966): 36-39.

1127 LEVITAN, S.A., AND TAGGART, R. THE PROMISE OF GREATNESS: THE SOCIAL PROGRAMS OF THE LAST DECADE AND THEIR MAJOR ACHIEVEMENTS. CAMBRIDGE: HARVARD U PR., 1976, PP. 316.

A DEFENSE OF THE GREAT SOCIETY AND ITS PROGRAMS.

1128 MERANTO, P. THE POLITICS OF FEDERAL AID TO EDUCATION IN 1965. SYRACUSE, NEW YORK: SYRACUSE U PR, 1967, PP. 144.

1129 MOYNIHAN, D.P. MAXIMUM FEASIBLE MISUNDERSTANDING: COMMUNITY ACTION IN THE WAR ON POVERTY. NEW YORK: FREE PRESS, 1969, PP.218.

1130 PRESSMAN, J.L., AND WILDAVSKY, A. IMPLEMENTATION: HOW GREAT EXPECTATIONS IN WASHINGTON ARE DASHED IN OAKLAND; OR, WHY IT'S AMAZING THAT FEDERAL PROGRAMS WORK AT ALL, THIS BEING A SAGA OF THE ECONOMIC DEVELOPMENT ADMINISTRATION. BERKELEY, CALIF.: U OF CALIF PR, 1973, PP. 182.

EXAMINES THE EDA PROGRAM IN OAKLAND, STRESSING FAILURES IN IMPLEMENTATION RESULTING FROM A MULTIPLICITY OF DECISION POINTS.

1131 RAINWATER, L., AND YANCEY, W.L. THE MOYNIHAN REPORT AND THE POLITICS OF CONTROVERSY: A TRANS-ACTION SOCIAL SCIENCE AND PUBLIC POLICY REPORT. CAMBRIDGE, MASS.: MIT PRESS, 1967, PP.493.

1132 ROUCEK, J.S. "THE POLITICS OF PRESIDENT JOHNSON'S 'WAR ON POVERTY'." POLITICO 31 (1966):293-320.

1133 THOMAS, N.C. "POLICY FORMULATION FOR EDUCATION: THE JOHNSON ADMINISTRATION." IN THE PRESIDENCY IN CONTEMPORARY CONTEXT. EDITED BY N.C. THOMAS, NEW YORK: DODD, 1975: 318-330.

REVIEW OF JOHNSON'S USE OF TASK FORCES TO MAKE EDUCATIONAL POLICY.

1134 WAYS, M. "CREATIVE FEDERALISM AND THE GREAT SOCIETY." FORTUNE (JAN. 1966): 121+.

SEE ALSO 433, 862, 864, 962, 1029, 1092, 1180, 1773, 1917, 2004, 2013, 2016, 2498

2. FOREIGN AND NATIONAL SECURITY

1135 AUSTIN, A. THE PRESIDENT'S WAR: THE STORY OF THE TONKIN GULF RESOLUTION AND HOW THE NATION WAS TRAPPED IN VIETNAM. NEW YORK: J.P. LIPPINCOTT, 1971, PP. 368.

1136 BALL, G.W. "TOP SECRET: THE PROPHECY THE PRESIDENT REJECTED." ATLANTIC (JULY 1972): 35-49.

1137 CLIFFORD, C.M. "A VIETNAM REAPPRAISAL." FOREIGN AFFAIRS 47 (JULY 1969): 601-622.

1138 COOPER, C. THE LOST CRUSADE: AMERICA IN VIETNAM. NEW YORK: DODD, MEAD, 1970, PP.559.

1139 ELLSBERG, D. "THE QUAGMIRE MYTH AND THE STALEMATE MACHINE." PUBLIC POLICY 19 (1971):PP. 217-274.

ADVOCATES THAT U.S. POLICY-MAKERS WERE NOT INADVERTENTLY TRAPPED IN THE "MIND" OF VIETNAM, BUT CONSISTENTLY CHOSE TO ESCALATE OUT OF IDEOLOGICAL COMMITMENTS AND FEAR OF SHORT-RUN DOMESTIC REPERCUSSIONS OF DEFEAT."

1140 EPSTEIN, E.J. "THE PENTAGON PAPERS: REVISING HISTORY." IN BETWEEN FACT AND FICTION: THE PROBLEM OF JOURNALISM BY E.J. EPSTEIN, NEW YORK: RANDOM, 1975: 78-100.

MOST OF WHAT THE PAPERS CONTAIN WAS REPORTED AT THE TIME IN THE NEW YORK TIMES AND OTHER NEWSPAPERS.

1141 FAULKNER, S. "WAR IN VIETNAM: IS IT CONSTITUTIONAL?" GEORGETOWN LAW J 56 (1968):1132-1143.

1142 GALLOWAY, J. THE GULF OF TONKIN RESOLUTION. RUTHERFORD, N.J.: FAIRLEIGH DICKINSON UNIV. PRESS, 1970, PP. 578.

CLOSE CASE-HISTORY OF THE EVENTS IN THE GULF OF TONKIN IN AUGUST 1964, INCLUDING 15 APPENDED DOCUMENTS. QUESTIONS ADMINISTRATION'S ACCOUNT OF THE EPISODE, THE NEED FOR A CONGRESSIONAL RESOLUTION, AND THE GENERAL ASSUMPTIONS OF THE DAY ABOUT THE NATURE OF PRESIDENTIAL WAR-POWERS.

1143 GELB, L. "THE PENTAGON PAPERS AND THE VANTAGE POINT." FOREIGN POLICY NO. 6 (SPRING 1972): 25-41.

DIRECTOR OF PENTAGON PAPERS STUDY DISCUSSES THE PUBLISHED PENTAGON PAPERS AND LBJ'S BOOK, THE VANTAGE POINT.

1144 GEYELIN, P.L. LYNDON B. JOHNSON AND THE WORLD. NEW YORK: F.A. PRAEGER, 1966, PP. 309.

LEADING WASHINGTON JOURNALIST'S ANALYSIS OF THE JOHNSON APPROACH, AS IT APPLIED TO THE PROPOSED MULTILATERAL NUCLEAR FORCE, THE DOMINICAN INTERVENTION, AND THE EARLY STAGES OF MILITARY BUILDUP IN VIETNAM. STRESSES CONTRAST BETWEEN KENNEDY AND JOHNSON AND EXPRESSES CONCERN LEST JOHNSON'S DOMESTIC ACHIEVEMENTS BE ERASED BY HIS UNREALISTIC AND IMPRACTICAL ATTEMPTS TO IMPOSE HIS OWN, OFTEN ILL-DEFINED POLICIES ON AN INTRACTABLE INTERNATIONAL POLITICAL ARENA.

1145 GOULDEN, J. TRUTH IS THE FIRST CASUALTY. CHICAGO: RAND MCNALLY, 1969, PP. 285.

1146 GRAFF, H.F. "DECISION IN VIET NAM: HOW JOHNSON MAKES FOREIGN POLICY." N Y TIMES MAG (JULY 4, 1965): 4-7+.

1147 HOOPES, T. THE LIMITS OF INTERVENTION: AN INSIDE ACCOUNT OF HOW THE JOHNSON POLICY OF INTERVENTION WAS REVERSED. NEW YORK: DAVID MCKAY CO., 1969, PP. 245. REVISED EDITION, 1973, U.MD., PP. 264.

MEMOIR BY ONE WHO FROM 1965 TO 1967 WAS DEPUTY ASSISTANT SECRETARY OF DEFENSE FOR INTERNATIONAL SECURITY AFFAIRS AND FROM THEN UNTIL THE END OF THE JOHNSON ADMINISTRATION WAS UNDERSECRETARY OF THE AIR FORCE. A CASE-STUDY STRESSING DEFENSE SECRETARY CLARK CLIFFORD'S ROLE IN THE EVENTS DESCRIBED IN THE SUBTITLE. FOR CONTRARY VIEWS, SEE ROCHE'S ARTICLE AND BOOK IN THE PRESIDENTIAL ADVISERS SECTION OF THIS CHAPTER.

1148 KAHIN, G. MCT. "THE PENTAGON PAPERS: A CRITICAL EVALUATION." APSR 69, NO.2 (JUNE 1975): 675-684.

1149 LOWENTHAL, A.F. THE DOMINICAN INTERVENTION. CAMBRIDGE, MASS.: HARVARD U PR, 1972, PP. 246.

1150 MOYERS, B.D. "BILL MOYERS TALKS ABOUT THE WAR AND LBJ: AN INTERVIEW." ATLANTIC (JULY 1968): 29-37.

1151 ----------. "ONE THING WE LEARNED." FOREIGN AFFAIRS 46 (1968):657-664.

1152 PEARSON, N. "GHOSTS THAT HAUNTED LBJ; HIS DECISION TO WITHDRAW." LOOK 32:25-9 JL 23 '68.

1153 PFEFFER, R.M., ED. NO MORE VIETNAMS? THE WAR AND THE FUTURE OF AMERICAN FOREIGN POLICY. NEW YORK: HARPER AND ROW, 1968, PP. 299.

1154 RUBIN, R.A. "FOREIGN POLICY, SECRECY, AND THE FIRST AMENDMENT: THE PENTAGON PAPERS IN RETROSPECT." HOWARD LAW J 17, NO. 3, 1972: 579-612.

1155 SCHLESINGER, A.M., JR. THE BITTER HERITAGE: VIETNAM AND AMERICAN DEMOCRACY 1941-1966. BOSTON: HOUGHTON, 1967, PP. 126.

1156 SELLEN, R.W. "OLD ASSUMPTIONS VERSUS NEW REALITIES: LYNDON JOHNSON AND FOREIGN POLICY." INTERNATIONAL J 28 (SPRING 1973): 204-229.

A CRITICAL ASSESSMENT OF PRESIDENT JOHNSON'S FOREIGN POLICY.

1157 SHEEHAN, N., ET AL. THE PENTAGON PAPERS AS PUBLISHED BY THE NEW YORK TIMES. NEW YORK: QUADRANGLE BOOKS, 1971, PP. 810.

1158 SLATER, J. INTERVENTION AND NEGOTIATION: THE UNITED STATES AND THE DOMINICAN INTERVENTION. NEW YORK: HAR-ROW, 1970, PP. 254.

1159 THE PENTAGON PAPERS: THE DEFENSE DEPARTMENT HISTORY OF UNITED STATES DECISION MAKING IN VIETNAM. THE SENATOR GRAVEL EDITION. BOSTON: BEACON, 1971, 5 VOLS.

1160 ULLMAN, R.H. "THE PENTAGON'S HISTORY AS 'HISTORY'." FOREIGN POLICY 4 (FALL 1971): 150-156.

1161 WARNER, G. "ESCALATION IN VIETNAM, THE PRECEDENTS OF 1954." INTERNATIONAL AFFAIRS 41 (1965):266-277.

1162 WESTERFIELD, H.B. "WHAT USE ARE THREE VERSIONS OF THE PENTAGON PAPERS?" APSR 69 (JUNE 1975): 685-696.

1163 WINDCHY, E.G. TONKIN GULF. NEW YORK: DOUBLEDAY, 1971, PP. 358.

SEE ALSO 83, 84, 85, 703, 727, 734, 736, 946, 984, 994, 1105, 1106, 1112, 1614, 2140

3. OTHER

1164 CHRISTIAN, G. THE PRESIDENT STEPS DOWN, A PERSONAL MEMOIR OF THE TRANSFER OF POWER. NEW YORK: MACMILLAN, 1970, PP. 282.

JOHNSON'S PRESS SECRETARY AT THE TIME OF LBJ'S DECISION NOT TO RUN IN 1968 GIVES AN INSIDER'S ACCOUNT OF THE LAST 100 DAYS OF THE JOHNSON PRESIDENCY.

1165 DEAKIN, J. LYNDON JOHNSON'S CREDIBILITY GAP. WASHINGTON, D.C.: PUBLIC AFFAIRS PRESS, 1968, PP. 65.

1166 FRANKEL, M. "WHY THE GAP BETWEEN L.B.J. AND THE NATION: FAILURE TO COMMUNICATE." N Y TIMES MAG 26 (JANUARY 7, 1968): 7+.

1167 HALPERIN, M.H. "THE DECISION TO DEPLOY THE ABM: BUREAUCRATIC AND DOMESTIC POLITICS IN THE JOHNSON ADMINISTRATION." WORLD POLITICS 25 (1972):62-95.

1168 WISE, D. "TWILIGHT OF A PRESIDENT." N Y TIMES MAG (NOVEMBER 3, 1968): 27-29+.

1169 WOLFENSTEIN, E.V. "THE TWO WARS OF LYNDON JOHNSON." POLITICS & SOCIETY 4 (1974): 357-396.

MARXIST INQUIRY INTO THE REASONS FOR LBJ'S "CREDIBILITY GAP" IN HIS CONDUCT OF "TWO WARS"--VIETNAM AND THE WAR ON POVERTY. SEEING THE TWO WARS AS MANIFESTATIONS OF THE NATIONAL INTEREST AS DEFINED BY AMERICAN POLITICAL CLASS, THE AUTHOR CONCLUDES THE CREDIBILITY GAP WAS "NOTHING OTHER THAN AN IN-HOUSE DEBATE BETWEEN JOHNSON AND HIS LIBERAL CRITICS."

SEE ALSO 768, 974, 1732, 1917, 2287

G. ADDITIONAL ASPECTS AND THEMES

1170 BISHOP, J.A. <u>A DAY IN THE LIFE OF PRESIDENT JOHNSON</u>. NEW YORK: RANDOM HOUSE, 1967, PP. 274.

IN THIS SEQUEL TO HIS DAY-IN-THE-LIFE BOOK ON KENNEDY, BISHOP DESCRIBES JOHNSON'S ROUTINE AND WORK HABITS.

1171 BRANDON, H. "WHITE HOUSE IN TRANSITION: L.B. JOHNSON'S MYSTIFYING IMAGE." <u>SAT R</u> 49 (JUNE 11, 1966): 10.

1172 BRANYAN, R.L., AND LEE, R.A. "LYNDON B. JOHNSON AND THE ART OF THE POSSIBLE." <u>SOUTHWESTERN SOCIAL SCIENCE Q</u> (DEC. 1964): 213-225.

1173 BRODER, D.S. "THE FALLACY OF LBJ'S CONSENSUS." <u>WASHINGTON MONTHLY</u> DEC. 1971, PP. 7-13.

THE "ROOT OF JOHNSON'S FAILURE WAS IN HIS OWN FLAWED CONCEPT OF PRESIDENTIAL LEADERSHIP AND PARTY RESPONSIBILITY IN A DEMOCRACY."

1174 BROGAN, D.W. "L.B.J. & THE AMERICAN INTELLECTUALS." <u>ENCOUNTER</u> 32 (JUNE 1969): 68-77.

1175 CARPENTER, L. <u>RUFFLES AND FLOURISHES</u>. GARDEN CITY, N.Y.: DOUBLEDAY, 1970.

REMINISCENCES OF JOHNSON'S WASHINGTON BY LADY BIRD'S SOCIAL SECRETARY.

1176 CORNWELL, E.E. "THE JOHNSON PRESS RELATIONS STYLE." <u>JOURNALISM</u> 43 (SPRING 1966): 3-9.

1177 DAVIE, M. <u>L.B.J.: A FOREIGN OBSERVER'S VIEWPOINT</u>. NEW YORK: BALLANTINE, 1966, PP. 123. SECOND EDITION, 1967.

1178 FAIRLIE, H. "JOHNSON AND THE INTELLECTUALS." <u>COMMENTARY</u> 41 (JANUARY 1966): 4+; (FEBRUARY 1966): 6+.

1179 GIMLIN, H. "CREDIBILITY GAPS AND THE PRESIDENCY." <u>EDITORIAL RESEARCH REPORTS</u> (FEBRUARY 7, 1968): 83-100.

1180 GOLDEN, H.L. <u>MR. KENNEDY AND THE NEGROES</u>. CLEVELAND: WORLD PUBLISHING COMPANY, 1964, PP. 319.

A SYMPATHETIC ACCOUNT OF JFK'S COOPERATION WITH THE CIVIL RIGHTS MOVEMENT, DRAWING ON INFORMATION PROVIDED BY KENNEDY AND HIS ADVISERS.

1181 HALBERSTAM, D. "LYNDON." ESQUIRE 78 (AUG. 1972): 73-88.

1182 HALEY, J.E. A TEXAN LOOKS AT LYNDON: A STUDY IN ILLEGITIMATE POWER. CANYON, TEX.: PALO DURO PRESS, 1964, PP. 256.

A RADICAL RIGHT CRITIQUE OF JOHNSON WHICH RECEIVED WIDESPREAD ATTENTION DURING THE 1964 PRESIDENTIAL CAMPAIGN.

1183 HARREN, L. NO HAIL, NO FAREWELL. NEW YORK: 1970.

A FOREIGNER'S VIEW OF JOHNSON'S PRESIDENCY.

1184 JANOS, L. "THE LAST DAYS OF THE PRESIDENT: LBJ IN RETIREMENT." ATLANTIC 232 (JULY 1973): 35-41.

AN INTIMATE GLIMPSE INTO THE LIFE OF THE 36TH PRESIDENT EMERGES FROM AN INTERVIEW WITH MRS. JOHNSON AT THE LBJ RANCH IN TEXAS.

1185 JOHNSON, C.A.T. (LADY BIRD JOHNSON) A WHITE HOUSE DIARY. NEW YORK: HOLT. 1970. PP. 806.

1186 ----------. "THE LBJ NOBODY KNEW: A CONVERSATION WITH LADY BIRD JOHNSON." U S NEWS (DEC. 24, 1973): 34-38.

1187 KEARNS, D. "LYNDON JOHNSON'S POLITICAL PERSONALITY," POLITICAL SCIENCE QUARTERLY 91 (FALL 1976):385-409.

BASED PRIMARILY ON EXTENDED CONVERSATIONS THE AUTHOR HELD WITH LBJ ABOUT HIS CHILDHOOD AND HIS POLITICAL CAREER AND ON JOHNSON'S PERSONAL PAPERS.

1188 LADD, B. CRISIS IN CREDIBILITY. NEW YORK: NEW AMERICAN LIBRARY, 1968, PP. 247.

1189 LEVITT, T. "JOHNSON TREATMENT." HARVARD BUS R 45 (JANUARY 1967): 114-118.

1190 MAGRATH, C.P. "LYNDON JOHNSON AND THE PARADOX OF THE PRESIDENCY: CONCERNING PRESIDENT AS NONPARTISAN LEADER." YALE R 54 (JUNE 1965): 481-493.

IN THE IMMEDIATE AFTERMATH OF JOHNSON'S ELECTORAL TRIUMPH

IN 1964, MAGRATH FELT THAT JOHNSON HAD THE POTENTIAL TO BE A SUCCESSFUL "CONSENSUS PRESIDENT," MAINTAINING WIDESPREAD SUPPORT FROM BOTH PARTIES YET SUCCEEDING TO INTRODUCE INNOVATIVE POLICIES.

1191 MOONEY, B. LBJ: AN IRREVERENT CHRONICLE. NEW YORK: CROWELL, 1976, PP. 290.

1192 MORGENTHAU, H.J. "TRUTH AND POWER: THE INTELLECTUALS AND THE JOHNSON ADMINISTRATION." NEW REPUBLIC 155 (NOVEMBER 26, 1966): 8-14; "DISCUSSION," 155 (DECEMBER 24, 1966): 35-36; 156: 42-43.

1193 NELSON, B. "COMMUNICATION GAP: LBJ'S MONOLOGUE WITH THE INTELLECTUALS." SCIENCE 157 (JULY 14, 1967): 173-176.

1194 NEUSTADT, R.E. "HOW LBJ IS DOING HIS JOB: INTERVIEW ANALYZING USE OF PRESIDENTIAL POWER." U S NEWS 57 (AUGUST 3, 1964): 34-37.

1195 O'DONNELL, K. "LBJ AND THE KENNEDYS." LIFE 69 (AUG. 7, 1970): 44-56.

RECOLLECTIONS OF A KENNEDY ADVISER.

1196 PHILLIPS, C. "JOHNSON HAS THE KIND OF TROUBLES TRUMAN HAD." N Y TIMES MAG 34 (OCTOBER 22, 1967): 34-35+.

1197 ROSENBLUM, S. LBJ LAMPOONED: CARTOON CRITICISM OF LYNDON B. JOHNSON. NEW YORK: COBBLE HILL PRESS, 1968, PP. 128.

1198 ROSTOW, E.V. "LBJ RECONSIDERED." ESQUIRE 75 (APRIL 1971): 118-119.

ANALYSIS OF PRESIDENT JOHNSON'S POLICY TOWARD VIETNAM BY A FORMER FOREIGN POLICY ADVISER.

1199 SEMPLE, R.B. "WHITE HOUSE ON THE PEDERNALES." N Y TIMES MAG (OCTOBER 31, 1965): 54-55+.

1200 SHERRILL, R. "LOOKING BACK AT JOHNSON." NATION 208 (JANUARY 13, 1969): 42-45.

1201 ----------. "POLITICS ON THE KING'S RANCH." N Y TIMES

MAG (JUNE 5, 1966): 43+.

1202 TYLER, G. "JOHNSON AND THE INTELLECTUALS: DUEL IN THE ADA
(AMERICANS FOR DEMOCRATIC ACTION)." MIDSTREAM 13
(AUGUST/SEPTEMBER 1967): 35-45.

1203 WILLIAMS, J.M. THE CONSTITUTIONAL BASIS FOR THE
IMPEACHMENT OF LYNDON B. JOHNSON. MINNEAPOLIS: CITIZENS
FOR GOVERNMENTAL RESTRAINT, 1968, PP. 28.

1204 WILLIAMS, T.H. "HUEY, LYNDON, AND SOUTHERN RADICALISM." J
OF AMERICAN HISTORY 60 (SEPT 1973): 267-293.

SEE ALSO 286, 289, 290, 297, 301, 1494, 1770, 1814, 1859,
1866, 1869, 2485, 2502

12
RICHARD M. NIXON AND HIS ADMINISTRATION

A. GENERAL HISTORICAL ACCOUNTS AND BIOGRAPHIES

1205 ALLEN, G. RICHARD NIXON: THE MAN BEHIND THE MASK. BELMONT, MASS.: WESTERN ISLANDS, 1971, PP. 433.

ALLEN'S EXPANSION OF HIS 1950 BOOK OF THE SAME TITLE WHICH CONSISTS OF ANECDOTES.A RIGHT-WING CRITIQUE OF NIXON BY A SOMETIME CONTRIBUTOR TO SUCH PERIODICALS AS THE JOHN BIRCH SOCIETY'S AMERICAN OPINION.

1206 DRURY, A. COURAGE AND HESITATION: NOTES AND PHOTOGRAPHS OF THE NIXON ADMINISTRATION. GARDEN CITY, N.Y.: DOUBLEDAY, 1971, PP. 416.

A SYMPATHETIC, COPIOUSLY ILLUSTRATED POPULAR ACCOUNT OF NIXON'S PRESIDENCY.

1207 EVANS, R., AND NOVAK, R. NIXON IN THE WHITE HOUSE: THE FRUSTRATION OF POWER. NEW YORK: RANDOM HOUSE, 1971, PP. 431.

AN ACCOUNT OF NIXON'S FIRST YEARS IN OFFICE BASED ON REPORTING BY 2 PARTICULARLY WELL CONNECTED WASHINGTON CORRESPONDENTS.

1208 HOFFMAN, P. THE NEW NIXON. NEW YORK: TOWER PUBLICATIONS, 1970, PP. 224.

1209 NIXON. 5 VOLS. CONGRESSIONAL QUARTERLY, WASHINGTON, D.C., 1970-1974.

THE PORTION OF THE SIXTH YEAR OF OFFICE THAT HE SERVED IS COVERED IN THE SERIES ENTITLED PRESIDENCY CITED IN THE CHAPTER ON PRESIDENT FORD.

1210 "NIXON: A FOUR-YEAR RECORD OF PLUSES AND MINUSES," CONG Q W REPT 30 (AUGUST 26, 1972): 2121-2140.

INCLUDES BACKGROUND, FINANCIAL, AND CAMPAIGN INFORMATION ON NIXON, HIS ACTIVITIES REGARDING THE ENVIRONMENT, HEALTH, EDUCATION, WELFARE, CRIME, JUSTICE, BUSING, DEFENSE, AND THE ECONOMY, AND HIS LEGISLATIVE RECORD.

1211 OSBORNE, J. 1.THE FIRST TWO YEARS OF THE NIXON WATCH. NEW YORK: LIVERIGHT, 1971, PP. 218.

THIS AND THE FOLLOWING OSBORNE VOLUMES CONTAIN THE FULL TEXT OF THE WIDELY RESPECTED "NIXON WATCH," PUBLISHED WEEKLY IN THE NEW REPUBLIC. IN A FEW INSTANCES, OSBORNE HAS ADDED TERSE COMMENTS ON THE RECEPTION OF COLUMNS.

1212 ----------. 2.THE THIRD YEAR OF THE NIXON WATCH. NEW YORK: LIVERIGHT, 1972, PP. 216.

1213 ----------. 3.THE FOURTH YEAR OF THE NIXON WATCH. NEW YORK: LIVERIGHT, 1973, PP. 218.

1214 ----------. 4.THE LAST NIXON WATCH. WASHINGTON, D.C.: NEW REPUBLIC, 1975, PP.246.

1215 "THE NIXON YEARS." WASH POST (AUG 9, 1974): SUPPL. 1-24.

FIFTEEN ARTICLES BY WASHINGTON POST STAFF WRITERS, INCLUDING CARL BERNSTEIN, BOB WOODWARD, DAVID BRODER, HAYNES JOHNSON, AND JULES WITCOVER DISCUSS THE PERSONALITY, POLITICAL STYLE, AND CAREER OF PRESIDENT NIXON, THE WATERGATE AND AGNEW AFFAIRS, THE FIRST LADY, THE POLITICAL, DOMESTIC, DIPLOMATIC, AND MORAL LEGACIES AND ACCOMPLISHMENTS OF THE ADMINISTRATION, AND THE PROSPECTS FOR THE FORD ADMINISTRATION. INCLUDES BIOGRAPHIES OF PRESIDENTIAL AIDES AND A CHRONOLOGY OF SIGNIFICANT EVENTS.

1216 VOORHIS, J. THE STRANGE CASE OF RICHARD MILHOUS NIXON. NEW YORK: POPULAR LIBRARY, 1972, PP. 350.

A CRITICAL ANALYSIS OF NIXON BY THE CALIFORNIA CONGRESSMAN DEFEATED FOR REELECTION IN NIXON'S FIRST RUN FOR OFFICE.

SEE ALSO 629, 1227, 1564, 1568, 1569

B. PRESIDENT'S PAPERS, MEMOIRS

1217 JACOBS, R.F. "THE STATUS OF THE NIXON PRESIDENTIAL HISTORICAL MATERIALS." AMERICAN ARCHIVIST 38 (JULY 1975): 337-338.

1218 NIXON, R.M. SETTING THE COURSE: THE FIRST YEAR. NEW YORK: FUNK AND WAGNALLS, 1970, PP. 500.

1219 ----------. SIX CRISES. NEW YORK: DOUBLEDAY, 1962; REPUBLISHED WITH NEW PREFACE, PYRAMID BOOKS, 1968, PP. 482.

PSYCHOLOGICALLY FASCINATING MEMOIR IN WHICH NIXON DESCRIBES HIS CAREER AS BESET BY CRISES, EACH OF WHICH IS

CHARACTERIZED BY A TYPICAL SEQUENCE OF EVENTS AND RESPONSES ON NIXON'S PART. PUBLISHED AFTER NIXON'S 1960 DEFEAT AND REPUBLISHED IN PAPERBACK AFTER HIS 1968 ELECTION WITH TEXT OF ACCEPTANCE SPEECH AND NEW PREFACE ADDED.

1220 ----------. THE CHALLENGES WE FACE. NEW YORK: MCGRAW-HILL, 1960, PP. 253.

SEE ALSO 54, 2033

C. COMPENDIA AND BIBLIOGRAPHIES

1221 HERBERS, J. "THE OTHER PRESIDENCY." N Y TIMES MAG 3 (MARCH 1974).

OMB CONTINUES TO IMPLEMENT NIXON POLICIES IN SPITE OF THE WATERGATE IMMOBILIZATION OF THE PRESIDENT. ASSERTS THAT OMB SERVED AS A SURROGATE PRESIDENT DURING THE WATERGATE PERIOD. SPECIAL FOCUSES ON THE POLICY MAKING INFLUENCE OF OMB'S DIRECTOR, ROY ASH.

SEE ALSO 1411, 1412, 1463

D. SELECTED MATERIAL ON PRE-PRESIDENTIAL BACKGROUND

1222 ALSOP, S. NIXON AND ROCKEFELLER: A DOUBLE PORTRAIT. GARDEN CITY: DOUBLEDAY, 1960, PP. 240.

IN THIS PRE-CONVENTION BIOGRAPHY OF THE TWO CONTENDERS FOR THE 1960 REPUBLICAN NOMINATION, ALSOP FOCUSES ON THE CONTRAST IN THE FORMATIVE YEARS AND THE EARLY CAREER OF THE THEN VICE PRESIDENT NIXON AND THE THEN GOVERNOOR ROCKEFELLER IN AN ENDEAVOR TO PREDICT THE KIND OF PRESIDENT EACH WOULD MAKE.

1223 COSTELLO, W. THE FACTS ABOUT NIXON: THE UNAUTHORIZED BIOGRAPHY OF RICHARD M. NIXON; THE FORMATIVE YEARS: 1913-1959. NEW YORK: VIKING PRESS, 1960, PP. 306.

A SCATHING CRITIQUE.

1224 DE TOLEDANO, R. ONE MAN ALONE: RICHARD NIXON. NEW YORK: FUNK AND WAGNALLS, 1969, PP. 386.

A CONSERVATIVE JOURNALIST'S ACCOUNT OF NIXON'S PRE-PRESIDENTIAL CAREER, PORTRAYING HIM AS THE VICTOR OVER ALMOST INSURMOUNTABLE ODDS, AMONG WHICH WERE HUMBLE ORIGINS, POLITICAL MISFORTUNE, AND A SERIES OF CONSPIRACIES TO PREVENT HIS ADVANCE.

1225 HARRIS, M. MARK THE GLOVE BOY; OR, THE LAST DAYS OF RICHARD NIXON. NEW YORK: MACMILLAN, 1964, PP. 147.

A CRITICAL ACCOUNT OF THE THEN FORMER VICE PRESIDENT NIXON'S ILL FATED 1962 GUBERNATORIAL CAMPAIGN.

1226 JACKSON, D. "THE YOUNG NIXON." LIFE (NOV. 6, 1970): 54+.

INTERVIEWS WITH NIXON'S FRIENDS, TEACHERS, CLASSMATES AND RIVALS--FROM HIS EARLIEST DAYS IN YORBA LINDA TO THE MOMENT HE ENTERED POLITICS.

1227 KORNITZER, B. THE REAL NIXON: AN INTIMATE BIOGRAPHY. NEW YORK: RAND MCNALLY, 1960, PP. 352.

AN ACCOUNT OF THE PEOPLE AND THE FORCES WHICH SHAPED VICE PRESIDENT NIXON'S LIFE. PARTICULAR ATTENTION IS PAID TO NIXON'S MOTHER AND HER IMPACT ON THE NIXON FAMILY. HANNAH NIXON WAS INTERVIEWED IN DEPTH BY THE AUTHOR, AS WERE WILLIAM ROGERS, ALICE ROOSEVELT, AND NIXON HIMSELF.

1228 MAZO, E. RICHARD NIXON: A POLITICAL AND PERSONAL PORTRAIT. NEW YORK: AVON BOOK DIVISION, HEARST CORP., 1960, PP. 270.

A SYMPATHETIC CAMPAIGN BIOGRAPHY RECOUNTING SEVERAL ASPECTS OF NIXON'S CAREER AMONG WHICH IS THE ILL FATED "DUMP NIXON" MOVEMENT OF 1956.

1229 MAZO, E., AND HESS, S. NIXON: A POLITICAL PORTRAIT. NEW YORK: HARPER & ROW, 1968, PP. 326.

AN UPDATE OF MAZO'S EARLIER BOOK. INCLUDES NIXON'S 1960 AND 1962 CAMPAIGNS AS WELL AS HIS EXPERIENCES IN NEW YORK.

1230 MCGINNISS, J. THE SELLING OF THE PRESIDENT, 1968. NEW YORK: TRIDENT PRESS, 1969, PP. 253.

A PARTICIPANT-OBSERVER'S ACCOUNT OF NIXON'S 1968 CAMPAIGN STRATEGY, FOCUSING ON THE CAREFUL USE OF TELEVISION AND THE RELATIVE ISOLATION OF THE CANDIDATE.

1231 "NIXON'S PARTICIPATION IN DECISIONS EXAMINED." CONG Q W REPT 18 (SEPTEMBER 16, 1960): 1577-1580.

1232 VIORST, M. "NIXON OF THE O.P.A." N Y TIMES MAG (OCT. 3, 1971): 70+.

ON NIXON'S BRIEF SERVICE IN THE WARTIME PRICE CONTROL AGENCY.

1233 WHITE, T.H. THE MAKING OF THE PRESIDENT 1968. NEW YORK: ATHENEUM, 1969,

THIS 3RD OF WHITE'S STUDIES OF AMERICAN PRESIDENTIAL ELECTIONS PROVIDES THE AUTHOR'S OBSERVATIONS AND INTERPRETATIONS OF THE PREVIOUS PRESIDENT (LBJ) AND HIS SUCCESSOR.

1234 WITCOVER, J. THE RESURRECTION OF RICHARD NIXON. NEW YORK: PUTNAM, 1970, PP. 473.

EXAMINES HOW NIXON RECOVERED FROM HIS 1960 PRESIDENTIAL AND 1962 GUBERNATORIAL DEFEATS AND WON THE 1968

PRESIDENTIAL NOMINATION.

SEE ALSO 939, 1100, 1248, 2447, 2493

E. ADVISERS AND ADVISORY RELATIONS

1235 ANDERSON, P. "THE PRESIDENT'S ACCUSER." N Y TIMES MAG (JULY 8, 1973): 8-9.

BIOGRAPHICAL SKETCH OF JOHN DEAN.

1236 APPLE, R.W. "HALDEMAN THE FIERCE, HALDEMAN THE FAITHFUL, HALDEMAN THE FALLEN." N Y TIMES MAG (MAY 6, 1973): 38-39+.

DISCUSSION OF HALDEMAN'S ROLE AS SPECIAL ASSISTANT TO THE PRESIDENT.

1237 BELOFF, N. "PROF. BISMARCK GOES TO WASHINGTON: KISSINGER ON THE JOB." ATLANTIC 224 (DEC 1969): 77-89.

1238 BLUMENFELD, R., ET AL. HENRY KISSINGER: THE PRIVATE AND PUBLIC STORY. NEW YORK: THE NEW AMERICAN LIBRARY, 1974, PP. 326.

AUTHORS INCLUDE THE STAFF AND EDITORS OF THE NEW YORK POST.

1239 BONAFEDE, D. "ADMINISTRATION REALIGNS HILL LIAISON TO GAIN TIGHTER GRIP ON FEDERAL POLICY." NATIONAL J 5 (1973):35-43.

ON THE ASSIGNMENT OF WILLIAM E. TIMMONS AS CHIEF CONGRESSIONAL LIAISON OFFICIAL AND THE CONSEQUENCES EXPECTED FROM THAT CHANGE.

1240 ----------. "CHARLES W. COLSON, PRESIDENT'S 'LIAISON WITH OUTSIDE WORLD'." NATIONAL J 2 (19730):1689-1694.

1241 ----------. "DUAL CAPACITY BRINGS POWER TO RONALD ZIEGLER." NATIONAL J 6 (1974):324-327.

ZIEGLER'S ROLE AS A WHITE HOUSE PRESS SECRETARY AND ASSISTANT TO THE PRESIDENT.

1242 ----------. "EHRLICHMAN ACTS AS A POLICY BROKER IN NIXON'S FORMALIZED DOMESTIC COUNCIL." NATIONAL J 3 (1971):1235-1244.

COMPREHENSIVE STUDY OF EHRLICHMAN AND HIS ACTIVITIES AS CHIEF PRESIDENTIAL ADVISOR ON DOMESTIC AFFAIRS.

1243 ----------. "HALDEMAN DIRECTS STAFF AS PRESIDENT'S ALTER EGO." NATIONAL J 3 (1971):513-522.

1244 ----------. "HALDEMAN, EHRLICHMAN DEPARTURES TO BRING MAJOR CHANGES IN ADMINISTRATION." NATIONAL J 5 (1973):633-636.

AS MR. NIXON SEARCHES FOR REPLACEMENTS FOR HIS 2 CLOSEST AIDES, "HE IS TURNING TO OLD AND TRUSTED ASSOCIATES WHO HAVE DEMONSTRATED BOTH THEIR INTEGRITY AND THEIR POLITICAL ACUMEN."

1245 ----------. "HARRY S. DENT DIGS IN AS KEY WHITE HOUSE POLITICAL LEGMAN." NATIONAL J 2 (SEPTEMBER 19, 1970): 2030-2035.

"HARRY S. DENT, FORMER AIDE TO SOUTH CAROLINA'S SEN. THURMOND, AND LATER PRESIDENT NIXON'S SOUTHERN SPOKESMAN, HAS EMERGED AS A KEY WHITE HOUSE LEGMAN FOR THE 1970 ELECTIONS."

1246 ----------. "HERBERT G. KLEIN: SPOKESMAN FOR THE ADMINISTRATION." NATIONAL J 1 (1969):258-262.

ON KLEIN'S ASSUMPTION OF THE NEWLY CREATED POSITION OF DIRECTOR OF COMMUNICATIONS.

1247 ----------. "JOHN MITCHELL, NIXON'S LEGAL ADVISOR, PLAYS POLICY ROLE FAR BEYOND HIS OFFICE." NATIONAL J 3 (1971):2005-2015.

NIXON'S ATTORNEY GENERAL AS AN OVERALL POLICY ADVISOR.

1248 ----------. "MURRAY CHOTINER: EARLY TUTOR, POLITICAL COUNSELOR." NATIONAL J 2 (1970):1130-1135.

ON A NIXON ADVISER WHO SERVED HIM FROM HIS INITIAL ADVENT INTO POLITICS.

1249 ----------. "NEW TASK FORCES SEEK IDEAS FOR PRESIDENT'S 1970 PROGRAM." NATIONAL J 1 (1969):2-6.

AN ANALYSIS OF 16 TASK FORCES SET UP BY PRESIDENT NIXON TO ANALYZE DOMESTIC PROBLEMS.

1250 ----------. "NIXON'S FIRST-YEAR APPOINTMENTS REVEAL PATTERN OF HIS ADMINISTRATION." NATIONAL J 2 (1970):182-192.

IN FILLING THE ROUGHLY 2000 PATRONAGE POSTS AVAILABLE, NIXON WAS MORE LIKELY THAN RECENT PRESIDENTS TO CHOOSE BUSINESSMEN AND ELECTED OFFICIALS AS WELL AS SOUTHERNERS. HE WAS LESS LIKELY TO EMPLOY ACADEMICIANS AND MEMBERS OF THE "EASTERN ESTABLISHMENT."

1251 ----------. "NIXON'S TROUBLES BRING ENHANCED ROLE FOR CABINET, BETTER WORKING RELATIONSHIPS." NATIONAL J 5 (1973):1472-1478.

1252 ----------. "PRESIDENT STILL SEEKS TO RESTORE STAFF
EFFICIENCY, MORALE." NATIONAL J 6 (1974):1-6.

1253 ----------. "PRESIDENT'S INNER CIRCLE OF FRIENDS SERVES
AS INFLUENTIAL "KITCHEN CABINET"." NATIONAL J 4 (1972):
126-135.

SUCH CLOSE PERSONAL NIXON FRIENDS AS ELMER H. BOBST,
DONALD M. KENDALL, W. CLEMENT STONE, AND ROBERT H.
ABPLANALP "HAVE DIRECT ACCESS TO THE WHITE HOUSE AND
EXERCISE AN INDIRECT, THOUGH VITAL, IMPACT ON PRESIDENT
NIXON'S OFFICIAL LIFE."

1254 ----------. "SPEECHWRITERS PLAY STRATEGIC ROLE IN
CONVEYING, SHAPING NIXON'S POLICIES." NATIONAL J 4
(1972):311-320.

1255 ----------. "ZIEGLER'S ADDED RESPONSIBILITY INCLUDES
KEEPING PRESIDENT INFORMED." NATIONAL J 5
(1973):866-873.

FIRST OF TWO-PART SERIES ON ADMINISTRATION PRESS-PUBLIC
RELATIONS ACTIVITIES COVERS THE UPGRADING OF ZIEGLER'S
TITLE AND RESPONSIBILITIES AND AN INFORMAL SURVEY OF WHITE
HOUSE CORRESPONDENTS REVEALING MOST THINK HE SHOULD STAY.

1256 BONAFEDE, D., AND GLASS, A.J. "HAIG REVAMPING STAFF,
SHIFTS IN PATRONAGE POLICY LIKELY." NATIONAL J 6 (1974):
495-511.

ON HAIG'S PLAN TO MODIFY WHITE HOUSE STAFF PROCEDURES SO
AS TO DEPART FROM VARIOUS PRACTICES OF HIS PREDECESSOR,
H. R. HALDEMAN. SPECIAL EMPHASIS ON PLANS TO REDUCE THE
STAFF'S SIZE.

1257 BONAFEDE, D., AND IGLEHART, J.K. "END OF COUNSELOR SYSTEM
ENLARGES POLICY-FORMING ROLE OF CABINET." NATIONAL J 5
(1973):726-729.

PRESIDENT NIXON'S "SURPRISE JUNKING OF THE WHITE HOUSE
COUNSELOR SYSTEM PRESAGES A RETURN...TO THE TRADITIONAL
PRACTICE OF CONDUCTING GOVERNMENTAL BUSINESS THROUGH THE
CABINET."

1258 BOYD, J. "HARRY DENT, THE PRESIDENT'S POLITICAL
COORDINATOR." N Y TIMES MAG 1 FEB. 1960.

1259 BUCHAN, A. "THE IRONY OF HENRY KISSINGER." INTERNAT
AFFAIRS 50 (JULY 1974): 367-379.

KISSINGER'S SUCCESSES OWE LITTLE TO HIS INTELLECTUAL
TRAINING; INSTEAD, THEY ARISE FROM HIS PRAGMATISM,

PHYSICAL ENERGY, AND HIS EYE FOR POLITICAL OPPORTUNITY.

1260 BURBY, J.F., AND LENHART, H., JR. "NIXON'S CHANGE IN GAME PLAN REFLECTS CONFIDENCE IN CEA, MCCRACKEN." NATIONAL J 3 (1971):1743-1753.

UNTIL NIXON'S ANNOUNCEMENT OF DRAMATIC CHANGES IN ECONOMIC POLICY ON AUGUST 15, 1971, IT WAS ASSUMED THAT THE MCCRACKEN-LED COUNCIL OF ECONOMIC ADVISERS WOULD BE LESS INFLUENTIAL THAN TREASURY SECRETARY JOHN B. CONNALLY AND OMB'S DIRECTOR GEORGE SHULTZ.

1261 COLLIER, B.L. "THE ROAD TO PEKING, OR, HOW DOES THIS KISSINGER DO IT?" NY TIMES (NOV 14,1971): 34-35,104-112.

1262 COLSON, C.W. BORN AGAIN. OLD TAPPAN, N.J.: CHOSEN BOOKS, 1976, PP. 351.

NIXON'S FORMER "HATCHET MAN" TURNED CHRISTIAN EVANGELIST RECOUNTS BOTH THE NATURE OF NIXON'S WHITE HOUSE AND HIS CHRISTIAN BELIEF AND COMMITMENT.

1263 COYNE, J.R., JR. THE IMPUDENT SNOBS: AGNEW VS. THE INTELLECTUAL ESTABLISHMENT. NEW ROCHELLE, N.Y.: ARLINGTON, 1972, PP. 524.

A CONSERVATIVE DEFENSE OF AGNEW. INCLUDES VERBATIM TRANSCRIPTS OF 94 SPEECHES, REPORTING HIS AD LIB SAYINGS AS WELL AS PREPARED TEXTS.

1264 CRAWFORD, A.F., AND KEEVER, J., JOHN B. CONNALLY: PORTRAIT IN POWER. AUSTIN: JENKINS, 1973, PP. 460.

A SYMPATHETIC ACCOUNT BY 2 TEXAS JOURNALISTS.

1265 DEAN, J.W., III. "PLAYBOY INTERVIEW: JOHN DEAN." PLAYBOY 22 (JAN. 1975) 65+.

1266 DUSCHA, J. "WHITE HOUSE WATCH OVER TV AND THE PRESS." N Y TIMES MAG (AUGUST 20, 1972): 9+.

PATRICK BUCHANAN'S ROLE AS "TV CRITIC-IN-RESIDENCE" AT THE WHITE HOUSE; HIS RELATIONSHIP WITH PRESIDENT NIXON.

1267 EPHRON, N. "KEN CLAWSON IS NO JOKE." NEW YORK (JUNE 3, 1974): 58-64, 67.

PROFILES THE FORMER WASHINGTON POST REPORTER WHO BECAME WHITE HOUSE COMMUNICATIONS DIRECTOR. DISCUSSES CLAWSON'S ALLEGED AUTHORSHIP OF THE "CANUCK LETTER" USED AGAINST SENATOR MUSKIE IN 1972 AND HIS ACTIVITIES DEFENDING THE PRESIDENT'S ROLE IN WATERGATE.

1268 ETTLINGER, C. "NIXON'S HEAD HUNTER: JERRY JONES CLAIMS THE WHITE HOUSE FILLS ITS VACANCIES RAPIDLY." GOVT EXECUTIVE

6 (JAN. 1974): 50-53.

COMPARES JONES' ASSERTION THAT PRESIDENTIAL APPOINTMENTS ARE MADE PROMPTLY WITH GAO'S CLAIM THAT APPOINTED POSITIONS LIE VACANT FOR MONTHS AT A TIME BECAUSE RECRUITMENT HAS BEEN AFFECTED BY WATERGATE.

1269 FOWLKES, F.V. "CONNALLY REVITALIZES TREASURY, ASSUMES STEWARDSHIP OF NIXON'S NEW ECONOMIC POLICY." NATIONAL J 3 (1971): 1988-1997.

"JOHN B. CONNALLY HAS RISEN IN LESS THAN 8 MONTHS FROM NEW BOY IN THE CABINET TO PRESIDENTIAL ADVISER AND CONFIDANT WITH INFLUENCE BEYOND HIS OFFICIAL JURISDICTION."

1270 GOLAN, M. THE SECRET CONVERSATIONS OF HENRY KISSINGER. NEW YORK: BANTAM, 1976, PP. 280.

1271 GOLDMAN, P. "THE PRESIDENT'S PALACE GUARD." NEWSWEEK (MAR. 19, 1973): 24-28.

DESCRIBES THE JOB, PHILOSOPHY, AND IMAGE OF THE PRESIDENT'S AIDE H. R. HALDEMAN.

1272 GRAUBARD, S. KISSINGER: PORTRAIT OF A MIND. NEW YORK: W.W. NORTON, 1973, PP. 288. SECOND EDITION, 1974, PP. 312.

A FAITHFUL, CHRONOLOGICAL SUMMARY OF KISSINGER'S WRITINGS ON INTERNATIONAL POLITICS PRIOR TO HIS CAREER IN THE NIXON AND THE FORD ADMINISTRATIONS.

1273 HALLETT, D. "A LOW-LEVEL MEMOIR OF THE NIXON WHITE HOUSE." N Y TIMES MAG (OCT. 20, 1974): 39-42+.

A FORMER MEMBER OF CHARLES COLSON'S STAFF RECOUNTS HIS EXPERIENCES WORKING WITH THE WHITE HOUSE.

1274 HAVEMANN, J. "SIMONS' EFFORTS TAKE EFFECT, ORDER EMERGES FROM CHAOS." NATIONAL J 6 (1974):153-158.

"IN A SPAN OF WEEKS, ADMINISTRATOR WILLIAM E. SIMON HAS BUILT A NEW FEDERAL ENERGY OFFICE BY RAIDING OTHER AGENCIES AND PULLING IN SPECIALISTS FROM PRIVATE INDUSTRY."

1275 "HOW NIXON HANDLES WORLD'S BIGGEST JOB; INTERVIEW WITH H.R. HALDEMAN, ASSISTANT TO THE PRESIDENT." U S NEWS 69 (SEPTEMBER 14, 1970): 56-62.

1276 "HOW NIXON'S WHITE HOUSE WORKS." TIME MAG 8 JUNE 1970, PP. 15-20.

DISCUSSION OF NIXON'S PERSONAL STAFF.

1277 IGLEHART, J.K. "RICHARDSON FACES BIG JOB CHANGING NEW RELATIONS WITH WHITE HOUSE, CONGRESS." NATIONAL J 2

(1970):1978-1988.

"HEW SECRETARY RICHARDSON WANTS TO CHANGE THE WAY HIS DEPARTMENT RELATES TO ITS 2 MOST IMPORTANT FEDERAL CLIENTS--CONGRESS AND THE WHITE HOUSE."

1278 INGRAM, T.H. "ITT AND WATERGATE: THE COLSON CONNECTION." WASHINGTON MONTHLY 5 (NOV. 1973): 32-36.

HYPOTHESIZES THAT THE WATERGATE BURGLARS BROKE INTO THE DEMOCRATIC NATIONAL COMMITTEE OFFICES IN SEARCH OF THE MISSING MEMORANDA ON THE ITT ANTITRUST SETTLEMENT, LISTED IN A MEMORANDUM WRITTEN BY PRESIDENTIAL AIDE CHARLES COLSON.

1279 "JOHN CONNALLY: MR. NIXON'S NO. 2 MAN?" NEWSWEEK (AUG. 9, 1971): 16-20.

EXAMINES CONNALLY'S RELATIONSHIP WITH PRESIDENT NIXON AND HIS POLITICAL FUTURE.

1280 KALB, M., AND KALB, B. KISSINGER. BOSTON: LITTLE, BROWN AND COMPANY, 1974, PP. 577.

TWO CBS REPORTERS WHO COVERED SOME OF KISSINGER'S MOST ACTIVE PERIPATETIC STATESMANSHIP PRESENT A DETAILED AND LARGELY FAVORABLE ACCOUNT OF HIS ACTIVITIES AND HIS STYLE.

1281 KILPATRICK, C. "LEONARD GARMENT IS BRIGHT, MUSICAL, A KNOWN NEW YORK LIBERAL AND A MAN CLOSE TO RICHARD NIXON." POTOMAC (WASH POST) (JUNE 7 1970): 17+.

1282 KOHL, W.L. "THE NIXON-KISSINGER FOREIGN POLICY SYSTEM AND U.S.-EUROPEAN RELATIONS." WORLD POLITICS 28 (OCT 1975): 1-43.

PRESENTS SIX MODELS FOR FOREIGN POLICY MAKING, SURVEYS "THE RULES OF THE FOREIGN POLICY GAME IN WASHINGTON," REVIEWS THE CHARACTERISTICS OF THE SYSTEM OF FOREIGN POLICY DEVELOPED BY PRESIDENT NIXON AND SECRETARY OF STATE KISSINGER, AND USES THE MODELS TO EXPLAIN "SPECIFIC CASES OF POLICYMAKING ON ISSUES OF U.S.-EUROPEAN RELATIONS."

1283 LANDAU, D. KISSINGER: THE USES OF POWER. BOSTON: HOUGHTON MIFFLIN, 1972, PP. 270.

EXPANDED FROM AN EXERCISE IN UNDERGRADUATE JOURNALISM, THIS WORK BY A FORMER HARVARD STUDENT DRAWS ON INTERVIEWS WITH KISSINGER'S COLLEAGUES IN ACADEMIC POLITICS. VERY CRITICAL OF HIS FAILURE TO ACHIEVE AMERICAN DISENGAGEMENT FROM INDOCHINA.

1284 LEACACOS, J.P. "KISSINGER'S APPARAT" FOREIGN POLICY (WINTER 1971-72): 3-28.

PART OF A SYMPOSIUM ON NIXON'S NATIONAL SECURITY COUNCIL. THE OTHER ARTICLE IN THAT SYMPOSIUM IS I.M. DESTLER, "WHAT

CAN ONE MAN DO?"

1285 LEINSTER, C. "NIXON'S FRIEND BEBE." LIFE (JULY 31, 1973): 18+.

1286 MAZLISH, B. KISSINGER: THE EUROPEAN MIND IN AMERICAN POLICY. SCRANTON, PA: BASIC BOOKS, 1976, PP. 400.

A PSYCHOBIOGRAPHY.

1287 NAUGHTON, J. "HOW THE SECOND BEST-INFORMED MAN IN THE WHITE HOUSE BRIEFS THE SECOND WORST-INFORMED GROUP IN WASHINGTON." N Y TIMES MAG (MAY 30, 1971): 9+.

RELATIONSHIP BETWEEN NIXON'S PRESS SECRETARY RONALD ZIEGLER AND THE WHITE HOUSE PRESS CORPS.

1288 NIHART, B. "NEW STAFF SYSTEM AFTER ONE YEAR." ARMED FORCES J 107 (APRIL 4, 1970): 25-29.

"THE NEW NSC SYSTEM IS THE CULMINATION OF 23 YEARS OF EXPERIENCE ADAPTED TO THE NEEDS OF A NEW PRESIDENT. VIEWED IN ISOLATION THE NIXON NSC SYSTEM MAKES A LOT OF SENSE. IN CONJUNCTION WITH THE EXECUTIVE AGENCIES OF GOVERNMENT THE FLOW OF INFORMATION, DELIBERATION, DECISION, AND IMPLEMENTATION SEEMS TO WORK SMOOTHLY."

1289 "NIXON CABINET." CONG Q W REPT 30 (DEC. 2, 1972): 3075-3083.

1290 "NIXON'S INNER CIRCLE OF BUSINESSMEN." BUS WK (JULY 31, 1971): 52-56.

1291 "NIXON'S PRIVATE CIRCLE." U S NEWS 74 (MAY 1973): 23-25.

BRIEFLY IDENTIFIES TEN OF NIXON'S FRIENDS WHO SHARE HIS POLITICAL PHILOSOPHY AND MOST OF WHOM ARE SELF-MADE BUSINESS SUCCESSES. AMONG THOSE DISCUSSED ARE CHARLES REBOZO, ROBERT H. ABPLANALP, BILLY GRAHAM AND DONALD M. KENDALL.

1292 NUTTER, G.W. KISSINGER'S GRAND DESIGN. WASHINGTON: AMERICAN ENTERPRISE INSTITUTE FOR PUBLIC POLICY RESEARCH, 1975, PP. 110.

A BRIEF DISCUSSION OF KISSINGER'S POLICIES FOLLOWED BY COPIOUS QUOTATIONS FROM HIS PUBLIC STATEMENTS.

1293 "ON NIXON APPOINTMENTS (TO THE EXECUTIVE OFFICE OF THE PRESIDENT AND THE VARIOUS EXECUTIVE DEPARTMENTS)." CONG Q W REPT 27 (JANUARY 31, 1969): 191-196.

1294 PETERSON, R.W., ED. <u>AGNEW: THE COINING OF A HOUSEHOLD WORD</u>. NEW YORK: FACTS ON FILE, 1972, PP. 181.

FOLLOWS AGNEW FROM 1968 THROUGH 1971, REPRINTING SUMMARY NEWS REPORTS OF HIS ACTIONS AND PORTIONS OF HIS PUBLIC UTTERANCES.

1295 RASKIN, A.H. "SAID NIXON TO GEORGE SHULTZ: 'I TRACK WELL WITH YOU.'" <u>N Y TIMES MAG</u> (AUG. 30, 1970): 24-25+.

1296 REEVES, R. "NIXON'S MEN ARE SMART BUT NO SWINGERS." <u>N Y TIMES MAG</u> (SEPTEMBER 29, 1968): 28-29+.

1297 ROSEN, G.R. "WATCH PETER FLANAGAN." <u>DUN'S R</u> 98 (JULY 1971): 28-31+.

"THE PRESIDENT'S LINK TO THE BUSINESS COMMUNITY IS A FORMER WALL STREET INVESTMENT BANKER WHO IS NOW 'THE MAN TO KNOW' IN THE WHITE HOUSE."

1298 SAFIRE, W. <u>BEFORE THE FALL: AN INSIDE VIEW OF THE PRE-WATERGATE WHITE HOUSE</u>. NEW YORK: DOUBLEDAY, 1975, PP. 704.

A SYMPATHETIC YET OBJECTIVE PORTRAYAL OF THE HUMAN SIDE OF NIXON'S WHITE HOUSE.

1299 ----------. "WHO'S WHAT AROUND THE WHITE HOUSE; LET HENRY AND AL AND GEORGE AND MEL DO IT." <u>N Y TIMES MAG</u> (NOV 11, 1973): 38-39+.

1300 SCHLAFLY, P., AND WARD, C. <u>KISSINGER ON THE COUCH</u>. NEW YORK: ARLINGTON HOUSE, 1975, PP. 846.

A CONSERVATIVE CRITIQUE OF KISSINGER'S STATECRAFT, ESPECIALLY WITH RESPECT TO HIS VIEWS ABOUT NUCLEAR STRATEGY.

1301 SCHOENFELD, A.F. "MRS. KNAUER, CONSUMER ENVOY--BOTH FOR AND TO THE WHITE HOUSE." <u>NATIONAL J</u> 2 (1970):90-98.

"MRS. KNAUER FACES A HOST OF INHIBITIONS INHERENT ... IN HER CAPACITY AS THE PRESIDENT'S ADVISER ON CONSUMER AFFAIRS."

1302 SEMPLE, R.B. "THE MIDDLE AMERICAN WHO EDITS IDEAS FOR NIXON." <u>N Y TIMES MAG</u> (APR. 12, 1970): 32-33+.

1303 SOBEL, L.A., ED. <u>KISSINGER AND DETENTE</u>. NEW YORK: FACTS ON FILE, 1975, PP. 202.

LARGELY REPRINTS THE WEEKLY, CHRONOLOGICAL <u>FACTS ON FILE</u>
NEWS SUMMARIES ON THIS TOPIC.

1304 SZULC, T. "HOW KISSINGER DID IT; BEHIND THE VIETNAM
CEASE-FIRE AGREEMENT." <u>FOREIGN POLICY</u> (SUMMER 1974):
21-69.

1305 "THE PRESIDENT'S CABINET." <u>CONG Q W REPT</u> (DEC 30, 1972):
3211+.

1306 "THE WHITE HOUSE PERSUADERS: TIMMONS AND HIS TEAM." <u>CONG
Q W REPT</u> (DEC. 1, 1973): 3122-3128.

DISCUSSES THE "PRESIDENT'S LOBBYISTS"(THE CONGRESSIONAL
LIAISON MEN), WILLIAM TIMMONS, MAX FRIEDERSDORF AND TOM
KOROLOGOS, AND THE ROLES THEY PLAY IN ATTEMPTING TO
PERSUADE CONGRESS TO VOTE THE WAY THE PRESIDENT WANTS.

1307 VIORST, M. "WILLIAM ROGERS THINKS LIKE RICHARD NIXON." <u>N
Y TIMES MAG</u> (FEB. 27, 1972): 12-13, 30-38.

"ROGERS HAS BEEN A GOOD AND VALUED FRIEND OF THE PRESIDENT
FAR LONGER THAN ANY OF THE OTHER MEN WHO SURROUND HIM AS
POLICY ADVISERS."

1308 WALLEN, H. "PAT BUCHANAN GETS IT RIGHT." <u>POTOMAC (WASH
POST MAG)</u> (DEC. 9, 1973): 12-13+.

1309 WALTERS, R. "WHAT DID ZIEGLER SAY, AND WHEN DID HE SAY
IT?" <u>COLUMBIA JOURNALISM R</u> 13 (SEPT-OCT 1974): 30-35.

EIGHT TECHNIQUES USED BY PRESS SPOKESMEN FOR THE WHITE
HOUSE TO FRUSTRATE QUERIES ON WATERGATE.

1310 WARD, D. "KISSINGER: A PSYCHOHISTORY." <u>J HISTORY OF
CHILDHOOD</u> 23 (1975):287-384.

1311 WATERS, C. "THE AGONY OF EGIL KROGH." <u>WASHINGTONIAN</u> 9
(MAY 1974): 60-67.

1312 WISE, D. "THE DEFENDING OF THE PRESIDENT." <u>N Y TIMES MAG</u>
(MAY 26, 1974): 10-11+.

FOCUSES ON 4 OF THE PRESIDENT'S DEFENDERS AND AIDES IN THE
IMPEACHMENT AND WATERGATE INVESTIGATIONS.

1313 WITCOVER, J. <u>WHITE KNIGHT: THE RISE OF SPIRO AGNEW</u>. NEW
YORK: RANDOM HOUSE, 1972. PP. 465.

1314 ----------. "THE TWO HATS OF HERBERT KLEIN." COLUMBIA
JOURNALISM R 9 (SPRING 1971): 26-30.

"CRITICIZING THE ADMINISTRATION'S COMMUNICATIONS DIRECTOR
IS UNFASHIONABLE, BUT HIS DUAL ROLE APPEARS TO INVOLVE
INHERENTLY CONFLICTING INTERESTS."

1315 ZUMWALT, E.R. ON WATCH: A MEMOIR. NEW YORK: QUADRANGLE,
1976, PP. 568.

ON ADMIRAL ZUMWALT'S SERVICE AS CHIEF OF NAVAL OPERATIONS
DURING THE NIXON ADMINISTRATION, HIS EFFORTS TO REFORM THE
NAVY, AND "NAVIGATE THE BUREAUCRATIC MAZES OF WASHINGTON."

SEE ALSO 89, 1221, 1322, 1338, 1351, 1355, 1357, 1367,
1370, 1389, 1400, 1428, 1429, 1627, 1715, 1788, 1792,
2004, 2013, 2016, 2432

F. SPECIFIC EVENTS, ACTIVITIES AND POLICIES

1. DOMESTIC

1316 BALZ, D.J. "JOCKEYING FOR TOP POSITION COMPLICATES
ECONOMIC POLICY MAKING." NATIONAL J 6 (1974):1027-1037.

"...THE STRUGGLE (BY SIMON AND ASH) TO BE FIRST AMONG
EQUALS IN GIVING MR. NIXON POLICY ADVICE HAS LED TO WHAT
ONE ADMINISTRATION OFFICIAL CALLED OUTRAGEOUS STATEMENTS
THAT TEND TO CREATE CONFUSION ABOUT THE ECONOMIC POLICIES
COURSE THE FEDERAL GOVERNMENT WILL FOLLOW."

1317 BARFIELD, C.E. "NIXON REORGANIZATION RAISES QUESTIONS
ABOUT ROLE OF SCIENCE IN FEDERAL POLICY-MAKING." NATIONAL
J 5 (1973):405-415.

"AT A TIME WHEN SCIENTIFIC AND TECHNOLOGICAL JUDGMENTS ARE
INCREASINGLY IMPORTANT TO PUBLIC POLICY DECISIONS,
PRESIDENT NIXON HAS ABOLISHED THE INSTITUTIONS ESTABLISHED
OVER THE PAST 15 YEARS TO PROVIDE THE WHITE HOUSE WITH
EXPERT ADVICE FROM TOP SCIENTISTS AND ENGINEERS."

1318 ----------. "PRESIDENTIAL REVAMPING OF SCIENCE TASKS
UPGRADES NATIONAL SCIENCE FOUNDATION ROLE." NATIONAL J 5
(1973):460-466.

QUESTIONS WHETHER THE NSF, "A SECOND LINE AGENCY THAT HAS
BEEN PRIMARILY DISPENSER OF GRANTS," WILL BE ABLE TO TAKE
ON THE ROLE OF OVERALL GOVERNMENTAL SCIENCE ADVISING
ASSIGNED TO IT UNDER THE NIXON REORGANIZATION.

1319 BOCK, E.A. POLITICAL EXECUTIVES AND THE WHITE HOUSE:
DRAFTING THE URBAN MASS TRANSIT ACT OF 1970.
INTER-UNIVERSITY CASE PROGRAM: BOX 229, SYRACUSE, N.Y.,
1976.

1320 BONAFEDE, D. "AGENCIES RESIST NIXON DIRECTIVE TO CUT BACK
SPENDING ON PUBLIC RELATIONS." NATIONAL J 3
(1971):1551-1556.

"A NUMBER OF FEDERAL DEPARTMENTS AND AGENCIES ARE IGNORING
OR CIRCUMVENTING A YEAR-OLD PRESIDENTIAL DIRECTIVE TO
CURTAIL PUBLIC RELATIONS SPENDING."

1321 ----------. "BUREAUCRACY, CONGRESS, INTERESTS SEE THREAT
IN NIXON REORGANIZATION PLAN." NATIONAL J 3 (MAY 8,
1971): 977-986.

"PRESIDENT NIXON'S PROPOSAL TO REORGANIZE THE EXECUTIVE
BRANCH ACCORDING TO FUNCTION AND GOAL RATHER THAN PROGRAM
IS STRONGLY OPPOSED BY SOME POWERFUL MEMBERS OF CONGRESS,
PRIVATE INTEREST GROUPS AND MANY OF THE FEDERAL AGENCIES
THAT WOULD BE REORGANIZED."

1322 ----------. "NIXON PERSONNEL STAFF WORKS TO RESTRUCTURE
FEDERAL POLICIES." NATIONAL J 3 (1971): 2440-2448.

ON NIXON'S EFFORT TO REORGANIZE THE EXECUTIVE BRANCH AND
MAKE IT MORE RESPONSIVE TO WHITE HOUSE LEADERSHIP.

1323 ----------. "PRESIDENT NIXON'S EXECUTIVE REORGANIZATION
PLANS PROMPT PRAISE AND CRITICISM." NATIONAL J 5
(1973):329-344.

1324 BONAFEDE, D., AND ALLIN, L. "PRESIDENT'S NEWS DIGEST IS A
POTPOURRI IN TWO DAILY DOSES." NATIONAL J 6 (JAN 1974):
131-136.

1325 BONAFEDE, D., AND COTTIN, J. "NIXON, IN REORGANIZATION
PLAN, SEEKS TIGHTER REIN ON BUREAUCRACY." NATIONAL J 2
(1970):620-626.

1326 BOWLER, M.K. THE NIXON GUARANTEED INCOME PROPOSAL.
CAMBRIDGE: BALLINGER PUBLISHING COMPANY, 1974, PP. 201.

1327 BUCHANAN, P.J. THE NEW MAJORITY: PRESIDENT NIXON AT
MID-PASSAGE. PHILADELPHIA: GIRARD BANK, 1973, PP. 79.

1328 BURBY, J.F. "NO LETUP FOR PRESIDENT'S ECONOMIC ADVISORS
DESPITE GOOD SECOND QUARTER." NATIONAL J 4
(1972):1279-1288.

ON THE ROLE OF HERBERT STEIN, CHAIRMAN OF THE PRESIDENT'S

COUNCIL OF ECONOMIC ADVISERS, IN PRESSING FOR A "TIGHT-FISTED" ADMINISTRATION POLICY TOWARD GOVERNMENTAL SPENDING.

1329 ----------. "PRESIDENT'S BUDGET REQUESTS SEEK TO RESHAPE DOMESTIC GOVERNMENT." NATIONAL J 5 (1973):139-145.

AN ANALYSIS OF THE CONTENT AND POLICY-MAKING BACKGROUND OF PRESIDENT NIXON'S FISCAL YEAR 1974 BUDGET, STRESSING THE ROLE OF CASPER W. WEINBERGER AND GEORGE P. SHULTZ AS BUDGET-DRAFTERS.

1330 ----------. "WHITE HOUSE SEES FIGHT TO CURB SPENDING AS BOTH GOOD POLITICS AND GOOD ECONOMICS." NATIONAL J 4 (1972):1313-1322.

ON THE STRUGGLE BETWEEN PRESIDENT NIXON AND CONGRESSIONAL LEADERS OVER THE NIXON ADMINISTRATION'S EFFORT TO IMPOSE A CEILING ON GOVERNMENT SPENDING FOR FISCAL YEAR 1973.

1331 BURKE, V., AND BURKE, V. NIXON'S GOOD DEED: WELFARE REFORM AND SUPPLEMENTAL SECURITY INCOME. NEW YORK: COLUMBIA UNIVERSITY PRESS, 1974, PP. 243.

1332 CHADWIN, M.L. "NIXON'S EXPROPRIATION POLICY SEEKS TO SOOTHE ANGRY CONGRESS." NATIONAL J 4 (1972):148-156.

ON PRESIDENTIAL-CONGRESSIONAL NEGOTIATIONS ABOUT THE APPROPRIATE AMERICAN RESPONSES TO FOREIGN NATIONS THAT EXPROPRIATE AMERICAN INDUSTRIES.

1333 CLARK, T.B., IGLEHART, J.K., AND LILLEY, W., III. "NEW FEDERALISM REPORT." NATIONAL J 4 (1972): 1908-1940.

1334 CURRIGAN, R. "OFFSHORE ISLAND FOR GIANT OIL TANKERS GAINING FAVOR OF WHITE HOUSE STAFF." NATIONAL J 49 (1971):2389-2398.

THE EFFORTS OF A "HIGH-LEVEL WHITE HOUSE GROUP" TO DEVISE TECHNOLOGICAL PROCEDURES THAT WOULD ALLOW OIL SUPERTANKERS TOO BIG FOR U.S. PORTS TO DELIVER OIL TO MAN-MADE OFF-SHORE ISLANDS.

1335 COTTIN, J. "ASH COUNCIL, GOVERNORS FAULT NIXON'S INTERGOVERNMENTAL RELATIONS OFFICE." NATIONAL J 4 (1971):182-185.

"SOME OF THE NATION'S GOVERNORS AND THE PRESIDENT'S INFLUENTIAL ASH COUNCIL ARE DISSATISFIED WITH THE PERFORMANCE OF THE OFFICE CREATED TO BRIDGE THE GAP BETWEEN FEDERAL AND STATE AND LOCAL GOVERNMENTS."

1336 DEWITT, K. "ADMINISTRATION TASK FORCE DEVELOPS PLANS TO OVERHAUL THE WELFARE SYSTEM." NATIONAL J 5 (1973):1315-1320.

ON THE ADMINISTRATION'S READINESS TO THREATEN TO USE THE VETO TO BLOCK ALL SCHOOL AID UNLESS ITS REQUEST FOR SPECIAL EDUCATIONAL REVENUE WAS APPROVED BY CONGRESS.

1337 DOCTORS, S.I., AND HUFF, A.S. MINORITY ENTERPRISE AND THE PRESIDENT'S COUNCIL. CAMBRIDGE, MASS.: BALLINGER, 1973, PP. 201.

A CASE-STUDY OF THE NIXON ADMINISTRATION'S ATTEMPT TO IMPLEMENT "BLACK CAPITALISM." DOCTORS PLAYED A PART IN THE SPECIAL PRESIDENTIAL COMMISSION SET UP FOR THAT PURPOSE. INCLUDES REMARKS ON THE JOB OF ADVISING COUNCILS IN GENERAL, AND ON THE ACTIVITIES OF THE PRESIDENT'S ADVISORY COUNCIL ON MINORITY BUSINESS ENTERPRISE.

1338 FOWLKES, F.V., AND HAVEMANN, J. "PRESIDENT FORMS FEDERAL ENERGY BODY WITH BROAD REGULATION, PRICE CONTROL POWERS." NATIONAL J 5 (1973):1830-1838.

"TO COPE WITH THE PETROLEUM SHORTAGE, PRESIDENT NIXON CONSOLIDATED SEVERAL FEDERAL ENERGY OFFICES INTO A FEDERAL ENERGY ADMINISTRATION."

1339 FOX, D.M., ED. "PRESIDENT NIXON'S PROPOSALS FOR EXECUTIVE REORGANIZATION: A MINI-SYMPOSIUM." PUBLIC ADMINISTRATION R 33 (SEPT.-OCT. 1973): 487-495 AND 34 (SEPT.-OCT. 1974): 487-495.

INCLUDES COMMENTS BY ALAN L. DEAN, HAROLD SEIDMAN, HARVEY MANSFIELD, JAMES FESLER, AND ROBERT GILMOUR CONCERNING NIXON'S PROPOSALS.

1340 GLASS, A.J. "CONGRESS WEIGHS NOVEL PROCEDURES TO OVERTURN NIXON IMPOUNDMENT POLICY." NATIONAL J 5 (1973):236-242.

1341 HAVEMANN, J. "CONGRESS AND COURTS BOOST BUDGET, REBUFF NIXON'S COST-CUTTING METHODS." NATIONAL J 5 (1973):1277-1286.

COURT DECISIONS AGAINST IMPOUNDMENT OF FUNDS, INFLATION, AND CONGRESSIONAL RESISTANCE HAVE HAMPERED PRESIDENTIAL EFFORTS TO REDUCE SPENDING IM FISCAL 1974.

1342 ----------. "REVENUE SHARING PLAN LIKELY TO BE EXTENDED, CHANGED." NATIONAL J 6 (1974):1074-1082.

ON DIFFERENCES BETWEEN A COALITION OF STATE AND LOCAL OFFICIALS AND ADMINISTRATION LEADERS AND "CONGRESSIONAL DOUBTERS" OVER THE NIXON REVENUE SHARING PROGRAM.

1343 IGLEHART, J.K. "GOVERNORS LOSE ENTHUSIASM FOR NIXON'S REVENUE-SHARING PROGRAMS." NATIONAL J 5 (1973):935-943.

"MANY OF THE NATION'S GOVERNORS HAVE SOURED ON PRESIDENT

NIXON'S CONCEPT OF A "NEW FEDERALISM"." BASED ON INTERVIEWS WITH GOVERNORS.

1344 IGLEHART, J.K., LILLEY, W., III, AND CLARK, T.B. "BUDGET STRAINS ALLIANCE BETWEEN NIXON AND STATE-LOCAL OFFICIALS." NATIONAL J 5 (1973):215-225.

"THE LOOSE ALLIANCE PRESIDENT NIXON BUILT WITH GOVERNORS, MAYORS, AND COUNTY EXECUTIVES IN SUPPORT OF HIS NEW FEDERALISM REVENUE-SHARING PROGRAM IS SHOWING SIGNS OF STRAIN OVER THE FACTS OF THE FISCAL 1974 BUDGET."

1345 IGLEHART, J.K., ROBINSON, J., SCHOENFELD, A.F., AND WILLINGHAM, E. "HEW'S AGENCY HEADS GAIN POWER AS NIXON PHILOSOPHY BRINGS TURMOIL AND CHANGE." NATIONAL J 2 (1970):2036-2051.

ON THE EFFECT OF THE NIXON ADMINISTRATION'S POLICIES AND HEW SECRETARY RICHARDSON'S PHILOSOPHY ON THIS "TURBULENT DEPARTMENT AND ITS 7 AGENCIES."

1346 LANZILLOTTI, R.F., HAMILTON, M.T., AND ROBERTS, R.B. PHASE II IN REVIEW: THE PRICE COMMISSION EXPERIENCE. WASHINGTON, D.C.: BROOKINGS, 1975. PP. 209.

1347 LILLEY, W., III. "HOSTILE COMMITTEE CHAIRMEN, LOBBIES PLEDGE FIGHT AGAINST REORGANIZATION PLAN." NATIONAL J (OCT. 16, 1971): 2072-2081.

1348 ----------. "NIXON INROADS AMONG DEMOCRATIC MAYORS WEAKEN PARTY'S OLD COALITION." NATIONAL J (JULY 15, 1972): 1143-1150.

"IN-DEPTH INTERVIEWS WITH 38 MAYORS DISCLOSED A SURPRISING DEGREE OF SUPPORT AMONG DEMOCRATS FOR PRESIDENT NIXON'S URBAN POLICIES."

1349 MILLER, R.L., AND WILLIAMS, R.M. THE NEW ECONOMICS OF RICHARD NIXON: FREEZES, FLOATS, AND FISCAL POLICY. NEW YORK: HARPER'S MAGAZINE PRESS, 1972. PP. 88.

1350 MITCHELL, C. "MOODS AND CHANGES: THE CIVIL RIGHTS RECORD OF THE NIXON ADMINISTRATION." NOTRE DAME LAWYER 49 (OCT. 1973): 63-77.

1351 MITCHELL, D.J.B., AND WEBER, A.R. "WAGES AND THE PAY BOARD." AMER ECON ASSOC 64 (MAY 1974): 88-92.

1352 MOYNIHAN, D.P. THE POLITICS OF A GUARANTEED INCOME: THE

NIXON ADMINISTRATION AND THE FAMILY ASSISTANCE PLAN. NEW
YORK: RANDOM HOUSE, 1973, PP. 579.

1353 MURPHY, R., AND GULLIVER, H. THE SOUTHERN STRATEGY. NEW
YORK: SCRIBNER, 1971, PP. 273.

1354 NATHAN, R. THE PLOT THAT FAILED: NIXON AND THE
ADMINISTRATIVE PRESIDENCY. NEW YORK: WILEY, 1975, PP.
193.

NIXON'S EFFORTS TO COPE WITH LONG-RUN DOMESTIC PROBLEMS BY
EXERCISING TIGHTER CONTROL OVER THE BUREAUCRACY,
PARTICULARLY WITH RESPECT TO "THE NEW FEDERALISM." NATHAN
WAS DEPUTY UNDER SECRETARY OF HEW AND ASSISTANT DIRECTOR
OF OMB 1969 TO 1971.

1355 NICHOLAS, H.G. "THE INSULATION OF THE PRESIDENCY."
GOVERNMENT AND OPPOSITION 8 (1973):156-176.

THE INCREASING ISOLATION OF PRESIDENTS SINCE EISENHOWER
RESULTS FROM CHANGES IN PRESIDENTIAL RELATIONS WITH PARTY,
CONGRESS AND CABINET AND IN THE DEVELOPMENT OF THE WHITE
HOUSE STAFF AND TREATMENT OF THE MASS MEDIA.

1356 ORR, S.C. "NATIONAL SECURITY COUNCIL NETWORK GIVES WHITE
HOUSE TIGHT REIN OVER SALT STRATEGY." NATIONAL J 3
(1971):877-886.

1357 PANETTA, L.E. BRING US TOGETHER: THE NIXON TEAM AND THE
CIVIL RIGHTS RETREAT. PHILADELPHIA: LIPPINCOTT, 1971, PP.
380.

1358 PHILLIPS, J.G. "FEDERAL BUDGET CUTS TURN MAYORS AGAINST
ADMINISTRATION REVENUE-SHARING PLANS." NATIONAL J 5
(1973):1099-1108.

INTERVIEWS WITH 41 MAYORS SHOW THEIR DISAFFECTION WITH THE
NIXON ADMINISTRATION BECAUSE OF ITS POLICY OF CUTTING
DOMESTIC FUNDING PROGRAMS.

1359 REAGAN, M. THE NEW FEDERALISM. NEW YORK: OXFORD
UNIVERSITY PRESS, 1972, PP.175.

CRITICAL OF REVENUE SHARING FROM A LIBERAL PERSPECTIVE.

1360 SEYMOUR, W.N., JR. UNITED STATES ATTORNEY. AN INSIDE VIEW
OF "JUSTICE" IN AMERICA UNDER THE NIXON ADMINISTRATION.
NEW YORK: MORROW, 1975, PP. 248.

1361 SHEAHAN, J. THE WAGE PRICE GUIDEPOSTS. WASHINGTON, D.C.: BROOKINGS, 1972, PP. 219.

1362 SILK, L.S. NIXONOMICS. NEW YORK: PRAEGER, 1973, PP. 224.

A REVIEW OF NIXON'S ECONOMIC POLICY BY A NEW YORK TIMES FINANCIAL CORRESPONDENT.

1363 SMITH, L. "PRESIDENT NIXON'S REGULATORY APPOINTMENTS." PUB UTILITIES FORTNIGHTLY (DEC. 9, 1971): 34-39.

1364 SOBEL, L.A., ED. INFLATION AND THE NIXON ADMINISTRATION: VOL I, 1969-71; VOL II, 1972-74. NEW YORK: FACTS ON FILE, 1974-75, PP. 635.

UNDER SEVERAL HEADINGS, THIS WORK REPRINTS THE WEEKLY FACTS ON FILE NEWS SUMMARIES ON THIS TOPIC.

1365 WEBER, A.R. IN PURSUIT OF PRICE STABILITY: THE WAGE-PRICE FREEZE OF 1971. WASHINGTON, D.C.: BROOKINGS, 1973, PP. 137.

A CASE STUDY OF "PHASE ONE" OF WAGE AND PRICE CONTROLS BY ONE OF THE KEY OFFICIALS INVOLVED IN FRAMING AND IMPLEMENTING THE POLICY.

SEE ALSO 86, 92, 96, 97, 105, 122, 160, 433, 864, 1260, 1276, 1336, 1352, 1427, 1469, 1727, 1745, 1854, 1892, 2004, 2013, 2016, 2287, 2291, 2297

2. FOREIGN AND NATIONAL SECURITY

1366 BENDER, J.C. "SELF-DEFENSE AND CAMBODIA: A CRITICAL APPRAISAL." BOSTON UNIVERSITY LAW R 50 (1970):130-139.

1367 BRENNER, M.J. "THE PROBLEM OF INNOVATION AND THE NIXON-KISSINGER FOREIGN POLICY." INTERNATIONAL STUDIES Q 17 (SEPT 1973): 255-294.

1368 BRZEZINSKI, Z. "HALF PAST NIXON." FOREIGN POLICY 3 (SUMMER 1971): 3-21.

CONCLUDES THAT NIXON DOCTRINE PRIORITIES ARE RIGHT BUT THAT THERE IS AN EXTREMELY LIMITED INTEREST IN THE THIRD WORLD.

1369 CHACE, J. "FIVE-POWER WORLD OF RICHARD NIXON." N Y TIMES MAG (FEBRUARY 20, 1972):14-15+.

1370 DESTLER, I.M. "THE NIXON SYSTEM, A FURTHER LOOK." FOR

SERVICE J 51 (FEB. 1974): 9-15, 28-29.

ON THE NIXON-KISSINGER PERFORMANCE IN FOREIGN POLICY. THEIR "CLOSED POLICY-MAKING APPROACH SEEMS EFFECTIVE ONLY IN A VERY LIMITED RANGE OF FOREIGN POLICY SITUATIONS." EXAMINES WHETHER THE DESIGNATION OF HENRY KISSINGER AS SECRETARY OF STATE BROUGHT ABOUT CHANGES IN THE MAKING OF NIXON ADMINISTRATION FOREIGN POLICY.

1371 FOX, D.T. THE CAMBODIAN INCURSION: LEGAL ISSUES. DOBBS FERRY, N.Y.: OCEANA, 1971, PP. 89.

1372 GARDNER, L.C., ED. THE GREAT NIXON TURNAROUND: AMERICA'S NEW FOREIGN POLICY IN THE POST-LIBERAL ERA (HOW A COLD WARRIOR CLIMBED CLEAN OUT OF HIS SKIN). NEW YORK: NEW VIEWPOINTS, 1973, PP. 350.

ESSAYS ON NIXON'S SHIFT ONCE IN OFFICE FROM HIS LONG-TERM ANTI-COMMUNISM TO A POLICY OF RAPPROCHEMENT WITH THE U.S.S.R. AND CHINA.

1373 GARRETT, S.A. "NIXONIAN FOREIGN POLICY: A NEW BALANCE OF POWER—OR A REVIVED CONCERT?" POLITY 8 (SPRING 1976): 389-421.

1374 HAHN, W.F. "THE NIXON DOCTRINE: DESIGN AND DILEMMAS." ORBIS 16 (SUMMER 1972): 361-376.

THE NIXON DOCTRINE SIGNALS AN ADJUSTMENT OF AMERICAN POLICY TO PROFOUND GLOBAL CHANGES.

1375 HUBBELL, J.G. "PRESIDENT NIXON, CAMBODIA AND NEW CHANCES FOR PEACE." READER'S DIGEST 97 (JULY 1970): 54-63.

"A BEHIND-THE-SCENE REPORT ON THE EVENTS AND REASONS THAT LED THE PRESIDENT TO HIS MOMENTOUS DECISION TO STRIKE AT NORTH VIETNAM'S MILITARY SANCTUARIES IN CAMBODIA."

1376 KAPLAN, M.A., ET AL. VIETNAM SETTLEMENT: WHY 1973, NOT 1969?(DEBATE). WASHINGTON, D.C.: AMERICAN ENTERPRISE INSTITUTE FOR PUBLIC POLICY RESEARCH, 1973, PP. 208.

A 3-PART, ORIGINALLY TELEVISED DEBATE ON THE TOPIC.

1377 MAFFRE, J. "SENATE ATTEMPTS TO LIMIT PRESIDENT'S POWER TO MAKE WAR." NATIONAL J 4 (1972): 443-450.

1378 MAXEY, D.R. "HOW NIXON DECIDED TO INVADE CAMBODIA." LOOK 34 (AUG. 11, 1970): 22-28.

1379 OSGOOD, R.E., ET AL. RETREAT FROM EMPIRE? THE FIRST NIXON

ADMINISTRATION. BALTIMORE: JOHNS HOPKINS PRESS, 1973, PP. 350.

1380 PORTER, G. A PEACE DENIED: THE UNITED STATES, VIETNAM AND THE PARIS AGREEMENT. BLOOMINGTON: INDIANA U PR, 1976, PP. 416.

1381 ROBERTS, C. "FOREIGN POLICY UNDER A PARALYZED PRESIDENCY." FOREIGN AFFAIRS 52 (JULY 1974): 675-689.

ON WHETHER WATERGATE WAS AFFECTING "BOTH THE SUBSTANCE AND CONDUCT OF U.S. FOREIGN POLICY AND WHETHER, AND IF SO TO WHAT DEGREE, OTHER NATIONS MAY HAVE ALTERED, OR PLAN TO ALTER, THEIR POSTURES TOWARD AND DEALINGS WITH WASHINGTON."

1382 SMITH, R.H. "THE PRESIDENTIAL DECISION ON THE CAMBODIAN OPERATION." AIR U R 22 (SEPT-OCT 1971): 45-53.

DISCUSSES MILITARY AND POLITICAL CONSIDERATIONS WHICH SEEMED TO INDICATE THE ADVISABILITY OF ACTION.

1383 "SYMPOSIUM ON THE UNITED STATES MILITARY ACTION IN CAMBODIA." AMER J OF INTERNAT LAW 65 (JAN 1971): 1-83.

CONTENTS INCLUDE "THE CAMBODIAN OPERATION AND INTERNATIONAL LAW," BY R. FALK; "THE CONSTITUTIONALITY OF THE CAMBODIAN INCURSION," BY W. ROGERS; "LEGAL DIMENSIONS OF THE DECISION TO INTERVENE IN CAMBODIA," BY J. MOORE.

1384 "UNITED STATES INTERVENTION IN CAMBODIA: LEGAL ANALYSES OF THE EVENT AND ITS DOMESTIC REPERCUSSIONS." BOSTON UNIVERSITY LAW R (SPRING 1970): WHOLE ISSUE.

1385 VAN DER LINDEN, F. NIXON'S QUEST FOR PEACE. WASHINGTON, D.C.: R.B. LUCE, 1972, PP. 247.

A SYMPATHETIC ACCOUNT OF NIXON'S FOREIGN POLICY UP TO THE TIME OF HIS TRIP TO CHINA BY A WHITE HOUSE CORRESPONDENT. BASED ON INTERVIEWS WITH ADMINISTRATION POLICY-MAKERS.

SEE ALSO 87, 88, 89, 93, 95, 100, 101, 102, 727, 1286, 1292, 1303, 1304, 1379, 1385, 1614, 1627, 1739, 1892, 2060, 2075, 2160

3. WATERGATE IMPEACHMENT PROCEEDINGS AND RESIGNATION

1386 AMERICAN CIVIL LIBERTIES UNION, THE. WHY PRESIDENT NIXON SHOULD BE IMPEACHED. WASHINGTON, D.C.: PUBLIC AFFAIRS PRESS, 1974, PP. 56.

1387 BELLUSH, J., AND WALLING, A. "WATERGATE: A PRELIMINARY BIBLIOGRAPHY." NATIONAL CIVIC R 63 (FEB 1974): 110-114.

SELECTED, PARTIALLY ANNOTATED BIBLIOGRAPHY IS DIVIDED INTO AN OVERVIEW, CIVIL LIBERTIES AND THE RULE OF LAW, IMPEACHMENT, THE ELECTION PROCESS, AND THE CONCENTRATION OF PRESIDENTIAL POWER.

1388 BERGER, R., ET AL. "SYMPOSIUM: UNITED STATES V. NIXON." UCLA LAW R 22 (1974):4-140.

1389 BERNSTEIN, C., AND WOODWARD, B. ALL THE PRESIDENT'S MEN. NEW YORK: SIMON & SCHUSTER, 1974, PP. 349.

REPORT BY THE WELL-KNOWN WASHINGTON POST REPORTORIAL TEAM OF THEIR EFFORTS TO DISCOVER WHO ORDERED THE WATERGATE BREAK-IN.

1390 BICKEL, A.M. "WATERGATE AND THE LEGAL ORDER." COMMENTARY 57 (1974):19-25.

1391 BONAFEDE, D. "ADMINISTRATION TRIES PUBLIC RELATIONS TO REESTABLISH IMAGE AND PROMOTE ITS EFFORTS." NATIONAL J 5 (JUNE 1973): 908-912.

"HOW THE WHITE HOUSE EXERCISES CENTRALIZED CONTROL OVER THE GOVERNMENT'S PRESS AND INFORMATION OPERATIONS," WITH SPECIAL EMPHASIS ON EFFORTS TO ELIMINATE THE "PUBLIC RELATIONS" DAMAGE OF WATERGATE.

1392 ----------. "NIXON LEGAL DEFENSE INCREASES OFFICE COSTS, STAFF." NATIONAL J 6 (JUNE 1974): 976-977.

1393 CARALEY, D., ET AL. "AMERICAN POLITICAL INSTITUTIONS AFTER WATERGATE--A DISCUSSION." PSQ 89 (WINTER 1974-75): 713-749.

TRANSCRIPT OF DISCUSSION BETWEEN THE EDITOR--CARALEY--AND EIGHT MEMBERS OF THE POLITICAL SCIENCE QUARTERLY EDITORIAL ADVISORY BOARD.

1394 CHAFFEE, S.H., ED. "THE WATERGATE EXPERIENCE." AMER POL Q 3 (OCT 1975): 355-472.

1395 CHESTER, L., MCCRYSTAL, C., ET AL. WATERGATE: THE FULL INSIDE STORY NEW YORK: BALLANTINE, 1973, PP. 280.

A RAPIDLY PACED JOURNALISTIC ACCOUNT WRITTEN ORIGINALLY FOR A BRITISH AUDIENCE.

1396 CHURCH, F. "THE WATERGATE FALLOUT." WORLD STUDIES 1 (SPRING 1974): 27-55.

WATERGATE RESULTS FROM THE EXTRA-CONSTITUTIONAL EXPANSION OF PRESIDENTIAL WAR AND EMERGENCY POWERS.

1397 COMMAGER, H.S. "THE PRESIDENCY AFTER WATERGATE." NEW YORK REVIEW OF BOOKS 20 (OCT. 18, 1973):49-53.

INQUIRES INTO THE PRESIDENCY IN THE CONSTITUTIONAL SETTING. ARGUES THAT FROM THE BEGINNING THE POWERS OF THE OFFICE HAVE BEEN INADEQUATELY AND THEREFORE DANGEROUSLY DEFINED.

1398 COX, A. "SOME REFLECTIONS ON POSSIBLE ABUSES OF GOVERNMENTAL POWER." RECORD OF THE BAR OF THE CITY OF NEW YORK 28 (DEC. 1973): 811-827.

FORMER SPECIAL PROSECUTOR DISCUSSES HIS INVESTIGATION OF THE WATERGATE AFFAIR AND RECOMMENDS MEASURES FOR ENSURING THAT THE INQUIRY IS CARRIED TO A SUCCESSFUL CONCLUSION.

1399 DASH, S. CHIEF COUNSEL: INSIDE THE ERVIN COMMITTEE--THE UNTOLD STORY OF WATERGATE. NEW YORK: RANDOM, 1976, PP. 275.

ACTIVITIES OF SENATE WATERGATE COMMITTEE DESCRIBED BY ITS MAJORITY COUNSEL.

1400 DEAN, J.W., III. BLIND AMBITION: THE WHITE HOUSE YEARS. NEW YORK: SIMON AND SCHUSTER, 1976, PP. 415.

1401 DREW, E. WASHINGTON JOURNAL. THE EVENTS OF 1973-1974. NEW YORK: RANDOM, 1974, PP. 428.

A REFLECTIVE JOURNALIST'S DIARY OF THE MOOD AS WELL AS OF THE EVENTS ON CAPITOL HILL DURING THE PERIOD OF THE IMPEACHMENT HEARINGS AND THE MONTHS IMMEDIATELY PRECEDING THEM.

1402 DWORKIN, R. "THE JURISPRUDENCE OF RICHARD NIXON." N Y REVIEW OF BOOKS (MAY 4, 1972): 27-35.

DEALS WITH PRESIDENTIAL APPOINTMENTS, POLITICAL QUESTIONS AND JUDICIAL POWER.

1403 EDELSTEIN, A.S., AND TEFFT, D.P. "MEDIA CREDIBILITY AND RESPONDENT CREDULITY WITH RESPECT TO WATERGATE." COMMUNICATION RESEARCH 1 (OCT 1974): 426-439.

1404 EPSTEIN, E.J. "DID THE PRESS UNCOVER WATERGATE?" IN BETWEEN FACT AND FICTION: THE PROBLEM OF JOURNALISM.

NEW YORK: RANDOM, 1975, PP. 19-32.

1405 FAIRLIE, H. "THE LESSONS OF WATERGATE." ENCOUNTER
     (OCTOBER 1974): 8-26.

     DISCUSSES THE MEANING AND SIGNIFICANCE OF THE WATERGATE
     AFFAIR, FOCUSING ON THE ROLE OF MORALITY IN POLITICS.

1406 FINCH, G.B. "IMPEACHMENTS AND THE DYNAMICS OF PUBLIC
     OPINION: A COMMENT ON 'GUILTY, YES; IMPEACHMENT, NO'."
     PSQ 89 (1974):301-3249.

     THIS COMMENT ON MCGEEVER'S "'GUILTY YES; IMPEACHMENT NO':
     SOME EMPIRICAL FINDINGS" ADVANCES A "CROSS PRESSURES"
     THEORY OF WHY, AT THAT TIME, CITIZENS WHO DISAPPROVED OF
     NIXON'S BEHAVIOR NEVERTHELESS WERE SUFFICIENTLY FEARFUL OF
     THE UNSETTLING CONSEQUENCES OF AN IMPEACHMENT TO REACH THE
     CONCLUSION SUMMARIZED IN THE ARTICLE'S TITLE.

1407 FRIEDMAN, L., ED. UNITED STATES V. NIXON: THE PRESIDENT
     BEFORE THE SUPREME COURT. NEW YORK: CHELSEA HOUSE, 1974,
     PP. 619.

     REPRINTS THE DECISIONS, BRIEFS ON BOTH SIDES, AND ORAL
     ARGUMENTS TAKEN DIRECTLY FROM THE SPECIAL REPORT OF
     JOINT COMMITTEE ON GOVERNMENT OPERATIONS THAT CONTAINS THE
     SAME MATERIAL.

1408 GLASS, A.J. "WATERGATE DIMINISHES NIXON'S LEVERAGE, FORCES
     SERIES OF LEGISLATIVE COMPROMISES." NATIONAL J 5
     (1973):1049-1056.

     "THE SENATE IS ASSERTING FRESH AUTHORITY IN REVERSE RATIO
     TO THE PRESIDENT'S DROP IN PUBLIC APPROVAL. THE RESULT IS
     A GENERAL STALEMATE IN POLICY-MAKING INITIATIVES DURING
     THE UNFOLDING WATERGATE INVESTIGATION."

1409 GRAHAM, B. "WATERGATE." CHRISTIANITY TODAY (JAN. 4,
     1974): 8-10+.

     INTERVIEW WITH BILLY GRAHAM ON WATERGATE AND GRAHAM'S
     ASSOCIATION WITH PRESIDENT NIXON.

1410 GUNTHER, G. "JUDICIAL HEGEMONY AND LEGISLATIVE AUTONOMY:
     THE NIXON CASE AND THE IMPEACHMENT PROCESS." UCLA LAW R
     22 (1974):30-39.

     CONTENDS THAT IN U.S. V. NIXON, THE SUPREME COURT
     MANAGED TO OVER-SHADOW THE IMPEACHMENT PROCESS WHICH HAD
     BEEN, AND SHOULD HAVE CONTINUED TO BE, PRIMARY.

1411 HALPERN, P.J., ED. WHY WATERGATE?. PACIFIC PALISADES,
     CAL.: PALISADES PUBLISHERS, 1975, PP. 233.

     ANTHOLOGY OF BRIEF ITEMS ON WATERGATE AND PRESIDENCY
     GENERALLY. BIBLIOGRAPHY.

1412 HARWARD, D.W., ED. CRISIS IN CONFIDENCE: THE IMPACT OF

WATERGATE. BOSTON: LITTLE, BROWN AND COMPANY, 1974, PP. 200.

ADDRESSES GIVEN BY 16 NATIONAL LEADERS IN THE CONTEXT OF WATERGATE. INCLUDES, FOR EXAMPLE, SENATOR SAM ERVIN, JR., RAMSEY CLARK, AND DANIEL ELLSBERG.

1413 HENKIN, L. "EXECUTIVE PRIVILEGE: MR. NIXON LOSES BUT THE PRESIDENCY LARGELY PREVAILS." UCLA LAW R 22 (1974):40-46.

ARTICLE STATES THAT WHILE U.S. V. NIXON HAS PROVED TO BE OF MAJOR POLITICAL IMPORTANCE, ITS CONSTITUTIONAL SIGNIFICANCE IS "LESS OBVIOUS."

1414 HOLM, J., KRAUS, S., AND BOCHNER, A.P. "COMMUNICATION AND OPINION FORMATION: ISSUES GENERATED BY WATERGATE." COMMUNICATION RESEARCH 1 (OCT 1974): 368-390.

DURING THE WATERGATE HEARINGS "THE IMAGE OF THE MAJOR POLITICAL ACTOR INVOLVED (NIXON) CHANGED AMONG SOME IN THE PUBLIC TO A MORE NEGATIVE CHARACTER. SECOND, THOSE AFFECTED BECOME MORE INVOLVED IN DISCUSSIONS WITH PERSONS AROUND THEM. FINALLY, THAT DISCUSSION LEADS TO A CHANGE IN OPINION ON ISSUES GENERATED BY THE POLITICAL EVENT."

1415 HUGHES, E.J. "A WHITE HOUSE TAPED." N Y TIMES MAG 9 (JUNE 1974): 17+.

A FORMER EISENHOWER AIDE ANALYZES THE WATERGATE TAPE TRANSCRIPT AND FINDS THE NIXON WHITE HOUSE A "JOYLESS" AND "AIMLESS" PLACE, CHARACTERIZED BY A "FORTRESS SPIRIT" AND "SPIRITUAL BLEAKNESS."

1416 "IMPEACHMENT LOBBY: EMPHASIS ON GRASS-ROOTS PRESSURE." CONG Q W REPT (MAY 25, 1974): 1368-1373.

1417 JAWORSKI, L. THE RIGHT AND THE POWER: THE PROSECUTION OF WATERGATE. NEW YORK: READER'S DIGEST PRESS, GULF PUBLISHING CO., 1976, PP. 305.

A MEMOIR BY THE 2ND WATERGATE SPECIAL PROSECUTOR REPORTING VARIOUS BEHIND THE SCENES ASPECTS OF THE WATERGATE INVESTIGATION AND PROSECUTIONS.

1418 KRAFT, J. "WHO'S RUNNING THE COUNTRY." ATLANTIC 233 (APR. 1974): 57-60+.

"AS WASHINGTON'S POWER CENTER WEAKENS IN A SEASON OF ABSTRACTION, THE BARONS TAKE OVER. HERE IS THE STORY OF HOW KISSINGER, SCHLESINGER, SHULTZ, AND WEINBERGER MOVED INTO THE VOID."

1419 KRAUS, S., AND CHAFFEE, S.H. "THE ERVIN COMMITTEE HEARINGS AND COMMUNICATION RESEARCH." COMMUNICATION RESEARCH 1 (OCT 1974): 339-344.

1420 KURLAND, P.B. "THE WATERGATE INQUIRY, 1973." IN CONGRESS INVESTIGATES: A DOCUMENTED HISTORY, EDITED BY A.M. SCHLESINGER, JR., AND R. BURNS. NEW YORK: CHELSEA HOUSE, 1975, PP. 3923-4064.

1421 ----------. "UNITED STATES V. NIXON: WHO KILLED COCK ROBIN?" UCLA LAW R 22 (1974):68-75.

1422 ----------. "WATERGATE, IMPEACHMENT, AND THE CONSTITUTION." MISS LAW J 45 (MAY 1974): WHOLE ISSUE.

1423 LANG, K., AND LANG, G.E. "TELEVISED HEARINGS: THE IMPACT OUT THERE." COLUMBIA JOURNALISM R 12 (NOV.-DEC. 1973): 52-57.

   SUMMARY OF SOME 20 STUDIES OF THE IMPACT OF THE SENATE WATERGATE HEARINGS.

1424 LARSON, C.V. "A CONTENT ANALYSIS OF MEDIA REPORTING OF THE WATERGATE HEARINGS." COMMUNICATION RESEARCH 1 (OCT 1974): 440-448.

1425 LEROY, D.J., WOTRING, E.C., AND LYLE, J. "THE PUBLIC TELEVISION VIEWER AND THE WATERGATE HEARINGS." COMMUNICATION RESEARCH 1 (OCT 1974): 406-425.

1426 LEWIS, F. "SOME ERRORS AND PUZZLES IN WATERGATE COVERAGE." COLUMBIA JOURNALISM R 12 (NOV.-DEC. 1973): 26-32.

   ASSERTS THAT JOURNALISTIC ERRORS TOOK PLACE DURING THE REPORTING OF WATERGATE AND THAT "THE FUMBLES OF JOURNALISTS DESERVE TO BE REPORTED AS DO THE FOLLIES OF PUBLIC OFFICIALS--AND FOR MUCH THE SAME REASONS."

1427 LUKAS, J. A. NIGHTMARE: THE UNDERSIDE OF THE NIXON YEARS. NEW YORK: VIKING, 1976, PP. 626.

1428 MAGRUDER, J.S. AN AMERICAN LIFE: ONE MAN'S ROAD TO WATERGATE. NEW YORK: ATHENEUM, 1974, PP. 338.

1429 ----------. "MEANS; WATERGATE REFLECTIONS." N Y TIMES MAG 31 (MAY 20, 1974): 103-104+.

1430 MCCARTNEY, J. "THE WASHINGTON POST AND WATERGATE: HOW TWO DAVIDS SLEW GOLIATH." COLUMBIA JOURNALISM R 12 (JULY-AUG 1973): 8-22.

1431 MCGEEVER, P.J. "GUILTY YES: IMPEACHMENT, NO: SOME EMPIRICAL FINDINGS." POL SCI R 89 (JUNE 1974): 289-299.

RESULTS OF A SURVEY CONDUCTED IN SEPTEMBER AND OCTOBER 1973 SHOWING THAT, AT THAT STAGE OF THE WATERGATE AFFAIR, CITIZENS BELIEVED THAT THE PRESIDENT HAD BEEN INVOLVED IN THE WATERGATE EVENTS BUT THAT HIS IMPEACHMENT WAS NOT WARRANTED.

1432 MILLER, W.L. "SOME NOTES ON WATERGATE AND AMERICA." YALE R 63 (MAR 1974): 321-322.

REFLECTIONS ON MORAL AND RELIGIOUS ASSUMPTIONS OF THE WATERGATE DEFENDANTS AND LONG-RUN IMPLICATIONS OF WATERGATE FOR THE TONE OF AMERICAN POLITICS.

1433 MOSHER, F.C., ET AL. WATERGATE: IMPLICATIONS FOR RESPONSIBLE GOVERNMENT. NEW YORK: BASIC BOOKS, 1974, PP. 137.

THE COMMERCIALLY PUBLISHED VERSION OF A SPECIAL STUDY COMMISSIONED BY THE SENATE WATERGATE COMMITTEE. PARTICIPANTS INCLUDE LEADING SCHOLARS IN THE FIELD OF PUBLIC ADMINISTRATION.

1434 NEW YORK TIMES, THE STAFF OF. THE END OF A PRESIDENCY. NEW YORK: BANTAM BOOKS, 1973, PP. 353.

"INSTANT JOURNALISM"--AN ACCOUNT OF THE EVENTS LEADING TO NIXON'S RESIGNATION, PRODUCED BY A NEWSPAPER STAFF AND PUBLISHED WITHIN DAYS AFTER THE EVENT.

1435 ----------. THE WATERGATE HEARINGS. NEW YORK: BANTAM BOOKS, 1973, PP. 886.

AN ANTHOLOGY OF CHOICE PASSAGES FROM THE SENATE WATERGATE HEARINGS.

1436 ----------. THE WHITE HOUSE TRANSCRIPTS. NEW YORK: BANTAM BOOKS, 1973, PP. 877.

PAPERBACK REPRINT WITH A BRIEF INTRODUCTION NOT IN THE GPO DUPLICATION.

1437 PETERS, C. "WHY THE WHITE HOUSE PRESS DIDN'T GET THE WATERGATE STORY." WASHINGTON MONTHLY 5 (JULY-AUG. 1973): 7-15.

THE WHITE HOUSE PRESS WAS OVERLY ATTENTIVE TO THE "REGULAR FLOW OF PRESIDENTIAL NEWS ANNOUNCEMENTS."

1438 POLSBY, N.W. "WATERGATE: ALIENATION AND ACCOUNTABILITY IN

THE NIXON ADMINISTRATION," IN POLITICAL PROMISES: ESSAYS AND COMMENTARY ON AMERICAN POLITICS, NEW YORK: OXFORD U PR. 1974: 3-14.

1439 PYNN, R.E., ED. WATERGATE AND THE AMERICAN POLITICAL PROCESS. NEW YORK: PRAEGER, 1975, PP. 246.

ESSAYS BY SCHOLARS AND JOURNALISTS, MANY OF THEM EXCERPTED.

1440 RANGELL, L. "LESSONS FROM WATERGATE: A DERIVATIVE FOR PSYCHOANALYSIS." PSYCHOANALYTIC Q 35 (1976): 37-61.

1441 REDFORD, E.S. "WATERGATE: A TEST OF CONSTITUTIONAL DEMOCRACY," IN PROSPECTS FOR CONSTITUTIONAL DEMOCRACY. ED. JOHN H. HALLOWELL. 1976.

WATERGATE "HAS LOWERED THE FAITH OF THE PEOPLE IN GOVERNMENT AND THE POLITICIANS WHO SERVE IN IT. YET THIS LACK OF FAITH IS TRADITIONAL AND A HEALTHY DEGREE OF SKEPTICISM HAS POSITIVE AS WELL AS NEGATIVE ASPECTS." THE RESULT MAY BE "A LONG-RUN EFFECT OF SUBSTANTIALLY STRENGTHENING THE SYSTEM OF CONSTITUTIONAL DEMOCRACY."

1442 "RICHARD M. NIXON: END OF A REMARKABLE CAREER." CONG Q W REPT (AUG. 10, 1974): 2083-2126.

1443 ROBINSON, M.J. "THE IMPACT OF THE TELEVISED WATERGATE HEARINGS." J COMMUNICATION SPRING 1974, PP. 17-30.

1444 ROSENBERG, K.C., AND ROSENBERG, J.K., EDS. WATERGATE: AN ANNOTATED BIBLIOGRAPHY. LITTLETON: LIBRARIES UNLIMITED, 1975, PP. 141.

A CHRONOLOGICAL MONTH-BY-MONTH LISTING FROM JUNE 1972 TO AUGUST 1974 EMPHASIZING NEWSPAPER AND MAGAZINE ARTICLES. THE ANNOTATIONS ARE BRIEF, AND THE CRITERIA FOR INCLUSION ARE UNCLEAR.

1445 ROTHENBERG, A.B. "WHY NIXON TAPED HIMSELF." PSYCHOANALYTIC R 62 (1975):201-223.

1446 SAFFELL, D.C., ED. WATERGATE: ITS EFFECTS ON THE AMERICAN POLITICAL SYSTEM. CAMBRIDGE, MASS.: WINTHROP, 1974, PP.371.

READINGS ON WATERGATE WITH A FEW GENERAL WRITINGS ON THE PRESIDENCY.

1447 SAFIRE, W. "LAST DAYS IN THE BUNKER." N Y TIMES MAG

(AUG. 18, 1974): 6+.

AMBIENCE OF NIXON WHITE HOUSE IN THE FINAL DAYS OF THE ADMINISTRATION.

1448 SCHUCK, V. "WATERGATE--THREE YEARS OF DOCUMENTS AND WRITING." KEY REPORTER 40 (SPRING 1975): 2+; 41 (WINTER 1975-1976): 2-4+.

1449 SUNDQUIST, J.L. "REFLECTIONS ON WATERGATE: LESSONS FOR PUBLIC ADMINISTRATION." PUB ADM R 34 (SEPT-OCT 1974): 453-461.

EXAMINES PREVALENT NOTIONS ABOUT PRESIDENTIAL POWERS WHICH ARE FOUND AMONG MANY PUBLIC ADMINISTRATORS, CLAIMING THAT THE PROFESSION OF PUBLIC ADMINISTRATION HAS CONSISTENTLY SOUGHT TO STRENGTHEN THE PRESIDENT AT THE EXPENSE OF OTHER ELEMENTS IN THE GOVERNMENTAL SYSTEM.

1450 "THE ERVIN COMMITTEE HEARINGS AND COMMUNICATION RESEARCH." COMMUNICATION RESEARCH (OCT 1974): WHOLE ISSUE.

1451 THOMPSON, F.D. AT THAT POINT IN TIME: THE INSIDE STORY OF THE SENATE WATERGATE COMMITTEE. NEW YORK: QUADRANGLE, 1975, PP. 275.

ACTIVITIES OF THE SENATE WATERGATE COMMITTEE AS VIEWED BY ITS CHIEF MINORITY COUNSEL.

1452 TODD, J.T. "WATERGATE AS A MANAGEMENT PROBLEM." MANAGEMENT R 62 (DEC. 1973): 18-23.

"...TRADITIONAL MANAGEMENT PRINCIPLES AS WELL AS SYSTEMS THEORY ARE APPLIED TO THE WATERGATE SITUATION IN ORDER TO RELATE IT TO MANAGERIAL APPROACHES COMMONLY USED IN MANY ORGANIZATIONS."

1453 TODD, W.B. "THE WHITE HOUSE TRANSCRIPTS." THE PAPERS OF THE BIBLIOGRAPHICAL SOCIETY OF AMERICA 68 (1974):267-296.

1454 VAN ALSTYNE, W. "THE THIRD IMPEACHMENT ARTICLE: CONGRESSIONAL BOOTSTRAPPING." ABA J 60 (OCT 1974): 1199-1202.

"JUST HOW ELASTIC A CONGRESSIONAL BOOTSTRAP IS THE IMPEACHMENT CLAUSE? WHEN CONGRESS FAILED EVEN TO ASK THE COURTS TO SUSTAIN ITS OWN VIEW OF ITS OWN POWERS AGAINST THOSE OF THE PRESIDENCY, COULD IT NEVERTHELESS PRESUME TO IMPEACH THE PRESIDENT FOR RESISTING ITS CLAIM? THE QUESTION WAS RAISED BY THE THIRD ARTICLE OF IMPEACHMENT VOTED AGAINST FORMER PRESIDENT NIXON BY THE HOUSE JUDICIARY COMMITTEE."

1455 VAN VALKENBERG, W.E. "IMPEACHMENT: GOD SAVE THE KING FROM

OVERZEALOUS SUBORDINATES." <u>UTAH LAW R</u> (SPRING 1974): 71-91.

ARGUES THAT PRESIDENTIAL FAILURE TO PREVENT ILLEGAL ACTS OF SUBORDINATES WHICH FURTHER HIS POLITICAL INTERESTS CONSTITUTES AN IMPEACHABLE OFFENSE.

1456 WASHINGTON POST WRITERS GROUP. <u>YEAR OF SCANDAL</u>. WASHINGTON, D.C.: WASHINGTON POST, 1973, PP. 110.

DOCUMENTS THE <u>WASHINGTON POST</u>'S ROLE IN REPORTING AND UNCOVERING THE WATERGATE STORY.

1457 WASHINGTON POST, THE STAFF OF. <u>THE FALL OF A PRESIDENT</u>. NEW YORK: DELACORTE PRESS, 1974, PP. 232.

SIMILAR TO THE <u>NEW YORK TIMES</u> RAPIDLY PRODUCED <u>THE END OF A PRESIDENCY</u>.

1458 ----------. <u>THE PRESIDENTIAL TRANSCRIPTS</u>. NEW YORK: DELACORTE PRESS, 1974, PP. 693.

SIMILAR TO THE <u>NEW YORK TIMES</u>'S REPRINT OF THE OFFICIALLY PUBLISHED TAPES, INTRODUCED BY <u>WASHINGTON POST</u> REPORTERS.

1459 <u>WATERGATE AND THE WHITE HOUSE</u>. VOL. 1: ED. EDWARD W. KNAPPMAN. NEW YORK: FACTS ON FILE, 1973, PP. 246. VOL. 2: ED. EVAN DROSSMAN AND EDWARD W. KNAPPMAN. NEW YORK: FACTS ON FILE, 1974, PP. 288. VOL. 3: ED. EDWARD W. KNAPPMAN AND EVAN DROSSMAN. NEW YORK: FACTS ON FILE, 1974, PP. 416.

VOLUME 1 COVERS THE PERIOD FROM JUNE 1972 THROUGH JULY 1973. VOLUME 2 COVERS THE PERIOD FROM JULY THROUGH DECEMBER 1973. VOLUME 3 COVERS THE PERIOD FROM JANUARY THROUGH SEPTEMBER 1974. CONTENTS INCLUDE CHRONOLOGY, BIOGRAPHICAL SKETCHES OF KEY PERSONS, WATERGATE DEVELOPMENTS, AND EDITORIAL REACTIONS.

1460 "WATERGATE: A HARD LOOK AT PRESIDENTIAL IMPEACHMENT." <u>CONG Q W REPT</u> (OCT. 27, 1973): 2831-2853.

1461 "WATERGATE: A HISTORIC CONSTITUTIONAL CONFRONTATION." <u>CONG Q W REPT</u> (JULY 28, 1973): 2031-2051.

1462 <u>WATERGATE: CHRONOLOGY OF A CRISIS</u>. WASHINGTON, D.C.: CONG Q, 1975, PP. 1039.

1463 "WATERGATE: THE CONSTITUTIONAL ISSUES." <u>CENTER MAG</u> 7 (MAR.-APR. 1974): 9-52.

1464 WHITE, T.H. <u>BREACH OF FAITH: THE FALL OF RICHARD NIXON</u>.

NEW YORK: ATHENEUM, 1975, PP. 373.

JOURNALIST'S BLOW-BY-BLOW ACCOUNT OF THE END OF NIXON'S PRESIDENCY, WITH BACKGROUND ON NIXON'S CAREER. COMPARE WOODWARD AND BERNSTEIN, THE FINAL DAYS.

1465 ----------. THE MAKING OF THE PRESIDENT 1972. NEW YORK: ATHENEUM, 1973.

THE 4TH OF WHITE'S STUDIES OF PRESIDENTIAL ELECTIONS. PROVIDES A GENERAL DESCRIPTION OF PRESIDENT NIXON.

1466 WHITEHEAD, R., JR. "POLL WATCHING: DO WE REALLY KNOW HOW THE PUBLIC FEELS ABOUT IMPEACHMENT?" COLUMBIA JOURNALISM R 12 (MAR-APR 1974): 3-6.

ASSERTS THAT PUBLIC OPINION POLLS DID NOT DETECT "UNDERLYING PUBLIC VALUES AND MISCONCEPTIONS" ABOUT IMPEACHMENT OF THE PRESIDENT BECAUSE THEY DID NOT ASK THE PROPER QUESTIONS.

1467 WIGGINS, C.E., AND WALDIE, J.R. "WATERGATE AND IMPEACHMENT IN PERSPECTIVE." CONG Q W REPT (DEC. 28, 1974): 3444-3449.

1468 WILLS, G. "RICHARD NIXON'S SEVENTH CRISIS." N Y TIMES MAG (JULY 8, 1973): 7+.

INTERPRETS PRESIDENT NIXON'S REACTION AND APPROACH TO THE WATERGATE AFFAIR.

1469 WINTER, R.K., JR. WATERGATE AND THE LAW: POLITICAL CAMPAIGNS AND PRESIDENTIAL POWER. WASHINGTON, D.C.: AMERICAN ENTERPRISE INSTITUTE FOR PUBLIC POLICY RESEARCH, 1974, PP. 85.

1470 WOODWARD, B., AND BERNSTEIN, C. THE FINAL DAYS. NEW YORK: S&S, 1976, PP. 476.

THE BEST SELLING, INTERVIEW-BASED RECONSTRUCTION OF THE WATERGATE PHENOMENON BY THE 2 WASHINGTON POST JOURNALISTS WHO PERSISTENTLY FOLLOWED THE CASE BEFORE IT CAME TO TRIAL. SIMILAR TO WHITE'S BREACH OF FAITH. SEE ALSO THE AUTHORS' EARLIER ALL THE PRESIDENT'S MEN.

SEE ALSO 90, 91, 94, 98, 99, 104, 768, 983, 983, 1214, 1221, 1235, 1236, 1278, 1311, 1312, 1354, 1457, 1467, 1478, 1810, 1855, 1892, 1912, 1974, 2022, 2035, 2209, 2213, 2329, 2333, 2334, 2344, 2454, 2459

4. OTHER

1471 BONAFEDE, D. "THE MAKING OF THE PRESIDENT'S BUDGET: POLITICS AND INFLUENCE IN A NEW MANNER (OPERATION OF THE

OFFICE OF MANAGEMENT AND BUDGET)." NATIONAL J 3 (JANUARY 23, 1971): 151-165.

1472 GLASS, A.J. "DEMOCRATIC CHALLENGE TO NIXON BUDGET BOGS DOWN OVER LACK OF ALTERNATE PROPOSALS." NATIONAL J 5 (1973):527-534.

ON THE STATUS OF LEGISLATIVE-EXECUTIVE CONFLICT OVER CONTROL OF THE BUDGET-SETTING PROCESS.

1473 ----------. "NIXON GIVES ISRAEL MASSIVE AID BUT REAPS NO JEWISH POLITICAL HARVEST." NATIONAL J 4 (1972):57-72.

"THE PRESIDENT'S LINKS TO THE ORGANIZED JEWISH COMMUNITY REMAIN TENUOUS,...EVEN THOUGH HIS ADMINISTRATION HAS BEEN MORE GENEROUS THAN ANY OTHER IN SUPPLYING ISRAEL WITH THE WEAPONS OF WAR."

1474 HENDERSON, C.P. THE NIXON THEOLOGY. NEW YORK: HARPER, 1972, PP. 210.

1475 SUNDQUIST, J.L. "FOUR MORE YEARS: IS DEADLOCK THE ONLY PROSPECT?" PUBLIC ADMINISTRATION R 33 (MAY-JUNE 1973): 279-284.

PROBLEMS THAT PRESIDENT NIXON EXPERIENCED WITH AN OPPOSITION CONGRESS THROUGHOUT HIS FIRST TERM. COMPARISON OF NIXON'S EXPERIENCES WITH THOSE OF OTHER PRESIDENTS.

1476 WITCOVER, J. "SALVAGING THE PRESIDENTIAL PRESS CONFERENCE." COLUMBIA JOURNALISM R 9 (FALL 1970): 27-34.

LAMENTING THE SHARP DECREASE IN PRESIDENTIAL PRESS CONFERENCES UNDER NIXON, WITCOVER PROPOSES THAT THE WHITE HOUSE PRESS CORPS URGE THE PRESIDENT TO HAVE MORE NEWS CONFERENCES. ACCOMPANIED ARE THE RESULTS OF A SURVEY ON THIS TOPIC ADMINISTERED TO 16 LEADING WASHINGTON BUREAU CHIEFS AND SENIOR WHITE HOUSE CORRESPONDENTS.

SEE ALSO 768, 1268, 1844, 1874, 1880, 1886, 1892, 1965, 2126, 2166, 2204, 2253

G. ADDITIONAL ASPECTS AND THEMES

1477 BARBER, J.D. "PRESIDENT NIXON AND RICHARD NIXON: CHARACTER TRAP." PSYCHOLOGY TODAY (OCT. 1974):113-18.

IN HIS BOOK CLASSIFYING PRESIDENTS BY PERSONALITY TYPE (THE PRESIDENTIAL CHARACTER), BARBER PREDICTED, PRIOR TO PRESIDENT NIXON'S REELECTION, THAT NIXON WAS LIKELY TO EXPERIENCE A "CHARACTER-BASED" TRAGEDY IN HIS SECOND TERM. HERE, AFTER NIXON'S RESIGNATION, BARBER RECAPITULATES HIS ORIGINAL ARGUMENT AND LINKS HIS THESIS TO THE DEMISE OF NIXON'S PRESIDENCY.

1478 BROWN, T.M. "THE EXILE: ONE YEAR OF SAN CLEMENTE." N Y TIMES MAG (AUGUST 3, 1975): 8-9+.

1479 CHESEN, E.S. PRESIDENT NIXON'S PSYCHIATRIC PROFILE: A PSYCHODYNAMIC-GENETIC INTERPRETATION.. NEW YORK: P.H. WYDEN, 1973, PP. 245.

A WEAKLY DOCUMENTED WORK THAT MIXES PARTISAN POLEMIC WITH AD HOC PSYCHO-HISTORICAL INTERPRETATION.

1480 EISENHOWER, D., AND EISENHOWER, J. "INTERVIEW WITH DAVID AND JULIE EISENHOWER." U S NEWS (OCT. 8, 1973): 34-40.

THE YOUNG EISENHOWERS TALK OF THE WHITE HOUSE PAST AND PRESENT AND FUTURE.

1481 GOLDWATER, B.M. "BARRY GOLDWATER SPEAKS HIS MIND ON RICHARD NIXON." U S NEWS 76 (FEB 1974): 38-42.

INTERVIEW WITH SENATOR GOLDWATER, WHO COMMENTS ON NIXON'S PERSONALITY.

1482 HART, R.P. "ABSOLUTISM AND SITUATION: PROLEGOMENA TO A RHETORICAL BIOGRAPHY OF RICHARD M. NIXON." COMMUNICATION MONOGRAPHS 43 (AUGUST 1976): 204-228.

1483 KEOGH, J. PRESIDENT NIXON AND THE PRESS. NEW YORK: FUNK, 1972, PP. 212.

1484 LURIE, L. THE RUNNING OF RICHARD NIXON. NEW YORK: COWARD, MCCANN,GEOGHEGAN, 1972, PP. 409.

1485 MAZLISH, B. IN SEARCH OF NIXON: A PSYCHOHISTORICAL INQUIRY. SCRANTON, PA.: BASIC BOOKS, 1972, PP. 187.

AN ANALYSIS OF THE EFFECTS OF NIXON'S FAMILY AND UPBRINGING ON HIS PERSONALITY. AUTHOR SPECULATES THAT NIXON SUFFERED FROM INSECURITY, GUILT, AND PERSONAL AGGRESSION WHICH CARRIES OVER TO HIS POLITICAL LIFE.

1486 ----------. "TOWARD A PSYCHOHISTORICAL INQUIRY: THE 'REAL' RICHARD NIXON." J OF INTERDISCIPLINARY HIST 1 (AUTUMN 1970): 49-105.

1487 OSBORNE, T.M. "EISENHOWER AGONISTES." POTOMAC (WASH POST) (MAR. 30, 1975): 8-11+.

ON DAVID EISENHOWER.

1488 ROGIN, M., AND LOTTIER, J. "THE INNER HISTORY OF RICHARD MILHOUS NIXON." TRANS-ACTION (1971):19-28.

PSYCHOLOGICAL ANALYSIS OF NIXON AND HIS BACKGROUND.

1489 SAFIRE, W. "THE PRESS IS THE ENEMY." NEW YORK (JAN 27, 1975): 41-44, 47-50.

NIXON'S HATRED OF THE PRESS WAS RESPONSIBLE FOR HIS DOWNFALL.

1490 SCHEER, R. AMERICA AFTER NIXON. NEW YORK: MCGRAW-HILL, 1974, PP. 326.

NIXON "ENDED THE COLD WAR" BECAUSE AMERICAN RESOURCES HAD BECOME OVEREXTENDED AND BECAUSE HE WAS SEEKING TO RESPOND TO THE NEEDS OF MULTINATIONAL CORPORATIONS, WHICH ARE HEAVILY DEPENDENT ON POORER NATIONS FOR RESOURCES AND CHEAP LABOR. ALSO INCLUDES DISCUSSION OF KISSINGER AND OF THE ROCKEFELLER FAMILY.

1491 SHERRILL, R. "ZEALOTS FOR NIXON; GAUDY NIGHT AT THE WATERGATE." NATION 215 (SEPTEMBER 25, 1972): 230-234.

1492 "THE NIXON ADMINISTRATION AND THE NEWS MEDIA." CONG Q W REPT 30 (JAN. 1, 1973): 3-7.

DISCUSSES PRESIDENTIAL PRESS CONFERENCES, OFFICIAL SECRETS, CONFIDENTIAL COMMUNICATIONS AND REPORTERS AND REPORTING--AS WELL AS THE PENTAGON PAPERS.

1493 WHALEN, R.J. CATCH THE FALLING FLAG: A REPUBLICAN'S CHALLENGE TO HIS PARTY. BOSTON: HOUGHTON-MIFFLIN, 1972, PP. 308.

A CONSERVATIVE REPUBLICAN AND ONE TIME NIXON CAMPAIGN AIDE CONFESSES HIS DISILLUSIONMENT WITH THE NIXON ADMINISTRATION. UNLIKE OTHER CONSERVATIVE APPRAISALS OF THE NIXON YEARS, WHALEN'S APPEARS LESS CONCERNED WITH FOREIGN POLICY THAN WITH THE DOMESTIC BETRAYAL OF THE CONSERVATIVE IDEAL OF LIMITED GOVERNMENT. FOCUS ON EARLY IMPERIALISTIC OVERTONES IN NIXON'S WHITE HOUSE.

1494 WILLS, G. NIXON AGONISTES; THE CRISIS OF THE SELF-MADE MAN. BOSTON: HOUGHTON MIFFLIN, 1970, PP. 617.

NIXON, AS THE "LEAST AUTHENTIC MAN ALIVE," WAS ESSENTIALLY A TACTICIAN WHO WAS UNAFFECTED BY THE GREAT DEPRESSION OR THE NEW DEAL. NIXON'S 1968 VICTORY IS SEEN AS AN ADMISSION THAT WE HAVE "NO POLITICS LEFT, BUT OLD LIBERAL INDIVIDUALISM." NIXON IS PORTRAYED AS THE ARCHETYPE SELF-MADE MAN. WILLS ALSO CRITICALLY ANALYZES KENNEDY.

1495 ----------. "THE HISS CONNECTION THROUGH NIXON'S LIFE." N Y TIMES MAG (AUG. 25, 1974): 8-9+.

1496 WOODSTONE, A. NIXON'S HEAD. NEW YORK: ST. MARTINS, 1972, PP. 248.

POPULARIZED PSYCHOBIOGRAPHY OF NIXON WHICH ARGUES THAT HE IS AN "ANAL-IMPULSIVE CHARACTER" WITH A DESIRE TO HUMILIATE HIMSELF AND THEN HUMILIATE THE WORLD AROUND HIM. DISCUSSES HIS EARLY LIFE AND CAREER AND HIS FIRST TERM, WITH STRONG EMPHASIS ON POLITICAL CAMPAIGNS AND INCIDENTS DESCRIBED IN NIXON'S BOOK SIX CRISES.

SEE ALSO 297, 301, 1275, 1356, 1572, 1588, 1814, 1866, 1869, 1982, 2363, 2485, 2502

13
GERALD R. FORD AND HIS ADMINISTRATION

A. GENERAL HISTORICAL ACCOUNTS AND BIOGRAPHIES

1497 MOLLENHOFF, C. THE MAN WHO PARDONED NIXON. NEW YORK: ST. MARTIN'S, 1976, PP. 312.

1498 PRESIDENCY. 3 VOLS. CONGRESSIONAL QUARTERLY, WASHINGTON, D.C., 1975-1977.

1499 REEVES, R. A FORD, NOT A LINCOLN. NEW YORK, HARCOURT, 1975, PP. 212.

B. PRESIDENT'S PAPERS, MEMOIRS

SEE ALSO 54.

C. COMPENDIA AND BIBLIOGRAPHIES

1500 BONAFEDE, D. AND COHEN, R., EDS. "THE FORD PRESIDENCY." NATIONAL J REPRINTS (1975-1976): WHOLE ISSUE.

D. SELECTED MATERIAL ON PRE-PRESIDENTIAL BACKGROUND

1501 JONES, C.O. MINORITY PARTY LEADERSHIP IN CONGRESS. BOSTON: LITTLE, BROWN, 1970.

1502 PEABODY, R.L. "POLITICAL PARTIES: HOUSE REPUBLICAN LEADERSHIP." IN AMERICAN POLITICAL INSTITUTIONS AND PUBLIC POLICY, EDITED BY A.P. SINDLER, BOSTON: LITTLE BROWN, 1969.

COVERS THE FORD-HALLECK LEADERSHIP CONTEST.

1503 "PRESIDENT FORD: THE MAN AND HIS RECORD." CONG Q, INC (1974): 79.

1504 TERHORST, J.F. GERALD FORD AND THE FUTURE OF THE

<u>PRESIDENCY</u>. NEW YORK: THE THIRD PRESS, 1975, PP. 245.

1505 ----------. "THE SHAPING OF THE PRESIDENT: FORD'S EARLY YEARS." <u>NEW YORK</u> (AUG. 26, 1974): 25-34.

TREATS PRESIDENT FORD'S LIFE FROM HIS BIRTH IN NEBRASKA THROUGH HIS WEDDING AND FIRST CAMPAIGN FOR CONGRESS.

1506 "THE PUBLIC RECORD OF GERALD R. FORD." <u>CONG Q W REPT</u> 31 (OCT 20, 1973): 2759-2771.

1507 VESTAL, B. <u>JERRY FORD, UP CLOSE: AN INVESTIGATIVE BIOGRAPHY</u>. NEW YORK: COWARD, MCCANN AND GEOGHEGAN, 1974, PP. 214.

SEE ALSO 1021, 1464

E. ADVISERS AND ADVISORY RELATIONS

1508 BONAFEDE, D. "FORD AND STAFF TEND TO BUSINESS... AND WAIT." <u>NATIONAL J</u> 6 (1974): 1179-1190.

"EIGHT MONTHS AFTER BEING TAPPED FOR THE VICE PRESIDENCY, GERALD FORD HAS SETTLED INTO THE ROLE THAT REQUIRES HIM TO BE READY TO TAKE OVER THE PRESIDENCY SHOULD PRESIDENT NIXON LEAVE OFFICE. FORD HAS SOUGHT TO KEEP HIMSELF INFORMED OF WHAT IS GOING ON, AND HAS BEEN PARTICULARLY ANXIOUS TO IMPROVE HIS UNDERSTANDING OF ECONOMICS AND FOREIGN POLICY."

1509 ----------. "FORD BEGINS MOVES TO RESHAPE HIS ADMINISTRATION." <u>NATIONAL J</u> 6 (1974):1825-1830.

"THE WHITE HOUSE HAS BEGUN AN URGENT TALENT HUNT FOR NEW FACES TO PUT A GERALD FORD STAMP ON THE ADMINISTRATION."

1510 ----------. "FORD LEAVES OFFICE STRUCTURE INTACT." <u>NATIONAL J</u> 7 (1975): 974.

ON THE ABSENCE OF BASIC CHANGES IN WHITE HOUSE ORGANIZATION BETWEEN THE NIXON AND THE FORD ADMINISTRATIONS.

1511 ----------. "FORD REVERSES TREND IN STRENGTHENING CABINET ROLE." <u>NATIONAL J</u> 7 (1975):652-656.

"FORD MEETS WITH THE CABINET MORE OFTEN THAN HIS PREDECESSORS DID AND HAS MORE INDIVIDUAL CONTACT WITH THE SECRETARIES OF THE DEPARTMENTS."

1512 ----------. "FORD'S LOBBYISTS EXPECT DEMOCRATS TO REVISE TACTICS." <u>NATIONAL J</u> 7 (JUNE 1975): 923-927.

"WHITE HOUSE AIDES, ELATED OVER THEIR RECENT SERIES OF
TRIUMPHS IN CONGRESS, THINK A TURNING POINT HAS BEEN
REACHED IN PRESIDENT FORD'S RELATIONS WITH THE DEMOCRATIC
MAJORITY ON CAPITOL HILL."

1513 ----------. "INSIDE THE WHITE HOUSE." <u>WASHINGTONIAN</u> 10
(SEPT 1975): 80-83.

COMPARES THE PERSONNEL EMPLOYED BY FORD WITH PREVIOUS
PRESIDENTIAL STAFFS.

1514 ----------. "NESSEN STILL SEEKS 'SEPARATE PEACE' WITH
PRESS." <u>NATIONAL J</u> 7 (1975): 1409.

1515 ----------. "PRESIDENTIAL STAFF CONTINUES GROWTH UNDER
FORD." <u>NATIONAL J</u> 7 (AUG. 2, 1975): 1110-1111.

"PRESIDENT FORD HAS PLEDGED HIMSELF TO REDUCE 'THE WHITE
HOUSE STAFF' BY TEN PERCENT. BUT A YEAR AFTER TAKING
OFFICE, FORD'S STAFF IS LARGER THAN NIXON'S WAS."

1516 ----------. "ROCKEFELLER'S ROLE FAILS TO MATCH FORD
PROMISE." <u>NATIONAL J</u> 7 (1975): 1191.

1517 ----------. "RUMSFELD LOOKS FOR EFFICIENCY IN DECISION
MAKING." <u>NATIONAL J</u> 7 (APR 1975): 518-521.

1518 ----------. "SPEECH WRITERS SHUN FLOURISHES IN MOLDING
FORD'S IMAGE." <u>NATIONAL J</u> 7 (1975):123-127.

DISCUSSION OF PROCEDURES USED IN WRITING PRESIDENTIAL
SPEECHES, AND OF PRESIDENT FORD'S STAFF OF SPEECH WRITERS
AND EDITORS. FORD'S OWN PREFERENCES IN REGARD TO SPEECHES,
AND SPEAKING STYLE.

1519 ----------. "STAFF IS ORGANIZED TO ENSURE ACCESSIBILITY
TO FORD." <u>NATIONAL J</u> 6 (1974):1954-1958.

"THE SHAPE OF THE FORD WHITE HOUSE STAFF STRUCTURE IS
RECTANGULAR RATHER THAN PYRAMIDAL IN AN EFFORT TO AVOID
SOME OF THE EXCESSES OF THE NIXON STAFF STRUCTURE AND
ENSURE THE OPENNESS OF HIS ADMINISTRATION AND AVAILABILITY
OF PRESIDENT FORD TO HIS CABINET AND OTHER MEMBERS OF HIS
OFFICIAL FAMILY. UNDER THE ORGANIZATIONAL PLAN NINE AIDES
SHARE GENERALLY EQUAL STATUS AS THEY OVERSEE THEIR SPECIAL
RESPONSIBILITIES. FOUR OF THE NINE ALSO HOLD CABINET RANK
AND WILL BE AVAILABLE TO FORD FOR GENERAL ADVICE OUTSIDE
THEIR OWN SPECIAL AREAS OF RESPONSIBILITY."

1520 CAMERON, J. "NELSON ROCKEFELLER'S METAMORPHOSIS AS VICE
PRESIDENT." <u>FORTUNE</u> 92 (OCT 1975): 118-123+.

1521 ----------.   "THE MANAGEMENT PROBLEM IN FORD'S WHITE
HOUSE," FORTUNE (JULY 1975): 74-81.

1522 CANNON, L. "NESSEN'S BRIEFINGS: MISSING QUESTIONS (AND
ANSWERS)." COLUMBIA JOURNALISM R 14 (MAY-JUNE 1975):
12-16.

1523 CAPLAN, J.F. "THE PRAGMATIC WORLD OF DONALD RUMSFELD."
SUNDAY   MAG   (WASHINGTON   STAR)   (SEPT   1971):
6-7,10-11,14-16.

ON RUMSFELD'S POLITICAL BACKGROUND, WRITTEN DURING HIS
PERIOD AS COUNSELOR TO PRESIDENT NIXON.

1524 EVANS,   R.,   AND   NOVAK,   R.   "JERRY FORD'S FRIEND MELVIN
LAIRD." NEW YORK (SEPT. 2, 1974): 31-35.

AN ACCOUNT OF LAIRD'S POLITICAL CAREER FROM ITS BEGINNING
IN 1946, EMPHASIZING HIS STYLE AND POSSIBLE POLITICAL ROLE
IN THE FUTURE.

1525 "EXECUTIVE   SHUFFLE."   CONG Q W REPT   (NOV. 8, 1975):
2347-2367.

1526 "FORD'S ECONOMIC TEAM: A FIRM WITH ONE CLIENT." CONG Q W
REPT (NOV. 23, 1974): 3173-3179.

ON FORD ECONOMIC AIDES L. WILLIAM SEIDMAN, WILLIAM E.
SIMON, ALAN GREENSPAN, AND ARTHUR BURNS.

1527 HARTMANN, R., ET AL. "HOW FORD RUNS THE WHITE HOUSE:
INTERVIEW WITH PRESIDENT'S THREE TOP ADVISORS." U S NEWS
(SEPT. 23, 1974): 28-33.

INTERVIEW WITH PRESIDENT FORD'S TOP ADVISORS DELVES INTO
SUCH MATTERS AS PRESIDENT FORD'S WORK HABITS, HIS METHOD
OF MAKING DECISIONS, AND WHETHER ANY INTERNAL FRICTION
EXISTS WITHIN THE WHITE HOUSE STAFF.

1528 HAVEMANN, J. "OMB'S NEW FACES." NATIONAL J 7 (JULY 26,
1975): 1071-1077.

"THE STYLE OF THE BOSS IS DIFFERENT AND SOME OF THE FACES
HAVE CHANGED, BUT NEARLY A YEAR AFTER PRESIDENT FORD'S
ADVISERS TOLD HIM THE POLICY ROLE OF THE OFFICE OF
MANAGEMENT AND BUDGET SHOULD BE REDUCED, OMB IS THE SAME
POWERFUL OFFICE."

1529 SOBEL,   L.A.,   ED.   PRESIDENTIAL   SUCCESSION: FORD,
ROCKEFELLER AND THE 25TH AMENDMENT. NEW YORK: FACTS ON
FILE, 1975, PP. 225.

ONE OF THE MANY CHRONOLOGICAL COMPENDIA OF THE WEEKLY
FACTS ON FILE REPORTS ON PUBLIC INTERESTS AND FIGURES.

SEE ALSO 1270, 1292, 1303, 1512, 1638, 1715, 2432

F. SPECIFIC EVENTS, ACTIVITIES AND POLICIES

1. DOMESTIC

1530 BALZ, D.J. "FORD CONTINUES TO REFINE LEGISLATIVE PROPOSALS
FOR MESSAGE." NATIONAL J 7 (1975):39-46.

A REPORT ON THE DELIBERATIONS BY PRESIDENT FORD AND HIS
SENIOR ADVISERS ON THE ECONOMIC AND ENERGY PROPOSALS TO BE
SUBMITTED TO CONGRESS.

1531 CORRIGAN, R. "FORD POSITION STRENGTHENED BY LACK OF
CONSENSUS IN CONGRESS." NATIONAL J 7 (1975):837-841.

"PRESIDENT FORD ENJOYS A MUCH STRONGER POSITION ON ENERGY
POLICY THAN HE HAD AT THE BEGINNING OF THE YEAR BECAUSE
CONGRESSIONAL DEMOCRATS, DESPITE THEIR COMMANDING
MAJORITIES IN BOTH CHAMBERS, HAVE NOT BEEN ABLE TO AGREE
ON A POSITION AND THERE IS LITTLE LIKELIHOOD THEY WILL."

1532 HAVEMANN, J. "FORD ENDORSES 172 GOALS OF 'MANAGEMENT BY
OBJECTIVE' PLAN." NATIONAL J (OCT. 26, 1974): 1597-1605.

SEE ALSO 1529, 1892

2. FOREIGN AND NATIONAL SECURITY

1533 FRANK, R. "FORD ECONOMIC AIDES SEEK TO SOLVE EXPORT POLICY
DISPUTE." NATIONAL J 7 (APRIL 26, 1975):609-611.

1534 FRANK, R.S. "U.S. TAKES FIRST HESITANT STEPS TOWARD SHIFT
IN COMMODITIES POLICY." NATIONAL J 7 (JUNE 21, 1975):
913-922.

1535 PHILLIPS, J.G. "CONTROVERSY SURROUNDS PROPOSED NUCLEAR
EXPORT POLICIES." NATIONAL J 7 (MAY 10, 1975): 685-689.

A BILL TO PROHIBIT EXPORTS OF NUCLEAR MATERIALS TO
COUNTRIES THAT DO NOT HAVE THE SAME SAFEGUARDS AGAINST
THEFT THAT APPLY WITHIN THE UNITED STATES HAS IRRITATED
FOREIGN GOVERNMENTS, ANNOYED THE U.S. NUCLEAR INDUSTRY AND
DIVIDED THE FORD ADMINISTRATION."

1536 ROWAN, R. THE FOUR DAYS OF MAYAGUEZ. NEW YORK: NORTON,
1975, PP. 224.

SEE ALSO 106, 107, 727, 1286, 1303, 1892

3. OTHER

1537 BONAFEDE, D. "FORD ADMINISTRATION PROMISES REFORMATION, RESTORATION." <u>NATIONAL J</u> 6 (1974):1217-1222.

"THE NEW STYLE AND APPROACH OF GERALD R. FORD WAS CLEARLY EVIDENT AS THE FIRST NON-ELECTED PRESIDENT TOOK OVER THE WHITE HOUSE. THE SMOOTH TRANSITION FROM PRESIDENT NIXON TO PRESIDENT FORD WAS AIDED BY FORD'S 25 YEARS IN THE HOUSE AND THE PERSONAL RAPPORT THAT EXISTED BETWEEN HIM AND CONGRESS--A RAPPORT HE MADE CLEAR HE HOPES WILL CONTINUE."

1538 ----------. "FORD'S FIRST 100 DAYS FIND SKEPTICISM REPLACING EUPHORIA." <u>NATIONAL J</u> 6 (1974):1711-1714.

"THE DISTINCTIVE QUALITY THAT CHARACTERIZES ONE PRESIDENCY FROM ANOTHER CONTINUES TO ELUDE THE FORD ADMINISTRATION AS IT COMPLETES ITS FIRST 100 DAYS IN OFFICE. ALTHOUGH GERALD FORD RETAINS MUCH OF THE SAME BASIC GOOD WILL HE HAD WHEN HE TOOK OFFICE ON AUG. 8, A DEGREE OF SKEPTICISM ABOUT THE KIND OF LEADERSHIP HE COULD PROVIDE ALSO REMAINS. MUCH OF THE CRITICISM FORD RECEIVES STEMS FROM HIS UNWILLINGNESS--OR INABILITY--TO SHAKE HIMSELF FREE FROM THE PERSONNEL AND POLICIES INHERITED FROM PRESIDENT NIXON."

1539 ----------. "FORD'S LOBBYISTS EXPECT DEMOCRATS TO REVISE TACTICS." <u>NATIONAL J</u> 7 (JUNE 21, 1975): 923-927

"PRESIDENT FORD IS BEING GIVEN MUCH OF THE CREDIT BY HIS WHITE HOUSE LOBBYISTS FOR THEIR SUCCESS IN HAVING HIS VETOES SUSTAINED BY AN OVERWHELMINGLY DEMOCRATIC CONGRESS. THEY SAY FORD'S WILLINGNESS TO PRESS FOR SUPPORT ON CAPITOL HILL HAS MADE THE DIFFERENCE."

1540 HAVEMANN, J. "CONGRESS, OMB PLAY BUDGET NUMBERS GAME." <u>NATIONAL J</u> 8 (APRIL 3, 1976): 446.

"THE FORD ADMINISTRATION ALREADY IS ACCUSING CONGRESS OF BUSTING THE PRESIDENT'S BUDGET. BUT CONGRESSIONAL BUDGET EXPERTS SAY THE ADMINISTRATION BUSTED ITS OWN BUDGET BY PACKING IT WITH PHONY FIGURES SO THAT IT APPEARS TO BE SMALLER THAN IT REALLY IS."

1541 ----------. "FORD, CONGRESS SEEK HANDLE ON 'UNCONTROLLABLE' SPENDING." <u>NATIONAL J</u> 7 (NOV 29, 1975): 1619-1626.

"FEDERAL SPENDING IS APPROACHING FOUR BILLION. PRESIDENT FORD IS PLANNING TO PROPOSE MAJOR POLICY CHANGES IN HIS FISCAL 1977 BUDGET TO HALT THE GROWTH OF SO-CALLED UNCONTROLLABLE SPENDING. BUT LITTLE IN PAST CONGRESSIONAL BEHAVIOR POINTS TO THE LIKELIHOOD OF LEGISLATORS ACCEPTING THESE PROPOSALS."

SEE ALSO 768, 1459, 1478, 1892

G. ADDITIONAL ASPECTS AND THEMES

1542 BARBER, J.D. "FORD: WILL HE TURN TOUGH?" <u>U S NEWS</u>

(SEPTEMBER 1974): 22-26.

1543 "GERALD FORD: A NEW CONSERVATIVE PRESIDENT." CONG Q W REPT 32 (AUG. 10, 1974): 2077-2082.

1544 HERSEY, J. THE PRESIDENT: A MINUTE-BY-MINUTE ACCOUNT OF A WEEK IN THE LIFE OF GERALD FORD. NEW YORK: KNOPF, 1975, PP. 153.

1545 LAIRD, M. "AMERICA'S NEW LEADERSHIP: THE PRESIDENT I KNOW." READER'S DIGEST (NOVEMBER 1974): 1-21.

A SYMPATHETIC BIOGRAPHICAL SKETCH OF PRESIDENT FORD BY A LONG-TIME CONGRESSIONAL ASSOCIATE AND INFORMAL ADVISER.

1546 MASHER, J. "A DAY IN THE LIFE OF THE PRESIDENT; MINUTE-BY-MINUTE REPORT FROM INSIDE THE WHITE HOUSE." U S NEWS 78 (FEB. 24, 1975): 12-19.

SEE ALSO 1901, 2363

14
PRESIDENTIAL RECRUITMENT

1547 BURKE'S PRESIDENTIAL FAMILIES OF THE UNITED STATES OF AMERICA. LONDON: BURKE'S PEERAGE LIMITED, 1975, PP. 676.

CONTAINS A CHAPTER ON EACH PRESIDENT, PROVIDING A SHORT BIOGRAPHICAL STUDY, CHRONOLOGY OF IMPORTANT EVENTS, AND THE PRESIDENT'S WRITINGS. FOCUSES ON TRACING THE PRESIDENT'S FAMILY, WITH SECTIONS ON LINEAGE, DESCENDENTS, BROTHERS, AND SISTERS.

1548 CAVAIOLI, F.J. WEST POINT AND THE PRESIDENCY. NEW YORK: ST. JOHN'S UNIVERSITY PRESS, 1962, PP. 154.

AN ACCOUNT OF THE ROLE OF WEST POINT GRADUATES IN PRESIDENTIAL POLITICS.

1549 ELAZAR, D.J. "WHICH ROAD TO THE PRESIDENCY?" SOUTHWESTERN SOCIAL SCIENCE Q (JUNE 1965): 37-46.

CAREER BACKGROUNDS OF PRESIDENTS STATISTICALLY ANALYZED.

1550 FERREE, M.M. "A WOMAN FOR PRESIDENT? CHANGING RESPONSES: 1958-1972." POQ 38 (FALL 1974): 390-399.

ARGUES THAT NEGATIVE RESPONSES IN PUBLIC OPINION POLLS TOWARD VOTING FOR A WOMAN PRESIDENTIAL CANDIDATE SUDDENLY DROPPED IN 1972, AFTER 15 YEARS OF LITTLE CHANGES, IN LARGE PART BECAUSE OF "THE EMERGENCE OF THE WOMEN'S MOVEMENT AND THE CONSEQUENT RECOGNITION ON THE PART OF MANY PEOPLE THAT WOMEN, TOO, ARE A DISADVANTAGED 'MINORITY.'"

1551 GORDON, C. "WHO CAN BE PRESIDENT OF THE UNITED STATES: THE UNRESOLVED ENIGMA." MARYLAND LAW R 28:1-32 WINTER '68.

ON THE AMBIGUITIES OF THE CONSTITUTIONAL PRESCRIPTIONS REGARDING WHO IS AND WHO IS NOT ELIGIBLE TO BE PRESIDENT.

1552 GRAFF, H.F. "PLAYING POLITICAL POSSUM ISN'T EASY." NEW YORK TIMES MAGAZINE (OCTOBER 2, 1960): 13+.

1553 HARRIS, L. "WHY THE ODDS ARE AGAINST A GOVERNOR'S BECOMING PRESIDENT." POQ 23 (1959):361-370.

BASING HIS CONCLUSION ON PUBLIC OPINION POLLS CONDUCTED IN THE LATE 1950'S WHICH REFLECTED A TENDENCY FOR CITIZENS TO HOLD GOVERNORS RESPONSIBLE FOR VARIOUS SOURCES OF POPULAR

DISCONTENT SUCH AS TAX INCREASES, HARRIS CONCLUDES THAT THE GOVERNORSHIP WAS NO LONGER A PROMISING SPRINGBOARD FOR ATTAINING THE PRESIDENCY.

1554 HECLO, H. "PRESIDENTIAL AND PRIME MINISTERIAL SELECTION." IN PERSPECTIVES ON PRESIDENTIAL SELECTION, EDITED BY D.R. MATTHEWS, WASHINGTON, D.C.: BROOKINGS, 1973: 19-48.

PRESIDENTIAL "SELECTION IN THE UNITED STATES IS HEAVILY WEIGHTED TOWARD ELECTORAL RATHER THAN OTHER PERFORMANCE CRITERIA. IN BRITAIN THE SUCCESSFUL APPRENTICE HAS ADVANCED THROUGH EXACTLY THE WORKING RELATIONSHIPS BY WHICH HE WILL ONE DAY GOVERN."

1555 HESS, S. AMERICA'S POLITICAL DYNASTIES FROM ADAMS TO KENNEDY. NEW YORK: DOUBLEDAY, 1966, PP. 736.

ACCOUNTS OF AMERICAN FAMILIES IN WHICH MORE THAN ONE INDIVIDUAL AND OFTEN MEMBERS OF MORE THAN ONE GENERATION HAVE BEEN NATIONALLY POLITICALLY INFLUENTIAL AND OF PRESIDENTIAL TIMBER.

1556 KEECH, W.R., AND MATTHEWS, D.R. THE PARTY'S CHOICE. WASHINGTON, D.C.: BROOKINGS, 1976, PP. 258.

MOST OF THIS BOOK DEALS WITH ASPECTS OF THE NOMINATING PROCESS AND, THEREFORE, DOES NOT FALL WITHIN THE COMPASS OF THE PRESENT BIBLIOGRAPHY. CHAPTER 7, HOWEVER, PRESENTS INFORMATION ON THE BACKGROUND CHARACTERISTICS OF MODERN PRESIDENTIAL CANDIDATES. ALSO SEE MATTHEWS' ESSAY "PRESIDENTIAL NOMINATIONS: PROCESS AND OUTCOMES."

1557 LASKI, H.J. "QUALIFICATIONS FOR THE PRESIDENCY." CURRENT HISTORY (MAY 1940): 28-30+.

"TODAY THE U.S. DEMANDS THAT ITS PRESIDENTS SUPPLY A LEADERSHIP WHICH IS POSITIVE IN THOUGHT AND ACTION."

1558 MATTHEWS, D.R. "PRESIDENTIAL NOMINATIONS: PROCESS AND OUTCOMES." IN CHOOSING THE PRESIDENT, EDITED BY J.D. BARBER, ENGLEWOOD CLIFFS, N.J.: PRENTICE-HALL, 1974: 35-70.

A FASCINATING USE OF GALLUP POLL DATA SINCE THE 1930'S TO IDENTIFY THE POPULATION OF "ELIGIBLE" PRESIDENTIAL CANDIDATES AND IDENTIFY THEIR CHARACTERISTICS. GALLUP POLLS, BY THE TIME OF THE FIRST PRESIDENTIAL PRIMARY IN AN ELECTION YEAR, HAVE ALMOST INVARIABLY INCLUDED BOTH MAJOR PARTY NOMINEES IN RESPONSES TO AN EXTENSIVE CANDIDATE PREFERENCE CHECK LIST ITEM. THIS ITEM SHOWS THAT BETWEEN 1936 AND 1972 THE TOTAL POPULATION OF ELIGIBLES (BY MATTHEWS' CRITERION) WAS MERELY 102. FOR FURTHUR DISCUSSION OF THIS STUDY, SEE MATTHEWS' BOOK ON THE TOPIC.

1559 NOVAK, M. CHOOSING OUR KING. NEW YORK: MACMILLAN, 1974, PP. 324.

A POPULAR BOOK COMMENTING CRITICALLY ON THE ROLE OF "MONARCHICAL" SYMBOLISM CONNECTED WITH THE PRESIDENT'S

STATUS AS CHIEF OF STATE AS A CRITERION FOR SELECTING SUCCESSFUL PRESIDENTIAL CANDIDATES.

1560 PEABODY, R.L., AND LUBALIN, E. "THE MAKING OF PRESIDENTIAL CANDIDATES." IN THE FUTURE OF THE AMERICAN PRESIDENCY, EDITED BY C.W. DUNN, MORRISTOWN, N.J.: GENERAL LEARNING PR, 1975: 26-65.

AN HISTORICAL ANALYSIS OF THE CAREER PATTERNS THAT HAVE LED TO PRESIDENTIAL NOMINATIONS.

1561 PEABODY, R.L., ORNSTEIN, N.J., AND ROHDE, D.W. "THE UNITED STATES SENATE AS A PRESIDENTIAL INCUBATOR: MANY ARE CALLED BUT FEW ARE CHOSEN." POLITICAL SCIENCE QUARTERLY 91 (SUMMER 1976): 237-258.

1562 RUSSELL, F. THE PRESIDENT MAKERS: FROM MARK HANNA TO JOSEPH P. KENNEDY. BOSTON: LITTLE BROWN, 1976, PP. 407.

1563 TUGWELL, R.G. HOW THEY BECAME PRESIDENT: THIRTY-SIX WAYS TO THE WHITE HOUSE. NEW YORK: SIMON & SCHUSTER, 1964, PP. 587.

VIGNETTES OF THE CAREER PATTERNS AND THE PATHS TO OFFICE OF ALL PRESIDENTS FROM GEORGE WASHINGTON THROUGH LYNDON JOHNSON, FOLLOWED BY A GENERAL OBSERVATION ABOUT THE STRENGTHS AND WEAKNESSES OF ALTERNATIVE MEANS OF SEEKING NOMINATION AND ELECTION.

SEE ALSO 1574, 2424

15
PRESIDENTIAL STYLE AND PERSONALITY

1564 BARBER, J.D. THE PRESIDENTIAL CHARACTER: PREDICTING PERFORMANCE IN THE WHITE HOUSE. ENGLEWOOD CLIFFS, N.J.: PRENCTICE-HALL, 1972, PP. 479.

EXTENDS BARBER'S EARLIER WORK ON LEADERSHIP, MOST OF WHICH IS LISTED ON PAGE 495 OF THIS BOOK. BARBER VIEWS PRESIDENTS AS RESPONDING TO ENVIRONMENTAL CIRCUMSTANCES (THE "POWER SITUATION" AND "PUBLIC MOOD") IN TERMS OF THEIR CONSCIOUS IDEOLOGIES AND THEIR UNDERLYING CHARACTER STRUCTURES. IN DOING SO THEY DEVELOP POLITICAL STYLES WHICH EMPHASIZE TO VARYING DEGREES RHETORIC, MANAGEMENT OF OTHER INDIVIDUALS IN A FACE-TO-FACE SETTING, AND ADMINISTRATIVE WORK. HIS FAMOUS CLASSIFICATION OF FOUR CHARACTER TYPES, WHICH FORM IN CHILDHOOD AHD BECOME ENTRENCHED AT THE TIME OF THE LEADER'S FIRST POLITICAL SUCCESS, IS BASED ON A CROSS-CLASSIFICATION OF THE LEADER'S LEVEL OF POLITICAL ACTIVITY AND CAPACITY TO GENUINELY ENJOY POLITICS. EXAMPLES COVER PRESIDENTS FROM TAFT THROUGH NIXON. TWO ESSAYS ON BARBER'S WORK ARE ALEXANDER GEORGE'S "ASSESSING PRESIDENTIAL CHARACTER," AND ERWIN HARGROVE'S "PRESIDENTIAL PERSONALITY AND REVISIONIST VIEWS OF THE PRESIDENCY."

1565 ----------. "CLASSIFYING AND PREDICTING PRESIDENTIAL STYLES: TWO "WEAK" PRESIDENTS." J OF SOCIAL ISSUES 24 (1968):51-80.

BASIS OF BARBER'S DISCUSSION OF COOLIDGE AND HOOVER IN HIS THE PRESIDENTIAL CHARACTER.

1566 ----------. "MAN, MOOD, AND THE PRESIDENCY." IN THE PRESIDENCY REAPPRAISED, EDITED BY R.G. TUGWELL AND T.E. CRONIN, NEW YORK: PRAEGER, 1974: 205-214.

ON THE RESONANCE BETWEEN PRESIDENTS' COMMUNICATIONS TO THE PUBLIC AND THE VARIATIONS OVER THE YEARS IN OFTEN IMPLICIT PUBLIC EXPECTATIONS OF WHAT IS NEEDED IN THE WAY OF PRESIDENTIAL LEADERSHIP.

1567 ----------. "STRATEGIES FOR UNDERSTANDING POLITICIANS." AMER J POL SCI (SPRING 1974): 443-467.

BARBER'S FULLEST METHODOLOGICAL EXPOSITION OF HIS PROCEDURES FOR CLASSIFYING PRESIDENTIAL CHARACTER AND STYLE. BARBER DOES NOT REFER TO GEORGE'S "ASSESSING PRESIDENTIAL CHARACTER," BUT HE DOES IN FACT RESPOND TO A NUMBER OF GEORGE'S CRITICISMS OF HIS METHODOLOGY IN THE PRESIDENTIAL CHARACTER.

1568 ----------. "THE INTERPLAY OF PRESIDENTIAL CHARACTER AND
STYLE: A PARADIGM AND FIVE ILLUSTRATIONS." IN SOURCEBOOK
FOR THE STUDY OF PERSONALITY AND POLITICS, EDITED BY F.I.
GREENSTEIN AND M. LERNER, CHICAGO: MARKHAM, 1971: 384-408.

BARBER'S EARLY REPORT OF OBSERVATIONS LATER EXPANDED ON IN
THE PRESIDENTIAL CHARACTER, CONTAINING HIS FULLEST
EXPOSITION OF WHAT HE MEANS BY "STYLE" AND OF HOW
DIFFERENT COMPONENTS OF A LEADER'S PSYCHE TEND TO BECOME
SHAPED AT LIFE'S DIFFERENT STAGES.

1569 ----------. "THE QUESTION OF PRESIDENTIAL CHARACTER."
SAT R 55 (SEPT 1972): 62-66.

A BRIEF GENERAL DISCUSSION."NEITHER THE WAR NOR THE ECONOMY
IS THE KEY CAMPAIGN ISSUE, SAYS A NOTED POLITICAL
SCIENTIST, BUT RATHER THE CHARACTER OF THE NEXT PRESIDENT.
THE AUTHOR EXAMINES THE PASTS OF RICHARD NIXON AND GEORGE
MCGOVERN TO DETERMINE HOW WELL EACH CANDIDATE WOULD
PERFORM IN OFFICE."

1570 BRODIE, B. "A PSYCHOANALYTIC INTERPRETATION OF WOODROW
WILSON." WORLD POLITICS 9 (APR 1957): 413-422.

REVIEW ARTICLE ON THE PSYCHOLOGICAL BIOGRAPHY OF AN
AMERICAN PRESIDENT WHICH GENERALLY ENJOYS THE MOST
FAVORABLE REPUTATION AMONG SUCH CONTROVERSIAL
WORKS--GEORGE AND GEORGE'S WOODROW WILSON AND COLONEL
HOUSE.

1571 BRODIE, F.M. THOMAS JEFFERSON: AN INTIMATE HISTORY. NEW
YORK: NORTON, 1974, PP. 591.

CONTROVERSIAL PSYCHO-BIOGRAPHY STRESSING JEFFERSON'S
ALLEGED SLAVE-CONCUBINE AS A SOURCE OF HIS AMBIVALENCE
WITH RESPECT TO SLAVERY.

1572 DIAMOND, E. "PSYCHOJOURNALISM: NIXON ON THE COUCH."
COLUMBIA JOURNALISM R 12 (MAR-APR 1974): 7-11.

CRITICIZES "PSYCHOJOURNALISTIC STYLE" OF PRESS ANALYSIS OF
PRESIDENT FOR USING "BLIND ITEMS, INNUENDO, MURKY
ATTRIBUTION AND SHIFTING OF THE BURDEN OF DISCUSSION ONTO
OTHERS. THE OVERALL TONE RAISES APPREHENSIONS WITHOUT
EXPLICITLY CONFRONTING THEM."

1573 DONLEY, R.E., AND WINTER, D.L. "MEASURING THE MOTIVES OF
PUBLIC OFFICIALS AT A DISTANCE: AN EXPLORATORY STUDY OF
AMERICAN PRESIDENTS." BEHAVIORAL SCIENCE 15
(1970):227-36.

USES TECHNIQUES OF PSYCHOLOGIST DAVID MCCLELLAN TO
CLASSIFY THE METAPHORIC IMAGERY OF THE THEMES "NEED FOR
ACHIEVEMENT" AND "NEED FOR POWER." CROSS-CLASSIFIED, THE
PRESIDENTS FALL INTO FOUR CATEGORIES THAT ARE RATHER
CONSISTENT WITH HISTORIANS' JUDGMENTS.

1574 FABER, D. THE MOTHERS OF AMERICAN PRESIDENTS. NEW YORK:

NEW AMERICAN LIBRARY, 1968, PP.271.

1575 FREUD, S. W., AND BULLITT, W.C. THOMAS WOODROW WILSON. BOSTON: HOUGHTON, 1967, PP. 307.

CONTROVERSIAL PSYCHOBIOGRAPHY; FREQUENTLY COMPARED UNFAVORABLY TO THE GEORGE AND GEORGE PERSONALITY STUDY OF WILSON.

1576 GEORGE, A. "ASSESSING PRESIDENTIAL CHARACTER." WORLD POLITICS 26 (1974):234-282.

A COMPREHENSIVE CRITIQUE OF THE EMPIRICAL, CONCEPTUAL, AND THEORETICAL ASSUMPTIONS OF BARBER'S INFLUENTIAL THE PRESIDENTIAL CHARACTER. EXTENSIVELY DISCUSSES PROBLEMS OF ANALYZING LEADERS' PSYCHOLOGIES.

1577 ----------. "POWER AS A COMPENSATION VALUE FOR POLITICAL LEADERS." J OF SOCIAL ISSUES 24 (JULY 1968): 29-49.

A SYSTEMATIC METHODOLOGICAL AND THEORETICAL DISCUSSION.

1578 GEORGE, A., AND GEORGE, J. WOODROW WILSON AND COLONEL HOUSE. NEW YORK: DAY, 1956, PP. 362. REPUBLISHED, NEW YORK: DOVER, 1964, PP. 361.

THE CLOSELY, BUT NOT EXPLICITLY, CONCEPTUALIZED QUALITY OF THIS WORK, THE PRODUCT OF MANY YEARS OF RESEARCH AND ANALYSIS, HAS LED TO ITS WIDESPREAD ACCEPTANCE AS THE MOST RIGOROUS PSYCHOBIOGRAPHY OF AN AMERICAN PRESIDENT. ALSO EXCELLENT ON THE WILSON AND HOUSE PRESIDENT-ADVISER RELATIONSHIP. THE GEORGES' METHODOLOGY IS DISCUSSED IN AN APPENDIX TO THE BOOK AND IN ESSAYS BY GEORGE CITED IN THIS VOLUME.

1579 HARGROVE, E.C. PRESIDENTIAL LEADERSHIP: PERSONALITY AND POLITICAL STYLE. NEW YORK: MACMILLAN, 1966, PP. 153.

TAKING AS HIS PREMISE THAT A FORCEFUL PRESIDENT IS NEEDED TO PROVIDE THE SPUR FOR INNOVATIVE ACTION BY THE AMERICAN GOVERNMENT, HARGROVE ANALYZES THE PERSONALITIES AND POLITICAL STYLES OF SIX TWENTIETH-CENTURY PRESIDENTS. ONE OF THE FIRST STUDIES TO CLASSIFY PRESIDENTS PSYCHOLOGICALLY.

1580 ----------. "PRESIDENTIAL PERSONALITY AND REVISIONIST VIEWS OF THE PRESIDENCY." AMER J POL SCI 17 (NOV. 1973): 819-835.

CRITICAL REAPPRAISAL OF LITERATURE ON PRESIDENTIAL CHARACTER, INCLUDING BARBER'S BOOK AND HARGROVE'S OWN WORK.

1581 HARRIS, I.D. "THE PSYCHOLOGIES OF PRESIDENTS." HIST OF CHILDHOOD Q 3 (WINTER 1976): 337-350.

AN ATTEMPT AT "A THEORETICAL FRAMEWORK WHEREBY MEN LIKE

NIXON AND MEN LIKE JOHNSON ARE BETTER UNDERSTOOD."
UTILIZING A THEORY "OF TWO PSYCHOLOGICAL TYPES ARISING OUT
OF EARLY FAMILY EXPERIENCES: THE ADULT-CIVILIZED AND THE
PEER-CIVILIZED." A FIRST-BORN CHILD, MARKED BY THE VALUES
OF THE PREVIOUS GENERATION, LBJ "CAN BE REGARDED AS HAVING
BEEN ADULT-CIVILIZED." LESS INFLUENCED BY ADULT VALUES,
HAVING MODELS IN OLDER SIBLINGS, NIXON "CAN BE REGARDED AS
HAVING BEEN PEER-CIVILIZED."

1582 ROGIN, M. FATHERS AND CHILDREN: ANDREW JACKSON AND THE
SUBJUGATION OF THE AMERICAN INDIAN. NEW YORK: KNOPF,
1975, PP. 373.

A PSYCHOBIOGRAPHICAL CRITIQUE OF JACKSON "THE INDIAN
KILLER" AS A REPRESENTATION OF THE CONTINUING THEME OF
RACIAL OPPRESSION IN AMERICAN SOCIETY.

1583 ROGOW, A.A., AND LASSWELL, H.D. POWER, CORRUPTION, AND
RECTITUDE. ENGLEWOOD CLIFFS: PRENTICE-HALL, 1963, PP.
138.

1584 SCHLESINGER, A.M., JR. "CAN PSYCHIATRY SAVE THE REPUBLIC?"
SAT R (SEPT. 7, 1974): 10-16.

1585 WEINSTEIN, E.A. "DENIAL OF PRESIDENTIAL DISABILITY: A CASE
STUDY OF WOODROW WILSON." PSYCHIATRY 30 (1967):376-91.

SEE ALSO 665, 913, 1070, 1083, 1300, 1310, 1440, 1445,
1477, 1479, 1481, 1485, 1486, 1488, 1496, 1542, 2450

16
ADVISORY INSTITUTIONS
AND PROCESSES

A. GROWTH OF INSTITUTIONALIZED ADVICE AND STAFFING

1586 BONAFEDE, D. "SCHOLARS TACKLE PROBLEM OF PRESIDENTIAL ADVISORY SYSTEM." NATIONAL J 7 (1975): 1607-1610.

SUMMARY OF A CONFERENCE OF PRESIDENTIAL ADVISERS AND ACADEMIC AUTHORITIES ON THE TOPIC.

1587 CARBONE, D.J. "THE EXECUTIVE OFFICE OF THE PRESIDENT AS A MANAGEMENT TOOL." PERSPECTIVES DEFENSE MGT P 27 (FEB 1967): 38.

1588 COHEN, R. ""INFORMATION GAP" PLAGUES ATTEMPT TO GRAPPLE WITH GROWING EXECUTIVE STRENGTH." NATIONAL J 5 (1973):379-388.

1589 CRONIN, T.E. "THE SWELLING OF THE PRESIDENCY." SAT R (FEB 1973): 30-36.

"THE NUMBER OF GOVERNMENT EMPLOYEES WORKING DIRECTLY UNDER THE PRESIDENT HAS GROWN AN ALARMING 20 PER CENT IN THE LAST 4 YEARS, AND NOW APPROACHES THE SIZE OF THE STATE DEPARTMENT'S DOMESTIC BUREAUCRACY."

1590 CRONIN, T.E., AND GREENBERG, S.D., EDS. THE PRESIDENTIAL ADVISORY SYSTEM. NEW YORK: HARPER AND ROW, 1969, PP. 375.

ANTHOLOGY PUBLISHED JUST BEFORE THE EXTENSIVE LITERATURE, INCLUDING CRONIN'S OWN, ON WHITE HOUSE STAFFING PROCESSES. INCLUDES MANY WRITINGS FROM 1950'S AND 1960'S STRESSING NEED FOR GREATER WHITE HOUSE CONTROL OVER POLICY DIRECTION AND COORDINATION OF EXECUTIVE AGENCIES.

1591 CRONIN, T.E., AND THOMAS, N.C. "FEDERAL ADVISORY PROCESSES: ADVICE AND DISCONTENT." SCIENCE 171 (1971):771-779.

1592 GAUS, J. "THE HOOVER COMMISSION: III. THE PRESIDENCY." APSR 43 (1949): 952-958.

1593 GILMOUR, R.S. "THE INSTITUTIONALIZED PRESIDENCY: A

CONCEPTUAL CLARIFICATION." IN THE PRESIDENCY IN CONTEMPORARY CONTEXT, EDITED BY N.C. THOMAS, NEW YORK: DODD, 1975: 147-159.

THOUGHTFUL, ANALYTIC DISCUSSION OF A WIDELY READ, BUT RARELY DEFINED PHRASE, "THE INSTITUTIONALIZED PRESIDENCY."

1594 GRAHAM, G.A. "THE PRESIDENCY AND THE EXECUTIVE OFFICE OF THE PRESIDENT." JP 12 (1950):599-621.

1595 HOBBS, E.H. BEHIND THE PRESIDENT: A STUDY OF EXECUTIVE OFFICE AGENCIES. WASHINGTON: PUBLIC AFFAIRS PRESS, 1954, PP. 248.

AN HISTORICAL ACCOUNT OF THE EXECUTIVE OFFICE OF THE PRESIDENT.

1596 MCREYNOLDS, W.H. "THE EXECUTIVE OFFICE OF THE PRESIDENT: THE OFFICE FOR EMERGENCY MANAGEMENT." PUBLIC ADMINISTRATION R 1 (1941):131-138.

1597 MORSTEIN MARX, F. THE PRESIDENT AND HIS STAFF SERVICES. CHICAGO: PUBLIC ADMINISTRATION SERVICE, 1947, PP. 26.

1598 NEUSTADT, R.E. "PRESIDENCY AND LEGISLATION: PLANNING THE PRESIDENT'S PROGRAM." APSR 49 (1955):980-1021.

1599 ----------. "PRESIDENCY AND LEGISLATION: THE GROWTH OF CENTRAL CLEARANCE." APSR 48 (SEPT 1954): 641-647.

1600 PASCHAL, J.F. "PRESIDENTIAL OFFICE: A SYMPOSIUM." LAW AND CONTEMPORARY PROBLEMS 21 (AUTUMN 1956): WHOLE ISSUE.

SPECIAL ISSUE COMPARABLE TO THE ISSUE OF THE SAME JOURNAL ABOUT A DECADE LATER THAT APPEARS IN BOOK FORM AS N. THOMAS AND H. BAADE, THE INSTITUTIONALIZED PRESIDENCY. INCLUDES NEUSTADT'S "THE PRESIDENCY AT MID-CENTURY." SELIGMAN ON THE PRESIDENT AND PARTY LEADERSHIP, AND STEELMAN AND KREAGER ON "THE EXECUTIVE OFFICE AS COORDINATOR."

1601 PRICE, D.K. "STAFFING THE PRESIDENCY." APSR 40 (1946):1154-1168.

1602 ROSSITER, C.L. "THE CONSTITUTIONAL SIGNIFICANCE OF THE EXECUTIVE OFFICE OF THE PRESIDENT." APSR 43 (1949):1206-17.

1603 THOMAS, N.C. "PRESIDENTIAL ADVICE AND INFORMATION: POLICY AND PROGRAM FORMULATION." IN THE INSTITUTIONALIZED PRESIDENCY. EDITED BY N.C. THOMAS AND H.W. BAADE, DOBBS FERRY, N.Y.: OCEANA, 1972: 114-146.

1604 THOMAS, N.C., AND BAADE, H.W., EDS. THE INSTITUTIONALIZED PRESIDENCY. DOBBS FERRY, N.Y.: OCEANA, 1971, PP. 239.

A SYMPOSIUM ON THE INSTITUTIONALIZED PRESIDENCY. ORIGINALLY PUBLISHED AS THE SUMMER 1970 ISSUE OF LAW AND CONTEMPORARY PROBLEMS (VOL. 35, NO.3). INCLUDES CRONIN'S "EVERYBODY BELIEVES IN DEMOCRACY UNTIL THEY GET TO THE WHITE HOUSE" AND SCHICK'S "THE BUDGET BUREAU THAT WAS," AMONG OTHERS.

1605 WISE, S., AND SCHIER, R.F. THE PRESIDENTIAL OFFICE. NEW YORK: CROWELL, 1968, PP. 248.

SEE ALSO 108, 109, 110, 111, 112, 113, 114, 115, 116, 199, 206, 216, 239, 439, 1776, 1781, 1798, 1982, 2033, 2446

B. SPECIFIC ADVISORY AND STAFFING INSTITUTIONS

1. CABINET

1606 FENNO, R.F. THE PRESIDENT'S CABINET: AN ANALYSIS IN THE PERIOD FROM WILSON TO EISENHOWER. CAMBRIDGE, MASS.: HARVARD UNIV. PRESS, 1959, PP. 327.

FOR THE WILSON THROUGH EISENHOWER ADMINISTRATIONS, FENNO WINNOWS THROUGH MASSES OF MEMOIRS AND OTHER HISTORICAL MATERIALS, SHOWING THAT THE CABINET HAS RARELY SERVED DELIBERATIVE FUNCTIONS EXCEPT UNDER VERY NONACTIVIST PRESIDENTS, BUT THAT INDIVIDUAL DEPARTMENT SECRETARIES OFTEN ARE POLITICALLY IMPORTANT. PROPOSALS TO RESHAPE THE CABINET INTO A COLLECTIVE DECISION-MAKING ORGAN ALONG BRITISH LINES RUN AFOUL OF THE GREATER HETEROGENEITY OF AMERICAN POLITICS AND SOCIETY.

1607 HORN, J.S. THE CABINET AND CONGRESS. NEW YORK: COLUMBIA UNIVERSITY PRESS, 1960, PP. 310.

ON THE RELATIONSHIP BETWEEN LEGISLATIVE AND EXECUTIVE POWER IN THE FEDERAL GOVERNMENT WITH DETAILED ATTENTION TO PROPOSALS FOR ADMITTING CABINET MEMBERS TO PARTICIPATE IN CONGRESSIONAL DEBATES AND HOLDING BRITISH-STYLE QUESTION PERIODS.

1608 PATTERSON, B.H. THE PRESIDENT'S CABINET: ISSUES AND QUESTIONS WASHINGTON: AMERICAN SOCIETY FOR PUBLIC

ADMINISTRATION, 1976, PP. 116.

ON THE RELATIONSHIPS OF CABINET MEMBERS WITH EACH OTHER AND WITH THE WHITE HOUSE.

SEE ALSO 356, 382, 386, 388, 396, 401, 413, 653, 845, 882, 947, 949, 1105, 1251, 1257, 1264, 1270, 1286, 1289, 1292, 1303, 1511, 1617, 1631, 1788

2. FOREIGN AND NATIONAL SECURITY

1609 BORKLUND, C.W. MEN OF THE PENTAGON: FROM FORRESTAL TO MCNAMARA. NEW YORK, PRAEGER, 1966, PP. 236.

1610 BRESICA, P.F. "THE NATIONAL SECURITY COUNCIL: INTEGRATION OF AMERICAN FOREIGN POLICY." APSR 34 (1946):295-300.

1611 CLARK, K.C., AND LEGERE, L.J., EDS. THE PRESIDENT AND THE MANAGEMENT OF NATIONAL SECURITY. NEW YORK: PRAEGER, 1969, PP. 274.

HISTORICAL REVIEW OF THE DEVELOPMENT OF NATIONAL SECURITY ADVISING UP TO THE ADVENT OF THE NIXON ADMINISTRATION.

1612 CUTLER, R. "THE DEVELOPMENT OF THE NATIONAL SECURITY COUNCIL." FOREIGN AFFAIRS 34 (1956):441-458.

FORMER DIRECTOR OF THE NSC DESCRIBES THE COUNCIL'S ROLE, FUNCTIONS, ORGANIZATION, AND EVOLUTION.

1613 DAVIS, V. "AMERICAN MILITARY POLICY: DECISION MAKING IN THE EXECUTIVE BRANCH." NAVAL WAR COLLEGE R 22 (1970):4-23.

1614 DESTLER, I.M. PRESIDENTS, BUREAUCRATS, AND FOREIGN POLICY. PRINCETON: PRINCETON UNIVERSITY PRESS, 1974, PP. 355.

DESCRIPTIVE AND PRESCRIPTIVE ANALYSIS OF HOW WHITE HOUSE NATIONAL SECURITY ADVISING WAS ORGANIZED FROM THE KENNEDY THROUGH THE NIXON ADMINISTRATIONS. ADVOCATES MORE SYSTEMATIC AND BETTER USE OF THE STATE DEPARTMENT BY PRESIDENTS.

1615 FALK, S.L. "THE NATIONAL SECURITY COUNCIL UNDER TRUMAN, EISENHOWER, AND KENNEDY." PSQ 79 (1964):403-434.

1616 FIGLIOLA, C.L. "CONSIDERATIONS OF NATIONAL SECURITY ADMINISTRATION: THE PRESIDENCY, POLICY MAKING AND THE MILITARY." PUBLIC ADMINISTRATION R 34 (JAN-FEB 1974): 82-88.

REVIEWS AND BOOKS DEALING WITH THE DEFINITION OF NATIONAL
SECURITY, PRESIDENTIAL ADMINISTRATION AND DECISION
MAKING,AND CIVIL-MILITARY RELATIONS.

1617 GRAEBNER, N.A. AN UNCERTAIN TRADITION: AMERICAN
SECRETARIES OF STATE IN THE TWENTIETH CENTURY. NEW YORK:
MCGRAW-HILL, 1961, PP.341.

1618 HAMMOND, P.Y. ORGANIZING FOR THE DEFENSE: THE AMERICAN
MILITARY ESTABLISHMENT IN THE TWENTIETH CENTURY.
PRINCETON: PRINCETON UNIVERSITY PRESS, 1961, PP.403.

A STUDY OF THE ORGANIZATION OF MILITARY PLANNING AND
ADVISING WITH BRIEF ATTENTION TO THE PRE-WORLD WAR II
EXPERIENCE AND DETAILED ANALYSIS OF WORLD WAR II AND THE
POST-WAR PERIOD THROUGH THE EISENHOWER YEARS. STRESSES
WHITE HOUSE-CONGRESS-DEFENSE DEPARTMENT RELATIONS.

1619 ----------. "PRESIDENTS, POLITICS, AND INTERNATIONAL
INTERVENTION." ANNALS 386 (1969):10-18.

EARLY NIXON ADMINISTRATION ESSAY SPECULATING ON WHETHER
VIETNAM HAS PERMANENTLY VITIATED PRESIDENTIAL CAPACITY TO
EXERCISE MILITARY POWER TO ADVANCE INTERNATIONAL POLICY
GOALS.

1620 ----------. "THE NATIONAL SECURITY COUNCIL AS A DEVICE
FOR INTERDEPARTMENTAL COORDINATION: AN INTERPRETATION AND
APPRAISAL." APSR 54 (1960):899-910.

A HISTORICAL OVERVIEW OF THE NSC'S ROLE, FOCUSING ON THE
QUESTION OF WHETHER COORDINATION IS BEST ACHIEVED THROUGH
LATERAL CLEARANCE OR LINE COMMAND.

1621 HASSLER, W.W. THE PRESIDENT AS COMMANDER IN CHIEF. MENLO
PARK,CALIFORNIA: ADDISON-WESLEY PUBLISHING CO., 1971, PP.
168.

AN HISTORICAL ACCOUNT, DEALING WITH EPISODES IN THE
WASHINGTION THROUGH NIXON ADMINISTRATIONS.

1622 HESS, S. "THE PRESIDENTIAL ADVISORY SYSTEM IN FOREIGN
POLICY." ROCKEFELLER FOUNDATION SEMINARS IN DIPLOMACY.
WASHINGTON, D.C.: JOHNS HOPKINS U. SCHOOL OF ADVANCED
INTERNATIONAL STUDIES, (NOV. 11, 1975): 1-35.

1623 HUZAR, E. "REORGANIZATION FOR NATIONAL SECURITY." JP 12
(1950):128-152.

1624 IRISH, M.D. "THE PRESIDENT'S FOREIGN POLICY MACHINE." IN
THE FUTURE OF THE AMERICAN PRESIDENCY, EDITED BY C.W.

DUNN, MORRISTOWN, N.J.: GENERAL LEARNING PRESS, 1975:
130-178.

THOROUGH SYNTHETIC REVIEW OF FOREIGN AND NATIONAL SECURITY
POLICY-MAKING PRACTICES FROM WASHINGTON THROUGH FORD
ADMINISTRATIONS.

1625 JACKSON, H.M., ED. THE NATIONAL SECURITY COUNCIL: JACKSON
SUBCOMMITTEE PAPERS ON POLICY-MAKING AT THE PRESIDENTIAL
LEVEL. NEW YORK: PRAEGER, 1965, PP. 311.

COMMERCIAL REPRINT OF MATERIAL ASSEMBLED IN CONNECTION
WITH THE SENATE COMMITTEE "ORGANIZING FOR NATIONAL
SECURITY" CHAIRED BY SENATOR JACKSON. THE JACKSON
COMMITTEE CRITICIZED EISENHOWER FOREIGN POLICY MACHINES AS
UNWIELDY AND WAS CONCERNED WITH WHETHER SUFFICIENT
PREPARATIONS WERE BEING MADE FOR CONVENTIONAL AS WELL AS
FOR NUCLEAR WARFARE.

1626 JOHNSON, R.H. "THE NATIONAL SECURITY COUNCIL: THE
RELEVANCE OF ITS PAST TO ITS FUTURE." ORBIS 13
(1969):709-735.

A REVIEW OF HOW PREVIOUS PRESIDENTS USED THE NSC WRITTEN
IN THE CONTEXT OF EARLY NIXON ADMINISTRATION PLANS TO
"REVIVE" THE COUNCIL.

1627 KISSINGER, H.A. AMERICAN FOREIGN POLICY. (EXPANDED ED.),
NEW YORK: NORTON, 1974.

THE FIRST EDITION(1969) CONTAINED THREE ESSAYS WRITTEN
BEFORE KISSINGER BECAME ASSISTANT TO THE PRESIDENT FOR
NATIONAL SECURITY AFFAIRS. THE EXPANDED EDITION APPEARED
AFTER KISSINGER BECAME SECRETARY OF STATE (1973) AND ADDS
NINE POLICY STATEMENTS AND GENERAL ANALYTIC DISCUSSION OF
FOREIGN POLICY THAT HE MADE BETWEEN JUNE 1972 AND DECEMBER
1973.

1628 MAY, E.R. "LESSONS" OF THE PAST: THE USE AND MISUSE OF
HISTORY IN AMERICAN FOREIGN POLICY. NEW YORK: OXFORD,
1973, PP. 220.

PRESIDENTS AND THEIR ADVISORS UNCRITICALLY USED MISLEADING
HISTORICAL ANALOGIES IN SHAPING AMERICAN FOREIGN POLICY IN
CONNECTION WITH PLANNING THE POST-WORLD WAR II POLITICAL
ARRANGEMENTS, CONDUCTING THE COLD WAR, AND MAKING MILITARY
COMMITMENTS BEARING ON KOREA AND VIETNAM.

1629 ----------. "THE DEVELOPMENT OF POLITICAL-MILITARY
CONSULTATION IN THE UNITED STATES." PSQ 70
(1955):161-180.

A REVIEW OF WORLD WAR I AND II PRESIDENTIAL-MILITARY
RELATIONS, PLUS THE POST WORLD WAR II FORMATION OF THE
NATIONAL SECURITY COUNCIL. BASED ON PRIMARY DOCUMENTS.

1630 MURDOCK, C.A. DEFENSE POLICY FORMATION: A COMPARATIVE
ANALYSIS OF THE MCNAMARA ERA. ALBANY: STATE U OF N.Y. PR,
1974, PP. 209.

ANALYZES DEFENSE POLICY-MAKING BY COMPARING EISENHOWER ADMINISTRATION AND MCNAMARA PRACTICES WITH POLICY-MAKING UNDER DEFENSE-SECRETARY MELVIN LAIRD. LAIRD IN MANY RESPECTS RESTORED THE PRACTICES OF THE 1950'S.

1631 PRICE, D.K., ED. THE SECRETARY OF STATE. ENGLEWOOD CLIFFS, N.J.: PRENTICE HALL, 1960, PP.200.

PAPERS BY DON K. PRICE, PAUL NITZE, DEAN ACHESON, ROBERT BOWIE, HENRY WRISTON, W.Y. ELLIOT, JOHN DICKEY. PREPARED FOR A CONFERENCE OF THE AMERICAN ASSEMBLY. SEE ESPECIALLY ACHESON'S "THE PRESIDENT AND THE SECRETARY OF STATE."

1632 SOUERS, S.W. "POLICY FORMULATION FOR NATIONAL SECURITY." APSR 43 (JUNE 1949): 534-543.

1633 STUPAK, R.J. THE SHAPING OF FOREIGN POLICY: THE ROLE OF SECRETARY OF STATE AS SEEN BY DEAN ACHESON. INDIANAPOLIS, IND.: ODYSSEY, 1969.

1634 WATERS, M. "SPECIAL DIPLOMATIC AGENTS OF THE PRESIDENT." ANNALS 307 (1956):124-133.

HISTORICAL ESSAY FOCUSING ON SEVERAL SUCH AGENTS, ESPECIALLY FDR'S USE OF HARRY HOPKINS IN WORLD WAR II.

1635 WYETH, G.A., JR. "THE NATIONAL SECURITY COUNCIL: CONCEPT OF OPERATIONS; ORGANIZATION; ACTUAL OPERATIONS." J INTERNATIONAL AFFAIRS 8 (1954):185-195.

SEE ALSO 118, 119, 120, 666, 760, 832, 1105, 1270, 1284, 1286, 2140

3. BUREAU OF BUDGET/OFFICE OF MANAGEMENT AND BUDGET

1636 APPLEBY, P. "HAROLD D. SMITH--PUBLIC ADMINISTRATION." PAR 7 (SPRING 1947): 77-81.

1637 BOMBARDIER, G. "THE MANAGERIAL FUNCTION OF OMB: INTERGOVERNMENTAL RELATIONS AS A TEST CASE." PUBLIC POLICY 23 (SUMMER 1975): 317-354.

EXAMINES OMB'S ACTIVITIES IN THE FIELD OF INTERGOVERNMENTAL RELATIONS AS AN ILLUSTRATION OF OMB'S MANAGEMENT FUNCTION.

1638 BONAFEDE, D. "LYNN SEEKS COMPROMISE IN HIS ROLE AS OMB

DIRECTOR." <u>NATIONAL J</u> 21 (1975):767.

A COMPARISON OF OMB DIRECTOR JAMES LYNN WITH HIS PREDECESSOR, ROY ASH. DISCUSSES LYNN'S CONCEPTION OF THE OMB'S ROLE AND HIS WORKING RELATIONSHIP WITH PRESIDENT FORD.

1639 BRUNDAGE, P.F. <u>THE BUREAU OF THE BUDGET</u>. NEW YORK: PRAEGER, 1970, PP. 387.

A FORMAL, STATIC ACCOUNT OF THE BUREAU WRITTEN BY FORMER EISENHOWER BUDGET DIRECTOR. THE BOOK WAS WRITTEN BEFORE BOB WAS RECONSTITUTED AS OMB. APPENDIX REPRINTS MAJOR EXECUTIVE ORDERS AND STATUTES APPLICABLE TO THE BOB'S RESPONSIBILITIES.

1640 ----------. "THE FEDERAL BUDGET: RECENT TRENDS AND FUTURE OPPORTUNITIES (AND ROLE OF THE OFFICE OF MANAGEMENT AND BUDGET)." <u>PRICE WATERHOUSE R</u> 15 (AUTUMN 1970): 6-21.

1641 BURKLAND, J.V. "FEDERAL BUDGETING DEVELOPMENTS: 1947-1948." <u>PAR</u> 8 (AUTUMN 1948): 267-74.

1642 CAREY, W.D. "ROLES OF THE BUREAU OF THE BUDGET." <u>SCIENCE</u> 156 (APRIL 14, 1967): 206-208+.

1643 COOK, D.O. "DOD LEGISLATIVE PROPOSALS AND THE BUREAU OF THE BUDGET." <u>JAG J</u> (OCT 1959): 13+.

1644 CULLITON, B.J. "OFFICE OF MANAGEMENT AND BUDGET: SKEPTICAL VIEW OF SCIENTIFIC ADVICE." <u>SCIENCE</u> (FEB. 1, 1974): 392-396.

1645 DAVIS, D.A., DEMPSTER, M.A., AND WILDAVSKY, A. "A THEORY OF THE BUDGETARY PROCESS." <u>APSR</u> (SEPT 1966): 529-547.

1646 DAWES, C.G. <u>THE FIRST YEAR: THE BUDGET OF THE UNITED STATES</u> NEW YORK: HARPER, 1921.

1647 DOTSON, A. <u>PRODUCTION PLANNING IN THE PATENT OFFICE</u>. INTER-UNIVERSITY CASE PROGRAM: BOX 229, SYRACUSE, N.Y., 1952, PP. 13. ALSO REPRINTED IN STEIN, H., ED. <u>PUBLIC ADMINISTRATION AND POLICY DEVELOPMENT: A CASE BOOK</u>. N.Y.: HARCOURT, BRACE, 1952.

HOW OFFICIALS OF THE PATENT OFFICE AND OF THE BUREAU OF THE BUDGET'S DIVISION OF ADMINISTRATIVE MANAGEMENT COOPERATED IN DEVISING A MORE EFFECTIVE ADMINISTRATIVE PROCEDURE FOR DISTRIBUTING PATENT COPIES.

1648 FOX, M. "THE PRESIDENT'S PROPOSALS FOR EXECUTIVE REORGANIZATION: A CRITIQUE," PAR 33 (SEPTEMBER/OCTOBER 1973): 401-406.

1649 GILMOUR, R.S. "CENTRAL LEGISLATIVE CLEARANCE: A REVISED PERSPECTIVE." PUBLIC ADMINISTRATION R 31 (1971):150-158.

A DISCUSSION OF CHANGES IN THE LEGISLATIVE CLEARANCE PROCESS AS A RESULT OF ACTIVIST PRESIDENTIAL LEADERSHIP SINCE THE 1960'S. THERE HAS BEEN A SHORT CIRCUITING OF USUAL BOB/OMB INSTITUTIONAL CHANNELS ON MATTERS DEEMED CENTRAL TO THE PRESIDENT'S PROGRAM, WITH MEMBERS OF THE WHITE HOUSE STAFF ASSUMING RESPONSIBILITY FOR KEY PIECES OF LEGISLATION.

1650 GLASER, N. "ON TASK FORCING," PUBLIC INTEREST 15 (SPRING 1969): 40-45.

1651 GORDON, G.J. "OFFICE OF MANAGEMENT AND BUDGET CIRCULAR A-95: PERSPECTIVES AND IMPLICATIONS." PUBLIUS 4 (1974):45-68.

1652 GREENHOUSE, S. "THE PLANNING-PROGRAMMING-BUDGETING SYSTEM," PAR 26 (DEC 1966): 271-77.

1653 GROSS, B.M. "THE NEW SYSTEMS BUDGETING," PAR 29 (MARCH/APRIL 1969): 113-136.

1654 HAMILL, K. "THIS IS A BUREAUCRAT." FORTUNE (NOV. 1953): 156-158+.

PROFILE OF VETERAN BUDGET BUREAU OFFICIAL, ROGER JONES.

1655 HARLOW, R.L. "ON THE DECLINE AND POSSIBLE FALL OF PPBS." PUBLIC FINANCE Q 1 (JAN. 1973): 85-105.

1656 HARPER, E.L., KRAMER, F.A., AND ROUSE, A.M. "IMPLEMENTATION AND USE OF PPB IN SIXTEEN FEDERAL AGENCIES." PUBLIC ADMINISTRATION R 29 (1969):623-632.

1657 HARRIS, J.P. "NEEDED REFORMS IN THE BUDGET SYSTEM." PAR (1952): 242-250.

1658 HAVEMANN, J. "BUDGET REFORM LEGISLATION CALLS FOR MAJOR PROCEDURAL CHANGE." NATIONAL J 6 (1974):734-742.

THE REVISION OF CONGRESS'S ANNUAL BUDGET PROCEDURE COULD DRASTICALLY ALTER THE LEGISLATIVE-EXECUTIVE BALANCE TO FAVOR THE FORMER.

1659 ----------. "OMB BEGINS MAJOR PROGRAM TO IDENTIFY AND ATTAIN PRESIDENTIAL GOALS." NATIONAL J 22 (1973):783-793.

1660 ----------. "OMB'S 'MANAGEMANT-BY-OBJECTIVE' PRODUCES GOALS OF UNEVEN QUALITY." NATIONAL J 5 (1973):1201-1210.

1661 ----------. "OMB'S LEGISLATIVE ROLE IS GROWING MORE POWERFUL AND MORE POLITICAL." NATIONAL J 43 (1973):1589-1598.

DESCRIBES THE SIGNIFICANT CHANGES IN OMB PRACTICE BY THE INTRODUCTION OF POLITICALLY APPOINTED ASSISTANT DIRECTORS("PADS") INTO ASPECTS OF THE LEGISLATIVE CLEARING PROCESS, TRADITIONALLY THE RESPONSIBILITY OF CAREER OFFICERS.

1662 HECLO, H. "OMB AND THE PRESIDENCY: THE PROBLEM OF NEUTRAL COMPETENCE." PUBLIC INTEREST (WINTER 1975): 80-98.

THE AUTHOR MAINTAINS THAT THE OLD BUREAU OF THE BUDGET WAS ONE OF THE FEW PLACES IN GOVERNMENT WHICH EXEMPLIFIED "NEUTRAL COMPETENCE." NEUTRAL COMPETENCE IS VIEWED AS THE HALLMARK OF A HIGHER CIVIL SERVICE WHICH PROVIDES RELATIVELY OBJECTIVE AND IMPARTIAL ADVICE TO A SUCCESSION OF PARTISAN LEADERS. THE IMPOUNDMENT CONTROVERSY OF THE 1970'S, WATERGATE, AND THE IMPOSITION OF POLICY LEVEL POLITICAL APPOINTEES IN BOB'S SUCCESSOR AGENCY, THE OFFICE OF MANAGEMENT AND BUDGET, HAVE THREATENED THE NEUTRAL COMPETENCE OF OMB.

1663 HELD, V. "PPBS COMES TO WASHINGTON." PUBLIC INTEREST (SUMMER, 1966):102-115.

AN EARLY DESCRIPTION AND DEFENSE OF WHAT LATER WAS TO BE A HIGHLY UNSUCCESSFUL AND RADICALLY ABANDONED BUDGETARY PROCEDURE.

1664 HELLER, D., AND HELLER, D. "THE EXTRAORDINARY POWERS OF THE BUREAU OF THE BUDGET." AMER LEGION M 79 (AUG 1965): 8-12+.

1665 HIRSCH, W. "TOWARD FEDERAL PROGRAM BUDGETING." PAR 26 (DEC 1966): 259-270.

1666 HOLCOMBE, A.N. "OVER-ALL FINANCIAL PLANNING THROUGH THE BUREAU OF THE BUDGET." PUBLIC ADMINISTRATION R 1 (1941):225-230.

REVIEWS THE BUDGET BUREAU'S ROLE IN PREPARING THE NATION'S BUDGET AND ECONOMIC PROGRAM.

1667 JONES, J.W. "THE EXECUTION OF THE FEDERAL BUDGET." ACCOUNTING REVIEW 17 (1942): 88.

1668 KEY, V.O. "THE LACK OF A BUDGETARY THEORY." APSR (DECEMBER 1940): 1137-1144.

1669 LATHAM, E. "EXECUTIVE MANAGEMENT AND THE FEDERAL FIELD SERVICE." PAR 5 (1945): 16.

1670 LAWTON, F.J. "IMPROVING THE BUDGETARY PROCESS." PAR 16 (SPRING 1956): 117-121.

1671 ----------. "LEGISLATIVE/EXECUTIVE RELATIONS IN BUDGETING AS VIEWED BY THE EXECUTIVE." PUBLIC ADMINISTRATION REVIEW 13 (1953):169-176.

A FORMER BUDGET DIRECTOR FOR PRESIDENT TRUMAN DESCRIBES THE ROLE OF THE BUDGET BUREAU AS A PRESIDENTIAL AGENT IN DEALING WITH CONGRESS ON LEGISLATIVE MATTERS. THE AUTHOR FOCUSES ON THE ISSUE OF ACCOUNTABILITY.

1672 LEWIS, F., AND ZARB, F. "FEDERAL PROGRAM EVALUATION FROM THE OMB PERSPECTIVE." PAR 34 (JULY-AUG 1974): 308-317.

1673 LONG, N. "POPULAR SUPPORT FOR ECONOMIC PROGRAMS." PAR 42 (APRIL 1948): 326-36.

1674 MERRIAM, R.E. "THE BUREAU OF THE BUDGET AS PART OF THE PRESIDENT'S STAFF." ANNALS 307 (1956):15-23.

BUDGET BUREAU OFFICIAL TRACES HISTORICAL DEVELOPMENT OF BOB SINCE 1921 AND DISCUSSES THE ROLE REQUIREMENTS OF WORKING AS A PRESIDENT'S STAFF AIDE, BUT NOT AS HIS PARTISAN ALLY.

1675 MORSTEIN MARX, F. "THE BUREAU OF THE BUDGET: ITS EVOLUTION AND PRESENT ROLE." APSR 39 (1945):869-898.

THE LEGAL AUTHORITY OF THE BOB AND ITS FUNCTIONS ARE DESCRIBED.

1676 MOSHER, F.C. PROGRAM BUDGETING: THEORY AND PRACTICE. CHICAGO: PUBLIC ADMINISTRATIVE SERVICE, 1954.

1677 MULLANEY, T.R. "OMB PUSHES PLANS TO IMPROVE FEDERAL MANAGEMENT; STILL NO MIRACLES." NATIONAL J 49 (1971):2378-2388.

1678 ODIORNE, G.S. "THE POLITICS OF IMPLEMENTING MBO." BUS HORIZONS 17 (JUNE 1974): 13-21.

1679 PEARSON, N.M. "A GENERAL ADMINISTRATIVE STAFF TO AID THE PRESIDENT." PUBLIC ADMINISTRATION R 4 (1944):127-147.

1680 ----------. "THE BUDGET BUREAU: FROM WARTIME BUREAU TO GENERAL STAFF." PUBLIC ADMINISTRATION R 3 (1943):126-149.

1681 PRICE, D.K. "GENERAL DAWES AND EXECUTIVE STAFF WORK." PAR (SUMMER 1951): 167-172.

1682 RAPPAPORT, P. "THE BUREAU OF THE BUDGET: A VIEW FROM THE INSIDE." J ACCOUNTANCY (MAR 1956): 31-37.

A FORMER BOB ASSISTANT DIRECTOR DURING THE EISENHOWER ADMINISTRATION PROVIDES AN "INSIDER'S" VIEW OF THE BUDGET BUREAU'S STAFF FUNCTIONS, WITH SPECIAL EMPHASIS ON GENERAL ACCOUNTING PRACTICES.

1683 RAWSON, R.H. "THE FORMULATION OF THE FEDERAL BUDGET." PUBLIC POLICY 2 (1941): 117-135.

1684 REESE, J.H. "THE ROLE OF THE BUREAU OF THE BUDGET IN THE LEGISLATIVE PROCESS." J PUBLIC LAW 15 (1966): 63-93.

1685 RIPLEY, R.B., AND DAVIS, J.W. "THE BUREAU OF THE BUDGET AND EXECUTIVE BRANCH AGENCIES: NOTES ON THEIR

INTERACTION." JP 29 (NOV 1967): 749-769.

ANALYSIS OF BOB-EXECUTIVE BRANCH INTERACTION BASED ON OPEN-ENDED INTERVIEWS.

1686 ROSE, R. MANAGING PRESIDENTIAL OBJECTIVES. NEW YORK: FREE PR, 1976, PP. 180.

A COMPREHENSIVE CASE-STUDY OF THE 1975 MANAGEMENT BY OBJECTIVES IN THE FEDERAL GOVERNMENT BY THE NIXON ADMINISTRATION'S OMB.

1687 SALASIN, S., AND KIVENS, L. "FOSTERING FEDERAL PROGRAM EVALUATION: A CURRENT OMB INITIATIVE." EVALUATION 2 NO. 2 (1975): 37-41.

1688 SAMUELSON, R.J. "THE PEOPLE EVERYONE LOVES TO HATE." WASHINGTONIAN 11 (NOV 1975): 62+.

A JOURNALIST'S LOOK AT THE OFFICE OF MANAGEMENT AND BUDGET.

1689 SCHICK, A. "A DEATH IN THE BUREAUCRACY: THE DEMISE OF FEDERAL PPB." PAR 33 (MARCH/APRIL 1973): 146-156.

1690 ----------. "THE BUDGET BUREAU THAT WAS: THOUGHTS ON THE RISE, DECLINE, AND FUTURE OF A PRESIDENTIAL AGENCY." LAW AND CONTEMPORARY PROBLEMS 35 (1970):519-39.

WRITING ON THE OCCASION OF THE CHANGE FROM BOB TO OMB, SCHICK DISCUSSES THE SHIFTS IN THE BUREAU'S ROLE WITH RESPECT TO BUDGETING, ADMINISTRATIVE MANAGEMENT AND PROGRAM PLANNING.

1691 ----------. "THE ROAD TO PPB: THE STAGES OF BUDGET REFORM." PAR 29 (MARCH/APRIL 1969): 137-151.

1692 SHORT, L.M. "AN INVESTIGATION OF THE EXECUTIVE AGENCIES OF THE UNITED STATES GOVERNMENT." APSR 33 (FEB 1939): 60-66.

1693 SMITH, H.D. THE MANAGEMENT OF YOUR GOVERNMENT. N.Y.: MCGRAW-HILL, 1945.

1694 ----------. "THE BUDGET AS AN INSTRUMENT OF LEGISLATIVE CONTROL AND EXECUTIVE MANAGEMENT." PAR 4 (SUMMER 1944): 181-88.

1695 ----------. "THE BUREAU OF THE BUDGET." PUBLIC
ADMINISTRATION R 1 (1941):106-115.

THE FIRST DIRECTOR OF THE BUREAU OF THE BUDGET AFTER ITS
LOCATION IN THE EXECUTIVE OFFICE OF THE PRESIDENT
DESCRIBES ITS ROLE AS A GENERAL STAFF AGENCY IN THE AREA
OF ADMINISTRATIVE MANAGEMENT AND THE PRESIDENT'S NEED FOR
THE AGENCY'S STAFF SERVICES.

1696 STAFFORD, S. "'POLITICAL' OMB CUTS AGENCIES TO SIZE."
GOVT EXECUTIVE 7 (AUG. 1974): 48-53.

1697 STANS, M. "THE PRESIDENT'S BUDGET AND THE ROLE OF THE
BOB." FEDERAL ACCOUNTANT 9 (SEPT 1959): 5-16.

1698 STANTON, T.C. "CONCEPTUAL UNDERPINNINGS OF THE FEDERAL
BUDGET PROCESS." FEDERAL ACCOUNTANT 24 (DEC 1975):
44-51.

A BUSINESS SCHOOL PROFESSOR'S HISTORICAL ACCOUNT AND
ANALYSIS OF CHANGING FEDERAL BUDGETING PRACTICES AND
ASSUMPTIONS FROM THE FRAMING OF THE CONSTITUTION THROUGH
THE 1970'S. STRESSES THE CONTINUING CONFLICT BETWEEN
PRESIDENT AND CONGRESS OVER CONTROL OF THE BUDGET.

1699 STEELMAN, J.R., AND KREAGER, H.D. "THE EXECUTIVE OFFICE AS
ADMINISTRATIVE COORDINATOR." LAW AND CONTEMPORARY
PROBLEMS 21 (1956):688-709.

1700 TRUEBLOOD, R.M. "THE REPORT OF THE PRESIDENT'S COMMISSION
ON BUDGET CONCEPTS." FEDERAL ACCOUNTANT 17 (JUNE 1968):
4-15.

PARTICIPANT-OBSERVER REVIEWS THE COMMISSION'S MAJOR
RECOMMENDATIONS AND SEVERAL WHICH WERE CONSIDERED BUT NOT
PROPOSED.

1701 WADE, L.L. "THE U.S. BUREAU OF THE BUDGET: AS AGENCY
EVALUATOR; ORIENTATION TO ACTION," AMERICAN J. ECONOMICS
AND SOCIOLOGY 55 (1967).

1702 WALKER, R. "THE RELATION OF BUDGETING TO PROGRAM
PLANNING." PAR 4 (SPRING 1944).

1703 WALSH, J. "OFFICE OF MANAGEMENT AND BUDGET: THE VIEW FROM
THE EXECUTIVE OFFICE." SCIENCE (JAN. 18, 1974):
180-182+.

1704 ----------. "OFFICE OF MANAGEMENT AND BUDGET: NEW ACCENT ON THE "M" IN OMB." SCIENCE 183 (1974):286-290.

1705 WANAT, J. "BUREAUCRATIC POLITICS IN THE BUDGET FORMULATION ARENA." ADMINISTRATION AND SOCIETY 7 (AUGUST 1975).

1706 WANN, A.J. "FRANKLIN D. ROOSEVELT AND THE BUREAU OF THE BUDGET." UNIV MO BUS & GOV R 9 (MAR-APR 1968): 32-41.

1707 WEEKS, O.D. "INITIATION OF LEGISLATION BY ADMINISTRATIVE AGENCIES." BROOKLYN LAW R 9 (JUNE 1939): 117-131.

1708 WILDAVSKY, A. THE POLITICS OF THE BUDGETARY PROCESS, 2D ED. BOSTON: LITTLE, BROWN, 1974, PP. 271.

THE MOST AUTHORITATIVE DISCUSSION OF BUDGET-MAKING AT THE FEDERAL LEVEL FROM THE AGENCY THROUGH THE CONGRESSIONAL STAGE, INCLUDING THE ROLE OF THE BOB/OMB. REPRINT OF 1964 EDITION WITH ADDED PREFACE. CRITIQUE OF THE PPBS PROCEDURE ATTEMPTED IN THE 1960'S. SUGGESTIONS ABOUT HOW USE OF THE INCREMENTAL APPROACH THAT WILDAVSKY CONSIDERS BOTH INEVITABLE AND DESIRABLE CAN ENHANCE BUDGETARY CONTROL BY CONGRESS.

1709 ----------. "POLITICAL IMPLICATIONS OF BUDGETING REFORM." PAR 21 (AUTUMN 1961): 183-90.

1710 ----------. "RESCUING POLICY ANALYSIS FROM PPBS." PAR (MAR-APR 1969): 189-202.

1711 ----------. "THE ANNUAL EXPENDITURE INCREMENT--OR HOW CONGRESS CAN REGAIN CONTROL OF THE BUDGET." PUBLIC INTEREST (FALL 1973): 84-108.

1712 ----------. "THE POLITICAL ECONOMY OF EFFICIENCY: COST-BENEFIT ANALYSIS AND PROGRAM BUDGETING." PAR 26 (DEC 1966): 292-312.

1713 WILKIE, H. "LEGAL BASIS FOR INCREASED ACTIVITY OF THE FEDERAL BUDGET BUREAU." GEORGE WASHINGTON LAW R 11 (APRIL 1943): 265-301.

1714 YARMOLINSKY, A. "IDEAS INTO PROGRAMS." THE PUBLIC INTEREST 2 (WINTER 1966): 71-9.

SEE ALSO 121, 122, 686, 754, 771, 1221, 1295, 1329, 1471, 1528, 1532, 1598, 1599, 1718, 1786, 1916, 1959, 2018, 2256, 2281

4. DOMESTIC COUNCIL

1715 BONAFEDE, D. "DOMESTIC COUNCIL TRIES TO MATCH EARLY PROMISE." NATIONAL J 7 (1975): 1687-1696.

1716 KESSEL, J.H. THE DOMESTIC PRESIDENCY: DECISION-MAKING IN THE WHITE HOUSE. MASSACHUSETTS: DUXBURY PRESS, 1975, PP. 149.

ANALYSIS OF THE EFFECT AND FUNCTIONING OF THE DOMESTIC COUNCIL DURING PRESIDENT NIXON'S FIRST TERM. BASED IN PART ON QUANTIFIED INTERVIEW DATA.

1717 MOE, R.C. "THE DOMESTIC COUNCIL IN PERSPECTIVE." THE BUREAUCRAT 5 (OCTOBER 1976): 251-272.

"ULTIMATELY THE FUTURE OF THE DOMESTIC COUNCIL WILL DEPEND ON THE WORKING STYLE OF THE INCUMBENT PRESIDENT. BOTH PRESIDENTS NIXON AND FORD FOUND THE COUNCIL AND THE STAFF A USEFUL TOOL TO ASSIST THEM IN GETTING OPTIONS ON COMPLEX ISSUES THROUGH THE BUREAUCRACY TO THEM IN A MANNER THAT ASSISTED THEIR OWN DECISION-MAKING."

1718 SHANI, M. "U.S. FEDERAL GOVERNMENT REORGANIZATION: EXECUTIVE BRANCH STRUCTURE AND CENTRAL DOMESTIC POLICY-MAKING STAFF." PUBLIC ADMINISTRATION (ENGLAND) 52 (SUMMER 1974): 193-208.

1719 WALDMAN, R.J. "THE DOMESTIC COUNCIL: INNOVATION IN PRESIDENTIAL GOVERNMENT." PAR 36 (1976): 260-268.

SEE ALSO 121, 122, 1242

5. ECONOMIC

1720 BEMAN, L. "THE CHASTENING OF THE WASHINGTON ECONOMISTS." FORTUNE 93 (JAN 1976): 158-162+.

1721 COLM, G. "THE EXECUTIVE OFFICE AND FISCAL ECONOMIC

POLICY." LAW AND CONTEMPORARY PROBLEMS 21 (1956):710-723.

FORMER MEMBER OF TRUMAN COUNCIL OF ECONOMIC ADVISORS' STAFF REVIEWS EVOLUTION OF THE CEA IN ITS EARLY YEARS, STRESSING DIFFERENCES OF NOURSE, KEYSERLING, AND BURNS.

1722 FLASH, E.S. ECONOMIC ADVICE AND PRESIDENTIAL LEADERSHIP: THE COUNCIL OF ECONOMIC ADVISERS. NEW YORK: COLUMBIA UNIV. PRESS, 1965, PP. 382.

OVERVIEW OF CEA UNDER THREE OF ITS CHAIRMEN--LEON KEYSERLING, ARTHUR BURNS AND WALTER HELLER. FLASH DISCUSSES THE COUNCIL'S ROLE DURING THE KOREAN MOBILIZATION, THE 1953-1954 RECESSION AND THE 1963 TAX PROPOSAL.

1723 HARRIS, S.E. THE ECONOMICS OF THE POLITICAL PARTIES: WITH SPECIAL ATTENTION TO PRESIDENTS EISENHOWER AND KENNEDY. NEW YORK: MACMILLAN, 1962.

1724 HOOD, R.C. "REORGANIZING THE COUNCIL OF ECONOMIC ADVISERS." PSQ 69 (1954):413-437.

1725 "HOW POLITICAL MUST THE COUNCIL OF ECONOMIC ADVISORS BE?" CHALLENGE 17 (MAR.-APR. 1974): 28-42.

PANEL DISCUSSION BY HERBERT STEIN, JAMES TOBIN, HENRY WALLICH, ARTHUR OKUN, WALTER HELLER, HENDRIK HOUTHAKKER, MARINA WHITMAN, AND ROY BLOUGH.

1726 MITCHELL, D.J.B. "INFLATION: LONG-TERM PROBLEMS." ANNALS 31 (1975): 114-126.

1727 ----------. "PHASE II WAGE CONTROLS." IND AND LABOR REL R 27 (APR 1974): 351-375.

1728 NORTON, H.S. THE COUNCIL OF ECONOMIC ADVISORS: THREE PERIODS OF INFLUENCE. UNIVERSITY OF SOUTH CAROLINA: BUREAU OF BUSINESS AND ECONOMIC RESEARCH, 1973, PP.72.

1729 NOURSE, E.G., AND GROSS, B.M. "THE ROLE OF THE COUNCIL OF ECONOMIC ADVISERS." APSR 42 (APR 1948): 283-295.

1730 REES, A. "WAGE-PRICE POLICY." UNIVERSITY PROGRAMS MODULAR STUDIES MORRISTOWN, N.J.: GENERAL LEARNING PRESS, 1974, PP. 19.

COMPREHENSIVE REVIEW OF THE NIXON ADMINISTRATION'S WAGE-PRICE POLICY BETWEEN 1971-73. FINDS THAT WAGE-PRICE CONTROLS PLAYED A SIGNIFICANT ROLE IN RESTRAINING INFLATION.

1731 SILVERMAN, C. THE PRESIDENT'S ECONOMIC ADVISERS. INTER-UNIVERSITY CASE PROGRAM: BOX 229, SYRACUSE, N.Y., 1959, PP.18.

CASE CONSIDERS THE ACTIONS OF THE FIRST THREE MEMBERS OF THE COUNCIL OF ECONOMIC ADVISERS, HOW THEY FACED THE PROBLEMS INVOLVED IN INCORPORATING PROFESSIONAL EXPERTISE IN MAJOR POLICY-MAKING DECISIONS, AND HOW ARTHUR BURNS TRIED TO RESOLVE THE SAME PROBLEMS AT THE BEGINNING OF THE EISENHOWER ADMINISTRATION.

1732 VON FURSTENBERG, G.M., AND BOUGHTON, J.M. "STABILIZATION GOALS AND THE APPROPRIATENESS OF FISCAL POLICY DURING THE EISENHOWER AND KENNEDY-JOHNSON ADMINISTRATIONS." PUBLIC FINANCE Q 1 (JAN. 1973): 5-28.

CONCLUDES THAT THE STABILIZATION RATIONALE HAD LITTLE TO DO WITH POLICY FORMATION IN THOSE YEARS.

SEE ALSO 657, 960, 967, 1260, 1316, 1338, 1351, 1526

6. SCIENCE AND TECHNOLOGY

1733 BARFIELD, C.E. "SCIENTISTS, CONGRESS SCRUTINIZE PRESIDENTIAL TECHNICAL ADVISORY PLAN." NAT J R 6 (AUG 1974): 1201-1204.

"LEADING U.S. SCIENTISTS AND SOME KEY MEMBERS OF CONGRESS ARE URGING CREATION OF A NEW APPROACH TO SCIENTIFIC ADVICE FOR THE WHITE HOUSE."

1734 BECKLER, D.Z. "THE PRECARIOUS LIFE OF SCIENCE IN THE WHITE HOUSE." DAEDALUS (SUMMER 1974): 115-134.

EXCELLENT HISTORICAL SURVEY OF THE RISE OF THE PRESIDENT'S SCIENCE ADVISORY COUNCIL AS AN EXECUTIVE OFFICE OF THE PRESIDENT AND THE TERMINATION OF THAT OFFICE UNDER NIXON. AUTHOR SERVED AS EXECUTIVE DIRECTOR OF THE COUNCIL THROUGHOUT ITS LIFE SPAN.

1735 BRONK, D.W. "SCIENCE ADVICE IN THE WHITE HOUSE." SCIENCE 186 (OCT 1974): 116-121.

1736 BROOKS, H. "THE SCIENTIFIC ADVISOR." IN SCIENTISTS AND NATIONAL POLICY-MAKING, EDITED BY R. GILPIN AND C. WRIGHT, PP. 73-96. NEW YORK: COLUMBIA UNIVERSITY PRESS, 1964.

BALANCED GENERAL DISCUSSION. ON LATER VICISSITUDES OF PRESIDENTIAL SCIENCE ADVISING, SEE D. BECKLER, "THE PRECARIOUS LIFE OF SCIENCE IN THE WHITE HOUSE."

1737 CAHN, A.H. EGGHEADS AND WARHEADS: SCIENTISTS AND THE ABM. CAMBRIDGE, MASS.: CENTER FOR INTERNAT STUDIES, MIT, 1971, PP. 261.

1738 DADDARIO, E.Q. "SCIENCE POLICY: RELATIONSHIPS ARE THE KEY." DAEDALUS 103 (SUMMER 1974): 135-142.

ASSERTS NEED FOR A CENTRAL FOCAL POINT, CLOSE TO THE PRESIDENT, OF SCIENTIFIC ADVICE AND COORDINATION.

1739 DOTY, P. "CAN INVESTIGATIONS IMPROVE SCIENTIFIC ADVICE? THE CASE OF THE ABM." MINERVA 10 (APR. 1972): 280-294.

FOR A FURTHER ACCOUNT OF THIS EPISODE, SEE CHAPTER 5 OF PRIMACK AND VON HIPPEL,ADVICE AND DISSENT: SCIENTISTS IN THE POLITICAL ARENA.

1740 GILPIN, R. AMERICAN SCIENTISTS AND NUCLEAR WEAPONS POLICY. PRINCETON: PRINCETON UNIVERSITY PRESS, 1962, PP. 352.

1741 KILLIAN, J.R., JR., ET AL. "SCIENCE ADVICE FOR THE WHITE HOUSE." TECHNOLOGY R 76 (JAN. 1974): 8-19.

1742 KISTIAKOWSKY, G.B. "PRESIDENTIAL SCIENCE ADVISING." SCIENCE (APR. 5, 1974): 38-42.

A REVIEW OF SCIENTIFIC ADVICE TO THE PRESIDENT, FROM THE EISENHOWER ADMINISTRATION TO THE PRESENT, SUGGESTING A NEW COUNCIL ON SCIENCE AND TECHNOLOGY.

1743 LYONS, G.M. "THE PRESIDENT AND HIS EXPERTS." ANNALS 394:36-45 MAR '71.

DISCUSSES THE DILEMMA FACED BY SOCIAL SCIENTISTS WHEN THEY ARE COMPELLED TO CHOOSE BETWEEN THEIR ALLEGIANCE TO THE PRESIDENT AND THE PROFESSIONAL STANDARDS OF THEIR OWN EXPERTISE.

1744 NATIONAL ACADEMY OF SCIENCES, AD HOC COM. ON SCIENCE. "SCIENCE AND TECHNOLOGY IN PRESIDENTIAL POLICYMAKING." WASHINGTON, D.C., 1974, PP. 56.

"THE COMMITTEE HAS REACHED THE CONCLUSION THAT SCIENCE AND TECHNOLOGY CAN FULLY SERVE THE FEDERAL GOVERNMENT--AND THE NATION--ONLY IF ADEQUATE MEANS ARE INCLUDED WITHIN THE STAFF STRUCTURE OF THE EXECUTIVE OFFICE OF THE PRESIDENT TO PROVIDE A SOURCE OF SCIENTIFIC AND TECHNOLOGICAL ANALYSIS AND JUDGMENT TO THE PRESIDENT AND THE AGENCIES IN HIS OFFICE."

1745 NELSON, B. "NIXON FORMS ADVISORY PANELS ON SCIENCE, SPACE, HEALTH." SCIENCE 162 (DEC. 13, 1968): 1255.

REVIEWS TRANSITION TASK FORCES ESTABLISHED BY
PRESIDENT-ELECT NIXON IN 1968.

1746 PRICE, D.K. THE SCIENTIFIC ESTATE CAMBRIDGE: HARVARD U
PR, 1965.

PRESIDENTIAL SCIENCE ADVISING DISCUSSED ESPECIALLY ON PP.
257-269.

1747 ----------. "MONEY AND INFLUENCE: THE LINKS OF SCIENCE TO
PUBLIC POLICY." DAEDALUS (SUMMER 1974): 97-113.

1748 PRIMACK, J., AND VON HIPPEL, F. ADVICE AND DISSENT:
SCIENTISTS IN THE POLITICAL ARENA. NEW YORK: BASIC BOOKS,
1974, PP. 299.

1749 "SCIENCE: THE DOORS TO THE WHITE HOUSE REOPEN." CONG Q W
REPT (OCT. 12, 1974): 2834-2840.

A REVIEW OF SCIENTIFIC ADVICE TO THE PRESIDENT STRESSING
THE OUTLOOK IN THE FORD ADMINISTRATION.

1750 SHERWOOD, M. "FEDERAL POLICY FOR BASIC RESEARCH:
PRESIDENTIAL STAFF AND THE NATIONAL SCIENCE FOUNDATION,
1950-1956." J AMER HIST 55 (1968):599-615.

1751 SKOLNIKOFF, E.B., AND BROOKS, H. "SCIENCE ADVICE IN THE
WHITE HOUSE? CONTINUATION OF A DEBATE." SCIENCE (JAN.
10, 1975): 35-41.

FAVORS PROPOSAL FOR A THREE-MEMBER COUNCIL FOR SCIENCE AND
TECHNOLOGY WITH STRONG PRESIDENTIAL SUPPORT. THE
ORGANIZATIONAL STRUCTURE OF THE COUNCIL, HOWEVER, IS LESS
IMPORTANT THAN THE MANDATE GIVEN TO THE OFFICE BY THE
PRESIDENT.

1752 STAATS, E.B. "FEDERAL ORGANIZATION FOR SCIENCE AND
TECHNOLOGY." GAO R (FALL 1974): 1-10.

SUGGESTIONS BY A LONG TIME OFFICIAL OF THE EXECUTIVE
OFFICE OF THE PRESIDENT, THEN SERVING AS
COMPTROLLER-GENERAL.

1753 STRICKLAND, D.A. SCIENTISTS IN POLITICS: THE ATOMIC
SCIENTISTS' MOVEMENT, 1945-1946. LAFAYETTE, IND.: PURDUE
UNIVERSITY STUDIES, 1968, PP.149.

SEE ALSO 70, 355, 846, 984, 1046, 1317, 1318, 1644

7. AD HOC COMMISSIONS, TASK FORCES AND ADVISORY GROUPS

1754 APPLEBY, P. "THE SIGNIFICANCE OF THE HOOVER COMMISSION

REPORT." YALE REVIEW 32 (AUGUST 1949).

1755 BRADY, J.R. "THE PRESIDENTIAL TASK FORCE AS AN ACTION
INSTRUMENT TO ACHIEVE URGENT NATIONAL GOALS." IND J OF
PUBLIC ADMINISTRATION 14 (1968):322-332.

1756 DEAN, A.L. "AD HOC COMMISSIONS FOR POLICY FORMATION?" IN
THE PRESIDENTIAL ADVISORY SYSTEM, EDITED BY T.E. CRONIN
AND S.D. GREENBERG, NEW YORK: HARPER AND ROW, 1969:
101-116.

PROS AND CONS OF USE OF SUCH ADVISORY GROUPS BY
PRESIDENTS, WITH HISTORICAL EXAMPLES.

1757 HOOVER, H. THE HOOVER COMMISSION REPORT ON ORGANIZATION
OF THE EXECUTIVE BRANCH OF THE GOVERNMENT. NEW YORK:
MCGRAW-HILL, 1949, PP. 524.

COMMERCIAL REPRINT OF THE REPORT OF THE FIRST HOOVER
COMMISSION. SEE CHAPTER TWO (GOVERNMENT PUBLICATIONS) FOR
ANNOTATION AND FOR THE REPORT OF THE SECOND HOOVER
COMMISSION.

1758 HUMPHREY, H.H. "CITIZEN ADVICE AND A DOMESTIC POLICY
COUNCIL." IN THE PRESIDENTIAL ADVISORY SYSTEM, EDITED BY
T.E. CRONIN AND S.D. GREENBERG, NEW YORK: HARPER AND ROW,
1969: 312-317.

A PRE-1968 ELECTION RECOMMENDATION THAT THE NEW PRESIDENT
ESTABLISH A DOMESTIC POLICY COUNCIL FOR IMPROVING NATIONAL
DECISION-MAKING PROCESSES AND SERVICES.

1759 KOMAROVSKY, M., ED. SOCIOLOGY AND PUBLIC POLICY: THE CASE
OF THE PRESIDENTIAL COMMISSIONS. WASHINGTON, D.C.:
AMERICAN SOCIOLOGICAL ASSOCIATION, 1975, PP. 183.

1760 KRAINES, O. "THE PRESIDENT VERSUS CONGRESS: THE KEEP
COMMISSION, 1905 - 1909. FIRST COMPREHENSIVE PRESIDENTIAL
INQUIRY INTO ADMINISTRATION." WESTERN POLITICAL Q 23
(1970):5-54.

HISTORICAL ACCOUNT OF THE INITIAL ASSERTION OF
PRESIDENTIAL RESPONSIBILITY FOR THE ADMINISTRATION OF
GOVERNMENT. A MAJOR STEP WAS TAKEN IN ENDING CONGRESS'
FULL LEGISLATIVE AUTHORITY IN THE MANAGEMENT OF THE PUBLIC
BUSINESS.

1761 MARCY, C.M. PRESIDENTIAL COMMISSIONS. NEW YORK: KINGS
CROWN PRESS, 1945, PP. 141.

1762 ORFIELD, L.B. "HOOVER COMMISSION AND FEDERAL EXECUTIVE
REORGANIZATION." TEMPLE L Q 24 (OCT 1950): 162-217.

1763 POPPER, F. THE PRESIDENT'S COMMISSIONS. NEW YORK: TWENTIETH CENTURY FUND, 1970, PP. 73.

A SUMMARY ESSAY ON THESE BODIES AND THEIR FUNCTIONS.

1764 PRITCHETT, C.H. "THE REGULATORY COMMISSION REVISITED," APSR 43 (OCTOBER 1949): 978-989.

1765 RELYEA, H.C. "DEVELOPMENT AND ORGANIZATION OF WHITE HOUSE CONFERENCES" PRESIDENTIAL STUDIES QUARTERLY 6 (WINTER AND SPRING 1976): 36-39.

1766 STIEBER, J. "THE PRESIDENT'S (ADVISORY) COMMITTEE ON LABOR-MANAGEMENT POLICY." INDUSTRIAL RELATIONS 5 (FEB 1966): 1-19.

1767 STOREY, R.G. "SECOND HOOVER COMMISSION: ITS LEGAL TASK FORCE." ABA J 40 (JUNE 1954): 483-86, 536-39.

1768 SULZNER, G.T. "THE POLICY PROCESS AND THE USES OF NATIONAL GOVERNMENTAL STUDY COMMISSIONS." WESTERN POLITICAL Q 24, NO. 3 (1971):438-448.

FOCUSES ON NATIONAL STUDY GROUPS THAT HAVE INVESTIGATED MATTERS OF GENERAL PUBLIC INTEREST. DISCUSSES THE ACTUAL AND POTENTIAL FUNCTIONS OF COMMISSIONS IN THE POLITICAL PROCESSES.

1769 SUNDERLAND, L.V. OBSCENITY: THE COURT, THE CONGRESS AND THE PRESIDENT'S COMMISSION. WASHINGTON, D.C.: AMERICAN ENTERPRISE INSTITUTE FOR PUBLIC POLICY RESEARCH, 1974, PP. 127.

1770 THOMAS, N.C., AND WOLMAN, H.L. "POLICY FORMULATION IN THE INSTITUTIONALIZED PRESIDENCY: THE JOHNSON TASK FORCES." IN THE PRESIDENTIAL ADVISORY SYSTEM, EDITED BY T.E. CRONIN AND S.D. GREENBERG, NEW YORK: HARPER AND ROW. 1969: 124-143.

SURVEYS EXPANSION OF TASK FORCE APPROACH IN LBJ'S ADMINISTRATION.

1771 ----------. "THE PRESIDENCY AND POLICY FORMULATION: THE TASK FORCE DEVICE." PUBLIC ADMINISTRATION R 29 (1969):459-471.

1772 WOLANIN, T.R. <u>PRESIDENTIAL ADVISORY COMMISSIONS: TRUMAN TO NIXON</u>. MADISON: U OF WISC PR, 1975, PP. 298.

RELYING PRIMARILY ON INTERVIEWS WITH COMMISSION MEMBERS, COMMISSION STAFF, AND WHITE HOUSE STAFF, WOLANIN DESCRIBES AND ANALYZES THE PURPOSES, ORGANIZATION, PROCEDURES, AND IMPACT OF POST-WWII COMMISSIONS.

SEE ALSO 72, 109, 123, 702, 929, 1018, 1019, 1022, 1024, 1028, 1032, 1037, 1249, 1336, 1337, 1592

8. OTHER

1773 CRONIN, T.E., AND THOMAS, N.C. "EDUCATIONAL POLICY ADVISORS AND THE GREAT SOCIETY." <u>PUBLIC POLICY</u> 18 (FALL 1970): 659-686.

EXAMINES THE COMPOSITION, POLITICAL PERSPECTIVES, AND SELF-PERCEPTIONS OF MEMBERS OF 26 ADVISORY BODIES THAT HELPED GUIDE THE OFFICE OF EDUCATION, HEW, AND THE JOHNSON WHITE HOUSE BETWEEN 1966-1969.

1774 ETZIONI, A., AND ANDERSON, P. "WILLING HANDS FOR WHAT?" <u>WASHINGTON MONTHLY</u> (JUNE 1969): 44-51.

ARGUES THAT THE NIXON ADMINISTRATION FAILED TO KEEP ITS PROMISE TO DEVELOP AN EFFECTIVE PLAN FOR VOLUNTARY ACTION TO INCREASE PUBLIC PARTICIPATION IN GOVERNMENT.

1775 MACMAHON, A. "THE FUTURE ORGANIZATIONAL PATTERN OF THE EXECUTIVE BRANCH." <u>APSR</u> 38 (1944):1179-1191.

1776 MANSFIELD, H.C. "REORGANIZING THE FEDERAL EXECUTIVE BRANCH: THE LIMITS OF INSTITUTIONALIZATION." <u>LAW AND CONTEMPORARY PROBLEMS</u> 35 (1970):461-495.

1777 MERRIAM, C.E. "THE NATIONAL RESOURCES PLANNING BOARD: A CHAPTER IN AMERICAN PLANNING EXPERIENCE." <u>APSR</u> 38 (DEC 1944): 1075-1088.

1778 REAGAN, M. "TOWARD IMPROVING PRESIDENTIAL LEVEL POLICY PLANNING." <u>PUBLIC ADMINISTRATION R</u> 203 (MARCH 1963): 177-186.

1779 SOMERS, H.M. <u>PRESIDENTIAL AGENCY: OWMR, THE OFFICE OF WAR MOBILIZATION AND RECONVERSION</u>. CAMBRIDGE, MASS.: HARVARD UNIVERSITY PRESS, 1950, PP. 238. ALSO, NEW YORK: GREENWOOD PRESS, 1969, PP. 238.

THE DEFINITIVE STUDY OF THE MAJOR WARTIME DOMESTIC POLICY
LEADERSHIP AND COORDINATION INSTITUTION, THE OFFICE OF WAR
MOBILIZATION AND RECONVERSION, BY A FORMER OWMR STAFF
AIDE. INCLUDES PROPOSALS FOR REORGANIZING THE PRESIDENCY.

SEE ALSO 460, 857, 1321, 1595, 1789, 1916, 2297

C. WHITE HOUSE OFFICE

1780 ANDERSON, P. THE PRESIDENT'S MEN: WHITE HOUSE ASSISTANTS
OF FRANKLIN D. ROOSEVELT, HARRY S. TRUMAN, DWIGHT D.
EISENHOWER, JOHN F. KENNEDY, LYNDON B. JOHNSON. GARDEN
CITY: DOUBLEDAY, 1968, PP. 420.

A BRISKLY, INTELLIGENTLY WRITTEN BOOK BY A WASHINGTON
JOURNALIST DESCRIBING SOME OF THE MORE VISIBLE WHITE HOUSE
AIDES IN THE ADMINISTRATIONS INDICATED IN THE SUBTITLE.
INCLUDES BRIEF OBSERVATIONS ON EACH OF THE FIVE WHITE
HOUSE AMBIANCES. BASED ON THE BETTER-KNOWN SOURCES,
ESPECIALLY MEMOIRS, PLUS INTERVIEWS. THE LATTER ARE USED
FOR BACKGROUND AND NOT SPECIFICALLY ATTRIBUTED TO THE
INDIVIDUALS INTERVIEWED.

1781 BAILEY, S.K. "THE PRESIDENT AND HIS POLITICAL EXECUTIVES."
ANNALS 307 (1956):24-36.

COMPREHENSIVE DISCUSSION OF CAREER AND APPOINTIVE
EXECUTIVES IN THE FEDERAL BUREAUCRACY AND THEIR JOINT
PRESSURES TO BE RESPONSIVE BOTH TO PRESIDENT AND TO
CONGRESS. CALLS FOR A MORE CENTRALIZED PARTY SYSTEM IN
ORDER TO ENHANCE PRESIDENT'S POLICY INFLUENCE OVER HIS
APPOINTEES.

1782 CAREY, W.D. "PRESIDENTIAL STAFFING IN THE SIXTIES AND
SEVENTIES." PUBLIC ADMINISTRATION R 29 (1969):450-458.

1783 CLIFFORD, C.M. "COUNSELING THE PRESIDENT." CENTER MAG
(MAY 1974): 22-26.

AN INTERVIEW WITH LONGTIME ADVISER OF DEMOCRATIC
PRESIDENTS, CLARK M. CLIFFORD.

1784 COFFEY, J.I., AND ROCK, V.O. THE PRESIDENTIAL STAFF.
WASHINGTON: NATIONAL PLANNING ASSOC, 1961, PP. 102.

1785 CRONIN, T.E. "EVERYBODY BELIEVES IN DEMOCRACY UNTIL HE
GETS TO THE WHITE HOUSE: AN ANALYSIS OF WHITE
HOUSE-DEPARTMENTAL RELATIONS." IN THE INSTITUTIONALIZED
PRESIDENCY EDITED BY N.C. THOMAS AND H.W. BAADE, DOBBS
FERRY, N.Y.: OCEANA, 1972: 147-199.

1786 GEORGE, A. "THE CASE FOR MULTIPLE ADVOCACY IN FOREIGN
POLICY." WITH "COMMENT: MULTIPLE ADVOCACY: SOME 'LIMITS

AND COSTS'" BY I.M. DESTLER AND REJOINDER BY THE AUTHOR. APSR 66 (1972): 751-795.

GEORGE DISCUSSES "PRESCRIPTIVE THEORIES OF POLICY MAKING IN COMPLEX ORGANIZATIONS WITH PARTICULAR REFERENCE TO FOREIGN POLICY MAKING IN THE EXECUTIVE BRANCH" THAT "INSTEAD OF UTILIZING CENTRALIZED MANAGEMENT PRACTICES TO DISCOURAGE OR NEUTRALIZE INTERNAL DISAGREEMENTS OVER POLICY...USE A MULTIPLE ADVOCACY MODEL TO HARNESS DIVERSITY OF VIEWS AND INTERESTS IN THE INTEREST OF RATIONAL POLICY MAKING." DESTLER ARGUES (INTER ALIA) THAT PRESIDENTS WILL INEVITABLY ADAPT THEIR POLICY MAKING PROCEDURES TO THEIR PREFERRED MODES OF INTERPERSONAL BEHAVIOR RATHER THAN TO PRESCRIPTIVE THEORIES SUCH AS THAT ADVANCED BY GEORGE.

1787 GUTHRIE, C.L. "INFORMING THE NATION'S PRESIDENT." SAM ADVANCE MGT J34:25-34 JA '69.

1788 HESS, S. ORGANIZING THE PRESIDENCY. WASHINGTON: BROOKINGS, 1976, PP. 228.

1789 HOBBS, E.H. "AN HISTORICAL REVIEW OF PLANS FOR PRESIDENTIAL STAFFING." LAW AND CONTEMPORARY PROBLEMS 21 (1956):663-688.

1790 HOXIE, R.G., ED. THE WHITE HOUSE ORGANIZATION AND OPERATIONS. NEW YORK: CENTER FOR THE STUDY OF THE PRESIDENCY, 1971, PP. 218.

TRANSCRIPT OF A CONFERENCE BY INDIVIDUALS WHO HAVE SERVED AS PRESIDENTIAL AIDES.

1791 JANIS, I.L. VICTIMS OF GROUPTHINK: A PSYCHOLOGICAL STUDY OF FOREIGN-POLICY DECISIONS AND FIASCOES. BOSTON: HOUGHTON MIFFLIN, 1972, PP.277.

SOCIAL PSYCHOLOGICAL ANALYSIS OF POLICY DECISIONS THAT WERE FAULTY BECAUSE GROUPS FAILED TO EXAMINE THE PREMISES ON WHICH THEY REACHED CONCLUSIONS (E.G., BAY OF PIGS) AND OF DECISIONS IN WHICH THE DECISIONMAKING GROUP ACTIVELY DEBATED AND CONSEQUENTLY AVERTED MISCALCULATIONS (E.G., THE CUBAN MISSILE CRISIS). THE FIRST TYPE OF DECISION RESULTS FROM MEMBERS' EXCESSIVE DEFFERENCE TO EACH OTHER ("GROUPTHINK").

1792 JOHNSON, R.T. MANAGING THE WHITE HOUSE: AN INTIMATE STUDY OF THE PRESIDENCY. NEW YORK: HARPER AND ROW, 1974, PP. 270.

BUSINESS SCHOOL PROFESSOR AND FORMER MEMBER OF NIXON'S ASH COUNCIL FOR FEDERAL REORGANIZATION PRESENTS SKETCHES OF DECISION-MAKING PRACTICES IN THE FDR THROUGH NIXON WHITE HOUSES.

1793 KRAFT, J. PROFILES IN POWER; A WASHINGTON INSIGHT. NEW
     YORK: NEW AMERICAN LIBRARY, 1966, PP. 192.

1794 MONDALE, W.F. "SOCIAL ADVISORS, SOCIAL ACCOUNTING, AND THE
     PRESIDENCY." LAW AND CONTEMPORARY PROBLEMS 35
     (1970):496-505.

     ADVOCATES A SOCIAL SCIENCE ADVISORY COUNTERPART TO THE
     PRESIDENT'S SCIENCE ADVISORY COUNCIL.

1795 PETERS, C. "THE PRINCE AND HIS COURTIERS: AT THE WHITE
     HOUSE, THE KREMLIN, AND THE REICHSCHANCELLERY."
     WASHINGTON MONTHLY 4 (FEB 1973): 30-39.

     COMPARES FORMER PRESIDENTIAL PRESS SECRETARY GEORGE
     REEDY'S DESCRIPTION OF THE PRESIDENCY AS INCREASINGLY
     ISOLATED BY A "SELF-SERVING COURT" OF UNDERLINGS WITH
     ALBERT SPEER'S ACCOUNT OF NAZI GERMANY AND KHRUSHCHEV'S
     ALLEGED MEMOIRS AND CONCLUDES "THAT THE STYLES OF
     GOVERNMENT BEING DESCRIBED BY ALL THREE ARE REMARKABLY
     ALIKE."ARGUES, DEPARTING FROM BAKER'S FORMULATION IN THE
     WATERGATE INQUIRY, THAT THE QUESTION TO BE ANSWERED WAS
     NOT WHETHER THE PRESIDENT "KNEW," BUT WHETHER HE "MUST
     HAVE KNOWN." THIS IS BECAUSE THE "PRIMARY RULES" OF
     BUREAUCRATIC CULTURE ARE THAT A SUPERIOR MUST ALWAYS HAVE
     "DENIABILITY" AND A SUBORDINATE KNOWS WHAT IS EXPECTED TO
     BE DONE WITHOUT BEING EXPLICITLY TOLD.

1796 RAVEN, B.H. "THE NIXON GROUP." J OF SOCIAL ISSUES 30 NO.
     4 (1974): 297-320.

     SOCIOMETRIC ANALYSIS GRAPHICALLY REPRESENTING
     RELATIONSHIPS AMONG PRESIDENT NIXON'S ADVISERS. RAVEN
     DRAWS ON THE WHITE HOUSE TRANSCRIPTS AND HEARINGS OF THE
     SENATE AND HOUSE WATERGATE COMMITTEES TO SHOW THAT THIS
     GROUP WAS NOT A CLOSELY KNIT TEAM WITH HIGH ESPRIT DE
     CORPS AND MUTUAL RESPECT. RATHER, THEY WERE HELD TOGETHER
     BY A COMMON DEPENDENCE ON THE PRESIDENT.

1797 REEDY, G. "ON THE ISOLATION OF PRESIDENTS." IN THE
     PRESIDENCY REAPPRAISED, EDITED BY R.G. TUGWELL AND T.E.
     CRONIN, NEW YORK: PRAEGER, 1974: 119-132.

     ARGUING THAT THE PRESIDENCY IS RAPIDLY LOSING ITS
     CAPABILITY TO FOSTER A DEMOCRATIC CONSENSUS, REEDY
     RECOMMENDS ESTABLISHMENT OF A CONGRESSIONAL COMMITTEE WITH
     AUTHORITY TO REQUIRE REPORTS AND INFORMATION FROM THE
     EXECUTIVE OFFICE OF THE PRESIDENT.

1798 SELIGMAN, L.G. "PRESIDENTIAL LEADERSHIP: THE INNER CIRCLE
     AND INSTITUTIONALIZATION." JP 18 (1956):410-426.

     PIONEERING DISCUSSION OF THE DEVELOPMENT OF WHITE HOUSE
     OFFICE STAFF AND OF OTHER ADVISORY AGENCIES IN THE
     EXECUTIVE OFFICE OF THE PRESIDENT.

1799 THOMPSON, J.C. "GETTING OUT AND SPEAKING OUT." FOREIGN POLICY (WINTER 1973): 49-69.

1800 WEISBAND, E., AND FRANK, T.M. RESIGNATION IN PROTEST: POLITICAL AND ETHICAL CHOICES BETWEEN LOYALTY TO TEAM AND LOYALTY TO CONSCIENCE IN AMERICAN PUBLIC LIFE. NEW YORK: GROSSMAN, 1975. PP. 236.

1801 WILLIAMS, C.D. "OFFICE OF THE PRESIDENT: A REORGANIZATION IS NEEDED." ABA J 40 (APR 1954): 285-8, 348-51.

THE PRESIDENTS' PERSONAL ASSISTANTS EXERCISE VAST POWER WITH LITTLE ACCOUNTABILITY. DISCUSSES THE CONTROVERSY OVER HARRY DEXTER WHITE TO ILLUSTRATE THE DANGERS OF HAVING PRESIDENTIAL AIDES OVERRULE CABINET OFFICIALS.

1802 ZORIN, V. "WHITE HOUSE GREY EMINENCES." NEW TIMES MOSCOW (APRIL 17, 1963): 7-10.

SEE ALSO 234, 244, 294, 356, 411, 596, 669, 1114, 1119, 1139, 1147, 1236, 1239, 1240, 1241, 1242, 1243, 1244, 1245, 1246, 1252, 1254, 1255, 1256, 1257, 1282, 1287, 1288, 1292, 1298, 1299, 1303, 1415, 1510, 1512, 1513, 1514, 1515, 1517, 1518, 1519, 1525, 1526, 1803, 1805, 2056

D. ADDITIONAL ASPECTS AND THEMES

1803 ACHESON, D. SKETCHES FROM LIFE OF MEN I HAVE KNOWN. NEW YORK: HARPER, 1961, PP. 206.

1804 HEREN, L. "KING'S MEN: A BRITISH VIEW OF THE WHITE HOUSE." HARPER'S 230 (FEB 1965): 105+.

COMPARES ADVISING ARRANGEMENTS IN THE UNITED STATES WITH THOSE IN GREAT BRITAIN.

1805 KOENIG, L.W. THE INVISIBLE PRESIDENCY. NEW YORK: RINEHART, 1960, PP. 438.

CASE STUDIES OF PRESIDENTIAL GREY EMINENCES, BEGINNING WITH ALEXANDER HAMILTON AND INCLUDING BOTH HARRY HOPKINS AND SHERMAN ADAMS.

1806 SPARKS, W. WHO TALKED TO THE PRESIDENT LAST?. NEW YORK: W.W. NORTON, 1971, PP. 127.

FACETIOUS BUT PERCEPTIVE COMMENTS ON "GETTING THE PRESIDENT'S EAR."

1807 ----------. "WHAT DO SPECIAL ASSISTANTS SPECIALIZE IN?"

ATLANTIC 227 (FEB 1971): 64-66+.

OBSERVATIONS OF A PRESIDENTIAL ASSISTANT FROM THE JOHNSON ADMINISTRATION.

1808 TUGWELL, R.G. "PRESIDENT AND HIS HELPERS: A REVIEW ARTICLE." PSQ 82 (JUNE 1967): 253-67.

1809 WOOD, R. "WHEN GOVERNMENT WORKS." THE PUBLIC INTEREST 18 (WINTER 1970): 39-51.

SEE ALSO 43, 89, 193, 290, 348, 350, 351, 352, 353, 355, 357, 358, 359, 360, 361, 362, 363, 365, 367, 368, 369, 371, 372, 374, 377, 379, 380, 382, 383, 385, 387, 388, 389, 390, 393, 394, 395, 398, 399, 400, 402, 403, 405, 408, 409, 410, 412, 413, 448, 611, 652, 653, 654, 655, 661, 662, 663, 664, 665, 667, 668, 669, 742, 798, 827, 828, 829, 831, 832, 833, 834, 837, 838, 839, 840, 841, 842, 843, 844, 847, 848, 849, 850, 851, 852, 940, 942, 945, 948, 951, 952, 956, 958, 959, 977, 1102, 1103, 1104, 1106, 1107, 1110, 1111, 1115, 1116, 1117, 1118, 1164, 1235, 1237, 1238, 1247, 1248, 1250, 1253, 1258, 1259, 1261, 1262, 1265, 1267, 1268, 1269, 1271, 1272, 1273, 1274, 1277, 1279, 1280, 1281, 1282, 1283, 1285, 1286, 1289, 1290, 1293, 1296, 1297, 1301, 1305, 1306, 1307, 1308, 1309, 1310, 1311, 1312, 1314, 1328, 1364, 1370, 1428, 1429, 1432, 1516, 1522, 1523, 1524, 1527, 1562, 1596, 1615, 1633, 1635, 1699, 1735, 1781, 1803, 1978, 2378, 2432, 2446

17

PRESIDENTIAL CONSTITUENCIES

A. GENERAL PUBLIC; SYMBOLIC ASPECTS OF THE PRESIDENCY

1810 ARTERTON, F.C. "THE IMPACT OF WATERGATE ON CHILDREN'S ATTITUDES TOWARD POLITICAL AUTHORITY." PSQ 89 (JUNE 1974): 269-288.REPRINTED IN AMERICAN POLITICAL INSTITUTIONS IN THE 1970S: A 'POLITICAL SCIENCE QUARTERLY' READER. NEW YORK: COLUMBIA U PR., 1976, PP. 29-48.

REPORTS RESULTS OF STUDY OF CHILDREN'S POLITICAL ATTITUDES AT HEIGHT OF WATERGATE CRISIS; AND FINDS THAT,IN CONTRAST TO THE CHILDREN STUDIED IN THE EARLY 1960'S WHO HAD RATHER POSITIVE PERCEPTIONS OF THE PRESIDENT, CHILDREN IN DECEMBER 1973 EXPRESSED "WHOLLY NEGATIVE" ATTITUDES AND "HAVE COME TO VIEW THE PRESIDENT AS A FIGURE TO BE STRENUOUSLY REJECTED." ARTERTON'S CONCERN IS WITH THE SUPPOSED CONNECTION BETWEEN LEGITIMACY AND CHILDREN'S EARLY ATTITUDES: "SHOULD EASTON AND DENNIS' ARGUMENTS PROVE THE MORE ADEQUATE EXPLANATION OF CHILDREN'S ATTITUDES IN THE LONG RUN, THEN FOR A GENERATION WE SHOULD SEE A SUBSTANTIAL IMPAIRMENT OF THE LEGITIMACY UPON WHICH THE STABILITY OF OUR POLITICAL SYSTEM IS BASED."

1811 ----------. "WATERGATE AND CHILDREN'S ATTITUDES TOWARD POLITICAL AUTHORITY REVISITED." PSQ 90 (FALL 1975): 477-496.

AFTER FORD BECAME PRESIDENT, CHILDREN'S ATTITUDES TOWARD THE PRESIDENT BECAME MORE FAVORABLE.

1812 BERENDT, J. "TEN YEARS LATER: A LOOK AT THE RECORD; WHAT THE SCHOOL BOOKS ARE TEACHING OUR KIDS ABOUT JFK." ESQUIRE 80 (NOV 1973): 140+.

A POPULAR REVIEW OF THE WIDESPREAD IDEALIZATION OF KENNEDY IN RECENT PRIMARY AND SECONDARY SCHOOL TEXTBOOKS.

1813 BINKLEY, W.E. "THE PRESIDENT AS A NATIONAL SYMBOL." ANNALS 283 (SEPT. 1952): 86-93.

1814 BRODY, R.A., AND PAGE, B.I. "THE IMPACT OF EVENTS ON PRESIDENTIAL POPULARITY: THE JOHNSON AND NIXON ADMINISTRATIONS." IN PERSPECTIVES ON THE PRESIDENCY, EDITED BY A. WILDAVSKY, BOSTON: LITTLE BROWN, 1975: 136-148.

CORRELATES THE PRESIDENTIAL POPULARITY AS MEASURED IN

SURVEYS WITH THE RATIO OF FAVORABLE TO UNFAVORABLE NEWS STORIES ON THE PRESIDENT, REACHING DIFFERENT CONCLUSIONS FROM THOSE IN MUELLER'S WAR, PRESIDENTS AND PUBLIC OPINION.

1815 BROWN, W.B. THE PEOPLE'S CHOICE: THE PRESIDENTIAL IMAGE IN THE CAMPAIGN BIOGRAPHY. BATON ROUGE: LOUISIANA STATE UNIVERSITY PRESS, 1960. PP. 177.

A HISTORY OF CHANGES OVER THE YEARS IN THE THEMES EMPHASIZED IN "AUTHORIZED" BIOGRAPHIES OF PRESIDENTIAL CANDIDATES WRITTEN FOR CAMPAIGN PURPOSES. DURING ALL HISTORICAL PERIODS, CAMPAIGN BIOGRAPHERS HAVE IDEALIZED THEIR SUBJECTS, BUT THE PARTICULAR NATURE OF THE IDEALIZATION SEEMS TO REFLECT CHANGES IN PUBLIC VALUES. INCLUDES A SELECTED LIST OF CAMPAIGN BIOGRAPHIES.

1816 CASEY, G. "THE THEORY OF PRESIDENTIAL ASSOCIATION: A REPLICATION." AMER J POL SCI 19 (FEB 1975): 19-25.

VOTERS WHO FAVOR THE INCUMBENT PRESIDENT TEND TO GENERALIZE THEIR VIEW AND ALSO FAVOR THE PERFORMANCE OF THE SUPREME COURT.

1817 CLEVELAND, H. "THE EXECUTIVE AND THE PUBLIC." ANNALS 307 (1956):37-54.

IN DISCUSSING THE PRESIDENT'S NEED TO SELECT AND BACK UP IMAGINATIVE, ENTREPRENEURIAL EXECUTIVES, CLEVELAND ASSERTS: "AS ANYONE KNOWS WHO HAS WORKED IN WASHINGTON, IT IS NOT 'NEUTRALITY' BUT VIGOROUS ADVOCACY THAT OVERCOMES INERTIA IN OUR BIG BUREAUCRACY."

1818 CRONIN, T.E. "THE TEXTBOOK PRESIDENCY AND POLITICAL SCIENCE." IN PERSPECTIVES ON THE PRESIDENCY: A COLLECTION. EDITED BY S. BACH AND G.T. SULZNER, LEXINGTON, MASS.: HEATH, 1974: 54-74.

ON THE IDEALIZATION OF PRESIDENTS IN AMERICAN GOVERNMENT TEXTBOOKS AND IN ACADEMIC STUDIES OF THE PRESIDENCY DURING THE 1950'S AND THE EARLY 1960'S.

1819 DRIGGS, D.W. "THE PRESIDENT AS CHIEF EDUCATOR ON FOREIGN AFFAIRS." WESTERN POLITICAL Q 11 (1958):813-819.

"GIVEN THE WORLD SITUATION TODAY...A STRONG CHIEF EXECUTIVE MUST...BE WILLING TO EXPLOIT THE PREROGATIVES OF THE PRESIDENT AS PRINCIPLE AGENT OF THE COUNTRY IN THE CONDUCT OF ITS FOREIGN RELATIONS." STRESSES THE NEED FOR ASSERTIVE PRESIDENTIAL "EDUCATION" OF "CONGRESS AND THE PEOPLE AT LARGE ON THE WHYS AND THE WHEREFORES" OF WHAT THE PRESIDENT CONSIDERS APPROPRIATE FOREIGN POLICY.

1820 EASTON, D., AND DENNIS, J. CHILDREN IN THE POLITICAL SYSTEM: ORIGINS OF POLITICAL LEGITIMACY. NEW YORK: MCGRAW-HILL, 1969, PP. 440.

SURVEY COVERING NUMEROUS ASPECTS OF CHILDREN'S PERCEPTIONS OF POLITICS, INCLUDING PROMINENTLY IN ITS ANALYSIS A

DISCUSSION OF THE EARLY AWARENESS OF THE PRESIDENCY. AT THE TIME OF THIS RESEARCH WHICH WAS JOINTLY CONDUCTED BY EASTON AND R.D. HESS IN THE LATE 1950'S AND THE EARLY 1960'S THE CHILDREN DISPLAYED HIGHLY POSITIVE VIEWS OF THE PRESIDENCY.

1821 EASTON, D., AND HESS, R.D. "THE CHILD'S POLITICAL WORLD." MIDWEST J POLITICAL SCIENCE 6 (1962):229-246.

A SYNTHETIC ACCOUNT OF THE SEQUENCE OF POLITICAL LEARNING IN AMERICAN CHILDREN. THE CHILD BEGINS BY ACQUIRING A SENSE OF NATIONALITY. THE FIRST SPECIFICALLY POLITICAL OBJECT TO COME INTO THE CHILD'S AWARENESS IS THE PRESIDENCY.

1822 ERSKINE, H. "THE POLLS: PRESIDENTIAL POWER." POQ 37 (1973):488-503.

1823 GRABER, D.A. PUBLIC OPINION, THE PRESIDENT, AND FOREIGN POLICY: FOUR CASE STUDIES FROM THE FORMATIVE YEARS. NEW YORK: HOLT, RINEHART AND WINSTON, 1968, PP. 374.

1824 ----------. "PERSONAL QUALITIES IN PRESIDENTIAL IMAGES: THE CONTRIBUTION OF THE PRESS." MIDWEST J POLITICAL SCIENCE 16 (FEB. 1972): 46-76.

1825 GREENSTEIN, F.I. "POPULAR IMAGES OF THE PRESIDENT." AMER J PSYCHIATRY 122 (NOV 1965): 523-529.

AS OF JOHNSON'S EARLY YEARS IN OFFICE, IT WAS EVIDENT THAT AMERICAN ADULTS TENDED TO SEE INCUMBENT PRESIDENTS IN A FAVORABLE LIGHT AND TO VIEW THE GOVERNMENT IN SIMPLIFIED TERMS AS AN EXTENSION OF THE PRESIDENT'S LEADERSHIP.

1826 ----------. "THE BENEVOLENT LEADER REVISITED: CHILDREN'S IMAGES OF POLITICAL LEADERS IN THREE DEMOCRACIES." APSR 69 (DEC 1975): 1371-1398.

COMPARES AMERICAN, BRITISH AND FRENCH CHILDREN'S VIEWS OF THEIR NATIONAL EXECUTIVES (U.S., PRESIDENT; U.K., QUEEN AND PRIME MINISTER; FRANCE, PRESIDENT AND PREMIER). CITES NUMEROUS STUDIES OF THE AMERICAN PRESIDENT, INCLUDING SOME NOT LISTED IN THIS CHAPTER.

1827 ----------. "THE BENEVOLENT LEADER: CHILDREN'S IMAGES OF POLITICAL AUTHORITY." APSR 54 (1960):934-43.

A QUESTIONNAIRE STUDY OF CHILDREN CONDUCTED DURING THE EISENHOWER ADMINISTRATION SHOWING THEIR HIGHLY FAVORABLE VIEWS OF THE PRESIDENT.

1828 ----------. "THE PSYCHOLOGICAL FUNCTIONS OF THE PRESIDENCY FOR CITIZENS." IN THE AMERICAN PRESIDENCY:

VITAL CENTER, EDITED BY E. CORNWALL, JR., GLENVIEW, ILL.:
SCOTT FORESMAN, 1966: 30-36.

SIMILAR TO GREENSTEIN'S "POPULAR IMAGES OF THE PRESIDENT,"
BUT PLACING MORE EMPHASIS ON POLITICAL THAN ON
PSYCHOLOGICAL THEMES.

1829 ----------. "WHAT THE PRESIDENT MEANS TO AMERICANS:
PRESIDENTIAL 'CHOICE' BETWEEN ELECTIONS." IN CHOOSING THE
PRESIDENT, EDITED BY J.D. BARBER, ENGLEWOOD CLIFFS, N.J.:
PRENTICE-HALL, 1974: 121-47.

REVISES GREENSTEIN'S MID-1960'S ESSAYS ON THE MEANING OF
PRESIDENTS TO CITIZENS IN THE LIGHT OF THE DISENCHANTMENT
THAT ATTENDED THE JOHNSON AND NIXON PRESIDENCIES.

1830 GUSTAFSON, M. "THE RELIGIOUS ROLE OF THE PRESIDENT."
MIDWEST J 14: 708-722.

1831 HESS, R.D., AND EASTON, D. "THE CHILD'S CHANGING IMAGE OF
THE PRESIDENT." POQ 24 (WINTER 1960): 632-44.

PIONEERING STUDY OF CHILDREN'S VIEWS OF THE PRESIDENT,
CONDUCTED DURING EISENHOWER YEARS. FINDS JUVENILE
IDEALIZATION OF THE PERIOD.

1832 HESS, R.D., AND TORNEY, J.V. THE DEVELOPMENT OF POLITICAL
ATTITUDES IN CHILDREN. CHICAGO: ALDINE, 1967.

FINDINGS ON PRE-ADULT IDEALIZATION OF THE PRESIDENT FROM
THE SAME STUDY REPORTED IN EASTON'S AND DENNIS'S CHILDREN
IN THE POLITICAL SYSTEM, BUT DISCUSSED MORE FROM THE
PERSPECTIVE OF DEVELOPMENTAL PSYCHOLOGY THAN THAT OF
POLITICAL SCIENCE.

1833 JAROS, D., AND KOLSON, K.L. "THE MULTIFARIOUS LEADER:
POLITICAL SOCIALIZATION OF AMISH, 'YANKS', BLACKS." IN
THE POLITICS OF FUTURE CITIZENS BY R.G. NIEMI, ET AL,
SAN FRANCISCO: JOSSEY-BASS, 1974: 41-62.

BLACK CHILDREN HAD NEGATIVE IMAGES OF THE PRESIDENT.
CHILDREN FROM TRADITIONALLY AUTHORITARIAN AMISH FAMILIES
HAD EXCEPTIONALLY POSITIVE IMAGES AND "MAINSTREAM" WHITE
CHILDREN'S IMAGES WERE CLOSER TO THOSE OF THE BLACKS THAN
THE AMISH.

1834 JAROS, D., HIRSCH, H., AND FLERON, F.J., JR. "THE
MALEVOLENT LEADER: POLITICAL SOCIALIZATION IN AN AMERICAN
SUB-CULTURE." APSR 62 (1968):564-595.

1835 KERNELL, S., SPERLICH, P.W., AND WILDAVSKY, A. "PUBLIC
SUPPORT FOR PRESIDENTS." IN PERSPECTIVES ON THE
PRESIDENCY, EDITED BY A. WILDAVSKY. BOSTON: LITTLE,BROWN,
1975: 148-181.

1836 LANDECKER, M. THE PRESIDENT AND PUBLIC OPINION. WASHINGTON, D.C.: PUBLIC AFFAIRS PRESS, 1968, PP. 133.

1837 MUELLER, J.E. WAR, PRESIDENTS, AND PUBLIC OPINION. NEW YORK: JOHN WILEY & SONS, 1973, PP. 300.

MUCH OF THIS BOOK CONSISTS OF SURVEY DATA ON TRENDS IN THE POPULARITY OF MODERN AMERICAN PRESIDENTS AND AN EFFORT TO CORRELATE THE UPS AND DOWNS OF PRESIDENTIAL POPULARITY WITH OTHER TREND DATA--FOR EXAMPLE, ECONOMIC INDICATORS. FOR A SIMILAR ANALYSIS USING DIFFERENT INDICATORS AND REACHING SOMEWHAT DIFFERENT FINDINGS, SEE BRODY AND PAIGE, "THE IMPACT OF EVENTS ON PRESIDENTIAL POPULARITY."

1838 PARKER, G.R. "POLITICAL BELIEFS ABOUT THE STRUCTURE OF GOVERNMENT: CONGRESS AND THE PRESIDENCY." SAGE PROFESSIONAL PAPERS IN AMERICAN POLITICS. VOL. 2, SERIES NO. 04-018. BEVERLY HILLS, CA.: SAGE PUBLICATIONS, 1974, PP. 42.

1839 ROSEN, C.M. "A TEST OF PRESIDENTIAL LEADERSHIP OF PUBLIC OPINION: THE SPLIT-BALLOT TECHNIQUE." POLITY 6 (WINTER 1973): 174-196.

A 1971 "SPLIT HALF SAMPLE SURVEY" SHOWING THAT COMPARABLE GROUPS OF THE ELECTORATE ASKED ABOUT VARIOUS POLICY ISSUES ARE MORE LIKELY TO APPROVE OF A POSITION IF THE QUESTIONNAIRE ADDS THE INFORMATION THAT THE PRESIDENT FAVORS THAT POSITION.

1840 SANFORD, F.H. "PUBLIC ORIENTATION TO ROOSEVELT." POQ 15 (SUMMER 1951): 189-216.

1841 SELIGMAN, L.G., AND BAER, M.A. "EXPECTATIONS OF PRESIDENTIAL LEADERSHIP IN DECISION-MAKING." IN THE PRESIDENCY. EDITED BY A. WILDAVSKY. BOSTON, MASS.: LITTLE, BROWN, 1969: 18-35.

INTERESTING EMPIRICAL STUDY OF LOCAL OREGON POLITICIANS' PERCEPTIONS OF LIKELY PRESIDENTIAL BEHAVIOR UNDER VARIED POLITICAL CIRCUMSTANCES.

1842 SIGEL, R.S. "IMAGE OF THE AMERICAN PRESIDENCY-PART II OF AN EXPLORATION INTO POPULAR VIEWS OF PRESIDENTIAL POWER." MIDWEST J POL SCI 10 (1966): 123-137.

REPORT OF AN EARLY 1960'S SURVEY FINDING THAT CITIZENS "WANT STRONG PRESIDENTS BUT WANT A TIME LIMIT ON THEIR TERMS OF OFFICE." PART 1 OF THE REPORT, COAUTHORED BY BUTLER, DEALS WITH THE THIRD TERM TRADITION AND IS CITED IN CHAPTER 18, SECTION 9.

1843 ----------. "IMAGES OF A PRESIDENT: SOME INSIGHTS INTO
THE POLITICAL VIEWS OF SCHOOL CHILDREN." APSR 62 (MARCH
1968): 216-226.

A SURVEY OF CHILDREN'S RESPONSES TO KENNEDY'S DEATH
INDICATED THAT CHILDREN HAVE MORE COMPLEX AND VARIEGATED
PERCEPTIONS OF THE PRESIDENT THAN WAS SUGGESTED IN EARLIER
RESEARCH.

SEE ALSO 199, 264, 568, 595, 607, 609, 888, 890, 1014,
1025, 1035, 1043, 1394, 1403, 1414, 1423, 1425, 1431,
1440, 1466, 1566, 1856, 1913

B. SPECIFIC ORGANIZED AND UNORGANIZED GROUPS

1844 HIRSCHBERG, V. "ADMINISTRATION HEADS FOR CLASH WITH
INDUSTRY OVER DEREGULATION PROPOSAL." NATIONAL J 3
(1971):1349-1359.

1845 KLEILER, F.M. "WHITE HOUSE INTERVENTION IN LABOR
DISPUTES." PSQ 68 (1953):227-241.

LEGISLATION ON THE PRESIDENT'S RESPONSIBILITIES IN
CONNECTION WITH LABOR DISPUTES IS SO VAGUE AND
INCONSISTENT THAT THIS POLICY AREA IS ONE IN WHICH THE
PRESIDENT MUST EXERCISE DECISION-MAKING DISCRETION.

1846 ROSSITER, C.L. "THE PRESIDENT AND LABOR DISPUTES." JP 2
(1949):93-120.

HISTORICAL ACCOUNT AND CONSTITUTIONAL DEFENSE OF
PRESIDENTIAL INVOLVEMENT IN LABOR DISPUTES. STRESSES THE
VAST POTENTIAL POWER OF PRESIDENTS IN LABOR DISPUTES,
ARGUING THAT BECAUSE THEY HAVE SO MUCH DISCRETION
PRESIDENTS SHOULD BE CAREFUL TO EXHAUST ALTERNATIVE
CHANNELS BEFORE ENTERING LABOR-MANAGEMENT CONFLICTS.

1847 TYLER, G. "THE PRESIDENCY AND LABOR." ANNALS 307
(1956):82-91.

SEE ALSO 71, 382, 416, 421, 441, 446, 447, 453, 497, 554,
561, 602, 682, 687, 688, 701, 765, 774, 864, 881, 885,
963, 966, 968, 972, 974, 976, 1174, 1178, 1180, 1192,
1202, 1278, 1334, 1337, 1473, 2283, 2284, 2372

C. POLITICAL PARTIES

1848 COOPER, J., AND BOMBARDIER, G. "PRESIDENTIAL LEADERSHIP
AND PARTY SUCCESS." JP 30 (1968):1012-1027.

A CLOSE, COMPARATIVE ANALYSIS OF ROLL CALL VOTING BY
DIFFERENT CATEGORIES OF MEMBERS OF THE HOUSE OF

REPRESENTATIVES ON ISSUES ADVOCATED BY KENNEDY DURING THE
87TH CONGRESS AND BY JOHNSON DURING THE 90TH CONGRESS.

1849 GOLDMAN, R.M. "TITULAR LEADERSHIP OF PRESIDENTIAL
PARTIES." IN THE PRESIDENCY, EDITED BY A. WILDAVSKY,
BOSTON: LITTLE, BROWN, 1969, PP. 384-410.

1850 HELMS, E.A. "THE PRESIDENT AND PARTY POLITICS." JP 11
(1949):42-64.

PRESIDENTS SHOULD BE GIFTED PARTY POLITICIANS IN ORDER TO
BE BETTER ABLE TO BRIDGE THE SEPARATION OF POWERS.

1851 HOLCOMBE, A.N. "PRESIDENTIAL LEADERSHIP AND THE PARTY
SYSTEM." YALE LAW R 43 (1954):321-335.

EFFECTIVE PRESIDENTIAL LEADERSHIP CALLS FOR EXERCISE OF
LEADERSHIP OF HIS OWN PARTY BY THE PRESIDENT WHILE
SIMULTANEOUSLY DRAWING UPON THE SUPPORT OF SOME MEMBERS OF
THE OTHER PARTY.

1852 ODEGARD, P.H. "PRESIDENTIAL LEADERSHIP AND PARTY
RESPONSIBILITY." ANNALS 307 (1956):66-81.

1853 SELIGMAN, L.G. "THE PRESIDENTIAL OFFICE AND THE PRESIDENT
AS PARTY LEADER." LAW AND CONTEMPORARY PROBLEMS 21
(1956):724-734.

COMPLEXITIES OF "LEADING" A DECENTRALIZED PARTY.

SEE ALSO 366, 1287, 1954

D. MASS MEDIA

1854 BAGDIKIAN, B.H. THE EFFETE CONSPIRACY. NEW YORK:
HARPER-COLOPHON, 1974, PP. 159.

ESSAYS BY A JOURNALIST ON THE PRESS, SEVEN OF WHICH DEAL
WITH FACETS OF PRESIDENTIAL PRESS RELATIONS (INCLUDING
RELATIONS WITH THE ELECTRONIC MEDIA) IN THE KENNEDY
THROUGH NIXON ADMINISTRATIONS.

1855 BARRETT, M., ED. MOMENTS OF TRUTH? NEW YORK: CROWELL,
1975, PP. 274.

A VOLUME IN THE ANNUAL SERIES OF COLUMBIA UNIVERSITY
SURVEYS OF BROADCAST JOURNALISM WHICH PAYS SPECIAL
ATTENTION TO PRESIDENTIAL RELATIONSHIPS WITH THE MASS
MEDIA, PARTICULARLY DURING WATERGATE.

1856 BLAISDELL, T.C., JR., SELZ, P., ET AL. THE AMERICAN
PRESIDENCY IN POLITICAL CARTOONS: 1776-1976. SALT LAKE
CITY, UTAH: PEREGRINE SMITH, INC., 1976, PP. 278.

1857 BOGARDUS, E.S. "SOCIOLOGY OF THE PRESIDENTIAL TV CONFERENCE." SOCIOLOGY AND SOCIAL RESEARCH 46 (1962):181-85.

1858 CATER, D. "THE PRESIDENT AND THE PRESS." ANNALS 307 (1956):55-65.

"AT HIS REGULAR PRESS CONFERENCE, THE PRESIDENT PRESENTS HIS VIEWS ON A COUNTLESS NUMBER OF MATTERS. IT HAS BEEN A SOURCE OF AMAZEMENT TO ME HOW SLIPSHOD, OCCASIONALLY, ARE THE METHODS OF INTERROGATING OUR HEAD OF STATE."

1859 CHILDS, M. WITNESS TO POWER. NEW YORK: MCGRAW-HILL, 1975, PP. 277.

A LONGTIME JOURNALIST'S ANECDOTAL RECOLLECTIONS OF HIS OBSERVATIONS OF MODERN PRESIDENTS.

1860 CORNWELL, E.E. PRESIDENTIAL LEADERSHIP OF PUBLIC OPINION. BLOOMINGTON: INDIANA UNIVERSITY PRESS, 1965, PP. 370.

DEALS HISTORICALLY FROM THE EARLY 20TH CENTURY TO THE TIME OF PUBLICATION.

1861 ----------. THE PRESIDENCY AND THE PRESS. MORRISTOWN, N.J.: GENERAL LEARNING PRESS (UNIVERSITY PROGRAMS MODULAR STUDIES), 1974, PP. 32.

A BRIEF REVIEW WHICH DRAWS UPON CORNWELL'S WORK IN HIS PRESIDENTIAL LEADERSHIP AND PUBLIC OPINION, HIS OTHER EARLY WRITINGS, AND ASPECTS OF PRESIDENTIAL PRESS-RELATIONS FROM THE MID-1960'S THROUGH THE NIXON ADMINISTRATION.

1862 ----------. "PRESIDENTIAL NEWS: THE EXPANDING PUBLIC IMAGE." JOURNALISM R 36 (1959):275-85.

PRESS COVERAGE OF GOVERNMENT FOCUSED ON CONGRESS AT THE TURN OF THE CENTURY AND ON THE PRESIDENT BY MID-CENTURY.

1863 ----------. "THE PRESIDENTIAL PRESS CONFERENCE: A STUDY IN INSTITUTIONALIZATION." MIDWEST J OF POLITICAL SCIENCE 4 (1960):370-389.

A DESCRIPTIVE COMPARISON OF THE FREQUENCY OF PRESS CONFERENCES AND THE EVALUATION OF PRESS CONFERENCE PROCEDURES UNDER ROOSEVELT, TRUMAN, AND EISENHOWER.

1864 CRONIN, T.E. "THE PRESIDENCY PUBLIC RELATIONS SCRIPT." IN THE PRESIDENCY REAPPRAISED, EDITED BY R.G. TUGWELL AND T.E. CRONIN, NEW YORK: PRAEGER, 1974: 168-183.

PRESIDENTS HAVE COME TO OVERSTRESS IMAGE-MAKING AND ACQUIRED THE STAFF TO DO SO.

1865 DIAMOND, E. "HOW THE WHITE HOUSE KEEPS ITS EYE ON THE

NETWORK NEWS SHOWS." <u>NEW YORK</u> (MAY 10, 1971): 45-49.

EXAMINES THE ORIGIN AND INFLUENCE ON THE PRESIDENT'S DAILY BRIEFING BOOK, A WHITE HOUSE PRODUCED "4,000 TO 10,000-WORD COMPENDIUM OF WHAT TELEVISION, NEWSPAPERS AND MAGAZINES ARE SAYING ABOUT THE WORLD, THE NATION, AND THE NIXON ADMINISTRATION."

1866 DICKERSON, N. <u>AMONG THOSE PRESENT: A REPORTER'S VIEW OF THE TWENTY-FIVE YEARS IN WASHINGTON</u>. NEW YORK: RANDOM HOUSE, 1976, PP. 256.

1867 FRANKEL, M. "THE PRESS AND THE PRESIDENT." <u>COMMENTARY</u> (JULY, 1971): 6+.

1868 GROSSMAN, M.B., AND ROURKE, F.E. "THE MEDIA AND THE PRESIDENCY: AN EXCHANGE ANALYSIS." <u>POLITICAL SCIENCE QUARTERLY</u> 91 (FALL 1976):455-470.

"ALTHOUGH THE VESTMENTS OF THE OFFICE MAY NO LONGER BE SUFFICIENT TO ASSURE A PRESIDENT THAT THE CREDIBILITY OF HIS MESSAGES WILL BE ACCEPTED WITHOUT QUESTION BY REPORTERS, THE TERMS OF THE EXCHANGE RELATIONSHIP ARE STILL FUNDAMENTALLY IN THE PRESIDENT'S FAVOR....BUT...AS A RESULT OF THEIR INCREASED ORGANIZATIONAL CAPABILITY AND GROWING PROFESSIONALIZATION, THE MEDIA ARE BECOMING SIGNIFICANTLY STRONGER IN THEIR ABILITY TO COVER THE WHITE HOUSE. EACH PARTY NOW TENDS TO DOMINATE THE AGENDA OF THE OTHER. IF IT IS CREDIBLE TO SPEAK OF AN IMPERIAL PRESIDENCY AS A SHORT-HAND DESCRIPTION OF THE GROWTH OF EXECUTIVE POWER IN AMERICAN SOCIETY, IT MAY BE NO LESS PLAUSIBLE TO THINK OF THE EMERGING CITADELS OF POWER IN THE AMERICAN PRESS AS AN IMPERIAL MEDIA.

1869 HALBERSTAM, D. "PRESS AND PREJUDICE." <u>ESQUIRE</u> 81 (APR. 1974): 109-114+.

KENNEDY, JOHNSON, AND NIXON WERE TREATED BY JOURNALISTS IN WAYS QUITE CONSISTENT WITH THEIR OWN VIEWS ABOUT THE PRESS AND HOW TO DEAL WITH IT.

1870 JOHNSON, M.B. <u>GOVERNMENT SECRECY CONTROVERSY: A DISPUTE INVOLVING THE GOVERNMENT AND THE PRESS IN THE EISENHOWER, KENNEDY, AND JOHNSON ADMINISTRATIONS</u>. NEW YORK: VANTAGE, 1967, PP. 136.

1871 JOSEPH, T. "HOW WHITE HOUSE CORRESPONDENTS FEEL ABOUT BACKGROUND BRIEFINGS." <u>JOURNALISM Q</u> 50 (AUTUMN 1973): 509+.

QUANTITATIVE ANALYSES OF "ATTITUDES RELATED TO BRIEFINGS PRODUCING THREE TYPES AMONG WHITE HOUSE NEWSMEN AND SELECTED OFFICIALS--ADVERSARY, POLITICO AND ETHICAL INDEPENDENT."

1872 KAMPELMAN, M.M. "CONGRESS, THE MEDIA, AND THE PRESIDENT."
IN CONGRESS AGAINST THE PRESIDENT, EDITED BY H.C.
MANSFIELD. NEW YORK: ACADEMY OF POL SCI. 1975: 85-97. ALSO
NEW YORK: PRAEGER, 1975.

1873 KELLEY, S., JR. PRESIDENTIAL PUBLIC RELATIONS AND
POLITICAL POWER. BALTIMORE, MD.: JOHNS HOPKINS U PR,
1956, PP. 247.

1874 KNAPPMAN, E.W. GOVERNMENT AND THE MEDIA IN CONFLICT,
1970-74. NEW YORK: FACTS ON FILE, 1974, PP. 204.

INCLUDES CHRONOLOGICAL NEWS SUMMARIES OF THE RELATIONS
BETWEEN POLITICS AND THE MEDIA IN GENERAL, THE PENTAGON
PAPERS CONTROVERSY, AND WATERGATE. ALSO INCLUDES A
SAMPLING OF NEWSPAPER EDITORIALS ON EACH ISSUE.

1875 MINOW, N.N., MARTIN, J.B., AND MITCHELL, L.M.
PRESIDENTIAL TELEVISION. NEW YORK: BASIC BOOKS INC.,
1973.

HOW PRESIDENTS FROM ROOSEVELT THROUGH NIXON USED THEIR
ACCESS TO THE ELECTRONIC MEDIA AS A VEHICLE FOR ADVANCING
THEIR POWER. ACCOMPANIED BY USEFUL TABULAR INFORMATION.

1876 MORGAN, E.P., WAYS, M., MOLLENHOFF, C., LISAGOR, P., AND
KLEIN, H.G. THE PRESIDENCY AND THE PRESS CONFERENCE.
WASHINGTON, D.C.: AMERICAN ENTERPRISE INSTITUTE FOR PUBLIC
POLICY RESEARCH, 1971, PP. 56.

1877 MOYNIHAN, D.P. "THE PRESIDENCY AND THE PRESS."
COMMENTARY (MAR 1971): 41-52.

CONTENDS THAT IF THE BALANCE OF POWER BETWEEN THE
PRESIDENCY AND THE PRESS SHOULD "TIP TOO FAR IN THE
DIRECTION OF THE PRESS, OUR CAPACITY FOR EFFECTIVE
DEMOCRATIC GOVERNMENT WILL BE SERIOUSLY AND DANGEROUSLY
WEAKENED."

1878 POLLARD, J.E. THE PRESIDENTS AND THE PRESS: TRUMAN TO
JOHNSON. WASHINGTON, D.C.: PUBLIC AFFAIRS PRESS, 1964,
PP. 125.

1879 ----------. "THE WHITE HOUSE NEWS CONFERENCE AS A CHANNEL
OF COMMUNICATION." POQ 15 (1951):663-678.

1880 PORTER, W.E. ASSAULT ON THE MEDIA: THE NIXON YEARS. ANN

ARBOR: U OF MICH PR, 1975, PP. 320.

A YEAR-BY-YEAR ACCOUNT OF THE EFFORTS BY THE NIXON ADMINISTRATION TO ENGAGE IN LITIGATION AGAINST JOURNALISTS WHO SOUGHT TO PROTECT THE CONFIDENTIALITY OF NEWS SOURCES, TO ENGAGE IN ANTITRUST ACTION AGAINST TELEVISION NETWORKS AND OTHERWISE TO HARASS REPRESENTATIVES OF THE MEDIA. A SELECTION OF RELEVANT DOCUMENTS IS APPENDED.

1881 RESTON, J.B. "THE PRESS, THE PRESIDENT, AND FOREIGN POLICY." FOREIGN AFFAIRS 44 (JULY 1966): 553-573.

1882 RINN, F.J. "THE PRESIDENTIAL PRESS CONFERENCE." IN THE PRESIDENCY, EDITED BY A. WILDAVSKY. BOSTON, MA: LITTLE, BROWN, 1969: 327-336.

1883 SESSIONS, C. "AGNEW'S ATTACK ON THE MEDIA: INTIMIDATION OR A PLEA FOR 'SELF-EXAMINATION'?" NATIONAL J 1 (1969):183-192.

1884 SMITH, A.M. THANK YOU, MR. PRESIDENT: A WHITE HOUSE NOTEBOOK. NEW YORK: HARPER, 1946, PP. 304.

AN ENTHUSIASTIC ACCOUNT BY THE UNITED PRESS'S WHITE HOUSE CORRESPONDENT ABOUT THE REGULAR EXCHANGES BETWEEN THE PRESIDENT AND THE PRESS CORPS ASSIGNED TO THE WHITE HOUSE.

1885 STEIN, M.L. WHEN PRESIDENTS MEET THE PRESS. NEW YORK: JULIAN MESSNER, 1969, PP. 190.

BRIEF, POPULAR SKETCHES OF PRESIDENTIAL PRESS RELATIONS THROUGHOUT AMERICAN HISTORY.

1886 "THE FAIRNESS PROBLEM REEXAMINED: HAS THE PRESS DONE A JOB ON NIXON?" COLUMBIA LAW R 12 (JAN.-FEB. 1974): 50-58.

DISCUSSIONS HELD AT THE COLUMBIA SCHOOL OF JOURNALISM BY HERBERT KLEIN, BILL MOYERS, BENJAMIN BRADLEE, FRED FRIENDLY, STEPHEN HESS, BENNO SCHMIDT, ELIE ABEL, TOM WICKER, FRANCES DALE AND WILLIAM RUSHER.

1887 THE PUBLIC INTEREST AND THE RIGHT TO KNOW. ACCESS TO GOVERNMENT INFORMATION AND THE ROLE OF THE PRESS. A SELECTIVE BIBLIOGRAPHICAL GUIDE. BOSTON: BOSTON PUBLIC LIBRARY, 1971, PP. 59.

1888 THOMAS, H. DATELINE: WHITE HOUSE. NEW YORK: MACMILLAN, 1975, PP. 298.

THE ANECDOTAL MEMOIRS OF A VETERAN UPI JOURNALIST. THOMAS BEGAN COVERING THE WHITE HOUSE DURING THE KENNEDY

ADMINISTRATION AT WHICH TIME SHE COVERED MRS. KENNEDY, AND SINCE THEN HAS COVERED THE PRESIDENTS THEMSELVES.

1889 WISE, D. "THE PRESIDENT AND THE PRESS." ATLANTIC 231 (APR 1973): 55-64.

DETAILS RELATIONS BETWEEN NIXON AND THE PRESS, WITH EMPHASIS ON TELEVISION NEWS REPORTERS, NETWORKS, AND THE ROLE OF THE PRESIDENTIAL AIDES.

1890 WITCOVER, J. "HOW WELL DOES THE WHITE HOUSE PRESS PERFORM?" COLUMBIA JOURNALISM R 12 (NOV-DEC 1973): 39-43.

SEE ALSO 318, 496, 547, 570, 572, 654, 786, 788, 892, 893, 914, 1049, 1073, 1176, 1188, 1190, 1230, 1241, 1266, 1309, 1314, 1389, 1424, 1426, 1430, 1437, 1443, 1476, 1489, 1492, 1514, 1522

E. CONGRESS

1891 ACHESON, D. "LEGISLATIVE-EXECUTIVE RELATIONS." YALE REVIEW 45 (1956):481-495.

PART OF THE DISCUSSION THAT WAS BROUGHT TOGETHER IN ACHESON'S A CITIZEN LOOKS AT CONGRESS. NO DOUBT INFLUENCED BY HIS OWN EXPOSURE AS SECRETARY OF STATE TO FREQUENT CONGRESSIONAL CRITICISM, ACHESON ARGUES THAT CONGRESS SHOULD ALLOW ADMINISTRATORS MORE LEEWAY IN CARRYING OUT THEIR EXECUTIVE RESPONSIBILITIES.

1892 AIKEN, G.D. AIKEN: SENATE DIARY JANUARY 1972 - JANUARY 1975. BRATTLEBORO, VT: STEPHEN GREENE, 1976, PP. 370.

A WEEK-BY-WEEK JOURNAL KEPT BY A SENIOR MEMBER OF THE SENATE DURING HIS LAST 3 YEARS IN OFFICE. INCLUDES A NUMBER OF OBSERVATIONS AND REFLECTIONS ON EXECUTIVE-LEGISLATIVE RELATIONS AND THE SPECIFIC EVENTS (E.G., WATERGATE) OF THE TIME.

1893 ARMSTRONG, W.P. "THE PRESIDENT AND THE CONGRESS: UNSOLVED PROBLEMS OF LEADERSHIP AND POWERS." ABA J 33 (MAY 1947): 417-20+.

1894 ARNOLD, P., AND ROOS, L.J. "TOWARD A THEORY OF CONGRESSIONAL-EXECUTIVE RELATIONS." R OF POLITICS 36 (JULY 1974): 410-429.

CONCLUDES THAT THE CONCEPT OF AN INDEPENDENT PRESIDENT OR AN INDEPENDENT CONGRESS BOTH "SHARE THE SAME, ZERO-SUM FALLACY. A PRESIDENT WITHOUT CONGRESS ENDS UP IN THE BOURBON TENDENCIES OF JOHNSON AND NIXON. HENCE WE CANNOT AGAIN ACCEPT THE MYTH OF SOLITARY PRESIDENTIAL POWER. BUT CONGRESS, WITHOUT THE LEGITIMATE ENERGIES OF A FORCEFUL

AND PROBING EXECUTIVE, WILL GIVE US AN AIMLESS DOMINATION
BY LOCAL AND SPECIAL INTERESTS."

1895 BERGER. R. "THE PRESIDENT, CONGRESS, AND THE COURTS."
YALE LAW J 83 (MAY 1974): 1111-1155.

DISCUSSES THREE ISSUES: THE IMPLICATIONS OF THE ATTEMPT TO
SUBPOENA PRESIDENT JEFFERSON IN THE TREASON TRIAL OF AARON
BURR AS HISTORICAL PRECEDENT; WHETHER IMPEACHMENT MUST
PRECEDE INDICTMENT; AND THE ALLEGED INACCURATE "INSTANT
HISTORY" ON WHICH THE BRIEF BY PRESIDENT NIXON'S ATTORNEY
ON THE APPROPRIATE GROUNDS FOR IMPEACHMENT WAS BASED.

1896 BICKEL. A.M. "CONGRESS, THE PRESIDENT AND THE POWER TO
WAGE WAR." CHICAGO-KENT LAW R 48 (FALL-WINTER 1971):
131.

1897 BINKLEY, W.E. PRESIDENT AND CONGRESS. NEW YORK: A.A.
KNOPF, 1947.

A CHRONOLOGICAL EXAMINATION OF EXECUTIVE-LEGISLATIVE
RELATIONS FROM WASHINGTON TO TRUMAN, EMPHASIZING THE WAYS
STRONG PRESIDENTS HAVE ECLIPSED CONGRESS. A CHAPTER ON
EISENHOWER, "THE SECOND ERA OF GOOD FEELING," WAS ADDED TO
THE 1962 VINTAGE PAPERBACK EDITION.

1898 ----------. "THE PRESIDENT AND CONGRESS." JP 11 (FEB
1949): 65-79.

DOCUMENTS THE SHIFT FROM CONGRESSIONAL TO PRESIDENTIAL
LEGISLATIVE LEADERSHIP, STRESSING THE CONTINUING
PULL-AND-HAUL BETWEEN THE BRANCHES.

1899 ----------. "THE PRESIDENT AS CHIEF LEGISLATOR." ANNALS
307 (1956):92-105.

CLEAR HISTORICAL ACCOUNT OF CHANGES FROM THE 19TH TO THE
20TH CENTURIES IN PRESIDENT'S LEGISLATIVE ROLE.HISTORICAL
INSTANCES, FROM JACKSON THROUGH EISENHOWER, OF THE
INCREASING ROLE OF THE PRESIDENT AS INITIATOR OF
LEGISLATION.

1900 ----------. "THE RELATION OF THE PRESIDENT TO CONGRESS."
PARLIAMENTARY AFFAIRS 3 (WINTER, 1949):7-20.

NOTING THE RECURRENT DISAGREEMENTS BETWEEN THE EXECUTIVE
AND THE LEGISLATIVE BRANCHES, BINKLEY REFLECTS UPON
WHETHER MORE DISCIPLINED POLITICAL PARTIES AND THE
FORMATION OF A LEGISLATIVE-EXECUTIVE COUNCIL MIGHT BE A
REFORM THAT WOULD ENHANCE THE EFFECTIVENESS OF
POLICY-MAKING IN THE UNITED STATES.

1901 BONAFEDE, D., ET AL. "THE PRESIDENT VERSUS CONGRESS: THE
SCORE SINCE WATERGATE." NATIONAL J 8 (1976): 730-748.

1902 BONAFEDE, D., RAPOPORT, D., AND HAVEMANN, J. "THE

PRESIDENT VERSUS CONGRESS: THE SCORE SINCE WATERGATE." NATIONAL J 8 (1976): 730-748.

AFTER INTERVIEWING "A WIDE RANGE OF PAST AND PRESENT GOVERNMENT OFFICIALS AND WELL RESPECTED ACADEMICIANS," A TEAM OF REPORTERS CONCLUDED THAT THE POSTWATERGATE PRESIDENCY "HAS BEEN COMPELLED TO LIVE WITHIN ITS CONSTITUTIONAL BOUNDS, BUT IS STILL AN OFFICE WITH ESSENTIALLY UNCURBED POWERS." THE PRESIDENT REMAINS "THE SINGLE MOST IMPORTANT FIGURE IN GOVERNMENT."

1903 BUCK, J.V. "PRESIDENTIAL COATTAILS AND CONGRESSIONAL LOYALTY." MIDWEST J POLITICAL SCIENCE 16 (AUG 1972): 460-472.

"THIS PAPER EXAMINES THE JOINT RETURNS OF PRESIDENTIAL AND CONGRESSIONAL RACES IN NON-SOUTHERN DISTRICTS FOR FOUR RECENT ELECTIONS AND THE RESULTS INDICATE THAT A BETTER SHOWING ON THE PART OF THE PRESIDENT RESULTS IN GREATER CONGRESSIONAL SUPPORT FOR HIS PROGRAMS. IT WOULD SEEM THEREFORE THAT THE SUCCESS OF THE PRESIDENT'S PROGRAM DEPENDS NOT ONLY ON HIS PARTY'S STRENGTH IN CONGRESS, BUT ON HOW WELL HE RUNS VIS-A-VIS EACH INDIVIDUAL CONGRESSMAN."

1904 CHAMBERLAIN, L.H. THE PRESIDENT, CONGRESS AND LEGISLATION. NEW YORK: COLUMBIA UNIVERSITY PRESS, 1946, PP. 478. ALSO, NEW YORK: AMS DRESS, 1967, PP. 478.

HISTORICAL ANALYSIS OF NUMEROUS LEGISLATIVE ENACTMENTS FROM THE LATE 19TH CENTURY THROUGH THE MID-1940'S, WITH SPECIAL ATTENTION TO THE DEGREE TO WHICH EACH BRANCH WAS RESPONSIBLE FOR INITIATING LEGISLATION. THE BOOK LACKS A SPECIFIC CRITERION FOR DETERMINING THE ORIGINAL SOURCE OF LEGISLATION AND FAILS TO DISTINGUISH BETWEEN THE PRE- AND POST-FDR PERIODS. THE LATTER OF COURSE WERE FAR MORE MARKED BY EXPLICIT EFFORTS AT AND EXPECTATIONS OF PRESIDENTIAL INITIATIVE.

1905 ----------. "THE PRESIDENT AS LEGISLATOR." ANNALS 283 (1952):94-101.

UNLIKE CHAMBERLAIN'S BETTER KNOWN STATISTICAL ANALYSIS OF WHICH BRANCH INITIATES LEGISLATION, THIS IS A GENERAL ESSAY -- LARGELY AN INVENTORY OF WAYS PRESIDENTS HAVE COME TO INFLUENCE LAW-MAKING.

1906 ----------. "THE PRESIDENT, CONGRESS, AND LEGISLATION." PSQ 61 (1946):42-60.

1907 COOPER, J. "THE LEGISLATIVE VETO AND THE CONSTITUTION." GEORGE WASHINGTON LAW R 30 (1962):467-516.

1908 COTTER, C.P. "ADMINISTRATIVE ACCOUNTABILITY TO CONGRESS: THE CONCURRENT RESOLUTION." WESTERN POLITICAL Q 9

(1956):955-966.

1909 DAVIDSON, R.H. "CONGRESS AND THE EXECUTIVE: THE RACE FOR REPRESENTATION." IN CONGRESS: THE FIRST BRANCH OF GOVERNMENT. EDITED BY A. DE GRAZIA, WASHINGTON, D.C.: AMER ENTERPRISE INSTITUTE, 1966: 1-22.

1910 DE GRAZIA, A. CONGRESS AND THE PRESIDENCY: THEIR ROLE IN MODERN TIMES. WASHINGTON, D.C.: AMERICAN ENTERPRISE INSTITUTE, 1967, PP. 192.

1911 -----------. REPUBLIC IN CRISIS: CONGRESS AGAINST THE EXECUTIVE FORCE. NEW YORK: FEDERAL LEGAL PUBLICATIONS, 1965, PP. 303.

1912 DREW, E. "WHY CONGRESS WON'T FIGHT." N Y TIMES MAG (SEPT. 23, 1973): 18-19+.

1913 EDWARDS, G.C., III. "PRESIDENTIAL INFLUENCE IN THE HOUSE: PRESIDENTIAL PRESTIGE AS A SOURCE OF PRESIDENTIAL POWER." APSR 70 (MAR 1976): 101-113.

1914 EGGER, R., AND HARRIS, J.P. THE PRESIDENT AND CONGRESS. NEW YORK: MCGRAW, 1963, PP. 128.

1915 FISHER, L. PRESIDENT AND CONGRESS: POWER AND POLICY. NEW YORK: FREE PRESS, 1972, PP. 347.

REVIEWS PRESIDENTIAL-CONGRESSIONAL RELATIONSHIPS IN THE SHARING OF LEGISLATIVE POWER, SPENDING POWER, TAXING POWER, AND THE WAR POWER.

1916 -----------. "PRESIDENTIAL SPENDING DISCRETION AND CONGRESSIONAL CONTROLS." LAW AND CONTEMPORARY PROBLEMS (WINTER 1972): 135-172.

CONGRESS LACKS EFFECTIVE POWER OVER THE PURSE, BOTH BECAUSE THE EXECUTIVE BRANCH HAS OFTEN CHOSEN TO REALLOCATE OR NOT TO SPEND CONGRESSIONAL APPROPRIATIONS AND BECAUSE SO-CALLED "UNCONTROLLABLE" EXPENDITURES RESULT FROM PROGRAM-COMMITMENT WITH INFLATIONARY COMPONENTS. THE MOST COMPREHENSIVE DISCUSSION OF THIS IS IN FISHER'S PRESIDENTIAL SPENDING POWER.

1917 FOX, D.M., AND CLAPP, C.H., EDS. "THE HOUSE RULES COMMITTEE AND THE PROGRAMS OF THE KENNEDY AND JOHNSON

ADMINISTRATIONS." MIDWEST J POLITICAL SCIENCE 14 (1970):667-672.

ARGUES THAT THE HOUSE COMMITTEE ON RULES DID NOT HAVE A SIGNIFICANT EFFECT IN PREVENTING PRESIDENTIAL PROPOSALS FROM REACHING THE FLOOR OF THE HOUSE IN THE 87TH THROUGH THE 90TH CONGRESSES.

1918 GALLAGHER, H.G. "PRESIDENTS, CONGRESS AND THE LEGISLATIVE FUNCTIONS." IN THE PRESIDENCY REAPPRAISED, EDITED BY R.G. TUGWELL AND T.E. CRONIN, NEW YORK: PRAEGER, 1974: 217-233.

1919 HARRIS, J.P. ADVICE AND CONSENT OF THE SENATE. BERKELEY, CALIF.: UNIV. OF CALF. PRESS, 1953, PP. 457.

1920 HERRING, E.P. PRESIDENTIAL LEADERSHIP: THE POLITICAL RELATIONS OF CONGRESS AND THE CHIEF EXECUTIVE. NEW YORK: RINEHART, 1940, PP. 173. REPRINTED WESTPORT, CONN.: GREENWOOD PR., 1972.

1921 ----------. "EXECUTIVE-LEGISLATIVE RESPONSIBILITIES." APSR 38 (1944):1153-1165.

1922 HILSMAN, R. "CONGRESSIONAL-EXECUTIVE RELATIONS AND THE FOREIGN POLICY CONSENSUS." APSR 52 (1958):725-744.

AGREEMENT BETWEEN PRESIDENT AND CONGRESS IS MORE LIKELY ON FOREIGN THAN ON DOMESTIC POLICIES. A DETAILED ANALYSIS OF REASONS WHY.

1923 ----------. "THE FOREIGN POLICY CONSENSUS: AN INTERIM RESEARCH REPORT." J OF CONFLICT RESOLUTION 11 (1968):361-382.

1924 HOLTZMAN, A. LEGISLATIVE LIASON: EXECUTIVE LEADERSHIP IN CONGRESS. CHICAGO: RAND MCNALLY, 1970, PP. 308.

1925 HOPKINS, B.R. "CONGRESSIONAL RELATIONS WITH EXECUTIVE AND JUDICIAL." ABA J 59 (FEB 1973): 145-149.

1926 HUITT, R.K. "WHITE HOUSE CHANNELS TO THE HILL." IN CONGRESS AGAINST THE PRESIDENT. EDITED BY H.C. MANSFIELD. NEW YORK: ACADEMY OF POL SCI, 1975: 71-84. ALSO NEW YORK: PRAEGER, 1975.

1927 JOHANNES, J.R. "CONGRESS AND THE INITIATION OF LEGISLATION." PUBLIC POLICY 20 (SPRING 1972): 281-309.

FOCUSES ON LEGISLATIVE INITIATIVE BY (1)ARGUING THAT CONGRESS DOES INDEED INITIATE--PROBABLY MORE OFTEN AND ON MORE IMPORTANT MATTERS THAN IS COMMONLY REALIZED; (2)SHOWING THAT CONGRESS HAS AVAILABLE DIFFERENT STRATEGIES FOR LEGISLATIVE INITIATIVE; AND (3)SPECIFYING SOME REASONS WHY AND WHEN CONGRESS IS ABLE TO INITIATE AND WHAT CONDITIONS FACILITATE SUCCESSFUL CONGRESSIONAL LEADERSHIP IN LAWMAKING."

1928 ----------. "THE PRESIDENT PROPOSES AND CONGRESS DISPOSES--BUT NOT ALWAYS: LEGISLATIVE INITIATIVE ON CAPITOL HILL." R OF POLITICS 36 (JULY 1974): 356-370.

"CONGRESS DOES INITIATE LEGISLATION, THANKS MAINLY TO ITS PLURALISTIC AND PERMEABLE COMMITTEE AND SUBCOMMITTEE STRUCTURE AND TO ITS INDIVIDUAL POLICY ADVOCATES, ESPECIALLY THE SENATE. GRANTED, CONGRESS DOES DEMAND RECOMMENDATIONS FROM THE PRESIDENT; BUT IN THEIR ABSENCE IT CAN AND DOES LEAD--NOT CONSISTENTLY, NOT PROGRAMMATICALLY, BUT AS A RESERVE INITIATOR EMPLOYING SEVERAL MEANS TO ITS END."

1929 ----------. "WHERE DOES THE BUCK STOP?-CONGRESS, PRESIDENT, AND THE RESPONSIBILITY FOR LEGISLATIVE INITIATION." WESTERN POLITICAL Q 25 (1972):396-415.

ANALYZES A NUMBER OF JOHNSON ADMINISTRATION POLICY MAKING CASES STIPULATING CIRCUMSTANCES UNDER WHICH LEGISLATIVE INITIATIVES TEND TO BE TAKEN BY THE PRESIDENT AND THOSE UNDER WHICH CONGRESS TAKES THE INITIATIVE.

1930 JONES, H.W. "THE PRESIDENT, CONGRESS, AND FOREIGN RELATIONS." CALIFORNIA LAW R 29 (1941):565-585.

A LEGAL AND CONSTITUTIONAL ANALYSIS OF THE DISTRIBUTION OF EXPENDITURE AND LEGISLATIVE POWER IN FOREIGN RELATIONS WITH SPECIAL ATTENTION TO THE ISSUES THAT AROSE OVER NEUTRALITY, LEND-LEASE, AND RELATED MATTERS DURING THE ROOSEVELT ADMINISTRATION PRIOR TO PEARL HARBOR.

1931 KEFAUVER, E. "THE NEED FOR BETTER EXECUTIVE-LEGISLATIVE TEAMWORK IN THE NATIONAL GOVERNMENT." APSR 38 (1944):317-24.

1932 KELLEY, S., JR. "PATRONAGE AND PRESIDENTIAL LEGISLATIVE LEADERSHIP." IN THE PRESIDENCY, EDITED BY A. WILDAVSKY, BOSTON: LITTLE,BROWN, 1969: 268-277.

1933 KELLY, J.B. "PROPOSED LEGISLATION CURBING THE WAR POWERS OF THE PRESIDENT." DICKINSON LAW R 76 (SPRING 1972): 411.

1934 KENT, F.R. "WHITE HOUSE TECHNIQUE." VIRGINIA Q R 9 (JULY 1933): 372-379.

A BRIEF ESSAY BY A WELL KNOWN JOURNALIST OF THE TIME ON PATRONAGE, POPULAR SUPPORT, AND PRESIDENTIAL PARTY STRENGTH IN CONGRESS AS RESOURCES FOR PRESIDENTIAL INFLUENCE OVER CONGRESS WITH SPECIAL REFERENCE TO ROOSEVELT'S "HUNDRED DAYS."

1935 KESSELMAN, M. "PRESIDENTIAL LEADERSHIP IN CONGRESS AND FOREIGN POLICY: A REAPPLICATION OF A HYPOTHESIS." MIDWEST J POLITICAL SCIENCE 9 (1965): 401-406.

1936 KOENIG, L.W. CONGRESS AND THE PRESIDENT. CHICAGO: SCOTT, FORESMAN & CO., 1965, PP. 197.

1937 LANE, G. THE PRESIDENT VERSUS CONGRESS: FREEDOM OF INFORMATION. JAMAICA, N.Y.: LANCO PRESS, 1971, PP. 61.

1938 LEHMAN, J. THE EXECUTIVE, CONGRESS, AND FOREIGN POLICY. NEW YORK: PRAEGER, 1976, PP. 275.

1939 LEVINE, R.C. "THE CONGRESSIONAL ROLE IN FORMULATING NATIONAL POLICY: SOME OBSERVATIONS ON THE FIRST SESSION OF THE NINETY-THIRD CONGRESS." HARVARD J ON LEGISLATION 11 (FEB. 1974): 161-180.

1940 LEVINSON, L.H., AND MILLS, J.L. "BUDGET REFORM AND IMPOUNDMENT CONTROL." VANDERBILT LAW R 27 (1974): 615-666.

1941 MACLEAN, J.C. PRESIDENT AND CONGRESS: THE CONFLICT OF POWERS. NEW YORK: H.W. WILSON, 1955, PP. 218.

1942 MACMAHON, A. "CONGRESSIONAL OVERSIGHT OF ADMINISTRATION." PSQ 58 (1943):161-190, 380-414.

1943 ----------. "SENATORIAL CONFIRMATION." PUBLIC ADMINISTRATION R 3 (1943):281-296.

1944 MANLEY, J.F. "THE PRESIDENCY, CONGRESS, AND NATIONAL POLICY-MAKING." IN POLITICAL SCIENCE ANNUAL, EDITED BY C.P. COTTER. NEW YORK: BOBBS-MERRILL, 1974: 227-273.

1945 MANSFIELD, H.C., ED. CONGRESS AGAINST THE PRESIDENT. NEW YORK: ACADEMY OF POL SCI, 32 NO. 1, 1975, PP. 200. ALSO NEW YORK: PRAEGER, 1975.

A COLLECTION OF THIRTEEN ESSAYS ON RECENT DEVELOPMENTS IN CONGRESS THAT BEAR UPON THE RELATIONSHIP BETWEEN EXECUTIVE AND LEGISLATIVE BRANCHES WITH SPECIAL EMPHASIS ON CONGRESSIONAL EFFORTS TO RESTRAIN THE PRESIDENT DURING THE JOHNSON AND KENNEDY ADMINISTRATIONS. ORIGINALLY PUBLISHED AS VOLUME 32, NUMBER 1 OF THE PROCEEDINGS OF THE ACADEMY OF POLITICAL SCIENCE.

1946 MOE, R.C., AND TEEL, S.C. "CONGRESS AS POLICY MAKER." IN CONGRESS AND THE PRESIDENT, EDITED BY R.C. MOE. PACIFIC PALISADES, CALIF.: GOODYEAR, 1971: 32-52.

ARGUES AGAINST STANDARD VIEW THAT CONGRESS HAS INCREASINGLY LEFT POLICY DEVELOPMENT AND INITIATION TO THE PRESIDENT.

1947 MOE, R.C., ED. CONGRESS AND THE PRESIDENT: ALLIES AND ADVERSARIES. PACIFIC PALISADES: GOODYEAR PUBLISHING COMPANY, 1971, PP. 324.

THE TITLE OF THIS ANTHOLOGY ADEQUATELY EXPLAINS WHAT IS COVERED IN ITS 24 SECTIONS. A VALUABLE COLLECTION OF ARTICLES AND BOOK SELECTIONS, PLUS SOME ORIGINAL CONTRIBUTIONS.

1948 MORGAN, T.D. "THE GENERAL ACCOUNTING OFFICE: ONE HOPE FOR CONGRESS TO REGAIN PARITY OF POWER WITH THE PRESIDENT." NORTH CAROLINA LAW R 51 (1973):1279-1368.

1949 PARRIS, J.H. "CONGRESS AND THE AMERICAN PRESIDENTIAL SYSTEM." CURRENT HISTORY 66 (1974):259-263.

1950 PATTERSON, J.T. "A CONSERVATIVE COALITION FORMS IN CONGRESS." J AMER HIST 52 (MARCH 1966): 757-72.

1951 PIPE, G.R. "CONGRESSIONAL LIAISON: THE EXECUTIVE BRANCH CONSOLIDATES ITS RELATIONS WITH CONGRESS...." PAR 26 (MAR 1966): 14-24.

1952 POLSBY, N.W. CONGRESS AND THE PRESIDENCY. ENGLEWOOD CLIFFS, N.J.: PRENTICE-HALL, 1971, PP. 162.

1953 RANDOLPH, R.C., AND SMITH, D.C. "EXECUTIVE PRIVILEGE AND THE CONGRESSIONAL RIGHT OF INQUIRY." HARVARD J ON LEGISLATION 10 (1973):621-671.

1954 RIKER, W.H., AND BAST, W. "PRESIDENTIAL ACTION IN CONGRESSIONAL NOMINATIONS." IN THE PRESIDENCY, EDITED BY A. WILDAVSKY. BOSTON: LITTLE, BROWN, 1969: 250-267.

1955 RODINO, P.W., JR. "CONGRESSIONAL REVIEW OF EXECUTIVE ACTION." SETON HALL LAW R 5 (SPRING 1974): 489-525.

ARTICLE BY CHAIRMAN OF THE HOUSE JUDICIARY COMMITTEE ON CONGRESSIONAL RESPONSE TO PRESIDENTIAL IMPOUNDMENT OF FUNDS, INCREASED MILITARY ACTIVITIES AND PROPOSED LEGISLATION TO LIMIT PRESIDENTIAL POWER.

1956 ROGERS, W.P. "CONGRESS, THE PRESIDENT, AND THE WAR POWERS." CALIFORNIA LAW R 59 (SEPT 1971): 1194-1214.

HISTORICAL DISCUSSION BY NIXON'S SECRETARY OF STATE OF THE CONFLICT OVER WAR POWERS AND A DISCUSSION OF THE "ISSUES WHICH BEAR UPON THE EXERCISE OF PRESIDENTIAL AND CONGRESSIONAL POWERS NOW AND IN THE FORESEEABLE FUTURE."

1957 SAPP, C.R. "EXECUTIVE ASSISTANCE IN THE LEGISLATIVE PROCESS." PUBLIC ADMINISTRATION REVIEW 6 (1946):10-19.

A GENERAL VIEW OF THE THEN NOT WIDELY KNOWN PROCEDURES FOR LEGISLATIVE CLEARANCE AND THE OTHER EXECUTIVE BRANCH CONTRIBUTIONS TO LAWMAKING. SPECIAL EMPHASIS ON THE ROLE OF THE BUREAU OF THE BUDGET.

1958 SCHICK, A. "BUDGET REFORM LEGISLATION: REORGANIZING CONGRESSIONAL CENTERS OF FISCAL POWER." HARVARD J ON LEGISLATION 2 (1974):303-350.

1959 ----------. "THE BATTLE OF THE BUDGET." IN CONGRESS AGAINST THE PRESIDENT, EDITED BY H.C. MANSFIELD. NEW YORK: ACADEMY OF POL SCI, 1975: 51-70. ALSO NEW YORK: PRAEGER, 1975.

1960 SCHLESINGER, A.M., JR., AND DE GRAZIA, A. CONGRESS AND THE PRESIDENCY: THEIR ROLE IN MODERN TIMES. WASHINGTON, D.C.: AMERICAN INSTITUTE FOR FOREIGN POLICY RESEARCH, 1967, PP. 189.

1961 SCRIBNER, J.L. "THE PRESIDENT VERSUS CONGRESS ON WARMAKING AUTHORITY." MILITARY REVIEW 52 (1972):87-96.

1962 SMITH, J.M., AND COTTER, C.P. "ADMINISTRATIVE ACCOUNTABILITY: REPORTING TO CONGRESS." WESTERN POLITICAL Q 10 (1957):405-415.

1963 TAPIA, R.R., JAMES, J.P., ET AL. "CONGRESS VERSUS THE EXECUTIVE: THE ROLE OF THE COURTS." HARVARD J ON LEGISLATION 11 (FEB 1974): 352-403.

DISCUSSES REASONS FOR "INCREASING CONGRESSIONAL USE OF COURTS...EXAMINES JUDICIAL WILLINGNESS TO DECIDE THE MERITS....AND CONCLUDES THAT THESE CONGRESSIONAL SUITS SHOULD BE SUBJECT TO A CAREFUL ANALYSIS THAT NO COURT HAS YET PROVIDED."

1964 "THE PRESIDENT, CONGRESS, AND THE COURTS." YALE LAW J 83 (1974):1111-1155.

1965 THOMPSON, F., JR., AND POLLITT, D.H. "CONGRESSIONAL CONTROL OF JUDICIAL REMEDIES: PRESIDENT NIXON'S PROPOSED MORATORIUM ON 'BUSING' ORDERS." NORTH CAROLINA LAW R 50 (JUNE 1972): 810-841.

1966 TIDMARCH, C.M., AND SABATT, C.M. "PRESIDENTIAL LEADERSHIP CHANGE AND FOREIGN POLICY ROLL-CALL VOTING IN THE U.S. SENATE." WESTERN POLITICAL Q 24 (DEC. 1972): 613-625.

1967 TRUMAN, D. "PRESIDENCY AND CONGRESSIONAL LEADERSHIP." PROCEEDINGS OF THE AMERICAN PHILOSOPHICAL SOCIETY 103 (1959):687-692.

CAREFUL HISTORICAL DISCUSSION, INCLUDING AN ANALYSIS OF THE EFFECTS OF SINGLE PARTY CONTROL OF THE PRESIDENCY AND CONGRESS VS. DIVIDED CONTROL OF THE TWO BRANCHES.

1968 WHITE, H. "EXECUTIVE RESPONSIBILITY TO CONGRESS VIA CONCURRENT RESOLUTION." APSR 36 (OCT 1942): 895-900.

ON THE EVOLUTION OF THE PROCEDURE THROUGH WHICH CONGRESS DELEGATES POLICY-MAKING AUTHORITY TO THE EXECUTIVE BUT "THAT AUTHORITY IS EXPRESSLY SUBJECT TO REVOCATION AT ANY TIME BY CONCURRENT RESOLUTIONS OF THE CONGRESS."

1969 YOUNGER, I. "CONGRESSIONAL INVESTIGATIONS AND EXECUTIVE SECRECY: A STUDY IN THE SEPARATION OF POWERS." U

<u>PITTSBURGH LAW R</u> 20 (JUNE 1959): 755.

1970 ZURCHER, A.J. "THE PRESIDENCY, CONGRESS AND SEPARATION OF POWERS: A REAPPRAISAL." <u>WESTERN POLITICAL Q</u> 3 (1950):75-97.

SEE ALSO 77, 86, 92, 97, 105, 153, 154, 155, 156, 157, 159, 160, 170, 184, 295, 385, 404, 463, 482, 510, 569, 575, 576, 647, 651, 682, 685, 723, 740, 757, 779, 884, 953, 1045, 1048, 1062, 1108, 1239, 1306, 1321, 1332, 1340, 1341, 1347, 1377, 1408, 1410, 1472, 1531, 1607, 1661, 1671, 1684, 1711, 1733, 1760, 1769, 2044, 2060, 2074, 2075, 2085, 2089, 2090, 2091, 2100, 2102, 2105, 2106, 2107, 2108, 2114, 2116, 2123, 2135, 2136, 2137, 2141, 2145, 2147, 2160, 2162, 2163, 2165, 2172, 2178, 2200, 2212, 2221, 2237, 2238, 2242, 2254, 2256, 2263, 2268, 2274, 2345, 2350, 2356, 2389, 2443, 2461

F. EXECUTIVE BRANCH

1971 ABERBACH, J.D., AND ROCKMAN, B.A. "CLASHING BELIEFS WITHIN THE EXECUTIVE BRANCH: THE NIXON ADMINISTRATION." <u>APSR</u> 70 (1970): 456-468.

SURVEY OF FEDERAL ADMINISTRATORS SHOWING SHARP POLICY DIFFERENCES BETWEEN HIGH LEVEL POLITICAL APPOINTEES AND SUPERGRADE CIVIL SERVANTS.

1972 BROWN, D.S. "THE PRESIDENT AND THE BUREAUS: TIME FOR A RENEWAL OF RELATIONSHIPS?" <u>PUBLIC ADMINISTRATION R</u> 26 (1966):174-182.

FOCUSSES ON ADMINISTRATION RELATIONS WITH EXECUTIVE BRANCH AGENCIES.

1973 CRONIN, T.E. "PRESIDENTS AS CHIEF EXECUTIVES." IN <u>THE PRESIDENCY REAPPRAISED</u>, EDITED BY R.G. TUGWELL AND T.E. CRONIN. NEW YORK: PRAEGER, 1974: 234-265.

1974 GOULDEN, J. "THE HOSTILE BUREAUCRACY." <u>WASHINGTONIAN</u> 9 (MAY 1974): 155-168.

1975 HALPERIN, M.H. "PRESIDENT AND THE MILITARY." <u>FOREIGN AFFAIRS</u> 50 (JAN 1972): 310-24.

REVIEWS RECENT PROPOSALS AND ORGANIZATIONAL EFFORTS TO ENHANCE PRESIDENT'S CAPACITY TO EVALUATE DEMANDS OF THE MILITARY.

1976 ----------. "THE PRESIDENCY AND ITS INTERACTION WITH THE CULTURE OF BUREAUCRACY." IN <u>THE SYSTEM: THE FIVE BRANCHES</u>

OF AMERICAN GOVERNMENT, EDITED BY C. PETERS AND J. FALLOWS. NEW YORK: PRAEGER, 1976: 1-54.

1977 HARRIS, J.P. CONGRESSIONAL CONTROL OF ADMINISTRATION. WASHINGTON, D.C.: BROOKINGS, 1964.

1978 HENRY, L.L. "THE PRESIDENCY, EXECUTIVE STAFFING, AND THE FEDERAL BUREAUCRACY." IN THE PRESIDENCY, EDITED BY A. WILDAVSKY. BOSTON: LITTLE, BROWN, 1969: 529-557.

1979 HUNTINGTON, S.P. THE COMMON DEFENSE: STRATEGIC PROGRAMS IN AMERICAN POLITICS. NEW YORK: COLUMBIA U PR, 1961.

1980 ----------. THE SOLDIER AND THE STATE: THE THEORY AND POLITICS OF CIVIL-MILITARY RELATIONS. NEW YORK: RANDOM HOUSE, 1964, PP. 534.

1981 KANTER, A. "PRESIDENTIAL LEADERSHIP OF THE MILITARY SERVICES." INST OF PUBLIC POLICY STUDIES U OF MICH. 1973, PP. 39.

1982 NATHAN, R. "THE "ADMINISTRATIVE PRESIDENCY"," PUBLIC INTEREST 44 (SUMMER 1976): 40-54.

TRADITIONAL ADMINISTRATIVE REFORM THEORY WHICH PRESCRIBED THAT THE PRESIDENT SHOULD HAVE STRONG CONTROL OVER ADMINISTRATIVE AGENCIES CAME CLOSE TO BEING PUT INTO ACTUAL PRACTICE DURING THE PRE-WATERGATE PHASE OF THE NIXON ADMINISTRATION. NATHAN CONSIDERS SUCH AN "ADMINISTRATIVE PRESIDENCY" UNDESIRABLE. AS AN ALTERNATIVE, HE PROPOSES CAREFUL PRESIDENTIAL ATTENTION TO APPOINTING EXECUTIVES WHO WILL COOPERATE WITH THE PRESIDENT WITHOUT, HOWEVER, YIELDING COMPLETELY TO HIS CONTROL.

1983 PARKER, R. "THE PRESIDENT AS HEAD OF THE EXECUTIVE-ADMINISTRATIVE HIERARCHY: A SURVEY." J PUBLIC LAW 8 (1959):437-461.

REVIEWS LEADING CONSTITUTIONAL LAW CASES AND OTHER PRECEDENTS BEARING ON THE EXTENT OF PRESIDENTIAL POWER OVER EXECUTIVE AGENCIES.

1984 PATTERSON, C.P. "THE PRESIDENT AS CHIEF ADMINISTRATOR." JP 11 (1949):213-235.

EXTENSIVE INVENTORY OF PRESIDENTIAL ADMINISTRATIVE POWERS

AND RESPONSIBILITIES. LARGELY DRAWING UPON SUPREME COURT
DECISIONS.

1985 REDFORD, E.S. "THE PRESIDENT AND THE REGULATORY
COMMISSIONS." TEXAS LAW R 44 (1965).

1986 RINEHART, J.C., AND BERNICK, E.L. "POLITICAL ATTITUDES AND
BEHAVIOR PATTERNS OF FEDERAL CIVIL SERVANTS." PAR
(NOV/DEC 1976): 603-611.

1987 SOMERS, H.M. "THE FEDERAL BUREAUCRACY AND THE CHANGE OF
ADMINISTRATION." APSR 158 (1954):131-151.

1988 STEELE, R.W. "POLITICAL ASPECTS OF AMERICAN MILITARY
PLANNING." MILITARY AFFAIRS 35 (1971):68-74.

1989 STEIN, H. AMERICAN CIVIL-MILITARY DECISIONS: A BOOK OF
CASE STUDIES. UNIVERSITY: UNIVERSITY OF ALABAMA PRESS,
1963, PP.705.

ELEVEN CASE STUDIES PROVIDING ACCOUNTS OF CIVIL-MILITARY
DECISIONS DURING THE YEARS 1932-1962. THE EDITOR PROVIDES
AN INTRODUCTORY ESSAY AND BRIEF INTRODUCTIONS TO EACH
CASE. IN A NUMBER OF CASES, PRESIDENTS FIGURE
SIGNIFICANTLY IN THE EVENTS DESCRIBED.

1990 WELBORN, D.M. "PRESIDENTS, REGULATORY COMMISSIONERS AND
REGULATORY POLICY." J PUBLIC LAW 15 (1960):1-29.

AN EMPIRICAL STUDY OF EISENHOWER'S AND KENNEDY'S
APPOINTMENTS TO INDEPENDENT REGULATORY COMMISSIONS AND OF
THE RELATIONSHIPS BETWEEN COMMISSION DECISIONS AND
PRESIDENTIAL POLICY GOALS.

1991 WOLL, P., AND JONES, R. "THE BUREAUCRACY AS A CHECK UPON
THE PRESIDENT." BUREAUCRAT 3 (APR 1974): 8-20.

SEE ALSO 76, 664, 670, 742, 760, 820, 853, 865, 872, 942,
957, 959, 1315, 1321, 1322, 1325, 1345, 1363, 1418,
1420, 1449, 1616, 1643, 1781, 1991, 2044, 2056

G. JUDICIARY

1992 ABRAHAM, H.J. JUSTICES AND PRESIDENTS. NEW YORK: OXFORD
U PR, 1974, PP. 310.

POLITICAL HISTORY OF APPOINTMENTS TO THE SUPREME COURT,
SEEKING TO EXPLAIN THE PRESIDENTIAL MOTIVES BEHIND EVERY

NOMINATION FOR THE POST OF SUPREME COURT JUSTICE SINCE 1789.

1993 CARRINGTON, P.D. "POLITICAL QUESTIONS: THE JUDICIAL CHECK ON THE EXECUTIVE." VIRGINIA LAW R 42 (FEB 1956): 175.

1994 CHOPER, J.H. "THE SUPREME COURT AND THE POLITICAL BRANCHES: DEMOCRATIC THEORY AND PRACTICE." U PENNSYLVANIA LAW R 122 (APRIL 1974): 810-858.

1995 KAHN, M.A. "ON THE APPOINTMENT OF JUSTICES TO THE SUPREME COURT." STANFORD LAW R 26 (FEB 1974): 689-715.

1996 PATTERSON, C.P. "THE PRESIDENT OVER THE JUDICIARY." BROOKLYN LAW R 11 (OCT 1941, APR 1942): 1-29, 155-86.

1997 PRITCHETT, C.H. "THE PRESIDENT AND THE SUPREME COURT." JP 11 (1949):80-92.

"ON THE WHOLE THERE IS LITTLE REASON TO ANTICIPATE THAT THE SUPREME COURT WILL EXERCISE SIGNIFICANT INFLUENCE ON THE BOUNDARIES OF PRESIDENTIAL POWER IN THE FUTURE."

1998 RAFFEL, B. "PRESIDENTIAL REMOVAL POWER: THE ROLE OF THE SUPREME COURT." U MIAMI LAW R 13 (FALL 1958): 69.

1999 ROSSITER, C.L. THE SUPREME COURT AND THE COMMANDER IN CHIEF. ITHACA,N.Y.: CORNELL UNIVERSITY PRESS, 1951, PP. 145.

IN A DISCUSSION FOCUSSING LARGELY ON COURT DECISIONS RELATING TO USE OF WAR POWERS BY PRESIDENTS LINCOLN AND FRANKLIN ROOSEVELT, ROSSITER REACHES THE CONCLUSION THAT "FOR MOST MARTIAL PURPOSES" THE DEFENSE OF THE CONSTITUTION LIES NOT IN ACTIONS OF THE COURT BUT "IN THE GOOD SENSE AND THE GOOD WILL OF THE POLITICAL BRANCHES OF THE NATIONAL GOVERNMENT."

2000 SCHUBERT, G.A. THE PRESIDENCY IN THE COURTS. MINNEAPOLIS, MINN.: U OF MINN. PR, 1957, PP. 391. ALSO BALTIMORE, MD.: DA CAPO PR, 1972, PP. 391.

A COMPREHENSIVE RESUME OF SUPREME COURT CASES DEALING WITH THE EXTENT OF PRESIDENTIAL POWER. SCHUBERT'S CONCLUSION WAS THAT THE COURT RARELY HAD CHALLENGED PRESIDENTIAL DECISIONS, THAT MOST OF THE CHALLENGES WHICH HAD OCCURRED LED TO DECISIONS AUGMENTING PRESIDENTIAL POWER, AND THAT THOSE DECISIONS CONTRARY TO A BROAD INTERPRETATION OF EXECUTIVE POWER OFTEN HAD BEEN MADE ONLY AFTER THE EVENTS

TO WHICH THEY APPLIED WERE A MATTER OF HISTORY.

2001 SCIGLIANO, R. THE SUPREME COURT AND THE PRESIDENCY. NEW YORK: FREE PRESS, 1971, PP. 233.

AN ANALYSIS OF THE DYNAMICS OF CONFLICT AND COOPERATION BETWEEN PRESIDENTS AND THE COURT, TAKING ACCOUNT BOTH OF THE COURT AS AN INSTITUTION AND OF PRESIDENTIAL RELATIONSHIPS WITH INDIVIDUAL JUSTICES. ARGUES AGAINST THE THESIS THAT PRESIDENTS TEND GENERALLY TO DOMINATE THE SUPREME COURT, TAKING ACCOUNT OF THE HISTORICAL EBB AND FLOW OF INFLUENCE RELATIONS BETWEEN THE 2 INSTITUTIONS.

2002 TAUBENECK, F.D., AND SEXTON, J.J. "EXECUTIVE PRIVILEGE AND COURT'S RIGHT TO KNOW - DISCOVERY AGAINST THE UNITED STATES IN CIVIL ACTIONS IN FEDERAL DISTRICT COURTS." GEORGETOWN LAW J 48 (1960):486.

SEE ALSO 77, 374, 417, 418, 434, 442, 443, 606, 658, 761, 770, 772, 773, 775, 776, 777, 1341, 1390, 1407, 1410, 1769, 1816, 1895, 1963, 1964, 1965, 2079, 2114, 2135, 2201, 2202, 2221, 2249, 2268, 2270, 2352, 2398

H. FOREIGN AND INTERNATIONAL

2003 CHURCHILL, W.S. THE SECOND WORLD WAR. 6VOLS. NEW YORK: HOUGHTON, 1948- 1953.

2004 DEGAULLE, C. MEMOIRS OF HOPE. LONDON: WEIDENFELD AND NICOLSON, 1971.

2005 ----------. THE COMPLETE WAR MEMOIRS OF CHARLES DEGAULLE. 3 VOLS. NEW YORK: SIMON AND SCHUSTER, 1964.

2006 EDEN, A. FACING THE DICTATOR. BOSTON: HOUGHTON, MIFFLIN, 1962, PP. 746.

2007 ----------. FULL CIRCLE: THE MEMOIRS OF ANTHONY EDEN. BOSTON: HOUGHTON MIFFLIN, 1960, PP.676. ALSO, LONDON: CASSELL, PP. 619.

2008 EUBANK, K. THE SUMMIT CONFERENCES: 1919-1960. NORMAN: UNIVERSITY OF OKLAHOMA PRESS, 1966, PP.225.

2009 LONGAKER, R.P. "THE PRESIDENT AS INTERNATIONAL LEADER."

LAW AND CONTEMPORARY PROBLEMS 21 (1956):735-752.

2010 MACMILLAN, H. AT THE END OF THE DAY: 1961-63. LONDON: MACMILLAN, 1973, PP. 572.

2011 ----------. POINTING THE WAY: 1959-61. LONDON: MACMILLAN, 1972, PP. 504.

2012 ----------. RIDING THE STORM: 1956-59. LONDON: MACMILLAN, 1971, PP. 786.

2013 MEIR, G. MY LIFE. NEW YORK: PUTNAM, 1975, PP. 480.

2014 NITZE, P.H. "THE MODERN PRESIDENT AS A WORLD FIGURE." ANNALS 307 (1956):114-123.

AS HEAD OF "THE WESTERN COALITION," THE MODERN PRESIDENT IS INESCAPABLY A WORLD, NOT JUST A DOMESTIC, LEADER.

2015 WARREN, S. THE PRESIDENT AS WORLD LEADER. PHILADELPHIA: LIPPINCOTT, 1964, PP. 480,

ON THE GROWING ROLE OF 20TH CENTURY PRESIDENTS AS LEADERS NOT ONLY DOMESTICALLY BUT IN THE INTERNATIONAL ARENA. CASE STUDIES OF ACTIVITIES BY PRESIDENTS FROM THEODORE ROOSEVELT THROUGH JOHN F. KENNEDY.

2016 WILSON,H. A PERSONAL RECORD: THE LABOR GOVERNMENT, 1964-70. BOSTON: LITTLE, BROWN, 1971, PP. 836.

2017 WORSNOP, R.L. "PRESIDENTIAL DIPLOMACY." EDITORIAL RESEARCH REPORTS 2 NO. 12 (1971): 737-758.

SEE ALSO 490, 512, 516, 527, 543, 574, 581, 593, 598, 704, 733, 870

1. OTHER CONSTITUENCIES

2018 MACDONALD, S. "POWER TO THE PEOPLE: FUEL, NEW FEDERALISM AND THE OMB." GOVT EXECUTIVE 6 (FEB. 1974): 24-25+.

SEE ALSO 440, 458, 459, 1130, 1263, 1335, 1342, 1343, 1344, 1348, 1358, 1359, 1637

18
PRESIDENTIAL POWERS
AND RESTRAINTS

A. SCOPE OF PRESIDENTIAL POWER; SEPARATION OF POWERS

2019 BACH,   S.,   AND   SULZNER,   G.T.   "INTRODUCTION."   IN
     PERSPECTIVES ON THE PRESIDENCY. LEXINGTON, MASS.:   HEATH,
     1974: 1-11.

     DEMOCRACY IN THE UNITED STATES AND ELSEWHERE IS AT BEST A
     FRAGILE FORM OF GOVERNMENT. THREE GENERAL "MODELS," ALL OF
     THEM IMPERFECT, ARE RELEVANT TO   RESTRAINING   PRESIDENTIAL
     AUTOCRACY--RESTRAINT OF PRESIDENTS (1) BY CITIZENS, (2) BY
     OTHER POLITICAL LEADERS, AND (3) BY THEMSELVES.

2020 BURNS,   J.M. "IS THE PRESIDENCY TOO POWERFUL?". N Y TIMES
     MAG12+ JL 16 '50.

     GROWTH OF PRESIDENTIAL POWER UNDER FDR AND TRUMAN FOLLOWS
     FROM HISTORICAL PRECEDENTS ESTABLISHED, FOR EXAMPLE, BY
     LINCOLN AND THEODORE ROOSEVELT AND, THEREFORE, IS NOT
     UNPRECEDENTED. STRONG PRESIDENCIES ARE TOLERABLE ONLY IF
     THE INDIVIDUAL INCUMBENTS HAVE A BASIC COMMITMENT TO
     DEMOCRACY AND ARE RESPONSIVE TO THE PUBLIC.

2021 CALL,   J.L.   "EXECUTIVE   POWER   VS.   LIMITED   GOVERNMENT."
     BAYLOR LAW R9:322 SUMMER '57.

2022 CLARY, E.B. "'EACH BRANCH SHALL BE INDEPENDENT': THE
     BURR-WATERGATE SYNDROME." CALIF STATE BAR J 49 (JAN-FEB
     1974): 17-18,20,22-23,78-81.

2023 COMMAGER, H.S. "ARE WE   CREATING A DICTATOR? ANSWER IS
     SOUGHT IN THE HISTORY OF THE PRESIDENCY." N Y TIMES MAG
     3+ MR 2 '41.

     A SYMPATHETIC ACCOUNT OF THE INCREASE IN THE POWER OF
     MODERN PRESIDENTS.

2024 ----------.   "CAN WE LIMIT PRESIDENTIAL POWER?". NEW
     REPUBLIC 158:15-18 AP 6 '68.

2025 ----------. "MISUSE OF POWER." NEW REPUBLIC 164:17-21
     AP 17 '71.

AN ATTACK ON "THE JOHNSON-NIXON THEORY OF EXECUTIVE AUTHORITY" BY A HISTORIAN WHO IN EARLIER YEARS VIEWED EXPANSIONS IN EXECUTIVE POWER FAVORABLY. COMPARE COMMAGER'S "ARE WE CREATING A DICTATOR?"

2026 "COMMITTEE LIST 'UNLIMITED' PRESIDENTIAL POWERS." CONG Q W REPT 31 (OCT 1973): 2732-2733.

REPORTS ON THE CATALOGUE OF 470 EMERGENCY STATUTES ISSUED SEPT. 30, 1973, BY THE SENATE SPECIAL COMMITTEE ON TERMINATION OF THE NATIONAL EMERGENCY.

2027 DAVENPORT, F.M. "THE GROWING POWER OF THE PRESIDENCY." BOSTON UNIVERSITY LAW R 14:655-67 JE '34.

2028 ECKHARDT, B., AND BLACK, C.L., JR. THE TIDES OF POWER. NEW HAVEN, YALE U PR, 1976, PP. 225.

A DIALOGUE BETWEEN A LEADING PROFESSOR OF CONSTITUTIONAL LAW AND A CONGRESSMAN TOUCHING UPON SUCH TOPICS AS GENERAL SCOPE OF PRESIDENTIAL POWER, IMPEACHMENT, AND IMPOUNDMENT.

2029 ELY, J.H. "UNITED STATES V. LOVETT: LITIGATING THE SEPARATION OF POWERS." HARVARD CIVIL RIGHTS-CIVIL LIBERTIES LAW R 10 (WINTER 1975): 1-32.

2030 FISHER, L. "THE EFFICIENCY SIDE OF SEPARATED POWERS." J OF AMERICAN STUDIES 5 (1971): 113-131.

THE FOUNDING FATHERS WERE NOT EXCLUSIVELY PREOCCUPIED WITH CURBING THE EXECUTIVE. RATHER THEY SOUGHT A MORE EFFECTIVE EXECUTIVE THAN EXISTED UNDER THE ARTICLES OF CONFEDERATION. SEE FISHER'S FURTHER DISCUSSION IN PRESIDENT AND CONGRESS: POWER AND POLICY.

2031 FROHNMAYER, D.B. "THE SEPARATION OF POWERS: AN ESSAY IN THE VITALITY OF A CONSTITUTIONAL IDEA." OREGON LAW R 52 (1973):211-235.

"THERE IS A GROWING SENSE OF AGREEMENT THAT ONE OF THE MOST CRUCIAL UNSETTLED CONSTITUTIONAL ISSUES CONCERNS THE ALLOCATION BETWEEN THE EXECUTIVE AND LEGISLATIVE BRANCHES OF THE AWESOME ARRAY OF NATIONAL GOVERNMENTAL POWERS. THIS ARTICLE ADDRESSES A RECURRING QUESTION REGARDING THE PROPER MANNER FOR RESOLVING JURISDICTIONAL DISPUTES BETWEEN THESE CONSTITUTIONALLY COORDINATE BRANCHES OF THE NATIONAL GOVERNMENT."

2032 GIBBONS, J.J. "THE INTERDEPENDENCE OF LEGITIMACY: AN INTRODUCTION TO THE MEANING OF SEPARATION OF POWERS." SETON HALL LAW R 5 (SPRING 1974): 435-488.

2033 GOLDSMITH, W.M. THE GROWTH OF PRESIDENTIAL POWERS. 3

VOLS. NEW YORK: CHELSEA HOUSE, 1974.

A HISTORY OF PRESIDENTIAL POWER AND RESTRAINTS BASED LARGELY ON EXTENSIVE REPRINTING OF DOCUMENTS BEGINNING WITH PRE-1789 WRITINGS ON EXECUTIVE POWER AND EXTENDING TO FORD'S PARDON OF NIXON. VOLUME I COVERS "THE FORMATIVE YEARS" THROUGH THE VAN BUREN PRESIDENCY; VOLUME II, "DECLINE AND RESURGENCE," SURVEYS THE YEARS FROM HARRISON'S PRESIDENCY THROUGH THAT OF THEODORE ROOSEVELT; VOLUME III, "TRIUMPH AND REAPPRAISAL," DEALS WITH SUBSEQUENT PRESIDENCIES. A COMPREHENSIVE INDEX TO ALL 3 VOLUMES IS INCLUDED IN THE FINAL VOLUME. PREFACE BY ARTHUR SCHLESINGER, JR.

2034 GOLDSTEIN, S.M. GROWTH OF THE EXECUTIVE POWER IN THE UNITED STATES. WASHINGTON, D.C.: GEORGETOWN UNIV. PRESS, 1938.

2035 HENDEL, S. "SEPARATION OF POWERS REVISITED IN THE LIGHT OF 'WATERGATE'." WESTERN POLITICAL Q 27 (DEC. 1974): 575-588.

WATERGATE DEMONSTRATES THE NEED TO LIMIT THE PRESIDENT'S "PRIVATE," COVERT POWER, NOT HIS PUBLIC POWER, IN ORDER TO PRESERVE THE PRESIDENTIAL CAPACITY FOR LEGISLATIVE LEADERSHIP AND SAFEGUARD AGAINST ABUSE OF POWER.

2036 HIRSCHFIELD, R.S. "THE POWER OF THE CONTEMPORARY PRESIDENCY." PARLIAMENTARY AFFAIRS 14 (SUMMER 1961): 353-377.

2037 JACOB, C. "THE LIMITS OF PRESIDENTIAL LEADERSHIP." SO ATLAN Q 62 (1963):461-473.

DRAWS EXTENSIVELY ON RICHARD NEUSTADT'S WORK TO ILLUSTRATE LIMITS ON THE PRESIDENT, ESPECIALLY THOSE BY CONGRESS, CITING HISTORICAL EXAMPLES.

2038 KENDALL, W. "THE TWO MAJORITIES." MIDWEST J OF POLITICAL SCIENCE 4 (1960):317-345.

CONSERVATIVE POLITICAL THEORIST'S ESSAY CONTRASTING LIBERAL PREFERENCE FOR THE EXECUTIVE BRANCH AND CONSERVATIVE PREFERENCE FOR CONGRESS. ACCURATE FOR TIME OF ESSAY, BUT DATED FOR EARLIER AND POST-VIETNAM PERIODS.

2039 KOENIG, L.W. "MORE POWER TO THE PRESIDENT." N Y TIMES MAG (JAN. 3, 1965):7.

2040 LARSON, A. "SOME MYTHS ABOUT THE EXECUTIVE BRANCH." CENTER MAG 7 (SEPT.-OCT. 1974): 53-60.

EXAMINES COMMON BELIEFS AND MISCONCEPTIONS ABOUT THE

NATURE AND SCOPE OF THE EXECUTIVE BRANCH, AS WELL AS THE POWERS THAT A PRESIDENT HAS IN RELATION TO IT AND THE TWO OTHER BRANCHES OF GOVERNMENT.

2041 LEVI, E.H. "SOME ASPECTS OF SEPARATION OF POWERS." COLUMBIA LAW R 76 (APR 1976): 371-391.

FORD ATTORNEY GENERAL DISCUSSES POWERS, LIMITATIONS AND RESPONSIBILITIES OF THE THREE BRANCHES.

2042 LOWI, T.J. "PERMANENT RECEIVERSHIP." CENTER MAG (MAR-APR 1974): 33-42.

A CONCISE SUMMARY, DRAWING ON EXAMPLES OF MODERN PRESIDENTIAL DECISION-MAKING, OF LOWI'S THESIS THAT CONGRESS SHOULD BE EXTREMELY PRECISE IN DRAFTING LEGISLATION THAT DELEGATES RULE-MAKING POWER TO THE EXECUTIVE. LOWI'S FULL ARGUMENT IS TO BE FOUND IN HIS THE END OF LIBERALISM (1969).

2043 LYNN, N.B. , AND MCCLURE, A.F. THE FULBRIGHT PREMISE: SENATOR J. WILLIAM FULBRIGHT'S VIEWS ON PRESIDENTIAL POWER. CRANBURY, N.J.: BUCKNELL UNIV. PRESS, 1973, PP. 224.

DOCUMENTS FULBRIGHT'S SHIFT IN VIEW SINCE THE 1950'S FROM THE POSITION THAT EXECUTIVE LEADERSHIP IN FOREIGN AFFAIRS SHOULD BE RELATIVELY UNRESTRAINED TO HIS LATER ADVOCACY OF CURBS ON PRESIDENTIAL POWER.

2044 MCKINLEY, C. "FEDERAL ADMINISTRATIVE PATHOLOGY AND THE SEPARATION OF POWERS." PUBLIC ADMINISTRATION R 11 (WINTER 1951): 18-25.

A CRITICAL VIEW OF THE ADMINISTRATIVE CONSEQUENCES OF JOINT PRESIDENTIAL AND CONGRESSIONAL CONTROLS OVER EXECUTIVE BRANCH AGENCIES.

2045 MILTON, G.F. THE USE OF PRESIDENTIAL POWER: 1789-1943. BOSTON: LITTLE, BROWN , 1945, PP. 349.

2046 MORRIS, R., ED. GREAT PRESIDENTIAL DECISIONS: STATE POWERS THAT CHANGED THE COURSE OF HISTORY. REV. ED. NEW YORK: HARPER AND ROW, 1973.

COLLECTION OF IMPORTANT PRESIDENTIAL DECISIONS.

2047 NEUSTADT, R.E. "THE CONSTRAINING OF THE PRESIDENT: THE PRESIDENCY AFTER WATERGATE." BRITISH J OF POLITICAL SCIENCE 4 (1974):383-397; ALSO IN N Y TIMES MAG (OCT. 14, 1973): 38+.

A TRUMAN WHITE HOUSE ALUMNUS DESCRIBES THE WAYS IN WHICH TRUMAN'S WORK HABITS (E.G. ACCESSIBILITY) AND THE POLITICAL SYSTEM (E.G. DECLINE IN THE STRENGTH OF POLITICAL PARTIES) CHANGED BETWEEN THE TRUMAN AND THE NIXON YEARS. TO THE DEGREE THAT SUCH TRENDS CAN BE

REVERSED, THE LATTER-DAY GROWTH OF UNILATERAL PRESIDENTIAL
POWER CAN BE LIMITED.

2048 PEPPERS, D.A. "'THE TWO PRESIDENCIES': EIGHT YEARS LATER."
IN PERSPECTIVES ON THE PRESIDENCY, EDITED BY A.
WILDAVSKY, BOSTON: LITTLE BROWN, 1975: 462-471.

2049 PIOUS, R.M. "IS PRESIDENTIAL POWER "POISON"?" PSQ   89
(1974):627-43.

"WE NO LONGER NAIVELY ASSUME THAT THE KEY TO VIABLE
POLICIES IS THE WISDOM AND TEMPERAMENT OF THE SORT OF MEN
WE ELECT TO THE PRESIDENCY. BUT IT IS STILL OUR FUNCTION,
IN ATTEMPTING TO MAKE THE PRESIDENT ACCOUNTABLE TO THE
PEOPLE, TO DESCRIBE ACCURATELY WHAT HE DOES-AND WHY."

2050 PRITCHETT, C.H. "THE PRESIDENT'S CONSTITUTIONAL POSITION."
IN THE PRESIDENCY REAPPRAISED, EDITED BY R.G. TUGWELL
AND T.E. CRONIN, PP. 12-31. NEW YORK: PRAEGER, 1974.

BRIEF REVIEW OF THE CONSTITUTIONAL AMBIGUITIES THAT HAVE
PERMITTED BOTH EXPANSIVE AND RESTRICTED JUSTIFICATIONS FOR
PRESIDENTIAL   POLICY   LEADERSHIP   AND   AUTONOMOUS
DECISION-MAKING IN VARIOUS POLICY SPHERES.

2051 REEDY, G. "THE PRESIDENCY IN 1976: FOCAL POINT OF
POLITICAL UNITY?" THE JOURNAL OF POLITICS 38 (AUGUST
1976):228-238.

EVEN AFTER VIETNAM AND WATERGATE, THE PRESIDENCY WILL
REMAIN POWERFUL. BUT THE MEMORY OF THESE EVENTS IS LIKELY
TO RESTRAIN FUTURE PRESIDENTS FROM EXERCISING UNILATERAL
POWER.

2052 SHAFFER, H.B. "SEPARATION OF POWERS." EDITORIAL RESEARCH
REPORTS 2 (1973):691-708.

2053 "THE POWERS OF THE PRESIDENT OF THE UNITED STATES."
CONGRESSIONAL DIGEST SPECIAL ISSUE JANUARY, 1947.

2054 TUGWELL, R.G. THE ENLARGEMENT OF THE PRESIDENCY. GARDEN
CITY: DOUBLEDAY, 1960, PP. 508.

AN HISTORICAL ACCOUNT OF THE GROWTH OF PRESIDENTIAL POWER
FROM THE WASHINGTON THROUGH EISENHOWER ADMINISTRATIONS.

2055 WAYNE, S.J. "CHECKS WITHOUT BALANCES: CONTAINING
PROMETHEUS." THE GEORGE WASHINGTON LAW REVIEW   43
(JANUARY 1975):485-500.

2056 WILDAVSKY, A. "SALVATION BY STAFF: REFORM OF THE
PRESIDENTIAL OFFICE." IN THE PRESIDENCY EDITED BY A.

WILDAVSKY, BOSTON: LITTLE BROWN, 1969, PP. 694-700.

2057 ----------. "THE TWO PRESIDENCIES." TRANS-ACTION DEC.
1966, PP. 7-14.

2058 WILMERDING, L. "THE PRESIDENT AND THE LAW." PSQ 67
(1952): 321-338.

2059 WORSNOP, R.L. "PRESIDENTIAL POWER." EDITORIAL RESEARCH
REPORTS (OCT 2, 1968): 723-740.

SEE ALSO 64, 90, 179, 186, 197, 277, 605, 1402, 1441,
1901, 1937, 1960, 1969, 1970, 1993, 2118, 2214, 2290,
2399, 2441

B. SPECIFIC POWERS

1. FOREIGN RELATIONS AND WAR

2060 ALSTYNE, W.V. "CONGRESS, THE PRESIDENT, AND THE POWER TO
DECLARE WAR: A REQUIEM FOR VIETNAM." U PENNSYLVANIA LAW
R 121 (1972):1-28.

2061 BARRETT, R.J. "THE WAR POWERS: CONSTITUTIONAL CRISIS." U
S NAVAL INST PROCEEDINGS 99 (NOV 1973): 18-25.

"TO PRESERVE BOTH OUR DEMOCRACY AND OUR SECURITY IN A
DANGEROUS AND COMPLEX WORLD WE NEED TO REVITALIZE THE
CONSTITUTIONAL WAR POWERS. THE FORMAL DECLARATION OF WAR
IS NO LONGER A VIABLE INSTRUMENT OF GOVERNMENT. THE NEW
ARRANGEMENTS MUST INCLUDE PRESIDENTIAL FLEXIBILITY TO MEET
EMERGENCIES AND AN EFFECTIVE CONGRESSIONAL VOICE AS THE
LEGISLATIVE EXPRESSION OF THE PEOPLE."

2062 BERDAHL, C.A. WAR POWERS OF THE EXECUTIVE IN THE UNITED
STATES. URBANA: UNIVERSITY OF ILLINOIS PRESS, 1921.
REPRINTED NEW YORK: JOHNSON REPRO CORP, 1971.

2063 BERGER, R. "ON WARS AND TREATIES: THE CONSTITUTION IS
CLEAR ENOUGH." NATION 216:393-8 MR 26 '73.

2064 ----------. "PRESIDENTIAL MONOPOLY OF FOREIGN RELATIONS."
MICHIGAN LAW R 71:1 N '72.

ESSAYS ON "PRESIDENTIAL EXECUTIVE AGREEMENTS, AND WHETHER THE SENATE MAY BE EXCLUDED FROM KNOWLEDGE OF, AND PARTICIPATION IN, NEGOTIATIONS WITH FOREIGN NATIONS AS PART OF THE TREATY-MAKING PROCESS."

2065 ----------. "WAR-MAKING BY THE PRESIDENT." U PA L REV 121:29 N '72.

ASSERTS THAT PRESIDENT NIXON'S UNILATERAL ACTS IN VIETNAM COULD NOT BE JUSTIFIED BY EITHER THE CONSTITUTION OR PAST PRESIDENTIAL PRACTICE.

2066 BERLE, A. "POWER IN FOREIGN RELATIONS." IN THE PRESIDENCY REAPPRAISED, EDITED BY R.G. TUGWELL AND T.E. CRONIN, PP. 74-82. NEW YORK: PRAEGER, 1974.

POSTHUMOUSLY PUBLISHED PAPER OF AN FDR BRAIN TRUSTER ARGUING THAT LIBERAL OPPONENTS TO PRESIDENTIAL AUTONOMY IN FOREIGN RELATIONS ARE MOVED BY SHORT-RUN POLICY CONCERNS RATHER THAN ENDURING PROCEDURAL VIEWS. DEFENDS PRESIDENTIAL FOREIGN POLICY AUTONOMY.

2067 BICKEL, A.M. "THE CONSTITUTION AND THE WAR." COMMENTARY 54 (1972):49-55.

DEALS WITH DECLARATION OF WAR, THE PRESIDENT AS COMMANDER-IN-CHIEF, CONGRESSIONAL-PRESIDENTIAL RELATIONS, CONGRESSIONAL POWERS, AND PRESIDENTIAL POWERS.

2068 BROWER, C.N. "THE GREAT WAR POWERS DEBATE." INTERNAT LAWYER 7 (OCT. 1973): 746-751.

CONCLUDES THAT JAVITS' BILL ON WAR POWERS DOES NOT PROVIDE RELIEF FROM THE PROBLEM.

2069 CALL, J.L. "GOVERNMENT BY DECREE THROUGH EXECUTIVE AGREEMENT." BAYLOR LAW R 6:277-90 SPRING '54.

2070 CAMPISI, D.J. "HONORED IN THE BREACH: PRESIDENTIAL AUTHORITY TO EXECUTE THE LAWS WITH MILITARY FORCE." YALE LAW J 83 (NOV.1973): 130-152.

"ACTION BY CONGRESS IS NECESSARY IF IT IS TO PREVENT THE CONTINUED EROSION OF ITS POWER TO CONTROL THE USE OF MILITARY FORCE IN DOMESTIC AFFAIRS. THE GENERAL AGGRANDIZEMENT OF THE POWER OF THE PRESIDENT MIGHT APPROPRIATELY BE CHECKED IN THIS AREA WHERE THE CLAIM OF CONGRESS IS STRONG AND THAT OF THE PRESIDENT IS BASED ON A FAULTY INTERPRETATION OF THE CONTROLLING STATUTES AND A MISCONCEPTION OF THE CONSTITUTIONAL PRECEDENTS." JOHNSON AND NIXON "IGNORED STATUTORY RESTRICTIONS ON THE USE OF MILITARY FORCE IN DOMESTIC AFFAIRS IN COMMITTING TROOPS TO THE STREETS ON A NUMBER OF OCCASIONS."

2071 CHEEVER, D.S., AND HAVILAND, H.F. AMERICAN FOREIGN POLICY AND THE SEPARATION OF POWERS. CAMBRIDGE: HARVARD UNIVERSITY PRESS, 1952, PP. 244.

2072 COHEN, R. "SELF-EXECUTING EXECUTIVE AGREEMENTS: A SEPARATION OF POWERS PROBLEM." BUFFALO LAW R 24 (FALL 1974): 137-158.

"AS A MATTER OF DOMESTIC LAW, THE PRESIDENT MAY MAKE INTERNATIONAL AGREEMENTS OTHER THAN TREATIES." ARTICLE EVALUATES "THE VARIOUS APPROACHES WHICH HAVE BEEN USED TO ASCERTAIN THE ORIGIN AND NATURE OF THE QUALIFICATIONS LIMITING PRESIDENTIAL POWER TO MAKE SELF-EXECUTING EXECUTIVE AGREEMENTS."

2073 COMMAGER, H.S. "WAR POWERS OF THE PRESIDENT; CHARGE OF DICTATORSHIP." N Y TIMES MAG3+ O 19 '41.

2074 "CONGRESS, THE PRESIDENT, AND THE POWER TO COMMIT TROOPS TO COMBAT." HARVARD LAW R 81 (1968):1771-1805.

2075 "CONSTITUTIONAL LAW—STANDING OF MEMBERS OF CONGRESS TO CHALLENGE EXECUTIVE ACTION IN THE WAR IN INDOCHINA—MITCHELL V. LAIRD." MARYLAND LAW R 33 (MARCH 1973): 504-511.

2076 COOLIDGE, F.L., JR., AND SHARROW, J.D., EDS. "PRESIDENTIAL VS. CONGRESSIONAL WAR-MAKING POWERS." BOSTON UNIVERSITY LAW R 50 (1970): 5-116.

2077 CORWIN, E.S. THE PRESIDENT'S CONTROL OF FOREIGN RELATIONS. PRINCETON: PRINCETON UNIV. PRESS, 1917, PP. 216. REPRINTED BY JOHNSON REPRINT CORP., NEW YORK, 1970.

2078 ----------. TOTAL WAR AND THE CONSTITUTION. WESTMINSTER, MARYLAND: KNOPF, 1947, PP. 182.

2079 D'AMATO, A. "MASSACHUSETTS IN THE FEDERAL COURTS: THE CONSTITUTIONALITY OF THE VIETNAM WAR." J LAW REFORM 29 (1970):11-21.

AN EXAMINATION OF AN ATTEMPT THROUGH LEGISLATION TO CURB PRESIDENTIAL MILITARY COMMITMENT.

2080 DEUTSCH, E.P. "THE PRESIDENT AS COMMANDER IN CHIEF." ABA J 57:27-32 JA '71.

"A STATE OF WAR MAY EXIST UNDER THE CONSTITUTION WITHOUT A

FORMER DECLARATION BY CONGRESS, AND AS COMMANDER-IN-CHIEF,
THE PRESIDENT HAS FULL PLENARY POWER TO CONDUCT MILITARY
OPERATIONS DURING A WAR, DECLARED OR UNDECLARED."

2081 EAGLETON, T.F. WAR AND PRESIDENTIAL POWER. NEW YORK:
LIVERIGHT, 1974, PP. 240.

ARGUES THAT THE 1973 WAR POWERS RESOLUTION PROVIDES
INSUFFICIENT POWER TO CONGRESS OVER PRESIDENTIAL AUTONOMY
IN WAR-MAKING.

2082 EMERSON, J.T. "WAR POWERS LEGISLATION. AN ADDENDUM." WEST
VIRGINIA LAW R 74:53, 367 AG-N '71 S '72.

2083 ----------. "WAR POWERS: AN INVASION OF PRESIDENTIAL
PREROGATIVES." AMERICAN BAR ASSOCIATION J 58
(1972):809-814.

"CONGRESS DOES NOT NEED NEW LEGISLATION TO GIVE IT A
POLICY-MAKING POSITION IN THE FIELD OF MAKING WAR."

2084 FAIRMAN, C. "THE PRESIDENT AS COMMANDER IN CHIEF." JP 11
(1949):145-170.

2085 FISHER, L. "WAR POWERS: A NEED FOR LEGISLATIVE
REASSERTION." IN THE PRESIDENCY REAPPRAISED, EDITED BY
R.G. TUGWELL AND T.E. CRONIN, NEW YORK: PRAEGER, 1974:
56-73.

2086 FORKUSCH, M.D. "TREATIES AND EXECUTIVE AGREEMENTS."
CHI-KENT L REV 32:201-25 JE '54.

2087 FRANKLIN, M. "WAR POWER OF THE PRESIDENT: AN HISTORICAL
JUSTIFICATION OF MR. ROOSEVELT'S MESSAGE OF SEPTEMBER 7,
1942." TULSA LAW R 17:217-55 N '42.

2088 ----------. "WAR-TIME POWERS OF THE AMERICAN PRESIDENCY
AS CONCEIVED BY THOMAS JEFFERSON." LAW GUILD R 2: 13-20
S '42.

2089 FRYE, A. A RESPONSIBLE CONGRESS: THE POLITICS OF NATIONAL
SECURITY. NEW YORK: MCGRAW-HILL, 1975, PP. 238.

DESPITE POPULAR ASSUMPTIONS TO THE CONTRARY, CONGRESS HAS
BECOME INCREASINGLY INVOLVED IN COOPERATING WITH THE
EXECUTIVE BRANCH IN MAKING NATIONAL SECURITY AND FOREIGN
POLICY. THE AUTHOR BELIEVES THAT FURTHER DEVELOPMENTS

ALONG THESE LINES ARE LIKELY AND DESIRABLE.

2090 FULBRIGHT, J.W. "CONGRESS, THE PRESIDENT AND THE WAR
POWER." ARKANSAS LAW R 25 (1971):71-84.

2091 GARDNER, J. "MEMBERS SEEK VETO OVER EXECUTIVE AGREEMENTS."
CONG Q W REPT 33 (AUG. 2, 1975): 1712-1717.

2092 GARNER, J.W. "EXECUTIVE DISCRETION IN THE CONDUCT OF
FOREIGN RELATIONS." AMER J INT LAW 31:289-93 AP '37.

2093 GOLDMAN, E.F. "THE PRESIDENT, THE PEOPLE, AND THE POWER TO
MAKE WAR." AMER HERITAGE 21:28-35 AP '70.

2094 GOLDWATER, B.M. "THE PRESIDENT'S ABILITY TO PROTECT
AMERICA'S FREEDOMS: THE WARMAKING POWER." LAW AND THE
SOCIAL ORDER (1971):423-449.

A LEADING AMERICAN CONSERVATIVE EXPRESSES RESERVATIONS
ABOUT RECENT LIMITATIONS PLACED ON PRESIDENTIAL INITIATIVE
IN FOREIGN AFFAIRS.

2095 ----------. "THE PRESIDENT'S CONSTITUTIONAL PRIMACY IN
FOREIGN RELATIONS AND NATIONAL DEFENSE." VIRGINIA J OF
INTERNATIONAL LAW 13 (1973):463-489.

2096 GRAEBNER, N.A. "PRESIDENTIAL POWER AND FOREIGN AFFAIRS."
IN THE FUTURE OF THE AMERICAN PRESIDENCY, EDITED BY C.W.
DUNN, MORRISTOWN, N.J.: GENERAL LEARNING PRESS, 1975:
179-203.

2097 GRUNDSTEIN, N.D. PRESIDENTIAL DELEGATION OF AUTHORITY IN
WARTIME. PITTSBURGH: UNIV. OF PITTSBURGH PRESS, 1961, PP.
106.

AN EXTENSIVE HISTORICAL AND LEGAL REVIEW GATHERING
TOGETHER THREE ARTICLES CALLED "PRESIDENTIAL SUBDELEGATION
OF ADMINISTRATIVE AUTHORITY IN WARTIME." GEORGE
WASHINGTON LAW REVIEW 15 AND 16 (1947 AND 1948).

2098 HARRIS, L. "WAR POWERS OF THE PRESIDENT." FLORIDA LAW J
19:221-7 JL '45.

2099 HENKIN, L. FOREIGN AFFAIRS AND THE CONSTITUTION.
MINEOLA, N.Y.: FOUNDATION PRESS, 1972, PP. 553.

A COMPREHENSIVE CONSTITUTIONAL LAW TEXTBOOK INCLUDING AN INDEX OF CASES AND NUMEROUS INDEXED PASSAGES DEALING WITH PRESIDENTIAL POWERS.

2100 "HISTORICAL AND STRUCTURAL LIMITATIONS ON CONGRESSIONAL ABILITIES TO MAKE FOREIGN POLICY." BOSTON UNIVERSITY LAW R 50 (1970):64-69.

2101 HOUGHTON, N.D. "WAR-MAKING AND THE CONSTITUTION." SOCIAL SCIENCE 39 (1964):67-78.

THE AUTHOR SUMMARIZES EXAMPLES OF HOW PRESIDENTIAL WAR-MAKING POWERS HAVE COME TO BE INCREASINGLY ACCEPTED AS CONSTITUTIONAL.

2102 JAVITS, J.K. WHO MAKES WAR: THE PRESIDENT VERSUS CONGRESS. NEW YORK: WILLIAM MORROW, 1973, PP.300.

2103 JENKINS, G.L. "THE WAR POWERS RESOLUTION: STATUTORY LIMITATION ON THE COMMANDER-IN-CHIEF." HARVARD J ON LEGISLATION 11 (1974):181-204.

WHY CONGRESS REASSERTED ITS WARMAKING ROLE AND ANALYZES HOW THE WAR POWERS RESOLUTION OF NOV. 1973 RESPONDS TO THIS GOAL.

2104 "JUSTICIABILITY OF PRESIDENTIAL WAR POWER." ST. JOHN'S LAW R 48 (DEC. 1973): 309-316.

2105 KATZENBACH, N.D. "CONGRESS AND FOREIGN POLICY." CORNELL INTERNATIONAL LAW J 3 (1970):33.

2106 KEOWN, S.S. "THE PRESIDENT, THE CONGRESS, AND THE POWER TO DECLARE WAR." UNIVERSITY OF KANSAS LAW R 16 (1967):82-97.

2107 KESSELMAN, M. "PRESIDENTIAL LEADERSHIP IN CONGRESS ON FOREIGN POLICY: A REPLICATION OF A HYPOTHESIS." MIDWEST J OF POLITICAL SCIENCE 9 (1965):401-406.

2108 ----------. "PRESIDENTIAL LEADERSHIP IN CONGRESS ON FOREIGN POLICY." MIDWEST J POLITICAL SCIENCE 5 (1961):284-289.

2109 KOENIG, L.W. THE PRESIDENCY AND THE CRISIS: POWERS OF THE

OFFICE FROM POLAND TO PEARL HARBOR. NEW YORK: KING'S
CROWN PR, 1944, PP. 166.

2110 LASKI, H.J. "THE AMERICAN PRESIDENT AND FOREIGN RELATIONS"
JP (FEBRUARY 1949).

WIDE-RANGING ESSAY ON AMERICAN FOREIGN POLICY MAKING AND
ITS SUBSTANCE, CRITICIZING THE COLD WAR POLICIES OF
TRUMAN.

2111 LOFGREN, C.A. "UNITED STATES V. CURTIS-WRIGHT EXPORT
CORPORATION: AN HISTORICAL REASSESSMENT." YALE LAW J 83
(NOV 1973): 1-32.

COMMENTING ON A MAJOR SUPREME COURT CASE JUSTIFYING
SWEEPING PRESIDENTIAL WAR POWERS, LOFGREN CONCLUDES "IT IS
INCORRECT TO DISMISS MAJOR SEGMENTS OF 'THE DECISION' AS
DICTA. BUT THE HISTORY ON WHICH THESE SEGMENTS REST IS
'SHOCKINGLY INACCURATE'."

2112 ----------. "WAR-MAKING UNDER THE CONSTITUTION: THE
ORIGINAL UNDERSTANDING." YALE LAW J 81:672 MR '72.

AN ATTEMPT TO ASCERTAIN THE FOUNDING FATHERS' INTENT.

2113 LYNCH, H.F. "PRESIDENTIAL CONTROL OF NUCLEAR WEAPONS IN
LIMITED WAR SITUATIONS." NAVAL WAR COLLEGE R 23
(1971):71-88.

ONLY THE PRESIDENT HAS THE AUTHORITY TO RELEASE NUCLEAR
WEAPONS FOR COMBAT OPERATIONS: SUCH A DECISION IS
CONDITIONED BY MANY FACTORS.

2114 MACIVER, K.F., JR., WOLFF, B.M., LOCKE, L.B. "THE SUPREME
COURT AS ARBITRATOR IN THE CONFLICT BETWEEN PRESIDENTIAL
AND CONGRESSIONAL WAR-MAKING POWERS." BOSTON UNIVERSITY
LAW R 50 (1970):78-116.

2115 MALAWER, S.S. "THE VIETNAM WAR UNDER THE CONSTITUTION." U
PITTSBURGH LAW R 31 (WINTER 1969): 205-241.

2116 MANLEY, J.F. "THE RISE OF CONGRESS IN FOREIGN
POLICY-MAKING." ANNALS 397 (SEPT 1971): 60-70.

"CONGRESS, BY FULFILLING ITS CONSTITUTIONAL
RESPONSIBILITIES IN THE FOREIGN POLICY FIELD, AND BY
RESISTING THE TEMPTATION TO APPROVE AUTOMATICALLY
PRESIDENTIAL INITIATIVES IN FOREIGN POLICY, MAY HELP
PREVENT THE UNITED STATES FROM REPEATING THE ERRORS OF
VIETNAM."

2117 MATHEWS, C. "THE CONSTITUTIONAL POWER OF THE PRESIDENT TO
CONCLUDE INTERNATIONAL AGREEMENTS." YALE LAW J 64

(1955):345-89.

A BRIEF AGAINST EFFORTS TO RESTRAIN THIS PRESIDENTIAL POWER.

2118 MAY. E.R. THE ULTIMATE DECISION: THE PRESIDENT AS COMMANDER IN CHIEF. NEW YORK: G. BRAZILLER, 1960, PP. 200.

NINE HISTORICAL CASE STUDIES BY SEVERAL AUTHORS. 8 DEAL WITH MILITARY DECISIONS MADE BY MADISON, POLK, LINCOLN, MCKINLEY, WILSON, FDR, TRUMAN, AND EISENHOWER. THE INTRODUCTORY DISCUSSION IS ON THE PRESIDENT'S ROLE AS COMMANDER-IN-CHIEF AS VIEWED BY THE CONSTITUTION'S FRAMERS.

2119 MCCLURE. W. INTERNATIONAL EXECUTIVE AGREEMENTS. NEW YORK: COLUMBIA UNIVERSITY PRESS, 1941.

2120 ----------. "THE PRESIDENCY AND WORLD AFFAIRS: MOBILIZATION OF ASSISTANCE." JP 2 (1949):206-217.

A STATE DEPARTMENT OFFICIAL'S DESCRIPTIVE ACCOUNT OF RECENT FOREIGN POLICY DECISIONS AND OF THE EXECUTIVE BRANCH'S FOREIGN POLICY MAKING MACHINERY.

2121 MCGHEE, G.W. "EXECUTIVE POWER IN FOREIGN POLICY-MAKING: EXPANSION OR CURTAILMENT?" CAPITOL STUDIES 1 (FALL 1972): 3-8.

2122 MONAGHAN, H.P. "PRESIDENTIAL WAR-MAKING." BOSTON UNIVERSITY LAW R 50 (1970):19-33.

2123 MOORE, J.N. "CONTEMPORARY ISSUES IN AN ONGOING DEBATE: THE ROLES OF CONGRESS AND THE PRESIDENT IN FOREIGN AFFAIRS." INTERNAT LAWYER 7 (OCT. 1973): 733-745.

EXAMINES 3 DEBATES RELATING TO CONGRESSIONAL-PRESIDENTIAL AUTHORITY: WAR POWERS, EXECUTIVE PRIVILEGE, AND THE PRESIDENT'S AUTHORITY TO MAKE EXECUTIVE AGREEMENTS.

2124 ----------. "THE NATIONAL EXECUTIVE AND THE USE OF ARMED FORCES ABROAD." NAVAL WAR COLLEGE R 21 (1969).

2125 MOORE. J.W. "EXECUTIVE POWERS AND FOREIGN RELATIONS: THE NEUTRALITY ACTS REVISITED." PROC S.C. HIST ASSOC (1971): 24-43.

2126 NESSON. C.R. "ASPECTS OF THE EXECUTIVE'S POWER OVER NATIONAL SECURITY MATTERS: SECRECY CLASSIFICATIONS AND

FOREIGN INTELLIGENCE WIRETAPS." INDIANA LAW J 49 (SPRING 1974): 399-421.

FOCUSES ON TWO EXECUTIVE POWERS AS THEY BEAR ON THE ELLSBERG CASE: THE POWER OF NATIONAL SECURITY CLASSIFICATION AND THE POWER TO USE WARRANTLESS WIRETAPS IN CONNECTION WITH FOREIGN INTELLIGENCE.

2127 NOBLEMAN, E.E. "THE DELEGATION OF PRESIDENTIAL FUNCTIONS: CONSTITUTIONAL AND LEGAL ASPECTS." ANNALS 307 (1956):134-143.

"THE PRESIDENT HAS ADEQUATE LEGAL AUTHORITY TO FREE HIMSELF FROM THE PERFORMANCE OF THE MULTITUDE OF FUNCTIONS AND DUTIES WHICH MAY IMPAIR THE PROPER DISCHARGE OF HIS VITAL HISTORIC CONSTITUTIONAL POWERS AND OBLIGATIONS."

2128 ODELL, T. WAR POWERS OF THE PRESIDENT. WASHINGTON, D.C.: WASHINGTON SERVICE BUREAU, 1942.

2129 PAOLUCCI, H. WAR, PEACE, AND THE PRESIDENCY. NEW YORK: MCGRAW, 1968, PP. 241.

2130 PATCH, B.W. "THE WAR POWERS OF THE PRESIDENT." EDITORIAL RESEARCH REPORTS 147-64 S 12 '40.

2131 PERLMUTTER, A. "THE PRESIDENTIAL POLITICAL CENTER AND FOREIGN POLICY: A CRITIQUE OF THE REVISIONIST AND BUREAUCRATIC-POLITICAL ORIENTATIONS." WORLD POLITICS 27 (1974):87-106.

"FOREIGN POLICY--IDEOLOGICALLY, INSTITUTIONALLY, AND BEHAVIORALLY--HAS BEEN AND PROBABLY WILL REMAIN THE AREA OF "COMPETENCE" OF THE FEW WHOSE COHESION(1.E., POLITICAL POWER) IS DERIVED FROM THEIR PROXIMITY TO THE PRESIDENTIAL POLITICAL CENTER, RATHER THAN (ACCORDING TO MILLS) FROM CLASS, SOCIAL, AND INSTITUTIONAL PROXIMITY."

2132 PLISCHKE, E. SUMMIT DIPLOMACY: PERSONAL DIPLOMACY OF THE PRESIDENT OF THE UNITED STATES. COLLEGE PARK: UNIVERSITY OF MARYLAND, 1958, PP. 125.

EXAMINES THE ROLE OF THE PRESIDENT IN FOREIGN POLICY MAKING, GIVING EXAMPLES OF PRESIDENTIAL INVOLVEMENT IN SUMMIT DIPLOMACY.

2133 POTTER, P.B. "POWER OF THE PRESIDENT OF THE UNITED STATES TO UTILIZE ITS ARMED FORCES ABROAD." AMER J INT LAW 48:458-9 JL '54.

2134 PUSEY, M.J. THE WAY WE GO TO WAR. BOSTON: HOUGHTON,

1969, PP. 314.

A SUMMARY OF HISTORICAL PRECEDENTS AND POSSIBLE NEW WAR-POWERS LEGISLATION. THE HISTORICAL DISCUSSION EMPHASIZES EVENTS IN THE TRUMAN THROUGH JOHNSON ADMINISTRATIONS.

2135 RATNER, L.G. "THE COORDINATED WARMAKING POWER--LEGISLATIVE, EXECUTIVE, AND JUDICIAL ROLES." SOUTHERN CALIFORNIA LAW R 44 (1971):461-489.

2136 REED, R.P. "FOREIGN POLICY AND THE INITIATION OF WAR: THE CONGRESS AND THE PRESIDENCY IN THE DISPUTE OVER WAR POWERS." POTOMAC R 6 (1973):1-29.

2137 REVELEY, W.T., III. "CONSTITUTIONAL ALLOCATION OF THE WAR POWERS BETWEEN THE PRESIDENT AND CONGRESS: 1787-1788." VIRGINIA J OF INTERNAT LAW 15 (FALL 1974): 93-147.

REVIEWS THE HISTORICAL CONSIDERATIONS AND INTENTIONS OF THE FRAMERS AND RATIFIERS OF THE CONSTITUTION IN REGARD TO WAR POWERS.

2138 ----------. "PRESIDENTIAL WAR-MAKING: CONSTITUTIONAL PREROGATIVE OR USURPATION?" VIRGINIA LAW R 55 (1969):1243-1305.

2139 ROBINSON, D.L. "THE PRESIDENT AS COMMANDER IN CHIEF." CENTER MAG (SEPT./OCT., 1971):58-67.

STRESSES UNILATERAL POWER OF THE PRESIDENT TO COMMIT MILITARY FORCES AND URGES STRENGTHENING OF FORCES TO COUNTERVAIL THE PRESIDENT.

2140 ROBINSON, E.E., ET AL. POWERS OF THE PRESIDENT IN FOREIGN AFFAIRS, 1945-1965: HARRY S. TRUMAN, DWIGHT D. EISENHOWER, JOHN F. KENNEDY, LYNDON B. JOHNSON. SAN FRANCISCO: COMMONWEALTH CLUB OF CALIF., 1966, PP. 279.

2141 ROSENBERG, J.A., WEINBERG, P., PINZLER, W.M. "HISTORICAL AND STRUCTURAL LIMITATIONS ON CONGRESSIONAL ABILITIES TO MAKE FOREIGN POLICY." BOSTON UNIVERSITY LAW R 50 (1970):51-77.

2142 ROSTOW, E.V. "GREAT CASES MAKE BAD LAW: THE WAR POWERS ACT." TEXAS LAW R 50 (1972):833-900.

CRITICIZES SENATOR JAVITS' BILL TO RESTRICT PRESIDENTIAL WAR-MAKING POWERS.

2143 SCHWARZER, W., AND WOOD, R.R. "PRESIDENTIAL POWER AND AGGRESSION ABROAD: A CONSTITUTIONAL DILEMMA." AMERICAN BAR ASSOCIATION JOURNAL 40 (1954):394-397.

2144 SHAFFER, L.A. "PRESIDENTIAL POWER TO MAKE WAR." INDIANA LAW R 7 (1974): 900-924.

ON THE PROCEDURAL DIFFICULTIES FACING PLAINTIFFS AND THE DIFFERING DISPOSITIONS OF CASES REGARDING THE PRESIDENT'S AUTHORITY TO WAGE WAR FOR AN EXTENDED PERIOD WITHOUT A CONGRESSIONAL DECLARATION OF WAR.

2145 "SHOWDOWN ON WAR--CONGRESS VS. NIXON (ON ENDING THE VIETNAM WAR IN PARTICULAR AND ON THE AUTHORITY OF THE PRESIDENT AS COMMANDER-IN-CHIEF GENERALLY)." U S NEWS 68:35 MY 25 '70.

2146 SMITH, J.M., AND JURIKA, S. THE PRESIDENT AND NATIONAL SECURITY: HIS ROLE AS COMMANDER IN CHIEF. IOWA: KENDALL/HUNT, 1972, PP. 303.

DISCUSSES CONSTITUTIONAL PRECEDENTS FOR PRESIDENTIAL ACTION IN THIS SPHERE AND SPECIFIC EVENTS DURING THE ROOSEVELT, TRUMAN, AND EISENHOWER ADMINISTRATIONS.

2147 SPONG, W.B., JR. "CAN BALANCE BE RESTORED IN THE CONSTITUTIONAL WAR POWERS OF THE PRESIDENT AND CONGRESS?" UNIVERSITY OF RICHMOND LAW R 6 (1971):1-47.

2148 STEVENSON, J.R. "THE CONSTITUTION AND THE PRESIDENT'S WAR POWERS." NY STATE BAR J 45 (APR 1973): 172-176.

2149 ----------. "WAR POWERS LEGISLATION: PRACTICAL AND CONSTITUTIONAL PROBLEMS: STATEMENT." DEPT STATE BUL 64: 833-6 JE 28 '71.

2150 STUART, G.H. "PRESIDENTIAL CONTROL OF FOREIGN POLICY." CURRENT HIST 22 (APR 1952): 207-210.

2151 SWISHER, C.B. "THE CONTROL OF WAR PREPARATIONS IN THE UNITED STATES." APSR 34 (1940):1085-1104.

2152 TANSILL, C.C. "WAR POWERS OF THE PRESIDENT OF THE UNITED STATES WITH SPECIAL REFERENCE TO THE BEGINNING OF

HOSTILITIES." <u>PSQ</u> 45 (1930):1-55.

2153 <u>THE PRESIDENT'S POWERS IN THE FIELD OF FOREIGN POLICY-SHOULD THEY BE CURTAILED (COLLEGE DEBATE SERIES).</u> WASHINGTON, D.C.: AMERICAN ENTERPRISE INSTITUTE, 1968, PP. 148.

2154 TOBIN, R.L. "WHO MAKES OUR FOREIGN POLICY?". <u>SAT R</u> 53:28 F 14 '70.

2155 TOMAIN, J.P. "EXECUTIVE AGREEMENTS AND THE BYPASSING OF CONGRESS." <u>J OF INT LAW AND ECON</u> 8 (JUNE 1973): 129-139.

BY INCREASED USE OF EXECUTIVE AGREEMENTS, THE EXECUTIVE BRANCH HAS SIGNIFICANTLY INCREASED ITS POWER IN FOREIGN POLICY.

2156 VELVEL, L.R. "THE CONSTITUTION AND THE WAR: SOME MAJOR ISSUES." <u>J OF URBAN LAW</u> 40 (1971):231-295.

2157 WALLACE, D. "PART 1: THE PRESIDENT'S EXCLUSIVE FOREIGN AFFAIRS POWERS OVER FOREIGN AID." <u>DUKE LAW J</u> (1970):293-328.

AN EXTENSIVELY DOCUMENTED HISTORICAL DISCUSSION AND LEGAL BRIEF, ARGUING THAT, ALTHOUGH CONGRESS CAN EXERCISE NUMEROUS RESTRAINTS UPON PRESIDENTIAL FOREIGN AFFAIRS POWERS, THE LEGISLATIVE BRANCH SHOULD BE WARY OF CURBING PRESIDENTIAL GRANTS OF FOREIGN AID.

2158 ----------. "PART 2: THE PRESIDENT'S EXCLUSIVE FOREIGN AFFAIRS POWERS OVER FOREIGN AID." <u>DUKE LAW J</u> 19 (1970):293-494.

SEE PART 1 OF WALLACE'S DISCUSSION, ALREADY NOTED ABOVE.

2159 ----------. "THE WAR-MAKING POWERS: A CONSTITUTIONAL FLAW." <u>CORNELL LAW R</u> 57:719-76 MY '72.

2160 WEBB, R.E. "TREATY-MAKING AND THE PRESIDENT'S OBLIGATION TO SEEK THE ADVICE AND CONSENT OF THE SENATE WITH SPECIAL REFERENCE TO THE VIETNAM PEACE NEGOTIATION." <u>OHIO STATE LAW J</u> 31 (SUMMER 1970): 490-515.

2161 WELLS, J.M. <u>THE PEOPLE VS. PRESIDENTIAL WAR.</u> NEW YORK: DUNELLEN COMPANY, 1970, PP. 199.

A COLLECTION OF 30 PERSONAL ACCOUNTS BY INDIVIDUALS INVOLVED IN THE MASSACHUSETTS SHEA BILL CHALLENGING THE PRESIDENT'S RIGHT TO SEND TROOPS TO WAR WITHOUT CONGRESS'S CONSENT AND PROVIDING PROTECTION FOR MASSACHUSETTS RESIDENTS DRAFTED TO SERVE IN SUCH WARS (E.G., VIETNAM).

2162 WENNER, S.J. "THE INDOCHINA WAR CASES IN THE UNITED STATES COURT OF APPEALS FOR THE SECOND CIRCUIT: THE CONSTITUTIONAL ALLOCATION OF WAR POWERS." NYU J INT LAW AND POLITICS 7 (SPRING 1974): 137-161.

2163 WILCOX, F.O. CONGRESS, THE EXECUTIVE AND FOREIGN POLICY. NEW YORK: HAR-ROW, 1971, PP. 179.

2164 WILCOX, F.O., AND FRANK, R.A., EDS. THE CONSTITUTION AND THE CONDUCT OF FOREIGN POLICY. NEW YORK: PRAEGER, 1976, PP. 145.

"AN INQUIRY BY A PANEL OF THE AMERICAN SOCIETY OF INTERNATIONAL LAW." INCLUDES CHAPTERS ON "CONTROLLING SECRECY IN FOREIGN AFFAIRS," "SECRECY VERSUS NATIONAL UNITY," "PUBLIC PARTICIPATION IN THE FOREIGN POLICY PROCESS," "THE POWER TO MAKE WAR," AND "MAKING FOREIGN POLICY THROUGH INTERNATIONAL AGREEMENT."

2165 WILLIAMS, C.D. "COOPER-CHURCH AMENDMENT: IS IT CONSTITUTIONAL?". NATIONAL R 22:731-3 JL 14 '70; REPLY WITH REJOINDER. J. LOTTERMAN. 22: 1031+

2166 WORMUTH, F.D. "THE NIXON THEORY OF THE WAR POWER: A CRITIQUE." CALIFORNIA LAW R 60:623-703 MY '72.

2167 WORSNOP, R.L. "WAR POWERS OF THE PRESIDENT." EDITORIAL RESEARCH REPORTS 183-200 MR 14 '66.

SEE ALSO 51, 62, 65, 67, 69, 72, 73, 74, 75, 76, 78, 82, 83, 84, 85, 87, 93, 102, 118, 119, 124, 126, 127, 128, 129, 130, 131, 132, 133, 134, 135, 139, 482, 502, 510, 541, 721, 757, 870, 871, 872, 875, 880, 986, 994, 1135, 1141, 1154, 1371, 1377, 1823, 1881, 1896, 1922, 1923, 1930, 1933, 1935, 1938, 1956, 1979, 1981, 1999, 2009, 2017, 2063, 2095, 2109, 2116, 2118, 2125, 2278, 2286

2. VETO AND OTHER LAW-MAKING POWERS

2168 BECKMAN, A.E. "ITEM VETO POWER OF THE EXECUTIVE." TEMP L Q 31:27 FALL '57.

2169 BELLAMY, C. "GROWING POTENTIAL OF THE POCKET VETO: ANOTHER
     AREA OF INCREASING PRESIDENTIAL POWER." ILLINOIS BAR J
     61:85 O '72.

2170 BOECKEL,   R.M.   "THE   VETO   POWER   OF   THE   PRESIDENT."
     EDITORIAL RESEARCH REPORTS 407:23 D 16 '32 PRICE ON
     APPLICATION.

2171 CLINEBURG, W.A. "PRESIDENTIAL VETO POWER." SOUTH CAROLINA
     LAW R 18:732 FALL '66.

2172 CONDO, J.A. "THE VETO OF S.3418: MORE CONGRESSIONAL POWER
     IN THE PRESIDENT'S POCKET?" CATHOLIC UNIVERSITY LAW R 22
     (WINTER 1973): 385-402.

     THE KENNEDY V. SAMPSON CASE CHALLENGING THE POCKET VETO
     ARGUES THAT "IF ALLOWED TO PROCEED UNCHECKED, THE EXERCISE
     OF THE POCKET VETO DURING BRIEF RECESSES OF CONGRESS COULD
     GRADUALLY VEST IN THE EXECUTIVE A NEAR-ABSOLUTE NEGATIVE
     ON ANY CONGRESSIONAL ACTION TO WHICH IT COULD APPLY."

2173 DAMON, A.L. "VETO." AMER HERITAGE 25 (FEB. 1974):
     12-15+.

     REVIEWS PAST PRESIDENTS' USE OF THE VETO AND SUMMARIZES IN
     TABULAR FORM ITS USE THROUGH HISTORY.

2174 JACKSON, C. PRESIDENTIAL VETOES 1792- 1945. ATHENS:
     UNIV. OF GEORGIA PRESS, 1967, PP. 254.

     AN ACCOUNT OF THE EVOLVING PRACTICES IN THE USE OF THE
     VETO-POWER AND THE RATIONALE FOR ITS EXERCISE.

2175 KASS,   B.L. "THE POCKET VETO: AN ILLUSIVE BONE OF
     CONTENTION." ABA J 57 (OCT. 1971): 1033-1035.

2176 LEE, J.R. "PRESIDENTIAL VETOES FROM WASHINGTON TO NIXON."
     JP 37 (MAY 1975): 522-546.

     EXAMINES "A SERIES OF HYPOTHESES ON THE FREQUENCY OF
     PRESIDENTIAL VETOES AND CONGRESSIONAL REACTIONS. THE
     PATTERN IN VETO BEHAVIOR IS NOT EASILY DESCRIBED IN TERMS
     EITHER OF TRENDS OR OF LONG-TERM OR SHORT-TERM CYCLES. YET
     REGRESSION ANALYSIS SHOWS THAT A SIGNIFICANT AMOUNT OF
     VARIATION IN PRESIDENTIAL VETO BEHAVIOR IS EXPLAINED BY
     THE PRESIDENT'S BACKGROUND AND PARTISAN OR ELECTORAL
     FACTORS, WHEREAS CONGRESSIONAL BEHAVIOR IS WELL PREDICTED
     BY OBJECTIVE CHANGES IN POLITICAL AND SOCIO-ECONOMIC
     ENVIRONMENT."

2177 "PRESIDENTIAL VETO POWER: A SHALLOW POCKET." MICHIGAN LAW R 70:148 N '71.

ON THE CIRCUMSTANCES UNDER WHICH THE PRESIDENT MAY CONSTITUTIONALLY INVOKE THE POCKET VETO POWER.

2178 RIGGS, R.A. "SEPARATION OF POWERS: CONGRESSIONAL RIDERS AND THE VETO POWER." U OF MICHIGAN J OF LAW REFORM 6 (SPRING 1973): 735-759.

"THIS ARTICLE EXAMINES WHETHER THERE IS ANY CONSTITUTIONAL GROUND ON WHICH THE PRESIDENT COULD TAKE THE UNPRECEDENTED ACTION OF SEPARATELY VETOING CONGRESSIONAL RIDERS.

2179 "THE VETO POWER AND KENNEDY V. SAMPSON: BURNING A HOLE IN THE PRESIDENT'S POCKET." NORTHWESTERN UNIVERSITY LAW R 69 (SEPT-OCT 1974): 587-625.

EXAMINES JUDICIAL INTERPRETATION OF THE FEDERAL POCKET VETO AND THE POCKET VETO'S USE ON THE STATE LEVEL AND CONCLUDES THAT THE KENNEDY V. SAMPSON DECISION HAS BROUGHT THE POCKET VETO INTO LINE WITH MODERN LEG-ISLATIVE NEEDS.

2180 TOWLE, K.A. "THE PRESIDENTIAL VETO SINCE 1889." APSR 31 (FEB 1937): 51-56.

2181 VOSE, C.E. "THE MEMORANDUM POCKET VETO." JP 26 (1964):397-405.

A CLOSELY DOCUMENTED HISTORY OF THE EVOLVING PRESIDENTIAL PRACTICE OF ACCOMPANYING POCKET VETOES WITH VETO MESSAGES.

SEE ALSO 140, 141

3. EXECUTIVE ORDERS AND RULE MAKING

2182 BARBER, S.A. THE CONSTITUTION AND THE DELEGATION OF CONGRESSIONAL POWER. CHICAGO: U OF CHICAGO PR, 1975, PP. 153.

AN ANALYSIS BASED ON INTERPRETATION OF CONSTITUTIONAL WORDING ARGUING THAT THE CONSTITUTION PLACES DEFINITE LIMITS ON CONGRESSIONAL DELEGATION OF POWER TO THE EXECUTIVE, BUT THE COURTS HAVE FAILED TO FORCE THESE LIMITS.

2183 BROWN, E.S. "EXECUTIVE ORDERS: A BIBLIOGRAPHICAL NOTE." UNIVERSITY DEBATERS ANNUAL (1933-1934): 343-73.

2184 CASH, R.B. "PRESIDENTIAL POWER: USE AND ENFORCEMENT OF EXECUTIVE ORDERS." NOTRE DAME LAWYER 39 (DEC 1963): 44-55.

2185 "EXECUTIVE COMMANDEERING OF STRIKE-BOUND PLANTS." YALE LAW J 51 (1941):282-298.

2186 "EXECUTIVE ORDERS AND THE DEVELOPMENT OF PRESIDENTIAL POWER." VILLANOVA LAW R 17:688 MR '72.

2187 FISHER, L. "DELEGATING POWER TO THE PRESIDENT." J PUBLIC LAW 19 (1970):251-282.

"THE PURPOSE OF THIS ARTICLE IS TWOFOLD: TO EXPLAIN WHY CONGRESS DELEGATES POWER TO THE PRESIDENT AND TO EXECUTIVE OFFICIALS AND TO IDENTIFY SOME OF THE SAFEGUARDS THAT PREVENT DELEGATION FROM BECOMING ABDICATION." BASED IN LARGE PART ON FISHER'S PRESIDENT AND CONGRESS: POWERS AND PREROGATIVES.

2188 HART, J. THE ORDINANCE MAKING POWERS OF THE PRESIDENT OF THE UNITED STATES. BALTIMORE: JOHNS HOPKINS PRESS, 1925. REPRINTED, NEW YORK: DA CAPO, 1970, PP. 339.

2189 LEISING, J.E. "PRESIDENTIAL POWERS OVER THE AWARDING OF INTERNATIONAL AIR ROUTES." TULANE LAW R 48 (JUNE 1974): 1176-1208.

ON SECTION 801 OF THE CIVIL AERONAUTICS ACT AND THE REQUIREMENT FOR PRESIDENTIAL APPROVAL OF CAB DECISIONS CONCERNING THE AWARDING OF AIR ROUTES TO CARRIERS.

2190 LEVINE, D. "THE EXECUTIVE ORDER: A FORM OF PRESIDENTIAL PARTICIPATION IN THE LEGISLATIVE PROCESS." PH.D. DISSERT, AMERICAN U, 1955.

2191 MORGAN, R.P. THE PRESIDENT AND CIVIL RIGHTS: POLICY-MAKING BY EXECUTIVE ORDER. NEW YORK: ST. MARTIN'S PRESS, 1970, PP. 107.

2192 NIXON, R.M. "EXECUTIVE ORDERS AND THE ASSUMPTION OF LEGISLATIVE POWER." WASHINGTON AND LEE COMMERCE R 1 (1973):77-108.

2193 "PRESIDENTIAL POWER: USE AND ENFORCEMENT OF EXECUTIVE ORDERS." NOTRE DAME LAW R 39:44 D '63.

2194 STEBBINS, P.E. "TRUMAN AND THE SEIZURE OF STEEL: A FAILURE

IN COMMUNICATION." HISTORIAN (NOV 1971): 1-21.

A RETROSPECTIVE ANALYSIS OF THE MAIN EVENTS IN THE STEEL SEIZURE, INCLUDING AN EXTENSIVE BIBLIOGRAPHICAL SUMMARY OF WRITINGS ON THAT EPISODE AS WELL AS PRIMARY-SOURCE DOCUMENTATION FROM THE TRUMAN LIBRARY. ARGUES THAT TRUMAN'S ACTION WAS UNSUCCESSFUL BECAUSE HE FAILED TO COMMUNICATE TO THE NATION AT LARGE THE NECESSITY AND THE DESIRABILITY OF CONTINUING THE INFORMAL PRECEDENTS SET BY EARLIER PRESIDENTS FOR USE OF EMERGENCY POWERS.

SEE ALSO 142

4. APPOINTMENT AND DISCHARGE

2195 CIRILLO, R.A. "ABOLITION OF FEDERAL OFFICES AS AN INFRINGEMENT ON THE PRESIDENT'S POWER TO REMOVE FEDERAL EXECUTIVE OFFICERS: A REASSESSMENT OF CONSTITUTIONAL DOCTRINES." FORDHAM LAW R 42 (MAR 1974): 562-610.

CONSIDERS S. 518 AND SIMILAR BILLS THROUGH WHICH CONGRESS SEEKS "TO RECAPTURE LEGISLATIVE POWERS LOST TO THE EXECUTIVE BRANCH" BY REQUIRING SENATE CONFIRMATION OF PRESIDENTIALLY APPROVED FEDERAL OFFICIALS.

2196 CORWIN, E.S. PRESIDENT'S REMOVAL POWER UNDER THE CONSTITUTION. NEW YORK: NATIONAL MUNICIPAL LEAGUE, 1927, PP. 70.

2197 CROSS, C.B. "THE REMOVAL POWER OF THE PRESIDENT AND THE TEST OF RESPONSIBILITY." CORNELL LAW Q 40 (1954):81-93.

2198 DONOVAN, W.J., AND RALSTONE, R.I. "THE PRESIDENT'S POWER TO REMOVE MEMBERS OF ADMINISTRATIVE AGENCIES." CORNELL LAW Q 21 (1936):215-248.

"THE CONSTITUTIONAL DIVISION OF POWERS REQUIRES, ON THE ONE HAND, THAT CONGRESS SHALL NOT INTERFERE WITH THE PREROGATIVE OF THE PRESIDENT TO CONTROL PURELY EXECUTIVE OFFICERS, AND, ON THE OTHER HAND, THAT THE PRESIDENT THROUGH THE EXERCISE OF HIS REMOVAL POWER SHALL NOT INTERFERE WITH THE LAWFUL ACTS OF CONGRESS IN CREATING ADMINISTRATIVE OFFICES HAVING QUASI-LEGISLATIVE OR QUASI-JUDICIAL FUNCTIONS."

2199 JACOBSON, J.M. "INHERENT EXECUTIVE POWER OF REMOVAL: A REEXAMINATION IN THE LIGHT OF THE NEW DEAL." NEW JERSEY LAW R 1 (JAN 1935): 32-64.

2200 JAMES, L.C. "SENATORIAL REJECTIONS OF PRESIDENTIAL NOMINATIONS TO THE CABINET: A STUDY IN CONSTITUTIONAL CUSTOM." ARIZONA LAW R 3:232. WINTER '61.

2201 KAHN, M.A. "THE POLITICS OF THE APPOINTMENT PROCESS: AN ANALYSIS OF WHY LEARNED HAND WAS NEVER APPOINTED TO THE SUPREME COURT." STANFORD LAW R 25 (JAN 1973): 251-285.

COMMENT CONCLUDES THAT BECAUSE POLITICAL AFFINITY WITH THE PRESIDENT IS THE OVERRIDING CHARACTERISTIC OF SUPREME COURT APPOINTEES, APPEALS JUDGE LEARNED HAND, WITH HIS UNCLEAR BUT COMPLEX JUDICIAL AND POLITICAL PHILOSOPHY, "WAS NOT A POLITICALLY LIKELY APPOINTMENT AT ANY TIME DURING HIS CAREER."

2202 KURLAND, P.B. "THE APPOINTMENT AND DISAPPOINTMENT OF SUPREME COURT JUSTICES." ARIZONA STATE U LAW J 2 (1972): 183-237.

DISCUSSES "THE IMPORTANT QUALITIES THAT A SUPREME COURT JUSTICE SHOULD POSSESS, THE VARIOUS COMPETING PRESSURES THAT OFTEN INFLUENCE PRESIDENTIAL SELECTIONS, THE SENATE'S PROPER ROLE IN THE CONFIRMATION PROCESS, AND FINALLY--WITH SPECIAL EMPHASIS UPON THE IMPEACHMENT PROCEEDINGS AGAINST JUSTICE DOUGLAS--THE AVAILABLE MEANS OF REMOVING INCUMBENT JUSTICES."

2203 LARSON, A. "HAS THE PRESIDENT AN INHERENT POWER OF REMOVAL OF HIS NON-EXECUTIVE APPOINTEES?." TENNESSEE LAW R 16 (1940): 259+.

2204 MOE, R.C. "SENATE CONFIRMATION OF EXECUTIVE APPOINTMENTS: THE NIXON ERA." IN CONGRESS AGAINST THE PRESIDENT, EDITED BY H.C. MANSFIELD, NEW YORK: ACADEMY OF POL SCI, 1975: 141-152. ALSO NEW YORK: PRAEGER, 1975.

2205 "MORGAN V. UNITED STATES--THE PRESIDENT'S POWER OF REMOVAL." HARVARD LAW R 51 (1938): 1246-51.

2206 PARKER, R. "REMOVAL POWER OF THE PRESIDENT AND INDEPENDENT ADMINISTRATIVE AGENCIES." INDIANA LAW J 36:63 FALL '60.

2207 REZNICK, L. "TEMPORARY APPOINTMENT POWER OF THE PRESIDENT." UNIVERSITY OF CHICAGO LAW R 41 (FALL 1973): 146-163.

2208 SWAIN, R.A. "THE PRESIDENT'S POWER OF REMOVAL AND THE T.V.A." GEORGE WASHINGTON LAW R 9 (1941): 703-13.

SEE ALSO 68, 76, 417, 442, 445, 1363, 1998

5. EXECUTIVE PRIVILEGE, SECRECY, CONFIDENTIALITY

2209 ALBERT, L.A., AND SIMON, L.G. "ENFORCING SUBPOENAS AGAINST
THE PRESIDENT: THE QUESTION OF MR. JAWORSKI'S AUTHORITY."
COLUMBIA LAW R 74 (MAY 1974): 545-560.

A CRITIQUE OF PRESIDENT NIXON'S ATTACK ON SPECIAL
PROSECUTOR LEON JAWORSKI'S AUTHORITY TO SUBPOENA THE
PRESIDENT.

2210 BECHT, A.C. "THE ABSOLUTE PRIVILEGE OF THE EXECUTIVE IN
DEFAMATION." VANDERBILT LAW R 15 (1962): 1127-1171.

2211 BERGER, R. "CONGRESSIONAL SUBPOENAS TO EXECUTIVE
OFFICIALS." COLUMBIA LAW R 75 (JUNE 1975): 865-891.

2212 ----------. "EXECUTIVE PRIVILEGE VS. CONGRESSIONAL
INQUIRY." UCLA LAW R 12 (1965): 1044-1364.

2213 BERGER, R. EXECUTIVE PRIVILEGE: A CONSTITUTIONAL
MYTH. CAMBRIDGE, MASS.: HARVARD UNIVERSITY PRESS, 1974,
PP. 430.

ON THE BASIS OF EXTENSIVE EXAMINATION OF BRITISH
PARLIAMENTARY AS WELL AS AMERICAN CONSTITUTIONAL
PRECEDENTS, BERGER ARGUES THAT THERE IS NO BASIS FOR THE
PRESIDENTIAL CLAIM OF AUTHORITY TO WITHHOLD INFORMATION.

2214 BISHOP, J.W., JR. "THE EXECUTIVE'S RIGHT OF PRIVACY: AN
UNRESOLVED CONSTITUTIONAL QUESTION." YALE LAW J 66
(1957).

"NEITHER THE EXECUTIVE NOR THE CONGRESS IS VERY SURE OF
ITS RIGHTS" WITH RESPECT TO PRESIDENTIAL POWER TO WITHHOLD
INFORMATION FROM THE LEGISLATURE, "AND BOTH USUALLY EVINCE
A TACTFUL DISPOSITION NOT TO PUSH THE ASSERTION OF THEIR
RIGHTS TO ABUSIVE EXTREMES."

2215 BRECKENRIDGE, A. THE EXECUTIVE PRIVILEGE. LINCOLN:
UNIVERSITY OF NEBRASKA PRESS, 1974, PP. 188.

TAKING EXPLICIT ISSUE WITH THE THESIS OF BERGER'S
EXECUTIVE PRIVILEGE (1974), BRECKENRIDGE ARGUES THAT THE
POLITICAL INDEPENDENCE OF THE EXECUTIVE CAN ONLY BE
PRESERVED IF PRESIDENTS ARE ALLOWED TO WITHHOLD AT LEAST
CERTAIN KINDS OF INFORMATION.

2216 CAPPELLETTI, M., AND GOLDEN, C.J., JR. "CROWN PRIVILEGE
AND EXECUTIVE PRIVILEGE: A BRITISH RESPONSE TO AN AMERICAN
CONTROVERSY." STANFORD LAW R 25 (1973):836-844.

2217 COLLINS, P.R. "POWER OF CONGRESSIONAL COMMITTEES OF INVESTIGATION TO OBTAIN INFORMATION FROM THE EXECUTIVE BRANCH: THE ARGUMENT FOR THE EXECUTIVE BRANCH." GEORGIA LAW J 39 (1951):563-598.

2218 COLTON, D. "FREEDOM OF INFORMATION ACT - THE DOCTRINE OF EXECUTIVE PRIVILEGE LIMITS STATUTORY ACCESS TO INFORMATION HELD WITHIN THE EXECUTIVE OFFICE OF THE PRESIDENT." TEXAS LAW R 49 (1970).

2219 COX, A. "EXECUTIVE PRIVILEGE." U PENNSYLVANIA LAW R 122 (1974):1383-1438.

A COMPREHENSIVE ESSAY BY THE WATERGATE SPECIAL PROSECUTOR DISCHARGED BY PRESIDENT NIXON, CALLING FOR GREATER JUDICIAL POWER OVER CLAIMS OF EXECUTIVE PRIVILEGE.

2220 DECHART, C.R. "DENIAL OF ACCESS TO INFORMATION IN THE EXECUTIVE." IN CONGRESS: THE FIRST BRANCH OF GOVERNMENT, EDITED BY A. DEGRAZIA, WASHINGTON, D.C.: AMER ENTERPRISE INST FOR PUBLIC POLICY RESEARCH, 1966.

2221 DORSEN, N., AND SHATTUCK, J.H.F. "EXECUTIVE PRIVILEGE, THE CONGRESS AND THE COURTS." OHIO STATE LAW J 35 (1974):1-40.

"AN ABSOLUTE CONGRESSIONAL POWER TO COMPEL INFORMATION SHOULD NOT BE SUBSTITUTED FOR AN ABSOLUTE EXECUTIVE POWER TO WITHHOLD IT."

2222 ERVIN, S.J. "CONTROLLING EXECUTIVE PRIVILEGE." LOYOLA LAW R 20, NO.1 (1974): 11-31.

OUTLINES THE PROVISIONS OF ERVIN'S BILL, S. 2432, FOR ESTABLISHING PROCEDURES FOR PRESIDENTIAL ASSERTIONS OF THE PRIVILEGE AND CONGRESSIONAL RESPONSE TO IT. TEXT OF S. 2432 IS APPENDED.

2223 ----------. "EXECUTIVE PRIVILEGE: THE NEED FOR CONGRESSIONAL ACTION." CASE AND COMMENT 79 (JAN.-FEB. 1974): 39-43, 45-48.

EXECUTIVE PRIVILEGE "MUST BE EXERCISED PERSONALLY BY THE PRESIDENT" AND DOES NOT BELONG "TO OTHER EXECUTIVE BRANCH OFFICERS."

2224 "EXECUTIVE PRIVILEGE - THE PRESIDENT DOES NOT HAVE AN ABSOLUTE PRIVILEGE TO WITHHOLD EVIDENCE FROM A GRAND JURY." HARVARD LAW R 87 (MAY 1974): 1557-1568.

2225 "EXTENSION OF EXECUTIVE PRIVILEGE TO EXECUTIVE OFFICERS OF

GOVERNMENT AGENCIES." <u>MARYLAND LAW R</u> 20 (1960):1368.

2226 "EXTENSION OF EXECUTIVE PRIVILEGE TO GOVERNMENT OFFICIALS OF LESS THAN CABINET RANK." <u>MINNESOTA LAW R</u> 44 (1960):547.

2227 FROHNMAYER, D.B. "AN ESSAY ON EXECUTIVE PRIVILEGE." <u>WEAVER CONSTITUTIONAL LAW SERIES</u> NO. 1. CHICAGO: AMERICAN BAR ASSOCIATION, 1974, PP. 1-17.

"THE FATE OF REPRESENTATIVE GOVERNMENT IN THE UNITED STATES WILL HINGE ON THE ABILITY OF OUR LEGISLATIVE AND JUDICIAL INSTITUTIONS TO RESIST AN UNCONTROLLED EXECUTIVE PREROGATIVE OVER THE LIFEBLOOD OF A DEMOCRATIC SOCIETY: ACCESS TO INFORMATION."

2228 "GOVERNMENT PRIVILEGE AGAINST DISCLOSURE OF OFFICIAL DOCUMENTS." <u>YALE LAW J</u> 58 (1949):993.

2229 HEY, H.W. <u>CONGRESSIONAL DEMANDS FOR EXECUTIVE INFORMATION</u>. CHICAGO: U OF CHICAGO (LIBRARY DEPT OF PHOTOGRAPHIC REPRODUCTION), 1956.

2230 HRUSKA, R.L. "EXECUTIVE RECORDS IN CONGRESSIONAL INVESTIGATIONS - DUTY TO DISCLOSE; DUTY TO WITHHOLD." <u>NEBRASKA LAW R</u> 35 (1956): 310.

2231 KRAMER, R., AND MARCUSE, H. "EXECUTIVE PRIVILEGE: A STUDY OF THE PERIOD 1953 - 1960." <u>GEORGE WASHINGTON LAW R</u> 29 (1961):623-717, 827-916.

2232 MALONE, D. "EXECUTIVE PRIVILEGE: JEFFERSON AND BURR AND NIXON AND EHRLICHMAN." <u>NY REVIEW OF BOOKS</u> 21 (JULY 18, 1974): 36-40.

2233 MCLAUGHON, H.K., JR. "CONSTITUTIONAL LAW--EXECUTIVE PRIVILEGE: TILTING THE SCALES IN FAVOR OF SECRECY." <u>N CAROLINA LAW R</u> 53 (DEC 1974): 419-430.

2234 MILES, C.W. "RIGHT OF THE PRESIDENT OF THE UNITED STATES TO WITHHOLD EXECUTIVE INFORMATION." <u>MD S B A</u> 59:230 '54.

2235 MILLER, A.S. "EXECUTIVE PRIVILEGE: ITS DUBIOUS CONSTITUTIONALITY." BUREAUCRAT 1 (SUMMER 1972): 136-141.

2236 "POLICING THE EXECUTIVE PRIVILEGE." UNIVERSITY OF MICHIGAN J OF LAW REFORM 5 (1972):568.

2237 "POWER OF THE EXECUTIVE TO WITHHOLD INFORMATION FROM CONGRESSIONAL INVESTIGATING COMMITTEES." GEORGIA LAW J 43 (1955):643.

2238 "PRESIDENT AND CONGRESS - POWER OF THE PRESIDENT TO REFUSE CONGRESSIONAL DEMANDS FOR INFORMATION." STANFORD LAW R 1 (1949):256-262.

2239 RAMIS, T.V. "EXECUTIVE PRIVILEGES: WHAT ARE THE LIMITS?" OREGON LAW R 54, NO. 1 (1975): 81-103.

EXECUTIVE PRIVILEGE CONSISTS OF "MANY LIMITED PRIVILEGES, EACH CONFINED TO A PARTICULAR TYPE OF COMMUNICATION: NO APPARENT DISTINCTION EXISTS BETWEEN ASSERTIONS OF PRIVILEGE IN LEGISLATIVE OR JUDICIAL FORUMS: AND STATUTES AND COMMON LAW SUPPORT THESE PRIVILEGES, NOT THE CONSTITUTION.

2240 ROURKE, F.E. "ADMINISTRATIVE SECRECY: A CONGRESSIONAL DILEMMA." APSR 54 (1960):684-694.

2241 ----------. "PRESIDENTIAL POWER: THE CONVENIENCE OF SECRECY." NATION 24 (JULY 1972): 39-42.

2242 SCHWARTZ, B. "EXECUTIVE PRIVILEGE AND CONGRESSIONAL INVESTIGATORY POWER." CALIFORNIA LAW R (1959):3-50.

2243 ----------. "EXECUTIVE PRIVILEGE: THE PUBLIC'S RIGHT TO KNOW AND PUBLIC INTEREST." FEDERAL BAR J 19 (1959): 7-17.

2244 SMITH, S.C. BIBLIOGRAPHY--EXECUTIVE PRIVILEGE. NEW HAVEN, CONN.: YALE LAW LIBRARY, 1973, PP. 41.

2245 SOFAER, A.D. "EXECUTIVE PRIVILEGE: AN HISTORICAL NOTE."

COLUMBIA LAW R 75 (NOV 1975): 1318-1321.

2246 STANTON, E.M. "EXECUTIVE PRIVILEGE: AN INSTITUTIONAL
PERSPECTIVE." WEAVER CONSTITUTIONAL LAW SERIES NO. 1.
CHICAGO: AMERICAN BAR ASSOCIATION, 1974, PP. 19-35.

INCLUDES CASE STUDIES OF INDIVIDUALS WHO DEVOTED MUCH TIME
TO "GROOMING" SOMEONE FOR THE PRESIDENCY -- E.G., L.M.
HOWE'S EXTENSIVE EFFORTS FOR FDR.

SEE ALSO 89, 99, 103, 127, 143, 144, 145, 146, 147, 148,
149, 150, 151, 152, 276, 1154, 1413, 1937, 1953, 1969,
2002, 2126

6. SPENDING, INCLUDING IMPOUNDMENT OF FUNDS

2247 ROBERTS, B. "TYING THE IMPERIAL PURSE STRINGS." WASHINGTON
MONTHLY 7 (SEPTEMBER 1975): 27-30.

2248 ABASCAL, R.S., AND KRAMER, J.R. "PRESIDENTIAL IMPOUNDMENT
PART I: HISTORICAL GENESIS AND CONSTITUTIONAL FRAMEWORK."
GEORGETOWN LAW J 62 (1974): 1549-1618. PART II, 63
(1974): 149-185.

"IN THE FIRST PART OF A TWO-PART ARTICLE, THE AUTHORS
ANALYZE THE HISTORY OF THE FEDERAL BUDGETARY SYSTEM AND
DEMONSTRATE THAT THE EXECUTIVE CANNOT DERIVE IMPOUNDMENT
AUTHORITY FROM ANY OF THE STATUTES ESTABLISHING BUDGET
PROCEDURES OR APPROPRIATION AUTHORIZATION." ACCORDING TO
THE FIRST OF THESE ARTICLES, CONGRESS HISTORICALLY HAS
REFUSED TO AUTHORIZE THIS SHIFT OF BUDGETARY POWER FROM
ITSELF TO THE PRESIDENT. THE SECOND ARTICLE ANALYZES THE
JUDICIAL AND THE LEGISLATIVE RESPONSES TO PRESIDENTIAL
IMPOUNDMENT.

2249 ARCHER, W.J. "PRESIDENTIAL IMPOUNDING OF FUNDS: THE
JUDICIAL RESPONSE." UNIVERSITY OF CHICAGO LAW R 44
(1973):328-356.

2250 BERKOVITCH, B.S., AND MEDINA, S.F., JR. "EXECUTIVE
IMPOUNDMENT OF APPROPRIATED FUNDS." RECORD OF THE
ASSOCIATION OF THE BAR AND THE CITY OF NEW YORK 28
(1973):508-524.

2251 CHURCH, F. "IMPOUNDMENT OF APPROPRIATED FUNDS: THE DECLINE
OF CONGRESSIONAL CONTROL OVER DISCRETION." STANFORD LAW
R 22 (1970):1240-1253.

2252 COHN, M.B. "IMPOUNDMENT OF FUNDS APPROPRIATED BY

CONGRESS." _OHIO STATE LAW J_ 34 (1973):416-427.

ON THE NATURE OF THE IMPOUNDMENT, THE GRAY AREA OF
LEGITIMATE IMPOUNDMENT, AND METHODS TO END IMPOUNDMENT.

2253 "CONTROVERSY OVER THE PRESIDENTIAL IMPOUNDMENT OF
APPROPRIATED FUNDS." _CONGRESSIONAL DIGEST_ 52 (APRIL
1973): 97-128.

2254 DAVID, G.W. "CONGRESSIONAL POWER TO REQUIRE DEFENSE
EXPENDITURE." _FORDHAM L R_ 33 (OCT 1964): 39-60.

2255 FISHER, L. _PRESIDENTIAL SPENDING POWER_. PRINCETON, N.J.:
PRINCETON UNIVERSITY PRESS, 1975, PP. 300.

THE MOST COMPREHENSIVE ACCOUNT OF THE WAYS A PRESIDENT CAN
CONTROL EXPENDITURES.

2256 ----------. "CONGRESS, THE EXECUTIVE AND THE BUDGET."
ANNALS 411 (1974):102-113.

DISCUSSES THE BUDGETARY CONFLICTS BETWEEN CONGRESS AND THE
PRESIDENT, FOCUSING ON THE SPENDING CEILING OF $250 BILLION
FOR FISCAL YEAR 1973.

2257 ----------. "DEMOCRACY AND SECRET FUNDING." _CENTER MAG_
7 (MAR.-APR. 1974): 54-56.

"WE HAVE NOW REACHED THE POINT WHERE A SUBSTANTIAL PORTION
OF THE FEDERAL BUDGET--POSSIBLY TEN BILLION DOLLARS OR
MORE--IS OBSCURED BECAUSE OF CONFIDENTIAL FUNDS, SECRET
FUNDS, OR CRYPTIC BUDGET JUSTIFICATIONS." REVIEWS THE
JUSTIFICATION FOR COVERT FUNDING AND SUGGESTS CONGRESS
SHOULD RESTRAIN ITS USE.

2258 ----------. "FUNDS IMPOUNDED BY THE PRESIDENT: THE
CONSTITUTIONAL ISSUE...." _GEORGE WASHINGTON LAW R_ 28
(1969): 124-37.

A REVIEW OF SUPREME COURT DECISIONS, EXPANDED UPON IN
FISHER'S _PRESIDENTIAL SPENDING POWER_.

2259 ----------. "IMPOUNDMENT OF FUNDS: USES AND ABUSES."
BUFFALO LAW R 23 (1973):141-200.

ATTEMPTS TO ESTABLISH CRITERIA FOR VALID AND INVALID USE
OF THE IMPOUNDMENT POWER.

2260 ----------. "REPROGRAMMING OF FUNDS BY THE DEFENSE
DEPARTMENT." _JP_ 36 (1974):77-102.

AN EXAMINATION OF A DEVICE FOR CIRCUMVENTING CONGRESSIONAL
STIPULATIONS ABOUT HOW APPROPRIATIONS SHOULD BE ALLOCATED.
SEE THE FURTHER DISCUSSION IN FISHER'S _PRESIDENTIAL
SPENDING POWER_.

2261 ----------. "THE POLITICS OF IMPOUNDED FUNDS." ADMIN SCI
Q 15 (1970):361-377.

"EXPLORES THE POLITICAL FACTORS WHICH GIVE RISE TO
DISPUTES OVER IMPOUNDED FUNDS." SEE FISHER'S BOOK
PRESIDENTIAL SPENDING POWER FOR HIS MOST EXTENSIVE
DISCUSSION OF IMPOUNDMENT.

2262 GOOSTREE, R.F. "THE POWER OF THE PRESIDENT TO IMPOUND
APPROPRIATED FUNDS: WITH SPECIAL REFERENCE TO GRANT-IN-AID
TO SEGREGATED ACTIVITIES." AMERICAN UNIVERSITY LAW R 2
(1962):32-47.

2263 HOPKINS, B.R. "CONGRESS CURTAILS PRESIDENTIAL
IMPOUNDMENTS." ABA J 60 (SEPT. 1974): 1053-1057.

AS A RESULT OF THE IMPOUNDMENT CONTROL ACT OF 1974, THE
EXECUTIVE MUST FOLLOW SPECIFIED IMPOUNDING PROCEDURES, AND
THE CONGRESS IS ABLE TO REVERSE PRESIDENTIAL ACTIONS.

2264 "IMPOUNDMENT OF FUNDS." HARVARD LAW R 86 (JUNE 1973):
1505-1535.

SKETCH OF THE HISTORY AND NATURE OF THE PRESENT
CONTROVERSY OVER IMPOUNDMENT. "THE ONLY POTENTIALLY VALID
JUSTIFICATIONS FOR IMPOUNDMENT ARISE WHEN PARTICULAR
IMPOUNDMENTS ARE BASED ON DEVELOPMENTS WITHIN THE AFFECTED
PROGRAM, AS AUTHORIZED BY THE ANTI-DEFICIENCY ACT, OR ON
PERMISSIVE LANGUAGE IN THE STATUTE GOVERNING THE
PARTICULAR PROGRAM ITSELF."

2265 "IMPOUNDMENT OF FUNDS." INDIANA LAW R 6 (1973):523-530.

2266 KRANZ, H. "A 20TH CENTURY EMANCIPATION PROCLAMATION:
PRESIDENTIAL POWER PERMITS WITHHOLDING OF FEDERAL FUNDS
FROM SEGREGATED INSTITUTIONS." AMERICAN UNIVERSITY LAW R
2 (1962):48-78.

2267 LEVINSON, H.L., AND MILLS, J.L. "IMPOUNDMENT: A SEARCH FOR
LEGAL PRINCIPLES." UNIVERSITY OF FLORIDA LAW R 26
(1974):191-220.

FIFTEEN RECOMMENDATIONS FOR LEGISLATION AFFECTING
BUDGETING AND IMPOUNDMENT.

2268 MIKVA, A.J., AND HERTZ, M.F. "IMPOUNDMENT OF FUNDS--THE
COURTS, THE CONGRESS AND THE PRESIDENT: A CONSTITUTIONAL
TRIANGLE." NORTHWESTERN UNIVERSITY LAW R 69 (JULY-AUG
1974): 335-389.

2269 MILLER, A.S. "PRESIDENTIAL POWER TO IMPOUND APPROPRIATED

FUNDS: AN EXERCISE IN CONSTITUTIONAL DECISION-MAKING." NORTH CAROLINA LAW R 43 (1965):502-547.

2270 MILLS, J.L., AND MUNSELLE, W.G. "UNIMPOUNDMENT: POLITICS AND THE COURTS IN THE RELEASE OF IMPOUNDED FUNDS." EMORY LAW S 24 (SPRING 1975): 313-353.

A LEGAL AND POLITICAL ANALYSIS OF THE PROCESS OF RELEASING IMPOUNDED FUNDS WITH SPECIAL REFERENCE TO THE BUDGET AND IMPOUNDMENT CONTROL ACT OF 1974.

2271 "PRESIDENTIAL IMPOUNDMENT: CONSTITUTIONAL THEORIES AND POLITICAL REALITIES." GEORGETOWN LAW J 61 (MAY 1973): 1295-1325.

2272 ROBERTS, B. "TYING THE IMPERIAL PURSE STRINGS." WASHINGTON MONTHLY 7 (SEPT. 1975): 29-30.

2273 SALOMON, R.A. "THE CASE AGAINST IMPOUNDMENT." HASTINGS CONSTIT LAW Q 2 (WINTER 1975): 277-308.

2274 SCHICK, A. "THE IMPOUNDMENT CONTROL ACT OF 1974." CONGRESSIONAL RESEARCH SERVICES 31 JAN. 1975, PP. 54.

2275 SOLTMAN, N.M. "THE LIMITS OF EXECUTIVE POWER: IMPOUNDMENT OF FUNDS." CATHOLIC UNIVERSITY LAW R 23 (1973):359-74.

2276 STANTON, N. "HISTORY AND PRACTICE OF EXECUTIVE IMPOUNDMENT OF APPROPRIATED FUNDS." NEBRASKA LAW R 53 (1974):1-30.

2277 ----------. "THE PRESIDENCY AND THE PURSE: IMPOUNDMENT 1802-1973." UNIVERSITY OF COLORADO LAW R 45 (1973):25-50.

CLAIMS THAT BOTH THE HISTORICAL RECORD AND THE RECENT CASES SHOW THE POWER TO IMPOUND FUNDS IS, EXCEPT UNDER LIMITED CIRCUMSTANCES, BEYOND THE SCOPE OF ANY INHERENT OR CONGRESSIONALLY DELEGATED PRESIDENTIAL POWER.

2278 STASSEN, J.H. "SEPARATION OF POWERS AND THE UNCOMMON DEFENSE: THE CASE AGAINST IMPOUNDING OF WEAPONS SYSTEM APPROPRIATIONS." GEORGETOWN LAW J 57 (JUNE 1969): 1159-1210.

2279 "THE LIKELY LAW OF EXECUTIVE IMPOUNDMENT." IOWA LAW R 59 (1972):50-90.

2280 WEINRAUB, S. "THE IMPOUNDMENT QUESTION - AN OVERVIEW." BROOKLYN LAW R 40 (1973):342-389.

2281 WILLIAMS, J.D. THE IMPOUNDING OF FUNDS BY THE BUREAU OF THE BUDGET. INTER-UNIVERSITY CASE PROGRAM: BOX 229, SYRACUSE, N.Y., 1955. PP. 33.

DESCRIBES DEVELOPMENT OF THE IDEA OF IMPOUNDING FUNDS FOR ENTIRE PROGRAMS, USE OF IMPOUNDMENT DURING WWII, AND HOW IT WAS DEFENDED AGAINST CONGRESSIONAL PROTESTS LED BY SENATORS MCCARRAN AND MCKELLER.

SEE ALSO 86, 92, 97, 105, 153, 154, 155, 156, 157, 159, 160, 161, 1340, 1341, 1939, 1940, 2028

7. MANAGEMENT OF THE ECONOMY

2282 BARTFELD, P.M. "U.S. TRADE LAW AT THE CROSSROADS: PRESIDENTIAL POWER IN THE TRADE AREA AFTER YOSHIDA INTERNATIONAL, INC. V. U.S. AND THE TRADE ACT OF 1974." NYU J INT LAW AND POLITICS 8 (SPRING 1975): 63-86.

2283 BERMAN, E. LABOR DISPUTES AND THE PRESIDENT OF THE UNITED STATES. NEW YORK: COLUMBIA U DEPT. OF POL SCI STUDIES IN HISTORY, ECONOMICS, AND PUBLIC LAW, 1924, VOL. 111, NO.2. REPRINTED NEW YORK: AMS PRESS, 1968, PP. 284.

2284 BLACKMAN, J.L. PRESIDENTIAL SEIZURE IN LABOR DISPUTES. CAMBRIDGE, MASS.: HARVARD UNIV. PRESS, 1967.

2285 CULLEN, D.E. NATIONAL EMERGENCY STRIKES. ITHACA: N Y STATE SCHOOL OF INDUSTRIAL AND LABOR RELATIONS, CORNELL U, 1968, PP. 134.

2286 DEKIEFFER, D.D.E., AND EASTON, E.R. "STAR INDUSTRIES: EXPANSION OF PRESIDENTIAL POWER TO SET TARIFFS?" UNIVERSITY OF COLORADO LAW R 45 (WINTER 1973): 149-161.

"WHAT STARTED AS A RELATIVELY UNCOMPLICATED TRADE WAR (THE "CHICKEN WAR") HAS RESULTED IN A SIGNIFICANT EXPANSION OF THE PRESIDENT'S AUTHORITY TO SET TARIFF BARRIERS, RAISING QUESTIONS OF CONSTITUTIONAL AS WELL AS INTERNATIONAL LAW."

2287 GOODWIN, C., ED. <u>EXHORTATION AND CONTROLS: THE SEARCH FOR A WAGE-PRICE POLICY, 1945-1971</u>. WASHINGTON, D.C.: BROOKINGS, 1975, PP. 432.

A REPORT OF A CONFERENCE ON WAGE-PRICE POLICY IN THE TRUMAN THROUGH NIXON ADMINISTRATIONS. THE CHAPTERS ON EACH ADMINISTRATION ARE BASED ON PRIMARY SOURCE RESEARCH BY ECONOMIC HISTORIANS. EACH CHAPTER AND A CONCLUDING ONE COMPARING THE 5 ADMINISTRATIONS WERE REVISED FOLLOWING THE CONFERENCE IN WHICH THE PAPER WRITERS DISCUSSED THEIR FINDINGS WITH NUMEROUS LEADING FORMER OFFICIALS FROM THOSE ADMINISTRATIONS.

2288 LARKIN, J.D. <u>THE PRESIDENT'S CONTROL OF THE TARIFF</u>. CAMBRIDGE: HARVARD UNIVERSITY PRESS, 1936, PP. 207.

2289 STEIN, H. <u>THE FISCAL REVOLUTION IN AMERICA</u>. CHICAGO: U OF CHICAGO PR, 1969, PP. 526.

SEE ALSO 63, 66, 71, 77, 82, 158, 762, 763, 764, 765, 860

8. ORGANIZATION AND REORGANIZATION OF THE EXECUTIVE

2290 ARNOLD, P. "THE FIRST HOOVER COMMISSION AND THE MANAGERIAL PRESIDENCY." <u>JP</u> 38 (FEB 1976): 46-70.

2291 ASH, R. "WHY THE FEDERAL GOVERNMENT NEEDS RESTRUCTURING." <u>FORTUNE</u> 83 (MAR 1971): 64+.

2292 BERNSTEIN, M. "THE PRESIDENCY AND MANAGEMENT IMPROVEMENT." <u>LAW AND CONTEMPORARY PROBLEMS</u> 35 (1970):505-519.

2293 COSTELLO, M. "PRESIDENTIAL REORGANIZATION." <u>EDITORIAL RESEARCH REPORTS</u> 2, NO.2 (1973): 519-536.

2294 COY, W. "FEDERAL EXECUTIVE REORGANIZATION REEXAMINED: BASIC PROBLEMS." <u>APSR</u> 40 (1946):1124-1137.

2295 EMMERICH, H. <u>FEDERAL ORGANIZATION AND ADMINISTRATIVE MANAGEMENT</u>. UNIVERSITY, ALABAMA: U OF ALABAMA PR, 1971, PP. 304.

A MAJOR HISTORICAL REVIEW OF PRESIDENTIAL COMMISSIONS AND STUDY GROUPS THAT HAVE PROPOSED GOVERNMENTAL

REORGANIZATION AND THE RESULTS OF THEIR EFFORTS. EXCELLENT
APPENDIX OF TEXTS OF REORGANIZATION PLANS. IMPORTANT
CONTRIBUTION TO INSTITUTIONALIZATION OF THE PRESIDENCY.

2296 FESLER, J.W. "ADMINISTRATIVE LITERATURE AND THE SECOND
HOOVER COMMISSION REPORTS." APSR 51 (1957): 135-157.

2297 FOX, M., ED. "A MINI-SYMPOSIUM: PRESIDENT NIXON'S
PROPOSALS FOR EXECUTIVE REORGANIZATION." PUBLIC
ADMINISTRATION R 34 (1974):487-495.

2298 GRAHAM, G.A. "REORGANIZATION: A QUESTION OF EXECUTIVE
INSTITUTIONS." APSR 32 (1938):599-621.

2299 HARRIS, J.P. "FEDERAL EXECUTIVE REORGANIZATION REEXAMINED:
WARTIME CURRENTS AND PEACETIME TRENDS." APSR 40
(1946):1137-1154.

2300 HART, J. "EXECUTIVE REORGANIZATION IN THE USA AND THE
GROWTH OF PRESIDENTIAL POWER." PUBLIC ADMINISTRATION
(ENGLAND) 52 (SUMMER 1974): 174-191.

2301 LEISERSON, A. "POLITICAL LIMITATIONS ON EXECUTIVE
REORGANIZATION." APSR 41 (FEB 1947): 68-84.

2302 MANSFIELD, H.C. "FEDERAL EXECUTIVE REORGANIZATION: THIRTY
YEARS OF EXPERIENCE." PAR 29:332-45 JL/AG '69.

2303 MORSTEIN MARX, F., ED. "FEDERAL EXECUTIVE REORGANIZATION
RE-EXAMINED: A SYMPOSIUM." APSR 40 (DEC. 1946):
1124-1168; 41 (FEB 1947): 48-84.

2304 ROGERS, L. "REORGANIZATION: POST MORTEM NOTES." PSQ
53:161-72 JE '38.

SEE ALSO 109, 375, 439, 460, 535, 1013, 1317, 1321, 1323,
1338, 1339, 1347, 1623, 1718, 1724, 2470

9. TENURE IN OFFICE: E.G., LENGTH OF TERM; DISABILITY

2305 BAILEY, H.A., JR. "PRESIDENTIAL TENURE AND THE TWO-TERM

TRADITION." PUBLIUS 2, NO.2 (FALL 1972): 95-106.

THIS RESTRICTION IS UNNECESSARY IN VIEW OF THE FREQUENT
FAILURE IN AMERICAN HISTORY OF PRESIDENTS TO RECEIVE
SECOND TERM REELECTION.

2306 BALDWIN, F.N., JR. "H.J. RES. 1111: WE WOULD RATHER SWITCH
THAN FIGHT?" THE GEORGE WASHINGTON LAW REVIEW 43
(JANUARY 1975):336-364.

2307 BARTHOLOMEW, P.C. "SUMMARY VIEW: THE PROBLEM OF
PRESIDENTIAL DISABILITY." ABA J 44 (1958): 542.

2308 BLACKMAN, P.H. "PRESIDENTIAL DISABILITY AND THE BAYH
AMENDMENT." WESTERN POLITICAL Q20:440-55 JE '67.

CONCLUDES THAT THE 25TH AMENDMENT IS NOT FLAWLESS, BUT IS
AN IMPROVEMENT OVER THE PREVIOUS STATE OF AFFAIRS.

2309 BROWN, E.S., AND SILVA, R.C. "PRESIDENTIAL SUCCESSION AND
DISABILITY." JP 11 (1949):236-256.

A SUMMARY OF HISTORICAL EPISODES OF INABILITY AND A
PROPOSED STATUTORY MEANS OF DEALING WITH THE PROBLEM.

2310 BROWNELL, H. "PRESIDENTIAL DISABILITY: THE NEED FOR A
CONSTITUTIONAL AMENDMENT." YALE LAW J 68 (1958):189-211.

BY EISENHOWER'S ATTORNEY GENERAL IN THE AFTERMATH OF
EISENHOWER'S SEVERAL EPISODES OF SERIOUS ILLNESS.

2311 CORWIN, E.S. "PRESIDENTIAL 'INABILITY'." NATIONAL R 26
NOV. 1955, PP. 9-16.

2312 DISHMAN, F.N. "REPORT ON PROBLEMS OF PRESIDENTIAL
INABILITY AND VACANCY IN THE OFFICE." ASSN BAR CITY NEW
YORK REC 19 (1964): 311-20..

2313 DOUB, G.C. "PRESIDENTIAL INABILITY: THE CONSTITUTIONAL
PROBLEM." MAINE S B A 48 (1959): 186.

2314 FEERICK, J.D. "PRESIDENTIAL INABILITY: THE PROBLEM AND A
SOLUTION." ABA J 50 (1964): 321.

2315 ----------. "VICE-PRESIDENCY AND THE PROBLEMS OF
PRESIDENTIAL SUCCESSION AND INABILITY." FORDHAM LAW R 32
(1964): 457.

2316 GASPERINI, E.L. "PRESIDENTIAL INABILITY RIDDLE." NEW YORK STATE BAR B 31 (1959): 258.

2317 GILLIAM, A.W., AND SLOAT, J.W. "PRESIDENTIAL INABILITY: THE PROBLEM AND A RECOMMENDATION." GEORGE WASHINGTON LAW R 24:448-64 MR '56.

2318 HANSEN, R.H. "ONE STRIKE AND YOU'RE OUT--THE CONSTITUTION AND EXECUTIVE DISABILITY." NEW HAMPSHIRE BAR J 5 (OCT 1962): 5.

2319 HEINLEIN, J.C. "PROBLEM OF PRESIDENTIAL INABILITY." U CINCINNATI LAW R 25 (SUMMER 1956): 310.

2320 KIRBY, J.C. "BREAKTHROUGH ON PRESIDENTIAL INABILITY: THE ABA CONFERENCE CONSENSUS." VANDERBILT LAW R 17 (1964): 463.

2321 KUHN, E.W. "PRESIDENTIAL INABILITY AND VICE PRESIDENTIAL VACANCY." TENNESSEE LAW R 32 (FALL 1964): 1.

2322 MARX, R. THE HEALTH OF THE PRESIDENTS. NEW YORK: PUTNAM, 1960.

A GENERAL STUDY OF THE PRESIDENTS AND THEIR HEALTH.

2323 PLESUR, M. "THE HEALTH OF PRESIDENTS." IN THE PRESIDENCY REAPPRAISED, EDITED BY R.G. TUGWELL AND T.E. CRONIN, PP. 187-204. NEW YORK: PRAEGER, 1974.

GOOD BRIEF REVIEW OF THE LITERATURE ON PRESIDENTIAL HEALTH, EXCELLENT BIBLIOGRAPHY, INCLUDING MEDICAL JOURNAL SOURCES.

2324 "PRESIDENT'S DISABILITY AND SUCCESSION." ST JOHN'S LAW R 32 (1958): 357.

2325 SIGEL, R.S., AND BUTLER, D. "THE PUBLIC AND THE NO THIRD TERM TRADITION." MIDWEST J POL SCI 8 (1964) PP. 39-54.

POPULAR OPINION SHOWING WIDESPREAD PUBLIC APPROVAL OF THE 22D AMENDMENT.

2326 WILDAVSKY, A. "CHOOSING THE LESSER EVIL: THE POLICY MAKER AND THE PROBLEM OF PRESIDENTIAL DISABILITY." PARLIAMENTARY AFFAIRS (WINTER, 1959-1960): 25-37.

2327 ----------. "PRESIDENTIAL SUCCESSION AND DISABILITY: POLICY ANALYSES FOR UNIQUE CASES." IN THE PRESIDENCY, EDITED BY A. WILDAVSKY. BOSTON: LITTLE BROWN, 1969, PP. 777-795.

2328 WILMERDING, L. "PRESIDENTIAL INABILITY." PSQ 72 (1957):161-181.

SEE ALSO 162, 266, 1431, 2362, 2367

10. IMPEACHMENT

2329 ASSOCIATION OF BAR OF CITY OF N.Y. "THE LAW OF PRESIDENTIAL IMPEACHMENT." RECORD OF THE BAR OF THE CITY OF NEW YORK 29 (FEB. 1974): 154-176.

REPORT ATTEMPTS TO DISCUSS THE LEGAL ISSUES CONCERNING PROPER GROUNDS FOR IMPEACHMENT WITHOUT TAKING "ANY POSITION ON THE CURRENT IMPEACHMENT CONTROVERSY." REPORT IS DIVIDED INTO 5 SECTIONS: PERTINENT CONSTITUTIONAL LANGUAGE, SUBSTANTIVE STANDARDS FOR IMPEACHMENT AND REMOVAL "AS FOUND IN THE LANGUAGE OF THE CONSTITUTION AND ILLUMINATED BY HISTORICAL EVIDENCE. THE 3RD AND 4TH SECTIONS DISCUSS THE RESPECTIVE PROCEDURES APPLICABLE TO AN IMPEACHMENT IN THE HOUSE OF REPRESENTATIVES, AND TO THE TRIAL OF AN IMPEACHMENT IN THE SENATE." THE LAST SECTION CONSIDERS THE PROPRIETY OF JUDICIAL REVIEW IN IMPEACHMENT CASES.

2330 BENEDICT, M.L. "A NEW LOOK AT THE IMPEACHMENT OF ANDREW JOHNSON." PSQ 88 (1973):349-367.

"THE VERSION OF THE JOHNSON IMPEACHMENT THAT AMERICANS HAVE FOUND IN TEXTBOOKS, STUDIES OF THE PRESIDENCY, AND HISTORIES OF THE RECONSTRUCTION ERA IS HARDLY LIKELY TO REASSURE THEM OF THE EFFICACY OF IMPEACHMENT PROCEEDINGS." HOWEVER, THE TEXTS ARE MISLEADING; "THE IMPEACHMENT OF PRESIDENT ANDREW JOHNSON WAS NO HASTY, PASSIONATE DECISION."

2331 BERGER, R. IMPEACHMENT: THE CONSTITUTIONAL PROBLEMS. CAMBRIDGE, MASS.: HARVARD UNIVERSITY PRESS, 1973, PP. 345.

2332 ----------. "IMPEACHMENT FOR HIGH CRIMES AND MISDEMEANORS." SOUTHERN CALIFORNIA LAW R 44 (1971).

2333 ----------. "IMPEACHMENT: AN INSTRUMENT OF REGENERATION; HOW IT WORKS AND WHY IT MUST BE USED- NOW." HARPER'S 248 (JAN 1974): 14,16,18-19,22.

2334 BLACK, C.L., JR. IMPEACHMENT. NEW HAVEN: YALE UNIVERSITY PRESS, 1974, PP. 80.

A BRIEF SUMMARY DISCUSSION BY A LEADING CONSTITUTIONAL AUTHORITY, ARGUING THAT IMPEACHABLE OFFENSES ARE THOSE "WHICH ARE PLAINLY WRONG IN THEMSELVES TO A PERSON OF HONOR, OR TO A GOOD CITIZEN, REGARDLESS OF WORDS ON THE STATUTE-BOOKS." UNLIKE RAOUL BERGER, BLACK BELIEVES THAT IMPEACHMENT CONVICTIONS ARE NOT SUBJECT TO JUDICIAL REVIEW.

2335 BRANT, 1. IMPEACHMENT: TRIALS AND ERRORS. NEW YORK: KNOPF, 1972, PP. 202.

2336 BRODERICK, A. "CITIZENS' GUIDE TO THE IMPEACHMENT OF THE PRESIDENT: PROBLEM AREAS." CATHOLIC UNIVERSITY LAW R 23 (WINTER 1973): 205-254.

THE "CITIZEN'S ROLE IN VOICING HIS VIEWS WITHIN THE POLITICAL FRAME OF IMPEACHMENT OF A PRESIDENT IS AS SIGNIFICANT AS IS EXERCISING HIS RIGHT TO VOTE FOR HIM."

2337 ----------. "WHAT ARE IMPEACHABLE OFFENSES?" ABA J 60 (APR 1974): 415-419.

2338 COMMITTEE ON THE JUDICIARY OF THE U.S. HOUSE OF REPRESENTATIVES, THE IMPEACHMENT INQUIRY STAFF. CONSTITUTIONAL GROUNDS FOR PRESIDENTIAL IMPEACHMENT. WASHINGTON, D.C.: PUBLIC AFFAIRS PRESS, 1974, PP. 62.

2339 COSTELLO, M. "PRESIDENTIAL IMPEACHMENT." EDITORIAL RESEARCH REPORTS 2, NO. 21 (1973): 925-946.

2340 ETRIDGE, G. "THE LAW OF IMPEACHMENT." MISSISSIPPI LAW J (1936).

2341 FENTON, P. "THE SCOPE OF THE IMPEACHMENT POWER." NORTHWESTERN UNIVERSITY LAW R 65 (1970).

2342 FIRMAGE, E.B. "THE LAW OF PRESIDENTIAL IMPEACHMENT." UTAH

LAW R (WINTER 1973): 681-704.

2343 FOSTER, L. "IMPEACHMENT: THE DOCTRINE OF SEPARATION OF
POWERS." FLORIDA BAR J 48 (APR. 1974): 254-258.

DISCUSSES THE DOCTRINE OF SEPARATION OF POWERS, FOCUSING
ON THE OUTLOOKS OF JEFFERSON, MADISON, AND OTHER EARLY
INTERPRETERS OF IT AND ON THE JOHNSON IMPEACHMENT.

2344 GLASS, A.J., AND HARRISON, S.L. "HOUSE ESTABLISHED
PROCEDURES TO HANDLE MOVES TO IMPEACH PRESIDENT."
NATIONAL J (OCT. 27, 1973): 1616-1620.

2345 GREENE, R.S. "THE BALANCE OF POWER, THE IMPEACHMENT POWERS
AND THE SUPREME POWER OF CONGRESS." FEDERAL BAR J 34
(1975):42-53.

CONGRESS SHOULD NOT FEAR TO USE THIS POWER WHEN
APPROPRIATE.

2346 IMPEACHMENT AND THE U.S. CONGRESS. WASHINGTON, D.C.:
CONGRESSIONAL Q, 1974, PP. 60.

2347 KINGSLEY, T.C. THE FEDERAL IMPEACHMENT PROCESS: A
BIBLIOGRAPHIC GUIDE. ITHACA: CORNELL UNIVERSITY
LIBRARIES, 1974, PP. 29.

2348 LEWIS, H.H. "IMPEACHMENT OF ANDREW JOHNSON: A POLITICAL
TRAGEDY." ABA J 40 (1954): 15-18, 80-87.

2349 MANGRUM, R.C. "REMOVAL OF THE PRESIDENT: RESIGNATION AND
THE PROCEDURAL LAW OF IMPEACHMENT." DUKE LAW J (JAN.
1974): 1023-1116.

ARTICLE ANALYZES THE AMERICAN PROCEDURE OF IMPEACHMENT,
OFFERING SOLUTIONS FOR IMPROVING THE PROCESS. DISCUSSES
VARIOUS IMMUNITIES, PRIVILEGES, RIGHTS, AND POWERS THAT
THOSE PARTY TO AN IMPEACHMENT MAY EXERCISE.

2350 MCWHINNEY, E. "CONGRESS AND THE PRESIDENCY AND THE
IMPEACHMENT POWER." INDIANA LAW R 8 (1974): 833-851.

2351 MORGAN, C., ET AL. "IMPEACHMENT: AN HISTORICAL OVERVIEW."
SETON HALL LAW R 5 (SPRING 1974): 689-719.

EXAMINES PRINCIPAL ENGLISH AND AMERICAN CASES IN WHICH
IMPEACHMENT HAS BEEN EMPLOYED IN ORDER TO CLARIFY AND

DEFINE THE TERM "IMPEACHABLE OFFENSE."

2352 REZNECK, D.A. "IS JUDICIAL REVIEW OF IMPEACHMENT COMING?"
ABA J 60 (JUNE 1974): 681-685.

2353 SCHNAPPER, M.B., ED. PRESIDENTIAL IMPEACHMENT: A
DOCUMENTARY OVERVIEW. WASHINGTON, D.C.: PUBLIC AFFAIRS
PRESS, 1974, PP. 144.

REPRINTS DOCUMENTS SUBMITTED TO THE HOUSE JUDICIARY
COMMITTEE AT THE TIME OF THE NIXON IMPEACHMENT HEARINGS,
INCLUDING PRO-IMPEACHMENT BRIEFS(E.G., BY THE AMERICAN
CIVIL LIBERTIES UNION) AND THE BRIEF AGAINST IMPEACHMENT
PREPARED BY PRESIDENT NIXON'S ATTORNEYS.

2354 SLOAN, G.R., AND GARR, I.E. "TREASON, BRIBERY, AND OTHER
HIGH CRIMES AND MISDEMEANORS: A STUDY OF IMPEACHMENT."
TEMPLE LAW Q 47 (1974):413-56.

2355 SMITH, S.C. "BIBLIOGRAPHY: SELECTED WRITINGS ON
IMPEACHMENT." YALE LAW LIBRARY (MAY 1973): 1-9.

2356 SWINDLER, W.F. "HIGH COURT OF CONGRESS: IMPEACHMENT
TRIALS, 1797-1936." AMER BAR ASSOC J 60 (APR 1974):
420-428.

"TWELVE 'CIVIL OFFICERS' OF THE U.S. HAVE BEEN SUBJECTED
TO TRIALS ON IMPEACHMENT ARTICLES IN THE SENATE. BOTH
COLORFUL AND COLORLESS FIGURES HAVE SUFFERED THROUGH THESE
TRIALS, AND THE NATION'S FABRIC HAS BEEN TESTED BY SOME OF
THE TRIALS. HISTORY SHOWS THAT IMPEACHMENT TRIALS HAVE
MOVED FROM BARELY DISGUISED POLITICAL VENDETTAS TO
QUASI-JUDICIAL PROCEEDINGS BEARING THE TRAPPINGS OF LEGAL
TRIALS."

2357 WALTHALL, T. "EXECUTIVE IMPEACHMENT: STEALING FIRE FROM
THE GODS." NEW ENGLAND LAW R 9 (WINTER 1974): 257-291.

REVIEWS THE DEVELOPMENT AND STATUS OF EXECUTIVE
IMPEACHMENT, CONCLUDING THAT A PRESIDENT MAY BE IMPEACHED
FOR NON-INDICTABLE OFFENSES AND THAT THE PROCESS FILLS THE
NEED FOR AN EFFECTIVE CHECK ON EXECUTIVE POWER.

2358 WOODWARD, C.V. "THAT OTHER IMPEACHMENT." N Y TIMES MAG
11 AUG. 1974, PP. 9+.

FINDS LITTLE OF USE IN THE JOHNSON IMPEACHMENT CASE FOR
LATER IMPEACHMENTS, LARGELY BECAUSE OF THE "RECKLESS
HASTE" OF THE PRESIDENT'S OPPONENTS.

2359 WRIGHT, F.X. "THE TRIAL OF PRESIDENTIAL IMPEACHMENTS:
SHOULD THE GHOST BE LAID TO REST?" NOTRE DAME LAWYER 44
(1969):1089-1103.

THE CONSTITUTIONAL PROVISIONS FOR IMPEACHMENT WERE POORLY CONCEIVED AT THE TIME THEY WERE FORMED AND ARE NOW GREATLY IN NEED OF REVISION.

2360 YANKWICH, L. "IMPEACHMENT OF CIVIL OFFICERS UNDER THE FEDERAL CONSTITUTION." GEORGETOWN LAW R 26 (1938).

SEE ALSO 91, 163, 164, 165, 1386, 1406, 1416, 1422, 1455, 1460, 2028, 2309

11. SUCCESSION

2361 COMMITTEE FOR ECONOMIC DEVELOPMENT. PRESIDENTIAL SUCCESSION AND INABILITY: A STATEMENT ON NATIONAL POLICY BY THE RESEARCH AND POLICY COMMITTEE OF THE COMMITTEE FOR ECONOMIC DEVELOPMENT. NEW YORK: 1965, PP. 41.

2362 FEERICK, J.D. FROM FAILING HANDS: THE STORY OF PRESIDENTIAL SUCCESSION. NEW YORK: FORDHAM UNIVERSITY PRESS, 1965. PP. 368.

HISTORICAL DISCUSSION OF PRESIDENTIAL SUCCESSION REFERRING TO THE CONSEQUENCES OF THE DEATHS AND ILLNESSES OF PRESIDENTS AND THE INCREASING IMPORTANCE OF THE VICE-PRESIDENCY.

2363 ----------. THE TWENTY-FIFTH AMENDMENT: ITS COMPLETE HISTORY AND EARLIEST APPLICATIONS NEW YORK: FORDHAM, 1976.

IN THIS SEQUEL TO HIS FROM FAILING HANDS(1965), FEERICK FOCUSES ON THE MEANING, THE LEGISLATIVE HISTORY, AND THE APPLICATION IN 1973 AND 1974 OF THE 25TH AMENDMENT.

2364 GREEN, T.F. "PRESIDENTIAL SUCCESSION." DICKINSON LAW R 61 (1957): 323.

2365 HEINLEIN, J.C. "PROBLEM OF CONTINUITY IN THE PRESIDENCY." U CINCINNATI LAW R 33 (1964): 447.

2366 LINDE, H.A. "REPLACING A PRESIDENT: RX FOR A 21ST CENTURY WATERGATE." THE GEORGE WASHINGTON LAW REVIEW 43 (JANUARY 1975):384-402.

2367 PERRY, B. "A MODEST PROPOSAL FOR A CHANGE IN THE LAW ON PRESIDENTIAL SUCCESSION AND PRESIDENTIAL DISABILITY." SOUTHWESTERN SOCIAL SCIENCE Q 47 (1966): 299-307.

2368 SILVA, R.C. PRESIDENTIAL SUCCESSION. ANN ARBOR: UNIVERSITY OF MICHIGAN PRESS, 1951, PP. 213. ALSO NEW YORK: GREENWOOD, 1968.

2369 ----------. "THE PRESIDENTIAL SUCCESSION ACT OF 1947." MICHIGAN LAW R 47 (1949):451-476.

2370 TOMPKINS, D.L. PRESIDENTIAL SUCCESSION: A BIBLIOGRAPHY. BERKELEY: UNIVERSITY OF CALIFORNIA, 1965, PP. 29.

2371 WILMERDING, L. "THE PRESIDENTIAL SUCCESSION." ATLANTIC MAY 1947, PP. 91-97.

SEE ALSO 94, 1529, 2308, 2315, 2321, 2412, 2421, 2424, 2428

12. OTHER: E.G., USE OF PERQUISITES OF OFFICE

2372 BARNHART, E.N. "THE INDIVIDUAL EXCLUSION OF JAPANESE AMERICANS IN WORLD WAR II." PACIFIC HISTORICAL R 24 (MAY 1960): 111-130.

2373 BECKER, S.L. "PRESIDENTIAL POWER: THE INFLUENCE OF BROADCASTING." Q J OF SPEECH 47 (1961):10-18.

2374 BROWN, E.S. "THE RESTORATION OF CIVIL AND POLITICAL RIGHTS BY PRESIDENTIAL PARDON." APSR 34 (1940):295-300.

2375 COHN, D.S. "ACCESS TO TELEVISION TO REBUT THE PRESIDENT OF THE UNITED STATES: AN ANALYSIS AND PROPOSAL." TEMPLE LAW Q 45 (WINTER 1972): 141-209.

SHOULD "A RIGHT OF ACCESS TO RADIO AND TELEVISION BE RECOGNIZED IN CERTAIN CIRCUMSTANCES...SO THAT SPOKESMEN FOR VIEWPOINTS CONTRASTING THOSE OF THE PRESIDENT WOULD BE ABLE TO REBUT HIM ON THE BROADCAST MEDIA AFTER HE HAD REQUESTED, RECEIVED, AND USED TIME THEREIN TO ADDRESS THE NATION"?

2376 CORDTZ, D. "THE IMPERIAL LIFESTYLE OF THE US PRESIDENT." FORTUNE 88 (OCT 1973): 142-147,220-222,224.

2377 CROTTY, W.S. "PRESIDENTIAL ASSASSINATIONS." SOCIETY (MAY 1972): 18-29.

COMPARISON OF AMERICAN AND FOREIGN PATTERNS OF POLITICAL VIOLENCE.

2378 DAMON, A.L. "PRESIDENTIAL EXPENSES." AMER HERITAGE 25 (JUNE 1974): 64-67, 94-95.

THE HISTORY OF VARIOUS ASPECTS OF PRESIDENTIAL EXPENSES: SALARY, HOUSING AND SERVANTS, PROTECTION, WHITE HOUSE OFFICE STAFF, TRANSPORTATION, RETIREMENT AND AN ADDITIONAL PERQUISITE: PRIVATE HOMES.

2379 DONOVAN, R.J. THE ASSASSINS. LONDON: ELEK BOOKS, 1956, PP. 302. SECOND EDITION, NEW YORK: POPULAR LIBRARY, 1969, PP. 254.

2380 FAUST, G.H. "PRESIDENT'S USE OF TROOPS TO ENFORCE FEDERAL LAW." CLEV-MAR L REV 7 (1958): 362.

2381 FISHER, L. "PRESIDENTIAL TAX DISCRETION AND EIGHTEENTH CENTURY THEORY." WESTERN POLITICAL Q 23 (1970):151-165.

2382 FRIEDMAN, D. "THE FAIRNESS DOCTRINE AND PRESIDENTIAL APPEARANCES." N Y LAW FORUM (FALL 1973): 398-407.

DISCUSSES RELATIVE MERITS, BENEFITS, AND DISADVANTAGES OF THE FAIRNESS DOCTRINE AND THE EQUAL TIME RULE WITH RESPECT TO THE RIGHT OF RESPONSE TO PRESIDENTIAL ADDRESSES.

2383 GANEK, J.P. "CONSIDERATION OF ONLY SELECTED PRESIDENTIAL SPEECHES IS ARBITRARY, AND THEREFORE IMPERMISSIBLE, WHERE RESPONSIVENESS TO PRIOR PRESIDENTIAL SPEECHES IS THE CRITERION FOR GRANTING TIME UNDER THE FAIRNESS DOCTRINE." J PUBLIC LAW 22 (1973): 257-270.

DISCUSSES REVERSAL OF AN FCC RULING THAT THE REPUBLICAN NATIONAL COMMITTEE WAS ENTITLED TO RELIEF FROM CBS BECAUSE OF ITS GRANT OF TIME TO THE DEMOCRATIC NATIONAL COMMITTEE FOR REPLY TO ISSUES RAISED IN EARLIER ADDRESSES OF PRESIDENT NIXON.

2384 GIBSON, R.M. "PRESIDENT'S INHERENT EMERGENCY POWERS." FED B J 12 (1951): 107-51.

2385 GIBSON, S.E. "PRESIDENTIAL PARDONS AND THE COMMON LAW." NORTH CAROLINA LAW R 43 (APR. 1975): 785-793.

REVIEWS SUPREME COURT DECISION HOLDING THAT "THE COMMUTATION OF A DEATH SENTENCE TO LIFE IMPRISONMENT WITHOUT THE POSSIBILITY OF PAROLE WAS A VALID EXERCISE OF THE PRESIDENT'S PARDONING POWER."

2386 GRUNDSTEIN, N.D. "PRESIDENTIAL POWER, ADMINISTRATION, AND ADMINISTRATIVE LAW." GEORGE WASHINGTON LAW R 18 (1950):285-326.

2387 LONGAKER, R.P. THE PRESIDENCY AND INDIVIDUAL LIBERTIES. ITHACA: CORNELL UNIVERSITY PRESS, 1961, PP. 239.

A SURVEY, BASED ON ARCHIVAL SOURCES, OF PRESIDENTIAL ACTIONS BEARING ON CIVIL RIGHTS AND CIVIL LIBERTIES, LARGELY FOCUSING ON THE TRUMAN AND THE EISENHOWER ADMINISTRATIONS.

2388 PATCH, B.W. "EMERGENCY POWERS OF THE PRESIDENT." EDITORIAL RESEARCH REPORTS (1938):87-100.

2389 PIOUS, R.M. "SOURCES OF DOMESTIC POLICY INITIATIVES." IN CONGRESS AGAINST THE PRESIDENT, EDITED BY H.C. MANSFIELD, NEW YORK: ACADEMY OF POL SCI, 1975: 98-111. ALSO NEW YORK: PRAEGER, 1975.

2390 PLISCHKE, E. "THE PRESIDENT'S RIGHT TO GO ABROAD." ORBIS 15 (FALL 1971): 755-783.

DISCUSSES CONSTITUTIONAL QUESTIONS INVOLVED IN PRESIDENTIAL FOREIGN TRIPS.

2391 POLLITT, D.H. "PRESIDENTIAL USE OF TROOPS TO EXECUTE THE LAWS: A BRIEF HISTORY." NORTH CAROLINA LAW R 36 (1958): 117.

2392 RANKIN, R.S., AND DALLMAYR, W.R. FREEDOM AND EMERGENCY POWERS IN THE COLD WAR. NEW YORK: APPLETON, 1964, PP. 277.

2393 RENO, L. "THE POWER OF THE PRESIDENT TO ACQUIRE AND GOVERN TERRITORY." GEORGE WASHINGTON LAW R 19 (1941):251-285.

2394 RICH, B.M. THE PRESIDENTS AND CIVIL DISORDER. WASHINGTON, D.C.: BROOKINGS INSTITUTION, 1941, PP. 235.

2395 ROCHE, J.P. "EXECUTIVE POWER AND DOMESTIC EMERGENCY: THE QUEST FOR PREROGATIVE." WESTERN POLITICAL Q 5 (1952): 592-618.

2396 ROSSITER, C.L. CONSTITUTIONAL DICTATORSHIP: CRISIS GOVERNMENT IN THE MODERN DEMOCRACY. PRINCETON, NEW JERSEY: PRINCETON UNIVERSITY PRESS, 1948, PP. 322. ALSO, NEW YORK: HARCOURT, BRACE, AND WORLD, 1963, PP. 322.

2397 ----------. "CONSTITUTIONAL DICTATORSHIP IN THE ATOMIC AGE." R OF POLITICS 2 (1949):395-418.

2398 SCHUBERT, G.A. "JUDICIAL REVIEW OF THE SUBDELEGATION OF PRESIDENTIAL POWER." JP 12 (1950):668-93.

2399 SHAFFER, H.B. "PRESIDENTIAL ACCOUNTABILITY." EDITORIAL RESEARCH REPORTS 1 (1973):167-184.

2400 SMITH, J.M., AND COTTER, C.P. POWERS OF THE PRESIDENT DURING CRISES. WASHINGTON, D.C.: PUBLIC AFFAIRS PR, 1960, (REPRINTED NEW YORK: DA CAPO PR, 1972), PP. 184.

A HISTORICAL AND ANALYTICAL ACCOUNT OF THE USE OF PRESIDENTIAL EMERGENCY POWERS, ARGUING THAT, WHILE THERE OUGHT TO BE PROCEDURAL LIMITATIONS ON SUCH POWERS, NEVERTHELESS THEY ARE A NECESSITY.

2401 SOMERS, H.M. "THE PRESIDENT AS ADMINISTRATOR." ANNALS 283 (1952):104-114.

2402 STOKE, H.W. "PRESIDENTIAL COORDINATION OF POLICY." ANNALS 221 (MAY 1942): 101-7.

"IN THE EMERGENCE OF THE EXECUTIVE OFFICE THERE APPEARS AN AGENCY IN WHICH THE PRESIDENCY IS LESS AN OFFICE OF DIRECTION THAN IT IS OF CO-ORDINATION IN WHICH THE PRESIDENT'S DECISIONS ARE THE COLLECTIVE REFLECTIONS OF MANY MINDS RATHER THAN OF ONE. IT IS A DEVELOPMENT WHICH MAKES ONE OF THE MOST IMPORTANT FUNCTIONS OF THE PRESIDENCY THE RATIFICATION AND COORDINATION OF OTHER MEN'S ADMINISTRATIVE ACTS AND POLICIES."

2403 STURM, A.L. "EMERGENCIES AND THE PRESIDENCY." JP 11 (1949):121-144.

INCREASING CRISES HAVE LED TO A NOTION NOT MENTIONED IN

THE CONSTITUTION--THAT THE PRESIDENT HAS EMERGENCY POWERS.

2404 SULLIVAN, R.R. "THE ROLE OF THE PRESIDENCY IN SHAPING LOWER LEVEL POLICY-MAKING PROCESS." POLITY 3 (1970):201-221.

2405 THOMPSON, C. "THE PRESIDENCY IN CRISIS: THE EMERGENCY POWERS OF OUR CHIEF EXECUTIVE AND ITS LIMITS." CURRENT HISTORY 8 (1945):33-38.

2406 WALDO, C.D., AND PINCUS, W. "THE STATUTORY OBLIGATIONS OF THE PRESIDENT: EXECUTIVE NECESSITY AND ADMINISTRATIVE BURDEN." PUBLIC ADMINISTRATION R 6 (1946):339-347.

SEE ALSO 302, 994, 1135, 1875, 1896, 1989, 2118, 2284

19
THE VICE PRESIDENCY

2407 BAKER, R. "THE BIGGEST BALTIMORE LOSER OF ALL TIME." N Y
TIMES MAG (OCT 1973): 34-35,107-108.

DISCUSSES THE CAREER, RESIGNATION, AND CONVICTION OF VICE
PRESIDENT AGNEW IN THE CONTEXT OF BALTIMORE'S POLITICAL
CULTURE.

2408 BARZMAN, S. MADMEN AND GENIUSES: THE VICE-PRESIDENTS OF
THE UNITED STATES. CHICAGO: FOLLETT PUBLISHING CO., 1974,
PP. 355.

2409 BAYH, B. ONE HEARTBEAT AWAY: PRESIDENTIAL DISABILITY AND
SUCCESSION. INDIANAPOLIS: BOBBS-MERRILL, 1968.

BAYH'S ACCOUNT OF THE 25TH AMENDMENT.

2410 BENDINER, R. "THE CHANGING ROLE OF THE VICE-PRESIDENT."
COLLIER'S (FEB. 17, 1956): 48-51+.

2411 BURNS, J.M. "A NEW LOOK AT THE VICE-PRESIDENCY." N Y
TIMES MAG 9 OCT. 1955.

2412 COHEN, M., AND WITCOVER, J. A HEARTBEAT AWAY: THE
INVESTIGATION AND RESIGNATION OF SPIRO T. AGNEW. NEW
YORK: THE VIKING PRESS, 1974, PP. 373.

ACCOUNT BY TWO REPORTERS FOR THE WASHINGTON POST OF THE
FULL STORY OF AND BEHIND THE RESIGNATION OF VICE PRESIDENT
AGNEW.

2413 CURTIS, R., AND WELLS, M. NOT EXACTLY A CRIME: OUR VICE
PRESIDENTS FROM ADAMS TO AGNEW. NEW YORK: DIAL, 1972, PP.
202.

BRIEF, ILLUSTRATED, HUMOROUS ACCOUNTS OF THE 39 VICE
PRESIDENTS FROM ADAMS TO AGNEW.

2414 DAVID, P. "THE VICE PRESIDENCY: ITS INSTITUTIONAL
EVOLUTION AND CONTEMPORARY STATUS." JP 29
(1967):721-748.

2415 DI SALLE, M.V., AND BLOCHMAN, L.G. SECOND CHOICE. NEW YORK: HAWTHORN BOOKS, 1966.

2416 DORMAN, M. THE SECOND MAN: THE CHANGING ROLE OF THE VICE-PRESIDENCY. NEW YORK: DELACORTE PRESS, 1968, PP. 305.

A HISTORY OF THE VICE PRESIDENCY FROM ADAMS TO AGNEW, WITH BIBLIOGRAPHY AND A FOREWORD BY FORMER VICE PRESIDENT HUBERT H. HUMPHREY.

2417 DURHAM, G.H. "THE VICE PRESIDENCY." WESTERN POLITICAL Q 1 (1948): 311-315.

2418 EVANS, M.S. "THE POLITICAL ODYSSEY OF SPIRO T. AGNEW." NATIONAL R (AUG. 18, 1972): 894-900, 914.

2419 GRAFF, H.F. "A HEARTBEAT AWAY." AMERICAN HERITAGE 15 (AUGUST 1964): 81-87.

A CONSIDERATION OF THE VICE PRESIDENT'S ROLE IN THE LIGHT OF 20TH CENTURY HISTORY.

2420 GRAHAM, D. "THE VICE PRESIDENCY: FROM CIGAR STORE INDIAN TO CROWN PRINCE." WASHINGTON MONTHLY 6 (APR. 1974): 41-44.

THE VICE PRESIDENCY HAS CHANGED FROM AN OFFICE OF LITTLE SIGNIFICANCE TO THE MOST FAVORED VEHICLE FROM WHICH TO ATTAIN A PRESIDENTIAL NOMINATION.

2421 HARWOOD, M. IN THE SHADOW OF PRESIDENTS: THE AMERICAN VICE PRESIDENCY AND SUCCESSION SYSTEM. PHILADELPHIA: LIPPINCOTT, 1966, PP. 239.

CONTAINS A BRIEF CHAPTER ON EACH OF THE 38 VICE-PRESIDENTS FROM ADAMS TO HUMPHREY, AN INTRODUCTORY CHAPTER ON THE VICE PRESIDENCY AT THE CONSTITUTIONAL CONVENTION, CHAPTERS ON THE 12TH AND THE 25TH AMENDMENTS, AND A BIBLIOGRAPHY.

2422 HATCH, L.C., AND SHOUP, E.L. A HISTORY OF THE VICE-PRESIDENCY OF THE UNITED STATES. NEW YORK: AMERICAN HISTORICAL SOCIETY, 1924. REVISED EDITION, 1934, PP. 437.

2423 HUMPHREY, H.H. "CHANGES IN THE VICE PRESIDENCY." CURRENT HISTORY 67 (AUG. 1974): 58-59, 89-90.

DISCUSSES THE VICE PRESIDENCY, CONCLUDING THAT THE PRESENT ROLE AND METHOD OF SELECTION OF THE VICE PRESIDENT BEST SERVE THE NEEDS OF THE AMERICAN POLITICAL SYSTEM.

2424 LEVIN, P.R. SEVEN BY CHANCE: THE ACCIDENTAL PRESIDENTS.
NEW YORK: FARRAR, STRAUS, 1948, PP. 374.

2425 MCCARTHY, E.J. "THE VICE PRESIDENT AS CROWN PRINCE." IN
THE HARD YEARS. BY E.J. MCCARTHY. NEW YORK: VIKING,
1975, PP. 15-18.

2426 "NAMING VICE PRESIDENTS: EFFORTS TO IMPROVE SYSTEM." CONG
Q W REPT (JAN. 12, 1974): 48-50.

POINTS OUT THAT THE NAMING OF FORD REVEALS SHORTCOMINGS IN
THE TRADITIONAL METHODS OF SELECTING VICE PRESIDENTS,
LISTS PROPOSALS TO IMPROVE THAT PROCESS, AND BRIEFLY
SUMMARIZES PARTY REFORM EFFORTS IN THAT AREA.

2427 SCHLESINGER, A.M., JR. "IS THE VICE-PRESIDENCY
NECESSARY?." ATLANTIC 233 (MAY 1974): 37-44.

2428 SINDLER, A.P. UNCHOSEN PRESIDENTS: THE VICE PRESIDENT AND
OTHER FRUSTRATIONS OF PRESIDENTIAL SUCCESSION. BERKELEY:
U OF CAL PR, 1976, PP. 118.

STUDY OF THE PROBLEM OF PRESIDENTIAL SUCCESSION AND THE
VICE PRESIDENCY AND OF POSSIBLE ALTERNATIVE APPROACHES.

2429 ----------. "MAKE THE VICE PRESIDENCY AN APPOINTIVE
OFFICE?" POLICY ANALYSIS 2 (1976): 351-356.

2430 STUDY GROUP ON VICE-PRESIDENTIAL SELECTION. REPORT.
CAMBRIDGE, MASS.: HARVARD UNIVERSITY INSTITUTE OF
POLITICS, 1976, PP. 67.

2431 TOMPKINS, D.L. THE OFFICE OF VICE PRESIDENT; A SELECTED
BIBLIOGRAPHY. BERKELEY: UNIVERSITY OF CALIFORNIA, 1957
PP. 19.

INCLUDES SECTIONS ON DISABILITY AND SUCCESSION AND ON
PROPOSALS TO CHANGE THE OFFICE.

2432 VEXLER, R.I. THE VICE-PRESIDENTS: BIOGRAPHICAL SKETCHES
OF THE VICE-PRESIDENTS AND CABINET MEMBERS. DOBBS FERRY,
N.Y.: OCEANA, 1975, 2 VOLS.

2433 WILLIAMS, I.G. THE AMERICAN VICE PRESIDENCY: NEW LOOK.
NEW YORK: DOUBLEDAY, 1954, PP. 82.

2434 ----------. THE RISE OF THE VICE-PRESIDENCY. WASHINGTON, D.C.: PUBLIC AFFAIRS PRESS, 1956.

2435 ----------. "THE AMERICAN VICE-PRESIDENCY AND FOREIGN AFFAIRS," WORLD AFFAIRS 120 (SUMMER 1957): 38-41.

2436 ----------. "THE AMERICAN VICE-PRESIDENCY." CURRENT HISTORY 66 (1974):254-258.

2437 WILMERDING, L. "THE VICE-PRESIDENCY." PSQ 68 (MAR. 1953): 17-41.

2438 WORSNOP, R.L. "VICE PRESIDENCY." EDITORIAL RESEARCH REPORTS 2 NO. 18 (1970): 835-856.

2439 YOUNG, D. AMERICAN ROULETTE: THE HISTORY AND DILEMMA OF THE VICE PRESIDENCY. NEW YORK: HOLT, RINEHART AND WINSTON, 1965, PP. 367.

2440 YOUNG, K., AND MIDDLETON, L. HEIRS APPARENT: THE VICE PRESIDENTS OF THE UNITED STATES. NEW YORK: PRENTICE-HALL INC., 1948.

SEE ALSO 94, 354, 407, 646, 651, 1098, 1263, 1294, 1313, 1516, 1520, 1529, 2315, 2363

20
PROPOSALS TO CHANGE
THE PRESIDENCY

2441 BEER, S.H. "GOVERNMENT AND POLITICS: AN IMBALANCE."
CENTER MAG 7 (MAR-APR 1974): 10-22.

UNDERLYING WATERGATE IS A FUNDAMENTAL TREND PRESENT IN
OTHER WESTERN NATIONS--THAT "TENDENCY TO AN ALMIGHTY
EXECUTIVE CONFRONTED BY AN ENFEEBLED SENSE OF SOCIAL
PURPOSE AND YET FRUSTRATED BY AN INCOHERENT PLURALISM."

2442 CHRISTOPHER, W. "A SPECIAL ELECTION TO FILL A PRESIDENTIAL
VACANCY." NYC BAR ASSOC.: RECORD 30 (JAN-FEB 1975):
47-54.

RECOMMENDS "THAT THE CONSTITUTION BE AMENDED TO PROVIDE
FOR A SPECIAL ELECTION WHEN THE PRESIDENT RESIGNS, DIES,
OR IS REMOVED MORE THAN A YEAR BEFORE THE END OF HIS TERM.
UNDER THIS PROPOSAL, THE VICE PRESIDENT WOULD BECOME AN
ACTING PRESIDENT FOR 90 DAYS UNTIL A NEW PRESIDENT COULD
BE ELECTED.

2443 "CONGRESSIONAL GOVERNMENT: CAN IT HAPPEN?" CONG Q W REPT
33 (JUNE 1975): 1331-1351.

2444 CRONIN, T.E. "PUTTING THE PRESIDENT BACK INTO POLITICS."
WASHINGTON MONTHLY SEPT. 1973, PP. 7-36.

RECENT PRESIDENTIAL "FAILURES," INCLUDING WATERGATE, HAVE
OCCURRED BECAUSE "PRESIDENTS HAVE TRIED TOO HARD TO HOLD
THEMSELVES ABOVE POLITICS--OR AT LEAST TO GIVE THAT
APPEARANCE--RATHER THAN ENGAGING IN IT DEEPLY ENOUGH."

2445 CUTLER, L.N., AND JOHNSON, D.R. "REGULATION AND THE
POLITICAL PROCESS." YALE LAW J 84 (JUNE 1975):
1395-1481.

CALLS FOR INTERVENTION BY BOTH PRESIDENT AND CONGRESS WHEN
AGENCIES FAIL TO SET PRIORITIES OR WHEN POLICIES ARE IN
CONFLICT.

2446 DRUCKER, P.F. "HOW TO MAKE THE PRESIDENCY MANAGEABLE."
FORTUNE 90 (NOV. 1974): 146-149.

PRESENTS GUIDELINES TO FACILITATE THE ADMINISTRATION OF
PRESIDENTIAL POWER -- E.G. ABANDONMENT OF A CENTRAL
OPERATING STAFF IN THE PRESIDENT'S OFFICE AND THE
ADMONITION THAT THE PRESIDENT FORGET ABOUT "STYLE" AND
FOCUS ON THE DECISION-MAKING SUBSTANCE.

2447 EISENHOWER, M.S. THE PRESIDENT IS CALLING. GARDEN CITY, N.Y.: DOUBLEDAY, 1974, PP. 598.

A VETERAN PRESIDENTIAL ADVISOR, WHO HAS SERVED IN SOME WAY EVERY PRESIDENT FROM COOLIDGE TO NIXON, AS WELL AS BEING BROTHER AND CONFIDANT TO PRESIDENT EISENHOWER, COMMENTS ON THE PRESIDENTS HE HAS SERVED AND THE ISSUES THEY CONFRONTED AND ALSO PROPOSES CHANGES IN THE PRESIDENCY AND IN PRESIDENTIAL SELECTION.

2448 GORHAM, W. "A SOCIAL REPORT AND SOCIAL POLICY ADVISORS." IN THE PRESIDENTIAL ADVISORY SYSTEM, EDITED BY T.E. CRONIN AND S.D. GREENBERG, PP. 68-74. NEW YORK: HARPER AND ROW, 1969.

2449 HARDIN, C.M. PRESIDENTIAL POWER AND ACCOUNTABILITY: TOWARD A NEW CONSTITUTION. CHICAGO: UNIV. OF CHICAGO PRESS, 1974, PP. 257.

EXAMINES THE GROWTH OF PRESIDENTIAL POWER, THE BUREAUCRACY, AND "THE TRAVAIL OF PUBLIC OPINION," AND ARGUES THAT A MAJOR CONSTITUTIONAL REFORM IS NEEDED. HE PROPOSES "PARTY GOVERNMENT" IN WHICH THE OPPOSITION LEADER WOULD RECEIVE A SEAT IN THE HOUSE OF REPRESENTATIVES AND IN WHICH THERE WOULD INDEED BE AN ORGANIZED OPPOSITION TO ANSWER THE PRESIDENT.

2450 HARGROVE, E.C. "WHAT MANNER OF MAN?" IN CHOOSING THE PRESIDENT. EDITED BY J.D. BARBER, ENGLEWOOD CLIFFS, N.J.: PRENTICE-HALL, 1974: 7-33.

PRESIDENTS NEED TO HAVE SUCH QUALITIES AS THE PSYCHOLOGICAL RESILIENCE ("DEMOCRATIC CHARACTER") TO ORGANIZE THEIR ADVISORS IN A "FLAT" RATHER THAN A HIERARCHICAL FASHION SO AS TO AVOID GETTING INTO SELF-DEFEATING IMPASSES SUCH AS THOSE OF THE JOHNSON AND NIXON ADMINISTRATIONS.

2451 HYMAN, S. "WHAT IS THE PRESIDENT'S TRUE ROLE?" N Y TIMES MAG 7 SEPT. 1958, PP. 108-109.

2452 KAUFMAN, H. "IN DEFENSE OF THE PRESIDENCY." BROOKINGS BULLETIN WINTER 1974, PP. 3-9.

2453 KOENIG, L.W. "THE PRESIDENT NEEDS NEW KINDS OF POWER." ANNALS 397 (SEPT 1971): 71-82.

2454 KRISLOV, S. "WATERGATE FALLOUT: SOME BIZARRE AND NOT-SO-BIZARRE PROPOSALS FOR CHANGES IN THE SYSTEM." CENTER REPORT 7 (APR. 1974): 10-15.

"LEADING POLITICAL SCIENTISTS, HISTORIANS AND LAWYERS ADDRESSED THEMSELVES TO THE PROBLEM OF IMPEACHMENT, PROPOSALS TO 'STRENGTHEN CONGRESS' AND 'CURB THE EXECUTIVE,' THE HOLDING OF PRESIDENTIAL ELECTIONS IN MID-TERM, THE PLACING OF THE OFFICE OF SPECIAL PROSECUTOR UNDER THE GAO, ELIMINATION OF 'POPULAR' ELECTION OF THE PRESIDENT, TO NAME BUT SOME."

2455 MACDONALD, D. "UPDATING THE CONSTITUTION OF THE UNITED STATES." ESQUIRE 81 (MAY 1974): 100-116.

PROPOSES TEN CONSTITUTIONAL AMENDMENTS REORGANIZING THE LEGISLATIVE AND EXECUTIVE BRANCHES AND THE STATES.

2456 MCCARTHY, E.J. "TOWARD A MORE RESPONSIBLE PRESIDENCY." IN THE HARD YEARS, BY E.J. MCCARTHY, NEW YORK: VIKING, 1975, PP. 3-27.

2457 MONDALE, W.F. THE ACCOUNTABILITY OF POWER: TOWARD A RESPONSIBLE PRESIDENCY. NEW YORK: MCKAY, 1975, PP. 284.

MONDALE'S FIRST BOOK. A POST-VIETNAM, POST-WATERGATE LIBERAL REACTION TO PRESIDENTIAL POWER ACCORDING TO WHICH "THE POTENTIAL FOR DISASTER IN THE PRESIDENTIAL OFFICE IS AS GREAT AS THE POTENTIAL FOR ACHIEVEMENT, AND UNLESS PRESIDENTS ARE CONTINUALLY CONFRONTED WITH THE POLITICAL PRICE OF ABUSING THEIR POWER, THAT DISASTER MAY ONCE AGAIN BECOME A REALITY."

2458 REESE, J.H. "NO CONFIDENCE REMOVAL OF THE PRESIDENT: THE WRONG SOLUTION TO A CONSTITUTIONAL PROBLEM." THE GEORGE WASHINGTON LAW REVIEW 43 (JANUARY 1975):416-436.

2459 SAFFELL, D.C., ED. AMERICAN GOVERNMENT: REFORM IN THE POST-WATERGATE ERA. CAMBRIDGE, MASS.: WINTHROP, 1976, PP. 267.

A COLLECTION OF ESSAYS ON POLITICAL REFORM, INCLUDING CONTRIBUTIONS BY, AMONG OTHERS, WILBUR J. COHEN, HENRY STEELE COMMAGER, C. WRIGHT MILLS, EUGENE MCCARTHY, ELIZABETH DREW, BEN WATTENBERG, DAVID BRODER, JAMES RESTON, GAYLORD NELSON, RICHARD ROVERE, AND NELSON POLSBY.

2460 SIMPSON, S.J. "CAN THE PRESIDENCY BE MADE SAFE FOR DEMOCRACY?" THE ANTIOCH REVIEW 33 (SUMMER 1975):60-72.

2461 SINDLER, A.P. "GOOD INTENTIONS, BAD POLICY: A VOTE OF NO CONFIDENCE ON THE PROPOSAL TO EMPOWER CONGRESS TO VOTE NO CONFIDENCE IN THE PRESIDENT." THE GEORGE WASHINGTON LAW REVIEW 43 (JANUARY 1975):437-458.

2462 SORENSEN, T.C. WATCHMEN IN THE NIGHT. CAMBRIDGE: MIT
PRESS, 1975, PP. 178.

ARGUES FOR A STRONG BUT ACCOUNTABLE PRESIDENCY.

2463 SUNDQUIST, J.L. "NEEDED: A WORKABLE CHECK ON THE
PRESIDENCY." BROOKINGS BULLETIN FALL 1973, PP. 7-11.

CALLS FOR A CONSTITUTIONAL AMENDMENT PROVIDING FOR A
PARLIAMENTARY VOTE OF "NO CONFIDENCE" AS A MORE EFFECTIVE
CHECK ON PRESIDENTIAL POWER THAN IMPEACHMENT.

2464 ----------. "THE CASE FOR AN EASIER METHOD TO REMOVE
PRESIDENTS." THE GEORGE WASHINGTON LAW REVIEW 43
(JANUARY 1975):472-484.

2465 "SYMPOSIUM ON THE REUSS RESOLUTION: A VOTE OF NO
CONFIDENCE IN THE PRESIDENT." GEORGE WASHINGTON LAW R 43
(JAN 1975): 327-500.

2466 "THE QUESTION OF A SINGLE SIX-YEAR PRESIDENTIAL TERM."
CONGRESSIONAL DIGEST 51 (MAR. 1972): 68-96.

PARTIAL CONTENTS.--ORIGIN OF THE PRESENT FOUR-YEAR
TERM.--PAST EFFORTS IN CONGRESS TO CHANGE THE LENGTH OF
TERM.--SIX-YEAR TERM PROPOSALS BEFORE THE 92ND CONGRESS.
INCLUDES STATEMENTS BY U.S. SENATOR GEORGE D. AIKEN, U.S.
SENATOR MIKE MANSFIELD, U.S. REPRESENTATIVE BILL FRENZEL,
JAMES MACGREGOR BURNS, CLARK M. CLIFFORD, AND JAMES C.
HAGERTY.

2467 TUGWELL, R.G. A MODEL CONSTITUTION FOR A UNITED REPUBLICS
OF AMERICA. SANTA BARBARA,CALIF.: FUND FOR THE REPUBLIC ,
1970, PP. 160.

AMONG TUGWELL'S PROPOSED REFORMS OF THE PRESIDENCY ARE THE
PROVISION FOR A SINGLE 9 YEAR TERM AND FOR SIMULTANEOUS
ELECTION OF THE PRESIDENT AND 2 VICE PRESIDENTS. "ONE TO
SUPERVISE GENERAL AFFAIRS AND THE OTHER TO SUPERVISE
INTERNAL AFFAIRS."

2468 ----------. "ON BRINGING PRESIDENTS TO HEEL." IN THE
PRESIDENCY REAPPRAISED. EDITED BY R.G. TUGWELL AND T.E.
CRONIN, PP. 266-293. NEW YORK: PRAEGER, 1974.

ORIGINAL FDR "BRAINTRUSTER" ADVOCATES BETTER CONTROL OF
PRESIDENTS BY THEIR POLITICAL PEERS. REFLECTS TUGWELL'S
GENERAL DISCONTENT WITH THE QUALITY OF POST-FDR
PRESIDENTS.

2469 VALENTI, J. "THE CASE FOR A SIX YEAR PRESIDENCY." SAT R
3 AUG. 1968,PP. 13-32.

2470 WOODS, E.C. "A PROPOSED REORGANIZATION OF THE EXECUTIVE
BRANCH OF THE FEDERAL GOVERNMENT." APSR 37 (1943):
476-90.

SEE ALSO 203, 1801, 2314, 2429

21

ADDITIONAL ASPECTS OF
THE PRESIDENCY

2471 AIKMAN. L. THE LIVING WHITE HOUSE. WASHINGTON D.C.:
NATIONAL GEOGRAPHIC SOCIETY, 1970, PP. 143.

2472 ALLEY, R.S. SO HELP ME GOD: RELIGION AND THE PRESIDENCY:
WILSON TO NIXON. RICHMOND, VA.: JOHN KNOX PR, 1972.

2473 BENEDICT. S. "CHANGING THE WATCH IN WASHINGTON (PROBLEMS
OF PRESIDENTIAL TRANSITION)." VIRGINIA Q R37:15-33
WINTER '61.

2474 BLOOM, M. "SHOULD THE HEALTH OF PRESIDENTIAL CANDIDATES BE
A CAMPAIGN ISSUE?" MEDICAL WORLD NEWS (FEB. 9, 1976):
13+.

2475 COYLE, D.C. ORDEAL OF THE PRESIDENCY. WASHINGTON, D.C.:
PUBLIC AFFAIRS PR, 1960. REPRINTED WESTPORT, CONN.,
GREENWOOD PR, 1973, PP. 408.

INCLUDES A RICH COLLECTION OF POLITICAL CARTOONS
CASTIGATING PRESIDENTS.

2476 DAVID, P., ED. THE PRESIDENTIAL ELECTION AND TRANSITION,
1960-1961. WASHINGTON: BROOKINGS INSTITUTION, 1961, PP.
353.

2477 FERSH, S.H. THE VIEW FROM THE WHITE HOUSE: A STUDY OF THE
UNION MESSAGES. WASHINGTON, D.C.: PUBLIC AFFAIRS PRESS,
1961, PP. 158.

2478 FURMAN. B. WHITE HOUSE PROFILE: A SOCIAL HISTORY OF THE
WHITE HOUSE, ITS OCCUPANTS AND FESTIVITIES. INDIANAPOLIS:
BOBBS MERRILL, 1951.

2479 GRAFF, H.F. "PROBLEM OF THE INTERREGNUM," THE NEW YORK

TIMES MAGAZINE (OCTOBER 2, 1960): 88+.

THE FIRST EXAMINATION OF THE MODERN (POST LAME-DUCK AMENDMENT) TRANSITION.

2480 ----------. "THE WEALTH OF PRESIDENTS." AMER HERITAGE 17 (OCT 1966): 4-5, 106-111.

2481 HALBERSTAM, M.J. "WHO'S MEDICALLY FIT FOR THE WHITE HOUSE." N Y TIMES MAG (OCT. 22, 1972): 39+.

PRESENTS ARGUMENTS FOR PHYSICAL AND MENTAL CHECKUP REQUIREMENTS FOR PRESIDENTS AND CANDIDATES.

2482 HECHT, M.B. BEYOND THE PRESIDENCY: THE RESIDUES OF POWER. NEW YORK: MACMILLAN, 1976, PP. 348.

THE POST-PRESIDENTIAL CAREERS OF AMERICAN PRESIDENTS.

2483 HENRY, L.L. PRESIDENTIAL TRANSITIONS. WASHINGTON: BROOKINGS INSTITUTION, 1960, PP. 755.

2484 ----------. TRANSFERRING THE PRESIDENCY: VARIATIONS, TRENDS, AND PATTERNS. WASHINGTON: BROOKINGS INSTITUTION, 1958, PP. 194.

2485 ----------. "PRESIDENTIAL TRANSITIONS: THE 1968-69 EXPERIENCE IN PERSPECTIVE." PUBLIC ADMINISTRATION R 29 (1969):471-482.

"THIS ARTICLE IS AN EARLY ASSESSMENT OF THE 1968-69 TRANSITION IN THE PERSPECTIVE OF PREVIOUS TRANSITION EXPERIENCE AND CONCLUDES WITH SOME OBSERVATIONS ABOUT THE INSTITUTIONALIZATION OF THE TRANSITION PROCESS AND SOME REMAINING AMBIGUITIES OF CONSTITUTIONAL USAGE AND RESPONSIBILITY."

2486 HURD, C. THE WHITE HOUSE STORY. NEW YORK: HAWTHORN BOOKS, 1966, PP. 240.

THE WHITE HOUSE "IS, AT ONE AND THE SAME TIME, THE NAME OF A BUILDING, THE NERVE CENTER OF AMERICAN GOVERNMENT, THE EXAMPLE OF THE NATION'S CONSTANT AND EVER-GROWING ASPIRATIONS, THE FOCAL POINT OF THE SOCIAL AND POLITICAL LIFE OF THE UNITED STATES, AND THE EXPRESSION OF A NATIONAL PERSONALITY."

2487 HYMAN, S. "THE ART OF THE PRESIDENCY." ANNALS 307 (SEPT. 1956): 1-9.

THE PRESIDENT'S "ART" CONSISTS OF REFLECTING AND CREATIVELY GUIDING THE VALUES OF THE PUBLIC, AS DID LINCOLN, RATHER THAN MANIFESTING THE OBDURATE PASSIVITY OF

A BUCHANAN OR THE BULL-HEADED, NEGATIVE, VETO-ORIENTED
ACTIVITY OF A CLEVELAND.

2488 INGRAM, T.H. "THE PRESIDENT'S ASYLUM: THE SECRET SERVICE'S
PREVENTIVE DETENTION." WASHINGTON MONTHLY 4 (OCT. 1972):
35-41.

ON PRESIDENTIAL PROTECTION.

2489 JOHNSON, J., AND JOHNSTON, F. THE WORKING WHITE HOUSE.
NEW YORK: PRAEGER, 1975, PP. 185.

2490 KITLER, G.D. HAIL TO THE CHIEF: THE INAUGURATION DAYS OF
OUR PRESIDENTS. PHILADELPHIA: CHILTON, 1965, PP. 242.

2491 LEISERSON, A. "SOCIAL UNREST AND THE PRESIDENCY." IN THE
FUTURE OF THE AMERICAN PRESIDENCY, EDITED BY C.W. DUNN,
PP. 287-305. MORRISTOWN, N.J.: GENERAL LEARNING PRESS,
1975.

2492 LEISH, K.W. THE WHITE HOUSE. NEW YORK: NEWSWEEK, 1972,
PP. 170.

2493 LINCOLN, F.B. "PRESIDENTIAL TRANSITION, 1968-1969." ABA
J 55 (1969): 529.

2494 MACDIARMID, J. "PRESIDENTIAL INAUGURAL ADDRESSES." POQ 1
(1937):72-85.

2495 PROTHRO, J.W. "VERBAL SHIFTS IN THE AMERICAN PRESIDENCY: A
CONTENT ANALYSIS." APSR 50 (1956):726-739.

2496 RAND, P. "COLLECTING MERIT BADGES: THE WHITE HOUSE
FELLOWS." WASHINGTON MONTHLY 6 (JUNE 1974): 47-56.

DISCUSSES THE WHITE HOUSE FELLOWS PROGRAM AND THE KIND OF
PEOPLE WHO ARE SELECTED.

2497 SHAFFER, H.B. "TRANSFER OF EXECUTIVE POWER:
EISENHOWER-NIXON-KENNEDY COOPERATION." EDITORIAL RESEARCH
REPORTS 23 NOV. 1960, PP. 865-82.

2498 STANLEY, D.T. CHANGING ADMINISTRATIONS: THE 1961 AND 1964

<u>TRANSITIONS IN SIX DEPARTMENTS</u>. WASHINGTON, D.C.: BROOKINGS INSTITUTION, 1965, PP. 147.

THIS STUDY FOCUSES LARGELY ON THE EISENHOWER-KENNEDY TRANSITION, CONCENTRATING ON THE MORE DETAILED TRANSITION PROBLEMS OF 5 DEPARTMENTS AND 1 INDEPENDENT AGENCY: STATE, DEFENSE, INTERIOR, AGRICULTURE, HEW, AND THE FAA. IT CONCLUDES WITH SOME FURTHER SUGGESTIONS FOR FUTURE TRANSITIONS.

2499 TOBIN, R.L. "VOICES FROM THE WHITE HOUSE; RECORDINGS OF FIVE PRESIDENTIAL VOICES." <u>SAT R</u> 51 (AUG 1968): 45.

2500 TUGWELL, R.G. "THE HISTORIANS AND THE PRESIDENCY: AN ESSAY REVIEW." <u>PSQ</u> 86 (JUNE 1971): 183-204.

FOCUSES ON HISTORIAN ERIC GOLDMAN'S STUDY OF PRESIDENT JOHNSON.

2501 WEAVER, P.H. "LIBERALS AND THE PRESIDENCY." <u>COMMENTARY</u> 60 (OCT 1975): 48-53.

NOTES THE SIGNIFICANCE OF THE "ABANDONMENT BY AMERICAN LIBERALS OF THEIR LONGSTANDING COMMITMENT TO THE STRONG PRESIDENCY."

2502 WEST, J.B. <u>UPSTAIRS AT THE WHITE HOUSE</u>. NEW YORK: WARNER, 1973, PP. 416.

THE REMINISCENCES OF THE CHIEF USHER OF THE WHITE HOUSE FROM 1941 TO 1969.

2503 WHITE, H.B. "VERBAL SHIFTS IN THE AMERICAN PRESIDENCY: A CONTENT ANALYSIS . <u>APSR</u>50: 726-50 S '56.

2504 WILDAVSKY, A. "WINNING THE ELECTION AND GOVERNING THE NATION." <u>TRANS-ACTION</u> 5 (1968):8-15.

SEE ALSO   479, 570, 571, 786, 830, 914, 944, 1863, 1864, 1879, 1882, 2444

INDEX OF AUTHORS

AMBROSE, S.E. 817, 818.

AMLUND, C.A. 281.

ANDERSON, P. 1235, 1774, 1780.

ANDREWS, R.B. 760.

ANDREWS, W.G. 184.

APPLE, R.W. 1236.

APPLEBY, P. 415, 1636, 1754.

ARCHER, W.J. 2249.

ARMBRUSTER, M.E. 34.

ARMSTRONG, A. 506.

ARMSTRONG, W.P. 1893.

ARNOLD, P. 1894, 2290.

ART, R.J. 942.

ARTERTON, F.C. 1810, 1811.

ASBELL, B. 562.

ASH, R. 2291.

AUERBACH, J.S. 579.

AUSTIN, A. 1135.

AWALT, F.G. 416.

BAADE, H.W. 1604.

BACH, S. 171, 185, 2019.

BAER, M.A. 1841.

BAGDIKIAN, B.H. 1103, 1854.

BAGNALL, J.A. 980.

BAILEY, H.A., JR. 2305.

BAILEY, S.K. 1121, 1781.

BAILEY, T.A. 282, 283.

BAKER, L. 417, 472, 1098.

BAKER, R. 2407.

BALCOM, M.N. 528.

BALDWIN, F.N., JR. 2306.

BALL, G.W. 1136.

BALZ, D.J. 1316, 1530.

BANKS, R.F. 761.

BARBER, J.D. 1477, 1542, 1564, 1565, 1566, 1567, 1568, 1569.

BARBER, S.A. 2182.

BARFIELD, C.E. 1317, 1318, 1733.

BARKLEY, A.W. 651.

BARNES, W.H. 418.

BARNHART, E.N. 2372.

BARRETT, M. 1855.

BARRETT, R.J. 2061.

BARRON, G.J. 473.

BARTFELD, P.M. 2282.

BARTHOLOMEW, P.C. 2307.

BARTLETT, C. 981.

BARTLEY, N.V. 854.

BARZMAN, S. 2408.

BAST, W. 1954.

BAYH, B. 2409.

BEAL, J.R. 828.

BEARD, C.A. 35, 474, 475, 580.

BECHT, A.C. 2210.

BECKER, S.L. 2373.

BECKLER, D.Z. 1734.

BECKMAN, A.E. 2168.

BEER, S.H. 2441.

BELL, J. 186, 187, 1078.

BELLAMY, C. 2169.

BELLUSH, B. 343.

BELLUSH, J. 1387.

BELOFF, N. 1237.

BEMAN, L. 1720.

BENDER, J.C. 1366.

BENDINER, R. 2410.

BENEDICT, M.L. 2330.

BENEDICT, S. 2473.

BENSON, E.T. 829.

BENSON, T.W. 545.

BERDAHL, C.A. 2062.

BERENDT, J. 1812.

BERGER, C. 697.

BERGER, H.N. 779.

BERGER, R. 1388, 1895, 2063, 2064, 2065, 2211, 2212, 2213,
    2213, 2331, 2332, 2333.

BERKOVITCH, B.S. 2250.

BERLE, A. 350, 830, 2066.

BERLIN, I. 581.

BERMAN, E. 2283.

BERMAN, W.C. 671.

BERNICK, E.L. 1986.

BERNSTEIN, B.J. 507, 630, 639, 672, 673, 698, 699, 700,
    762, 763, 764, 765, 866, 982, 983.

BERNSTEIN, C. 1389, 1470.

BERNSTEIN, I. 419, 420.

BERNSTEIN, M. 2292.

BERNSTEIN, M.H. 214.

BICKEL, A.M. 1390, 1896, 2067.

BICKERTON, I.J. 701.

BIDDLE, F. 351, 352.

BILLINGTON, M. 674, 675.

BINGHAM, W. 1049.

BINKLEY, W.E. 188, 189, 1813, 1897, 1898, 1899, 1900.

BISHOP, D.G. 476.

BISHOP, J.A. 563, 1015, 1050, 1170.

BISHOP, J.W., JR. 2214.

BLACK, C.L., JR. 2028, 2334.

BLACKMAN, J.L. 2284.

BLACKMAN, P.H. 2308.

BLAIR, C., JR. 900.

BLAIR, J. 900.

BLAISDELL, T.C., JR. 1856.

BLOCHMAN, L.G. 2415.

BLOOM, M. 2474.

BLUM, J.M. 353, 354, 508.

BLUMBERG, S.A. 867.

BLUMENFELD, R. 1238.

BOCHNER, A.P. 1414.

BOCK, E.A. 984, 1319.

BOECKEL, R.M. 2170.

BOGARDUS, E.S. 1857.

BOMBARDIER, G. 1637, 1848.

BONAFEDE, D. 1239, 1240, 1241, 1242, 1243, 1244, 1245,
        1246, 1247, 1248, 1249, 1250, 1251, 1252, 1253, 1254,
        1255, 1256, 1257, 1320, 1321, 1322, 1323, 1324, 1325,
        1391, 1392, 1471, 1508, 1509, 1510, 1511, 1512, 1513,
        1514, 1515, 1516, 1517, 1518, 1519, 1537, 1538, 1539,
        1586, 1638, 1715, 1901, 1902.

BONAFEDE, D. AND COHEN, R., EDS. 1500.

BORDEN, M. 284.

BORG, D. 477, 478.

BORKLUND, C.W. 1609.

BOSKIN, J. 461.

BOTTOME, E.M. 868.

BOUGHTON, J.M. 1732.

BOWLER, M.K. 1326.

BOYD, J. 1258.

BRADEN, W.W. 570, 582.

BRADLEE, B. 1051.

BRADSHAW, J. 943.

BRADY, J.R. 1755.

BRANDENBURG, E. 479, 570, 571, 582.

BRANDON, H. 1171.

BRANT, I. 2335.

BRANYAN, R.L. 1172.

BRANYON, R.L. 807.

BRECKENRIDGE, A. 2215.

BREMER, H.F. 329.

BRENNAN, J.A. 421.

BRENNER, M.J. 1367.

BRESICA, P.F. 1610.

BRESSLER, N. 3.

BRODER, D.S. 1173.

BRODERICK, A. 2336, 2337.

BRODIE, B. 1570.

BRODIE, F.M. 1571.

BRODY, R.A. 1814.

BROGAN, D.W. 1174.

BRONK, D.W. 1735.

BROOKS, H. 1736, 1751.

BROOKS, P.C. 631.

BROUGH, J. 312, 313.

BROWER, C.N. 2068.

BROWN, D.S. 702, 1972.

BROWN, E.C. 583.

BROWN, E.S. 2183, 2309, 2374.

BROWN, SEYOM 703.

BROWN, STEWART 190.

BROWN, T.M. 1478.

BROWN, W.B. 1815.

BROWNELL, H. 2310.

BROWNLOW, L. 191.

BRUENN, H.G. 564.

BRUNDAGE, P.F. 1639, 1640.

BRZEZINSKI, Z. 1368.

BUCHAN, A. 1259.

BUCHANAN, P.J. 1327.

BUCHANAN, T. 1016.

BUCHANAN, W.W. 4.

BUCK, J.V. 1903.

BULLITT, W.C. 1575.

BUNDY, M. 404, 985.

BURBY, J.F. 1260, 1328, 1329, 1330.

BURKE, J.G. 5.

BURKE, V. 1331, 1331.

BURKLAND, J.V. 1641.

BURLINGHAM, B. 944.

CHACE, J. 1369.

CHADWIN, M.L. 1332.

CHAFFEE, S.H. 1394, 1419.

CHALLENER, R.D. 831.

CHAMBERLAIN, J. 932.

CHAMBERLAIN, L.H. 1904, 1905, 1906.

CHANDLER, A.D., JR. 808.

CHARLES, S.F. 357.

CHASE, H.W. 914.

CHAYES, A. 986.

CHEEVER, D.S. 2071.

CHESEN, E.S. 1479.

CHESTER, L. 1395.

CHILDS, M. 795, 1859.

CHOPER, J.H. 1994.

CHRISTENSON, R.M. 676.

CHRISTIAN, G. 1164.

CHRISTOPHER, W. 2442.

CHURCH, F. 1396, 2251.

CHURCHILL, W.S. 2003.

CIRILLO, R.A. 2195.

CLAPP, C.H. 1917.

CLARK, K.C. 1611.

CLARK, T.B. 1333, 1344.

CLARY, E.B. 2022.

CLEMENS, D.S. 546.

CLEVELAND, H. 1817.

CLIFFORD, C.M. 1137, 1783.

CLIFTON, C.V. 1076.

CORDTZ, D. 2376.

CORNWELL, E.E. 172, 328, 780, 1176, 1860, 1861, 1862, 1863.

CORRIGAN, R. 1334, 1531.

CORRY, J. 1017.

CORWIN, E.S. 196, 197, 198, 510, 2077, 2078, 2196, 2311.

COSTELLO, M. 2293, 2339.

COSTELLO, W. 1223.

COSTIGAN, D. 646.

COTTER, C.P. 1908, 1962, 2400.

COTTIN, J. 1325, 1335.

COX, A. 1398, 2219.

COY, W. 2294.

COYLE, D.C. 2475.

COYNE, J.R., JR. 1263.

CRANE, R. 987.

CRAWFORD, A.F. 1264.

CREEL, G. 359.

CRIDER, J.H. 572.

CRONIN, T.E. 181, 199, 1589, 1590, 1591, 1773, 1785, 1818, 1864, 1973, 2444.

CROSS, C.B. 2197.

CROSSMAN, R.H. 285.

CROTTY, W.S. 2377.

CROWELL, L. 547.

CROWN, J.T. 922.

CROWNOVER, A.B. 424.

CULLEN, D.E. 2285.

CULLITON, B.J. 1644.

CUNLIFFE, M. 200.

DE GRAZIA, A. 1910, 1911, 1960.

DE SANTIS, V. 887.

DE TOLEDANO, R. 1224.

DEAKIN, J. 1165.

DEAN, A.H. 988.

DEAN, A.L. 1756.

DEAN, J.W., III. 1265, 1400.

DECHART, C.R. 2220.

DECTER, M. 1053.

DEGAULLE, C. 2004, 2005.

DEGLER, C.N. 330.

DEKIEFFER, D.D.E. 2286.

DEMPSTER, M.A. 1645.

DENNIS, J. 1820.

DESTLER, I.M. 1370, 1614.

DEUTSCH, E.P. 2080.

DEWART, L. 989.

DEWITT, K. 1336.

DI SALLE, M.V. 2415.

DIAMOND, E. 1572, 1865.

DIBACCO, T.V. 881.

DICKERSON, N. 1866.

DINEEN, J. 934.

DINERSTEIN, H.S. 990.

DISHMAN, F.N. 2312.

DIVINE, R.A. 481, 513, 768, 769, 991.

DOCTORS, S.I. 1337.

DONAHOE, B.F. 425.

DONALD, A.D. 924.

DONLEY, R.E. 1573.

DONOVAN, J.C. 482.

DONOVAN, R.J. 796, 935, 2379.

DONOVAN, W.J. 2198.

DORMAN, M. 2416.

DORSEN, N. 2221.

DOTSON, A. 1647.

DOTY, P. 1739.

DOUB, G.C. 2313.

DOUGLAS, W.O. 362.

DREIR, J.C. 992.

DREW, E. 1401, 1912.

DREWRY, E.B. 11.

DRIGGS, D.W. 1819.

DROZE, W.H. 426.

DRUCKER, P.F. 2446.

DRUKS, H. 706.

DRUMMOND, R. 833.

DRURY, A. 1206.

DULLES, E.L. 834.

DULLES, J.F. 835.

DUNN, C.W. 173.

DUPEUX, G. 261.

DURANT, A. 37.

DURANT, J. 37.

DURHAM, G.H. 2417.

DUSCHA, J. 1266.

DWORKIN, R. 1402.

EAGLETON, T.F. 2081.

FREED, F. 715.

FREEDMAN, M. 368.

FREELAND, R.M. 711.

FREESE, P.L. 1022.

FREIDEL, F. 38, 307, 331, 344, 345, 587.

FREUD, S. W. 1575.

FRIEDMAN, D. 2382.

FRIEDMAN, L. 1407.

FRIER, D.A. 856.

FRISCH, M.J. 588, 589.

FRITCHEY, C. 286.

FROHNMAYER, D.B. 2031, 2227.

FRYE, A. 2089.

FUCHS, L.H. 1058.

FULBRIGHT, J.W. 2090.

FURER, H.B. 640, 1093.

FURMAN, B. 2478.

FURNAS, H. 205.

FUSFELD, D.R. 590.

GADDIS, J.L. 518, 712, 713.

GALBRAITH, J.K. 945.

GALLAGHER, H.G. 1918.

GALLOWAY, J. 993, 1142.

GANEK, J.P. 2383.

GARDNER, J. 2091.

GARDNER, L.C. 431, 519, 714, 1372.

GARDNER, R.W. 432.

GARNER, J.W. 2092.

GARR, I.E. 2354.

GOLDSMITH, W.M. 2033.

GOLDSTEIN, S.M. 2034.

GOLDWATER, B.M. 1481, 2094, 2095.

GOODHART, A.L. 1024.

GOODHART, P. 488.

GOODWIN, C. 2287.

GOOLD-ADAMS, R. 838.

GOOSTREE, R.F. 2262.

GORDON, C. 1551.

GORDON, G.J. 1651.

GORHAM, W. 2448.

GORVINE, A. 984.

GOULDEN, J. 1145, 1974.

GOULDING, P.G. 1105.

GRABER, D.A. 716, 1823, 1824.

GRAEBNER, N.A. 717, 888, 1617, 2096.

GRAFF, H.F. 1106, 1146, 1552, 2419, 2479, 2480.

GRAHAM, B. 1409.

GRAHAM, D. 2420.

GRAHAM, G.A. 1594, 2298.

GRAHAM, O.L. 332, 433, 591.

GRAUBARD, S. 1272.

GRAY, R.K. 797.

GREEN, D. 718.

GREEN, T.F. 2364.

GREENBERG, B.S. 1025.

GREENBERG, S.D. 1590.

GREENE, R.S. 2345.

GREENHOUSE, S. 1652.

GREENSTEIN, F.I. 1825, 1826, 1827, 1828, 1829.

GREER, T. 592.

GRESSLEY, G.M. 434.

GRIFFITH, E.S. 206.

GROSS, B.M. 657, 1096, 1653, 1729.

GROSSMAN, M.B. 1868.

GROTH, A.J. 262.

GROVES, L. 520.

GRUBBS, D.H. 435.

GRUNDSTEIN, N.D. 2097, 2386.

GUEDALLA, P. 263.

GUERRANT, E.O. 287.

GUHIN, M.A. 839, 840.

GULLIVER, H. 1353.

GUNTHER, G. 1410.

GUNTHER, J. 309.

GUSTAFSON, M. 1830.

GUTHRIE, C.L. 1787.

HAM, C. 770.

HAHN, W.F. 1374.

HAIGHT, D.E. 174.

HALASZ, N. 593.

HALBERSTAM, D. 946, 1181, 1869.

HALBERSTAM, M.J. 2481.

HALEY, J.E. 1182.

HALL, D.K. 994.

HALLETT, D. 1273.

HALPERIN, M.H. 719, 872, 1167, 1975, 1976.

HALPERIN, S. 549.

HALPERN, P.J. 1411.

HAMBY, A.L. 333, 622, 679, 782, 783.

HAMILL, K. 1654.

HAMILTON, M.T. 1346.

HAMMOND, P.Y. 1618, 1619, 1620.

HANSEN, R.H. 2318.

HARDIN, C.M. 2449.

HARGROVE, E.C. 207, 264, 1579, 1580, 2450.

HARLOW, R.L. 1655.

HARMON, M.J. 369.

HARPER, A.D. 680.

HARPER, E.L. 1656.

HARREN, L. 1183.

HARRIMAN, W.A. 370.

HARRIS, I.D. 1581.

HARRIS, J.P. 1657, 1914, 1919, 1977, 2299.

HARRIS, L. 1553, 2098.

HARRIS, M. 1225.

HARRIS, S.E. 964, 1723.

HARRISON, S.L. 2344.

HART, J. 208, 2188, 2300.

HART, R.P., 1482.

HARTLEY, A. 995.

HARTMANN, R. 1527.

HARTMANN, S.M. 681, 720.

HARVEY, J.C. 965, 1122.

HARWARD, D.W. 1412.

HARWOOD, M. 2421.

HARWOOD, R. 1081.

HASSLER, W.W. 1621.

HATCH, L.C. 2422.

HATHAWAY, E.V. 39.

HAUGE, G. 889.

HAVARD, W.C. 209.

HAVEMANN, J. 1274, 1338, 1341, 1342, 1528, 1532, 1540,
    1541, 1658, 1659, 1660, 1661, 1902.

HAVILAND, H.F. 2071.

HAWLEY, E.W. 436.

HAYNES, R.F. 721.

HEATH, J.F. 521, 902, 966.

HECHT, M.B. 455, 2482.

HECLO, H. 1554, 1662.

HEINLEIN, J.C. 2319, 2365.

HELD, V. 1663.

HELLER, D. 841, 841, 1664, 1664.

HELLER, F.H. 210.

HELLER, W.W. 967.

HELMS, E.A. 1850.

HENDEL, S. 2035.

HENDERSON, B. 903.

HENDERSON, C.P. 1474.

HENKIN, L. 1413, 2099.

HENRY, L.L. 211, 371, 1978, 2483, 2484, 2485.

HERBERS, J. 1221.

HEREN, L. 1804.

HERRING, E.P. 1920, 1921.

HERRING, G.C., JR. 489.

HERSEY, J. 624, 936, 1544.

HERTZ, M.F. 2268.

HERZ, M.F. 722.

HESS, G.R. 522.

HESS, R.D. 1821, 1831, 1832.

HESS, S. 1229, 1555, 1622, 1788.

HEY, H.W. 2229.

HILLMAN, W. 632.

HILLS, R.M. 968.

HILSMAN, R. 996, 1922, 1923.

HIRSCH, H. 1834.

HIRSCH, W. 1665.

HIRSCHBERG, V. 1844.

HIRSCHFIELD, R.S. 175, 212, 2036.

HITCHENS, H.L. 723.

HOBBS, E.H. 857, 1595, 1789.

HOBBS, J.P. 821.

HOFFMAN, P. 1208.

HOFSTADTER, R. 594.

HOLCOMBE, A.N. 1666, 1851.

HOLLINGSWORTH, H.M. 334.

HOLM, J. 1414.

HOLMANS, A.E. 858.

HOLMES, W.F. 334.

HOLSTI, O.R. 842, 997.

HOLTZMAN, A. 1924.

HOOD, R.C. 1724.

HOOPES, R. 969.

HOOPES, T. 843, 1147.

HOOVER, H. 1757.

JACOB, C. 437, 2037.

JACOBS, R.F. 1217.

JACOBSEN, H.K. 523.

JACOBSON, H.K. 1045.

JACOBSON, J.M. 2199.

JACOBY, R.L. 319.

JAFFE, L.L. 374.

JAMES, D.B. 217.

JAMES, D.C. 524.

JAMES, J.P. 1963.

JAMES, L.C. 2200.

JAMESON, H.B. 799.

JANIS, I.L. 1791.

JANOS, L. 1184.

JAROS, D. 1833, 1834.

JAVITS, J.K. 2102.

JAWORSKI, L. 1417.

JENKINS, G.L. 2103.

JENSEN, A.L. 40.

JOESTEN, J. 1026.

JOHANNES, J.R. 1927, 1928, 1929.

JOHANNSEN, D.E. 566.

JOHNSON, C.A.T. (LADY BIRD JOHNSON) 1185, 1186.

JOHNSON, D.B. 176.

JOHNSON, D.R. 2445.

JOHNSON, H.B. 1081.

JOHNSON, J. 2489.

JOHNSON, L.B. 1088, 1089, 1090, 1091.

JOHNSON, M.B. 1870.

JOHNSON, R.H. 1626.

JOHNSON, R.T. 1792.

JOHNSON, S.H. 1082.

JOHNSON, W. 218.

JOHNSTON, F. 2489.

JOHNSTON, L.D. 174.

JONAS, M. 527.

JONES, A.H. 595.

JONES, B. 438.

JONES, C.O. 1501.

JONES, H.G. 17.

JONES, H.W. 1930.

JONES, J.M. 724.

JONES, J.W. 1667.

JONES, R. 1991.

JOSEPH, T. 1871.

JURIKA, S. 2146.

JUST, W. 1049.

KAHAN, J.H. 998.

KAHIN, G. MCT. 1148.

KAHN, H. 18.

KAHN, M.A. 1995, 2201.

KALB, B. 1280.

KALB, M. 1280.

KALLENBACH, J.E. 265, 266.

KAMPELMAN, M.M. 1872.

KANE, J.N. 41.

KANELY, E.A. 4.

KANTER, A. 1981.

KAPLAN, M.A. 1376.

KARL, B.D. 375, 439.

KASS, B.L. 2175.

KATEB, G. 1059.

KATZENBACH, N.D. 2105.

KAUFMAN, H. 2452.

KAUFMANN, W.W. 947.

KAZIN, A. 1060.

KEARNS, D. 1083, 1187.

KEECH, W.R. 1556.

KEEVER, J., 1264.

KEFAUVER, E. 1931.

KELLEY, S., JR. 1873, 1932.

KELLY, J.B. 1933.

KEMPTON, M. 891.

KENDALL, W. 2038.

KENNAN, G.F. 376.

KENNEDY, J.F. 916, 917, 918, 919, 920.

KENNEDY, ROBERT F. 1000.

KENNEDY, ROSE FITZGERALD 1061.

KENT, F.R. 1934.

KENYON, C.M. 219.

KEOGH, J. 1483.

KEOWN, S.S. 2106.

KERNELL, S. 1835.

KESSEL, J.H. 1716.

KESSELMAN, M. 1935, 2107, 2108.

KEY, V.O. 1668.

KILBORN, P. 784.

KILLIAN, J.R., JR. 1741.

KILPATRICK, C. 377, 1062, 1281.

KIMBALL, W.F. 490.

KING, A. 267.

KINGSLEY, T.C. 2347.

KINTNER, R. 349.

KIRBY, J.C. 2320.

KIRKENDALL, R.S. 19, 20, 335, 336, 440, 642, 643.

KISSINGER, H.A. 1627.

KISTIAKOWSKY, G.B. 846, 1742.

KITLER, G.D. 2490.

KIVENS, L. 1687.

KLEILER, F.M. 1845.

KLEIN, A.L. 921.

KLEIN, H.G. 1876.

KLIMAN, G. 1043.

KLUCKHOHN, F.L. 596.

KNAPP, D. 970.

KNAPPMAN, E.W. 1874.

KOENIG, L.W. 198, 220, 644, 771, 1063, 1805, 1936, 2039,
    2109, 2453.

KOHL, W.L. 1282.

KOLKO, G. 525, 725.

KOLKO, J. 725.

KOLSON, K.L. 1833.

KOMAROVSKY, M. 1759.

KORNITZER, B. 822, 1227.

KOSKOFF, D.E. 937.

KRAFT, J. 1001, 1418, 1793.

KRAINES, O. 1760.

KRAMER, F.A. 1656.

KRAMER, J.R. 2248.

KRAMER, R. 2231.

KRANZ, H. 2266.

KRAUS, S. 1414, 1419.

KREAGER, H.D. 1699.

KRISLOV, S. 2454.

KROCK, A. 288.

KUHN, E.W. 2321.

KUKLICK, B. 726.

KURLAND, P.B. 1420, 1421, 1422, 2202.

KYBAL, V. 347.

LADD, B. 1188.

LAFEBER, W. 289, 526, 727.

LAIRD, M. 1545.

LAMMERS, W.W. 221.

LANDAU, D. 1283.

LANDECKER, M. 1836.

LANDER, B.G. 1123.

LANDER, L. 1124.

LANDIS, J.M. 441.

LANE, G. 1937.

LANE, M. 1027.

LANG, G.E. 1423.

LANG, K. 1423.

LANGER, W.L. 491.

LANGLEY, H.D. 527.

LANZILLOTTI, R.F. 1346.

LOGSDON, J.M. 1046.

LONG, A.K. 998.

LONG, N. 224, 1673.

LONGAKER, R.P. 971, 2009, 2387.

LORENZ, A.L. 786.

LOSS, R. 225.

LOTTIER, J. 1488.

LOWENTHAL, A.F. 1149.

LOWI, T.J. 2042.

LUBALIN, E. 1560.

LUKAS, J. A. 1427.

LURIE, L. 1484.

LYLE, J. 1425.

LYNCH, H.F. 2113.

LYNN, N.B. 2043.

LYON, P. 801.

LYONS, G.M. 1743.

MACARTHUR, D. 660.

MACDIARMID, J. 2494.

MACDONALD, D. 2455.

MACDONALD, S. 2018.

MACIVER, K.F., JR. 2114.

MACLEAN, J.C. 1941.

MACMAHON, A. 1775, 1942, 1943.

MACMILLAN, H. 2010, 2011, 2012.

MAFFRE, J. 1377.

MAGRATH, C.P. 1190.

MAGRUDER, J.S. 1428, 1429.

MAILER, N. 1067.

MAIN, J.T. 226.

MAJOR, J. 339.

MALAWER, S.S. 2115.

MALLALIEU, W.C. 730.

MALONE, D. 2232.

MANCHESTER, W.R. 905, 1029.

MANGRUM, R.C. 2349.

MANLEY, J.F. 1944, 2116.

MANN, S.Z. 685.

MANSFIELD, H.C. 1776, 1945, 2302.

MARANELL, G.M. 291.

MARCUSE, H. 2231.

MARCY, C.M. 1761.

MARKEL, L. 625.

MARSH, J.F., JR. 686.

MARTIN, G. 382.

MARTIN, H.A. 664.

MARTIN, J.B. 1875.

MARX, R. 2322.

MASHER, J. 1546.

MATHEWS, C. 2117.

MATHEWS, J.M. 574.

MATTHEWS, D.R. 1556, 1558.

MATUSOW, A.J. 630, 687.

MAXEY, D.R. 1378.

MAXWELL, J.A. 528.

MAY, E.R. 529, 1628, 1629, 2118.

MAZLISH, B. 1286, 1485, 1486.

MAZO, E. 1228, 1229.

MCCARTHY, E.J. 2425, 2456.

MCCARTNEY, J. 1430.

MCCLURE, A.F. 646, 688, 2043.

MCCLURE, W. 2119, 2120.

MCCONNELL, B. 42.

MCCONNELL, G. 227, 772, 972.

MCCONNELL, J. 42.

MCCOY, D.R. 691.

MCCRYSTAL, C. 1395.

MCFADYEN, B.D. 731.

MCFARLAND, C.K. 446.

MCGEEVER, P.J. 1431.

MCGHEE, G.W. 2121.

MCGINNISS, J. 1230.

MCKINLEY, C. 2044.

MCKINZIE, R.D. 447.

MCLAUGHON, H.K., JR. 2233.

MCLELLAN, D.S. 732.

MCNEAL, R. 598.

MCNEILL, W.H. 530.

MCPHERSON, H. 1107.

MCREYNOLDS, W.H. 1596.

MCWHINNEY, E. 2350.

MEAGHER, S. 1030, 1031.

MEDINA, S.F., JR. 2250.

MEE, C.L. 733.

MEIR, G. 2013.

MERANTO, P. 1128.

MERMELSTEIN, D. 1094.

MERRIAM, C.E. 1777.

MERRIAM, R.E. 1674.

MEYER, K.E. 1003.

MEYERS, J. 1068.

MICHELSON, C. 383.

MIDDLETON, L. 2440.

MIKVA, A.J. 2268.

MILES, C.W. 2234.

MILLER, A.S. 2235, 2269.

MILLER, D.C. 567.

MILLER, M. 633.

MILLER, R.L. 1349.

MILLER, W.J. 847.

MILLER, W.L. 1432.

MILLIS, W. 599.

MILLS, J.L. 1940, 2267, 2270.

MILTON, G.F. 2045.

MINOW, N.N. 1875.

MIROFF, B. 1069.

MITCHELL, C. 1350.

MITCHELL, D.J.B. 1351, 1726, 1727.

MITCHELL, L.M. 1875.

MOE, R.C. 1717, 1946, 1947, 2204.

MOLEY, R. 292, 384, 448, 449, 450.

MOLLENHOFF, C. 1497, 1876.

MONAGHAN, H.P. 2122.

MONDALE, W.F. 1794, 2457.

MONGAR, T.M. 1070.

MYERS, H. 958.

NADICH, J. 823.

NASH, G.D. 340.

NATHAN, J.A. 1004.

NATHAN, R. 1354, 1982.

NAUGHTON, J. 1287.

NAVASKY, V.S. 949.

NELSON, B. 1193, 1745.

NELSON, D.M. 534.

NESSON, C.R. 2126.

NEUMANN, W.L. 550, 600.

NEUSTADT, R.E. 229, 230, 269, 270, 271, 294, 689, 1071,
      1194, 1598, 1599, 2047.

NICHOLAS, H.G. 1355.

NICHOLS, J.P. 494.

NIHART, B. 1288.

NITZE, P.H. 2014.

NIXON, E.B. 452.

NIXON, R.M. 1218, 1219, 1220, 2192.

NOBLE, G.B. 851.

NOBLEMAN, E.E. 2127.

NORTON, H.S. 1728.

NOURSE, E.G. 1729.

NOVAK, M. 1559.

NOVAK, R. 1079, 1207, 1524.

NUNNERLY, D. 1005.

NUTTER, G.W. 1292.

O'BRIEN, D.J. 453.

O'BRIEN, L. 950, 1108.

O'CONNER, J.F.T. 454.

O'DONNELL, K. 1072, 1195.

O'HARA, W.T. 973.

O'LEARY, P.M. 535.

ODEGARD, P.H. 1852.

ODELL, T. 2128.

ODIORNE, G.S. 1678.

OPOTOWSKY, S. 951.

ORFIELD, L.B. 1762.

ORLANSKY, H. 568.

ORNSTEIN, N.J. 1561.

ORR, S.C. 1356.

OSBORNE, J. 1211, 1212, 1213, 1214.

OSBORNE, T.M. 1487.

OSGOOD, R.E. 734, 1379.

OWENS, G. 867.

PACHTER, H.M. 1006.

PAGE, B.I. 1814.

PAIGE, G. 735, 752.

PAN, S.C.Y. 551.

PANETTA, L.E. 1357.

PAOLUCCI, H. 2129.

PAPER, L.J. 907.

PARK, C.J. 736.

PARKER, E.B. 1025.

PARKER, G.R. 1838.

PARKER, R. 1983, 2206.

PARMET, H.S. 455, 802.

PARRIS, J.H. 1949.

ROGOW, A.A. 665, 1583.

ROHDE, D.W. 1561.

ROHERTY, J.M. 952.

ROLLINS, A.B. 390, 927.

ROOS, L.J. 1894.

ROOSEVELT, ELEANOR. 391, 392.

ROOSEVELT, ELLIOTT. 312, 313, 322, 553.

ROOSEVELT, F.D. 323, 324, 325, 326.

ROOSEVELT, J. 314.

ROSE, L.A. 743, 744.

ROSE, R. 1686.

ROSEN, C.M. 1839.

ROSEN, E.A. 394, 577.

ROSEN, G.R. 1297.

ROSENBERG, J.A. 2141.

ROSENBERG, J.K. 1444.

ROSENBERG, K.C. 1444.

ROSENBLUM, S. 1197.

ROSENMAN, D. 296.

ROSENMAN, S.I. 296, 327, 395.

ROSS, D.R.B. 554.

ROSS, H. 464.

ROSS, T.B. 880.

ROSSITER, C.L. 236, 603, 1602, 1846, 1999, 2396, 2397.

ROSTEN, L.C. 604.

ROSTOW, E.V. 1198, 2142.

ROSTOW, W.W. 1114.

ROTHENBERG, A.B. 1445.

ROUCEK, J.S. 1132.

SKAU, G.H. 605.

SKOLNIKOFF, E.B. 1751.

SLATER, J. 1158.

SLOAN, G.R. 2354.

SLOAT, J.W. 2317.

SLUSSER, R.M. 1008.

SMALL, N.J. 242.

SMITH, A.M. 243, 806, 877, 1884.

SMITH, C.W. 606.

SMITH, D. 955.

SMITH, D.C. 1953.

SMITH, G. 540, 667, 790.

SMITH, H.D. 1693, 1694, 1695.

SMITH, J.M. 1962, 2146, 2400.

SMITH, L. 1363.

SMITH, R.H. 1382.

SMITH, S.C. 2244, 2355.

SMITH, W.B. 826.

SNELL, J.L. 555.

SNETSINGER, J. 774.

SNOWMAN, D. 751.

SNYDER, R.C. 752.

SOBEL, L.A. 1009, 1010, 1303, 1364, 1529.

SOBEL, R. 43.

SOFAER, A.D. 2245.

SOLOW, R.M. 1095.

SOLTMAN, N.M. 2275.

SOMERS, H.M. 1779, 1987, 2401.

SONTAG, R.J. 556.

SWINDLER, W.F. 277, 2356.

SWISHER, C.B. 405, 2151.

SZULC, T. 1003, 1304.

TAFT, W.H. 249.

TAGGART, R. 1127.

TANENHAUS, J. 775.

TANSILL, C.C. 498, 2152.

TANZER, L. 956.

TAPIA, R.R. 1963.

TAUBENECK, F.D. 2002.

TAYLOR, M.D. 853, 957.

TAYLOR, T. 44.

TEEL, S.C. 1946.

TEFFT, D.P. 1403.

TERCHEK, R.J. 1011.

TERHORST, J.F. 1504, 1505.

THACH, C.C. 250.

THEOHARIS, A.G. 558, 610, 668, 693, 694, 793.

THOMAS, H. 1888.

THOMAS, N.C. 180, 1133, 1591, 1603, 1604, 1770, 1771, 1773.

THOMPSON, C. 2405.

THOMPSON, F., JR. 1965.

THOMPSON, F.D. 1451.

THOMPSON, J.C. 1799.

THOMPSON, R.E. 958.

THOMPSON, W.C. 1039.

TIDMARCH, C.M. 1966.

TIMMONS, B.N. 407, 408.

TOBIN, J. 977.

VENKATARAMANI, M.S. 612.

VESTAL, B. 1507.

VEXLER, R.I. 816, 2432.

VINYARD, D. 254.

VIORST, M. 543, 1232, 1307.

VON HIPPEL, F. 1748.

VON FURSTENBERG, G.M. 1732.

VOORHIS, J. 1216.

VOSE, C.E. 32, 33, 2181.

WADE, L.L. 1701.

WAGNON, W.O., JR. 669.

WALDIE, J.R. 1467.

WALDMAN, R.J. 1719.

WALDO, C.D. 2406.

WALKER, J.L. 176.

WALKER, R. 1702.

WALKER, R.L. 413.

WALLACE, D. 2157, 2158, 2159.

WALLACE, H.L. 885.

WALLACE, W.V. 500.

WALLEN, H. 1308.

WALLER, G.M. 501.

WALLING, A. 1387.

WALSH, J. 1703, 1704.

WALTERS, R. 1309.

WALTHALL, T. 2357.

WALTON, R. 1012.

WANAT, J. 1705.

WANN, A.J. 613, 1706.

WARD, C. 1300.

WARD, D. 1310.

WARNER, G. 559, 1161.

WARREN, F.A. 468.

WARREN, S. 2015.

WATERS, C. 1311.

WATERS, M. 1634.

WATSON, R.L. 614.

WATSON, W.M. 1117.

WAYNE, S.J. 2055.

WAYS, M. 1134, 1876.

WEAVER, P.H. 2501.

WEBB, R.E. 2160.

WEBER, A.R. 1351, 1365.

WEEKS, O.D. 1707.

WEIDNER, E. 1013.

WEINBERG, P. 2141.

WEINRAUB, S. 2280.

WEINSTEIN, E.A. 1585.

WEINTHAL, E. 981.

WEISBAND, E. 1800.

WEISS, S.L. 502.

WELBORN, D.M. 1990.

WELLES, S. 615.

WELLS, J.M. 2161.

WELLS, M. 2413.

WENNER, S.J. 2162.

WEST, J.B. 2502.

WESTERFIELD, H.B. 1162.

WESTIN, A.F. 776.

WHALEN, R.J. 938, 1493.

WHITE, H. 1968.

WHITE, H.B. 2503.

WHITE, S. 1042.

WHITE, T.H. 939, 1100, 1233, 1464, 1465.

WHITE, W.S. 1101.

WHITEHEAD, D.F. 503.

WHITEHEAD, R., JR. 1466.

WHITNEY, C. 670.

WHITNEY, D.C. 45, 46.

WICKER, E. 469.

WICKER, R. 912.

WICKER, T. 913, 1077, 1118, 1119.

WIGGINS, C.E. 1467.

WILCOX, F.U. 2163, 2164.

WILCOX, J. 616.

WILDAVSKY, A. 182, 183, 255, 256, 863, 1130, 1645, 1708,
    1709, 1710, 1711, 1712, 1835, 2056, 2057, 2326, 2327,
    2504.

WILKIE, H. 1713.

WILKINS, B.H. 960.

WILLIAMS, C.D. 1801, 2165.

WILLIAMS, I.G. 2433, 2434, 2435, 2436.

WILLIAMS, J. 777.

WILLIAMS, J.D. 2281.

WILLIAMS, J.M. 1203.

WILLIAMS, O.P. 695.

WILLIAMS, R.M. 1349.

WILLIAMS, T.H. 1204.

WOODSTONE, A. 1496.

WOODWARD, B. 1389, 1470.

WOODWARD, C.V. 302, 2358.

WORMUTH, F.D. 2166.

WORSNOP, R.L. 2017, 2059, 2167, 2438.

WOTRING, E.C. 1425.

WRESZIN, M. 468.

WRIGHT, F.X. 2359.

WRONE, D. 1044.

WYETH, G.A., JR. 1635.

WYMON, D.S. 561.

YANCEY, W.L. 1131.

YANKWICH, L. 2360.

YARMOLINSKY, A. 1714.

YARNELL, A. 778.

YORK, H.F. 758.

YOUNG, D. 2439.

YOUNG, J.S. 259.

YOUNG, K. 2440.

YOUNGER, I. 1969.

ZARB, F. 1672.

ZINN, H. 342.

ZORIN, V. 1802.

ZUMWALT, E.R. 1315.

ZURCHER, A.J. 1970.